Plan

P9-EDX-669

with For Dummies

Covering the most popular destinations in North America and Europe, *For Dummies* travel guides are the ultimate user-friendly trip planners. Available wherever books are sold or go to www.dummies.com

And book it with our online partner, Frommers.com

- ✔ Book airfare, hotels and packages
- ✔ Find the hottest deals
- ✔ Get breaking travel news
- ✔ Enter to win vacations
- ✔ Share trip photos and stories
- ✔ And much more

Frommers.com, rated the #1 Travel Web Site by PC Magazine

FOR DUMMIES®

The fun and easy way™ to travel!

U.S.A.

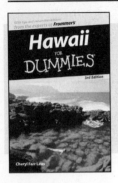

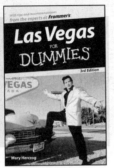

Also available:

Alaska For Dummies
Arizona For Dummies
Boston For Dummies
California For Dummies
Chicago For Dummies
Colorado & the Rockies For Dummies
Florida For Dummies
Los Angeles & Disneyland For Dummies
Maui For Dummies
National Parks of the American West For Dummies

New Orleans For Dummies
New York City For Dummies
San Francisco For Dummies
Seattle & the Olympic Peninsula For Dummies
Washington, D.C. For Dummies
RV Vacations For Dummies
Walt Disney World & Orlando For Dummies

EUROPE

A Travel Guide for the Rest of Us!

Also available:

England For Dummies
Europe For Dummies
Germany For Dummies
Ireland For Dummies
London For Dummies

Paris For Dummies
Scotland For Dummies
Spain For Dummies

OTHER DESTINATIONS

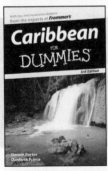

Also available:

Bahamas For Dummies
Cancun & the Yucatan For Dummies
Costa Rica For Dummies
Mexico's Beach Resorts For Dummies
Montreal & Quebec City For Dummies
Vancouver & Victoria For Dummies

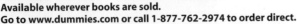

Australia
FOR
DUMMIES®
1ST EDITION

by Marc Llewellyn & Lee Mylne

WILEY

Wiley Publishing, Inc.

Australia For Dummies®, 1st Edition

Published by
Wiley Publishing, Inc.
111 River St.
Hoboken, NJ 07030-5774
www.wiley.com

For general information on our other products and services, please contact our Customer Care Department within the U.S. at 800-762-2974, outside the U.S. at 317-572-3993, or fax 317-572-4002.

For technical support, please visit www.wiley.com/techsupport.

Wiley also publishes its books in a variety of electronic formats. Some content that appears in print may not be available in electronic books.

Library of Congress Control Number: 2008922121

ISBN: 978-0-470-17834-8

Manufactured in the United States of America

10 9 8 7 6 5 4 3 2 1

WILEY

About the Authors

Sydney resident **Marc Llewellyn** is one of Australia's premier travel writers and the winner of several writing awards. He is the president of the Australian Society of Travel Writers. He's written two travelogues; *Riders to the Midnight Sun* tells of his journey from the Ukrainian Black Sea to the Russian Arctic on a cheap bicycle. His latest manuscript, with the working title *Islands of the Winds,* tells the story of a year working as a peasant farmer and shrimp fisherman on an island off Sicily. He is the coauthor of *Frommer's Australia.*

Lee Mylne has spent almost all her working life as a journalist — in newspapers, magazines, and radio — and has travelled to more than 40 countries. Born and raised in New Zealand, she has lived in Australia since 1986 and is currently based in Melbourne. In 2006, she was awarded Life Membership of the Australian Society of Travel Writers, of which she is a past president. She is the coauthor of *Frommer's Australia,* the author of *Frommer's Portable Australia's Great Barrier Reef,* and a contributor to *Frommer's Dream Vacations.* She is also the coeditor and a contributor to the anthology *Best Foot Forward, 30 Years of Australian Travel Writing.*

Publisher's Acknowledgments

We're proud of this book; please send us your comments through our Dummies online registration form located at www.dummies.com/register/.

Some of the people who helped bring this book to market include the following:

Editorial

Editors: Heather Wilcox, Production Editor; Cate Latting and Kathleen Warnock, Development Editors

Copy Editor: Elizabeth Kuball

Cartographer: Guy Ruggiero

Editorial Assistant: Jennifer Polland

Senior Photo Editor: Richard Fox

Cover Photos: © Eric Meola/ Getty Images

Cartoons: Rich Tennant (www.the5thwave.com)

Composition Services

Project Coordinator: Lynsey Stanford

Layout and Graphics: Claudia Bell, Carl Byers, Joyce Haughey, Stephanie D. Jumper

Proofreaders: Melanie Hoffman, Caitie Kelly, Lisa Stiers

Indexer: Slivoskey Indexing Services

Publishing and Editorial for Consumer Dummies

Diane Graves Steele, Vice President and Publisher, Consumer Dummies

Joyce Pepple, Acquisitions Director, Consumer Dummies

Kristin A. Cocks, Product Development Director, Consumer Dummies

Michael Spring, Vice President and Publisher, Travel

Kelly Regan, Editorial Director, Travel

Publishing for Technology Dummies

Andy Cummings, Vice President and Publisher, Dummies Technology/General User

Composition Services

Gerry Fahey, Vice President of Production Services

Debbie Stailey, Director of Composition Services

Contents at a Glance

Maps at a Glance

Table of Contents

Introduction

．．

So you want to go to the Land Down Under! We heartily concur with
your choice, because we live here, we love it, and we want to show
you what makes Australia such a special place.

Traveling halfway around the world (which most readers of this book
will be doing) is a big undertaking, and we're here to help you break it
into doable parts. We help you decide where in Australia you want to go,
tell you how to get there, and give you the scoop on what to do after you
arrive.

From the Outback to the Great Barrier Reef to glorious cities like Sydney
and Melbourne, we give you options so you can find the experiences
that are right for you — whether you want to cuddle a koala, explore a
shipwreck, or climb the Sydney Harbour Bridge (or all three!).

About This Book

Australia For Dummies is a concise and precise guide to the top destinations in Australia. In addition to the "Big Three" of Sydney, the Great
Barrier Reef, and Uluru (Ayers Rock), we offer an overview of the other
major cities, activities, and resorts throughout the country. We give you
information about all the Australian states, in case you find yourself
wanting to hop over to Tasmania or up to Kakadu, for example.

We've done the legwork for you. We give you only the info you need —
from what to do before you leave, to what you need to know when you
get here.

This is a guidebook and also a reference book. You can read it cover to
cover, or you can jump in anywhere to find the information you want
about a specific city or region. Whether you're sitting in your living room
figuring out how many vacation days you'll need for the trip, or looking
for a sushi restaurant in Sydney, *Australia For Dummies* is set up so you
can get the facts, descriptions, and recommendations you want, quickly.
You can open it to any chapter and dig in to get the information you
need without any hassles.

Please be advised that travel information is subject to change at any
time — and this is especially true of prices. We suggest that you write or
call ahead for confirmation when making your travel plans. The authors,

editors, and publisher cannot be held responsible for the experiences of readers while traveling. Your safety is important to us, so we encourage you to stay alert and be aware of your surroundings. Keep a close eye on cameras, purses, and wallets — all favorite targets of thieves and pickpockets.

Conventions Used in This Book

In this book, we include lists of hotels, restaurants, and attractions. As we describe each, we often use abbreviations for commonly accepted credit cards. Take a look at the following list for an explanation of each:

AE: American Express

DC: Diners Club

MC: MasterCard

V: Visa

Note: The Discover card is not accepted in Australia.

We divide the hotels into two categories — our personal favorites and those that don't make our preferred list but still get our hearty seal of approval. Don't be shy about considering the runner-up hotels if you can't get a room at one of the favorites or if your preferences differ from ours. The amenities that the runners-up offer, and the services that each provides, make all these accommodations good choices to consider as you determine where to rest your head at night.

We also include some general pricing information to help you decide where to unpack your bags or dine on the local cuisine. We use a system of dollar signs to show a range of costs for one night in a hotel (in a double room) or a meal at a restaurant (included in the cost of each meal is an appetizer, entree, and nonalcoholic beverage). Check out the following chart to see what range we're using (in U.S. dollars):

Cost	Hotel	Restaurant
$	Less than $80	Less than $25
$$	$81–$160	$26–$40
$$$	$161–$240	$41–$55
$$$$	$241–$320	$56 and over
$$$$$	$321 and over	

Prices in this guide for hotels, restaurants, attractions, and services are given first in Australian dollars (A$), and then converted into U.S. dollars (US$) and British pounds (£).

The exchange rate used throughout the book is A$1 = US$0.80/£0.40, US$1 = A$1.25, or £1 = A$2.45. You can find a chart giving examples of how much various things cost in all three currencies in Chapter 5.

Foolish Assumptions

As we wrote this book, we made some assumptions about you and what your needs may be as a traveler. Here's what we assumed about you:

- ✔ You may be an inexperienced traveler looking for guidance when determining whether to take a trip to Australia and how to plan it.

- ✔ You may be an experienced traveler who hasn't yet been to Australia and wants expert advice on how to best plan your trip and enjoy the country.

- ✔ You're not looking for a book that provides all the information available about Australia or that lists every hotel, restaurant, or attraction available to you. Instead, you're looking for a book that focuses on the places that give you the best or most unusual experience in Australia.

If you fit any of these criteria, *Australia For Dummies* gives you the information you're looking for!

How This Book Is Organized

This book is divided into eight parts covering the major aspects of your trip and the regions of Australia. Each part is broken down into specific components so you can go right to the subtopic you want. (If you want to go to the Great Barrier Reef, you don't have to read all about the Red Centre, for example.) Following are brief summaries of the parts.

Part 1: Introducing Australia

Get a panoramic view of Australia as we scan the continent's highlights, the not-to-be-missed attractions and activities. We give you a thumbnail sketch of Australia's history and culture. Then we help you decide when to go, based on the seasons and events, and offer some itineraries based on time and interests.

Part 11: Planning Your Trip to Australia

Australia isn't a spur-of-the-moment destination. And part of the fun of planning a trip to such a huge, remote place is figuring out where you want to go and what you want to do. Ah, the possibilities! We help you get off on the right foot, and let you know about things you need to do (like getting a visa) before you leave. We can give you ideas on how to budget for the trip, the different ways to get here, and how to get around after you're here. We also provide resources for those with special travel needs and interests.

Part III: Sydney, Melbourne, and the Australian Capital Territory

Sydney and Melbourne are two of the largest cities in Australia, each with world-class hotels, dining, arts, and nightlife. We have lots of good advice about visiting these cities and their environs. Located between Melbourne and Sydney is the nation's capital, Canberra, in a federal district called Australian Capital Territory.

Part IV: Brisbane, Queensland, and the Great Barrier Reef

Brisbane is the closest major city to the Great Barrier Reef; in this part, we give you the highlights. From Brisbane, you can make your way to one of the natural wonders of the world: the Great Barrier Reef. We give you the lowdown on the top resorts along the coast and on the Reef itself, as well as information about the many activities you can participate in.

Part V: The Red Centre and the Top End

Mysterious Uluru (Ayers Rock) stands tall in the Red Centre, where it's been the object of curiosity for thousands of years. We tell you the best way to get to this remote part of Australia, where to stay, and about the charming town of Alice Springs, as well as the other natural wonders in the area. The Northern Territory, just above the Red Centre, is known as the Top End, and we introduce you to its capital city of Darwin, as well as the mammoth Kakadu National Park.

Part VI: The South and West

These regions offer smart cities and great natural beauty, and they produce some of the finest wines in Australia (and the world). Adelaide is a great starting point for touring the south, and there's nowhere better than Kangaroo Island for seeing marsupials in the wild. Perth is the major city in Western Australia, providing an excellent base for wine tours and wildflower watching.

Part VII: Tasmania

The island-state is home to colonial cities, beautiful parks, and unique wildlife, including the endangered Tasmanian devil. It's also a more manageable size than some of the great expanses of the mainland.

Part VIII: The Part of Tens

Every *For Dummies* book has a Part of Tens. These fun and pithy chapters are a list of what makes a place special. In this case, we take a look at ten sites that are part of Australia's convict history, and then give you ten Australian expressions you need to know!

In the back of this book, we include an appendix — your Quick Concierge — containing lots of handy information you may need, ranging from area codes to customs regulations, electricity, and driving rules (there are individual "Fast Facts" sections in most chapters with important local information). Check out this appendix when searching for answers to lots of questions that may come up as you travel. You can find the Quick Concierge easily, because it's printed on yellow paper.

Icons Used in This Book

These icons appear in the margins throughout this book:

Keep an eye out for the Bargain Alert icon as you seek money-saving tips and/or great deals.

The Best of the Best icon highlights the best that Australia has to offer.

Watch for the Heads Up icon to identify annoying or potentially dangerous situations, such as tourist traps, unsafe neighborhoods, budgetary rip-offs, and other circumstances to beware of.

Look to the Kid Friendly icon for attractions, hotels, restaurants, and activities that are particularly hospitable to children or people traveling with kids.

This icon highlights those only-in-Australia places that are unique to the Land Down Under.

The Tip icon highlights useful advice on things to do and ways to schedule your time.

Where to Go from Here

Your next stop is Australia, a living, vibrant, wonderfully diverse country that offers something for every taste, inclination, or budget. It's a place that's worth traveling halfway around the world for!

Part I
Introducing Australia

The 5th Wave   By Rich Tennant

"I thought we should go to Australia! You know, the land down under. As an employee of the subway system, I thought that would appeal to you."

In this part . . .

1 t's a country . . . it's a continent . . . it's got beaches, deserts, mountains, and great cities. Australia is a place that's both ancient and modern, with remote wilderness and teeming urban areas. In this part, we give you glimpses of all the above, with some of our personal bests in lodging, dining, attractions, and activities. We also offer up a brief history of human presence on the continent, add some advice on the seasons (they go by opposites!), and provide four suggested itineraries for your stay.

Chapter 1

Discovering the Best of Australia

by Marc Llewellyn and Lee Mylne

In This Chapter

▶ Discovering the best lodgings, dining, and attractions
▶ Experiencing the best of Aboriginal culture
▶ Viewing the best Australian flora and fauna
▶ Kicking back on the best beaches and hiking the best trails

*B*est means different things to different people. So the best we can do is share with you our personal favorites. Australia's scenery, wildlife, culture, beaches, lodgings, food, and weather can all — in various guises — lay claim to being world-class. The landscape, in places, is almost unbelievable, all bathed in a special light that's found nowhere else in the world.

There are, of course, the "big three" — Sydney, the Great Barrier Reef, and the magnificent monolith Uluru, known affectionately as "the Rock." These *should* be on your list, but don't forget that Australia has so much more to offer: charming country towns, isolated and pristine beaches, rustic sheep stations, rain forest villages, and mountain lodges. To find out what you'll be missing if you don't — even occasionally — take the road less traveled, check out this chapter, in which we try to narrow our personal choices in the "Best of" stakes.

The Best Luxury Hotels

The big cities offer the high-end chains as well as boutique hotels. The resorts on the Great Barrier Reef, both onshore and on their own islands, are gorgeous and loaded with amenities as well as natural beauty.

> ✔ **Park Hyatt Sydney** (Sydney, New South Wales): This artistically curving property on The Rocks foreshore is the best-positioned hotel in town. It's right on the water, and some rooms have views

across the harbor to the Sydney Opera House. The building is a pleasure to look at, and from a ferry on the harbor, it looks like a wonderful addition to the toy-town landscape of The Rocks. Each of the 33 executive suites has two balconies equipped with a telescope. See Chapter 11.

✔ **Sebel Reef House** (Cairns, Queensland): Drop-dead gorgeous — that's the only way to describe this period piece from the colonial era. This is one of the most romantic hotels in Australia. The white walls are swathed in bougainvillea, and the beds with mosquito netting. Airy interiors feature rustic handmade artifacts and white wicker furniture. The Verandah Spa rooms, which have Jacuzzis on the balconies within earshot of the ocean, overlook the pool, waterfalls, and lush gardens. See Chapter 17.

✔ **Longitude 131** (Uluru/Ayers Rock, Red Centre): You can find this African-style luxury safari camp, with perfect views of Uluru, in the sand dunes a mile or two from the main complex. It offers 15 top-class air-conditioned tents, each with a private bathroom and a balcony overlooking the Rock. The resort is promoting them as "six star." A central facility, **Dune House,** holds a restaurant (with superb food), bar, library, and shop. See Chapter 18.

✔ **Hayman Island Resort** (Whitsunday Islands, Queensland): This is the most luxurious and glamorous resort in Australia. Check-in is done over a glass of bubbly aboard the resort's sleek launch as you travel from Hamilton Island Airport. You soon find your way through the open-air sandstone lanais, cascading ponds, and tropical foliage to the fabulous hexagonal complex of swimming pools by the sea. Dress is beachwear by day, smart casual at night. Every room, suite, villa, and penthouse has a balcony or terrace, bathrobes, and valet service (and butler service in the penthouses). See Chapter 17.

The Best Moderate and Alternative Accommodations

With a decent exchange rate and a good supply of moderately priced places to stay, you can find both comfort and bargains throughout Australia. We also include some unique places to stay.

✔ **North Adelaide Heritage Group** (Adelaide, South Australia): It's worth coming to Adelaide just for the experience of staying in one of these out-of-this-world apartments, cottages, or suites. Each of the 21 properties is fabulous. We particularly recommend the former Friendly Meeting Chapel Hall, once the headquarters of the "Albert Lodge No. 6 of the Independent Order of Oddfellows, Manchester Unity Friendly Society, and the Court Huntsman's Pride No. 2478 of the Ancient Order of Foresters Friendly Society." See Chapter 20.

✔ **Underground Motel** (Broken Hill, New South Wales): Making the trip out to White Cliffs is worth the effort, just to stay here for the night. All but two of the rooms are underground; they're reached by a maze of spacious tunnels dug out of the rock and sealed with epoxy resin. The temperature below ground is a constant 72°F (22°C), which is decidedly cooler than a summer day outside. Rooms are comfortable though basic, with shared toilets and showers. Turn the light off, and it's dark as a cave. See Chapter 12.

✔ **Freycinet Lodge** (Freycinet National Park, Tasmania): We can't praise this ecofriendly lodge enough. Comfortable one- and two-room cabins spread unobtrusively through the bush, connected by raised walking tracks. The main part of the lodge houses a lounge room and an excellent restaurant that sweeps out onto a veranda overlooking the limpid green waters of Great Oyster Bay. The lodge is right next to the white sands of Hazards Beach, and from here it's an easy stroll to the start of the Wineglass Bay walk. See Chapter 23.

✔ **Reef Retreat** (Cairns, Queensland): A low-rise collection of contemporary studios and suites built around a saltwater swimming pool in a peaceful grove of palms and silver Paperbarks, Reef Retreat has 36 units, including studios (which are much larger than the average hotel room and offer terrific value). See Chapter 17.

The Best Dining Experiences

From gloriously fresh seafood to traditional Australian "bush tucker," you'll find Australia's culinary offerings are as diverse as the landscape. Waves of immigration have brought tastes from around the world into the native cuisine, and you'll find ethnic restaurants all over. Don't forget to try the world-class wines, and hoist a brew or two!

✔ **Spirit House** (Yandina, Queensland): Walk along the jungle paths to the hidden building and you'll start to get an idea of what's in store at this amazing restaurant on the Sunshine Coast. Tables are set around a lagoon and among the trees, with massive statues and other artworks scattered throughout. The flavors that come out of this kitchen are mainly Thai but with other Asian influences. See Chapter 17.

✔ **Tetsuya's** (Sydney, New South Wales): Tetsuya's was named the fifth best restaurant in the world in *Restaurant Magazine*'s annual list of the world's 50 best eateries in 2007. So what makes Tetsuya's so good? On a recent visit, we secured a table next to the ceiling-to-floor windows and had an intimate view across a Japanese-inspired courtyard with maples and waterfall. The service is impeccable; the food, truly inspired. See Chapter 11.

✔ **e'cco bistro** (Brisbane, Queensland): Simple food, done exceptionally well and with passion. That's the winning philosophy behind the food at e'cco, one of Australia's top restaurants. Housed in a former tea warehouse on the city fringe, the bistro has large windows, bold colors, and modern furniture. Dishes include such delights as duck breast with Peking duck consommé, wombok, broccolini, chilli, and ginger; or grilled white fish with a cassoulet of white beans, clams, mussels, parsley, and peppers. See Chapter 16.

✔ **Mures Upper Deck** (Hobart, Tasmania): This large and bustling waterfront restaurant offers great views of bobbing yachts as well as very fine seafood caught on the owner's own fishing boats. I recommend starting with a bowl of the signature Mures Smokey Chowder or some local oysters. A real treat is the seafood platter. The best summer dessert is the restaurant's famous summer pudding, which almost bursts with berries. See Chapter 22.

The Best Museums

Australia charts its tumultuous history in some fine museums; here are a few of the ones we find most interesting:

✔ **National Museum of Australia** (Acton, Australian Capital Territory): Using state-of-the-art technology and hands-on exhibits, the museum concentrates on three themes: Australian society and its history since 1788; the interaction of people with the Australian environment; and Aboriginal and Torres Strait Islander cultures and histories. It relies more on images and sound than on historical objects to tell the stories. See Chapter 15.

✔ **The Australian Aviation Heritage Centre** (Darwin, Northern Territory): This museum has a B-52 bomber as its most prized exhibit but also boasts a B-25 Mitchell bomber, Mirage and Sabre jet fighters, and rare Japanese Zero fighter wreckage. Even if you aren't a military or aircraft buff, you may enjoy the funny, sad, heartwarming, and sometimes heart-wrenching displays on World War II and Vietnam. See Chapter 19.

✔ **The National Gallery of Victoria** (Melbourne, Victoria): The international branch of the National Gallery (in St. Kilda), and its Ian Potter Centre, off Federation Square, combine to offer a collection of international art, including works by Gainsborough, Constable, Bonnard, Delacroix, Van Dyck, El Greco, Monet, Manet, Magritte, and Rembrandt, and more than 20 rooms dedicated to Australian art. See Chapter 13.

The Best of Aboriginal Culture

Australia has many places in which you can learn more about the culture of the indigenous people who have lived on this land for millennia. The best places are in the Red Centre, at Alice Springs and Uluru-Kata

Tjuta, and in the Northern Territory. Some take the form of tours, others are cultural centers. Aboriginal art can also make a unique souvenir.

✔ You'll taste bush food, throw boomerangs, and learn about Aboriginal family values during a half-day tour of the Aborigine-owned **Aboriginal Art & Culture Centre** in Alice Springs. **Anangu Tours** run a series of walks around and near Uluru (Ayers Rock). The Anangu are the traditional owners of Uluru. Join them for walks around the Rock as you learn about the "snake men" who fought battles here, pick bush food off trees, throw spears, visit rock paintings, and watch the sun set. See Chapter 18.

✔ **Manyallaluk, The Dreaming Place,** is an Aboriginal community near Katherine, in the Northern Territory, which welcomes visitors and teaches them to paint, weave, throw boomerangs, and perform other tasks of daily life. It's a low-key day and the chance to chat one-on-one with Aboriginal people in their home. Mike Keighley of **Far Out Adventures** takes tours to Elsey Station (a ranch) near Katherine, where you can visit with the children of the Mangarrayi people, sample bush tucker, learn a little bush medicine, and swim in a natural "spa pool" in the Roper River. See Chapter 19.

✔ **Tjapukai Aboriginal Cultural Park,** in Cairns, is a multimillion-dollar center showcasing the history of the Tjapukai people — their Dreamtime creation history and their often-harrowing experiences since the white man arrived — using a film, superb theatrical work, and a dance performance. Its Aboriginal arts-and-crafts gift shop is one of the country's best, and there is also an outdoor "corroboree" experience at night. See Chapter 17.

✔ **Tandanya Aboriginal Cultural Institute** in the South Australian capital, Adelaide, is a good place to find out more about Aboriginal culture. At the Institute, they offer boomerang- and spear-throwing instruction, painting with natural ochers, discussions on Aboriginal culture, and guided walking tours. See Chapter 20.

The Best Natural Scenery

Australia offers some of the most diverse landscapes in the world. From long sweeps of pristine beach to the red dust of the Outback, the lush green rain forests of the Tropics, and rugged mountain ranges, somewhere you'll find a landscape to tear at your heart.

✔ The 74 islands of the **Whitsundays** are best seen from the deck of your own private yacht. Bareboat sailing (or skipper-yourself) is one of the most popular pastimes here, and it's easy to see why as you explore the deserted bays, snorkel over dazzling reefs, fish for coral trout, and feel the wind in your sails. It's on the same latitude as Tahiti, and on the same level of beauty. See Chapter 17.

✔ **Kata Tjuta** (the Olgas) and **Uluru** (Ayers Rock) are mysterious and magnetic. Uluru has an impact that's hard to describe — and even the photos you'll see won't prepare you for it. Just as awesome are the red domes of Kata Tjuta, just 50km (31 miles) from the Rock. These are even more significant to Aboriginal people than Uluru, and more intriguing to many visitors. See Chapter 18.

✔ Vast fields of **wildflowers** — pink, mauve, red, white, yellow, and blue — cover much of Western Australia every spring, from around August through October. Join the Australians who flock here for the spectacle, but make sure you book ahead. See Chapter 21.

The Best Places to Snorkel and Dive

It goes without saying that the best places to snorkel and dive in Australia are on the Great Barrier Reef, right? Well, not quite. It's true, but the important thing is to realize that Australia offers divers and snorkelers many other options, depending on which part of the country you're visiting. Second only to the Reef is the lesser-known Ningaloo Reef in Western Australia, so put that on your list, too.

✔ **Heron Island** is the top snorkel and dive site in Australia. If you stayed in the water for a week, you couldn't snorkel all the acres of coral stretching from shore. Take your pick of around 20 dive sites, about half of them within a 15-minute boat ride from the island's jetty: the Coral Cascades, with football trout and anemones; the Blue Pools, favored by octopus, turtles, and sharks; Heron Bommie, with its rays, eels, and more. See Chapter 17.

✔ Off **Cairns,** the gateway to the **Great Barrier Reef** for most people, are Moore, Norman, Hardy, Saxon, and Arlington reefs and Michaelmas and Upolu cays — all about 90 minutes by boat. You can explore them on a day trip from Cairns or join a live-aboard boat. Among the fabulous dive sites off **Port Douglas,** north of Cairns, are Split-Bommie, with its fan corals and schools of fusiliers; Barracuda Pass, with its coral gardens and giant clams; and the swim-through coral spires of the Cathedrals. See Chapter 17.

✔ **Lady Elliot Island,** off the Queensland coast near Bundaberg, is a coral cay island with gorgeous coral lagoons, perfect for snorkeling. Boats take you farther out to snorkel above manta rays, plate coral, and big fish. Divers can swim through the blowhole, 16m (52 ft.) down, and see gorgonian fans, soft and hard corals, sharks, barracudas, and reef fish. See Chapter 17.

The Best Wildlife Viewing

Australia's wildlife is unique. Isolation has given the continent some of the world's most unusual animals — the kangaroo, the platypus, and the koala to name just three. Add to that abundant birdlife, reptiles, and marine life and you've got more than enough to keep the most avid wildlife watchers happy.

✔ You'll see more native animals on South Australia's **Kangaroo Island** — including koalas, wallabies, birds, echidnas, reptiles, seals, and sea lions — than anywhere else in the country, apart from a wildlife park. And the distances between major points of interest are not great, so you won't spend half the day just getting from place to place. See Chapter 20.

✔ If cuddling a koala is high on your list, head to Brisbane's **Lone Pine Koala Sanctuary.** This is the world's first and largest koala sanctuary. Along with 130 koalas, lots of other Aussie wildlife — including wombats, Tasmanian devils, 'roos (which you can hand-feed), and colorful parakeets — are on show. You can even have your photo taken with a koala in your arms. See Chapter 16.

✔ **Kakadu National Park** in the Northern Territory is home to one-third of Australia's bird species. It's also the favored habitat of lots of **saltwater crocodiles,** which you can see on a cruise on the Yellow Water Billabong. See Chapter 19.

✔ Head into Queensland's World Heritage–listed **Wet Tropics Rainforest** behind Cairns or Port Douglas with **Wait-a-While Rainforest Tours** to spotlight possums, lizards, pythons, or even the shy and elusive **platypus.** Groups regularly spot the rare, bizarre Lumholtz's tree kangaroo. See Chapter 17.

The Best Beaches

Australia is blessed with thousands of beaches, some deserted and some more popular. So bring your *cozzie* (Australian for "swimsuit") and take the plunge!

✔ The sea is turquoise, the sun is warm, the palms sway, and the low-rise hotels beside **Four Mile Beach** can't spoil the feeling that it is a million miles from anywhere. But isn't there always a serpent in paradise? In this case, the "serpents" are North Queensland's seasonal, potentially deadly marine stingers. Come from June through September to avoid them. See Chapter 17.

✔ Azure water, islands dotting the horizon, and white sand edged by vine forests make **Mission Beach** a real winner. The bonus is that hardly anyone comes here. Cassowaries (giant emulike birds) hide in the rain forest, and the tiny town of Mission Beach makes itself invisible behind the leaves. See Chapter 17.

✔ Perth has 19 great beaches, but the petite crescent of **Cottesloe Beach** is the prettiest. After you've checked out the scene, join the fashionable set for brunch in the Indiana Tea House, a mock-Edwardian bathhouse fronting the sea. See Chapter 21.

The Best Places for a Bushwalk

✔ Many bushwalks in the **Blue Mountains National Park** offer awesome views of valleys, waterfalls, cliffs, and forest. You get to walk beneath dripping tree ferns, underneath pounding cascades, and through areas skirted by wilderness. All are easy to reach from Sydney. See Chapter 12.

✔ You can start from Alice Springs and walk the 250km (155-mile) semi-desert **Larapinta Trail,** which winds through the stark crimson McDonnell Ranges. You don't have to walk the entire length — plenty of day-length and multiday sections are possible. This one's for the cooler months only (Apr–Oct). See Chapter 18.

✔ Whether a wetlands stroll or an overnight hike in virgin bushland, you can find it in the World Heritage–listed **Kakadu National Park.** You'll see red cliffs, cycads, waterfalls, lagoons hiding man-eating crocodiles, what sometimes looks like Australia's entire bird population, and Aboriginal rock art. See Chapter 19.

✔ The 80km (50-mile) Overland Track between **Cradle Mountain & Lake St. Clair National Park** is arguably the best hike in Australia. The trek, from Cradle Mountain to Lake St. Clair, takes five to ten days, depending on your fitness level. Shorter walks, some lasting just half an hour, are also accessible. See Chapter 23.

Chapter 2

Digging Deeper into Australia

by Marc Llewellyn

- -

In This Chapter

▶ Checking out Australia's history
▶ Getting the lay of the land
▶ Meeting (and respecting) the unique animals
▶ Understanding the Aboriginals' role and today's diverse Australia

- -

*T*his chapter helps you find out more about Australia's history, culture, and people. Starting from prehistoric times, we give you a thumbnail sketch of Australian history, introduce some of the country's unique animals and landscapes, and talk about the people who make up the diverse Australian population. We also give you some tips on Australian cuisine and potent potables, because Australia is world famous (and rightly so!) for its fabulous beers and wines.

History 101: The Main Events

In the beginning, there was the **Dreamtime** — at least according to the Aborigines of Australia. Between then and now, perhaps, the supercontinent referred to as **Pangaea** split into two huge continents called **Laurasia** and **Gondwanaland.** Over millions of years, continental drift carried the landmasses apart. Gondwanaland divided into South America, Africa, India, Australia and New Guinea, and Antarctica. **Giant marsupials** evolved to roam the continent of Australia: Among them were a plant-eating animal that looked like a wombat the size of a rhinoceros; a giant squashed-face kangaroo standing 3m (10 ft.) high; and a flightless bird the same size as an emu, but four times heavier. The last of these giant marsupials is thought to have died out 40,000 years ago, possibly helped toward extinction by Aborigines.

The existence of Australia had been in the minds of Europeans since the Greek astronomer Ptolemy drew a map of the world in about A.D. 150

showing a large landmass in the south, which he believed had to be there to balance out the land in the Northern Hemisphere. He called it *Terra Australia Incognita* — the unknown southland.

Evidence suggests that Portuguese ships reached Australia as early as 1536 and even charted part of its coastline. In 1606, William Jansz was sent by the Dutch East India Company to open up a new route to the Spice Islands, and to find New Guinea, which was supposed to be rich in gold. Between 1616 and 1640, many more Dutch ships made contact with Australia as they hugged the west coast of "New Holland."

In 1642, the Dutch East India Company, through the governor general of the Indies, Anthony Van Diemen, sent Abel Tasman to find and map the southland. Over two voyages, he charted the northern Australian coastline and discovered Tasmania, which he named Van Diemen's Land.

Captain James Cook turned up in 1770 and charted the east coast in his ship H.M.S. *Endeavour*. He claimed the land for Britain and named it New South Wales, probably as a favor to Thomas Pennant, a Welsh patriot and botanist. Cook landed at Botany Bay, which he named after the discovery of scores of plants hitherto unknown to science. Turning northward, Cook passed an entrance to a possible harbor, which appeared to offer safe anchorage, and named it Port Jackson after the secretary to the admiralty, George Jackson. Back in Britain, King George III viewed Australia as a potential colony and repository of Britain's overflowing prison population, which could no longer be transported to the United States of America following the War of Independence.

The **First Fleet** left England in May 1787, made up of 11 store and transport ships (none of them bigger than the passenger ferries that ply modern-day Sydney Harbour) led by Arthur Phillip. Aboard were 1,480 people, including 759 convicts. Phillip's flagship, *The Supply,* reached Botany Bay in January 1788, but Phillip decided the soil was poor and the surroundings too swampy. On January 26, now celebrated as Australia Day, he settled on Port Jackson (Sydney Harbour) instead.

The convicts were immediately put to work clearing land, planting crops, and constructing buildings. The early food harvests were failures, and by early 1790, the fledgling colony was facing starvation.

Phillip decided to give some convicts pardons for good behavior and service, and grant small land parcels to those who were industrious. In 1795, coal was discovered; in 1810, Governor Macquarie began city building projects; and, in 1813, the explorers Blaxland, Wentworth, and Lawson forged a passage over the Blue Mountains to the fertile plains beyond.

When **gold** was discovered in Victoria in 1852, and in Western Australia 12 years later, hundreds of thousands of immigrants from Europe, America, and China flooded into the country. By 1860, over a million non-Aboriginal people were living in Australia.

The last 10,000 convicts were transported to Western Australia between 1850 and 1868, bringing the total shipped to Australia to 168,000.

On January 1, 1901, the six states that made up Australia proclaimed themselves to be part of one nation, and the **Commonwealth of Australia** was formed. In 1914, Australia joined the mother country in war. In April the following year, the Australian and New Zealand Army Corps (Anzac) formed a beachhead on the peninsula of Gallipoli in Turkey. The Turkish troops had been warned, and eight months of fighting ended with 8,587 Australian dead and more than 19,000 wounded.

Australians fought in World War II in North Africa, Greece, and the Middle East. In March 1942, Japanese aircraft bombed Broome in Western Australia and Darwin in the Northern Territory. In May 1942, Japanese midget submarines entered Sydney Harbour and torpedoed a ferry before being destroyed. Later that year, Australian volunteers fought an incredibly brave retreat through the jungles of Papua New Guinea on the Kokoda Track against much larger Japanese forces. Australian troops fought alongside Americans in subsequent wars in Korea and Vietnam and sent military support to the Persian Gulf conflicts.

Following World War II, mass immigration to Australia, primarily from Europe, boosted the population. In 1974 the left-of-center Whitlam government put an end to the White Australia policy that had largely restricted black and Asian immigration since 1901. In 1986, the Australian Constitution was separated from that of England.

In 1992, the High Court handed down the **"Mabo"** decision that ruled that Aborigines had a right to claim government-owned land if they could prove a continued connection with it.

The 2000 Olympic Games in Sydney put medal-winning Australian athletes Cathy Freeman and Ian Thorpe in the spotlight, and spurred a new wave of interest and tourism in the Land Down Under.

Australia is a modern nation coming to terms with its identity. The umbilical cord with Mother England has been cut, and the nation is still trying to find its position within Asia.

One thing Australia realized early on was the importance of tourism to its economy. Millions flock here every year. Factor in the landscape, the native Australian culture, the sunshine, the animals, and some of the world's best cities, and you've got a fascinating, accessible destination full of amazing diversity and variety.

Taking In Australia's Landscape

People wonder why such a huge country has a population of just 20 million people. The truth is, Australia can barely support that many. About 90 percent of those people live on only 2.6 percent of the continent.

Climatic and physical land conditions ensure that the only decent rainfall occurs along a thin strip of land around Australia's coast. It's been even tougher of late: Australia is in the grip of the worst drought in a century. The vast majority of Australia is harsh **Outback**. People survive where they can in this great arid land because of one thing: the **Great Artesian Basin.** This saucer-shaped geological formation stretches over much of inland New South Wales, Queensland, South Australia, and the Northern Territory. Beneath it are underground water supplies stored some 66 million to 208 million years ago, when the area was much like the Amazon basin is today. Bore holes bring water to the surface and allow sheep, cattle, and humans a respite from the dryness.

Just off the Queensland coast, The **Great Barrier Reef** stretches some 2,000km (1,240 miles) from off Gladstone, to the Gulf of Papua, near New Guinea. It's not more than 8,000 years old, although many fear that rising seawater, caused by global warming, will cause its demise. As it is, the nonnative Crown of Thorns starfish and a bleaching process believed to be the result of excessive nutrients flowing into the sea from Australia's farming land, is causing significant damage.

Meeting Australia's Unique Animals

Australia's isolation from the rest of the world over millions of years has led to the evolution of forms of life found nowhere else. Probably the strangest of all is the **platypus.** This *monotreme* (egg-laying marsupial) has webbed feet, a ducklike bill, and a tail like a beaver's. It lays eggs, and the young suckle from their mother. When a specimen was first brought back to Europe, skeptical scientists insisted it was a fake — a concoction of several different animals sewn together.

Then there's the **koala.** This fluffy marsupial eats virtually indigestible gum (eucalyptus) leaves and sleeps about 20 hours a day. There's only one koala species, although those found in Victoria are much larger than their brethren in more northern climes. Australia is also famous for **kangaroos.** There are 45 different kinds of kangaroos and wallabies, ranging from small rat-size kangaroos to the man-size red kangaroos.

The animal you're most likely to come across in your trip is the **possum,** named by Captain James Cook after the North American "opossum," which he thought they resembled. (They actually aren't related at all.) The brush-tailed possum is commonly found in suburban gardens, including those in Sydney. Then there's the **wombat.** There are four species of this bulky burrower in Australia, but the common wombat is most frequently found. You may come across the smaller hairy-nosed wombat in South Australia and Western Australia.

The **dingo,** thought by many to be a native of Australia, was, in fact, introduced — probably by Aborigines or traders from the north. They vary in color from yellow to a russet red and are despised by farmers. Commonly seen **birds** include the fairy penguin along the coast, black swans, parrots, cockatoos, and honeyeaters. **Tasmanian devils** can be found in — you guessed it — the island/state of Tasmania, though a virulent disease has decimated the wild population.

Snakes are common throughout Australia, but you'll rarely see one. The most dangerous land snake is the taipan, which hides in the grasslands in northern Australia. If, by the remotest chance, you're bitten by a snake, you must immediately immobilize the limb, wrapping it quite tightly (but not tight enough to restrict the blood flow) with a cloth or bandage, and head to the nearest hospital for antivenin.

There are two types of **crocodile** in Australia: the (relatively) harmless freshwater croc, which grows to 3m (10 ft.), and the dangerous estuarine (or saltwater) crocodile, which reaches 5 to 7m (16–23 ft.). Freshwater crocs eat fish; estuarine crocs aren't so picky.

Never swim in or stand on the bank of any river, swamp, or pool in northern Australia unless you know *for certain* it's croc-free.

Spiders are common all over Australia, with the funnel web spider and the red-back spider being the most aggressive. Funnel webs live in holes in the ground (they spin their webs around the hole's entrance) and stand on their back legs when they're about to attack. Red-backs have a habit of resting under toilet seats and in car trunks, generally outside the main cities. Caution is a good policy.

If you go bushwalking, check your body carefully. **Ticks** are common, especially in eastern Australia, and can cause severe itching and fever. If you find one on you, dab it with methylated spirits or another noxious chemical. Wait a while and pull it out gently with tweezers.

Fish to avoid are stingrays, porcupine fish, stonefish, lionfish, and puffer fish. Never touch an **octopus** if it has blue rings on it, or a cone shell, and be wary of the painful and sometimes deadly tentacles of the box **jellyfish** along the northern Queensland coast in summer. If you happen to brush past one of these creatures, pour vinegar over the affected site immediately — local authorities leave bottles of vinegar on the beach for this purpose. Vinegar deactivates the stingers that haven't already affected you, but doesn't affect the ones that already have.

In Sydney, you may come across "stingers" or "blue bottles" as they're also called. These long-tentacled blue jellyfish can inflict a nasty sting that can last for hours. Sometimes you'll see warning signs on patrolled beaches. The best remedy if you're stung is to wash the affected area with fresh water and have a hot bath or shower.

Meeting the People Down Under

It's thought that more races of people live in Australia than anywhere else in the world, including North America. High levels of immigration have led to people from some 165 nations making the country their home. In general, relations between the different groups have been peaceful. Today Australia is an example of a multicultural society, despite an increasingly vocal minority that believes that Australia has come too far in welcoming people from races other than their own.

The Aboriginal people

When Cook landed at Botany Bay to claim the land for the British Empire, at least 300,000 Aborigines were already on the continent. Whether you believe a version of history that suggests that the Aboriginal people were descendants of migrants from Indonesia, or the Aboriginal belief that they have occupied Australia since the beginning of time, there is scientific evidence that people were here at least 60,000 years ago.

At the time of the white "invasion" of their lands, there were at least 600 different, largely nomadic tribal communities, each linked to their ancestral land by **sacred sites** (certain features of the land, such as hills or rock formations). They were hunter-gatherers, spending about 20 hours a week harvesting the resources of the land, rivers, and the ocean. The rest of the time was taken up by a complex social and belief system, as well as by life's practicalities, such as making utensils, weapons, and musical instruments such as didgeridoos and clapsticks.

The basis of Aboriginal spirituality rests in the **Dreamtime** stories, in which spirits created everything — land, stars, mountains, the moon, the sun, the oceans, water holes, animals, and humans. Much Aboriginal art is related to their land and the sacred sites that are home to the Dreamtime spirits.

Dutch records from 1451 show that the Macassans, from islands now belonging to Indonesia, had a long relationship trading Dutch glass, pipes, and alcohol, for sea slugs from Australia's coastal waters, which they sold to the Chinese. Dutch, Portuguese, French, and Chinese vessels also encountered Australia — in fact, the Dutch fashion for pointy beards caught on long before the British First Fleet arrived in 1778.

When the British came, bringing their **diseases** with them, coastal communities were virtually wiped out by smallpox. As late as the 1950s, large numbers of Aborigines in remote regions succumbed to outbreaks of influenza and measles.

Although relationships between the settlers and local Aborigines were initially peaceful, conflicts over land and food soon led to skirmishes in which Aborigines were massacred and settlers and convicts attacked — Governor Phillip was speared in the back by an Aborigine in 1790.

Within a few years, some 10,000 Aborigines and 1,000 Europeans had been killed in Queensland alone, while in Tasmania, a campaign to rid the island entirely of Aborigines was successful, with the last full-blooded Tasmanian Aborigine dying in 1876. By the start of the 20th century, the Aboriginal people were considered a dying race. Most of them lived in government reservations or church-run missions.

Massacres of Aborigines continued to go largely or wholly unpunished into the 1920s, by which time it became government policy to remove light-skinned Aboriginal children from their families and to sterilize young Aboriginal women. Many children of the "stolen generation" were brought up in white foster homes or church refuges and never reunited with their biological families — many children with living parents were told that their parents were dead.

Today, there are some 283,000 Aborigines living in Australia, and, in general, a great divide still exists between them and the rest of the population. Aboriginal life expectancy is 20 years lower than that of other Australians, with overall death rates between two and four times higher. Aborigines make up the highest percentage of the country's prison population, and many Aborigines die while incarcerated.

A landmark in Aboriginal affairs occurred in 1992 when the High Court determined that Australia was not an empty land *(terra nullius)* as it had been seen officially since the British arrived. The **"Mabo" decision** resulted in the **1993 Native Title Act,** which allowed Aboriginal groups, and the ethnically distinct people in the Torres Strait islands, to claim government-owned land if they could prove continual association with it since 1788. The later **"Wik" decision** in 1996, determined that Aborigines could make claims on government land leased to agriculturists. The federal government, led by the right-leaning Prime Minister John Howard, curtailed these rights under pressure from farming and mining interests.

Issues currently facing the Aboriginal population include harsh mandatory sentencing laws, which came to international attention in 2000.

Added to this was the simmering issue of the federal government's decision not to apologize to the Aboriginal people for the "stolen generation." In March 2000, a government-sponsored report stated there was never a "stolen generation," while independent researchers believed that the report underestimated how many people were personally affected.

Before the Sydney 2000 Olympic Games, a popular movement involving people of all colors and classes called for reconciliation and an apology to the Aboriginal people. In Sydney, an estimated 250,000 people marched across the Sydney Harbour Bridge. The Liberal (which in Australia is actually a conservative party) Government refused to bow to public pressure. Despite threats of boycotts and rallies during the Olympics, the Games passed without major disturbance, and a worldwide audience watched as Aboriginal runner Cathy Freeman lit the Olympic cauldron.

How immigration has changed Australia's population

"White Australia" was a term used to distinguish the Anglo-Saxon population from the Aboriginal population, and until 1974 there existed a White Australia Policy — a result of conflict between European settlers and Chinese immigrants in the gold fields in the 1850s. This policy severely restricted the immigration of people who lacked European ancestry. These days, though, a walk through any of the major cities would show that things have changed dramatically.

About 100,000 people immigrate to Australia each year. Of these, the latest figures state that approximately 18 percent are from New Zealand, and 10 percent were born in the United Kingdom or Ireland. More than 28 percent hail from Asia, 6 percent from South Africa, and 2 percent from the United States and Canada.

Waves of immigration have brought in millions of people since the end of World War II. Results from the 2001 census show that more than 4.1 million Australian residents were born overseas — that's 22 percent of the population. New waves of immigration have come from countries such as Iraq and Somalia. So what's the typical Australian like? Well, he's hardly Crocodile Dundee.

Eating and Drinking in Australia

You can thank Australia's multicultural population for the fantastic cuisine developed over the past few decades. The food here is fresh and the chefs are innovative. Once a land of British-style "meat and three veg," Australia is now a place where you can get top-class food in any cuisine — Italian, Greek, Vietnamese, and other immigrants have seen to that.

The fusion of flavors and styles has melded into what's now commonly referred to as *Contemporary* or *Modern Australian* — a distinctive cuisine blending the spices of the East with the flavors of the West.

All about Australian wine

Winemaking has come a long way since the first grape vines were brought to Australia on the First Fleet in 1788. These days, more than 550 major companies and small winemakers produce world-class wines commercially in Australia. The demand for Australian wine overseas has increased so dramatically in the past few years that domestic prices have risen, and new vineyards are being planted at a frantic pace.

Of the white wines, big favorites include the fruity chardonnay and Riesling varieties, the herbaceous or grassy sauvignon blanc, and the dry sémillon. Of the reds, the dry cabernet sauvignon, the fruity merlot, the burgundy-type pinot noir, and the big and bold **Shiraz,** which has taken the world by storm, come out tops. Regions popular with wine-lovers include the Hunter Valley (New South Wales), the Barossa (South Australia), and Margaret River (Western Australia).

Australian for "beer," mate!

An Aussie likes nothing better on a hot day than a cold *tinnie* (can of beer). Barbecues would not be the same without a case of tinnies, or *stubbies* (small bottles).

Among the most popular Aussie beers are Victoria Bitter (known as VB), XXXX (pronounced "four-ex"), Fosters, and brews produced by the Tooheys company. Another popular choice is Cascade, a German-style beer that you'll usually find only in a bottle. It's light in color, strong in taste, and made from Tasmanian water straight off a mountain. If you want to get plastered, try Coopers — it's rather cloudy, very strong, and can cause a terrific hangover. Most Australian beers range from 4.8 percent to 5.2 percent alcohol.

In New South Wales (NSW), bars serve beer by the glass in a *schooner* or a smaller *midi* — though, in a few places, it's also served in British measurements, by pints and half pints. In Victoria you should ask for a *pot* or the smaller *glass.* In South Australia, a schooner is the size of a NSW midi, and in Western Australia a midi is the same size as a New South Wales midi, but a glass about half its size is called a *pony.* Confused? The easiest way to order is to point out the size you want.

Chapter 3

Deciding When and Where to Go

by Lee Mylne

In This Chapter

▶ Discovering Australia's major cities and regions
▶ Going opposite with the seasons
▶ Checking out Australia's calendar of events

*A*ustralia is a big country! Where do you start? For most people, it's Sydney. But Australia has much to offer, and after coming such a long way, you want to see as much as possible, even if your time is short. That said, trying to cram too much into your visit is a big mistake. You're better off settling on a couple of places and seeing them properly. Wherever you choose to explore, you'll have plenty to do; even small towns have a surprising amount to see. This chapter gives you the highlights of each region and lists the country's main events so you can work out the best time and place for your visit.

Going Everywhere You Want to Be

This book — of necessity — gives only the highlights of Australia. Covering it all is impossible. We concentrate on the major destinations, but we also tell you about the gems that abound in every part of the country. Yes, go to the Sydney Opera House and the Great Barrier Reef, but if you can, see some of the lesser-known attractions and meet the locals.

Most Australians live in coastal towns and cities, and it's in these that you'll likely stay. That said, getting into the Outback, which every state and territory has to some degree, is worth the effort. For many people, this is the "real" Australia — or at least one of the stereotypes. It shows you a side of Australia you won't see in the cities — both in the landscape and in the people.

Australia is blessed with one of the greatest natural attractions in the world: the Great Barrier Reef. It also has rain forests, mountains, wildflowers, wine country, fantastic scenic drives, bird-filled wetlands, and countless beautiful beaches.

Australia consists of six states — New South Wales (NSW), Queensland (QLD), Victoria (VIC), South Australia (SA), Western Australia (WA), and Tasmania (TAS) — and two internal territories, the Australian Capital Territory (ACT) and the Northern Territory (NT). The national capital is Canberra, in the ACT. We cover them all and hope that the following outline will help you decide which ones you want to visit.

Sydney and New South Wales

Most tourists come to Australia to see Sydney, and there's no denying it's one of the most spectacularly located cities in the world. Right on Sydney Harbour, with the iconic **Opera House** and **Harbour Bridge** framing the vast expanse of water, with dozens of harbor and ocean beaches in and around it, Sydney is hard to beat! It's also a good base for day trips or overnight excursions inland, especially to the scenic **Blue Mountains** and the wineries of the **Hunter Valley.**

A string of pretty beachside towns stretches down the southern coast of New South Wales to Victoria. North of Sydney is remnant rain forest and a more tropical air in the laid-back hangout of **Byron Bay.**

Inland highlights include the mining town of **Broken Hill** (known for wildlife, art galleries, and Aboriginal influences), and Outback opal-mining towns **White Cliffs** and **Lightning Ridge,** which exist in a wacky underground world of their own.

Melbourne and Victoria

Don't try to compare **Melbourne** with Sydney. There's an old rivalry between Australia's two largest cities, but they're worlds apart. Melbourne, the capital of Victoria, is more stately and old-world. It offers an exciting mix of ethnicities and the country's best fashion shopping. Victoria is also the site of one of Australia's great road trips, the **Great Ocean Road,** which stretches for 106km (66 miles) along the southern coast. Then there's the **inland High Country,** the stamping ground of the title character in Banjo Paterson's 1890 poem "The Man from Snowy River."

Canberra and the Australian Capital Territory

Surrounded by New South Wales is the Australian Capital Territory (ACT), home to the national capital, **Canberra.** A planned city similar in architectural concept to Washington, D.C., Canberra is surrounded by bushland and is home to some of the country's best national museums.

Australia

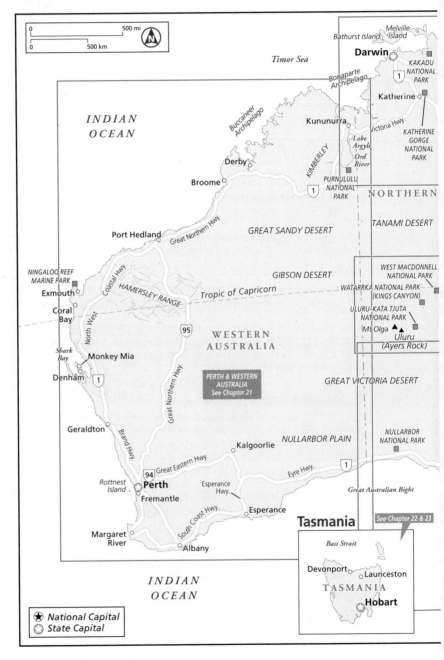

0 500 mi
0 500 km

Timor Sea

INDIAN OCEAN

Bathurst Island | Melville Island

Darwin

KAKADU NATIONAL PARK

Bonaparte Archipelago

Katherine

Buccaneer Archipelago

Kununurra

Victoria Hwy.

KATHERINE GORGE NATIONAL PARK

Lake Argyle

Ord River

Derby

KIMBERLEY

Broome

PURNULULU NATIONAL PARK

NORTHERN

TANAMI DESERT

Port Hedland

Great Northern Hwy.

GREAT SANDY DESERT

WEST MACDONNELL NATIONAL PARK

NINGALOO REEF MARINE PARK

Coastal Hwy.

GIBSON DESERT

WATARRKA NATIONAL PARK (KINGS CANYON)

Exmouth

HAMERSLEY RANGE

Tropic of Capricorn

Coral Bay

North West Coastal Hwy.

ULURU–KATA TJUTA NATIONAL PARK

Mt Olga

Uluru (Ayers Rock)

Shark Bay

Monkey Mia

95

WESTERN AUSTRALIA

Denham

1

PERTH & WESTERN AUSTRALIA See Chapter 21

GREAT VICTORIA DESERT

Geraldton

Great Northern Hwy.

Brand Hwy.

NULLARBOR PLAIN

NULLARBOR NATIONAL PARK

94

Great Eastern Hwy.

Kalgoorlie

Rottnest Island

Perth

Esperance Hwy.

Eyre Hwy.

1

Great Australian Bight

Fremantle

Esperance

Tasmania

See Chapter 22 & 23

South Coast Hwy.

Margaret River

Albany

INDIAN OCEAN

Bass Strait

Devonport

Launceston

TASMANIA

Hobart

★ National Capital
◯ State Capital

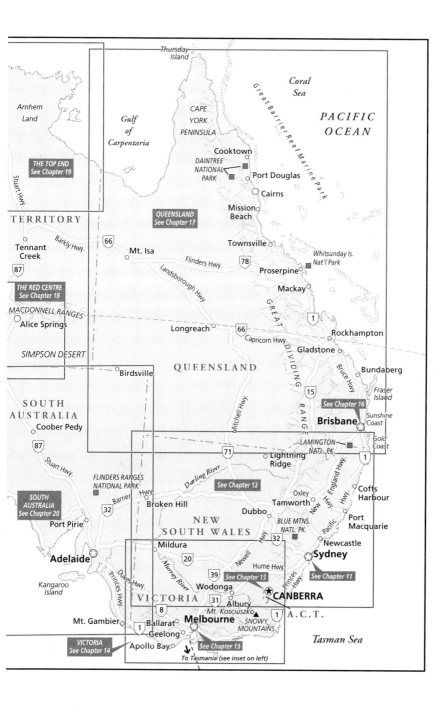

Brisbane, Queensland, and the Great Barrier Reef

Brisbane is a fun city to stay in and explore, as well as a great jumping-off point for the **Great Barrier Reef,** which stretches more than 2,000km (1,240 miles) along the coast. Alluring island resorts dot the coast — most rather expensive, but worth the money.

Queensland is also known for its lovely white-sand beaches. Many of the best and most accessible strands are on the **Gold Coast** in the state's south (about an hour's drive from the state capital, Brisbane), and the **Sunshine Coast** (a two-hour drive north of Brisbane).

Cairns and Port Douglas in the far north have their fair share of beaches, too, but swimming in their waters can be *very* hazardous to your health because deadly box jellyfish, or *stingers,* inhabit them from October through May, when you should stick to the waterfront lagoons at Airlie Beach and Cairns, or to your hotel pool. The jellyfish are mainly found in coastal waters and do not interfere with Great Barrier Reef activities like snorkeling or diving. Island swimming is mostly stinger-free, but be careful and ask a lifeguard before plunging into that inviting water.

Among the most appealing of Queensland's destinations are the 74 **Whitsunday Islands** in the Great Barrier Reef Marine Park. These mostly uninhabited islands are a paradise for sailing, as well as kayaking, snorkeling, diving, fishing, hiking, and bird-watching.

Another big attraction is the lush 110-million-year-old **Daintree Rainforest,** north of Port Douglas.

The Red Centre

The majestic presence of **Uluru,** also known as Ayers Rock, is what draws everyone to the ocher sands of the Red Centre, the heart of the Northern Territory. Many visitors discover that the lesser-known nearby domes of **Kata Tjuta,** or "the Olgas," are even more spectacular. A half-day's drive from the Rock brings you to **Kings Canyon,** a spectacular desert gorge. If you visit the Red Centre, try to spend at least a few days in **Alice Springs,** a laid-back Outback town with much to offer. It has Aboriginal arts and crafts, Aboriginal tours, a world-class desert wildlife park, hiking through the stark **MacDonnell Ranges,** and camel rides along a dry riverbed.

The Top End

The northwest reaches of the country encompass what Aussies call the Top End. This is a remote, vast, semidesert region where the cattle probably outnumber the people. The tropical city of **Darwin** is the Territory's capital. A few hours' drive will bring you to **Kakadu National Park,** where you can cruise past crocodiles on inland *billabongs* (ponds), bird-watch, and visit ancient Aboriginal rock-art sites.

Perth and Western Australia

Making it to Western Australia, one of Australia's most wild and beautiful regions, is worth the trouble. The seas teem with whales in season, and thrill-seekers can swim alongside gigantic but gentle whale sharks on the Northwest Cape every fall (Mar–June). The state's capital, **Perth,** has surf beaches. Nearby is the restored 19th-century port of **Fremantle.** In the southwest is the **Margaret River wine region,** punctuated by wild forests, thundering surf, cliffs, rich bird life, and kangaroos.

Adelaide and South Australia

Lying between Western Australia and Victoria is South Australia. The stately capital, **Adelaide,** is known for its conservatism, parks, and churches. It is an ideal base for exploring Australia's illustrious wine region, the **Barossa Valley,** dotted with big-name winemakers such as Penfolds, Seppelts, and Wolf Blass, all less than an hour from the city!

The greatest of South Australia's attractions — apart from wine — is **Kangaroo Island,** a place alive with native animals: wallabies, kangaroos, echidnas, koalas, sea lions and all sorts of birds, from black swans to kookaburras to penguins.

Tasmania

Last stop before Antarctica! Australia's lovely island state is best known for its beautiful national parks, expanses of alpine wilderness, ancient forests, and magnificent trout fishing. The capital is **Hobart,** a former penal town. If you're up for it, you could tackle the **Overland Track,** an 85km (53-mile) hiking trail between **Cradle Mountain** and **Lake St. Clair** that passes through highland moors, dense rain forests, and several mountains. A more leisurely option is a visit to the stone ruins of **Port Arthur,** where thousands of convicts brought in to settle the new British colony were imprisoned and died. All of Tasmania is spectacular, but you haven't seen anything until you've experienced **Freycinet National Park,** with its pink granite outcrops set against an emerald-green sea.

Scheduling Your Time

When planning your trip to Australia, keep reminding yourself that this is a huge continent with long distances between many major attractions. Australia is as big as Western Europe and about the same land mass as the 48 contiguous states of the United States. You'll most likely start your trip in Sydney, and from there it's a long day's drive (or two) to either Brisbane in the north or Melbourne to the south; Western Australia is a week's drive from Sydney!

Take into account how much time you have, and then prioritize your sightseeing. *Remember:* Even some domestic flights can take three hours (or more if you're going west), so don't try to do too much or you'll be exhausted. The better your planning, the more you'll enjoy your discovery of the best Australia has to offer.

Revealing the Secrets of the Seasons

Keep in mind that, when it's summer in the Northern Hemisphere, it's winter Down Under. So the peak travel season in the most popular parts of Australia is the Southern Hemisphere winter (June–Aug). Happily, airfares to Australia offered by U.S. airlines are usually lowest from mid-April to late August — the best time to visit the Red Centre, the Top End, and the Great Barrier Reef.

In much of the country — Queensland from around Townsville and northward, all of the Top End and the Red Centre, and most of Western Australia — the most pleasant time to travel is April through September, when daytime temperatures are 66°F to 88°F (19°C–31°C) and it rarely rains. June, July, and August are the busiest months in these parts; you'll need to book accommodations and tours well in advance, and you'll pay higher rates then, too.

Australia's summer is a nice time to visit the southern states — New South Wales, Victoria, South Australia, Western Australia from Perth to the south, and Tasmania. Even in winter, temperatures rarely dip below freezing, and snow falls only in parts of Tasmania, in the ski fields of Victoria, and in the Snowy Mountains of southern New South Wales.

The best months to visit Australia are September and October, when it's often still warm enough to enjoy the southern states, it's cool enough to tour Uluru (Ayers Rock), the wildflowers are in full bloom in Western Australia, and the humidity and rains have not come to Cairns and the Top End (although it will be very hot by Oct).

In summer (Oct–Mar), you can expect it to be hot, humid, and wet (or all three) if you're touring the Red Centre, the Top End, and Western Australia except Perth and the southwest. The Top End, the Kimberley, and North Queensland, including Cairns, are intensely hot and humid in the Wet season from November or December through March or April. In the Top End and Kimberley, the Wet season is preceded by a sticky build-up period in October and November. Some attractions close, floodwaters render others off-limits, and hotels drop their rates, often dramatically. So if you decide to travel in these areas at this time — and lots of people do — be prepared to take the heat, possible floods, and, in tropical coastal areas, the slight chance of cyclones.

Australia's summer holidays run from about mid-December to the end of January, when schools close and families head off on their vacations. Book well ahead if you're traveling then. The school year in Australia is usually broken into four semesters, with two-week holidays around Easter, the last week of June and the first week of July, and the last week of September and the first week of October.

Perusing a Calendar of Events

Almost everything shuts down on Good Friday, Christmas Day, and Boxing Day (Dec 26), and much is closed January 1, Easter Sunday, and Easter Monday. Most establishments close until 1 p.m., if not all day, on Anzac Day (Apr 25), a World War I commemorative day.

January

The Sydney Festival, a major performing arts festival, runs for most of January and features free jazz or classical music concerts held outdoors on two Saturday nights near the Royal Botanic Gardens. Take a picnic and arrive by 4 p.m. to get a good spot. Call ☎ **02/8248 6500** or check www.sydneyfestival.org.au for more details. First to third weeks in January.

In Perth, players from the world's top nine tennis nations line up for the **Hyundai Hopman Cup,** a seven-day mixed-doubles competition in late December/early January. For tickets, contact **Ticketek** (☎ **13 28 49** in Australia; www.ticketek.com), or check www.hopmancup.com.au. End of December to early January.

The whole country celebrates **Australia Day,** a public holiday on January 26. Australia Day marks the landing of the First Fleet of convicts at Sydney Cove in 1788. Every town puts on some kind of celebration; in Sydney, there are ferry races and tall ships in the harbor, food and wine stalls in Hyde Park, open days at museums and other attractions, and fireworks in the evening.

February

The Sydney Gay & Lesbian Mardi Gras (☎ **02/9568 8600;** www.mardi gras.org.au), a month-long event corresponding roughly to the dates of actual Mardi Gras, culminates in a spectacular parade of costumed dancers and decorated floats, watched by several hundred thousand onlookers, followed by a giant invitation-only warehouse party. Late February and/or early March.

March

Melbourne hosts the **Australian Formula One Grand Prix,** the first Grand Prix of the year on the international FIA Formula One World Championship circuit, over four days in March. For tickets, contact **Ticketek** (☎ **13 28 49** in Australia) or order online at http://cars. grandprix.com.au. First or second week of March.

April

Anzac Day is Australia's national day of mourning for servicepeople who have died in wars and conflict. It is a public holiday, but many attractions open in the afternoon. Moving services are held around the country, even in the smallest towns. Some are held at dawn, others later in the morning. Wreaths are laid in memory of the dead, from World War I onward. In major cities, there is usually a public parade of returned servicepeople through the streets. Huge crowds turn out to honor them. April 25.

May

For a real Outback experience, head to the **Back to the Never Never Festival** in Mataranka, about 100 km (62 miles) south of Katherine in the Northern Territory. Equestrian events, including a gymkhana, polocrosse (a cross between polo and lacrosse) matches, and a rodeo, are highlights. There's live entertainment on Saturday night and a Bushman's Breakfast for all comers on Sunday morning. For more details, contact the **Mataranka Community Government Council** (☎ 08/8975 4576; e-mail: council@mataranka.nt.gov.au). Usually held on the third weekend of May.

June

World and Australian premieres of Aussie and international movies take place in the State Theatre and other venues during the **Sydney Film Festival** (☎ 02/9318 0999; www.sydneyfilmfestival.org), held for two weeks from the first or second Friday in June.

July

The quirky **Imparja Camel Cup** (☎ 08/8952 6796; www.camelcup.com.au), held each year in Alice Springs, may be a nightmare for the riders, but it's great entertainment for spectators. Nine camel races are held around the dusty outback track throughout the day, with other entertainment including belly dancers, rickshaw rides, and more. Mid-July.

August

Sydneysiders by the thousands pound the pavement in the 14km (8 ¾-mile) **City to Surf** "fun run" from the city to Bondi Beach. For details, visit www.city2surf.sunherald.com.au (from June onward) or call ☎ 1800/555 514 in Australia. If slots are available, you can enter on race day. Second Sunday in August.

September

A million tulips, daffodils, hyacinths, and other blooms carpet the banks of Canberra's Lake Burley Griffin in stunning themed flower-bed designs during the annual **Floriade,** which features performing arts and other entertainment. Contact **Canberra & Region Visitors Centre** (☎ 1300/ **554 114** in Australia; www.visitcanberra.com.au) or check out the Web site www.floriadeaustralia.com. The festival runs for a month starting about mid-September.

October

The world's best Indy-car drivers race a street circuit around Surfers Paradise on the Queensland's Gold Coast for the **Lexmark Indy 300,** as part of the international FedEx Championship champ car motor-sport series. Contact **Ticketek** (☎ **1300/303 103** in Australia; www.ticketek. com), or check the event's Web site (www.indy.com.au). The carnival runs for four days in mid- or late October.

November

On the first Tuesday of November, Australia stops to watch its most famous horse race, the **Melbourne Cup.** Those who are not actually at Melbourne's Flemington racecourse to watch the A$3.5-million (US$2.8-million/£1.4-million) race, are glued to the TV or radio! It's a public holiday in Melbourne. For tickets, contact **Ticketmaster** (☎ **1300/136 122** in Australia; www.ticketmaster.com.au); for information, visit www.vrc.net.au.

December

On **New Year's Eve,** if you're in Sydney, the best entertainment is watching the Sydney Harbour Bridge light up with fireworks. The main show is at 9 p.m., not midnight, so children don't miss out. Pack a picnic and snag a harbor-side spot by 4 p.m., or even earlier at the best vantage point — Mrs. Macquarie's Chair in the Royal Botanic Gardens. December 31.

Chapter 4

Following an Itinerary: Four Great Options

by Marc Llewellyn and Lee Mylne

In This Chapter

▶ Seeing Australia's top attractions in one or two weeks
▶ Visiting Australia with kids
▶ Tasting wines and smelling the wildflowers in Western Australia

*P*lanning a trip to Australia is a daunting task, simply because of the distances you have to cover. For visitors from the Northern Hemisphere, it's a long way to come for just a week, but if that's all you can spare, you still want to see as much as possible. Our inclination is to immerse ourselves in one spot and soak it up, but we know that not everyone wants to do that. Seeing as much as you can is often a priority, especially when you've invested so much in getting here.

First-time visitors, with a week or two to explore, may find the first couple of itineraries most helpful. We've put together some suggestions for seeing the best of Australia in one or two weeks. You can, of course, fiddle with them to suit your own interests — for example, you could substitute the Cairns section of the one-week itinerary for the Uluru/Red Centre days in the two-week itinerary, flying from Sydney to Uluru.

If you've been to Australia, or you've already visited Sydney, the Great Barrier Reef, or Uluru (Ayers Rock), you may want explore places a little more off the beaten track. If you're bringing the young ones, our itinerary for traveling with kids may give you some ideas for the kids (without forgetting the parents).

Getting around this vast continent, where the major attractions are thousands of miles apart, is time-consuming. Flying is the only way to cover long distances efficiently, but it can also be expensive. Remember to allow flying time in your itineraries and don't try to pack too much in on the days you fly — even domestic flights can be around three hours and can be quite draining.

Our best tip is this: If the pace gets too hectic, just chill out and reorder your sightseeing priorities. Take time to meet the locals and ask their advice on what you should see as well. Australia is complex and fascinating place, and in a week or two you'll only just scratch the surface of everything it can offer.

Seeing Australia's Highlights in One Week

Careful planning will maximize the number of things you can see in a short time, but try not to overschedule yourself. Concentrate on a few things — perhaps one city and/or one of the natural wonders — and you'll go home having had a memorable time. Australians are a laid-back lot, generally, and in many places the pace is relaxed.

Use this one-week itinerary to make the most of a short time. One week provides barely enough time to see the best of Sydney, which for most people is their first stop. Your spectacular introduction to the city may well be from the window of your plane as you fly over the Sydney Harbour Bridge and the Opera House.

If you have only a week and want to head farther afield, there are two main choices, depending on your interests. The Great Barrier Reef is a "must" for divers, but don't forget that you must allow time on either side of your reef trip for flying (you can't fly within 24 hours of scuba diving). There are no such problems with Australia's other icon, Uluru (Ayers Rock), in the heart of the Red Centre. This well-travelled triangle of Sydney–Cairns–Uluru gives you a complete Australian experience.

On **Day One,** check into your **Sydney** hotel and start the jetlag-recovery process. If you arrive in the morning and have a full day ahead of you, try to stay up and hit the nearest cafe for a shot of caffeine to keep you going. Head to **Circular Quay,** where you'll have a fantastic view of **Sydney Harbour Bridge.** Then stroll over to the **Sydney Opera House** and soak up some history at **The Rocks.** If you have time, you can take the ferry from Circular Quay to **Manly** beach to round off a fairly relaxed day with fish and chips, and then get some much-needed sleep.

Start **Day Two** with a ride to the top of the **Sydney Tower** to experience Sydney's highest attraction, **Skywalk,** a breathtaking 260 meters (853 ft.) above the city. Harnessed onto a moving, glass-floored viewing platform that extends out over the edge of the tower, you can view it all — the Harbour Bridge, Opera House, Sydney Harbour, all the way to the **Blue Mountains.** It's not as scary as it sounds. Sydney Tower has several attractions, including **OzTrek** — a simulator ride the kids will love.

Then head to **Taronga Zoo** or the **Sydney Aquarium** for an introduction to Australia's wildlife. If you enjoy museums, put the **Australia Museum,** the **Australian National Maritime Museum** at Darling Harbour, or the **Powerhouse Museum** on your list. To learn more about Sydney's origins as a convict settlement, visit the **Hyde Park Barracks Museum,** a convict-built prison. Finish off your day with a twilight (or later on weekends) **Bridge Climb** or take the kids to **Luna Park,** a small traditional amusement park that's at its best when lit up at night.

On **Day Three,** take a day trip to the **Blue Mountains.** Take the train from Sydney's Central Station to **Katoomba,** two hours from Sydney. Then jump on the Blue Mountains Explorer Bus, which allows you to hop on and off wherever you please. There are also many day tours leaving from Sydney. Don't miss the spectacular **Three Sisters** rock formations, best viewed from Echo Point Road at Katoomba. If you're adventurous, you may want to take a tour from Katoomba to the **Jenolan Caves,** about a 90-minute drive southwest. Head back to Sydney and have dinner somewhere with a view of the harbor.

On **Day Four,** take the earliest flight you can from Sydney to **Cairns** to begin your discovery of the **Great Barrier Reef.** Flight time is three hours, which will wipe out most of your morning. On arrival, check into a hotel in the city center, which, on such a tight schedule, will make getting to the major attractions quicker and easier than staying on the northern beaches. Explore the city a little and see some wildlife — including a massive saltwater crocodile — in the bizarre setting of the **Cairns Rainforest Dome,** atop the Hotel Sofitel Reef Casino. You'll have time the rest of the day to head out to visit the **Tjapukai Aboriginal Cultural Park.** If you aren't going to the Red Centre, this is a great place to learn about Aboriginal culture and life, albeit in a theme-park way. You could also save the visit for the evening, when **Tjapukai by Night** tours give a different look at traditional ceremonies, including dinner and a fire-and-water outdoor show.

On **Day Five,** take a day trip to the **Great Barrier Reef.** Tour boats leave from the Reef Fleet Terminal, and the trip to the outer reef takes about two hours. After you're there, you'll spend your day on a pontoon with about 300 people (or in the water!). Experienced divers may prefer to take a day trip with one of the dive charter companies that take smaller groups and visit two or three reefs. The pontoons of the big operators also offer the chance to take a scenic flight — a spectacular experience. Divers must spend another 24 hours in Cairns before flying. If you're content to snorkel, ride the glass-bottom boats, and soak up the sun, you can fly out the next day. Back in Cairns, take a stroll along the Esplanade and eat at one of the busy cafes and restaurants that line the strip.

If you can't fly on **Day Six** consider a trip to the rain forest. Head for the mountain village of **Kuranda** aboard the steam train along the **Kuranda Scenic Railway,** past waterfalls and gorges. In Kuranda, explore the markets and the nature parks, and maybe take a **Kuranda Riverboat Tour,** which runs about 45 minutes. Make your return journey on the **Skyrail** cableway, which carries you over the rain forest (you can get to ground level at a couple of stations on the way) to the edge of Cairns, and provides sensational views of the coast and mountains.

Or, you could head to the World Heritage–listed **Daintree Rainforest,** two hours' drive north of Cairns. Many tour operators, including Port Douglas–based **Heritage & Interpretive Tours,** run day tours into the Daintree and Cape Tribulation national parks. If you're exploring on your own, make time for a one-hour cruise on the **Daintree River** with **Dan Irby's Mangrove Adventures,** where you'll travel in a small open boat and see lots of fascinating wildlife.

If you choose the Daintree option, overnight in the lovely resort town of **Port Douglas** and head to one of its great restaurants — **Salsa Bar & Grill** has a relaxed and lively atmosphere, and terrific food.

Unless you have a flight directly out of Cairns, you'll spend most of **Day Seven,** your last day in Australia, returning to Sydney. With the time you have left, treat yourself to dinner at a restaurant overlooking the harbor, with its bridge and the Opera House illuminated — it's a sight you'll always remember.

Seeing More of Australia in Two Weeks

You can make your visit much more relaxed if you have two weeks to spend. In two weeks, you have time to see all three icons — Sydney, the Great Barrier Reef, and Uluru — in more depth, and maybe even have time to go outside those areas if you see just two of the "Big Three."

For the first week, follow the itinerary in the preceding section. But instead of catching a plane from Cairns back to Sydney, on **Day Seven** take a flight to **Uluru (Ayers Rock).**

Leave Cairns as early as you can (this will probably mean spending the night in Cairns rather than Port Douglas). Your flight to Ayers Rock Airport will take around three hours or more. Make sure you book a direct flight, and not one that goes via Sydney! And make sure you remember to ask for a window seat, because the views as you fly over the Outback will be like nothing you've seen before.

If you take the early flight, you can be in **Uluru** by around 9 a.m., which gives you the whole day to take in the enormity of this fabulous mono-lith. Take the shuttle from Ayers Rock Resort to the Rock. If you decide to climb Uluru (remembering that the Aboriginal traditional owners would prefer you didn't), make sure you don't do it at the hottest time of day. A climb will take you between two and four hours, depending on your fitness. An alternative is to join **Anangu Tours** for a walk around it; one of the best is the late-afternoon Kuniya walk, which concludes with watching sunset over Uluru — an unforgettable sight. Spend some time in the impressive and interesting **Uluru-Kata Tjuta Cultural Centre** near the base of Uluru. And after doing all that in a day, you'll be ready for a quiet dinner at whatever hotel you've chosen to stay in.

Make the effort to get up for sunrise on **Day Eight.** This is one of the most magic times at Uluru, and is also a great time to do the 9.6km (6-mile) Base Walk circumnavigating Uluru, which takes two to three hours. There are a range of other ways to experience Uluru, including camel rides, Harley-Davidson tours, and helicopter joy-flights, but walking up close to the Rock beats them all, in our opinion. You'll also have time on Day Eight to head to **Kata Tjuta** (also called the Olgas) where you'll see that there is much more to the Red Centre than just one Rock. Kata Tjuta is about 48km (30 miles) west of Uluru, but plenty of tours go there if you don't have your own wheels. End your day in the desert with the **Sounds of Silence** dinner, run by Ayers Rock Resort. Sip champagne as the sun sets over Uluru, to the eerie music of the didgeridoo, then tuck into kangaroo, barramundi, and other native foods. But it's not the food you're here for — it's the silence and the stars. A short stargazing session with an astronomer ends a memorable evening.

On **Day Nine,** rent a four-wheel-drive and tackle the trip from Uluru to Alice Springs, stopping for a night at **Kings Canyon.** It is 306km (190 miles) from Uluru to Kings Canyon (also known as **Watarrka National Park**), which offers another unbeatable look at Outback Australia. You can spend the afternoon walking up the canyon and around the rim. It's very steep, and it'll take you around four hours. A gentler walk is the short and shady canyon floor walk. Stay over at the Kings Canyon Resort.

On **Day Ten,** start out early for **Alice Springs,** and take the unpaved but interesting **Mereenie Loop Road,** which leads you through the **Glen Helen Gorge** or the historic **Hermannsburg** mission settlement. Whichever road you take, the scenery is like nowhere else in Australia. You'll probably spend most of the day driving to Alice.

On arrival, check into a hotel and head out to one of the local restaurants, several of which offer sophisticated versions of bush tucker including kangaroo, emu, and crocodile dishes.

If you can stand another early start, on **Day 11,** take a **dawn balloon flight** over the desert, usually followed by a champagne breakfast. If you don't head back to bed for a few hours of catch-up sleep, there are plenty of attractions, including the **Alice Springs Desert Park** for a look at some unusual Australian creatures, the **School of the Air,** and the **Royal Flying Doctor Service** base. In the afternoon, take a half-day tour with an Aboriginal guide at the **Aboriginal Art & Culture Centre.** Alternatively, visit the **Alice Springs Telegraph Station Historical Reserve** set in an oasis just outside town for a look at early settler life. Finish the day with a **sunset camel ride** down the dry Todd River bed and have dinner at the camel farm.

On **Day 12,** fly back to Sydney. Direct flights from Alice Springs to Sydney leave in the early afternoon, so you have all morning to explore more of the town and perhaps buy some Aboriginal art. On arrival in

Sydney after an almost three-hour flight, check into your hotel and spend the night discovering some of the city's nightlife.

On **Day 13,** hit Sydney's famous beach, **Bondi.** Take the Bondi Explorer bus from Circular Quay, which gives you a choice of harbor-side bays and coastal beaches, or take the train to Bondi Junction and then a bus to the beach. Spend the day lazing on the sand or — in summer, at least — taking a dip in the surf. For the more energetic, the scenic cliff-top walk to **Bronte Beach,** or further on to **Coogee,** is worth doing.

Spend **Day 14** doing that last-minute shopping or seeing the Sydney sights you haven't had time for so far. Round it off with a fabulous seafood dinner somewhere with a fantastic view of the Harbour Bridge.

Discovering Australia with Kids

Australia is an unbelievable destination for kids — and not just for the kangaroos and koalas that almost every child (and parent!) wants to see. Our suggestion is to explore Sydney for two days with family in tow, and then head up to the Blue Mountains on a day trip to ride the cable car and the world's steepest railway. The climax comes with a few days exploring the Barrier Reef and the rain forest around Port Douglas.

On **Day One,** first off, head to Circular Quay to see the **Sydney Opera House.** A tour inside may be a bit much for younger kids, but you can walk around it. Go from here to the **Royal Botanic Gardens** to spot hundreds of fruit bats squabbling among the treetops. After lunch, take a ferry to **Taronga Zoo.** All the kids' favorites are here, from kangaroos and koalas to platypuses. A farmyard section edges onto a playground of sorts with lots of water features to give your kids a sprinkle on a hot day. On **Day Two** head to **Sydney Tower,** then on to **Sydney Aquarium,** where huge sharks swim right above your head.

On **Day Three,** take a day trip to the Blue Mountains. Several companies run tour buses to the area, stopping off at an animal park along the way. The best one is **Featherdale,** where you can get up close to kangaroos, koalas, and Tasmanian devils. The tour will also stop at Scenic World, where you can take the short ride on the **Scenic Railway.** It's very steep, so hold on tight. At the bottom you'll find yourselves in an ancient **tree fern forest** — it's remarkable. A short walk takes you to the **Skyway,** a cable car that goes 300m (984 ft.) above the Jamison Valley.

Now it's time to head north, up the Tropics. On **Day Four,** you need to fly to your Queensland destination, because it would take you several days to drive up the coast. Most people base themselves in **Port Douglas** rather than Cairns, because the beach is huge and uncrowded and some of the best trips originate from here. On **Day Five,** it's time to visit the **Reef.** Cruise boats take around 90 minutes to get from Port Douglas to the outer Reef, but after you're there, you're in for some amazing snorkeling. On **Day Six,** head (slightly) inland to explore **Daintree National Park** and the **Cape Tribulation Rainforests.** Usually included in the tour is a boat trip among the local crocodiles.

On **Day Seven,** you fly back to Sydney, and if you have time, take the kids by ferry to **Luna Park,** or walk there across the Harbour Bridge. The fun park is small, with a few rides suitable for younger kids, but it does boast a magnificent view across to the Harbour Bridge and Opera House, which look glorious after the sun's gone down.

Wining and Dining (and Wildflowers) in Margaret River, Western Australia

Getting to see more of Australia than its most famous icons and the East Coast beaches is not always easy. But if you have the time, there are many wonderful places off the beaten track, which will give another dimension to your image and memories of Australia. Here, we suggest a few days in the Margaret River region, a few hours' drive south of the Western Australia capital, Perth. You can add it on to the end of a week or so in the east, or change it with the latter part of the one- or two-week itineraries earlier in this chapter. You can fly to Western Australia from any of the other destinations, and you *should* fly, because it's a week's drive from Sydney to Perth!

Each year from August to mid-November, the southern half of Western Australia is blessed with a carpet of 12,000 species of white, yellow, mauve, pink, red, and blue **wildflowers.** Wildflower shows and festivals in country towns throughout the state accompany the annual blossoming. September and October are the peak months.

Starting from the pleasant, sunny city of Perth, you can tailor your trek to take in some great beaches and surfing, winery tours, excellent food and wine, and the chance to see kangaroos, whales, and dolphins.

Spend **Day One** in **Perth,** which has a superb climate, a great setting on the Swan River, a fabulous outdoor life of biking and beaches, excellent restaurants, and a historic port, Fremantle. If you'd like to spend a day or so recovering from jet lag as well as getting to know the city, you can overnight here before taking off on your exploration of Western Australia. A relaxing way to spend the day is at the port of **Fremantle,** about 19km (12 miles) southwest of Perth at the mouth of the Swan River.

"Freo" is a bustling district of 150 National Trust buildings, alfresco cafes, museums, galleries, pubs, markets, and shops in a masterfully preserved historical atmosphere. It's still a working port, so you'll see container ships and fishing boats unloading, and yachts gliding in and out of the harbor. It's a favorite destination for Perth's population every weekend, resulting in a wonderful hubbub of shoppers, merchants, cappuccino drinkers, tourists, and fishermen. You can enjoy the parade as you knock back a beer or two on the veranda of a gorgeous old pub.

On **Day Two,** a leisurely four-hour drive southwest from Perth will put you on the edge of the vineyards of **Margaret River,** one of Australia's finest and most scenic wine regions. En route, stop off at the town of Bunbury, where you may be lucky enough to see the **wild dolphins,** which regularly come in to "play" with visitors. The area is compact, so you can make your base at any of the boutique lodges or B&Bs. You can then take your choice from around 80 wineries, as well as numerous galleries and many gourmet produce outlets. Eat at one of the excellent local restaurants — perhaps try one of the local specialties, *marron* (a freshwater crustacean) or venison, with a bottle of Margaret River wine.

Spend **Day Three** traveling the winding country roads of the southwest "hook" of Western Australia. **Prevelly,** west of Margaret River, has some of Australia's best surfing. You can follow Caves Road south to **Augusta** to the historic lighthouse at **Cape Leeuwin,** where the Indian and Southern oceans meet. Augusta is one of the best places in the south to see migrating **whales** (both humpback and southern right) in season — with tours available. Your trip will take you through stands of massive karri and jarrah trees. Don't miss **Boranup Drive,** a scenic detour that cuts through a magnificent karri forest. For the adventurous, there is a maze of caves, some of which are open to the public. Have lunch at one of the winery restaurants or picnic in their lovely gardens. Wind your way back to your accommodations, with the car stocked with some new favorite wines to drink or take home, as well as local cheeses, olive oil, and perhaps some craftwork.

On **Day Four,** head to the area north of Margaret River town for the biggest concentration of **wineries** including some of Australia's big names, as well as the **Margaret River Chocolate Company.** Caves Road runs north from here, heading for **Dunsborough** and **Cape Naturaliste.** Don't hurry along the tree-lined country roads; take time to explore some of the local galleries and enjoy the scenery. At **Yallingup,** you swing northeast for Dunsborough, where — between September and November — you can do more whale-watching. Another stop on your way back to Perth should be at the seaside town of **Busselton,** where a visit to the underwater observatory at the end of the longest timber jetty in the Southern Hemisphere is well worthwhile.

Part II

Planning Your Trip to Australia

The 5th Wave

By Rich Tennant

"I bought all the adapters we'll need for our trip to Australia, including this one for your walking stick."

In this part . . .

*T*his part helps you plan your trip to Australia and deal with the practical side of traveling Down Under.

In Chapter 5, there are tips on how to budget for your trip and what things cost. Chapter 6 helps you to get there, and deal with your jet lag once you land; it also offers some suggestions for escorted and package tours. Chapter 7 looks at how to get around this vast continent and gives you some useful tips on traveling in the Outback.

The right choice of accommodations can make or break a holiday, so in Chapter 8 we look at the best way of choosing and booking your hotel, resort, or other roof over your head. (You can even stay on a farm!) We make sure to discuss plenty of family-friendly options.

So many activities, so little time! In Chapter 9, we cover some of the many active pursuits you can try, from bushwalking to scuba diving. We also give you some specialized travel resources for seniors, gays and lesbians, and people with mobility issues.

Chapter 10 is all about the remaining details — like how to get the essential visa and passport you'll need to travel to Australia, and what to expect from airport security. And, of course, don't forget to phone home (we tell you how).

Chapter 5

Managing Your Money

by Lee Mylne

In This Chapter

▶ Planning a realistic budget for your trip
▶ Figuring the value of the Australian dollar
▶ Using ATMs, traveler's checks, and credit cards

*A*ustralia is not a hugely expensive destination, once you get there. But it *is* far away from pretty much everywhere in the Northern Hemisphere, and you'll probably find the airfare to be your largest single expense. That said, Australia's exchange rate is a bonus for American and British visitors — although fluctuations mean you can never be sure just how much of a bonus it'll be.

Planning Your Budget

You know what's most important to you to make your trip a success. Do you want to stay in luxury hotels or resorts, or are you just as happy in more modest accommodations? Takeout or sit-down? Will your photos be your favorite souvenirs, or do you want to take home some Aboriginal art? All these factors will determine your total budget and how you allocate it. In this section, we give you an idea of your major expenses and offer some ideas on how to save money in each area.

Transportation

Australia is a long haul from pretty much everywhere. This means that the cost of getting here will probably take the largest chunk of your budget.

Many airlines fly to Australia from the United States and Europe, most of them via Asia. Consider a stopover along the way, so you arrive ready to hit the ground running. (In Chapter 6, we discuss airline options and give some tips on finding deals.)

When you get to Australia, you can choose to travel around most cities by public transport. Outside of the cities, you can use a combination of air, rail, and road to see the things that interest you most.

When traveling from region to region, the fastest way of getting around this vast continent is to **fly.** Qantas offers travelers from the United States a great deal with the **Aussie AirPass,** which allows you to fly to more than one Australian city for much less than you would pay for individual domestic airfares. (For more information on the Aussie AirPass, check out Chapter 7.)

Trains can take you the length of the eastern coast, and even across the Nullarbor Plain to Perth, and between Adelaide in South Australia and Darwin in the Northern Territory — a great Outback journey. **Rail passes** can also help save on your travel. A range of passes is available from Rail Australia, through its overseas agents, as well as from Great Southern Railway and Queensland's Traveltrain. (See Chapter 7 for details on travel in Queensland.)

Driving gives you flexibility to plan your journey as you go — stopping wherever you fancy, getting away from major routes, and seeing some of the country's lesser-known attractions that may not be as accessible via public transit. But gasoline is somewhat more expensive in Australia than in the United States and Canada, so it's something you'll have to build into your budget (on the bright side, for visitors from Great Britain and Europe, gasoline is *much* cheaper than at home), and there are additional driving challenges: In addition to having to drive on the left-hand side of the road (an unfamiliar experience for North Americans, not so much for Brits), when you're driving in the Outback, you run the risk of hitting kangaroos or breaking down far from anyone who can help.

Lodging

Whether you're looking for the ultimate in 5-star luxury or a budget backpacker's hostel, you can find it in Australia. A huge range of accommodations is available, and prices vary widely. The cost varies even more depending on your location — for example, Sydney and Melbourne prices will be well above those in a regional or country town in Western Australia, for the same quality. Tourist hot spots like Cairns and the Whitsunday Islands charge top price during their busy seasons.

Australia has a star rating system for hotels and motels, and we outline what you can expect for your stars in Chapter 8.

If you prefer a more personal experience, sometimes for less than the cost of a hotel room, you'll be glad to know that Australia has lots of bed-and-breakfasts (B&Bs). Aussie B&Bs are more likely to be upmarket places, with lots of amenities, almost on the level of a boutique hotel — quite a distance from their traditional origins as extra rooms in family homes. Another great way to get an inside look at how Australians live for not a great amount of money is to spend time on a farmstay, which gives you a taste of rural life.

Serviced apartments are very popular, and you can find agencies that manage and rent them all over the country. They provide much more space for your money than single hotel rooms. In a serviced apartment, you'll have furnished accommodations, including linens and maid service. If you're traveling with your family, you'll value that, along with a full kitchen. Even if you only make breakfast, you'll save a bundle on food costs.

 In major cities, you're most likely to get deals at hotels on weekends, when business travelers go home. Wherever you are, ask about deals or packages that include tours or other extras.

Dining

Australia's multicultural population is reflected in the variety of cuisines available all over the country. In most places — with a few backwater exceptions, perhaps — you'll find food that is fresh, innovative, and tasty. In most places, you'll find good-value eats, especially in ethnic cuisines.

Check out the many farmer's markets in major cities and regional centers for fresh produce. You may be able to buy the ingredients for money-saving picnics or meals you can prepare in your kitchenette.

Sydney and Melbourne vie for top honors in the restaurant trade. In both cities, you'll have trouble choosing among the many fabulous restaurants — in all price ranges — on offer. Ask the locals for their recommendations, and browse our suggestions in those chapters.

To complement your dining, try some of Australia's great wines. More than 550 major companies and small winemakers produce wine in Australia, and many have an international reputation for quality. Many good wines are available at reasonable prices in bottle shops and discount wholesalers.

 In restaurants, you'll pay much more for a bottle, but you can save money by looking for restaurants with a BYO (short for *bring your own*) policy, though there may be a corkage fee.

Sightseeing

Sightseeing is not part of your travel where we recommend you cut corners. See what you want to see, and be prepared to pay whatever it costs; these things are what you'll remember long after you've forgotten what your hotel room was like.

Many of Australia's greatest sights are free: Sydney Harbour, the fabulous beaches, walks, gardens, and many art galleries, including the

National Gallery of Victoria in Melbourne and the National Gallery of Australia in Canberra.

Of course, if you want to see the Great Barrier Reef, you'll have to pay a fairly hefty price to get to it. Most day trips cost between A$150 and A$200 (US$120–US$160/£60–£80 per person per day, up to around A$1,400 (US$1,100/£560) per person if you're overnighting on the reef on a live-aboard cruise.

At Uluru (Ayers Rock), the Uluru–Kata Tjuta National Park has an entrance fee of A$25 (US$20/£10) per person for three days. It's worth every cent.

The **See Sydney & Beyond Smartvisit card** (☎ 02/9247 6611; www. seesydneycard.com) packages more than 40 of the city's main attractions and tours. It's available for one, two, three, or seven days, and you can buy the card online in advance or pick it up after you arrive. A one-day pass costs A$65 (US$52/£26).

Seniors visiting from overseas do not usually qualify for discounts (discounts are reserved for Australian citizens), but it pays to ask because exceptions do exist.

Shopping and nightlife

Shopping and nightlife are two areas in which you can be really flexible with your budgeting. Whether you hit the sack or hit the town is up to you. Scan the nightlife options in each chapter and decide what will add to your Australian experience and what you can live without (depending on the cost). Most clubs outside Sydney have reasonable cover charges. Sydney and Melbourne offer all the shopping you'd expect in major international cities, from cheap souvenirs to high-end luxury goods. You can also spend significant amounts on Aboriginal art or such Australian specialties as opals and pearls, or you can come home with a relatively inexpensive but unique piece of art or jewelry.

Cutting Costs — But Not the Fun

Because going to Australia isn't an everyday event, you should plan to spend enough to make it a comfortable, fun trip. But you *can* have a memorable experience without going broke. Here are some suggestions:

- ✔ **Go off-season.** If you can travel at non-peak times, which can be easy when it's summer in Australia and winter in the Northern Hemisphere, you'll find hotel prices almost half the price of peak months. Look for shoulder season values during the transitional seasons of spring and fall.

- ✔ **Travel midweek.** If you can travel on a Tuesday, Wednesday, or Thursday, you may find cheaper flights to Australia. When you ask about airfares, see if you can get a cheaper rate by flying on a different day. (For more tips on getting a good fare, see Chapter 6.)

✔ **Try a package tour.** For many destinations, you can book airfare, hotel, ground transportation, and some sightseeing just by making one call to a travel agent or packager, for a price much less than if you put the trip together yourself. Several airlines offer excellent package deals. (See Chapter 6 for more on package tours.)

✔ **Reserve a room with a refrigerator and coffeemaker.** You don't have to slave over a hot stove to cut a few costs. Most hotels and motels in Australia have minifridges and coffeemakers. Just making your own breakfast will save you money.

✔ **Always ask for discount rates.** Membership in AAA, frequent-flier plans, trade unions, AARP, or other groups may qualify you for savings on car rentals, plane tickets, hotel rooms, and even meals. Ask about everything; you may be pleasantly surprised.

✔ **Ask whether your kids can stay in the room with you.** A room with two double beds usually doesn't cost any more than one with a queen-size bed. And many hotels won't charge you the additional-person rate if the additional person is pint-size and related to you. Even if you have to pay an extra charge for a rollaway bed, you'll save much more by not taking two rooms.

✔ **Try expensive restaurants at lunch instead of dinner.** Lunch tabs are usually a fraction of what dinner would cost at the same restaurant, and the menu often boasts many of the same specialties.

✔ **Get out of town.** In many places, big savings are just a short drive or taxi ride away. Hotels just outside the city, across the river, or less conveniently located can be great bargains. Outlying motels often have free parking, with lower rates than downtown hotels.

✔ **Don't rent a gas guzzler.** Renting a smaller car is cheaper, and you save on gas to boot. (*Remember:* Gas is somewhat more expensive in Australia than it is in the United States or Canada.) For more on car rentals, see Chapter 7.

✔ **Walk a lot.** And we're not just talking about bushwalking. In the relatively flat, compact city centers, a good pair of walking shoes can save you lots of money in taxis and other local transportation. As a bonus, you'll get to know your destination more intimately, as you explore at a slower pace.

✔ **Skip the souvenirs.** Your photographs and your memories may be the best mementos of your trip. If you're concerned about money, you can do without the T-shirts, key chains, snow globes, plastic boomerangs, and other cheesy trinkets.

Handling Money

You're the best judge of how much cash you feel comfortable carrying or what alternative is your favorite — and that's not going to change much on your vacation. True, you'll probably be moving around more and incurring more expenses than you generally do (unless you happen to eat out every meal when you're at home), and you may let your mind slip into vacation gear and not be as vigilant about your safety. But, those factors aside, the only type of payment that won't be quite as available to you away from home is your personal checkbook.

The Australian dollar is divided into 100¢. Coins are 5¢, 10¢, 20¢, and 50¢ pieces (silver) and $1 and $2 pieces (gold). Prices often end in a variant of 1¢ and 2¢ (for example, 78¢ or $2.71), a relic from the days before 1-cent and 2-cent pieces were phased out. Prices are rounded to the nearest 5¢ — so 77¢ rounds down to 75¢, and 78¢ rounds up to 80¢. Bank notes come in denominations of $5, $10, $20, $50, and $100.

Universal Currency Converter (www.xe.com/ucc) gives up-to-the-minute conversions for your dollar or pound. Table 5-1 offers a rough idea of how many Australian dollars you'll get for your home currency. The rate of exchange used for the U.S. dollar was US$1 = A$1.25 (or A$1 = US$0.80). The exchange rate for the British pound was £1 = A$2.45 (or A$1 = £0.40).

Exchange at least some money — just enough to cover airport incidentals and transportation to your hotel — before you leave home (though don't expect the exchange rate to be ideal), so you can avoid lines at airport ATMs.

When you change money, ask for some small bills or loose change. Petty cash will come in handy for tipping and public transportation. Consider keeping the change separate from your larger bills, so that it's readily accessible and you'll be less of a target for theft.

You can exchange money before you leave at your local American Express or Thomas Cook office or at most major banks. **American Express** offers traveler's checks and foreign currency (with a $15 order fee and additional shipping costs) at www.americanexpress.com or ☎ 800-807-6233.

Using ATMs and carrying cash

The easiest and best way to get cash away from home is from an ATM, sometimes referred to as a *cash machine* or *money machine* in Australia. The **Cirrus** (☎ 800-424-7787; www.mastercard.com) and **PLUS** (☎ 800-843-7587; www.visa.com) networks span the globe; look at the back of your bank card to see which network you're on, and then call or check online for ATM locations at your destination. Be sure you know your

Table 5-1	The Australian Dollar, U.S. Dollar, and British Pound				
A$	US$	£	A$	US$	£
0.25	0.20	0.10	30.00	24.00	12.00
0.50	0.40	0.20	35.00	28.00	14.00
1.00	0.80	0.40	40.00	32.00	16.00
2.00	1.60	0.80	45.00	36.00	18.00
3.00	2.40	1.20	50.00	40.00	20.00
4.00	3.20	1.60	55.00	44.00	22.00
5.00	4.00	2.00	60.00	48.00	24.00
6.00	4.80	2.40	65.00	52.00	26.00
7.00	5.60	2.80	70.00	56.00	28.00
8.00	6.40	3.20	75.00	60.00	30.00
9.00	7.20	3.60	80.00	64.00	32.00
10.00	8.00	4.00	85.00	68.00	34.00
15.00	12.00	6.00	90.00	72.00	36.00
20.00	16.00	8.00	95.00	76.00	38.00
25.00	20.00	10.00	100.00	80.00	40.00

personal identification number (PIN) before you leave home, and find out your daily withdrawal limit. Keep in mind that many banks impose a fee every time your card is used at a different bank's ATM, and that fee can be much higher for international transactions (up to $5 or more). On top of this, the bank from which you withdraw cash may charge its own fee. Check with your bank to find out what kind of fee will be added for international withdrawals, and plan your visits to ATMs accordingly.

Even with the international transaction fees, ATMs often offer the best exchange rates. Avoid exchanging money at commercial exchange bureaus and hotels, which often have the highest transaction fees.

Australian ATMs use four-digit PINs, so if you have a longer PIN, make sure you change yours to a four-digit one before you leave home. The major banks in Australia are the National Australia Bank, the Commonwealth Bank, ANZ, and Westpac.

Charging ahead with credit cards

Credit cards are a safe way to carry money: They also provide a convenient record of your expenses, and they generally offer good exchange
rates. You can also withdraw cash advances at banks or ATMs, if you
know your PIN. If you've forgotten yours, or didn't even know you had
one, call the number on the back of your credit card and ask the bank to
send it to you. It usually takes five to seven business days.

Keep in mind that many banks assess a 1 percent to 3 percent transaction fee on *all* charges you incur abroad (whether you're using the local
currency or your native currency). But credit cards still may be the
smart way to go when you factor in things like ATM fees and traveler's
check exchange rates (and service fees).

 Some credit card companies recommend that you notify them of any
impending trips abroad so that they don't become suspicious when the
card is used in a foreign destination and block your charges. Even if you
don't call your credit card company in advance, you can always call the
card's toll-free emergency number if a charge is refused — a good reason
to carry the phone number with you. Carry more than one card on your
trip; a card may not work for any number of reasons, so having a backup
is the smart way to go.

Visa and MasterCard are universally accepted in Australia; American
Express and Diners Club are considerably less common, and Discover is
not used. Always carry a little cash, because many merchants won't take
credit cards for purchases under A$15 (US$12/£6) or so.

Toting traveler's checks

Traveler's checks are not as widely accepted in Australia as they are in
many other countries. If you do opt for them, get them in Australian dollars. Checks in major currencies are often accepted at banks, big hotels,
currency exchanges, and some shops in major tourist regions, but
smaller shops, restaurants, and other businesses will have no idea what
the exchange rate is when you present a check denominated in a non-
Australian currency. Another advantage of Australian-dollar checks is
that the two largest Aussie banks, ANZ and Westpac, cash them free of
charge; it'll cost you around A$5 to A$11 (US$4–US$8.80/£2–£4.40) to
cash a check denominated in a foreign currency at most Australian
banks.

Taking into account ATM fees, if you're withdrawing money from an ATM
daily, you may be better off with traveler's checks.

You can buy traveler's checks at most banks in your home country.
They're offered in denominations of $20, $50, $100, $500, and sometimes
$1,000. Generally, you'll pay a service charge ranging from 1 percent to 4
percent. The most popular traveler's checks are offered by **American
Express** (☎ 800-807-6233); **Visa** (☎ 800-732-1322); and **MasterCard**

(☎ **800-223-9920**). If you're an American Express card holder, call ☎ **800-221-7282** — this number accepts collect calls, offers service in several foreign languages, and exempts Amex gold and platinum card-holders from the 1 percent fee. If you're a member of AAA, you can obtain Visa checks for a $9.95 fee (for checks up to $1,500) at most AAA offices or by calling ☎ **866-339-3378.**

If you choose to carry traveler's checks, be sure to keep a record of their serial numbers separate from your checks in case they're stolen or lost. You'll get a refund faster if you know the numbers.

American Express, Thomas Cook, Visa, and **MasterCard** offer **foreign currency traveler's checks,** which are useful when traveling to Australia.

Taking Taxes into Account

Australia applies a 10 percent Goods and Services Tax (GST) on most products and services. Your international airline tickets to Australia are not taxed, nor are domestic airline tickets for travel within Australia if you buy them outside Australia. If you buy Australian airline tickets after you arrive in Australia, you will pay tax on them.

Basic groceries are not taxed, but restaurant meals are. Items bought in duty-free stores will not be charged GST, nor will items you export — such as an Aboriginal painting that you buy in a gallery in Alice Springs and have shipped to your home outside Australia.

Other taxes include a departure tax of A$38 (US$30/£15) for every passenger 12 and over, which is included in the price of your airline ticket when you buy it; there are also landing and departure taxes at some airports, which are also included in the price of your ticket.

If you visit the Great Barrier Reef, you'll pay a "reef tax," officially called the Environmental Management Charge, of A$5 (US$4/£2) for every person over the age of 4. The charge, which goes toward park upkeep, may be included in the price of your tour, but often it is not, and you'll be asked for it when you board the boat.

Dealing with a Lost or Stolen Wallet

Contact your credit card company the minute you discover your wallet has been lost or stolen and file a report at the nearest police precinct. Your credit card company or insurer may require a police report number or record of the loss. Most credit card companies have toll-free numbers to call if your card is lost or stolen; your credit card company may be able to wire you a cash advance or deliver an emergency credit card in a day or two. Call the following toll-free numbers in Australia:

Getting your GST back

You can claim back the General Service Tax you've paid, through the **Tourist Refund Scheme** (TRS), when you leave Australia, on the taxes that you paid on purchases of A$300 (US$240/£120) or more from a single outlet, within the last 30 days before you leave. More than one item may be included in that A$300. You can also claim a 14.5 percent wine tax called Wine Equalisation Tax (WET)

For example, you can claim the GST you paid on ten T-shirts each worth A$30 (US$24/£12), as long as you bought them in the same store. Do this as you leave Australia by presenting your receipt, or *tax invoice,* to the Australian Customs Service's TRS booths, located beyond passport control in the international departure areas at most airports. If you buy several things on different days from one store, which together add up to A$300 or more, you must ask the store to total all purchases on one tax invoice — now there's a nice piece of bureaucracy to remember Australia by!

Pack the items you have purchased in Australia in your carry-on baggage, because you must show them to Customs. You can use the goods before you leave Australia (such as wearing clothes or jewelry you've purchased) and still claim the refund, but you cannot claim a refund on things you've actually consumed. You cannot claim a refund on alcohol other than wine (the Wine Tax, mentioned above). Allow a little extra time to stand in line at the airport and get your refund.

You can also claim a refund if you leave Australia as a cruise passenger from Circular Quay or Darling Harbour in Sydney, or from Brisbane, Cairns, Darwin, Hobart, or Fremantle (Perth). If your cruise departs from elsewhere in Australia, or if you're flying out from an airport other than Adelaide, Brisbane, Cairns, Darwin, the Gold Coast, Melbourne, Perth, or Sydney, call the **Australian Customs Service** (☎ **1300/363 263** in Australia, or 02/6275 6666) to see if you can still claim the refund.

- ✔ American Express: ☎ 1300/132 639
- ✔ MasterCard: ☎ 1800/120 113
- ✔ Visa: ☎ 1800/450 346

Visa's U.S. emergency number is ☎ **800-847-2911** or 410-581-9994. American Express cardholders and traveler's check holders should call ☎ **800-221-7282.** MasterCard holders should call ☎ **800-307-7309** or 636-722-7111. For other credit cards, call the toll-free number directory at ☎ **800-555-1212.**

 If you need emergency cash over the weekend when all banks and American Express offices are closed, you can have money wired to you via **Western Union** (☎ **800-325-6000;** www.westernunion.com).

Identity theft or fraud is a potential complication of losing your wallet, especially if you've lost your driver's license as well as cash and credit cards. Notify the major credit reporting bureaus as soon as you get home (or right away if you're on an extended trip); placing a fraud alert on your records may protect you against liability for criminal activity. The major U.S. agencies are **Equifax** (☎ **800-766-0008;** www.equifax.com), **Experian** (☎ **888-397-3742;** www.experian.com), and **TransUnion** (☎ **800-680-7289;** www.transunion.com).

If you've lost all forms of photo ID, call your airline and explain the situation; the airline's agents may allow you to board the plane if you have a copy of your passport or birth certificate and a copy of the police report.

Chapter 6

Getting to Australia

by Lee Mylne

* *

In This Chapter

▶ Coming to grips with long (long) distances
▶ Choosing which airport you'll arrive at
▶ Booking your flight (and getting the best price)
▶ Looking for escorted tours and package deals

* *

The first and most important thing to consider is that Australia is a long, long haul from the Northern Hemisphere. It is a nearly 15-hour nonstop flight from Los Angeles to Sydney, made even longer if you come via Honolulu. From the East Coast of North America, add five-and-a-half hours to that! If you're coming from the States via Auckland, add transit time in New Zealand plus another three hours for the Auckland–Sydney leg. If you're coming from the United Kingdom, you're in for a flight of around 12 hours from London to Asia, and then possibly a lay-over of quite a few hours (which is not a bad thing if you can find a hotel room to rest in), because flights to Australia have a habit of arriving in Asia early in the morning and departing around midnight; and finally another eight- to nine-hour flight to Australia. Still keen? Great, let's go!

Flying to Australia (and Stops along the Way)

Sydney, Cairns, Melbourne, Brisbane, Adelaide, Darwin, and Perth are all international gateways, but most major airlines fly only into Sydney. Not many long-haul flights to Australia are nonstop. On most flights you'll have at least one stop somewhere, such as Honolulu, Hong Kong, Singapore, or somewhere else in Asia. Although this will extend your flying time, you may be grateful for the chance to stretch your legs or have a stopover, sometimes at no extra cost (except for the hotel room in which you'll catch up on your sleep!).

The major airports (and which airlines fly into them)

✔ **Sydney:** Kingsford Smith Airport is Australia's main international airport. It is 8km (5 miles) from the city center and is served by **Air Canada** (U.S. flights from Los Angeles and Honolulu; Canadian flights from Toronto and Vancouver), **Air New Zealand** (U.S. flights from Los Angeles, San Francisco, and Honolulu), **Air Tahiti Nui** (flights from New York and Los Angeles), **British Airways** (U.K. flights from London), **Cathay Pacific** (U.S. flights from Los Angeles, New York, and San Francisco; Canadian flights from Vancouver; U.K. flights from London), **Emirates** (U.S. flights from New York; U.K. flights from London, Glasgow, Manchester, and Birmingham; New Zealand flights from Auckland and Christchurch), **Hawaiian Airlines** (U.S. flights from Seattle, Portland, Sacramento, San Francisco, San Jose, Las Vegas, Los Angeles, San Diego, Phoenix, and Honolulu), Qantas subsidiary **Jetstar** (U.S. flights from Honolulu; New Zealand flights from Christchurch), **Philippine Airlines** (U.S. flights from Los Angeles, San Francisco, Las Vegas, and Honolulu; Canadian flights from Vancouver), **Qantas** (U.S. flights from Los Angeles, New York, and San Francisco; Canadian flights from Vancouver; U.K. flights from London; New Zealand flights from Auckland, Wellington, and Queenstown), **Singapore Airlines** (U.S. flights from Los Angeles and New York; U.K. flights from London and Manchester), **Thai Airways** (U.S. flights from Los Angeles and New York; U.K. flights from London), **United Airlines** (U.S. flights from Los Angeles, New York, San Francisco, and Honolulu; Canadian flights from Toronto; U.K. flights from London), and **Virgin Atlantic** (U.K. flights from London). New Zealand airline **Freedom Air** flies from Hamilton, Palmerston North, and Dunedin, and **Pacific Blue** links Sydney and Christchurch.

✔ **Melbourne:** Often referred to as Tullamarine Airport, after the suburb in which it's located, Melbourne International Airport is 22km (14 miles) northwest of the city center (conveniently under the same roof as the domestic terminals). It's served by **Air New Zealand** (U.S. flights from Los Angeles, San Francisco, and Honolulu; U.K. flights from London; New Zealand flights from Auckland, Wellington, Christchurch, Dunedin, Hamilton, and Palmerston North), **British Airways** (U.K. flights from London), **Cathay Pacific** (U.S. flights from Los Angeles and San Francisco; Canadian flights from Vancouver and Toronto; U.K. flights from London), **Emirates** (U.S. flights from New York; U.K. flights from London, Glasgow, Manchester, and Birmingham; New Zealand flights from Auckland), **Qantas** (U.S. flights from Los Angeles, New York, San Francisco, and Honolulu; Canadian flights from Toronto and Vancouver; U.K. flights from London, Glasgow, and Manchester; New Zealand flights from Auckland, Wellington, and Christchurch), **Singapore Airlines** (U.S. flights from Los Angeles, New York, and San Francisco; Canadian flights from Vancouver; U.K. flights from London and Manchester), and **United Airlines** (U.S. flights from Los Angeles, New York, San Francisco, and Honolulu; Canadian flights from Toronto; U.K. flights from London). Direct flights to Melbourne from New York are also operated by **Thai Airways. China Southern Airlines, Malaysia Airlines,** and **Philippine Airlines** also fly direct from Los Angeles. Qantas subsidiary **Jetstar** flies direct from Honolulu, and from Christchurch in New Zealand. **Freedom Air** flies to Melbourne from Dunedin in New Zealand.

✔ **Brisbane:** About 20 international airlines serve Brisbane International Airport, which is about 16km (10 miles) from the city. The airport is undergoing a major expansion and modernization, expected to be finished by the end of 2008. Brisbane is served by **Qantas** with direct flights from Los Angeles. Otherwise, you'll probably arrive via Singapore or Bangkok on **Singapore Airlines** or **Thai Airways,** or on **Emirates** via Dubai. **Air New Zealand, Freedom Air, Qantas,** and **Jetstar** fly from New Zealand.

✔ **Cairns:** The airport is 8km (5 miles) north of the city center. You're only likely to arrive in Cairns if you're flying on **Jetstar** via Singapore and Darwin, on **Cathay Pacific** via Hong Kong, or on **United Airlines** or **Air New Zealand** from Auckland.

✔ **Darwin:** The airport is about 13km (8 miles) northeast of the city center. International flights into Darwin arrive via Singapore, served by budget carriers **Jetstar** and **Tiger Airways.**

✔ **Adelaide:** The airport is 5km (3 miles) west of the city center. It is served by **Air New Zealand** (flights from Auckland), **Cathay Pacific** (flights from Hong Kong), **Malaysia Airlines** (flights from Kuala Lumpur), **Qantas** (flights from Singapore), and **Singapore Airlines** (flights from Singapore).

✔ **Perth:** Perth Airport is 12km (7½ miles) northeast of the city. It is served by **Air New Zealand** (from Auckland, code-sharing with **United Airlines** and **Air Canada**), **Cathay Pacific** (from Hong Kong), **Emirates** (from Dubai), **Malaysia Airlines** (from Kuala Lumpur), **Qantas** (from Singapore, code-sharing with **British Airways**), **Singapore Airlines** (from Singapore), **Thai Airways** (from Bangkok), and **Tiger Airways** (from Singapore).

Getting the Best Deal on Your Airfare

Flexibility is the key to getting your ticket to Australia at the cheapest possible price. If you can book well in advance or at the last minute, or if you can fly midweek or at less-busy times, you may end up paying a fraction of the full fare.

Try to book a ticket in its country of origin. For example, if you're planning a one-way flight from Sydney to Auckland, an Australia-based travel agent such as **Flight Centre** (☎ **13 31 33** in Australia, or 07/3011 7830; www.flightcentre.com.au) will probably have the lowest fares. For multi-leg trips, book in the country of the first leg; for example, book Melbourne–Auckland–Los Angeles in Australia.

Travel agents specializing in cheap fares include **Austravel** (☎ 0870/166 2020 in the U.K.; www.austravel.net); **Downunder Direct,** a division of Swain Australia (☎ 800-642-6224 in the U.S. and Canada; www.down underdirect.com); and **Goway** (☎ 800-387-8850 in the U.S. and Canada; www.goway.com).

Keep an eye on television and newspaper ads for promotional specials or fare wars, which can be seasonal or suddenly break out when a carrier adds a new route.

Working with consolidators

Consolidators, also known as *bucket shops,* are wholesale brokers in the airline-ticket game. Consolidators buy deeply discounted tickets ("distressed" inventories of unsold seats) from airlines and sell them to online ticket agencies, travel agents, tour operators, corporations, and, to a lesser degree, the general public.

Consolidators advertise in Sunday newspaper travel sections (often in small ads with tiny type), in the United States and the United Kingdom. They can be great sources for cheap international tickets. On the downside, these tickets are often loaded with restrictions, such as cancellation penalties (as high as 50 percent to 75 percent of the ticket price). And keep in mind that most of what you see advertised is of limited availability.

Several reliable consolidators are worldwide and available online. **STA Travel** (www.statravel.com) has been the world's leading consolidator for students since it purchased Council Travel, but its fares are competitive for travelers of all ages. **Flights.com** (www.flights.com) has excellent fares worldwide. **Air Tickets Direct** (☎ 800-778-3447; www.air ticketsdirect.com) is based in Montreal and leverages the Canadian dollar for low fares.

Booking your flight online

The most popular online travel agencies in the United States are **Travelocity.com, Expedia.com,** and **Orbitz.com.** Other Web sites for booking airline tickets online include **Cheapflights.com, Smarter Travel.com,** and **Priceline.com.** Meta search sites (which find and then direct you to airline and hotel Web sites for booking) include **Sidestep. com** and **Kayak.com. Lastminute.com** is a great source for last-minute flights and getaways. In addition, most **airlines** offer online-only fares that even their phone agents know nothing about.

In the United Kingdom, go to **Opodo.com** or **Travelsupermarket** (☎ 0845/345-5708; www.travelsupermarket.com), a flight search engine that offers flight comparisons for the budget airlines whose seats often end up in bucket-shop sales. British travelers should also check **Flights International** (☎ 0800/0187050; www.flights-international. com) for deals on flights all over the world.

Avoiding economy-class syndrome

Deep vein thrombosis (DVT), or "economy-class syndrome," is a potentially fatal blood clot that develops in a deep vein. It can be caused by sitting in cramped conditions — such as an airplane seat — for too long. During a long-haul flight, be sure to get up, walk around, and stretch your legs every 60 to 90 minutes to keep your blood flowing. Other preventive measures include frequent flexing of the legs while sitting, drinking lots of water, and avoiding alcohol and sleeping pills. If you have a history of DVT, heart disease, or another condition that puts you at high risk, some experts recommend wearing compression stockings or taking anticoagulants when you fly. Consult your doctor about the best course for you. Symptoms of deep vein thrombosis include leg pain or swelling, or even shortness of breath.

Considering an Escorted or Package Tour

One of the great advantages of escorted tours, with a group leader to take care of everything for you, is that the price usually includes everything from airfare to hotels, meals, tours, admission costs, and local transportation. There are no nasty financial surprises along the way, and you can also get to see the greatest number of sights in the shortest available time, with the minimal chance — if your tour operator is reputable — of anything going very wrong.

Despite the fact that escorted tours require big deposits and give you little flexibility in the choice of hotels, restaurants, and itineraries, many people enjoy the structure they offer. Whether they're by bus, coach, train, or boat — or a combination — escorted tours let you sit back and relax without having to worry about the details. Tours are particularly convenient for people with limited mobility, and they can be a great way to make new friends, especially if you're traveling alone.

On the downside, you'll have little opportunity for much spontaneous interaction with the locals. The tours can be jam-packed with activities, leaving little room for individual sightseeing, and they often focus on the most popular sights, so you miss out on lesser-known gems.

When choosing an escorted tour, ask a few simple questions before you pay a deposit:

- ✔ What is the company's cancellation policy? Can you get your money back if you cancel? How late can you cancel? Can the tour operator cancel the trip if it doesn't get the required minimum passengers?

- ✔ What are the hotel choices and price options? Check them out online, and find out what types of rooms are offered.

✔ Is a complete schedule available? (You need to assess how jam-packed it is.) Is there free time to shop on your own or just lie by the pool with a book? Can you opt out of some activities if you want to? Are you going to be up before the roosters every day?

✔ How large is the group? Does the tour operator have a minimum and maximum number of people it'll take? What is the likely age group you'll be traveling with?

✔ What exactly does the tour include in the price? Ask about transfers to and from the airport, and whether drinks are included in the meal prices. What about tipping?

✔ Are airport departure fees and taxes included in the total cost (they rarely are)? Are there any other fees? Look for hidden fees so you know exactly how much the tour will cost.

Here are a few companies that offer escorted tours to Australia:

✔ **Connections Adventures** and **Connections Safaris** (call Australian Pacific Touring ☎ **800-290-8687** in the U.S., Goway ☎ **800-387-8850** in Canada, and ☎ **020/89464536** in the U.K.; www.connections.travel) offer two kinds of tours within Australia. **Connections Adventures** is aimed at the 18-to-39 age group, with tours in Queensland and the Northern Territory. **Connections Safaris** has an open age policy and runs small group tours in the Northern Territory, Western Australia, and Tasmania.

✔ **Contiki** (☎ **888-CONTIKI** [266-8454] in the U.S. and Canada, 1300/188 635 or 02/9511 2200 in Australia; www.contiki.com) specializes in escorted tours for 18- to 35-year-olds. It offers a wide range of Australian tours, from 3 days on the Great Barrier Reef to 25 days in the Northern Territory, Queensland, and New South Wales — and whole lot in between. Because they attract a lot of Australians, Contiki tours are a good way to meet locals.

✔ **Premier Vacations** (☎ **800-321-6720** in the U.S. and Canada; www.premierdownunder.com) is a reliable escorted tour operator, offering a 27-day "grand tour," which also takes in New Zealand, as well as an independent tour of Sydney, Melbourne, and Cairns.

✔ **Maupintour** (☎ **800-255-4266** in the U.S. and Canada; www.maupintour.com) offers a 15-day tour of Australia, covering Cairns, Uluru, Alice Springs, Melbourne, Hobart, and Sydney.

✔ **Collette Vacations** (☎ **800-340-5158** in the U.S., 800-468-5955 in Canada, or 0800/0921-888 in the U.K.; www.collettevacations.com) has been offering escorted tours since 1918! It offers trips of up to two weeks, including tours for people interested in the great train journeys of Australia and its wineries.

Coping with jet lag

Jet lag is the worst thing about traveling long distances across different time zones. If you're flying north–south and you feel sluggish when you touch down, your symptoms will be the result of dehydration and the general stress of air travel. But when you travel east–west or vice-versa, your body becomes hopelessly muddled about what time it is, and everything — from your digestive system to your brain — can become severely out of whack. Traveling east is more difficult on your internal clock than traveling west because most peoples' bodies are more inclined to stay up late than fall asleep early.

To help fight off the worst effects of jet lag try these suggestions:

- Reset your watch to your destination time before you board the plane.

- Drink lots of water before, during, and after your flight. Avoid alcohol.

- Exercise and sleep well for a few days before your trip.

- If you have trouble sleeping on planes, fly eastward on morning flights.

- Daylight is the key to resetting your body clock. At the Web site for **Outside In** (www.bodyclock.com), you can get a customized plan of when to seek and avoid light in order to cope with jet lag.

Choosing a package tour

Package tours are simply a way to buy the airfare, hotel, car rental, airport transfers, and sometimes activities at one time and often at prices far less than you'd pay for each thing separately. For people who don't want an escorted tour, this is a great way of saving money. You can get such a good price because the tour operators buy packages in bulk, so they can resell them for less.

Travel packages are also listed in the travel section of your local Sunday newspaper, or in national travel magazines such as *Arthur Frommer's Budget Travel Magazine, Travel + Leisure, National Geographic Traveler,* and *Condé Nast Traveler.*

One good source of package deals is the airlines themselves. Most major airlines offer air/land packages. Several big **online travel agencies** — Expedia, Travelocity, Orbitz, and Lastminute.com — also do a brisk business in packages.

Locating package tours

Information about package tours to Australia is available from a number of sources, including the following companies:

✔ **Austravel** (☎ **0870/166-2020** in the U.K.; www.austravel.net) has been packaging tours Down Under for more than 30 years.

✔ **ATS Tours** (☎ **888-781-5170** in the U.S. and Canada; www.ats tours.com). Another long-time operator (it's been around for 32 years), ATS offers independent and escorted tours throughout Australia and the South Pacific.

✔ **Goway** (☎ **800-387-8850** in the U.S. and Canada; www.goway.com), has been operating since 1970 and even has an office in Sydney.

✔ **Swain Tours** (☎ **800-22-SWAIN** [79246] in the U.S. and Canada; www.swaintours.com) and Swain's budget-travel division, **Downunder Direct** (☎ **800-642-6224** in the U.S. and Canada; www.downunderdirect.com), are also good sources. Swain is operated and largely staffed by Aussies and has an office in Sydney.

Checking out airline and hotel packages

Airlines are a good source for package tours because they package their flights together with accommodations. The following airlines offer packages to Australia:

✔ **American Airlines Vacations** (☎ **800-321-2121;** www.aa vacations.com).

✔ **Continental Airlines Vacations** (☎ **800-301-3800;** www.co vacations.com).

✔ **United Vacations** (☎ **888-854-3899;** www.unitedvacations.com).

✔ **Qantas Vacations** (☎ **800-348-8145** in the U.S., or 800-348-8137 in Canada; www.qantasvacations.com). Qantas also offers great discounts on flights within Australia with its Aussie AirPass (see Chapter 7).

Chapter 7

Getting Around Australia

by Lee Mylne

● ●

In This Chapter

▶ Flying around the country
▶ Taking the train or the bus
▶ Driving yourself, and learning the rules of the road

● ●

*V**ast.* That's the best word to describe Australia. Make no mistake, the distances to cover if you're going to see even a fraction of the best of this country are enormous. Don't think you'll be able to travel easily and quickly between the major sights — because you simply won't. For example, Uluru (Ayers Rock) is more than 2,800km (1,760 miles) northwest of Sydney, and the Great Barrier Reef is a similar distance northeast of Sydney — that's roughly the distance from New York City to Denver, Colorado. Possibly the biggest mistake visitors make is underestimating how long it takes to get around.

Flying is the best way to travel between most points. If you have the time or the inclination, you can travel by train, bus, or car, but the landscape is often unchanging. A good compromise is to fly when the distances between your chosen destinations are long and use land travel for shorter hops.

Making Your Way Around Australia

By plane

Airfares within Australia have always been expensive. In recent years, greater competition between domestic airlines has brought the prices down a bit, but you still need to plan ahead and budget. Australia's air network is not as well developed as that of North America or Europe, so don't assume there's a direct flight to your chosen destination, or that there's a flight every hour or even every day.

Between them, the three major airlines serve every state capital, as well as most major regional towns on the east coast, Tasmania, and places like Broome in Western Australia. Competition is getting fiercer, so all airlines will likely have added to their route networks by the time you read this.

Melbourne has two airports: the main international and domestic terminals at Tullamarine, and Avalon Airport, about 50km (31 miles) from the city, which is used by Jetstar. Make sure you check which one your flight leaves from before you book.

The main players are

- ✔ **Qantas** (☎ **800-227-4500** in the U.S. and Canada; 0845/7747767 in the U.K. or 208/600 4300 in London; 1/407 3278 in Ireland; 0800/ 808 767 in New Zealand or 09/357 8900 in Auckland; 13 13 13 in Australia; www.qantas.com.au)

- ✔ **Virgin Blue** (☎ **13 67 89** in Australia, or 07/3295 2296; www. virginblue.com.au)

- ✔ **Jetstar** (☎ **13 15 38** in Australia, or 03/8341 4901; **0800 800 995** in New Zealand; www.jetstar.com.au), a Qantas-owned no-frills airline.

- ✔ **Regional Express** (☎ **13 17 13** in Australia; www.regional express.com.au) serves regional New South Wales, South Australia, Victoria, and northern Tasmania.

Low-cost Asian carrier **Tiger Airways** (www.tigerairways.com), already flying into Darwin and Perth from Singapore, started offering Australian domestic flights from Melbourne in late 2007.

Saving money on airfares

Qantas typically offers **international travelers** a discount of around 30 percent off the full price for domestic flights bought within Australia. To qualify, show your passport and international ticket number when making your booking. But confirm that the fare for international travelers is the best deal you can get, because the latest deal in the market that day (or a package deal with accommodations thrown in) may be even cheaper.

If you're visiting from the United States and plan on traveling to more than one Australian city, buying a Qantas **Aussie AirPass** is much cheaper than buying regular fares. The pass is good for travel on certain flights between Los Angeles, San Francisco, or Honolulu and Sydney, Melbourne, or Brisbane, and also gives you up to another three destinations within Australia (or more, for an extra US$100 each).

AirPass prices starts from US$1,099 to US$1,599 depending on the season, for economy-class travel. Prices vary according to which "zone" you're traveling to. Zone 1 covers travel to Sydney, Canberra, Melbourne, Brisbane, the Gold Coast, Adelaide, Hobart, and Launceston. Zone 2, which costs an extra US$200, will take you to Cairns, Townsville, Hamilton Island, Rockhampton, Mackay, Gladstone, Alice Springs, Ayers Rock (Uluru), and Darwin. Zone 3 costs an extra US$400 or US$500 and will get you to Perth, Broome, and Hayman Island.

If you're starting your trip in the United States from somewhere other than Los Angeles or Honolulu, special fares are available — but only from San Jose, San Diego, Seattle, Portland, Las Vegas, Dallas, Denver, St. Louis, Chicago, New York (JFK and Newark), Washington, D.C., Miami, and Boston. Check with Qantas (☎ **800-227 4603;** www.qantas.com) for details.

The AirPass is also only available on certain flights, but you can pay a US$300 surcharge to travel on other flights and still get an AirPass. You must stay for a minimum of 7 days and a maximum of 21 days from your first transatlantic flight, and must buy the pass before you arrive in Australia. Australia and New Zealand residents can't purchase this pass.

Flight-seeing

Aerial touring allows you to miss all the boring bits of traveling by land. Many of the most fascinating landscapes, such as the weird Bungle Bungles formations in the Kimberley, are best seen from the air. **Aircruising Australia** (☎ **1800/252 053** in Australia, or 02/9693 2233; 0800/445 700 in New Zealand; www.aircruising.com.au) operates luxury aerial tours of 8 to 12 days in a private aircraft, usually a 38-passenger Dash 8, traveling as low as 300m (1,000 ft.). The company mainly markets within Australia, so your fellow passengers are likely to be Aussies. And because the tours are expensive for Australians, most passengers are over 55. The tours are very well organized and allow lots of time for land-based sightseeing, some free time, and a maximum two hours in the air most days. Accommodations are usually the best available, and the itineraries include "fun extras." Fares in 2007 ranged from A$8,949 to A$12,695 (US$7,160–US$10,160/£3,500–£5,000) per person sharing a double or twin room.

If your timing is right, you may also be able to take in Antarctica as part of your Australian vacation. **Antarctica Sightseeing Flights** (☎ **1800/633 449** in Australia, or 03/9725 8555; www.antarcticaflights.com.au) offers once-in-a-lifetime flights over the icy continent. The 12-hour journey offers spectacular viewing of the frozen beauty of Antarctica — a truly memorable experience. Flights are seasonal (Nov–Feb) and include a New Year's Eve flight. Most leave from Sydney or Melbourne, with connections from Brisbane, Canberra, and Adelaide. You reach the Antarctic coastline after about four hours flying and spend the next four hours above pristine glaciers, mountain ranges, soaring coastal cliffs, and ice floes. In 2007 and 2008, fares ranged from A$999 (US$799/£400) in an economy center seat to A$5,499 (US$4,399/£2,199) in first class.

By train

Australia's rail network links Perth to Adelaide, and continues on to Melbourne and north to Canberra, Sydney, Brisbane, and up the coast to Cairns. There's a line right up the middle, from Adelaide to Alice Springs and Darwin. Some rural towns, such as Broken Hill, also have rail service. Trains generally cost more than buses but are still reasonably priced, and offer a comfortable, safe way of getting around.

Most long-distance trains have sleepers with windows, air-conditioning, electric outlets, wardrobes, sinks, and fresh linens. First-class sleepers have attached bathrooms, and fares often include meals. Second-class sleepers use shared shower facilities, and meals are not included. Some second-class sleepers are private cabins; on other trains you share with strangers. Single cabins are usually of broom-closet dimensions but surprisingly comfy, with their own toilets and basins. The food ranges from mediocre to pretty good. Smoking is usually banned, or allowed only in the club cars or special "smoking rooms."

There are several different authorities that run the trains. They are:

- ✔ **Countrylink** (☎ **13 22 32** in Australia; www.countrylink.info), which manages travel within New South Wales and from Sydney to Canberra, Melbourne, Brisbane, and a number of New South Wales country towns

- ✔ **Great Southern Railway** (☎ **13 21 47** in Australia, or 08/8213 4592; www.gsr.com.au), a private enterprise that runs the long-distance *Indian Pacific,* the *Overland,* and the *Ghan*

- ✔ **Public Transport Authority,** or PTA (☎ **1300/662 205** in Western Australia, or 08/9326 2600; www.transwa.wa.gov.au), which operates trains in Western Australia

- ✔ **Traveltrain,** the long-distance train division of Queensland Rail (☎ **1300/131 722** in Australia, or 07/3235 1133; www.traveltrain.com.au), which handles rail within that state

Outside Australia, the umbrella organization **Rail Australia** (www.rail australia.com.au) handles inquiries and makes reservations for all long-distance trains, with the exception of PTA routes, through its overseas agents: **ATS Tours** (☎ **800-423-2880**) in the United States; **Goway** (☎ **800-387-8850**) in Canada; **International Rail** (☎ **0870/751-5000**) in the United Kingdom; and **Tranz Scenic** (☎ **0800/808 900** or 03/339 3809) in New Zealand.

Two long-distance trains — the *Indian Pacific* and the *Ghan* — are experiences in themselves rather than just a way of getting between two points. They can also be expensive, but if you're a train buff, they're not to be missed.

The *Indian Pacific,* run by Great Southern Railway, is a glamorous train linking Sydney, Broken Hill, Adelaide, Kalgoorlie, and Perth in a three-day Outback run twice a week. Slightly less glam, but still comfortable, the *Ghan* (named after Afghani camel trainers who traveled the Outback in the 19th century) travels between Adelaide and Darwin twice a week via Alice Springs, with connections from Sydney and Perth on the *Indian Pacific* and from Melbourne on Great Southern Railway's third train, the newly refurbished *Overland.* It travels in daylight between Adelaide and Melbourne three times a week. All three trains offer a choice of economy seats and second- or first-class sleepers.

Queensland Rail's Traveltrain operates two trains on the Brisbane–Cairns route: The *Sunlander* runs twice a week from Brisbane to Cairns, offering a choice of the premium, all-inclusive Queenslander class; single-, double-, or triple-berth sleepers; or economy seats. Two services also run as far as Townsville on this route without Queenslander class. The high-speed **Tilt Train** operates two weekly trips on the same route in less time — by about eight hours — with business-class-style seating. Tilt Trains also serve Rockhampton daily (except Sat) from Brisbane. Traveltrain also operates trains to Outback towns. All Traveltrain and most Countrylink long-distance trains stop at most towns en route, so they're useful for exploring the eastern states.

Saving with rail packages and passes

Rail passes are available from Rail Australia, through its overseas agents. Passes are not valid for first-class travel, but upgrades are available. The **Austrail Flexipass** is good for economy seats and second-class sleepers on all long-distance trains (except PTA service in Western Australia) and is even good for suburban city train networks. It allows you to travel for 15 or 22 days, consecutive or not, within a 6-month period. Prices range from A$862 (US$690/£345) for a 15-day Flexipass to A$1,210 (US$968/£484) for a 22-day Flexipass.

This pass, and the Great Southern Railway **Rail Explorer Pass,** which gives you six months of unlimited travel aboard the *Ghan,* the *Indian Pacific,* and the *Overland* for A$590 (US$472/£236) must be bought before you arrive in Australia.

Queensland's **Traveltrain Holidays** (☎ 1300/131 722 in Australia, or 07/3235 1133; www.traveltrain.com.au), has the Wanderer and Stopover rail passes. The **Wanderer** pass costs A$266 (US$213/£106) and provides six months of unlimited one-way travel in economy seating on Queensland's coastal trains, with departures from Brisbane or Cairns. Pass holders also receive up to 50 percent discounts for return journeys on any of the Queensland's Outback rail services. The **Stopover** fare lets travelers choose to stop up to four times in four weeks when traveling on the Tilt Train. Prices vary depending on the number of stops.

Great Southern Railway, Countrylink, and Queensland Rail Traveltrain all offer rail packages that include accommodations and sightseeing.

By bus

Australian bus or "coach" terminals are centrally located and well lit, and buses are usually clean and air-conditioned, with adjustable seats, TV monitors, and sometimes toilets. Drivers are polite and sometimes even give a bit of a commentary. Buses are all nonsmoking.

Australia has one national long-distance coach operator, **Greyhound Australia** (☎ **13 14 99** in Australia, or 07/4690 9950; www.greyhound.com.au) — not to be confused with Greyhound in the United States. The company does not operate in Tasmania, which is serviced by **Redline Coaches** (☎ **1300/360 000** in Australia; www.redlinecoaches.com.au). In addition to point-to-point services, Greyhound Australia also offers a limited range of tours at popular locations on its networks, including Uluru, Kakadu, Monkey Mia in Western Australia, and the Great Ocean Road in Victoria.

Fares and some passes are considerably cheaper for students, backpacker cardholders, and Hostelling International/YHA members.

Several kinds of bus passes are available, including day passes (for between 3 and 30 days), preset itinerary passes, and distance-based passes. You may need to book the next leg of your trip 12 to 24 hours ahead; during school vacation periods, which are always busy, booking as much as seven days ahead is a good idea.

If you know where you're going and you're willing to obey a "no backtracking" rule, consider Greyhound Australia's **Aussie Explorer** predetermined itinerary pass. This allows unlimited stops in a generous time frame on a preset one-way route (you can travel the route in either direction). There is a huge range of itineraries to choose from. For example, the **Aussie Reef and Rock** pass takes in Alice Springs, Katherine, Darwin, Mount Isa, Cairns, and the whole east coast down to Sydney. The pass is valid for six months and costs A$1,293 (US$1,034/£517) from Sydney, including tours to Uluru (Ayers Rock), Kakadu National Park, and Kings Canyon. You don't have to start in Sydney; you can start at any point along any of the pass routes, in which case the pass may be cheaper. In the case of the Reef and Rock pass, you could start in Brisbane (in which case the pass costs A$1,176/US$941/£470) or Cairns (from where the pass costs A$943/US$754/£377). The **All Australian Pass** costs A$2,827 (US$2,262/£1,131) and is valid for a year.

The **Aussie Kilometre Pass** allows unlimited stops in any direction within the distance you buy. Passes are available in increments of 1,000km (620 miles). Prices range from A$360 (US$288/£144) for 2,000km (1,240 miles) — enough to get you from Cairns to Brisbane — to A$2,597 (US$2,078/£1,039) for 20,000km (6,200 miles).

By car

There are definitely some great drives in Australia, and you can set the pace if you're the one behind the wheel, and even reach some places that may not be as accessible via public transportation. So here's the lowdown on getting around on your own four wheels.

 First of all: *Drive on the left, pass on the right.* This is the most important thing to remember. There are regular fatalities involving tourists from Europe and North America who stray onto the "wrong" side and into the path of an oncoming vehicle. Don't let it be you.

When you're outside the major centers, Australian roads — even some main highways — are two-lane affairs. In remote and country areas, they can be rutted and potholed, often with no outside line markings, and sometimes no shoulders. Remember that what looks like a road on a map may actually be an "unsealed" (unpaved) track suitable for four-wheel-drive vehicles only. Many roads in the Top End are passable only in the Dry season (about Apr–Nov). If you plan long-distance driving, get a road map that indicates paved and unpaved roads.

Much of the center of Australia is desert, with no roads. The north–south Stuart Highway links Adelaide and Darwin, but that's about the extent of it. In most places you must travel around the edge of the country on Highway 1.

You can use your current driver's license or an international driver's permit in every state of Australia. You must carry your license when driving. The minimum driving age is 16 or 17, depending on which state you visit, but some car rental companies require you to be 21, or even 26, if you want to rent a four-wheel-drive vehicle.

As we've already mentioned, there are some vast distances between major cities and attractions in Australia. Take a look at Table 7-1 below for some examples.

Table 7-1	Sample Driving Distances in Australia	
Route	*Distance*	*Approximate Driving Time*
Cairns–Sydney	2,495km (1,547 miles)	29 hours (allow 4–5 days)
Sydney–Melbourne	873km (541 miles)	15 hours (allow 1–2 days)
Sydney–Perth	4,131km (2,561 miles)	51 hours (allow 6–7 days)
Adelaide–Darwin	3,024km (1,875 miles)	31 hours (allow 4–6 days)
Perth–Darwin	4,163km (2,581 miles)	49 hours (allow 6–8 days)

Renting a car

In tourist towns like Cairns, most tour operators will pick you up and drop you off at your hotel door, making a rental car unnecessary. A regular car will get you to most places in this book, but in some areas with unpaved roads, renting a four-wheel-drive vehicle makes sense. All the major car rental companies rent them. Many companies offer specials, especially in tourist areas with off seasons. Advance purchase rates, usually 7 to 21 days, can offer significant savings.

The "big four" car rental companies and two other large companies in Australia all have offices and networks across the country:

- ✔ **Avis** (☎ **13 63 33** in Australia; 800-230-4898 in the U.S. and Canada; 8445/81 81 81 in the U.K.; www.avis.com.au)

- ✔ **Budget** (☎ **1300/362 848** in Australia; 800-472-3325 in the U.S.; 800-268-8900 in Canada; 8701/56 56 56 in the U.K.; www.budget.com.au)

- ✔ **Europcar** (☎ **1300/13 13 90** in Australia, or 03/9330 6160; 877-940-6900 in the U.S. and Canada; 0870/607-5000 in the U.K.; www.europcar.com.au)

- ✔ **Hertz** (☎ **13 30 39** in Australia; 800-654-3001 in the U.S. and Canada; 0870/844 844 in the U.K.; www.hertz.com.au)

- ✔ **Red Spot Car Rentals** (☎ **1300/668 810** in Australia, or 02/8303 2222; www.redspotrentals.com.au; in Sydney, Melbourne, Brisbane, Perth, Cairns, the Gold Coast, Hobart, and Launceston)

- ✔ **Thrifty** (☎ **1300/367 227** in Australia, www.thrifty.com.au; 800-847-4389 in the U.S. and Canada; 01494/751-540 in the U.K.).

Damage to a rental car caused by an animal (hitting a kangaroo, for example) is not covered by car rental companies' insurance policies, nor is driving on an unpaved road. Insurance for loss of, or damage to, the car, and third-party property insurance are usually included, but read the agreement carefully, because the fine print contains information that the staff may not tell you. For example, damage to the car body may be covered, but not damage to the windshield or tires, or damage caused by water or driving too close to a bushfire.

The deductible, known as *excess* in Australia, on insurance may be as high as A$2,000 (US$1,600/₤800) for regular cars and up to A$5,500 (US$4,400/₤2,200) on four-wheel-drives and motor homes. You can reduce it, or avoid it altogether, by paying a premium of between about A$20 to A$50 (US$16–US$40/₤8–₤20) per day on a car or four-wheel-drive, and around A$25 to A$50 (US$20–US$40/₤10–₤20) per day on a motor home. The amount of the excess reduction premium depends on the vehicle type and the extent of reduction you choose. Your rental company may bundle personal accident insurance and baggage insurance into this premium. And again, check the conditions; some excess reduction payments don't reduce excesses on single-vehicle accidents, for example.

Australia's extreme distances often make one-way rentals a necessity, for which car rental companies can charge a hefty penalty amounting to hundreds of dollars. A one-way fee usually applies to motor-home rentals, too — usually around A$200 to A$220 (US$160–US$176/£80–£88), more for remote outback areas such as Broome and Alice Springs. And there's a seven-day rental minimum.

By motor home

Motor homes (Aussies call them *camper vans*) are popular for traveling in Australia. Smaller than American RVs, they come in two-, three-, four-, or six-berth versions, and usually have everything you need, such as a minifridge/freezer, microwave, gas stove, utensils, linens, and touring information, including maps and campground guides. All have showers and toilets, except some two-berthers. Most have air-conditioned driver's cabins, but not all have air-conditioned living quarters, a necessity in most parts of the country from November through March. Four-wheel-drive campers are available, but they tend to be small, and some lack hot water, toilet, shower, and air-conditioning. The minimum driver age for motor homes is usually 21.

Australia's major camper van rental firms are **Apollo Motorhome Holidays** (☎ **1800/777 779** in Australia, or 07/3265 9200; www.apollo camper.com.au), **Britz Campervan Rentals** (☎ **1800/331 454** in Australia, or 03/8379 8890; www.britz.com), and **Maui** (☎ **1300/363 800** in Australia, or 03/8379 8891; www.maui.com.au).

Rates vary with the seasons. May and June are the slowest months; December and January are the busiest. You can sometimes get better rates by booking in your home country. Renting for longer than three weeks might reduce the daily rate by a few dollars. Most companies require a minimum four- or five-day rental. Give the company your itinerary before booking, because some routes, such as the ferry to Tasmania — or, in the case of a four-wheel-drive motor home, the Gibb River Road in the Kimberley — may need the company's permission. Companies may not permit you to drive their two-wheel-drive motor home on unpaved roads, although they may make an exception for relatively short, unsealed access roads to recognized campgrounds. Check first.

Australians navigate by road name, not road number. The easiest way to get where you're going is to familiarize yourself with the major towns along your route and follow the signs toward them.

Following the rules of the road, Australian style

Here are some driving tips you should know before you take to the road:

✔ **Drive on the left.** (Yes, we know we said that before, but it bears repeating.) You yield, or "give way" to the right when a faster car approaches. Left turns on a red light are not permitted unless a sign says so.

✔ **Approach roundabouts (traffic circles) slowly enough to stop if you have to, and yield to all traffic on the roundabout.** Flash your indicator as you leave the roundabout even if you're going straight, because, technically, that's a left turn.

✔ **Do not drink and drive.** Drunken driving laws are *strictly* enforced. The maximum permitted blood alcohol level when driving is 0.05 percent. Police set up random breath-testing units (RBTs) all the time, so getting caught is easy. You'll face a court appearance if you do.

✔ **Observe the speed limit.** The speed limit is 50kmph (31 mph) or 60kmph (37 mph) in urban areas, 100kmph (62 mph) in most country areas, and sometimes 110kmph (68 mph) on freeways. In the Northern Territory, the speed limit is set at 130kmph (80 mph) on the Stuart, Arnhem, Barkly, and Victoria highways, while rural roads are designated 110kmph (68 mph) speed limits unless otherwise signposted. But be warned — the Territory has a high road death toll. Speed-limit signs are black numbers circled in red on a white background.

✔ **Wear your seat belt — it's required by law.** Drivers and passengers, including taxi passengers, must wear a seat belt when the vehicle is moving forward. Children must sit in the back seat in a child-safety seat or harness; car rental companies will rent these to you, but be sure to book them in advance. Tell the taxi company you have a child when you book a cab so it can send a car with the right restraints.

Staying safe on the road

Fatigue is a major killer on Australia's roads. A good rule to follow is to take a short break every hour or two, even if you don't feel tired. In some states, "driver reviver" stations operate on major roads during holiday periods. They serve free tea, coffee, and cookies, and are often at roadside picnic areas that have restrooms.

 Kangaroos and other wildlife are a common road hazard outside the cities. Try to avoid driving in country areas between dusk and dawn, when it's cooler and 'roos are most active. If you hit one, always stop and check its pouch for live *joeys* (baby kangaroos); females usually have one in the pouch. Wrap the joey tightly in a towel or old sweater, don't feed or overhandle it, and take it to a vet in the nearest town. Most vets will treat native wildlife for free.

Organizations that can help with injured wildlife include the following:

- ✔ RSPCA Wildlife in the **Australian Capital Territory** (☎ **02/6287 8100** or 0413/495 031)

- ✔ Wildcare in **Western Australia** (☎ **08/9474 9055**) and **Tasmania** (☎ **03/6233 2852**)

- ✔ Wildlife Information & Rescue Service (WIRES) in **New South Wales** (☎ **02/8977 3333**)

- ✔ Wildlife Rescue in **Queensland** (☎ **0418/792 598**) and the **Northern Territory** (☎ **0409/090 849**)

- ✔ Wildlife Rescue Fauna Rescue of S.A. in **South Australia** (☎ **08/ 8289 0896**)

- ✔ Wildlife Victoria (☎ **0500/540 000** or 03/9663 9211) in **Victoria**.

Some highways run through unfenced *stations* (ranches), where sheep and cattle pose a threat. Cattle like to rest on the warm paved road at night, so put your lights on high to spot them. If an animal does loom, slow down — but never swerve, or you may roll. If you have to, hit it. Tell ranchers within 24 hours if you've hit their livestock.

Car rental companies will not insure for animal damage to the car, which should give you an inkling of how common an occurrence this is.

Another major hazard is the **road train.** A road train can be as many as three big truck containers linked together to make a "train" up to 54m (177 ft.) long. If you're in front of one, give the driver plenty of warning when you brake, because drivers need a lot of space to slow down. When passing a road train, allow at least 1 kilometer (⅔ mile) of clear road before you pass, but don't expect the driver to make it easy — "truckies" are notorious for their lack of concern for motorists.

Unsealed (unpaved) country roads can also be hazardous. They're usually bone dry, which makes them more slippery than they look, so travel at a moderate speed — 35kmph (22 mph) is not too cautious, and anything over 60kmph (37 mph) is dangerous. Don't overcorrect if you veer to one side. Keep well behind any other vehicles, because the dust they throw up can block your vision.

Floods are common in the Top End and far north Queensland (north of Cairns) from November or December through March or April (the Wet season). Never cross a flooded road unless you're sure of its depth. Crocodiles may be lurking, so do not wade in to test it! Fast-flowing water is dangerous, even if it's shallow. When in doubt, stay where you are and wait for the water to drop; most flash floods subside in 24 hours. Check the road conditions ahead at least once a day in the Wet season. We list the phone numbers for road conditions in the individual destination chapters.

Coping with emergencies on the road

The **emergency** breakdown assistance telephone number for every Australian auto club is ☎ **13 11 11** from anywhere in Australia. If you aren't a member of an auto club that has a reciprocal agreement with the Australian clubs, you'll have to join the Australian club on the spot before it will tow or repair your car. The cost of this varies between the clubs in each state. Basic membership usually costs somewhere around A$80 (US$64/£32), and you may also have to pay a special "on-road joining fee" (in New South Wales, it is A$159/US$127/£64) and in some cases — depending on distances involved — a towing fee, which could get pricey if you are stranded somewhere in the Outback. Make sure you get the emergency assistance number for your car rental company, too.

If you break down or get lost in the Outback, never leave your vehicle. There have been many cases of stranded drivers — even Aussies who should have known better — dying after wandering off for help or water, when neither is to be found for many miles. If you get lost in the Outback, conserve your body moisture and energy by doing as little as possible and staying in the shade of your car. Put out distress signals in patterns of three — three yells, three columns of smoke, and so on. The traditional Outback call for help is "coo-*ee*" (with the accent on the *ee*), yodeled in a high pitch; the sound travels a long way.

State auto clubs provide free breakdown emergency assistance to members of many affiliated automobile associations around the world. Even if you're not a member, the clubs are a good source of advice on local regulations, touring advice, road conditions, traveling in remote areas, and any other motoring questions you may have. They share a Web site: www.aaa.asn.au. You can drop into numerous regional offices, as well as the locations listed here:

- ✔ **New South Wales & ACT: National Roads and Motorists' Association (NRMA),** 388 George St., Sydney, NSW 2000 (☎ **13 11 22** in New South Wales, or 02/8741 6000).

- ✔ **Northern Territory: Automobile Association of the Northern Territory (AANT),** 79–81 Smith St., Darwin, NT 0800 (☎ **08/8981 3837**).

- ✔ **Queensland: Royal Automobile Club of Queensland (RACQ),** 300 St. Pauls Terrace, Fortitude Valley, QLD 4006 (☎ **13 19 05** in Australia, or 07/3361 2444); also in the General Post Office (GPO) building, 261 Queen St., Brisbane (☎ **07/3872 8465**).

- ✔ **South Australia: Royal Automobile Association of South Australia (RAA),** 55 Hindmarsh Sq., Adelaide, SA 5000 (☎ **08/8202 4600**).

- ✔ **Tasmania: Royal Automobile Club of Tasmania (RACT),** corner of Murray and Patrick streets, Hobart, TAS 7000 (☎ **13 27 22** in Tasmania, or 03/6232 6300).

- ✔ **Victoria: Royal Automobile Club of Victoria (RACV),** 550 Princes Hwy., Noble Park, VIC 3174 (☎ **13 13 29** in Australia, or 03/9790 2211).

- ✔ **Western Australia: Royal Automobile Club of WA (RACWA),** 228 Adelaide Terrace, Perth, WA 6000 (☎ **13 17 03** or 08/9436 4444).

Filling up the tank

Petrol (gasoline) stations are mostly self-service in the cities, but you may find a full-service operation in country towns. Prices go up and down, but at press time it was around A$1.21 ($0.48) a liter, which is the equivalent of US$3.65 per gallon, for unleaded petrol in Sydney, and A$1.45 ($0.58) per liter (US$4.38 per gallon) or more in the Outback. (One U.S. gallon equals 3.78 liters.) Most rental cars take unleaded gas, and motor homes run on diesel.

Gas stations (also called *roadhouses* in rural areas) can be few and far between in the Outback, so fill up whenever you can.

Chapter 8

Booking Your Accommodations

by Lee Mylne

. . . .

In This Chapter

▶ Seeing stars in hotel ratings

▶ Choosing hotels, motels, B&Bs, apartments . . . or farms?

▶ Saving money on accommodations

. . . .

*W*hether you're looking for a luxury resort on the Great Barrier Reef, a hideaway bed-and-breakfast, a city apartment where you can cook for yourself, or the chance to meet the locals, you can find whatever accommodations you need in Australia. From top-class hotels in the cities, to budget hostels almost everywhere, Australia has a wide range of accommodations to suit almost every traveler.

Most hotel rooms have reverse-cycle air-conditioning for heating and cooling, a telephone, a color TV, a clock radio, a minifridge (if not a mini-bar), an iron and ironing board, and self-serve coffee and tea. Private bathrooms are standard, although they often have only showers, not tubs. Air-conditioning is essential for any room you're booking in Queensland, the Red Centre, and the Top End, including the northern parts of Western Australia. If you aren't staying in a major hotel, make sure you ask about air-conditioning when you book, because it isn't always standard in lower-priced establishments — and in some places, some rooms may have it, while others do not.

Smoking and nonsmoking rooms are usually available in most major hotels, so if you can't stand the smell of stale cigarette smoke, make sure you book a nonsmoking room.

Breakfast is often (but not always) included in the room rate, so ask when you book. If breakfast isn't included, hotel breakfasts are notoriously expensive, so you may want to head to a cafe down the street.

Australian accommodations properties carry **star ratings** given by AAA Tourism, which has been awarding ratings since the 1950s. Independent assessments are based on facilities, amenities, maintenance, and cleanliness. Ratings run from 1 to 5 stars. Stars are featured in AAA Tourism guides, and recent research shows that 70 percent of travelers use the star ratings when choosing their accommodations. (These star ratings are noted in Table 8-1 using asterisks.) The rating scheme covers more than 18,000 accommodations throughout every state and territory.

Table 8-1	Key to Hotel Star Rating System
Stars	*What You'll Find*
*	A basic standard of accommodations, simply furnished, with a resident manager.
**	More comfort and value with additional features. Well-maintained properties offering an average standard of accommodations with average furnishings, bedding, and floor coverings.
***	Well appointed, with a comfortable standard of accommodations, and above-average furnishings and floor coverings.
****	Exceptionally well-appointed establishments with high-quality furnishings, a high degree of comfort, high standard of presentation, and guest services.
*****	International standard establishments offering superior appointments, furnishings, and décor, with an extensive range of first-class guest services. Reception, room service, and housekeeping are available 18 hours a day, with restaurant/bistro facilities available nightly. A number and variety of room styles, suites, or both are available. A choice of dining facilities, 24-hour room service, housekeeping, and valet parking are offered. Porter and concierge services are available, as are dedicated business centers and conference facilities.

Staying in Style

Perhaps you're someone who prefers the quality and consistency of a hotel. You'll have lots of styles and price ranges to choose from.

Hotels

The largest hotel group in Australia is the French chain **Accor,** which has more than 100 properties (that's about 15,000 rooms) under its Sofitel, Novotel, Mercure, All Seasons, Ibis, and Formule 1 brands. The high-end Sofitels can only be found in Sydney, Melbourne, and Brisbane, but the other brands are spread throughout Australia, even in remote Outback towns such as Kalgoorlie in Western Australia. Many other international chains, such as Marriott, Sheraton, and Hilton, have properties in Australia, mostly in the capital cities.

There is also a large range of smaller, independent and boutique hotels, which offer a more personal service but perhaps less extensive facilities. These are often charming and stylish, tucked away in quiet streets but still within easy reach of the city centers.

In this book, listed rack rates are based on double occupancy for one night. Sometimes this rate changes according to the season; in that case, we list each season's rates when possible. Some hotel groups — including Accor — use a "dynamic" room rate, which means the rate changes on a daily basis, according to occupancy and demand. In these case, we list rates as "from $x." The best way of finding out the rate for the time you want to stay is to go to the hotel's Web site, which lists exact prices for your stay, on the day you check. In Table 8-2, we give you an idea of what you can expect in the way of furnishings and amenities based on the cost of your room.

Table 8-2	Key to Hotel Dollar Signs	
Dollar Signs	*Price Range (US$)*	*What to Expect*
$	Less than $100	These accommodations are relatively simple and inexpensive. Rooms will likely be small, and televisions are not necessarily provided. Parking is not provided — it's catch-as-you-can on the street.
$$	$101–$200	A bit classier, these midrange accommodations offer more room, more extras (such as irons, hair dryers, or a microwave), and a more convenient location than the preceding category.
$$$	$201–$300	Higher class still, these accommodations begin to look plush. Think chocolates on your pillow, a classy restaurant, underground parking garages, maybe even expansive views of the water.
$$$$	$301–$400	These top-rated accommodations come with luxury amenities such as valet parking, on-site spas, and in-room hot tubs and CD players — but you're starting to pay through the nose for 'em.
$$$$$	$401 and up	This is pure, unadulterated luxury, where your every whim is catered to, the bar is free, and privacy is assured. Mostly found in island resorts and exclusive retreats.

Serviced apartments

Serviced apartments are popular with Australians, for their space and flexibility. Families can to cook for themselves and business travelers have space to entertain or hold meetings. Basically, a serviced apartment is fully furnished, with one, two, or three bedrooms, a living room, a kitchen or kitchenette, a laundry, and often two bathrooms — in other words, all the facilities of a hotel suite and more, often for less than the cost of a 4-star hotel room. (Not every apartment kitchen has a dishwasher, so check if that's important to you.) Cleaners will come in daily (or in some cases weekly) to make your beds and clean.

Australia's huge supply of apartments ranges from clean and comfortable, if a little dated, to luxurious. Most can be rented for one night, especially in cities, but in popular vacation spots, some proprietors will insist on a minimum three-night stay, or a week in high season.

Two of the biggest serviced apartment chains are

- ✔ **Medina Serviced Apartments** (☎ 1300/633 462 in Australia, or 02/9356 1000; www.medinaapartments.com.au), which has a chain of midrange to upscale properties in Sydney, Melbourne, Brisbane, Canberra, Adelaide, and Perth. A new property is scheduled to open in Darwin in 2008.

- ✔ **Quest Serviced Apartments** (☎ 1800/334 033 in Australia, or 03/9645 8357; www.questapartments.com.au), has more than 100 properties in every state and territory, making it Australia's largest apartment chain.

You can also find apartment hotels, which offer similar services.

Motels and motor inns

Australia's plentiful motels are neat and clean, if often a little dated. They usually have air-conditioning, telephones, color TVs, clock radios, minifridges or minibars, and self-serve tea and coffee. Most have only showers, not bathtubs. Some have restaurants attached, and many have swimming pools. Motor inns offer a greater range of facilities and, generally, a higher standard of rooms than motels. They're a great option if you're driving long distances between destinations and want somewhere affordable and basic to spend the night.

Bed-and-breakfast inns (B&Bs)

B&Bs range from cheap and cheerful family homes to luxury retreats where breakfast is provided. You can easily find charming rooms for under A$100 (US$80/£40) for a double. Bathroom facilities are sometimes shared, although more properties now offer private, if not always en-suite (attached), bathrooms.

The Australian Bed & Breakfast Book (www.bbbook.com.au) lists more than 400 B&Bs across Australia. Although the B&Bs pay to be in the book, they have to meet certain standards to be included. The entire book is posted on the Web site, and in Australia, it's widely available in bookshops and newsdealers, or you can order it direct (☎ **02/6658 5701**) for A$20 (US$16/£8) plus A$15 (US$12/£6) for overseas express postage.

What Next? Productions Pty. Ltd. (☎ **0438/600 696** cell phone; www.beautifulaccommodation.com) publishes a series of *Beautiful Accommodation* color guides listing around 500 exquisite properties in every state and territory, many in charming country areas. The properties listed are rather upscale, roughly in the A$150 to A$300 (US$120–US$240/£60–£120) range. Each book sells for A$30 (US$24/£12) in Australian bookstores and can be ordered online.

Another good Web site is that of **Bed & Breakfast and Farmstay Australia** (www.australianbedandbreakfast.com.au), which has links to all state B&B organizations.

Staying on an Aussie farm

For a truly Australian experience, and a chance to interact with families who make their living from the land, opt for a farmstay. Most are farms first, tourist operations second, but for many people — after years of drought — diversifying into tourism has kept them going. You'll find your hosts eager to share their way of life and to learn about yours.

Accommodations may be anything from a basic bunkhouse (ask if it's air-conditioned, because most farms are in hot areas) to rustically luxurious digs in a cottage or guesthouse. Do some research on the farm — many activities are seasonal, some farmers will not allow you to get involved in dangerous work because of insurance issues, not all will offer horseback riding, and *farm* means different things in different parts of Australia. If you like green fields and dairy cows, Victoria may be the place for you. If checking fences on a 500,000-hectare (200,000-acre) Outback *station* (ranch) sounds wildly romantic, head to Western Australia, Queensland, or the Northern Territory.

Bed & Breakfast and Farmstay Australia's Web site (www.australian bedandbreakfast.com.au) is a good place to start. Another good contact is **Accommodation Getaways Victoria** (☎ **1300/132 358** in Australia, or 03/9431 5417; www.agv.net.au). **Bed & Breakfast and Farmstay NT** (www.bed-and-breakfast.au.com) lists about 20 Northern Territory properties in Darwin, the Top End, and the Red Centre.

Meals are usually included, as you're in a remote area, distant from the nearest cafe or restaurant. Allow yourself a few days to get to know how rural Australia lives.

Finding the Best Room at the Best Rate

The *rack rate* is the maximum rate that a hotel charges for a room and is what you pay if you walk in off the street without a reservation. Hardly anybody pays this price, however, except in high season or on holidays, and there are many ways to lower the cost of your room.

Find out if there are special rates or other discounts that you may qualify for, such as corporate, student, military, senior, frequent flier, or other discounts. Your hotel may also offer special rates at weekends, midweek, or other off-peak times. You can save big on hotel rooms by traveling in a destination's off season or shoulder seasons, when rates typically drop, even at luxury properties.

When booking a room in a chain hotel, you often get a better deal by calling the individual hotel's reservation desk rather than the chain's main number. Booking online can also reap rewards, as many hotels offer Internet-only discounts, or supply rooms to Priceline, Hotwire, or Expedia at rates lower than the ones you can get through the hotel itself.

If you're planning to stay in one place for a few days, ask about long-stay discounts. Anything over about three days can attract a discount at certain resorts, especially in Queensland. Many offer "Stay 5, Pay 4" deals and similar for differing lengths of stay. Many B&B operators also offer weekly rates as well as nightly.

Watch out for hidden costs. Ask about local taxes and service charges, which can increase the cost of a room by 10 percent or more. When you book a room, ask what's included in the room rate and what's extra. If you're staying in a resort, ask if you'll be charged for beach chairs, towels, sports equipment, and other amenities.

Consider the pros and cons of all-inclusive packages, usually offered at resorts. *All-inclusive* means different things at different places. Many all-inclusive packages include three meals daily, sports equipment, spa treatments, and other amenities; others may include most alcoholic drinks. In general, you save money going the all-inclusive way — as long as you use the facilities provided. The downside is that your choices are limited to what the resort has to offer.

Sign up to a hotel chain's frequent-stay loyalty program, in which you can accumulate points or credits to earn free hotel nights, airline miles, in-room amenities, merchandise, tickets to concerts and events, and discounts on sporting facilities. Many hotels operating in Australia, including Hilton and Marriott, offer rewards programs.

Surfing the Web for hotel deals

In addition to online travel booking sites such as **Travelocity, Expedia, Orbitz, Priceline,** and **Hotwire,** you can book hotels through **Hotels.com, Quikbook** (www.quikbook.com), and **Travelaxe** (www.travelaxe.net).

Swapping houses with an Aussie

You stay in their house, and they stay in yours. House-swapping is becoming a more popular and viable means of travel, and it's certainly the case with Australians. You both get an authentic and personal view of the area you're visiting.

To find a compatible swap, try **HomeLink International** (www.homelink.org), the largest and oldest home-swapping organization, founded in 1952, with over 11,000 listings worldwide (US$90 for a yearly membership). There is a branch of HomeLink in Australia. Others with lots of Australian properties to choose from are **Homefor Exchange.com** (US$59 for six months), **InterVac.com** (US$95 for one year), and the U.K.-based **Home Base Holidays** (www.homebase-hols.com), where you can browse the listings for free but must pay £29 for a year to view the contact details or to list your home.

HotelChatter.com is a daily Webzine offering smart coverage and critiques of hotels worldwide. Go to **TripAdvisor.com** or **HotelShark.com** for independent consumer reviews of hotels and resorts.

Be sure to get a confirmation number and make a printout of any online booking transaction, just in case you show up at the hotel and it doesn't have a record of your reservation.

Reserving the best room

Somebody has to get the best room in the house, so it may as well be you. Start by joining the hotel's frequent-guest program, which may make you eligible for upgrades. A hotel-branded credit card usually gives its owner silver or gold status in frequent-guest programs.

Make sure you ask lots of questions when you're making your booking. Ask about a corner room, which is often larger and quieter, with more windows and light, but for the same price as a standard room. Ask if the hotel is renovating; if it is, request a room away from the construction. Ask for a room that has been recently renovated or refurbished. Ask about nonsmoking rooms and rooms with views. Be sure to request your choice of twin, queen-, or king-size beds. If you're a light sleeper, ask for a quiet room away from vending or ice machines, elevators, restaurants, bars, and discos.

If you aren't happy with your room when you arrive, ask for a different one. Most places will happily oblige.

In resort areas such as Queensland, ask the following questions before you book a room:

✔ **What's the view like?** If you're on a budget, you may be willing to pay less for a room with no view (or with a view of the parking lot), especially if you don't plan to spend much time in your room.

✔ **Does the room have air-conditioning or ceiling fans? Do the windows open?** If the room has no air-conditioning, you want windows that open. But if the windows open, and the nighttime entertainment is nearby, you may want to find out when showtime is over.

✔ **How far is the room from the beach and other amenities?** If it's far, is there transportation to and from the beach, and is it free?

Chapter 9

Catering to Special Needs or Interests

by Lee Mylne

. . . .

In This Chapter

▶ Traveling with children
▶ Finding the senior discounts
▶ Accessing Australia: Resources for the physically challenged
▶ Looking for lavender: GLBT resources
▶ Diving, bushwalking, kayaking, and more: Finding active Australia

. . . .

*W*hether you want to find out how easy it will be to travel with kids in Australia, or how you can get a senior discount, this section has information designed to help travelers with special needs work out the best options for their visit. Or maybe you're just keen to find out where the best bird-watching or diving is? We cover that as well.

Traveling with the Brood: Advice for Families

Australians travel widely with their own kids, so the whole country is pretty family-friendly. Generally, facilities for families are good and you'll find most tourist attractions offer money-saving family passes. I've taken my kids to all sorts of places and have generally found little to complain about (despite mixed reviews from them!). Make it fun, and everyone has a good time.

Some online resources for planning family travel include **Family Travel Forum** (www.familytravelforum.com), a comprehensive site that offers customized trip planning; **Family Travel Network** (www.family travelnetwork.com), an online magazine providing travel tips; and **TravelWithYourKids.com** (www.travelwithyourkids.com), a site written by parents for parents offering sound advice for long-distance and international travel with children. Australian travel magazine ***Holidays with Kids*** has a comprehensive Web site listing great options for family travel in Australia at www.holidayswithkids.com.au. **Rascals in Paradise** (☎ 415-921-7000; www.rascalsinparadise.com) sells family vacation packages to Australia.

For accommodations, families can't do better than to book into one of the huge range of serviced or unserviced apartments (with or without daily maid service). Usually less expensive than a hotel room, they offer a lot more living space — a living room, a kitchen, a bathroom or two, and the privacy of a separate bedroom for adults.

Many Australian resorts have kids' clubs with extensive programs designed for under-12s and, in some cases, teenagers. The French-owned Accor chain of hotels and resorts has kids' clubs, kids' menus designed by a nutritionist, and other family-friendly facilities including family rooms. Other resorts, such as Hamilton Island, have "kids stay, eat, and play free" offers, particularly during holiday periods. Many hotels offer connecting units or family rooms. Ask when booking.

International airlines and domestic airlines in Australia charge 75 percent of the adult fare for kids under 12. Most charge 10 percent for infants under 2 not occupying a seat. Australian transport companies, attractions, and tour operators usually charge half-price for kids under 12 or 14 years.

Children entering Australia with their parents still need their own visas, as well as passports.

Making Age Work for You: Tips for Seniors

Visiting seniors from other countries often don't qualify for discounted entry to tours, attractions, and events in Australia; that privilege is usually reserved only for Australian seniors (also called *pensioners*). But it always pays to inquire about discounts when booking hotels, flights, and train or bus tickets. The best ID to bring is something that shows your date of birth or something that marks you as an "official" senior, like a membership card from AARP.

Members of **AARP,** 601 E St. NW, Washington, DC 20049 (☎ 888-687-2277; www.aarp.org), get discounts on hotels, airfares, and car rentals. AARP offers members a wide range of benefits, including *AARP: The Magazine* and a newsletter. Anyone over 50 can join.

Many reliable agencies and organizations target the 50-plus market. **Elderhostel** (☎ 800-454-5768; www.elderhostel.org) arranges worldwide study programs for those aged 55 and over.

In Australia, pick up a copy of *Get Up & Go,* the only national travel magazine for those over 50 and the official Seniors Card travel magazine (www.getupandgo.com.au). It's a glossy quarterly, available at most newsdealers for A$4.95 (US$3.95/£2), and has an extensive section called Destination Australia, which covers a region in each state or territory in every issue.

Accessing Australia: Advice for Travelers with Disabilities

Most hotels, major stores, attractions, and public restrooms in Australia have wheelchair access. Many smaller lodges and even B&Bs are starting to cater to guests with disabilities, and some diving companies cater to scuba divers with disabilities. National parks make an effort to include wheelchair-friendly pathways, too. Taxi companies in bigger cities can usually supply a cab equipped for wheelchairs.

TTY facilities are still limited largely to government services. For information on all kinds of facilities and services (not just travel-related organizations) for people with disabilities, contact **National Information Communication Awareness Network,** P.O. Box 407, Curtin, ACT 2605 (☎ **1800/806 769** voice and TTY in Australia, or 02/6285 3713; www. nican.com.au). This free service can put you in touch with accessible accommodations and attractions throughout Australia, as well as with travel agents and tour operators who understand your needs.

Organizations that offer a vast range of resources and assistance to disabled travelers include **MossRehab** (☎ **800-CALL-MOSS** [2255-6677]; www.mossresourcenet.org); the **American Foundation for the Blind** (AFB; ☎ **800-232-5463;** www.afb.org); and the **Society for Accessible Travel & Hospitality** (SATH; ☎ **212-447-7284;** www.sath. org). **AirAmbulanceCard.com** is now partnered with SATH and allows you to preselect top-notch hospitals in case of an emergency.

Access-Able Travel Source (☎ **303-232-2979;** www.access-able.com) offers a comprehensive database on travel agents from around the world with experience in accessible travel; destination-specific access information; and links to such resources as service animals, equipment rentals, and access guides.

Many travel agencies offer customized tours and itineraries for travelers with disabilities. Among them are **Flying Wheels Travel** (☎ **507-451-5005;** www.flyingwheelstravel.com) and **Accessible Journeys** (☎ **800-846-4537** or 610-521-0339; www.disabilitytravel.com).

Flying with Disability (www.flying-with-disability.org) is a comprehensive information source on airplane travel.

Avis Rent a Car (☎ **888-879-4273**) has an "Avis Access" program that offers services for customers with special travel needs. These include specially outfitted vehicles with swivel seats, spinner knobs, and hand controls; mobility scooter rentals; and accessible bus service. Reserve well in advance.

Also check out the quarterly magazine *Emerging Horizons* (www.emerginghorizons.com), available by subscription ($17/year in the U.S.; $22/year outside the U.S).

The "Accessible Travel" link at **Mobility-Advisor.com** offers a variety of travel resources to disabled persons.

British travelers should contact **Holiday Care** (☎ **0845/124-9971** in the U.K. only; www.holidaycare.org.uk) to access a wide range of travel information and resources for disabled and elderly people.

Following the Rainbow: Resources for Gay and Lesbian Travelers

Sydney is one of the most gay-friendly cities in the world. There are plenty of gay and lesbian bars, and most Saturday nights see a privately operated gay dance party taking place in an inner-city warehouse somewhere. The cafes and pubs of Oxford Street in Darlinghurst, a short cab ride or long stroll from Sydney's downtown area, are the liveliest areas. The annual Sydney Gay & Lesbian Mardi Gras, culminating in a huge street parade and party in late February or early March, is a high point on the city's calendar and is attended by huge crowds.

In rural areas, you still find some resistance to gays and lesbians, but Australians are generally tolerant. Noosa, on Queensland's Sunshine Coast, is a favored destination for revelers after the Sydney Mardi Gras, and a couple of resorts in North Queensland cater to gay and lesbian travelers. One of the best known is **Turtle Cove Resort & Spa** (☎ **1300/727 979** in Australia, or 07/4059 1800; www.turtlecove.com.au), on a private beach between Cairns and Port Douglas.

The LGBT community has lots of support services in Australia. The **Gay & Lesbian Counselling Service of NSW** (☎ **02/8594 9500** for the administration office) runs a national hot line (☎ **1800/184 527** in Australia, or 02/8594 9596) from 7:30 to 10 p.m. daily. Its Web site (www.glccs.org.au) has contact information for each state. In Sydney, the **Albion Street Centre** (☎ **02/9332 9600** administration, or 02/9332 9700 information line) is an AIDS clinic and information service.

The International Gay and Lesbian Travel Association (IGLTA; ☎ 800-448-8550 or 954-776-2626; www.iglta.org) is the trade association for the gay and lesbian travel industry, and offers an online directory of gay- and lesbian-friendly travel businesses and tour operators. **Gay & Lesbian Tourism Australia** (www.galta.com.au) also has listings of useful businesses in each state.

Many agencies offer tours and travel itineraries for gay and lesbian travelers. **Above and Beyond Tours** (☎ 800-397-2681; www.abovebeyond tours.com) are gay Australia tour specialists. **Now, Voyager** (☎ 800-255-6951; www.nowvoyager.com) offers worldwide trips, and **Olivia** (☎ 800-631-6277; www.olivia.com) offers lesbian cruises and resort vacations.

Gay.com Travel (☎ 800-929-2268 or 415-644-8044; www.gay.com/travel), is the online successor to *Out & About* magazine. It provides information about gay-owned, gay-oriented, and gay-friendly lodging, dining, sightseeing, nightlife, and shopping establishments in every major destination worldwide. British travelers should click on the "Travel" link at www.uk.gay.com for advice and gay-friendly trip ideas. The Canadian Web site **GayTraveler** (http://gaytraveler.ca) offers ideas and advice for gay travel all over the world.

The following travel guides are available in bookstores and online: *Spartacus International Gay Guide* (Bruno Gmünder Verlag; www.spartacusworld.com/gayguide); *Odysseus: The International Gay Travel Planner* (www.odyusa.com); and the *Damron* guides (www.damron.com), with annual books for gay men and lesbians.

Active Australia: Where to Go for the Gusto

Outdoor pursuits are high on the list of many visitors to Australia, lured by the wide-open spaces and a climate ideal for exploring and experiencing the great activities on offer. Whether it's a gentle occupation like bird-watching, or the thrill of white-water rafting, Australia is sure to have an activity that suits you.

Most operators and outfitters listed in this book specialize in adventure vacations for small groups. The **Great Outdoor Recreation Pages (GORP)** site (http://gorp.away.com) not only has links to adventure-tour operators in Australia, but also contains articles, sells books and maps, and has links to heaps of sites on Australia with an action slant.

Outer Edge Expeditions (☎ 800-322-5235 or 517-552-5300; www.outer-edge.com) and **The World Outdoors** (☎ 800-488-8483 or 303-413-0938; www.theworldoutdoors.com) offer ecologically minded multisport diving, hiking, biking, canoeing, and kayaking packages to the Great Barrier Reef and North Queensland rain forest.

Meals, accommodations, equipment rental, and guides are usually included, though international airfares are not. Where you end up resting your head at night varies depending on the package — on a sea-kayaking trip, you'll likely be camping on a beach; on a hiking expedition, you may stay at a wilderness lodge; and on a biking trip you often stop at B&B-style lodgings. Remember to check the regional chapters in this book for more information on the outdoor activities in the area you're visiting.

Scuba diving

Diving on the Great Barrier Reef is a major attraction for visitors to Australia — whether they're experienced divers or not. What is less well known is that there are good dive sites all around the Australian coast, not just off Queensland. A second barrier reef, in Ningaloo Reef Marine Park, stretches 260km (161 miles) off the coast of Western Australia. In Tasmania, you can dive kelp beds popular with seals, and in South Australia you can cage-dive with great white sharks.

Wherever you find coral in Australia, you find dive companies offering learn-to-dive courses, day trips, and, in some cases, extended journeys on live-aboard vessels. Most international dive certificates, including PADI, NAUI, SSI, and BSAC, are recognized. You can rent gear and wet suits wherever you go.

Remember to allow time in your itinerary for a medical exam in Australia. If you're already a certified diver, be sure to bring your "C" card and log book. If you're going to take a dive course, you'll need a medical certificate from an Australian doctor stating that you're fit for scuba diving. (An all-purpose physical is not enough.) Almost all the dive schools will arrange the medical exam for you.

You must complete your last dive 24 hours before you fly in an aircraft. This catches a lot of people off-guard when they're preparing to fly to their next destination the day after a visit to the Reef. You won't be able to helicopter off the Reef back to the mainland, either.

Check to see if your travel insurance covers diving. **The Divers Alert Network** (☎ **800-446-2671;** www.diversalertnetwork.org) sells diving insurance and has diving and nondiving medical emergency hot lines, and an information line for dive-related medical questions.

If you've never been diving and don't plan to become qualified, you can see what all the fuss is about on an "introductory" dive that lets you dive in the company of an instructor on a one-time basis, with a briefing beforehand. Most dive operators on the Great Barrier Reef and other dive locations offer introductory dives.

For information on dive regions and operators, try the state tourism marketing boards' Web sites. Tourism Queensland's Web site (www.queenslandholidays.com.au) has information on most dive operators to the Great Barrier Reef. **Dive Queensland** (☎ **07/4051 1510;** fax 07/4051 1519; www.dive-queensland.com.au), the Queensland Dive Tourism Association, requires its member operators to abide by a code of ethics. Its Web site has a list of members and the services they offer. Another good source is **Diversion Dive Travel** (☎ **1800/607 913** in Australia, or 07/4039 0200; www.diversionoz.com), a Cairns-based travel agent that specializes in dive holidays on the Great Barrier Reef and other places. It books day trips and extended excursions on a choice of live-aboard vessels, as well as dive courses, island resorts with diving, accommodations, and non-diving tours. It also sells diving insurance. Its proprietors are dive instructors, and one of them is trained as a handicapped diving instructor for divers with disabilities.

Bushwalking (hiking)

Australia has many national parks crisscrossed with hiking trails. You're never far from a park with a bushwalk, whether it's an easy stroll, or a six-day odyssey on the Cape-to-Cape trail in Western Australia. A good Australian bushwalking Web site is www.bushwalking.org.au.

Some parks charge an entry fee, ranging from A$6 to A$18 (US$4.80–US$14/£2.40–£7.20). The best place to get information about bushwalking is the National Parks & Wildlife Service, or its equivalent in each state:

- **Environmental Protection Agency** (Queensland Parks & Wildlife Service; ☎ 07/3227 8185; www.epa.qld.gov.au).

- **New South Wales National Parks & Wildlife Service** (www.nationalparks.nsw.gov.au). It has a visitor information center at Cadmans Cottage, 110 George St., The Rocks, Sydney (☎ 02/9247 5033).

- **Parks & Wildlife Commission of the Northern Territory** (☎ 08/8999 4555; www.nt.gov.au/nreta/parks). The Northern Territory Tourist Commission is the official source of information on parks and wildlife matters.

- **Parks Victoria** (☎ 13 19 63; www.parkweb.vic.gov.au).

- **South Australian Department for Environment and Heritage** (☎ 08/8204 9010; www.environment.sa.gov.au).

- **Tasmania Parks and Wildlife Service** (☎ 1300/368 550 in Australia, or 03/6233 8011; www.dpiwe.tas.gov.au).

- **Western Australian Department of Environment and Conservation** (☎ 08/9334 0333; www.naturebase.net).

Auswalk (☎ 03/5356 4971; www.auswalk.com.au) offers self-guided or escorted/accommodated walking tours through picturesque parts of Australia such as the Great Ocean Road in Victoria, Lamington National Park Island in Queensland, and the Red Centre and the Blue Mountains in New South Wales.

World Expeditions (☎ 415-989-2212 in the U.S., 613-241-2700 in Canada, 1300/720 000 in Australia; www.worldexpeditions.com.au) runs expeditions to destinations less traveled, such as Hinchinbrook Island in the Great Barrier Reef Marine Park and the long-distance Bibbulmun Track in Western Australia's southwest. Some trips incorporate other pursuits, like rafting, sailing, or biking.

Biking

Much of Australia's countryside is flat and ideal for cycling (as Aussies call biking) and there are plenty of trails. Just remember that you often have to cope with heat and long distances. The rain forest hills behind Cairns hosted the world mountain-biking championships in 1996, and Sydney's Blue Mountains have good mountain-biking trails. All major towns and most resort centers rent regular bikes and mountain bikes.

Remote Outback Cycle Tours (☎ **08/9279 6969;** www.cycletours. com.au) takes novice and expert riders of all ages on tours across the country. The distances are vast, but the trip combines cycling with four-wheel-drive travel. Itineraries include trips in the Red Centre, including the Oodnadatta Track cattle-driving route from Alice Springs to Adelaide via the opal-mining town of Coober Pedy in South Australia.

Bird-watching

Australia's geography as an island continent means it also has unique bird species. It's probably best known for its brilliant parrots, but you'll see species from the wetlands, savanna, mulga scrub, desert, oceans, dense bushland, rain forest, mangroves, rivers, and other habitats. More than half of the country's species have been spotted in the Daintree Rainforest area in north Queensland, and one-third live in wetlands-rich Kakadu National Park in the Top End.

Kirrama Wildlife Tours (☎ **07/4065 5181;** www.kirrama.com.au) operates birding expeditions to remote regions in northern Australia from a base in North Queensland. Broome-based ornithologist George Swann of **Kimberley Birdwatching, Wildlife & Natural History Tours** (☎ **08/9192 1246;** www.kimberleybirdwatching.com.au) leads extended birding trips throughout the Kimberley and the Northern Territory. **Fine Feather Tours** (☎ **07/4094 1199;** www.finefeathertours.com.au), based near Port Douglas near the Daintree Rainforest, operates bird-watching day trips and afternoon river cruises. To get in touch with birding clubs all over Australia, contact **Birds Australia** (☎ **1300/730 075** in Australia, or 03/9347 0757; www.birdsaustralia.com.au).

Canoeing and sea kayaking

Katherine Gorge in the Northern Territory offers some spectacular flat canoeing, and you'll also find delightful canoeing on the bird-rich Ord River in the Top End. Both are full of generally harmless freshwater crocodiles, but *never* canoe in saltwater-crocodile territory. Operators all around the coastline rent kayaks and lead guided expeditions. Popular spots are the Whitsunday Islands in north Queensland, the cold southern seas around Tasmania, and Byron Bay, where you can take a three-hour "dolphin kayaking" trip to see wild dolphins (and whales June–Oct) and "kayak-surf" the waves.

Rivergods (☎ **08/9259 0749;** www.rivergods.com.au) conducts multi-day sea-kayaking, canoeing, and white-water-rafting adventures throughout Western Australia's pristine ocean and rivers, in which whales, sharks, *dugongs* (manatees), sea snakes, turtles, and dolphins abound. The company also runs a "sea kayak with wild seals" day outing from Perth. **Gecko Canoeing** (☎ **1800/634 319** in Australia, or 08/8972 2224; www.geckocanoeing.com.au) leads canoeing trips of one to seven days along remote Top End rivers between April and September.

Fishing

Reef, game, deep sea, beach, estuary, and river fishing — Australia's massive coastline lets you do it all. Drop a line for coral trout on the Great Barrier Reef; go for the world-record black marlin off Cairns; hook a fighting "barra" (barramundi) in the Northern Territory or the Kimberley; or cast for trout in Tasmania's highland lakes. Charter boats will take you out for the day from most towns all around the coast.

Golf

Australians are passionate about golf, and courses abound. Queensland has the lion's share of the stunning resort courses, such as the Sheraton Mirage in Port Douglas, Laguna Quays Resort near the Whitsundays, and the Hyatt Regency Sanctuary Cove Resort on the Gold Coast. The Gold Coast has more than 40 courses. One of the world's best desert courses is at Alice Springs.

Most courses rent clubs for around A$30 (US$24/£12). Greens fees start at around A$20 (US$16/£8) for 18 holes but average A$65 (US$52/£26) or more on a championship course. **Koala Golf** (☎ **1300/301 686** in Australia, or 02/9746 6646; www.koalagolf.com) offers escorted day trips and package tours to excellent golf courses in major cities and holiday areas around Australia.

Sailing

The 74 islands of the Whitsundays in Queensland provide a spectacular backdrop for a sailing holiday. And you don't have to join an organized cruise or tour; the Whitsunday region is Australia's **bareboating** capital, which means you can charter an unskippered yacht and sail yourself, even if you're not an experienced sailor (for more detailed information on bareboating, see Chapter 17).

Chapter 10

Taking Care of the Remaining Details

by Lee Mylne

In This Chapter

▶ Getting a passport and visa
▶ Insuring your trip
▶ Taking care of your health and safety
▶ Staying in touch by e-mail and phone

*B*efore you head off Down Under, you need to take care of some remaining details. Is your passport up to date? Have you taken out insurance in case of accidents? Are you wondering how you'll keep in touch with family and friends while you're gone? These points and more are easy to deal with when you know how, and we cover it all in this chapter.

Getting a Passport

You most definitely need a passport to go to Australia. Getting one takes some time, so if you don't have one, or if yours has expired, apply for one in the early stages of planning your trip. Processing has been particularly slow recently, so give yourself at least a couple months to get or renew yours. You *can* expedite it — by paying a hefty surcharge.

For an up-to-date, country-by-country listing of passport requirements around the world, go to the "Foreign Entry Requirement" Web page of the U.S. State Department at http://travel.state.gov.

To enter Australia, each person in your party (including children) will also need a **visa** (see information about getting a visa below).

Applying for a U.S. passport

If you're applying for a passport for the first time, follow these steps:

1. **Complete a passport application in person at a U.S. passport office; a federal, state, or probate court; or a major post office.**

   To find your regional passport office, check the U.S. State Department Web site or call the **National Passport Information Center (☎ 877-487-2778)** for automated information.

2. **Present a certified birth certificate as proof of citizenship.**

   You may also want to bring along your driver's license, state or military ID, or Social Security card.

3. **Submit two identical photos, measuring 2 x 2 inches.**

4. **Submit the processing fee at the time you apply.**

   For people 16 and over, a passport is valid for ten years and costs $85. For those travelers 15 and under, a passport is valid for five years and costs $70.

If you have a passport in your current name that was issued within the past 15 years (and you were over age 16 when it was issued), you can renew it by mail for $67. Whether you're applying in person or by mail, you can download passport applications from the U.S. State Department Web site at http://travel.state.gov.

Applying for passports in other countries

The following list offers information for citizens of Canada, the United Kingdom, and Ireland:

- ✔ **Canadians** can obtain passport applications from travel agencies throughout Canada or from the central **Passport Office,** Department of Foreign Affairs and International Trade, Ottawa, ON K1A 0G3 (☎ **800-567-6868;** www.ppt.gc.ca).

- ✔ **British** citizens can pick up an application for a standard ten-year passport (five-year passport for children under 16), visit your nearest passport office, major post office, or travel agency or contact the **United Kingdom Passport Service (☎ 0870/521-0410;** www.ukpa.gov.uk).

- ✔ **Irish** citizens can apply for a ten-year passport at the **Passport Office,** Setanta Centre, Molesworth Street, Dublin 2 (☎ **01/671-1633;** www.irlgov.ie/iveagh). Those under age 18 and over 65 must apply for a three-year passport. You can also apply at 1A South Mall, Cork (☎ **021/272-525**), or at most post offices.

Getting a visa for your trip to Australia

Along with a current passport valid for the duration of your stay, the Australian government requires a **visa** from visitors of every nation, except New Zealand, to be issued before you arrive. If you're a short-term visitor or business traveler, the process is easy and can be done in a few minutes on the Internet, using the Australian government's **Electronic Travel Authority (ETA),** an electronic visa that takes the place of a stamp in your passport.

Tourists should apply for a **Visitor ETA.** The visa is free (though there is a service charge for getting it via the Internet), and it's valid for visits to Australia of up to three months each within a one-year period. Tourists may not work in Australia. If you're visiting for business, you have two choices: Apply for a **Short Validity Business ETA,** which covers a single visit of three months within a one-year period, or pay A$70 (US$56/£28) to apply for a **Long Validity Business visa,** which entitles you to as many three-month stays in Australia as you like for the life of your passport but cannot be done online.

You can apply for an ETA yourself, or have your travel agent or airline do it when you book your plane ticket. (This service may incur an additional fee from the airline or travel agent.) To apply online, visit www. eta.immi.gov.au; the A$20 (US$16/£8) charge is payable by credit card (Amex, Diners Club, MasterCard, or Visa). Assuming you do not have a criminal conviction and are in good health, your ETA should be approved quickly. You can also apply for the visa at Australian embassies, high commissions, and consulates. Everyone traveling with you (including children) must have his own visa.

Fees mentioned in this section are in Australian dollars; the exact amount charged by the Australian embassy, consulate, or high commission in your country will depend on the foreign currency exchange rate.

In the United States, Canada, the United Kingdom, Ireland, and many other countries, most travel agents and airlines are ETA-compatible.

Guard your passport well. Keep it with you at all times, or keep it locked up in a hotel safe. You'll need it when converting traveler's checks or foreign currency, but otherwise kept it in a safe place.

Dealing with a lost passport

Losing your passport is not the end of the world, but replacing a lost or stolen passport should be dealt with immediately. First, report it to the police. Then contact the nearest consulate or high commission office and begin to take the necessary steps to get a new one. For the addresses of consulates and high commissions, see the appendix.

Playing It Safe: Travel and Medical Insurance

There are three kinds of travel insurance, and you should seriously consider them all: medical, trip cancellation, and lost luggage insurance. Costs vary widely, depending on the cost and length of your trip, your age and health, and the type of trip you're taking. There's an old saying: "If you can't afford the insurance, you can't afford to travel." Take it from me, as someone who once required emergency surgery while overseas, the insurance is well worth it!

✔ **Trip-cancellation insurance:** This insurance helps you retrieve your money if you have to back out of a trip, if you have to return home early, or if your travel supplier goes bankrupt. It usually covers such events as sickness, natural disasters, and State Department advisories that your destination is unsafe for travel. The latest news in trip-cancellation insurance is the availability of expanded hurricane coverage and the *any-reason cancellation coverage* — which costs more but covers cancellations made for any reason. You won't get back 100 percent of your prepaid trip cost, but you'll be refunded a substantial portion.

TravelSafe (☎ 888-885-7233; www.travelsafe.com) offers both types of coverage. Expedia also offers any-reason cancellation coverage for its air-hotel packages. For details, contact one of the following recommended insurers: **Access America** (☎ 866-807-3982; www.accessamerica.com), **Travel Guard International** (☎ 800-826-4919; www.travelguard.com), **Travel Insured International** (☎ 800-243-3174; www.travelinsured.com), or **Travelex Insurance Services** (☎ 888-457-4602; www.travelex-insurance.com).

✔ **Medical insurance:** For travel overseas, most U.S. health plans (including Medicare and Medicaid) do not provide coverage, and the ones that do often require you to pay for services upfront and reimburse you only after you return home. As a safety net, you may want to buy travel medical insurance, particularly if you're traveling to a remote or high-risk area where emergency evacuation may be necessary.

Australia's immense distances mean you can sometimes be a long way from a hospital or a doctor. Make sure your policy covers medical evacuation by helicopter or Australia's Royal Flying Doctor Service airlift. (You may well need this if you become sick or injured in the Outback.) Very few health insurance plans pay for medical evacuation back to the United States (which can cost US$10,000 and up). A number of companies offer medical evacuation services anywhere in the world.

If you're ever hospitalized more than 150 miles from home, **MedjetAssist** (☎ 800-527-7478; www.medjetassistance.com) will pick you up and fly you to the hospital of your choice anywhere in the world in a medically equipped and staffed aircraft 24 hours day,

7 days a week. Annual memberships are US$225 individual, US$350 family; you can also purchase short-term memberships.

Australia has a reciprocal medical-care agreement with Great Britain and a limited agreement with Ireland and New Zealand, which covers travelers for medical expenses for immediately necessary treatment in a public hospital (but not evacuation to your home country, ambulances, funerals, and dental care). Australia's national health system, called Medicare, is similar to the program by the same name in the United States. Having insurance is crucial, though, because medical care in Australia is expensive, and the national healthcare system typically covers only 85 percent of treatment (sometimes less). You won't be covered for treatment in a private hospital, and evacuation insurance is a must.

If you decide on additional medical insurance, try **MEDEX Assistance** (☎ 410-453-6300; www.medexassist.com) or **Travel Assistance International** (☎ 800-821-2828; www.travel assistance.com). For general information on Travel Assistance International services, call the company's **Worldwide Assistance Services, Inc.,** at ☎ 800-777-8710.

Canadians should check with their provincial health plan offices or call **Health Canada** (☎ 866-225-0709; www.hc-sc.gc.ca) to find out the extent of their coverage and what documentation and receipts they must take home in case they're treated overseas.

✔ **Lost luggage insurance:** On international flights (including U.S. portions of international trips), baggage coverage is limited to approximately US$9.07 per pound, up to approximately US$635 per checked bag. If you plan to check items more valuable than what's covered by the standard liability, see if your homeowner's policy covers your valuables, get baggage insurance as part of your comprehensive travel-insurance package, or buy Travel Guard's BagTrak product.

If your luggage is lost, immediately file a lost-luggage claim at the airport. Most airlines require that you report delayed, damaged, or lost baggage within four hours of arrival. The airlines are required to deliver luggage, once found, directly to your house or destination free of charge.

Staying Healthy When You Travel

Australian hygiene standards are high, hospitals are modern and well equipped, and doctors are well qualified, so you don't have to worry too much about illness on a trip Down Under. You don't need any vaccinations to enter Australia (unless you're coming via Africa or South America, when you'll need a Yellow Fever vaccination certificate).

But if you're traveling in remote Outback areas, you can sometimes be a long way from a hospital or a doctor. Even with the Royal Flying Doctor Service to help you, medical travel insurance (see the preceding section) may be advisable. Australian pharmacists may only fill prescriptions written by Australian doctors, so carry enough medication with you for your trip.

Spiders, snakes, and other beasties

Snake and spider **bites** may not be as common as the hair-raising stories you'll hear would suggest, but snakes are commonly encountered — especially if you're hiking or camping — and it pays to be wary. Australia's two deadly spiders are the large hairy funnel web and the tiny red-back, which has a distinctive red slash on its back. If you're bitten, keep calm; moving as little as possible may save your life. Immobilize the limb and wrap that whole section of the limb tightly (but not tight enough to restrict blood flow). Then head to the nearest hospital, where antivenin should be available.

Hikers should check for ticks, which are common. If you find one, dab it with methylated spirits or some other noxious chemical. Wait a while, and then gently and carefully pull it out with tweezers, ensuring you don't leave its head inside the wound.

Marine *stingers,* or box jellyfish, inhabit the coastal waters of the northern third of Australia in summer. Their painful sting can cause heart failure and death. If you're stung, pour vinegar over the affected site immediately — local authorities leave bottles of vinegar on the beach for this purpose. On beaches in Sydney and other areas, you may come across *blue bottles* (which are sometimes also called stingers but are not the same as the jellyfish found in northern waters). These long-tentacled blue jellyfish (also known as *Portuguese men-of-war*) inflict a generally harmless but painful sting that can last for hours. The best remedy is to rinse the stung area in seawater or fresh water to remove any tentacles. For intense pain, apply heat or cold, whichever feels better. If you experience breathing difficulties or disorientation following a jellyfish sting, seek medical attention immediately.

Other things to avoid in the water include stingrays, stonefish (which as their name suggests look like stones, so don't walk on underwater "rocks"), lionfish, puffer fish, blue-ringed octopus (it has blue circles all over its body), and *cone shells* (a shellfish shaped like a blunt cone).

There are two types of crocodiles in Australia: the freshwater crocodile, which grows to almost 3m (10 ft.), and the dangerous estuarine (or saltwater) crocodile, which reaches 5 to 7m (17–23 ft.). Freshwater crocs are considered harmless; estuarine crocs are definitely not. They are called "saltwater" crocs but live mostly in freshwater rivers, wetlands, gorges, and *billabongs* (ponds). Estuarine crocs are very dangerous, move quickly, and can remain unseen just below the surface of the water; few people survive an attack. Never swim into, or stand near the bank of, any river, swamp, or pool in the northern third of Australia, unless you know for certain it's croc-free, and don't swim at beaches near stream or river mouths.

Slip, slop, slap in the sun

 Australians have the world's highest death rate from skin cancer. So here, we say, "Slip on a shirt, slop on the sunscreen, and slap on a hat" to limit your exposure to the sun. This is especially important during the first few days of your trip, and from 11 a.m. to 3 p.m. in summer and 10 a.m. to 2 p.m. in winter. Remember that UV rays reflected off walls, water, and the ground can burn you even when you're not in direct sunlight. Use a broad-spectrum sunscreen with a high protection factor (SPF 30 or higher). Wear a broad-brimmed hat that covers the back of your neck, ears, and face (a baseball cap won't cut it), and a long-sleeved shirt. Remember that children need more protection than adults do. Don't even think about traveling without sunglasses, or you'll spend your entire vacation squinting into Australia's harsh light.

Staying Connected by Cellphone

Some people love the idea of getting away from it all and being in a place with no cellphone reception. For others, it's unthinkable. In some remote areas and a few island resorts, you'll be without reception whether you like it or not. But mostly, staying connected is easy.

The three letters that define much of the world's wireless capabilities are **GSM** (Global System for Mobile Communications), a big, seamless network that makes for easy cross-border cellphone use in many countries worldwide. In the United States, T-Mobile, AT&T Wireless, and Cingular use this quasi-universal system; in Canada, Microcell and some Rogers customers are GSM; and all Europeans and most Australians use GSM. GSM phones function with a removable plastic SIM card, encoded with your phone number and account information. If your cellphone is on a GSM system and you have a world-capable multiband phone such as many Sony Ericsson, Motorola, or Samsung models, you can make and receive calls across civilized areas around much of the globe. Just call your wireless operator and ask for international roaming to be activated on your account. Unfortunately, per-minute charges can be high.

If you decide to rent a cellphone — called *mobile phones* in Australia — you can do it easily. You can rent a phone from any number of overseas sites, including kiosks at airports and at car rental agencies, but we suggest renting the phone before you leave home. North Americans can rent one from **InTouch USA** (☎ 800-872-7626; www.intouchglobal.com) or **RoadPost** (☎ 888-290-1606 or 905-272-5665; www.roadpost.com). InTouch will also, for free, advise you on whether your existing phone will work overseas; simply call ☎ 703-222-7161 between 9 a.m. and 4 p.m. EST, or go to http://intouchglobal.com/travel.htm.

In Australia, mobile phone company **Vodafone** (☎ **1300/365 360;** www.vodarent.com.au) has outlets at Brisbane, Cairns, and Melbourne international airports, and at Sydney and Perth international and domestic airports, and a store in Southport on the Gold Coast. They cost A$5 to A$8 (US$4–US$6.40/£2–£3.20) per day, plus call charges and insurance, depending on the kind of phone and coverage you want. You can rent a SIM card for A$1 (US$0.80/£0.40) per day or A$15 (US$12/£6) per month.

Australia's cell network is digital, not analog. Calls to or from a mobile telephone are generally more expensive than calls to or from a land line. The price varies depending on the carrier, the time of day, the distance between caller and recipient, and the telephone's pricing plan.

Buying a prepaid phone can be a good deal. After you arrive, stop by a local cellphone shop and get the cheapest package; you'll probably pay less than $100 for a phone and a starter calling card.

Accessing the Internet away from Home

Aside from cybercafes, most youth hostels and public libraries have Internet access. Avoid hotel business centers unless you're willing to pay exorbitant rates. Cybercafes (also called *Internet cafes* in Australia) can be found almost everywhere. Major tourist cities like Cairns and Darwin have whole streets lined with them, and even smaller places like Broome have a few to choose from. To find cybercafes in your destination check www.cybercaptive.com and www.cybercafe.com.

Most major airports have Internet kiosks that provide basic Web access for a per-minute fee that's usually higher than cybercafe prices. Check out copy shops like Kinko's (http://fedex.kinkos.com), which offers computer stations with fully loaded software (as well as Wi-Fi). It has stores in Sydney and Melbourne.

More and more hotels, resorts, airports, cafes, and retailers are going Wi-Fi (wireless fidelity), becoming "hotspots" that offer free high-speed Wi-Fi access or charge a small fee for usage. Most laptops sold today have built-in wireless capability. To find public Wi-Fi hotspots at your destination, go to www.jiwire.com; its Hotspot Finder holds the world's largest directory of public wireless hotspots.

For dial-up access, most business-class hotels throughout Australia offer dataports for laptop modems, and some of them offer free high-speed Internet access. Even smaller bed-and-breakfasts these days often have Wi-Fi access or dial-up from the phone in your room.

Wherever you go, bring a **connection kit** of the right power and phone adapters, a spare phone cord, and a spare Ethernet network cable — or find out whether your hotel supplies them to guests (many don't, or will charge you a fee for them).

Australia's electricity supply is 240 volts, 50 Hz. North Americans and Europeans need to buy a converter before they leave home, because Australian stores usually only stock converters for Aussie appliances to fit American and European outlets.

Keeping Up with Airline Security Measures

If you arrive at the airport at least one hour before a domestic flight and two hours before an international flight, you'll generally have plenty of time to get through the security checkpoints. You can check the average wait times at your airport by going to the **Transportation Security Administration Security Checkpoint Wait Times** site (`http://wait time/tsa.dhs.gov`).

Beat the ticket-counter lines by using the self-service electronic ticket kiosks at the airport or printing out your boarding pass at home from the airline Web site. Using curbside check-in is also a smart way to avoid lines. If you're running late, tell an airline employee; they can usually get you to the front of the line.

Help speed up security before you're screened by knowing what you can carry on and what you can't. For the latest updates on items you're prohibited from bringing in carry-on luggage, go to `www.tsa.gov/travelers/airtravel`.

Remove jackets, shoes, metal belt buckles, heavy jewelry, and watches and place them either in your carry-on luggage or the security bins provided. Place keys, coins, cellphones, and pagers in a security bin. If you have metallic body parts, carry a note from your doctor. When possible, keep packing liquids in checked baggage.

Use a TSA-approved lock, which can be opened by luggage inspectors with a special code or key, for your checked luggage. Look for Travel Sentry–certified locks at luggage or travel shops and Brookstone stores (or online at `www.brookstone.com`).

Part III
Sydney, Melbourne, and the Australian Capital Territory

The 5th Wave   By Rich Tennant

"There were several injuries during the building of the Sydney Opera House. Most of them architects who inadvertently sat on the scale model."

In this part . . .

*W*e head for the bright lights, big cities of the Eastern part of Australia! In Chapter 11, we introduce you to Sydney, and its iconic sights (like the Opera House) and world-class hotels and restaurants. Sydney's the major city in New South Wales and in Chapter 12, we tell you about some of that territory's highlights, from mountain to beach to Outback.

In Chapter 13, we introduce you to Australia's most cosmopolitan and European-style city: Melbourne. Wander its cobblestone lanes to find the best coffee shops and bars, and get ready to shop-'til-you-drop. Then we take you out of the city to one of Victoria's most popular day-trip destinations: Phillip Island, where you can gaze upon the cute fairy penguins as they come ashore each night.

Chapter 14 takes you beyond the city, to some of Victoria's most appealing regional centers. We drive along the spectacular 94km (58-mile) Great Ocean Road, discover the mountains and forests of the High Country, and learn the story of famous outlaw Ned Kelly.

Like Washington, D.C., Canberra is a planned capital, and it's located in its own territory (the Australian Capital Territory, or ACT) between Sydney and Melbourne. In Chapter 15, we take a peek at the city that's the seat of the Australian government.

Chapter 11

Sydney

by Marc Llewellyn

In This Chapter

▶ Arriving in Sydney
▶ Getting around the city
▶ Finding the best room in Sydney
▶ Exploring the harbor and beyond

S ydney is a jewel of a city, set around one of the finest harbors in the world. This thriving, sunny metropolis is home to some famous architectural and natural icons — the Sydney Opera House, the Sydney Harbour Bridge, and Bondi Beach. Most of Sydney's main attractions are concentrated in a relatively compact area. Still, there's so much to do that you could easily spend a week here and still find yourself crashing into bed at night exhausted, having tried to see everything.

In summer head to one of Sydney's beaches — with over 20 strung along the city's oceanfront, and dozens more around the harbor, you'll be spoiled for choice. The most famous, of course, is Bondi, a strip of golden sand legendary for its Speedo-clad Lifesavers and surfboard riders. Another favorite is Manly, a 30-minute ferry trip from Circular Quay. Pick up some fish and chips and head for the main beach, which is flanked by a row of giant pines that chatter with hundreds of small, colorful parrots at dusk. The best time to return is in the early evening, when the lights of the skyscrapers around Circular Quay streak like rainbows across the water of the harbor, and the sails of the Opera House and the girders of the Harbour Bridge are lit up — it's magical.

Compared to many other major cities, Sydney offers good value. Food and public transport are cheap, and attractions are generally not prohibitively expensive. (Senior and student prices are almost always available with ID.) The price of a hotel room is comparatively cheaper than in other major cities such as New York and London.

Getting There

The city has one airport and a major train hub at Central Station. It's also served by highways from the north and south.

By air

All international flights arrive at **Sydney International Airport,** which is 8km (5 miles) from the city center. Free shuttle buses link the international and domestic terminals. In both terminals, you'll find luggage carts, wheelchairs, a post office (open Mon–Fri 9 a.m.–5 p.m.), mailboxes, currency exchange, duty-free shops, restaurants, bars, stores, showers, luggage lockers, a place where you can leave luggage, ATMs, and tourist information desks. You can rent mobile phones in the international terminal.

The airport is efficient, has extremely strict quarantine procedures — you must declare all food — and is completely nonsmoking.

On arrival, pick up a copy of *Sydney: The Official Guide,* from the rack just before passport control, which contains tear-out discount tickets for some of Sydney's major attractions. Luggage trolleys are free to hire in the international arrival terminal but cost A$4 (US$3/£1.50) outside departure terminals (you'll need coins).

By train

Central Station (☎ **13 15 00** for CityRail, or 13 22 32 for Countrylink interstate trains) is the main city and interstate train station. It's on George Street in downtown Sydney. All interstate trains depart from here, and it's a major CityRail hub. Many city buses leave from nearby Railway Square for places like Town Hall and Circular Quay.

By bus

Greyhound coaches operate from the **Sydney Coach Terminal** (☎ **02/ 9212 1500**), on the corner of Eddy Avenue and Pitt Street, bordering Central Station.

By cruise ship

Cruise ships dock at the **Overseas Passenger Terminal** in The Rocks, opposite the Sydney Opera House, or in Darling Harbour if The Rocks facility is already occupied.

By car

Drivers enter Sydney from the north on the Pacific Highway, from the south on the M5 and Princes Highway, and from the west on the Great Western Highway.

Getting from the Airport into Sydney

The **Airport Link** connects the international and domestic airports to the city stations of Central, Museum, St. James, Circular Quay, Wynyard, and Town Hall. You need to change trains for other Sydney stations. Unfortunately, the line has no dedicated luggage areas and, because it's on a scheduled route into the city from the suburbs, it gets very crowded during rush hours (approximately 7–9 a.m. and 4–6:30 p.m.). If you have lots of luggage and you're traveling into the city at these times, taking a taxi is probably best. Otherwise walk to the end of the platform, and there should be more room on board.

The train takes ten minutes to reach the Central Railway Station and continues to Circular Quay. Trains leave every 15 minutes or so and cost A$13 (US$10/£5) one-way adults, A$8.80 (US$7/£4.40) children. Round-trip tickets are only available if you really hate Sydney and want to return to the airport on the same day. Ask at the ticket office about group tickets and Family Fare tickets, which allow a second child — or more — to travel for free with an adult. (The first child pays the standard child fare.)

Sydney Airporter coaches (☎ **02/9666 9988;** http://kst.com.au) operate to the city center from bus stops outside the terminals every 15 minutes. This service will drop you off (and pick you up) at hotels in the city, Kings Cross, and Darling Harbour. This could be frustrating if you're staying at the last hotel on the route! Pickups from hotels require at least three hours' advance notice; you can book online. Tickets cost A$10 (US$8/£5) one-way and A$17 (US$14/£7) round-trip from the International Terminal; A$12 (US$9.60/£6) one-way and A$20 (US$16/£8) round-trip from the Domestic Terminal. The return portion can be used at any time in the future.

Both short-term and long-term parking are available at both terminals. An example is a four-day stay at the Domestic Terminal, which costs A$79 (US$63/£39).

Finding Information after You Arrive

The **Sydney Visitor Centre at The Rocks,** First Floor, The Rocks Centre, Corner of Argyle and Playfair streets, The Rocks (☎ **02/9240 8788;** www.sydneyvisitorcentre.com), is a good place to pick up maps, brochures, and tourist information about Sydney as well as other towns in New South Wales; it also sells books, T-shirts, DVDs, postcards, and the like. The office is open daily from 9 a.m. to 5 p.m.

Also in The Rocks is the **National Parks & Wildlife Centre,** in Cadmans Cottage (a sandstone building, built in 1816, set back from the water in front of The Rocks), 110 George St. (☎ **02/9247 5033**). This place has lots of national park information and runs boat tours to some of the islands in Sydney Harbour. It's open Monday through Friday from 9:30 a.m. to 4:30 p.m., and on Saturday and Sunday from 10 a.m. to 4:30 p.m.

There's also the **Sydney Visitors Centre — Darling Harbour,** 33 Wheat Rd., Darling Harbour (near the IMAX Theatre). It's open daily from 9:30 a.m. to 5:30 p.m.

If you want to inquire about destinations and holidays in Sydney or the rest of New South Wales, call **Tourism New South Wales**'s help line (☎ **13 20 77** in Australia).

In Manly, the **Manly Visitors Information Centre** (☎ **02/9976 1430**), is at Manly Wharf (where the ferries arrive). It's open Monday through Friday from 9 a.m. to 5 p.m., weekends from 10 a.m. to 4 p.m.

There are **City Host information kiosks** at Martin Place (between Elizabeth and Castlereagh streets), on George Street (next to Sydney Town Hall), and at Circular Quay (corner of Pitt and Alfred streets). They offer maps, brochures, and advice and are open daily from 9 a.m. to 5 p.m.

Orienting Yourself in Sydney

Sydney is one of the largest cities in the world by area, covering more than 1,730 sq. km (675 sq. miles) from the sea to the foothills of the Blue Mountains. Thankfully, the city center is compact. The jewel in Sydney's crown is its harbor, which empties into the South Pacific Ocean through headlands known simply as North Head and South Head. On the southern side of the harbor are the high-rises of the city center; the Sydney Opera House; a string of beaches, including Bondi; and the inner-city suburbs. The Sydney Harbour Bridge and a tunnel connect the city center to the high-rises of the North Sydney business district and the affluent northern suburbs and beautiful ocean beaches beyond.

The city's main thoroughfare, **George Street,** runs up from **Circular Quay** (pronounced key), past Wynyard CityRail station and Town Hall, to Central Station. A whole host of streets run parallel to George, including Pitt, Elizabeth, and Macquarie streets. **Macquarie Street** runs up from the Sydney Opera House, past the Royal Botanic Gardens and Hyde Park. **Martin Place** is a pedestrian thoroughfare that stretches from Macquarie to George streets. It's about halfway between Circular Quay and Town Hall — in the heart of the city center.

The easy-to-spot **Sydney Tower** (also known as Centrepoint Tower), facing onto pedestrian-only **Pitt Street Mall** on Pitt Street, is the main city-center landmark. Next to Circular Quay and across from the Opera House is **The Rocks,** a cluster of small streets that was once part of a larger slum and is now a tourist attraction. Roads meet at **Town Hall** from Kings Cross in one direction and Darling Harbour in the other. From Circular Quay to The Rocks it's a five- to ten-minute stroll; to Wynyard,

Sydney Harbour Area

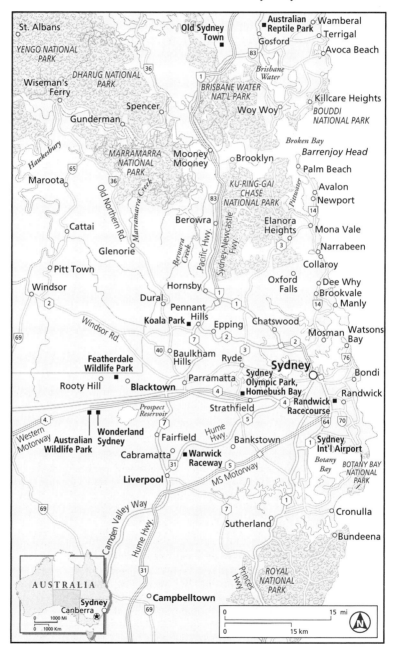

about ten minutes; and to Town Hall, about 20 minutes. From Town Hall to the near side of Darling Harbour it's about a ten-minute walk.

Introducing the Neighbourhoods

Circular Quay

This transport hub for ferries, buses, and CityRail trains is tucked between the Harbour Bridge and the Sydney Opera House. The Quay, as it's called, is a good spot for a stroll, and its outdoor restaurants and street performers are popular. The Rocks, the Royal Botanic Gardens, the Modern Australian Art Museum, and the start of the main shopping area (centered on Pitt and George streets) are a short walk away.

The Rocks

This historic area, a short walk west of Circular Quay, is packed with colonial buildings, intriguing back streets, boutiques, pubs, and top-notch restaurants and hotels. It's the most exclusive place to stay because of its beauty and its proximity to the Opera House and harbor. Shops are geared toward Sydney's yuppies and wealthy tourists — don't expect bargains. On weekends, a portion of George Street is blocked off for The Rocks Market, with stalls selling souvenirs and crafts.

Town Hall

In the heart of the city, this area is home to the main department stores and two Sydney landmarks, the Town Hall and a historic shopping mall called the Queen Victoria Building (QVB). In this area are Sydney Tower and the boutique-style chain stores of Pitt Street Mall. Farther up George Street are major movie houses, the entrance to Sydney's small Spanish district (around Liverpool Street), and the city's Chinatown.

Darling Harbour

Designed as a tourist precinct, Darling Harbour features Sydney's main convention, exhibition, and entertainment centers; a waterfront prome-nade; the Sydney Aquarium; the Panasonic IMAX Theatre; the Australian Maritime Museum; the Powerhouse Museum; Star City (Sydney's casino); a major food court; and plenty of shops. Nearby are the funky restau-rants of Cockle Bay and King Street Wharf.

Kings Cross and the suburbs beyond

"The Cross," as it's known, is the city's red-light district — though it's also home to some of Sydney's best-known nightclubs and restaurants. The area has plenty of hostels, a few bars, and some upscale hotels. The main drag, Darlinghurst Road, is short but crammed with strip joints, prostitutes, addicts, drunks, and such. Also in this area are cheap e-mail centers that offer discount overseas phone rates. There's a heavy police presence, but do take care.

Paddington/Oxford Street

This inner-city suburb, centered on trendy Oxford Street, is known for its expensive terrace houses, off-the-wall boutiques and bookshops, restaurants, pubs, and nightclubs. It's also the heart of Sydney's large gay community and has a liberal scattering of gay bars and dance spots.

Darlinghurst

Between grungy Kings Cross and upscale Oxford Street, this extroverted, grimy terraced suburb is home to some of Sydney's best cafes. It's probably not wise to wander around at night. Take the CityRail train to Kings Cross and head right from the exit.

Central

The congested and polluted crossroads around Central Station, the city's main train station, has little to recommend it. Buses run from here to Circular Quay, and it's a 20-minute walk to Town Hall.

Newtown

This popular student area centers on car-clogged King Street, which is lined with alternative shops, bookstores, and ethnic restaurants. People-watching is the thing to do — see how many belly-button rings, violently colored hairdos, and Celtic arm tattoos you can spot.

Glebe

Yuppies and students come to this inner-city suburb for the cafes, restaurants, pubs, and shops along Glebe Point Road. All this, plus a location 15 minutes from the city and 30 minutes from Circular Quay, makes it a good place for budget-conscious travelers.

Bondi and the southern beaches

Some of Sydney's most glamorous surf beaches — Bondi, Bronte, and Coogee — lie along the South Pacific coast southeast of the city center. Bondi has a wide sweep of beach, some interesting restaurants and bars, plenty of attitude, and beautiful bodies — and no CityRail station.

Watsons Bay

Watsons Bay is known for The Gap — a section of dramatic sea cliffs — as well as several good restaurants and the Watsons Bay Hotel beer garden. It's a terrific spot to spend a sunny afternoon. To reach it on public transportation, take bus no. 324 or 325 from Circular Quay.

The North Shore

Ferries and buses provide access to these wealthy neighborhoods across the Harbour Bridge. Gorgeous Balmoral Beach, Taronga Zoo, and upscale boutiques are the attractions in Mosman.

Manly and the northern beaches

Half an hour away by ferry, or 15 minutes by the faster JetCat, Manly is famous for its ocean beach — it gives Bondi a run for its money — and scores of cheap food outlets. Farther north are more beaches popular with surfers. CityRail train lines do not go to the northern beaches. The farthest beach from the city, Palm Beach, has magnificent surf and lagoon beaches, walking paths, and a golf course.

Balmain

West of the city center, a short ferry ride from Circular Quay, Balmain was once Sydney's main shipbuilding area. In the last few decades, the area has become trendy and expensive. The suburb has a village feel to it, abounds with restaurants and pubs, and stages a popular Saturday market at the local church.

Homebush Bay

Sydney Olympic Park was the main site of the 2000 Olympic games. You'll find Telstra Stadium (once named Stadium Australia), the Aquatic Center, and Homebush Bay Information Centre, parklands, and a water-bird reserve here.

Getting Around Sydney

The center of Sydney is compact enough to walk between most places of interest, but you'll have to catch public transport if you want to head farther out, to Manly or Bondi beaches perhaps. The nicest way to see the city is from the water, and there are frequent ferry services zipping back and forth across the harbor. Buses are relatively convenient, but you'll probably find yourself using the CityRail train system more.

By train

Sydney's CityRail trains travel both underground and overground — the double-decker carriages are a feature, as is the system's ability to self-combust as soon as a train breaks down or a driver calls in sick. Hence, timetables should be used as a *very* rough guide. The system is also limited; many tourist areas — including Manly, Bondi Beach, and Darling Harbour — are not connected to the network. Single tickets within the city center cost A$2.40 (US$1.90/£0.95) adults, A$1.20 (US$0.95/£0.50) children. Round-trip tickets cost A$4.80 (US$3.85/£1.90) adults, A$2.40 (US$1.90/£0.95) children, for travel starting before 9 a.m.; A$3.40 (US$2.70/£1.35) adults, A$2.40 (US$1.90/£0.95) children, after 9 a.m. Information is available from the **Infoline** (☎ **13 15 00** in Australia).

By bus

Buses are frequent and reliable and cover a wide area of metropolitan Sydney — though you may find the system a little difficult to navigate if

Transport/attraction passes

Sydney Ferries have teamed up with Taronga Zoo and Sydney Aquarium to provide two discount passes.

The **Zoo Pass** includes round-trip ferry trips from Circular Quay to Taronga Zoo, a trip on the Aerial Safari cable car at the zoo, and a bus trip back to the ferry if you somehow end up at the top (which is unlikely, because generally you start at the top of the hill and work your way down). It costs A$39 (US$31/£16) adults, A$21 (US$17/£8.40) children 4 to 15. A family ticket costs A$37 (US$30/£15) for the first adult, A$32 (US$26/£13) for a second adult, A$20 (US$16/£8) for the first child, A$12 (US$9.60/£4.80) for each additional child.

The **Aquarium Pass** includes round-trip ferry travel from Circular Quay to the Sydney Aquarium and also entry. It costs A$33 (US$26/£13) adults, A$17 (US$14/£6.80) children, A$81 (US$65/UK£32) families of two adults and two children. Buy tickets at Circular Quay.

you're visiting some of the outer suburbs. For a 4km (2½-mile) "section," the minimum fare, which covers most short hops in the city, is A$1.70 (US$1.40/$0.75) adults, A$0.80 (US$0.65/$0.35) children. The farther you go, the cheaper each section is. For example, the 44km (27-mile) trip to Palm Beach, way past Manly, costs A$5.40 (US$4.30/$2.15) adults, A$2.70 (US$2.15/$1) children. Sections are marked on bus-stand signs, but most Sydneysiders are as confused about the system as you will be — when in doubt, ask the bus driver.

To reach Bondi by public transport, ride bus no. 380 to Bondi Beach from Circular Quay; it takes up to an hour. A quicker alternative is taking a CityRail train to Bondi Junction to connect with the same buses. Bus no. 333 takes around 40 minutes from Circular Quay to Bondi Beach. It has limited stops, but you can catch it from Elizabeth Street near Martin Place, along Oxford Street, and from the bus terminal at Bondi Junction. You need to buy a ticket at newsdealers or 7-Eleven stores beforehand. A **Travel Ten** bus ticket (see "Using a travel pass to get around," later in this chapter) is a good option if you're staying in Bondi. Bus no. 378 from Railway Square, Central Station, goes to Bronte, and bus nos. 373 and 374 travel to Coogee from Circular Quay.

By car

Traffic restrictions, parking, and congestion can make getting around by car frustrating, but if you plan to visit some of the outer suburbs or take excursions elsewhere in New South Wales, then renting a car will give you more flexibility. The **National Roads and Motorists' Association** (NRMA) is the New South Wales auto club; for emergency breakdown service, call ☎ **13 11 11.**

Car rental agencies in Sydney include Avis, 214 William St., Kings Cross (☎ 1800/225 553); Budget, 93 William St., Kings Cross (☎ 13 27 27 in Australia, or 02/9339 8888); Hertz, corner of William and Riley streets, Kings Cross (☎ 13 30 39 in Australia); and Thrifty, 75 William St., Kings Cross (☎ 02/9380 5399). Avis, Budget, Hertz, and Thrifty also have desks at the airport. Rates average about A$60 (US$48/£24) per day for a small car. One of the best-value operations is Bayswater Car Rentals, 180 William St., Kings Cross (☎ 02/9360 3622; www.bayswatercarrentals.com.au), which has small cars for around A$40 (US$32/£16) a day with everything included.

By ferry

The best way to get a taste of a city that revolves around its harbor is to jump on a ferry. The main ferry terminal is at Circular Quay. Machines at each wharf dispense tickets. (There are also change machines.) For ferry information, call ☎ 13 15 00 or visit the ferry information office opposite Wharf 4. Timetables are available for all routes.

One-way trips within the inner harbor (which is everywhere except Manly and Parramatta) cost A$5.20 (US$4/£2.60) adults, A$2.60 (US$2/£1) children 4 to 15. Kids under 4 travel free.

The ferry to Manly takes 30 minutes and costs A$6.40 (US$5/£2.50) adults, A$3.20 (US$2.50/£1.75) children. It leaves from Wharf 3. The rapid **JetCat** service to Manly takes 15 minutes and costs A$8.20 (US$4/£2) for both adults and children. After 7 p.m. all trips to and from Manly are by JetCat at ferry prices. Ferries run from 6 a.m. to midnight.

By monorail and tram

The monorail, with its single overhead line, connects the central business district to Darling Harbour — though it's only a 15- to 20-minute walk from Town Hall. The system operates Monday through Thursday from 7 a.m. to 10 p.m., Friday and Saturday from 7 a.m. to midnight, and Sunday from 8 a.m. to 10 p.m. Tickets are A$4.50 (US$3.60/£1.80), free for children under 5. An all-day **monorail pass** costs A$9 (US$7.20/£4.50). The trip from the city center to Darling Harbour takes around 12 minutes. Look for the gray overhead line and the tubelike structures that are stations. Call **Metro Monorail** (☎ 02/8584 5288; www.metrolightrail.com.au) for information.

Meanwhile, a system of **trams** runs on a route that traverses a 3.6km (2¼-mile) track between Central Station and Wentworth Park in Pyrmont. It provides good access to Chinatown, Paddy's Markets, Darling Harbour, the Star City casino, and the Sydney Fish Markets. The trams run every ten minutes. The one-way fare is A$3 to A$4 (US$2.40–US$3.20/£1.20–£1.60) adults, A$1.80 to A$3 (US$1.40–US$2.40/£0.75–£1.20) children 4 to 15, depending on distance. Two-way tickets are also available. A day pass costs A$8.40 (US$6.70/£3.30) adults, A$6.50 (US$5.20/£2.60) children, A$20 (US$16/£8) families of five. Contact **Metro Light Rail** (☎ 02/8584 5288; www.metrolightrail.com.au) for details.

By taxi

Several taxi companies serve the city center and suburbs. All journeys are metered.

If you cross either way on the Harbour Bridge or through the Harbour Tunnel, it will cost you an extra A$3 (US$2.40/£1.20) — a rip-off considering there's only an official toll on the way into the city. If you take the Eastern Distributor from the airport (the most likely case), it's A$4.50 (US$3.60/£1.80). An extra 10 percent will be added to your fare if you pay by credit card.

Taxis line up at stands in the city, such as those opposite Circular Quay and Central Station. They're also frequently found in front of hotels. A yellow light on top of the cab means it's vacant. Cabs can be hard to get on Friday and Saturday nights and between 2 p.m. and 3 p.m. every day, when cabbies are changing shifts after 12 hours on the road. Some people prefer to sit up front, but it's certainly not considered rude if you don't. Passengers must wear seat belts in the front and back seats. The **Taxi Complaints Hotline** (☎ 1800/648 478 in Australia) deals with problem taxi drivers. Taxis are licensed to carry four people.

The main cab companies are **Taxis Combined** (☎ 13 33 00); **RSL Taxis** (☎ 02/9581 1111); **Legion Cabs** (☎ 13 14 51); and **Premier Cabs** (☎ 13 10 17).

By water taxi

Water taxis operate 24 hours a day and are a quick, convenient way to get to waterfront restaurants, harbor attractions, and some suburbs. You can also charter them for private cruises. Fares are based on an initial flag-fall for the hire of the vessel, then a charge per person traveling. On most trips, the more people who are traveling, the lower the fare per person. The typical fare for a group of six people would be A$10 to A$15 (US$8–US$12/£4–£6) per person for an inner harbor jaunt. Sometimes you can combine with other people if you call well in advance. The main operators are **Water Taxis Combined** (☎ 02/9555 8888; www.water taxis.com.au), **Beach Hopper** (☎ 0412 400 990 mobile; www.water taxi.net.au), and **Yellow Water Taxis** (☎ 02/9299 0199; www.yellow watertaxis.com).

Staying in Style

The best location for lodging in Sydney is in The Rocks and around Circular Quay — a short stroll from the Sydney Opera House, the Harbour Bridge, the Royal Botanic Gardens, and the ferry terminals.

Hotels around Darling Harbour offer good access to the local facilities, including museums, the Sydney Aquarium, and the Star City casino. Most Darling Harbour hotels are a 10- to 15-minute walk, or a short

Central Sydney Hotels

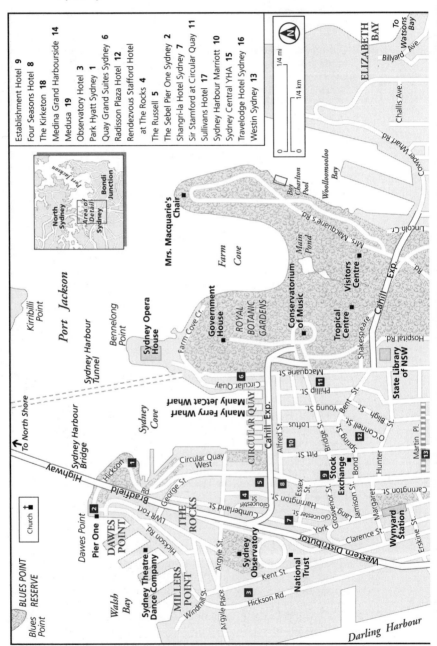

Establishment Hotel **9**
Four Seasons Hotel **8**
The Kirketon **18**
Medina Grand Harbourside **14**
Medusa **19**
Observatory Hotel **3**
Park Hyatt Sydney **1**
Quay Grand Suites Sydney **6**
Radisson Plaza Hotel **12**
Rendezvous Stafford Hotel
  at The Rocks **4**
The Russell **5**
The Sebel Pier One Sydney **2**
Shangri-la Hotel Sydney **7**
Sir Stamford at Circular Quay **11**
Sullivans Hotel **17**
Sydney Harbour Marriott **10**
Sydney Central YHA **15**
Travelodge Hotel Sydney **16**
Westin Sydney **13**

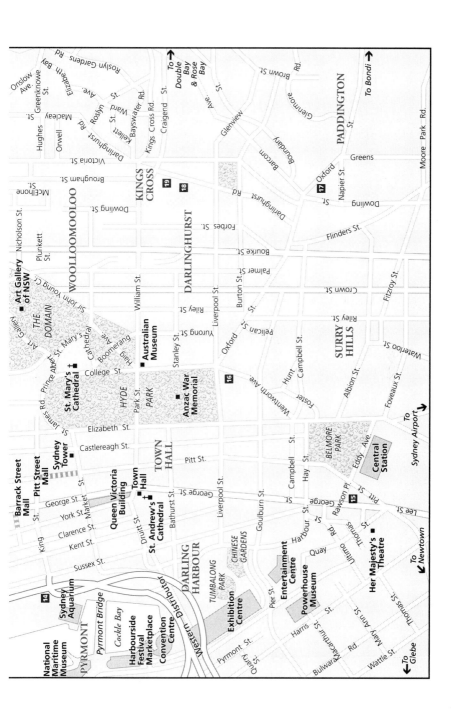

Using a travel pass to get around

Several passes are available for visitors who will be using public transportation frequently. All work out to be much cheaper than buying individual tickets.

- ✔ The **SydneyPass** includes unlimited travel on Sydney Explorer coaches, Bondi & Bay Explorer coaches, three Sydney Harbour cruises, the JetCat to Manly, the high-speed RiverCat to Parramatta (linking the city center to this important heritage and business center along a historic waterway), Sydney buses, Sydney Ferries, and CityRail trains (within the "Red TravelPass" travel zone, which includes the entire city center, as well as to Bondi Junction). For three days of travel over a seven-day period, the SydneyPass costs A$110 (US$88/£55) adults, A$55 (US$44/£22) children; for five days over a seven-day period, A$145 (US$116/£58) adults, A$70 (US$56/£28) children; and for seven consecutive days, A$165 (US$132/£66) adults, A$80 (US$64/£32) children. Family fares are also available. Buy tickets at the information desk at the airport, at the TransitShop at Circular Quay (near McDonald's), from the Sydney Ferries ticket offices at Circular Quay, and from Explorer bus drivers.

- ✔ A **Weekly Travel Pass** allows unlimited travel on buses, trains, and ferries. There are six different passes (each a different color) depending on the distance you need to travel. The passes most visitors use are the Red Pass and the Green Pass. The **Red Pass** costs A$33 (US$26/£13) adults, A$17 (US$13/£7.50) children; it covers all transportation within the city center and near surroundings. This pass gets you aboard inner harbor ferries, but not the ferry to Manly. The **Green Pass,** which costs A$41 (US$33/£17) adults, A$21 (US$16/£8) children, takes you to more distant destinations, including Manly (aboard the ferry but not the JetCat before 7 p.m.). You can buy either pass at newsdealers or bus, train, and ferry ticket outlets.

- ✔ The **Day Tripper** ticket gives you unlimited bus, train, and ferry travel for one day. Tickets cost A$15 (US$12/£6) adults, A$7.70 (US$6/£3) children. The pass is available at all bus, train, and ferry ticket outlets.

- ✔ The **City Hopper** allows unlimited all day CityRail travel around 11 stations within the city area. They include: Central, Martin Place, Museum, Town Hall, St James, Circular Quay, Kings Cross, Wynyard, Redfern, Milsons Point, and North Sydney. Before 9 a.m., tickets cost $7 (US$5.50/£2.75) adults, A$3 (US$2.50/£1.25) children; after 9 a.m., tickets cost A$5 (US$4/£2) adults, A$2.50 (US$2/£1) children.

- ✔ A **Travelten bus** ticket offers ten bus rides for a discounted price. A Blue Travelten covers two sections on the bus route and costs A$14 (US$11/£5.50) adults, A$6.80 (US$5.40/£2.70) children; a Brown Travelten covers up to nine sections and costs A$23 (US$19/£10) adults, A$12 (US$9.30/£4.50) children.

- ✔ The **Travelten ferry** ticket costs A$34 (US$27/£13) adults, A$17 (US$14/£7) children. It's good for ten trips within the inner harbor (this excludes Manly). You can buy Travelten tickets at newsdealers, bus depots, or the Circular Quay ferry terminal. Tickets are transferable, so if two or more people travel together, you can use the same ticket.

- ✔ A **Manly Ferry Ten** ticket (allowing ten journeys) costs A$48 (US$38/£19) adults, A$24 (US$19/£10) children; a weekly JetCat ticket costs A$68 (US$54/£27) per person. After 7 p.m. all trips to and from Manly are by JetCat at ferry prices. Ferries run from 6 a.m. to midnight.

monorail or light-rail trip, from Town Hall and the central shopping district in and around Sydney Tower and Pitt Street Mall.

More hotels are grouped around Kings Cross, Sydney's red-light district. Some of the hotels here are among the city's best, and you'll also find a range of cheaper lodgings. Kings Cross can be unnerving at any time, but especially on Friday and Saturday nights when the area's strip joints and nightclubs are jumping.

Glebe, with its ethnic restaurants, is another inner-city suburb popular with tourists. It's well served by local buses.

If you want to stay near the beach, check out the options in Manly and Bondi, though you should consider their distance from the city center and the lack of CityRail trains to these areas. A taxi to Manly from the city will cost around A\$37 (US\$29/£15) and to Bondi around A\$28 (US\$22/£11).

Always ask about discounts, package deals, and any other special offerings when booking a hotel, especially if you're traveling in winter when hotels are less likely to be full. Ask about weekend discounts, corporate rates, and family plans.

Almost all hotels offer nonsmoking rooms; inquire when you make a reservation if it's important to you. Most moderately priced to very expensive rooms will have tea- and coffeemaking facilities, and an iron. Coffeemakers as such are rare in Australian hotels.

Getting a deal on a good hotel

- ✔ The **Sydney Visitors Centre bookings desk** (☎ 02/9667 6050), in the arrivals hall of the airport's International Terminal, negotiates deals with many of Sydney's hotels and offers exceptional discounts on rooms that haven't been filled that day.

- ✔ Another way to hunt for discounted hotel rooms is through an independent hotel search site. The two most popular are www.last minute.com.au and www.wotif.com. LastMinute.com allows you to check prices at least a month in advance.

- ✔ Booking through a hotel's Web site can also yield savings. For example, a search of the **Accor** Web site (www.accorhotels.com.au), which has 31 hotels in and around Sydney, shows you can save up to 50 percent off the rack rate.

- ✔ **Serviced apartments** are well worth considering because you can save a bundle by cooking your own meals; many also have free laundry facilities.

The top hotels

Establishment Hotel
$$$$ **Wynyard**

Sydney's coolest hotel offers sleek modernist rooms in two styles: one with restored warehouse ceilings, Japan-black floorboards, and flashes of strong color, and the other more tranquil in color and softer in feel. All rooms come with generous-size marble or bluestone bathrooms. In the same building you'll find one of Sydney's best restaurants, est., and also the small-but-gorgeous Sushi E. Also here are a couple of trendy bars and the popular Tank nightclub. The building is a historic Sydney landmark, but the feel is "now" rather than then.

See map p. 118. 5 Bridge Lane, Sydney (off George Street, near Wynyard CityRail Station), Sydney, NSW 2000. ☎ *02/9240 3110. Fax: 02/9240 3101.* www.merivale. com. *Parking: A$35 (US$28/£14). Rack rates: A$350 (US$280/£140) Junior Room, A$415 (US$332/£166) Establishment Room, A$970–A$1,150 (US$776–US$920/£388–£460) penthouse. AE, DC, MC, V.*

Four Seasons Hotel Sydney
$$$$ **The Rocks**

The Four Seasons features impressive views of Sydney Harbour and the Opera House and is close to The Rocks and the Sydney Opera House. The rooms are elegantly decorated, with marble bathrooms and plenty of mahogany, and though neither a modern nor a historic hotel — a bit of a 1970s block from the outside — it still has a nice charm about it. The staff is helpful and efficient, the outdoor pool is the largest in any hotel in Sydney, the spa is one of the city's best, and the restaurant, Cables, is a high-standard eatery, too.

See map p. 118. 199 George St., The Rocks, Sydney, NSW 2000. ☎ *02/9238 0000. Fax: 02/9251 2851.* www.fourseasons.com/sydney. *Parking: A$27 (US$21/£10). Rack rates: A$350 (US$280/£140) city-view double, A$395 (US$316/£158 Opera House–view double, A$470 (US$376/£188) harbor-view double, A$530–A$1,050 (US$424–US$840/ £212–£420) suite. AE, MC, V.*

The Kirketon
$$ **Kings Cross**

If you want to stay somewhere a bit offbeat then this boutique hotel in Darlinghurst is a fascinating option. Rooms come with king-size, queen-size, double, or twin beds, and are lightly stocked with modernist furniture and custom-made fittings, including mirrored headboards, sleek bathrooms hidden away behind mirrored doors, and textured bedspreads and areas of wallpaper. All in all, the décor is fun if you like this sort of thing. Standard rooms are compact and each comes with a double bed; some come with a tub as well as shower. Premium rooms have a queen-size bed. Executive rooms are large with king-size beds; some have a balcony overlooking the main road (which can be noisy at night). The inside scoop is that the best standard room is no. 330, the best premium room no. 340, and the best executive room no. 323. I would definitely ask for a room away from the main road. The same company operates another boutique hotel, **Medusa,** 267 Darlinghurst Rd. (☎ **02/9331 1000;** www.medusa.com. au). Rooms start at A$270 (US$216/£108) there, and the overall size and quality of the rooms reflect the price jumps.

See map p. 118. 229 Darlinghurst Rd., Darlinghurst, NSW 2010. ☎ *02/9332 2011. Fax: 02/9332 2499.* www.kirketon.com.au. *Parking: A$25 (US$20/£10). Rack rates: A$145 (US$116/£58) junior room, A$175 (US$140/£70) premium double, A$175 (US$140/ £70) executive double. AE, DC, MC, V.*

Manly Pacific Hotel
$$$ **Manly**

Standing on your balcony in the evening with the sea breeze in your nostrils and the chirping of hundreds of lorikeets is nothing short of heaven. The Manly Pacific is the only hotel of its class in this beachside suburb. There's nothing claustrophobic here, from the broad expanse of glittering foyer to the wide corridors and spacious accommodations. Each standard room is light and modern, with two double beds, a balcony, limited cable TV, and all the necessities. The hotel is a ten-minute stroll, or a A$5 (US$4/£2) taxi ride, from the Manly ferry.

55 North Steyne, Manly, NSW 2095. ☎ *02/9977 7666. Fax: 02/9977 7822.* www. accorhotels.com.au. *Parking: A$10 (US$8/£4). Rack rates: A$283–A$327 (US$226–US$261/£113–£130) double, A$512 (US$409/£205) suite. AE, DC, MC, V.*

Medina Grand, Harbourside
$$$ **Darling Harbour**

This impressive serviced hotel (which is essentially a furnished apartment with maid service) offers modern, comfortable rooms at competitive prices. It's reached by an offshoot road and a short, unattractive walk from the Sydney Aquarium in Darling Harbour, but makes up for it by being close to all the Darling Harbour attractions and shops. You can choose between studio and one-bedroom apartments, which all come with Italian designer furniture, large windows, and balconies (some with good harbor views). Studio units come with a kitchenette, and one-bedroom units come with a fully equipped kitchen and a second TV. There's a small pool and an exercise room.

See map p. 118. Corner of Shelley and King streets, King Street Wharf, Sydney, NSW 2000. ☎ *1300/300 232 in Australia, or 02/9249 7000. Fax: 02/9249 6900.* www.medina apartments.com.au. *Secure parking available on-site. Check w/hotel for fee. Rack rates: A$238–A$254 (US$190–US$203/£95–£101) studio, A$265–A$330 (US$212– US$264/£106–£132) 1-bedroom apartment. Check Web site for packaged/weekend rates. AE, DC, MC, V.*

Observatory Hotel
$$$$$ The Rocks

This exclusive hotel, a 10-minute walk from The Rocks and 15 minutes from Circular Quay, is a turn-of-the-20th-century beauty competing for top-hotel-in-Sydney honors. It's fitted with antiques, objets d'art, and the finest carpets, wallpapers, and draperies. Plus, it's renowned for its personalized service. Rooms are plush and quiet, with huge bathrooms. Some rooms have city views; others look out over the harbor. The pool here is one of the best in Sydney; note the Southern Hemisphere constellations on the roof.

See map p. 118. 89–113 Kent St., Sydney, NSW 2000. ☎ *1800/806 245 in Australia, or 02/9256 2222. Fax: 02/9256 2233.* www.observatoryhotel.com.au. *Parking: A$30 (US$24/£12). Rack rates: A$415–A$450 (US$332–US$360/£165–£180) double, from A$510 (US$408/£204) suite; extra person A$66 (US$53/£26). AE, MC, V.*

Park Hyatt Sydney
$$$$$ The Rocks

This artistically curving property on The Rocks foreshore is the best-positioned hotel in Sydney. It's right on the water, and some rooms have fantastic views across the harbor to the Sydney Opera House. Its location and general appeal mean it's usually full and frequently has to turn guests away. The building itself is a pleasure to look at, and from a ferry on the harbor it looks like a wonderful addition to the toy-town landscape of The Rocks. The good-size rooms incorporate every possible luxury. Room rates here depend on views; the least expensive units have only glimpses of the harbor. (The most expensive rooms look over the Opera House.) Each of the 33 executive suites has two balconies with a telescope.

See map p. 118. 7 Hickson Rd., The Rocks, Sydney, NSW 2000. ☎ *800-633-7313 in the U.S. and Canada, or 02/9241 1234. Fax: 02/9256 1555.* www.sydney.hyatt.com. *Parking: A$22 (US$17/£9). Rack rates: A$650–A$700 (US$520–US$560/£260–£280) double, A$820–A$920 (US$656–US$736/£328–£368) executive studio, from A$1,000 (US$800/£400) suite. Ask about weekend discounts and packages. AE, DC, MC, V.*

Quay Grand Suites Sydney
$$$$ Circular Quay

The best serviced-apartment complexes, like this one, can outdo superior AAA-rated five-star hotels — even in price. The spacious, ultramodern rooms and apartments face the Botanic Gardens or have fantastic views across the ferry terminals and the Sydney Harbour Bridge. The fully equipped units have balconies so you can admire the views. The noises from the CityRail station and the ferry horns are captivating but can easily be shut out. Bathrooms are large and feature a good-size Jacuzzi.

See map p. 118. 61 Macquarie St., E. Circular Quay, Sydney, NSW 2000. ☎ *1800/091 954 in Australia, or 02/9256 4000. Fax: 02/9256 4040.* www.mirvachotels.com.au. *Valet parking: A$20 (US$16/£8). Rack rates: A$335–A$507 (US$268–US$405/£134–£202) 1-bedroom apartment. Ask about weekend packages and long-term discounts. AE, DC, MC, V.*

Radisson Plaza Hotel Sydney
$$$ Wynyard

In the heart of the city in a heritage building, the Radisson Plaza Hotel Sydney has chic rooms, with muted chocolate tones and sensual fabrics. Each room features a bathroom with marble vanity, separate shower, and extra-deep European-style bathtub. Premier Rooms feature a king-size, queen-size, or two double beds; Atrium Rooms overlook the light well, which is open to the sky; Deluxe Rooms are located on the 11th and 12th floors of the hotel and feature full-length glass doors, which open onto Juliet-style balconies. Studio Spa Suites are larger and open plan, while One-Bedroom Spa Suites have separate living areas and balconies.

See map p. 118. 27 O'Connell St., Sydney NSW 2000. ☎ *800-333-3333 in the U.S.; 1800/333 333 in Australia, or 02/8214 0000. Fax: 02/8214 1000.* www.radisson.com/sydneyau_plaza. *Parking: A$35 (US$28/£14). Rack rates: A$300 (US$240/£120) Premier and Atrium rooms. A$330 (US$264/£132) Deluxe Room, A$394 (US$315/£157) Studio Spa suite, A$430 (US$344/£174) One-Bedroom Spa Suite. AE, DC, MC, V. CityRail: Wynyard.*

Ravesi's on Bondi Beach
$$ Bondi Beach

On Australia's most famous golden sands, this AAA-rated three-star hotel offers modern, minimalist rooms with white marble bathrooms — all very chic, with African tribal wall hangings. Standard doubles are spacious; there's a one-bedroom suite, and a split-level one-bedroom option with the bedroom upstairs. Room nos. 5 and 6 and the split-level suite have the best views of the ocean. All rooms have Juliet balconies, and the split-level suite has its own terrace. If you're a light sleeper, request a room on the top floor, because the popular Ravesi's Restaurant can be noisy on busy nights. The bar is a great place to watch the outside street scene.

Corner of Hall Street and Campbell Parade, Bondi Beach, NSW 2026. ☎ *02/9365 4422. Fax: 02/9365 1481.* www.ravesis.com.au. *Parking: A$8 (US$6.40/£3.20) at the Swiss-Grand Hotel nearby. Rack rates: A$120 (US$96/£48) standard double, A$230 (US$184/£92) double with side view, A$295 (US$236/£118) beachfront room, A$275 (US$220/£110) 1-bedroom suite, A$275–A$350 (US$220–US$280/£110–£140) split-level suite with terrace; extra person A$30 (US$24/£12). AE, DC, MC, V.*

Rendezvous Stafford Hotel at The Rocks
$$$ The Rocks

The Stafford offers some of the best-positioned serviced apartments in Sydney, in the heart of The Rocks, close to the harbor and Circular Quay, and a short stroll from the Central Business District. The property consists of modern apartments in a six-story building (the best units, for their harbor and Opera House views, are on the top three floors) and seven two-story terrace houses dating from 1870 to 1895. The Stafford is recommended for its location, spacious rooms, and kitchen facilities. Studio rooms come with a choice of a queen-size bed or two single beds, a shower over a tub, a microwave, a toaster, and a refrigerator.

See map p. 118. 75 Harrington St., The Rocks, Sydney, NSW 2000. ☎ *02/9251 6711. Fax: 02/9251 3458.* www.rendezvoushotels.com. *Parking: A$15 (US$12/£6). Rack rates: A$235–A$275 (US$188–US$220/£94–110) studio double, A$280 (US$225/£112) 1-bedroom apartment, A$320 (US$256/£128) executive 1-bedroom apartment, A$295 (US$236/£118) terrace house, A$370 (US$295/£150) 1-bedroom penthouse. Ask about weekly discounts. AE, DC, MC, V.*

The Russell
$$ **The Rocks**

This is the coziest place to stay in The Rocks — perhaps in all of Sydney. It's more than 100 years old, and it shows its age wonderfully in the creaks of the floorboards and the ramshackle feel of the brightly painted corridors. Each of the 29 rooms is different in style, size, and shape; all come with a queen-size bed, and most have cable TV. All rooms have immense character, including a series of rooms added on in 1990 above the Fortune of War Hotel next door. There are no harbor views, but from some rooms you can see the tops of the ferry terminals at Circular Quay. Guests have the use of a sitting room, a living room, and a rooftop garden. The apartment is a large, open-plan unit with a king-size bed and small kitchen; it's suitable for three people. It overlooks Circular Quay.

See map p. 118. 143A George St., The Rocks, Sydney, NSW 2000. ☎ *02/9241 3543. Fax: 02/9252 1652.* www.therussell.com.au. *No parking available. Rack rates: A$140–A$195 (US$112–US$156/£62–£78) double without bathroom, A$235–A$270 (US$188–US$216/£94–£108) double with bathroom, A$280 (US$224/£112) suite or apartment; extra person A$30 (US$24/£12). Rates include continental breakfast. AE, DC, MC, V.*

The Sebel Pier One Sydney
$$$ **Walsh Bay**

A premier waterfront hotel, the Sebel is in the historic Woolloomooloo Wharf complex and has been painstakingly renovated, leaving as much of the original structure intact as possible. It's a wonderfully intoxicating blend of old wooden beams and modern art. The only drawback to staying in one of the tastefully appointed waterfront rooms is that the harbor views — through windows that run all the way to the polished wooden floorboards — could make you want to stay in for the rest of the day.

See map p. 118. 11 Hickson Rd., Walsh Bay, Sydney NSW 2000. ☎ *1800/780 485 in Australia. Fax: 02/8298 9777.* www.mirvachotels.com.au. *Parking: AS$25 (US$20/£10). Rack rates: A$235 (US$188/£94) double, A$290 (US$232/£116) waterfront room. Rates include breakfast. AE, DC, MC, V.*

Shangri-la Hotel Sydney
$$$$$ Circular Quay

For a room with a view, you're not going to do better than this ultramodern landmark hotel with a touch of Asian flair. It's a five-minute walk from Circular Quay. Try to book a room on the 20th floor or above: From here Sydney and its harbor is laid out at your feet. All rooms are contemporarily furnished and rely on the views perhaps more than the décor to impress. The top five room floors, from levels 29 to 34, have use of the Horizon Club lounge. This supplies breakfast and evening canapés.

See map p. 118. 176 Cumberland St., The Rocks, Sydney, NSW 2000. ☎ *1800/801 088 in Australia, or 02/9250 6000. Fax: 02/9250 6250.* www.shangri-la.com. *Parking: A$21 (US$17/£8). Rack rates: A$450–A$500 (US$360–US$400/£180–£200) double, A$750 (US$600/£300) corner room, A$550–A$4,900 (US$440–US$3,920/£220–£2,000) suite. Ask about package deals. AE, DC, MC, V.*

Sir Stamford at Circular Quay
$$$$$ Circular Quay

From the moment the doorman doffs his top hat to you, you enter the world of aristocracy, complete with the slight scent of cigar smoke and aged brandy in the air. This hotel has a prime location, a short walk from Circular Quay and the Opera House, and just across the road from the Royal Botanic Gardens. Rooms are exceptionally large and luxurious, with good-size marble bathrooms — though, to be honest, it may be time for a refurbishment. Most rooms have small balconies. The rooms on the east side of the hotel have the best views across the Botanic Gardens. Most rooms are accessible to wheelchairs.

See map p. 118. 93 Macquaire St., Sydney, NSW 2000. ☎ *1300/301 391 in Australia, or 02/9252 4600. Fax: 02/9252 4286.* www.stamford.com.au. *Parking: A$40 (US$32/£16). Rack rates: A$540 (US$432/£215) double, A$580 (US$464/£232) deluxe harbor-view double, A$705–A$3,000 (US$564–US$2,400/£280–£1,200) Sir Stamford presidential suite. AE, DC, MC, V.*

Star City Hotel
$$$$ Darling Harbour

This gambling and entertainment complex includes an AAA-rated five-star hotel, with rooms overlooking Darling Harbour and the architecturally interesting Pyrmont Bridge. Although the four split-level Royal Suites are spectacular — each with three TVs, a giant Jacuzzi, a full kitchen, two bathrooms, its own sauna, and the services of the former butler to the governor of Queensland — the standard rooms are somewhat small. Executive suites are very nice. If you win big, use your winnings to pay for a room with views over Darling Harbour.

80 Pyrmont St., Pyrmont, Sydney, NSW 2009. ☎ *1800/700 700 in Australia, or 02/9777 9000. Fax: 02/9657 8344.* www.starcity.com.au. *Parking: A$20 (US$16/£8). Rack rates: A$350–A$370 (US$280–US$296/£140–£150) double, from A$510 (US$408/£208) suite. AE, DC, MC, V.*

Swiss-Grand Hotel
$$$$ **Bondi Beach**

Right on Bondi Beach, overlooking the Pacific, the Swiss-Grand is the best hotel in Bondi. It occupies a unique position overlooking the waves and sand of one of Australia's most famous cultural icons. The lobby is grand, indeed, with high ceilings and stylish furniture. Each room is a suite, with separate bedroom and living room. All are spacious, and each comes with a luxurious bathroom. All rooms have two TVs; some have Jacuzzis. Oceanfront units have balconies. The sumptuousness of the accommodations and a terrific day spa help make this a fine place to stay.

Corner of Campbell Parade and Beach Rd. (P.O. Box 219, Bondi Beach, NSW 2026). ☎ *800-344-1212 in the U.S., or 02/9365 5666; 1800/655 252 in Australia; 0800/951 000 in the U.K.; 0800/056 666 in New Zealand. Fax: 02/9365 9710.* www.swissgrand. com.au. *Free parking. Rack rates: A$308 (US$246/£123) standard double, A$352 (US$281/£140) oceanview double, from A$396 (US$317/£158) suite. Packages are available on the hotel's Web site. AE, DC, MC, V.*

Sydney Central YHA
$ **Central**

This multiple-award-winning hostel is one of the biggest and busiest in the world. With a 98 percent year-round occupancy rate, you'll have to book early. It's in a historic nine-story building, and offers far more than standard basic accommodations. In the basement is the Scu Bar, a popular drinking hole with pool tables and occasional entertainment. There's also an entertainment room with more pool tables and e-mail facilities, TV rooms on every floor, and a movie room. Rooms are clean and basic. Three dorm rooms hold eight people each, 24 sleep up to six, and 70 accommodate four. The YHA is accessible to travelers with disabilities.

See map p. 118. 11 Rawson Place (at Pitt Street, outside Central Station), Sydney, NSW 2000. ☎ *02/9281 9111. Fax: 02/9281 9199.* www.yha.com.au. *Parking: A$12 (US$9.60/£4.80). Rack rates: A$28–A$33 (US$22–US$26/£11–£13) dorm bed, A$82 (US$66/£33) twin without bathroom, A$94 (US$75/£37) twin with bathroom; non-YHA members are charged an extra A$3.50 (US$2.80/£1.40) per night. MC, V.*

Sydney Harbour Marriott
$$$$ **Circular Quay**

This well-located property is a quick stroll to Circular Quay and The Rocks by foot. A third of the rooms have views over the harbor, with the Deluxe Bridge View rooms and the Deluxe Opera View rooms having the pick of the vantage points. The semi-indoor/outdoor pool is reasonable, the Modern Australian rooms are a fair size and nice and bright, each room features a large work desk area and a safe for your laptop. The Customs House Bar below has a nice courtyard for an outside drinkie.

30 Pitt St. (at Alfred Street), Sydney 2000. ☎ *1800/251 259 in Australia, or 02/9259 7000. Fax: 02/9251 1122.* www.marriott.com.au. *Parking: A$30 (US$24/£12). Rack rates: A$350 (US$280/£140) standard room, A$550 (US$440; £220) suite. AE, DC, MC, V.*

Tricketts Luxury Bed & Breakfast
$$ **Glebe**

In 2006, the *New York Times* described Tricketts as the best bed-and-breakfast accommodation in the Southern Hemisphere. Although that's quite a claim, as soon as I walked into this atmospheric old place, I wanted to ditch my modern Sydney apartment and move in. Your first impression as you enter the tessellated, tiled corridor of the 1880s Victorian mansion is the jumble of plants and ornaments, high ceilings, Oriental rugs, and leaded windows. Guests relax over a decanter of port or with a magazine on wicker furniture on the veranda overlooking fairly busy Glebe Point Road. The guest rooms are quiet and homey. Favorites are no. 2, with its wooden floorboards and king-size bed, and the Honey Room Suite — with an 1820s king-size four-poster bed.

270 Glebe Point Rd., Glebe (the water end), NSW 2037. ☎ *02/9552 1141. Fax: 02/9692 9462.* www.tricketts.com.au. *Free parking. Rack rates: A$198 (US$158/£78) double, A$220 (US$176/£88) honeymoon suite. Rates include continental breakfast. MC, V.*

Westin Sydney
$$$ **Martin Place**

One of Sydney's most celebrated AAA-rated five-star hotels, the Westin is in the center of the city, in the Martin Place pedestrian mall. Integrated into a 19th-century post office building, the Westin's charm is modern and classic. The large rooms have comfortable beds and floor-to-ceiling windows. The hotel is home to several bars, restaurants, and clothing shops. Just steps from the central shopping streets and the QVB, and a 10- to 15-minute walk to both the Sydney Opera House and Darling Harbour, the hotel features an impressive seven-story atrium, a wonderful two-level health club, and an exclusive day spa.

See map p. 118. 1 Martin Place, Sydney, NSW 2000. ☎ *800-937-8461 in the U.S., or 02/8223 1111. Fax: 02/8223 1222.* www.westin.com.au. *Parking: A$25 (US$20/£10). Rack rates: A$286 (US$229/£115) double. AE, DC, MC, V.*

Runner-up hotels

Alishan International Guest House

$–$$ **Glebe**   The Alishan is a quiet place with a real Aussie feel. It's at the city end of Glebe Point Road, just ten minutes by bus from the shops around Town Hall. It's a mixture of upmarket youth hostel and typical guesthouse. Standard dorm rooms are spotless, light, and bright, and come with two sets of bunks. Doubles have a double bed, a sofa and armchair, and a shower. *100 Glebe Point Rd., Glebe, NSW 2037.* ☎ *02/9566 4048. Fax: 02/9525 4686.* www.alishan.com.au. *Limited off-street parking available (free). Rack rates: A$27–A$33 (US$22–US$26/£11–£13) dorm bed, A$99–A$115 (US$79–US$92/£40–£46) double, A$154 (US$123/£62) family room. AE, MC, V.*

Periwinkle-Manly Cove Guesthouse

$$ **Manly** Across the road from one of Manly's two harbor beaches, the Periwinkle is a short walk from the ferry and the main ocean beach. Rooms are small and come with a double bed. Some have a shower and toilet (these go for higher prices), but otherwise you'll have to make do with one of four separate bathrooms (one has a tub). A full kitchen means you can save money by not eating out. Room nos. 5 and 10 are the nicest and have screened balconies overlooking the harbor (but no bathrooms). *18–19 E. Esplanade, Manly, NSW 2095. ☎ 02/9977 4668. Fax: 02/9977 6308.* www.periwinkle. citysearch.com.au. *Free parking. Rack rates: A$ 135 (US$ 108/£54) double without bathroom, A$ 165 (US$ 132/£66) double with bathroom; units with harbor views A$ 10 (US$ 8/£4) extra. Rates include continental breakfast. MC, V.*

Stamford Sydney Airport

$$$$ **Airport** This is the best airport hotel. Each room has a king-size bed or two doubles, access to airport information, and a good-size bathroom with tub. It's minutes from the airport, and pickup service is free. Day-use rates are A$ 85 (US$ 68/£34) for two to four hours, A$ 115 (US$ 92/£46) for four to eight hours. *Corner of O'Riordan and Robey streets (P.O. Box 353), Mascot, Sydney, NSW 2020. ☎ 1300/301 391 in Australia, or 02/9317 2200. Fax: 02/ 9317 3855.* www.stamford.com.au. *Parking: A$ 15 (US$ 12/£6). Rack rates: A$ 270 (US$ 216/£108) double, from A$ 370 (US$ 296/£149) suite. Ask about discount packages and weekend rates. AE, DC, MC, V.*

Sullivans Hotel

$$ **Paddington** Sullivans is in the heart of the action in one of Sydney's most popular shopping, entertainment, restaurant, and gay pub and club areas. The hotel is popular with Americans during Gay and Lesbian Mardi Gras. All rooms are simple and compact but are good for a few nights. Each comes with an attached shower. Standard rooms have two single beds, and each garden room has a queen-size bed and pleasant garden views. *See map p. 118. 21 Oxford St., Paddington, NSW 2021. ☎ 02/9361 0211. Fax: 02/9360 3735.* www.sullivans.com.au. *Limited free parking. Rack rates: A$ 165 (US$ 132/ £66) standard double, A$ 180 (US$ 144/£77) garden room double and triple, family room A$ 180 (US$ 144/£77), A$ 225 (US$ 128/£64) 2 connecting rooms. AE, DC, MC, V.*

Travelodge Hotel Sydney

$$ **City Centre** This three-and-one-half-star business-oriented hotel is cheap for Sydney, comfortable, and well located — making it a good option for travelers who just want to unpack and explore. The rooms are IKEA-like in appearance, with a choice of one queen-size bed or two twin beds. Each comes with a kitchenette with a microwave. From here it's a short walk to Oxford Street, Town Hall, Hyde Park, and the monorail to Darling Harbour. *See map p. 118. 27–33 Wentworth Ave., Sydney, NSW 2000. ☎ 1300/886 886 in Australia, or 02/8267 1700. Fax: 02/8267 1800.* www.travelodge.com.au. *Parking: A$ 17 (US$ 14/£7). Rack rates: A$ 119 (US$ 95/£47) double or twin; extra person A$ 16 (US$ 13/£7.50). AE, DC, MC, V.*

Dining Out

Sydney is a gourmet paradise, with an abundance of fresh seafood, a vast range of vegetables and fruit always in season, prime meats at inexpensive prices, and top-quality chefs making international names for themselves. Asian and Mediterranean cooking have had a major influence on the cuisine, with spices and herbs finding their way into most dishes. Immigration has brought with it almost every type of cuisine you can imagine, from African to Tibetan, from Russian to Vietnamese.

Sydney is a great place to try Modern Australian, or "Mod Oz," cuisine, which has been applauded by chefs and food critics around the world. Modern Australian cuisine emphasizes fresh ingredients and a creative blend of European styles with Asian influences. At its best, Modern Australian food is world-class, but you'll probably have to go to the best of Sydney's restaurants to see what the scene is all about.

By the way, in Australia, the first course is called the entree and the second course the main.

Australians think American-style coffee tastes like ditch water and favor a range of Italian-style coffee creations. Ask for a latte if you just want coffee with milk. "Bottomless" cups of coffee are rare in Australia.

Most moderate and inexpensive restaurants in Sydney are **BYO,** as in "bring your own" bottle, though some places also have extensive wine and beer lists. More moderately priced restaurants are introducing corkage fees, which means you pay anywhere from A$2 to A$8 (US$1.60–US$6.40/£0.80–£3.20) per person for the privilege of the waiter opening your bottle of wine. Very expensive restaurants discourage BYO.

Aria
$$$$ Circular Quay   MODERN AUSTRALIAN

With front-row views of the Harbour Bridge and the Sydney Opera House, Aria stands in one of the most enviable spots in the city. The windows overlooking the water are huge, the atmosphere is elegant and buzzy, and many of the tables have a stunning view. The food, created by Matthew Moran, one of Australia's great chefs, is imaginative and mouthwatering. Standout dishes include the pan-fried kingfish filets with a salad of white beans and hazelnut, with a red-wine sauce; and the sweet pork loin with lentil salad and black pudding.

See map p. 132. 1 Macquarie St., East Circular Quay. ☎ *02/9252 2555.* www.aria restaurant.com.au. *Reservations essential. Main courses: A$42–A$49 (US$34–US$39/£17–£20); pre-theater supper, 1 course A$36 (US$29/£18), 2 courses A$58 (US$46/£29), 3 courses A$72 (US$57/£28). AE, DC, MC, V. Open: Mon–Fri noon to 2:30 p.m., pre-theater daily 5:30–7 p.m., Mon–Sat 7–11:30 p.m.; Sun 6–11:30 p.m.*

Central Sydney Dining

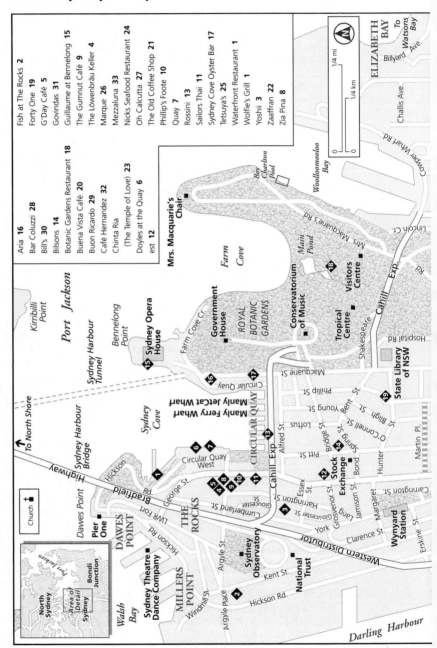

Fish at The Rocks **2**
Forty One **19**
G'Day Café **5**
Govindas **31**
Guillaume at Bennelong **15**
The Gumnut Café **9**
The Löwenbräu Keller **4**
Marque **26**
Mezzaluna **33**
Nicks Seafood Restaurant **24**
Oh Calcutta **27**
The Old Coffee Shop **21**
Phillip's Foote **10**
Quay **7**
Rossini **13**
Sailors Thai **11**
Sydney Cove Oyster Bar **17**
Tetsuya's **25**
Waterfront Restaurant **1**
Wolfie's Grill **1**
Yoshii **3**
Zaaffran **22**
Zia Pina **8**

Aria **16**
Bar Coluzzi **28**
Bill's **30**
Bilsons **14**
Botanic Gardens Restaurant **18**
Buena Vista Café **20**
Buon Ricardo **29**
Café Hernandez **32**
Chinta Ria
(The Temple of Love) **23**
Doyles at the Quay **6**
est **12**

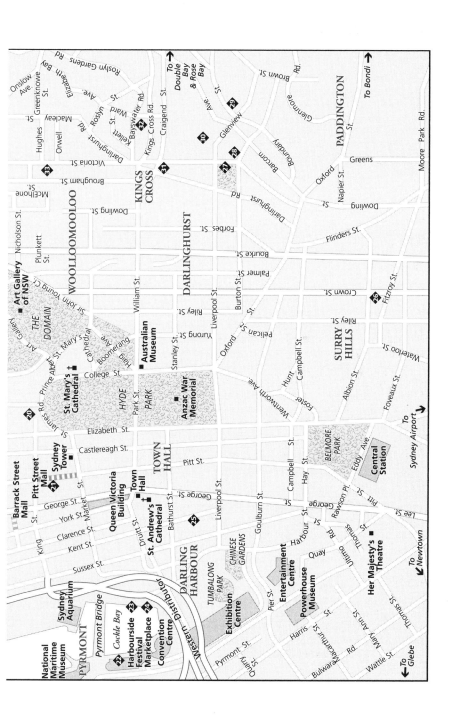

Bilsons
$$$$ Town Hall FRENCH/MODERN AUSTRALIAN

Tucked away at the back of the Radisson Plaza Hotel is a great restaurant that could compete with some of the Michelin-starred classics in Europe. Chef Tony Bilson, is a well-known Sydney personality and the quality of his French-influenced food is a testament to some 30 years in the business. The restaurant is modern in its look, but comfortable, and the service is impeccable. Expect something in the same vein as slow-roasted suckling pig with grilled pineapple, or grilled breasts of wild pigeon with foie gras.

See map p. 132. The Foyer, Radisson Plaza Hotel, 27 O'Connell St., Sydney. ☎ *02/8214 0496.* www.bilsons.com.au. *Reservations essential. Main courses: A$40 (US$32/£16); 8-course degustation menu A$120 (US$96/£48) per person without wine, A$200 (US$160/£80) per person with wine. AE, DC, MC, V. Open: Mon–Fri noon to 2:30 p.m.; Mon–Sat 6–10 p.m.*

The Boathouse on Blackwattle Bay
$$$$ Glebe SEAFOOD

Above Sydney University's rowing club and overlooking a working area of Sydney Harbour, this converted boat shed offers water views across to the city. It serves French-inspired seafood in an elegant, yet informal, atmosphere of white tablecloths and natural lighting. You can see the chefs at work in the open kitchen. You can't go wrong with the signature dish: the snapper fish pie with roasted tomatoes and mashed potatoes. Usually, nine varieties of oysters are on the menu. Head here for a lunchtime treat. Catch a taxi — it's a little hard to find.

End of Ferry Road, Glebe. ☎ *02/9518 9011.* www.theboathouse.net.au. *Reservations recommended. Main courses: A$37–A$43 (US$30–US$34/£15–£17). AE, DC, MC, V. Open: Tues–Sun noon to 2:30 p.m. and 6:30–10 p.m.*

Bondi Icebergs/Icebergs Dining Room & Bar
$$$$ Bondi Beach SEAFOOD/MEDITERRANEAN

This revamped swimming club complex overlooking Bondi Beach is a fabulous place to hang out. From its position on the cliffs, the Icebergs Bar looks across the beach and water, and its floor-to-ceiling windows make sure you get to experience what's probably the best view in Sydney. The bar features lots of cushions and even hammocks, and the views stretch on across the balcony and into the restaurant. Inside it's all frosted-glass dividers (to match the color of the ocean), and white tablecloths and napkins (to resemble the surf). Not surprisingly, seafood features highly on the menu. You may find wild scallops, risotto with coral trout and oregano, a fish stew from Livorno, and spaghetti with clams. Here too is the **Sundeck Café,** which boasts a variety of light snacks and meals ranging from focaccia, salads, and burgers to fresh local seafood and pasta, all served out on a terrace with fantastic views.

1 Notts Ave., Bondi Beach. ☎ *02/9365 9000. Reservations essential. Main courses: A$36–A$44 (US$29–US$35/£15–£18). AE, DC, MC, V. Open: Tues–Sat noon to 3 p.m. and 6.30–10:30 p.m., Sun noon to 3 p.m. and 6:30–9 p.m.*

Botanic Gardens Restaurant
$$$ Circular Quay   MODERN AUSTRALIAN

You couldn't ask for a better walk to a restaurant than through the Royal Botanic Gardens, next to the Sydney Opera House. Enjoying lunch on the wisteria-covered balcony in the middle of Sydney's most beautiful park is a treat every visitor should enjoy. Main courses often mix a bit of Mediterranean, French, and Asian. They include the very popular white sausage *(boudin blanc)* with lentils and braised fennel. Try perfect crème brûlée with underlying plum purée for dessert (A$ 12/US$ 9.20/£4.60).

See map p. 132. In the Royal Botanic Gardens. ☎ *02/9241 2419. Reservations recommended. Main courses: A$23–A$30 (US$18–US$24/£9–£12). AE, DC, MC, V. Open: Daily 8 a.m.–4:30 p.m. Bus or ferry: Circular Quay.*

Buena Vista Café
$ Town Hall   CAFE

If you happen to be in the city center, this fabulous, largely undiscovered restaurant and cafe is a must for the great value and the absolutely fantastic views reaching over Hyde Park and even to the harbor. It's very large inside, has panoramic windows, and serves meals from the counter. Hearty breakfasts include bacon and eggs, omelets, and cereals. All-day dishes run to sandwiches, Caesar salad, homemade pies, pastas, and lasagna. Even if you're not hungry, it's well worth popping in for a coffee.

See map p. 132. Level 14, Law Courts Building, 184 Phillip St. (Queens Square). ☎ *02/9230 8224. Main courses: A$8–A$13 (US$6–US$10/£3–£5); coffee and cake A$5 (US$4/£2). No credit cards. Open: Mon–Fri 7 a.m.–5 p.m.*

Buon Ricordo
$$$ Paddington   ITALIAN

With yellow walls pinned with antique plates and artwork, and padded wooden chairs and archways, Buon Ricordo oozes trattoria-style charm. The food is rich and the prices for main courses are high, but the food is just perfection. Dishes may include such seasonal specialties as crispy fried harbor prawns, or a delicious winter salad of raw fennel and artichoke hearts. A favorite is the polenta cake with grilled radicchio flavored with sweet vincotto. The house signature dish is *fettuccine al tartufovo* — fettuccine served in a cream sauce with lightly fried, truffle-infused eggs.

See map p. 132. 108 Boundary St., Paddington. ☎ *02/9360 6729.* www.buonricordo. com.au. *Reservations essential. Main courses: A$38–A$49 (US$30–US$39/£15–£20), pastas A$25–A$30 (US$20–US$24/£10–£12). AE, DC, MC, V. Open: Fri–Sat noon to 3 p.m., Tues–Sat 6:30–11 p.m.*

Chinta Ria (The Temple of Love)
$$ Darling Harbour   MODERN MALAYSIAN

Cockle Bay's star attraction for those who appreciate good food and fun ambience without paying a fortune, Chinta Ria is on the roof of the three-story development. In a round building dominated by a giant golden Buddha in the center, Chinta Ria serves fairly good "hawker-style" (read: cheap and delicious) Malaysian food. Although the food is good, the atmosphere is even more memorable. The service is slow, but who cares in such an interesting space, with plenty of nooks, crannies, and society folk to look at. There are seats outside (some within range of the noise of the highway), but the best views unfold inside.

See map p. 132. Cockle Bay Wharf Complex. ☎ 02/9264 3211. Main courses: A$13–A$26 (US$9.60–US$21/£4.70–£10). AE, DC, MC, V. Open: Daily noon to 2:30 p.m. and 6–11 p.m.

Doyles at the Quay
$$$ Circular Quay   SEAFOOD

Doyles is synonymous with seafood in Sydney. Most customers sit outside to enjoy the fabulous views across the harbor, though guardrails somewhat interrupt the view of the Opera House. The most popular dish is basically pricey fish and chips, which costs A$35 (US$28/£14). You can also get a dozen oysters for A$30 (US$24/£12) or half a lobster for A$65 (US$52/£26). One word of advice: Australian lobsters (crayfish in reality) aren't as tasty as lobsters in other parts of the world. Still, if it's a nice day, it's a nice place to sit.

A sister restaurant, **Doyles on the Beach (☎ 02/9337 2007)**, is over at Watsons Bay. Ferries run to Watsons Bay from Circular Quay Monday through Friday every half-hour from 10:35 a.m. to 3:35 p.m.; Saturday, Sunday, and public holidays, every 45 minutes from 9:20 a.m. to 6:15 p.m.

See map p. 132. Overseas Passenger Terminal, Circular Quay. ☎ 02/9252 3400. Main courses: A$30–A$60 (US$24–US$48/£12–£24). DC, MC, V. Open: Daily 11:30 a.m.– 3 p.m., Mon–Sat 5:30–10:30 p.m., Sun 5:30–9:30 p.m.

est.
$$$$ Wynyard   MODERN AUSTRALIAN

Upstairs in the trendy Establishment Hotel you'll find est., a restaurant that culinary luminary Peter Doyle has melded into a Sydney icon. The décor is a sensual masterpiece, with white columns and rich felt-brown carpets adding to an ambience already sexed up by cool lounge music. Dishes on the menu include grilled rock lobster with herbs and lemon butter, and juniper-crusted saddle of venison, with beetroot purée, potato, and semolina gnocchi. It's more laid-back on the top floor, where you'll find the city's best sushi bar — a trendy place with one long table bathed in natural light called **Sushi E.** This is partitioned off from **Hemisphere** — a moody drinking place with leather armchairs and comfy sofas.

See map p. 132. Level 1, 252 George St., Sydney. ☎ 02/9240 3010. www.merivale. com. *Reservations essential. Main courses: A$43–A$57 (US$34–US$46/£17–£23). AE, DC, MC, V. Open: Mon–Fri noon to 3 p.m., Mon–Sat 6–10 p.m.*

Fish at The Rocks
$$$ The Rocks   SEAFOOD

This midsize eatery a ten-minute stroll up the main hill leading from The Rocks, serves delicious food with a focus on fresh seafood. There are a few tables outside, and plenty inside below the photographs of sailing boats. The staff is friendly and the service professional. Portions are not huge, so don't expect to fill up on a single main course if you're starving. The dishes are well crafted, though. Favorites here are the Queensland scallops on polenta and braised peas, and the whiting filets in a beer-batter. Don't pass on the chocolate mud cake, either — it's stunning.

See map p. 132. 29 Kent St., The Rocks. ☎ *02/9252 4614.* www.fishattherocks. com.au. *Reservations recommended. Main courses: A$24–A$29 (US$19–US$23/ £9.50–£12). AE, MC, V. Open: Daily noon to 2:30 p.m. and 6–10:30 p.m.*

Forty One
$$$$ Wynyard   FRENCH/MODERN AUSTRALIAN

Powerful people, celebrities, and Sydneysiders out for a celebration all come here to feel exclusive. The 41st-floor views over the city and the harbor are terrific, the service is fun, the cutlery is the world's best, and Swiss chef and owner Dietmar Sawyere has given the food a wickedly good Asian slant. In all, it's a glamorous place to experience some of the best of Australian cuisine. The signature dish is roast wild hare, with celeriac and potato purée, Viennese carrots, and chartreuse jus.

See map p. 132. Level 42, Chifley Tower, 2 Chifley Sq. ☎ *02/9221 2500.* www.forty-one.com.au. *Reservations required. Main courses: 3-course menu A$125 (US$100/£50), 3-course menu with matched wine A$140 (US$112/£56), 6 courses with wine A$200 (US$160/£80). AE, DC, MC, V. Open: Tues–Fri noon to 4 p.m., Mon–Sat 6–10 p.m.*

G'Day Café
$ The Rocks   CAFE

According to the manager, half the tourists who visit Sydney eat at this little place in the heart of The Rocks. It offers simple, satisfying food at around half the price you'd expect to pay in a tourist precinct. The interior is uninspiring, but in back there's a leafy courtyard. Among the offerings are focaccia sandwiches, soups, salads, burgers, lasagna, chili, and curry.

See map p. 132. 83 George St., The Rocks. ☎ *02/9241 3644. Main courses: A$3–A$7 (US$2.40–US$5.60/£1.20–£2.80). AE. Open: Sun–Thurs 5 a.m. to midnight, Fri–Sat 5 a.m. to 3 a.m.*

Govindas
$ Kings Cross   VEGETARIAN

When I think of Govindas, I can't help smiling. Perhaps it's because I'm recalling the happy vibe from the Hare Krishna center it's based in, or maybe it's because the food is so cheap! Or maybe it's because the restaurant even throws in a decent movie with the meal. (The movie theater is on a different floor.) The food is simple vegetarian, served buffet-style and eaten in a basic room off black-lacquer tables. Typical dishes include pastas and salads, lentil dishes, soups, and casseroles. It's BYO and doctrine-free.

See map p. 132. 112 Darlinghurst Rd., Darlinghurst. ☎ *02/9380 5155.* www.govindas. com.au. *Main courses: Dinner A$16 (US$13/£6.50), including movie. AE, MC, V. Open: Daily 6–11 p.m.*

Guillaume at Bennelong
$$$$ **Circular Quay   FRENCH**

If you go to Bondi, you have to swim in the Pacific; if you see the Harbour Bridge, you have to walk across it; if you visit the Opera House, you must eat at Guillaume at Bennelong. The restaurant is as uniquely designed as the building itself, with tall glass windows that furrow around in an arch and grab the harbor and Circular Quay by the throat. Renowned French chef Guillaume Brahimi's offerings include sealed veal sweetbreads, or chicken breast with duck foie gras ravioli. Many would rather miss the first half of the opera than leave before dessert. The best bar in town is upstairs, where you can see over the water to the bridge and up to the other "sails." Good bar food is available until 11:30 p.m.

See map p. 132. In the Sydney Opera House, Bennelong Point. ☎ *02/9241 1999. Fax: 02/9241 3795.* www.guillaumeatbennelong.com.au. *Reservations recommended. Main courses: A$39 (US$31/£15). AE, DC, MC, V. Open: Thurs–Fri noon to 3 p.m., pre-theater menu Mon–Sat 5:30–7:45 p.m., dinner Mon–Sat 8–10:30 p.m.*

The Gumnut Café
$ **The Rocks   MODERN AUSTRALIAN**

A hearty lunch in a courtyard shaded by umbrellas — ah, heaven. With a great location in the heart of The Rocks, this 1890 sandstone cottage restaurant has an extensive indoor seating area, so it's a perfect place to take a break from sightseeing. On weekends, live jazz sets the mood. The breakfast specials are popular, and at lunchtime the cafe bustles with tourists and local office workers. The courtyard is heated in winter.

See map p. 132. 28 Harrington St., The Rocks. ☎ *02/9247 9591. Main courses: A$8.50–A$14 (US$6.80–US$11/£3.40–£5.50). AE, DC, MC, V. Open: Sun–Wed 8 a.m.– 5 p.m., Thurs–Sat 8 a.m.–10:30 p.m.*

The Löwenbräu Keller
$$ **The Rocks   BAVARIAN**

Renowned for celebrating Oktoberfest every day for 30 years, this is the place to watch Aussies let their hair down. Come for lunch and munch a club sandwich in the glassed-off atrium while watching the daytime action of The Rocks. For a livelier scene, head here on Friday or Saturday night, when *beer-sculling* (chugging) and yodeling are accompanied by a brass band, and costumed waitresses ferry foaming beer steins about the cellarlike space. Options include hearty southern German and Austrian fare and several varieties of German beers in bottle or on draft. A good bargain is the lunchtime special, for just A$12 (US$9.60/£4.80).

See map p. 132. 18 Argyle St. (at Playfair Street), The Rocks. ☎ *02/9247 7785.* www. lowenbrau.com.au. *Reservations recommended. Main courses: A$17–A$23 (US$9.60–US$18/£4.80–£9). AE, DC, MC, V. Open: Daily 9:30 a.m.–2 a.m. (kitchen closes at 11 p.m.).*

Marque
$$$$ Central FRENCH

Seriously sophisticated, Marque offers a small menu featuring classic French dishes with pizazz in an eggplant-colored room. Politicians, actors, and food critics all rave about the place. The *New York Times* wrote lyrically about the beet tart on flaky pastry, and suggested that the "sardine fillet, baked inside a thin, crisp, translucent crust until it looks like a fossil, then served with mackerel jelly" could only have been created by a "culinary wizard."

See map p. 132. 4–5/355 Crown St., Surry Hills. ☎ *02/9332 2225.* www.marque restaurant.com.au. *Reservations essential. Main courses: A$39–A$43 (US$31–US$34/£15–£17). AE, DC, MC, V. Open: Mon–Sat 6:30–10:30 p.m.*

Mezzaluna
$$$$ Kings Cross NORTHERN ITALIAN

Exquisite food, flawless service, and an almost unbeatable view across the city's western skyline have all helped Mezzaluna position itself among Sydney's top waterside eateries. An open, candlelit place with white walls and polished wooden floorboards, the dining room opens onto a huge all-weather terrace kept warm in winter by heaters. There's always a fabulous risotto on the menu. Whatever you choose, you can't really go wrong.

See map p. 132. 123 Victoria St., Potts Point. ☎ *02/9357 1988. Fax: 02/9357 2615.* www. mezzaluna.com.au. *Reservations recommended. Main courses: A$32–A$43 (US$26–US$34/£13–£17). AE, DC, MC, V. Open: Mon–Fri noon to 3 p.m., Mon–Sat 6–11 p.m.*

Nick's Seafood Restaurant
$$$ Darling Harbour SEAFOOD

This nice indoor and alfresco eatery overlooking the water offers good cocktails, and plenty of seafood. The best seats are outside in the sunshine, where you can watch the world go by over a bottle of wine. Our choice of dish is the seafood platter for two, which has enough crab, prawns, fish, oysters, and lobster to satisfy. It costs A$120 (US$96/£48). Otherwise, there are various fish, prawn, and octopus dishes to choose from. Nicks has another, equally nice eatery, on the other side of the Aquarium called **Nick's Bar & Grill** (☎ **02/9279 0122**) and yet another, called **Nick's Bar & Grill Bondi Beach** (☎ **02/9365 4122**) in the Bondi Pavilion (opposite the beach).

See map p. 132. The Promenade, Cockle Bay Wharf (on the city side of Darling Harbour). ☎ *02/9264 1212.* www.nicks-seafood.com.au. *Reservations recommended. Main* *courses: A$26–A$39 (US$21–US$31/£11–£15); A$5 (US$4/£2) per-person surcharge on weekends and public holidays. AE, MC, V. Open: Daily noon to 3 p.m. and 6–11 p.m.*

Phillip's Foote
$$ The Rocks   BARBECUE

Venture behind this historic pub and you'll find a courtyard strung with tables, benches, and large barbecues. Choose your own steak, lemon sole, trout, chicken, or pork, and throw it on the "barbie." It's fun, it's filling, and you may even make some new friends while your meal's sizzling. Some Sydneysiders think A$27 (US$21/£11) is a bit pricey, but then again you're eating in prime real estate land. Keep an eye on the meat — there's no excuse if you burn your own steak!

See map p. 132. 101 George St., The Rocks. ☎ *02/9241 1485.* www.phillips foote.com.au. *Main courses: A$27 (US$21/£11). AE, DC, MC, V. Open: Mon–Sat noon to midnight, Sun noon to 10 p.m.*

Pompei's
$ Bondi Beach   PIZZA/PASTA/ICE CREAM

Use good ingredients and you'll get good pizzas — regulars swear they're the best in Sydney. Toppings include figs, prosciutto, fresh goat cheese, and pumpkin. Pompei's also has a selection of pizzas without cheese. And leave some room for the homemade gelati, the best in Sydney. Try dense raspberry, thick chocolate, tiramisu, or limoncello. The water views and outside tables are another plus.

126–130 Roscoe St. (at Gould Street), Bondi Beach. ☎ *02/9365 1233. Reservations recommended. Main courses: Pizza A$13–A$17 (US$10–US$14/£5–£7). AE, DC, MC, V. Open: Tues–Sun 11 a.m.–11 p.m.*

Quay
$$$$ Circular Quay   MODERN AUSTRALIAN

With its enviable location on top of the cruise-ship terminal, Quay offers some of the loveliest views in the city. Some feel that it's Sydney's best restaurant (though we prefer Tetsuya's). In good weather, the sun sparkles off the water and through the large windows. At night, when the city lights wash over the harbor and bridge and the Opera House's sails are lit up, the view is even better. Chef Peter Gilmore's menu is a revelation of French, Italian, and Australian ideas. Signature dishes include crisped pressed duck with garlic purée and porcini mushrooms, and seared yellowfin tuna with tomato jelly, roasted eggplant, and basil oil.

See map p. 132. On the upper level of the Overseas Passenger Terminal, Circular Quay West, The Rocks. ☎ *02/9251 5600.* www.quay.com.au. *Reservations recommended well in advance. Main courses: A$38 (US$30/£15); A$6 (US$4.80/£2.40) per-person surcharge on public holidays. AE, DC, MC, V. Open: Mon–Fri noon to 2:30 p.m., daily 6–10 p.m.*

Ravesi's

$$$ Bondi Beach   MODERN AUSTRALIAN

Set on a corner beside a run of surf shops, Ravesi's is a kind of fish tank, with the water on the outside. Downstairs, it's all glass windows and bar stools — the perfect place to people-watch. On weekend nights, the place is packed. Upstairs is a fine casual restaurant with seating inside and out on the balcony overlooking the beach. On a recent visit, we had the smoked chicken salad with avocado, chile, mango, and peanuts and it easily out-classed any salad we've had for a long while. Weekend breakfast up here is a wonderful experience, too, and they do excellent bloody marys.

Corner of Campbell Parade and Hall Street, Bondi Beach. ☎ *02/9365 4422. Reservations recommended. Main courses: A$23–A$29 (US$18–US$23/£9–£12), breakfasts A$10–A$22 (US$8–US$18/£4–£9). AE, MC, V. Open: Mon–Fri noon to 3 p.m. and 6–10 p.m., Sat 9 a.m.–3 p.m. and 6–10 p.m., Sun 9 a.m.–4 p.m.*

Rossini

$ Circular Quay   ITALIAN

This cafeteria-style Italian restaurant opposite Ferry Wharf 5 at Circular Quay is great for people-watching. The outside tables are perfect for break-fast or a quick bite before a show at the Opera House. Breakfast croissants, Italian doughnuts, muffins, and gorgeous Danish pastries cost A$3 (US$2.40/£1.20); bacon and eggs with toast, A$12 (US$9.60/£4.80). Wait to be seated for lunch or dinner, make your choice, pay at the counter, take a ticket, and then pick up your food. Meals, including veal parmigiana, cannelloni, ravioli, chicken crepes, and octopus salad, are often huge. You could easily get away with one meal for two people — ask for an extra plate — and although it's not the best Italian you'll ever eat, it is tasty.

See map p. 132. Shop W5, Circular Quay. ☎ *02/9247 8026. Main courses: A$10–A$22 (US$8–US$18/£4–£9). No credit cards. Open: Daily 7 a.m.–10 p.m.*

Sailors Thai

$$$ The Rocks   THAI

With a reputation as hot as the chilies in its jungle curry, Sailors Thai can-teen attracts lunchtime crowds who come to eat noodles and pork and prawn wonton soup, and Thai salads at its one stainless steel table with some 40 chairs. Four other tables overlook the cruise-ship terminal and the quay. Downstairs, the a la carte restaurant serves inventive food that's a far cry from the fare at your average Thai restaurant, such as stir-fried pineapple curry with chilies and cashew nuts, and wonderfully glutinous coconut ash pudding, made from the ash of burned coconuts cooked with licorice root, coconut water, rice flour, and sugar.

See map p. 132. 106 George St., The Rocks. ☎ *02/9251 2466.* www.sailorsthai. citysearch.com.au. *Reservations required well in advance in restaurant, not accepted in canteen. Main courses: A$26–A$35 (US$21–US$28/£11–£14) restaurant, A$15–A$23 (US$12–US$18/£6–£9) canteen. AE, DC, MC, V. Open: Restaurant Mon–Fri noon to 2 p.m., Mon–Sat 6–10 p.m.; canteen daily noon to 9 p.m.*

Sydney Cove Oyster Bar
$$$ Circular Quay SEAFOOD

Just before you reach the Sydney Opera House, you'll notice a couple of small shedlike buildings with tables and chairs set up to take in the stunning views of the harbor and the Harbour Bridge. The first is a Sydney institution, serving some of the best oysters in town. Light meals such as Asian-style octopus and seared tuna steak are also on the menu.

See map p. 132. No. 1 Eastern Esplanade, Circular Quay East. ☎ *02/9247 2937.* www.sydneycoveoysterbar.com. *Main courses: A$25–A$35 (US$20–US$28/£10–£14); 10 percent surcharge weekends and public holidays. AE, DC, MC, V. Open: Mon–Sat 11 a.m.–11 p.m., Sun 11 a.m.–8 p.m.*

Tetsuya's
$$$$ Town Hall JAPANESE/FRENCH FUSION

Tetsuya's was named one of the best in the world in *Restaurant Magazine*'s annual list of the world's 50 best eateries in 2007. So what makes Tetsuya's so good? On a recent visit, we had an intimate view across a Japanese-inspired courtyard with maples and waterfall. We chose the wine-matching option to go with our ten courses (corkage costs A$20/US$16/£8 if you bring your own wine), and you get to taste ten wines, several made especially to complement Tetsuya's dishes. This option costs A$85 (US$68/£34 per head. The service is impeccable, the food inspired. Small delicate morsels appeared: an incredible shot of pea soup with bitter chocolate sorbet was first, followed by a roulette of chopped smoked ocean trout capped with caviar, then a leek and spanner crab custard, to the signature confit of Tasmanian ocean trout with a crust of konbu seaweed, on a bed of daikon radish and fennel. Getting a table is difficult; book four weeks in advance, and confirm a few days before.

See map p. 132. 529 Kent St. ☎ *02/9267 2900.* www.tetsuyas.com. *Reservations essential; accepted 4 weeks ahead. Main courses: 10-course degustation menu A$185 (US$148/£74) per person; drinks extra. AE, DC, MC, V. Open: Fri noon to 3 p.m., Tues–Sat 6–10 p.m.*

Waterfront Restaurant
$$$$ Circular Quay MODERN AUSTRALIAN

You can't help but notice the mast, rigging, and sails that mark this restaurant in a converted stone warehouse. It's right next to the water below the main spread of The Rocks. It's popular at lunchtime, when business-people snap up the best seats outside in the sunshine. At night, with the colors of the city washing over the harbor, it can be magical. You get a choice of such things as steaks, mud crab, fish filets, or prawns. The seafood platter, at A$132 (US$105/£52) for two, includes lobsters, Balmain bugs (small, odd-looking crayfish), prawns, scallops, baby squid, fish pieces, and octopus. The food is simple and fresh, at prices that reflect the glorious position and views. Come here instead of Doyles.

In the same building you'll find sister restaurants **Wolfie's Grill** (☎ 02/ 9241 5577), which serves good char-grilled beef and seafood, and **The Italian Village** (☎ 02/9247 6111), which serves regional Italian cuisine.

In Campbell's Storehouse, 27 Circular Quay West, The Rocks. ☎ *02/9247 3666.* www.waterfrontrestaurant.com.au. *Reservations recommended. Main courses: A$35–A$39 (US$28–US$31/£14–£16); A$3.50 (US$2.40/£1.20) per-person surcharge weekends and public holidays. AE, DC, MC, V. Open: Daily noon to 10:30 p.m.*

Yoshii
$$–$$$$ The Rocks   JAPANESE

Yoshii is about as far away from the popular conveyor-belt sushi service as you can imagine. Sit at the counter and watch the chef slice and dice, or in the more intimate, muted tone main restaurant and witness beautiful service. At lunchtime there are seven set menus to choose from, and at dinner two 13-course options: the Yoshii menu and the Saqura menu. Tastes from the latter include smoked salmon mousse wrapped in marinated dried apricot, a Tasmania oyster with plum wine jelly, and a grilled persimmon and scallop with saffron *sumiso* sauce.

See map p. 132. 115 Harrington St., The Rocks. ☎ *02/9247 2566.* www.yoshii.com. au. *Reservations essential. Main courses: Lunch A$45–A$50 (US$36–US$40/£18–£20); dinner, Yoshii menu A$120 (US$96/£48) per person, Saqura Menu A$100 (US$80/£40) per person. AE, DC, MC, V. Open: Tues–Fri noon to 3 p.m., Mon–Sat 6–9:30 p.m.*

Zaaffran
$$ Darling Harbour   MODERN AUSTRALIAN/INDIAN

Sydney certainly hasn't seen an Indian restaurant quite like this one before. Forget the dark interiors and Indian murals. Here you find white surfaces, a glass-fronted wine cellar, and magnificent views of the water and the Sydney skyline from the far side of Darling Harbour. (An outdoor terrace provides the best views.) Expect such delights as the famed chicken *biryani*, baked in a pastry case and served with mint yogurt, or the tiger prawns in coconut cream and a tomato broth. Even fans of traditional Indian food are impressed by the creations here.

See map p. 132. Level 2, 345 Harbourside Shopping Centre, Darling Harbour. ☎ *02/ 9211 8900. Reservations recommended. Main courses: A$20–A$26 (US$16–US$21/£8– £10). AE, DC, MC, V. Open: Daily noon to 2:30 p.m. and 6–11 p.m.*

Zia Pina
$$ The Rocks   PIZZA/PASTA

With 10 tables downstairs and another 24 upstairs, there's not much room to breathe in this cramped pizzeria and spaghetti house. But squeeze in between the bare-brick walls and wallow in the clashes and clangs coming from the chefs in the kitchen. Pizzas come in two sizes; the larger feeds two people. They cost between A$16 and A$20 (US$13–US16/£7–£8). There are several chicken dishes, seafood dishes, and salads, too.

See map p. 132. 93 George St., The Rocks. ☎ **02/9247 2255.** www.ziapina.com.au.
*Reservations recommended. Main courses: A$9–A$20 (US$7.20–US$16/£3.60–£8).
AE, DC, MC, V. Open: Daily noon to 3 p.m., Sun–Mon 5–9 p.m., Tues–Thurs 5–
10:30 p.m., Fri–Sat 5–11:30 p.m. CityRail, bus, or ferry: Circular Quay.*

Cafe culture

Debate rages over which cafe serves the best coffee in Sydney, which
has the best atmosphere, and which has the tastiest snacks. The main
cafe scenes center on **Victoria Street** in Darlinghurst, **Stanley Street** in
East Sydney, and **King Street** in Newtown. Other places, including
Balmoral Beach on the North Shore, Bondi Beach, and Paddington, all
have their own favored hangouts.

Americans will be sorry to learn that free refills of coffee are rare in
Australian restaurants and cafes. Expect a cup of coffee to cost from
A$2.50 to A$3 (US$2–US$2.40/£1–£1.40); main courses at the cafes in this
section run from about A$8 to A$15 (US$6.40–US$12/£3.20–£6).

Following are some of our favorites around town.

Bar Coluzzi
Kings Cross

Although it may no longer offer the best coffee in Sydney, this cafe's claim
to fame is that it served real espresso when the rest of the city was drinking Nescafé. People-watching is fun at this fashionably worn-around-the-
edges spot.

See map p. 132. 322 Victoria St., Darlinghurst. ☎ **02/9380 5420.** *MC, V. Open: Daily
5 a.m.–8 p.m. CityRail: Kings Cross.*

Bill's
Kings Cross

This bright, airy place, strewn with flowers and magazines, serves nou-
veau cafe-style food. It's so popular you may have trouble finding a seat.
The signature breakfast dishes — including ricotta hotcakes with honeycomb butter and banana, and sweet corn fritters with roast tomatoes and
bacon — are the stuff of legend.

See map p. 132. 433 Liverpool St., Darlinghurst. ☎ **02/9360 9631.** *Fax: 02/9360 7302. AE,
MC, V. Open: Mon–Sat 7:30 a.m.–3 p.m. CityRail: Kings Cross.*

Café Hernandez
Kings Cross

The walls of this tiny, cluttered cafe are crammed with eccentric fake mas-
terpieces, and the aroma of 20 types of coffee roasted and ground on the
premises permeates the air. It's almost a religious experience for discern-
ing inner-city coffee addicts. The Spanish espresso is a treat.

See map p. 132. 60 Kings Cross Rd., Potts Point. ☎ ***02/9331 2343.*** www.cafe
hernandez.com.au. *AE, MC, V. Open: Daily 24 hours.*

The Old Coffee Shop
Town Hall

Sydney's oldest coffee shop opened in the Victorian Strand Arcade in 1891.
The shop may or may not serve Sydney's best java, but the old-world feel
of the place and the sugary snacks, cakes, and pastries make up for it. It's
a good spot to take a break from shopping and sightseeing.

Ground floor, Strand Arcade. ☎ ***02/9231 3002.*** *MC, V. Open: Mon–Fri 7:30 a.m.–5 p.m.,
Sat 8:30 a.m.–5 p.m., Sun 10:30 a.m.–4 p.m. CityRail: Town Hall.*

Exploring Sydney

The only problem with visiting Sydney is fitting in everything you want
to do and see. Of course, you won't want to miss the iconic attractions:
the **Opera House** and the **Harbour Bridge.** Everyone seems to be climbing the arch of the bridge these days on the BridgeClimb Sydney Tour, so
look up for the tiny dots of people waving to the ferry passengers below.

You should also check out the native wildlife in **Taronga Zoo** and the
Sydney Aquarium, stroll around the tourist precinct of **Darling
Harbour,** and get a dose of Down Under culture at the not-too-large
Australian Museum. Also try to take time out to visit one of the nearby
national parks for a taste of the Australian bush. If it's hot, take your
cozzie (swimsuit) and towel to **Bondi Beach** or **Manly.**

Sydney Harbour

Officially called Port Jackson, **Sydney Harbour** is the focal point of
Sydney and one of the features that makes this city so special. It's
entered through the **Heads,** two bush-topped outcrops (you'll see them
if you take a ferry or JetCat to Manly). The harbor laps at some 240km
(149 miles) of shoreline before stretching out into the Parramatta River.
Visitors are awestruck by the harbor's beauty, especially at night, when
the sails of the Opera House and the girders of the Harbour Bridge are lit
up. During the day, it buzzes with green-and-yellow ferries pulling in and
out of busy Circular Quay, sleek tourist craft, fully rigged tall ships, giant
container vessels, and hundreds of white-sailed yachts.

The greenery along the harbor's edges is a surprising feature, thanks to
the **Sydney Harbour National Park,** a haven for native trees and plants,
and a feeding and breeding ground for lorikeets and other nectar-eating
bird life. In the center of the harbor is a series of islands; the most
impressive is the tiny isle supporting **Fort Denison,** which once housed
convicts and acted as part of the city's defense.

Sydney Attractions

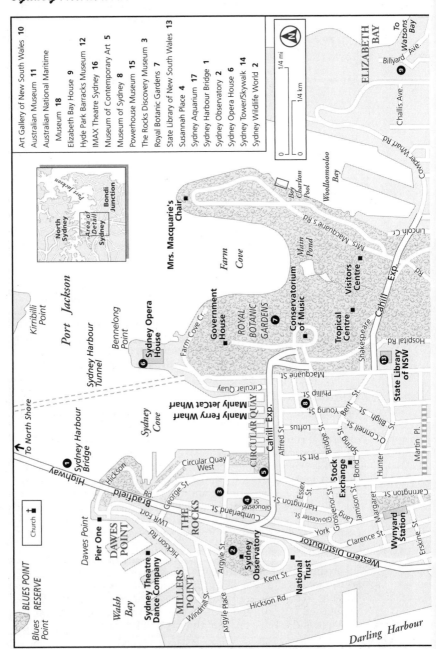

Art Gallery of New South Wales **10**
Australian Museum **11**
Australian National Maritime Museum **18**
Elizabeth Bay House **9**
Hyde Park Barracks Museum **12**
IMAX Theatre Sydney **16**
Museum of Contemporary Art **5**
Museum of Sydney **8**
Powerhouse Museum **15**
The Rocks Discovery Museum **3**
Royal Botanic Gardens **7**
State Library of New South Wales **13**
Susannah Place **4**
Sydney Aquarium **17**
Sydney Harbour Bridge **1**
Sydney Observatory **2**
Sydney Opera House **6**
Sydney Tower/Skywalk **14**
Sydney Wildlife World **2**

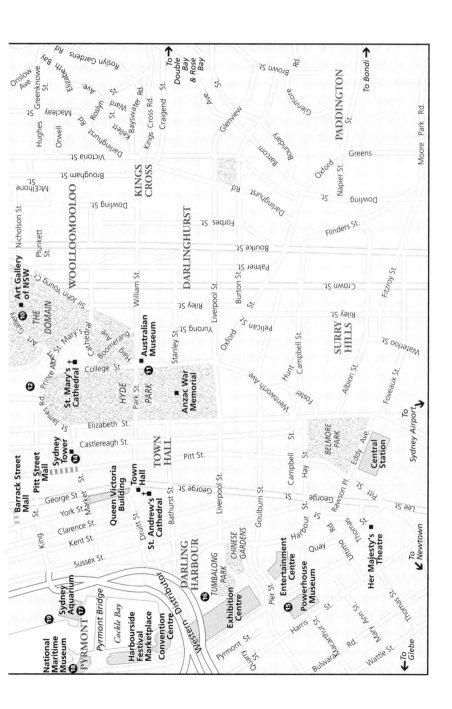

A couple of money-saving passes

If you'll be spending a few days in Sydney, check out the **See Sydney & Beyond Pass** (☎ **1300/661-711;** www.seesydneycard.com), which includes admission to over 40 of Sydney's major attractions, including the BridgeClimb, the Opera House, the Aquarium, several wildlife parks, a host of museums, and some farther-flung attractions, such as the Jenolan Caves in the Blue Mountains. The pass can be purchased for periods of one to seven days, with or without public transit (on the train, bus, and ferry). Prices range from A$69 (US$55/£28) for an adult over 16 (one day, no transport) to A$285 (US$228/£114) for an adult (seven days, with transport). There are also children's and family passes available. In addition, you can purchase a discount pass to Sydney Wildlife World, Sydney Aquarium, and Sydney Tower at any of these attractions or online at their Web sites for A$64 (US$51/£26) adults, A$35 (US$28/£14) children.

Attractions around Sydney Harbour

Royal Botanic Gardens

The gardens, next to the Sydney Opera House, were laid out in 1816 on the site of a farm that supplied food for the colony. They're informal in appearance, with a scattering of duck ponds and open spaces, though several areas are dedicated to particular plant species. These include the rose garden, the cacti and succulent display, and the central palm and rain forest groves (watch out for the thousands of large fruit bats, which chatter and argue among the rain forest trees). **Mrs. Macquarie's Chair,** along the coast path, offers superb views of the Opera House and the Harbour Bridge. The "chair" is a step cut out of sandstone with a huge stone plaque on top. It bears the name of Elizabeth Macquarie (1788–1835), the wife of Governor Lachlan Macquarie. (It's a favorite stop for tour buses.) The sandstone building dominating the gardens nearest to the Opera House is the **Government House,** once the official residence of the governor of New South Wales.

See map p. 146. Opposite Sydney Opera House. Admission: Free. Open: Daily 10 a.m.–4 p.m.

Sydney Harbour Bridge

Construction of the Sydney Harbour Bridge started in 1924, and it took 1,400 men eight years to complete. Today it rivals the Sydney Opera House as the most photographed structure in Australia. The bridge, is 1,150m (3,772 ft.) long and spans 503m (1,650 ft.) from the south shore to the north. It has pedestrian walkways, two railway lines, and an eight-lane road. The 30-minute stroll from one end to the other offers excellent harbor views. From the other side, you can take a CityRail train from Milsons Point back to the city (to Wynyard — change there for Circular Quay, Town Hall, or Central). As you walk across, stop off at the **Pylon Lookout.** From the top of this bridge support, 89m (292 ft.) above the water, you get panoramic views of Sydney Harbour, the ferry terminals of

Circular Quay, and beyond. Reach the pylon by walking to the far end of George Street in The Rocks toward the Harbour Bridge. Just past the Mercantile pub, you'll see some stone steps that take you onto Cumberland Street. From there, it's a two-minute walk to the steps underneath the bridge on your right. Climb four flights of stairs to reach the bridge's Western Footway, and then walk along to the first pylon. *Note:* Climbing up inside the pylon involves 200 steps.

See map p. 146. Pylon Lookout. ☎ *02/9247 3408. Admission: A$9 (US$7/£3.50) adults, A$3.50 (US$3/£1.50) children over 7. Open: Daily 10 a.m.–5 p.m.*

Sydney Opera House

Only a handful of buildings around the world are as architecturally and culturally significant as the Sydney Opera House. And this white-sailed construction caught midbillow over the waters of Sydney Cove is a working building. It's a full-scale performing arts complex with five major spaces. The biggest and grandest is the 2,690-seat **Concert Hall,** which has the best acoustics of any building of its type in the world. Come here to experience opera, chamber music, symphonies, dance, choral performances, and even rock 'n' roll. The **Opera Theatre** is smaller, seating 1,547, and books operas, ballets, and dance. The **Drama Theatre,** seating 544, and the **Playhouse,** seating 398, specialize in plays and smaller-scale performances. The **Boardwalk,** seating 300, is used for dance and experimental music.

Danish Architect Jørn Utzon won an international competition to design the Opera House. From the start, the project was controversial, with many Sydneysiders believing it was a monstrosity. Following a disagreement, Utzon returned home without ever seeing his finished project. Initially, the project was budgeted at a cool A$7 million (US$5.6 million/£2.8 million), but by the time it was finished in 1973 it had cost a staggering A$102 million (US$82 million/£41 million). Since then, continual refurbishment and the major task of replacing the asbestos-laden grouting between the hundreds of thousands of white tiles that make up its shell has cost many millions more. A long-overdue reconstruction is being completed, aimed at putting into practice what Jørn Utzon has long visualized. The Tourism Services Department at the Sydney Opera House can book **combination packages,** including dinner and a show; a tour, dinner, and a show; or a champagne interval performance.

See map p. 146. Bennelong Point. ☎ *02/9250 7250 for guided tours and information, or 02/9250 7777 box office. Fax: 02/9251 3943.* www.sydneyoperahouse.com. *Open: Box office Mon–Sat 9 a.m.–8:30 p.m., Sun 2 hours before performance. Tickets: A$12 to A$180 (US$9.60–US$144/£4.70–£72); plays average A$40 to A$60 (US$32–US$48/£16–£24). Guided one-hour tours A$26 (US$21/£11) adults, A$16 (US$13/£6.50) children. Tours daily 9 a.m.–5 p.m. (every 30 minutes), subject to theater availability. Backstage Tour A$150 (US$120/UK£60) starts daily at 7 a.m., for 2 hours, with breakfast.*

Exploring The Rocks

Sydney's historic district is on the Harbour Bridge side of Circular Quay hilly and cross-cut with alleyways. Some of Australia's oldest pubs are

Walk on the wild side: Climbing the Harbour Bridge

At one time, only bridge workers had the opportunity to view Sydney from the top of the main bridge arch. But now Sydneysiders and tourists can experience the spectacular view and the exhilarating achievement of climbing to the top of one of Australia's icons.

In addition to the original climb up one of the arches, you can also do one called the **Discovery Climb.** This takes climbers into the heart of the bridge. You traverse the suspension arch and then wind your way through a tangle of hatchways and girders suspended above the traffic. Both experiences take three hours from check-in at the BridgeClimb base, 5 Cumberland St., The Rocks (☎ **02/9240 1100** or 02/8274 7777; fax 02/9240 1122; www.bridgeclimb.com), to completion. The office is open daily from 8 a.m. to 6 p.m., and climbers leave in small groups every ten minutes or so.

Climbers wear "Bridge Suits" and are harnessed to a line. Participants are breath-tested for alcohol and are banned from carrying anything, including cameras. Climbs cost A$165 (US$132/£66) adults, A$100 (US$80/£40) children 12 to 16 on weekdays during the day and night; A$185 (US$148/£74) adults, A$125 (US$100/£50) children for climbs on Saturday and Sunday. Daily twilight climbs cost A$245 (US$196/£99) adults, A$185 (US$148/£74) children. Children under 12 are not allowed to climb. A dawn climb, on the first Saturday each month, costs A$295 (US$236/£118) adults, A$195 (US$156/£78) children. (Check first, as prices change often.)

here, as well as fine restaurants, stores, and hotels. Pick up a walking map from the visitor center and be sure to get off the main streets and see the original houses that survived the bulldozers.

The Eora Aboriginal people originally inhabited the headland now known as The Rocks for thousands of years. In 1788, British convicts and their guards arrived. A jail was built where the Four Seasons Hotel now stands, on George Street, and public hangings were common. Later it evolved into a vibrant port community, though its history is colored with outbreaks of plague, shanghaied sailors, and cut-throat gangs.

In 1973, bulldozers and protesters clashed with police over plans to tear down many of the buildings. These resulted in the Green Bans, which halted any further demolition. In 1975 a compromise was reached and the bans were lifted, in return for heritage protection and community consultation on future projects.

Today, there are 96 heritage buildings in The Rocks. The oldest is Cadmans Cottage, built in 1815, while the Dawes Point Battery, built in 1791, is the oldest remaining European structure. On Observatory Hill you'll find the three remaining walls of Fort Phillip, built in 1804.

Attractions in The Rocks

The Rocks Discovery Museum

This small but interesting museum is in a restored 1850s sandstone warehouse. It tells the story of The Rocks from pre-European days to the present. Learn about the area's traditional landowners, the establishment of the English colony, the sailors and traders who made the area their home, and the protests that saved this unique part of Sydney.

*See map p. 146. Kendall Lane, The Rocks. ☎ **1800/067 676**. Admission: Free. Open: Daily 10 a.m.–5 p.m.*

Museum of Contemporary Art (MCA)

This imposing sandstone museum set back from the water on The Rocks side of Circular Quay offers wacky, entertaining, inspiring, and befuddling displays of what's new (and dated) in modern art. It houses the J. W. Power Collection of more than 4,000 pieces, including works by Andy Warhol, Christo, Marcel Duchamp, and Robert Rauschenberg, as well as temporary exhibits. Free guided tours are conducted midweek at 11 a.m. and 1 p.m. and on weekends at noon and 1:30 p.m. The MCA cafe (☎ **02/9241 4253**) is a nice spot, with good views of the harbor and Opera House. It's serves up Contemporary food from 10 a.m. to 5 p.m. daily.

*See map p. 146. 140 George St., Circular Quay. ☎ **02/9245 2400**. www.mca.com.au. Admission: Free. Open: Daily 10 a.m.–6 p.m. (5 p.m. in winter).*

Susannah Place Museum

This museum, set around a terrace of four houses, built in 1844, is a real highlight of The Rocks area. It provides visitors with the opportunity to explore domestic working-class life from 1844 to 1990. The modest interiors and rear yards illustrate the restrictions of 19th-century inner-city life. The many layers of the paint finishes, wallpapers, and floor coverings that have survived provide a valuable insight into the tastes of the working class. The original brick privies and open laundries are some of the earliest surviving washing and sanitary amenities remaining in the city. There's also a delightful little shop.

*See map p. 146. 58–64 Gloucester St., The Rocks. ☎ **02/9241 1893**. www.hht. net.au. Admission: A$8 (US$6.40/£3.20) adults, A$4 (US$3.20/£1.60) children, A$17 (US$14/£7) families; free entry to shop. Open: Sat–Sun and Tues–Thurs 10 a.m.– 5 p.m.; Jan and NSW school holidays daily 10 a.m.–5 p.m.*

Darling Harbour attractions

Australian National Maritime Museum

Modern Australia owes almost everything to the sea, so it's not surprising that there's a museum dedicated to ships, from Aboriginal vessels to submarines. You'll find ships' logs and things to pull and tug at. Docked in the harbor are several ships and launches, including an Australian Navy destroyer, the *Vampire;* an Oberon Class submarine; and a replica of the *Endeavour,* the ship Captain James Cook commanded when he laid claim to Australia. You can clamber over many of them. Allow two hours.

See map p. 146. Darling Harbour. ☎ *02/9298 3777.* www.anmm.gov.au. *Admission: Main exhibition free; ships A$30 (US$24/£12) adults, A$16 (US$13/£6.50) children 5–15, A$65 (US$52/£26) families; Navy Package (includes museum and two ships) A$18 (US$14/£7) adults, A$9 (US$7/£3.50) children, A$40 (US$32/£16) families; single vessels A$10–A$15 (US$8–A$12/£4–£6) adults, A$8–A$16 (US$6.40–US$13/£3.20–6.50) children. Open: Daily 9:30 a.m.–5 p.m. (until 6:30 p.m. in Jan).*

Powerhouse Museum

Sydney's most interactive museum is also one of the largest in the Southern Hemisphere. In the postmodern industrial interior you'll find all sorts of displays and gadgets relating to the sciences, transportation, human achievement, decorative art, and social history. The many hands-on exhibits make this museum worthy of a couple of hours of your time.

See map p. 146. 500 Harris St., Ultimo (near Darling Harbour). ☎ *02/9217 0111.* www.powerhousemuseum.com. *Admission: A$10 (US$8/£4) adults, A$5 (US$4/£2) students and children 5–15, A$24 (US$19/£9.50) families. Open: Daily 9:30 a.m.–5 p.m.*

Sydney Aquarium

This aquarium is one of the world's best and should be near the top of your itinerary. The main attractions are the underwater walkways through two enormous tanks — one full of giant rays and gray nurse sharks and the other where you can see the seals in action. Other excellent exhibits include a magnificent section on the Great Barrier Reef, where thousands of colorful fish school around coral outcrops. A touch-pool allows you to stroke baby sharks. Try to visit during the week, when it's less crowded.

See map p. 146. Aquarium Pier, Darling Harbour. ☎ *02/8251 7800.* www.sydney aquarium.com.au. *Admission: A$27 (US$22/£11) adults, A$14 (US$11/£5.50) children 3–15, A$66 (US$53/£26) families. Open: Daily 9 a.m.–10 p.m.; Seal Sanctuary closes at 7 p.m. in summer.*

Other top attractions

Hyde Park Barracks Museum

These Georgian-style barracks were designed in 1819 by the convict and architect Francis Greenway. They were built by convicts and inhabited by prisoners. These days they house relics from those early days, including log books, early settlement artifacts, and a room full of ships' hammocks in which visitors can lie and listen to fragments of prisoner conversation. The displays are far more straightforward than those at the Museum of Sydney. The courtyard cafe is excellent.

See map p. 146. Queens Square, Macquarie Street. ☎ *02/8239 2311.* www.hht.nsw. gov.au. *Admission: A$10 (US$8/£4) adults, A$5 (US$4/£2) children, A$20 (US$16/£8) families. Open: Daily 9:30 a.m.–5 p.m.*

Wildlife at Featherdale

If you have time to visit only one wildlife park in Sydney, make it the wonderful **Featherdale Wildlife Park,** 217 Kildare Rd., Doonside (☎ **02/9622 1644;** www.feather dale.com.au). The park's newest addition is the Reptilian Pavilion, which houses 30 native species of reptiles in 26 exhibits. To get there, head to Blacktown station, then board bus no. 725 (ask the driver to tell you when to get off). By car: Take the M4 motorway to Reservoir Road and turn off; travel 4km (2½ miles), and turn left at Kildare Road. Admission is A$19 (US$15/£7.50) adults, A$9.50 (US$7.60/£3.80) children 3–15, A$55 (US$44/£22) families. It's open daily from 9 a.m. to 5 p.m.

Sydney Tower (Centrepoint Tower)

The tallest building in the Southern Hemisphere is not hard to miss — it resembles a giant steel pole skewering a golden marshmallow. Standing more than 300m (984 ft.) tall, the tower offers 360-degree views across Sydney and as far as the Blue Mountains. An elevator takes you to the indoor viewing platform on the top floor, so you don't have to climb 1,504 steps. The ticket price includes admission to **OzTrek,** where visitors are strapped into moving chairs in front of a 180-degree screen. On this simulator ride, you white-water raft in Queensland, climb Uluru (Ayers Rock), and have a close encounter with a saltwater crocodile. Don't be too concerned if you feel the building tremble slightly, especially in a stiff breeze — we're told it's perfectly natural. Below the tower are three floors of stores and restaurants.

See map p. 146. 100 Market St. (another entrance on Pitt Street Mall). ☎ *02/9333 9222.* www.sydneytoweroztrek.com.au. *Admission: A$24 (US$18/£9) adults, A$14 (US$11/£5.50) children 4–15, A$60 (US$48/£24) families. Open: Sun–Fri 9 a.m.– 10:30 p.m., Sat 9 a.m.–11:30 p.m.*

Sydney Tower Skywalk

You don a special suit, walk out onto a glass-floored platform 260m (853 ft.) above the city floor and walk around the building. The views are breathtaking (even between your feet!). You're harnessed to a safety rail with a sliding harness, so there's no chance of falling off, and funny, well-informed guides offer a helping hand to the nervous. Each Skywalk lasts approximately 90 minutes and operates daily from 9 a.m. to 10 p.m., with the last Skywalk departing at 8:15 p.m. Cameras aren't allowed for safety reasons, but group or individual shots cost from A$20 (US$16/$8). Children under 10 aren't allowed on the Skywalk.

See map p. 146. Centrepoint Podium Level, 100 Market St. (entrance also through Pitt Street Mall). ☎ *02/9333 9222.* www.skywalk.com.au. *Admission: Day Skywalk, daily A$109 (US$87/£43) adults (16 and over), A$85 (US$68/£34) children (aged 10–15); Dusk Skywalk, daily A$139 (US$111/£55) adults, A$105 (US$84/£42) children; Night Skywalk, Mon–Thurs A$109 (US$87/£43) adults, A$85 (US$68/£34) children; Night*

Skywalk, Fri–Sun A$129 (US$103/£51) adults, A$95 (US$76/£38) children. Open: Daily 9 a.m.–10 p.m. (last Skywalk departs 8:15 p.m.).

Attractions in the Sydney suburbs

Oceanworld Manly

Though not as impressive as Sydney Aquarium, you can combine Oceanworld with a visit to Manly Beach for a nice outing. There's a display of Barrier Reef fish, as well as giant sharks. Also here are the five most venomous snakes in the world. Shark feeding is at 11 a.m. on Monday, Wednesday, and Friday. There is a **"dive with the sharks"** program, where you can get in the tanks with gray nurse sharks. It costs A$175 (US$140/£70) for qualified divers, A$205 (US$164/£82) for divers who have logged less than 15 dives or haven't dived in the last six months, or A$235 (US$188/£94) for nonqualified divers (includes an introduction to scuba diving course). To sign up, download an application from the Web site.

West Esplanade, Manly. ☎ *02/8251 7878.* www.oceanworld.com.au. *Admission: A$18 (US$14/£7) adults, A$9.50 (US$7.60/£3.70) children, A$44 (US$35/£17) families; 15 percent off admission prices after 3:30 p.m. Open: Daily 10 a.m.–5:30 p.m.*

Taronga Zoo

Taronga has the best view of any zoo in the world. Set on a hill, it looks over Sydney Harbour, the Opera House, and the Harbour Bridge. It's easiest on the legs to explore the zoo from the top down. The main attractions are the chimpanzee exhibit, the gorilla enclosure, and the Nocturnal Houses, where you can see some of Australia's nighttime marsupials, including the platypus and the cuter-than-cute bilby (the Australian Easter bunny). There's an interesting reptile display, a couple of Komodo dragons, a scattering of indigenous beasties — including a few koalas, echidnas, kangaroos, dingoes, and wombats — and lots more. The kangaroo and wallaby exhibit is unimaginative; you'd be better off going to Featherdale Wildlife Park (see the "Wildlife at Featherdale" sidebar). Animals are fed at various times during the day. The zoo can get crowded on weekends, so we recommend visiting during the week or in the morning on weekends.

Bradley's Head Road, Mosman. ☎ *02/9969 2777. Admission: A$32 (US$26/£13) adults, A$18 (US$14/£7) children 4–15, A$84 (US$67/£33) families. Admission includes a trip on the Aerial Safari cable car. Open: Daily 9 a.m.–5 p.m. (until 9 p.m. Jan).*

More cool things to see and do

These are some other highly recommended things to see and do:

- In Darling Harbour is the **IMAX Theatre Sydney** (☎ **02/9281 3300;** www.imax.com.au), where, usually, four different IMAX films are showing on the gigantic eight-story-high screen. Admission is A$18 (US$15/£7.50) adults, A$13 (US$11/£5.50) children 3–15, A$50 (US$40/£20) families. It's open Sunday through Thursday from 10 a.m. to 10 p.m., Friday and Saturday from 10 a.m. to 11:30 p.m.

✔ The site of the 2000 Olympic Games, **Sydney Olympic Park,** Homebush Bay (☎ **02/9714 7888;** www.sydneyolympicpark.nsw. gov.au), is still very much a tourist attraction as well as a major sporting venue. Most of the Olympic venues are here, as well as plenty of bars and restaurants. Start at the **Homebush Bay Information Centre,** which has displays, walking maps, and tour tips. There are several tours available. It's open daily from 9 a.m. to 5 p.m.

✔ A trip to Australia should always include a bit of nature. If you like huge crocs and such, head to the **Australian Reptile Park,** Pacific Highway, Somersby (☎ **02/4340 1022;** www.reptilepark.com.au). What started as a one-man operation supplying snake antivenin in the early 1950s has become a nature park teeming with the slippery-looking creatures. But it's not all snakes and lizards; you'll also find saltwater crocodiles and American alligators, as well as plenty of somewhat cuddlier creatures, such as koalas, platypuses, wallabies, dingoes, and flying foxes. Admission is A$22 (US$18/£9) adults, A$12 (US$9/£4.50) children 3 to 15, A$60 (US$42/£21) families. It's open daily from 9 a.m. to 5 p.m.

✔ Sydney's latest wildlife addition is **Sydney Wildlife World,** Aquarium Pier, Darling Harbour (☎ **02/9333 9288;** www.sydney wildlifeworld.com.au). There are a few highlights here, including a *cassowary* (a flightless bird about the size of an emu, but armed with a dangerous spiked toe) and some endangered yellow-footed rock wallabies. Discount tickets are available if you book online, and you can buy a special Attractions Pass, which allows discounted entry to Sydney Wildlife World, Sydney Aquarium, and Sydney Tower. Admission is A$29 (US$23/£12) adults, A$14 (US$11/£5.50) children 3 to 15, A$68 (US$54/£27) families. It's open daily from 9 a.m. to 10 p.m.

✔ Stargazers will love **Sydney Observatory,** Observatory Hill, Watson Road, Millers Point, The Rocks (☎ **02/9241 3767**). The city's only major museum of astronomy offers visitors a chance to see the southern skies through modern and historic telescopes. The introduction of a new Space Theatre 3D ride, which takes you zooming through the stars, makes it worth visiting during the day as well as the evening. Admission during the day is A$7 (US$5.60/£2.80) adults, A$5 (US$4/£2) children, A$20 (US$16/£8) families; guided night tours (reservations required) cost A$15 (US$12/£6) adults, A$10 (US$8/£4) children, A$40 (US$32/£16) families. It's open daily from 10 a.m. to 10 p.m.

Getting a Tan on Sydney's Beaches

One of the big bonuses of visiting Sydney in the summer (Dec–Feb) is that you get to experience the beaches in their full glory. Most major city beaches, such as Manly and Bondi, have lifeguards (or "lifesavers" as they are called in Australia) on patrol. They check the water conditions and are on the lookout for *rips* — strong currents that can pull a swimmer far out to sea. Safe places to swim are marked by red and yellow flags.

One of the first things visitors wonder when they hit the water in Australia is, "Are there sharks?" The answer is yes, but they're rarely spotted inshore — you're far more likely to spy a migrating whale. Sharks have more reason to be scared of humans than we have to be scared of them; most sharks end up as the fish in your average packet of fish and chips. Though some beaches — such as the small beach next to the Manly ferry wharf and a section of Balmoral Beach in Mosman — have permanent shark nets, most rely on portable nets that are moved from beach to beach.

Another common problem are *blue bottles* — small blue jellyfish, often called *stingers* in Australia and *Portuguese-men-o'-war* elsewhere. Blue bottles deliver a hefty punch from their many stinging cells, causing a burning sensation almost immediately. Wearing a T-shirt in the water reduces the risk somewhat (though a pair of jeans isn't a good idea). If you're stung, rinse the area liberally with seawater or fresh water to remove any tentacles stuck in the skin. For intense pain, apply heat or cold, whichever feels better. If you experience breathing difficulties or disorientation, seek medical attention immediately.

Sydney's best beaches

Sydney's most famous beach is **Bondi.** In many ways, it's a raffish version of a California beach, with plenty of tanned skin and in-line skaters. Though the beach is nice, it's cut off from the cafe and restaurant strip that caters to beachgoers by a road that pedestrians have to funnel across in order to reach the sand. On summer weekend evenings it's popular with souped-up cars and groups of kids from the suburbs.

If you follow the water along to your right at Bondi, you'll come across a scenic cliff-top trail that takes you to **Bronte Beach** (a 20-minute walk), via gorgeous little **Tamarama,** nicknamed "Glamourama" for its trendy sun worshippers. This boutique beach is known for its dangerous rips. Bronte has better swimming than Bondi.

Clovelly Beach, farther along the coast, is blessed with a large rock pool carved into a rock platform and sheltered from the force of the Tasman Sea. This beach is wheelchair-accessible via a series of ramps.

The cliff walk from Bondi will eventually bring you to **Coogee,** which has a pleasant strip of sand with a couple of hostels and hotels nearby.

On the North Shore, you find **Manly,** a long curve of golden sand edged with Norfolk Island pines. Follow the crowds shuffling through the pedestrian Corso to the main ocean beach.

From Manley, looking at the ocean, head to your right along the beachfront and follow the coastal path to small, sheltered **Shelly Beach,** a nice area for snorkeling and swimming. (A small takeout outlet sells drinks and snacks.) Follow the path up the hill to the parking lot. Here, a track cuts up into the bush and leads toward a firewall, which marks the entrance to the **Sydney Harbour National Park.** Around here you have spectacular ocean views across to Manly and the northern beaches (the headland farther in the distance is Palm Beach).

Farther north along the coast are a string of ocean beaches. They include the surf spots of **Curl Curl, Dee Why, Narrabeen, Mona Vale, Newport, Avalon,** and **Palm Beach,** a long and beautiful strip of sand separated from the calmer waters of **Pittwater** by sand dunes and a golf course. Here you find the Barrenjoey Lighthouse, which offers fine views along the coast.

The best harbor beach is at **Balmoral,** a North Shore hangout with some good cafes and two good, upmarket beach-view restaurants — the **Bathers Pavilion (☎ 02/9969 5050)** and **The Watermark (☎ 02/9968 3433).** The beach is split into three parts. As you look toward the sea, the middle section is the most popular with sunbathers, and the wide expanse to your left and the sweep of beautiful sand to your right have a mere scattering. There's a caged pool area for swimming.

Sydney's Parks and National Parks

As well as the Botanic Gardens, Sydney is blessed with plenty of parks and green spaces. Further afield, to the south and the north, are two magnificent national parks.

In the center of the city is **Hyde Park,** a favorite with lunching business-people. Of note are the **Anzac Memorial** to Australian and New Zealand troops killed in the wars, and the **Archibald Fountain,** complete with spitting turtles and sculptures of Diana and Apollo. At night, lights illuminate avenues of trees, giving the place a lovely appearance.

Also popular is **Centennial Park,** usually entered from the top of Oxford Street. It opened in 1888 to celebrate the centenary of European settlement, and today it encompasses huge areas of lawn, several lakes, picnic areas with outdoor grills, cycling and running paths, and a cafe.

A hundred years later, **Bicentennial Park,** at Australia Avenue, in Home-bush Bay, came along. Forty percent of the park's total 100 hectares (247 acres) is general parkland reclaimed from a city dump; the rest is the largest existing remnant of wetlands on the Parramatta River and is home to many species of local and migratory birds.

You don't need to go far to experience Sydney's nearest national park. **The Sydney Harbour National Park** stretches around parts of the inner harbor and includes several small islands. The best walk through the Sydney Harbour National Park is the **Manly to Spit Bridge Scenic Walkway.** This 10km (6-mile) track winds its way from Manly (it starts near the Oceanarium) via Dobroyd Head to Spit Bridge, where you can catch a bus back to the city. The walk takes around three hours at a casual pace, and the views across Sydney Harbour are fabulous.

Other access points to the park include tracks around Taronga Zoo (ask the zoo staff to point you toward the obscured entrances) and above tiny Shelly Beach, opposite the main beach at Manly.

Also part of the national park is the restored **Fort Denison,** that tiny island fort you can see in the middle of the harbor between Circular Quay and Manly. The fort was built during the Crimean War in response to fears of a Russian invasion, and was later used as a penal colony. **Heritage Tours** of the island leave from Cadmans Cottage, 110 George St., The Rocks (☎ 02/9247 5033), at 11:30 a.m. and 2:30 p.m. Wednesday through Sunday. They cost A$22 (US$18/£9) adults, A$18 (US$14/£7) children, A$72 (US$58/£29) families. The return ferry trip, tour, and time spent on the island means you should plan on three hours or so.

To the northeast of the city center is **Ku-ring-gai Chase National Park** (☎ 02/9457 9322 or 02/9457 9310). It's a great place to take a bushwalk through gum trees and rain forest on the lookout for wildflowers, sandstone rock formations, and Aboriginal art. There are plenty of tracks through the park; one of our favorites is a relatively easy 2.5km (1½-mile) tramp to **The Basin** (Track 12). The well-graded dirt path takes you down to a popular estuary with a beach and passes some significant Aboriginal engravings. There are also wonderful water views over Pittwater from the picnic areas at **West Head.** The park is open from sunrise to sunset, and admission is A$11 (US$8.80/£4.40) per car. You can either drive to the park or catch a ferry from Palm Beach to The Basin (from there, you can walk up Track 12 and back). Ferries run on the hour (except at 1 p.m.) from 9 a.m. to 5 p.m. daily and cost A$4.50 (US$3.60/£1.80) one-way; call ☎ 02/9918 2747 for details.

South of Sydney is the **Royal National Park,** Farrell Avenue, Sutherland (☎ 02/9542 0648). It's the world's oldest national park, declared in 1879. There's a visitor center at Audley Weir (past the main park entrance). You have to pay a A$11 (US$8.80/£4.40) per-car fee to enter the park.

There are several ways to reach the park, but our favorites are the little-known access points from Bundeena and Otford. To get to **Bundeena,** take a CityRail train from Central Station to the seaside suburb of Cronulla (around one hour). Just below the train station, through an underpass, you'll find Cronulla Wharf. From there, hop on the delightful little ferry run by **National Park Ferries** (☎ 02/9523 2990) to Bundeena, which we highly recommend you visit. Ferries run on the half-hour from Cronulla (except 12:30 p.m. on weekdays). The last one back from Bundeena is at 7 p.m. (6 p.m. in winter). After you get off the ferry, the first turn on your left just up the hill will take you through part of the village to wonderful Jibbon Beach. Walk along the beach to the end, hop up some rocks, and follow the track (about 20 minutes) through the park to Jibbon Head, for some stunning ocean views.

Look for the Aboriginal rock carvings off to your right before you reach it (a sign points toward the headland, but the carvings are to your right). It's around a three-hour round-trip walk to Marley Beach (which has strong surf and dangerous rips) and a six-hour round-trip to beautiful Wattamolla, where there's safe swimming for children in the salty lagoon. The ferry returns to Cronulla from Bundeena hourly on the hour (except 1 p.m. on weekdays). The fare is A$5.20 (US$4/£2) each way.

An alternative way to reach the park is to take the train from Central Station to **Otford,** then climb the hill up to the sea cliffs. The entrance to the national park is a little tricky to find, so you may have to ask directions — but roughly, it's just to the left of a cliff top popular for hang gliding, radio-controlled airplanes, and kites. A two-hour walk from the sea cliffs through beautiful and varying bushland and a palm forest will take you to Burning Palms Beach. There is no water along the route. The walk back up is steep, so attempt this trek only if you're reasonably fit. Trains to the area from Central Station are irregular, and the last one departs around 4 p.m., so give yourself at least two-and-a-half hours for the return trip to the train station to make sure you don't get stranded.

You can walk the memorable 26km (16 miles) from Otford to Bundeena, or vice versa, in two days. (Take all your food, water, and camping gear.) The track sticks to the coast, crosses several beaches, and is relatively easy to follow.

Exploring Sydney by Guided Tour

Harbor tours and cruises

The best thing about Sydney is the harbor, and you shouldn't leave without taking a harbor cruise.

✔ **Sydney Ferries (☎ 13 15 00** in Australia, or 02/9245 5600; www. sydneyferries.info) offers a one-hour morning harbor cruise with commentary departing Circular Quay, Wharf 4, daily at 10:30 a.m. It costs A$18 (US$14/£7) adults, A$9 (US$7.20/£3.60) children under 16, A$45 (US$36/£18) families.

A two-and-a-half-hour afternoon cruise explores more of the harbor; it leaves from Wharf 4 at 1 p.m. on weekdays, 12:30 p.m. on weekends and public holidays. This tour costs A$24 (US$19/£9.50) adults, A$12 (US$9.60/£4.80) children, A$60 (US$48/£24) families.

The highly recommended one-and-a-half-hour **Evening Harbour Lights tour,** which takes in the city lights as far east as Double Bay and west to Goat Island, leaves Monday through Saturday at 8 p.m. from Wharf 4. The evening tour costs A$22 (US$18/£9) adults, A$11 (US$8.80/£4.49) children, A$55 (US$44/£22) families.

✔ **Captain Cook Cruises,** departing Jetty 6, Circular Quay (☎ 02/9206 1111; www.captaincook.com.au), offers several harbor excursions on its sleek vessels, with commentary along the way. Examples include a 2-hour-20-minute **Coffee Cruise** departing from Jetty 6, Circular Quay, at 10 a.m. and 2:15 p.m. daily. It costs A$46 (US$37/£18) adults, A$24 (US$19/£9.50) children, A$99 (US$80/£40) families.

Another is a **Seafood Buffet Lunch** cruise, which departs Circular Quay at 12:30 p.m. daily and costs A$62 (US$50/£25) adults, A$30 (US$24/£12) children.

The **Sydney Harbour Explorer** cruise is popular and stops off at The Rocks, Watson's Bay, Taronga Zoo, and Darling Harbour. You get on and off when you want. It costs A$29 (US$23/£12) adults, A$15 (US$12/£6) children, A$69 (US$55/£27) families. It leaves Circular Quay at 9:45 a.m., 11:30 a.m., 1:30 p.m., and 3:30 p.m. daily.

Captain Cooke cruises have ticket booths at Jetty 6, Circular Quay (open daily 8:30 a.m.–7 p.m.), and at 1 King Street Wharf, Darling Harbour (near the Sydney Aquarium). That booth has limited opening hours of 11 a.m. to 4 p.m. daily.

✔ **Matilda Cruises** (☎ 02/9264 7377; www.matilda.com.au) offers a one-hour **Rocket Harbour Express** narrated sightseeing tour leaving the pontoon at the far end of Sydney Aquarium at Darling Harbour eight times daily beginning at 9:30 a.m. (six times daily Apr–Sept, beginning at 10:30 a.m.). You can stay on for the full hour, or get off and on again at Circular Quay (opposite the Museum of Contemporary Art), the Opera House, Watsons Bay, and Taronga Zoo. The last boat leaves Taronga Zoo at 5:10 p.m. in summer (4:10 p.m. in winter). There's tea and coffee on board. The cruise costs A$25 (US$20/£10) adults, A$17 (US$14/£7) children 5 to 12, A$59 (US$47/£23) families. Boats also zip across from Darling Harbour and Circular Quay to Luna Park on the half-hour from 9:30 a.m. to 7 p.m. (and to 10 p.m. Fri–Sat). A one-way journey costs A$5.70 (US$4.50/£2.25) adults, A$2.80 (US$2.20/£1.10) children, A$14 (US$11/£5.70) families.

The company also offers a **Zoo Express,** including zoo entry, from both Darling Harbour and Circular Quay. It costs A$37 (US$29/£15) adults, A$20 (US$16/£8) children 5 to 14, A$110 (US$88/£44) families.

Matilda Cruises has a **ticket booth** at Jetty 6 at Circular Quay, and a ticket office next to the Sydney Aquarium at Darling Harbour.

Other cruise operators also have booths and information available at Circular Quay and Darling Harbour.

A cruise of Aboriginal origins

The *Deerubbun,* a former Australian navy torpedo recovery vessel, makes quite an impression as it pulls up to the dock near the Opera House concourse with speakers blaring out a recording of clap sticks and didgeridoos. The boat revolutionized the Sydney cruise industry in late 2006 by offering an Aboriginal perspective of the famous waterway.

Tourists learn that Circular Quay was once occupied by the Cadigal people. They also learn about Bennelong, the captured Aborigine who once lived on the point where the Opera House now stands, and his wife, Barangaroo, who opposed her husband's conciliatory efforts with the Europeans.

The boat putters past the Royal Botanic Gardens, and the guide tells stories of the early Europeans and their hopeless farms, and the smallpox epidemic of 1789, which the local Aborigines thought was caused by evil spirits. Mixed in with the observations of the landscape are tales of the first Aboriginal tour guides, who took early settlers inland from the harbor, as well as mentions of soldiers, statesmen, and farmers who came into contact with the Aborigines — and much more.

Tourists disembark at Clark Island to see cave shelters with roofs stained black from ancient fireplaces, convict engravings, and a natural fish trap. Two Aboriginal guides, their bodies plastered in ghostly white ocher, beat a rhythm with hardwood sticks and growl through a didgeridoo, as they beckon the tourists to the Welcoming Ceremony. Then comes a repertoire of haunting songs, music, and dance. Every visitor to Sydney should do this trip.

Aboriginal Cultural Cruises depart Tuesday through Saturday at 12:45 p.m. from the Eastern Pontoon (near the Sydney Opera House). The cost is A$55 (US$44/£22) adults, A$45 (US$36/£18) children 5 to 14. Tickets are available from Sydney Visitor Centres. For more information, call ☎ **02/9699 3491** or go to www.tribalwarrior.org.

The one-stop shop for tickets and information on all harbor cruises is the **Australian Travel Specialists** (☎ 02/9247 5151; www.atstravel. com.au). Checking Web sites before you come to Australia, or popping into a ticket office at Darling Harbour or Circular Quay, is a good idea, because cruise options, departure times, and prices change frequently.

Bus tours

Bright red **Sydney Explorer** buses operate every day, traveling a 28km (18-mile) circuit and stopping at 27 places. These include the Sydney Opera House, the Royal Botanic Gardens, the State Library, Mrs. Macquarie's Chair, the Art Gallery of New South Wales, Kings Cross, Elizabeth Bay House, Wynyard CityRail station, the Queen Victoria Building, Sydney Tower, the Australian Museum, Central Station, Chinatown, Darling Harbour, and The Rocks. Buses depart from Circular Quay at 18-minute intervals starting at 8:40 a.m., with the last "round-trip" service departing Circular Quay at 5:20 p.m. (and returning to

Circular Quay at 7 p.m.). Hop on and off anywhere along the route where you see the red Sydney Explorer sign, and leave at any attraction along the way. If you want to stay on the bus from start to finish, the full circuit takes one-and-a-half hours.

The **Bondi & Bay Explorer** also operates every day, traveling a 30km (19-mile) circuit around the eastern harborside bays and coastal beaches. Stops along the way include Kings Cross, Double Bay, Watsons Bay, Bondi Beach, Bronte Beach, Coogee Beach, Paddington, Oxford Street, and Martin Place. The bus departs from Circular Quay at 25-minute intervals starting at 9:15 a.m., with the last "round-trip" service departing Circular Quay at 4:20 p.m. (and returning to Circular Quay at 5:55 p.m.). Board anywhere along the route where you see the Bondi & Bay Explorer sign, and get off at any attraction along the way. If you want to stay on board from start to finish without making any stops, the entire circuit takes one-and-a-half hours.

 Tickets entitle you to free travel on regular blue and white Sydney Buses within the same zones covered by your Explorer tickets until midnight. You also get discounts on some attractions, such as a 15 percent discount on tickets to Sydney Aquarium.

Combined one-day tickets for both buses cost A$39 (US$31/£15) adults, A$18 (US$14/£7) children 4 to 16, A$97 (US$77/£39) families. Buy tickets on board the bus. You can also buy a two-day ticket for A$68 (US$54/£28) adults, A$34 (US$27/£13) children, A$170 (US$136/£68) families; you must use the second-day portion within eight days.

Walking tours

The center of Sydney is compact, and you can see a lot in a day on foot.

✔ If you want to find out more about Sydney's history, then book a guided tour with **The Rocks Walking Tour** (☎ 02/9247 6678; www.rockswalkingtours.com.au), based at 23 Playfair St., Rocks Square. Excellent walking tours leave Monday through Friday at 10:30 a.m., 12:30 p.m., and 2:30 p.m. (in Jan 10:30 a.m. and 2:30 p.m.), and Saturday and Sunday at 11:30 a.m. and 2 p.m. The one-and-a-half-hour tour costs A$20 (US$16/£8) adults, A$11 (US$8.20/£4.10) children 10 to 16, A$51 (US$40/£20) families, free for accompanied children under 10.

✔ Another fun experience is **The Rocks Pub Tour** (☎ 02/9240 8788; www.therockspubtour.com), a journey aimed at illuminating the lives of the sailors and whalers that once lived around here. You get to meet some of the locals, visit three historic pubs, wander around the alleyways, try a brew, and enjoy special offers for pub meals. The one-and-a-half-hour tour departs from Cadman's Cottage at 5 p.m. Monday, Wednesday, Friday, and Saturday. It costs A$35 (US$28/£14). You must be at least 18 (the legal drinking age in Australia) to take the tour.

✔ A journey with a difference is **Weird Sydney Ghost and History Tours (☎ 02/9943 0167;** www.destinytours.com.au). The tour — in a hearse — is fascinating and fun. It explores a section of historic Sydney and more modern additions, including a former VD clinic, the Sydney Opera House, and some buildings along Macquarie Street. The two-and-a-half-hour trip costs A$72 (US$58/£29) adults, A$36 (US$29/£14) children. The tour leaves nightly at 8 p.m. (7 p.m. in winter).

Shopping the Local Stores

You'll find plenty of places to keep your credit cards in action in Sydney. Generally speaking, it's not a particularly expensive place to shop, but if you're from foreign shores, a lot depends on how your currency is trading at the time.

The best shopping areas

Most shops of interest to the visitor are in **The Rocks** and along **George and Pitt streets** (including the shops below the Sydney Tower and along Pitt Street Mall). Other precincts worth checking out are **Mosman** on the North Shore and **Double Bay** in the eastern suburbs for boutique shopping, **Chatswood** for its general shopping centers, the **Sydney Fishmarket** for the sake of it, and **weekend markets,** listed here:

✔ Don't miss the **Queen Victoria Building (QVB),** on the corner of Market and George streets. This Victorian shopping arcade is one of the prettiest in the world and has some 200 boutiques — mostly men's and women's fashion — on four levels. The arcade is open 24 hours, but the shops do business Monday through Saturday from 9 a.m. to 6 p.m. (Thurs to 9 p.m.) and Sunday from 11 a.m. to 5 p.m.

✔ The **Strand Arcade** (between Pitt Street Mall and George Street) was built in 1892 and is interesting for its architecture and small boutiques, food stores, and cafes, and the Downtown Duty Free store on the basement level.

✔ **Oxford Street** runs from the city to Bondi Junction through Paddington and Darlinghurst and is home to countless clothing stores for the style conscious. You could spend anywhere from two hours to a whole day making your way from one end to the other. Detour down William Street once you get to Paddington to visit the headquarters of celebrated international Australian designer Collette Dinnigan. On the same street are the trendy boutiques Belinda and Corner Store (cutting-edge designs), and Pelle and Di Nuovo (luxury recycled goods).

What to look for and where to find it

Regular shopping hours are generally Monday through Wednesday and Friday from 8:30 a.m. or 9 a.m. to 6 p.m., Thursday from 8:30 a.m. or 9 a.m.

to 9 p.m., Saturday from 9 a.m. to 5 p.m. or 5:30 p.m., and Sunday from
10 a.m. or 10:30 a.m. to 5 p.m. Exceptions are noted in the store listings
in the following sections.

Aboriginal artifacts and crafts

Despite the reports you may have heard of Aboriginal art fetching
record prices, unless you know an awful lot about it you can only hope
to buy something that may look good on your wall, rather than something that will increase in value.

If we were in the market for a decent boomerang or didgeridoo we'd
head to **Gavala Aboriginal Art & Cultural Education Centre,** Shop 131,
Harbourside, Darling Harbour (☎ **02/9212 7232**). Gavala is owned and
operated by Aborigines, and it stocks plenty of authentic Aboriginal
crafts, including carved emu eggs, grass baskets, cards, and books. A
first-rate painted didgeridoo will cost anywhere from A$100 to A$450
(US$80–US$360/£40–£180). The store is open daily from 10 a.m. to 9 p.m.

Quality Aboriginal art from some of Australia's best-known painters is on
sale at **Original & Authentic Aboriginal Art,** 79 George St., The Rocks
(☎ **02/9251 4222**). Artists whose work is represented include Paddy
Fordham Wainburranga, whose paintings hang in the White House in
Washington. Expect to pay in the range of A$1,000 to A$4,000 (US$800–
US$3,200/£400–£1,600) for the larger paintings. There are some nice
painted pots here, too, costing A$30 to A$80 (US$24–US$64/£15–£32).
The gallery is open daily from 10 a.m. to 6 p.m.

Art prints and originals

The Rocks is the place to come for expensive things for your wall. Try
Billich, 104 George St., The Rocks (☎ **02/9252 1481**), a fine-art gallery
featuring Sydney scenes intermingled with Asian-influenced on a grand
scale. It's open daily from 9 a.m. to 8 p.m.

Ken Done is known for having designed his own Australian flag, which he
hopes to raise over Australia if it abandons its present one. The colorful
art at **Done Art and Design,** 1 Hickson Rd. (off George Street), The Rocks
(☎ **02/9247 2740**), is his. The clothing designs — which feature printed
sea- and beachscapes, the odd colorful bird, and lots of pastels — are by
his wife, Judy. It's open daily from 10 a.m. to 5:30 p.m.

Books

You'll find a good selection of books on Sydney and Australia at the **Art
Gallery of New South Wales,** the Garden Shop in the **Royal Botanic
Gardens,** the **Museum of Contemporary Art,** the **Australian Museum,**
and the **State Library of New South Wales.**

Among the best general bookstores are **Abbey's Bookshop,** 131 York St.,
behind the QVB (☎ **02/9264 3111**); **Angus & Robertson Bookworld,**
168 Pitt St., Pitt Street Mall (☎ **02/9235 1188**); and **Borders,** Skygarden,

77 Castlereagh St. (entrance also on Pitt Street Mall; ☎ 02/9235 2433). Borders has a wonderful magazine section as well as thousands of titles.

Goulds Book Arcade, 32 King St., Newtown (☎ 02/9519 8947), is bursting at the seams with many thousands of secondhand and new books; its open daily from 8 a.m. to midnight. You can find hundreds of travel guides, maps, Australiana titles, coffee-table books, and accessories at the **Travel Bookshop,** Shop 3, 175 Liverpool St. (across from the southern end of Hyde Park, near the Museum CityRail station; ☎ 02/9261 8200); it's open Monday through Friday from 9 a.m. to 6 p.m. and Saturday from 10 a.m. to 5 p.m. There's also an Amex counter at the Travel Bookshop.

Crafts

Some of Australia's most respected craft artists and designers are represented at **Collect,** 88 George St., The Rocks (☎ 02/9247 7984). There are some wonderful glass, textile, ceramic, jewelry, metal, and wood-turned items for sale. It's open daily from 9:30 a.m. to 5:30 p.m.

Department stores

The two big names in Sydney shopping are David Jones and Myer. Both stores are open Monday through Wednesday and Friday through Saturday from 9 a.m. to 6 p.m., Thursday from 9 a.m. to 9 p.m., and Sunday from 11 a.m. to 5 p.m.

David Jones (☎ 02/9266 5544) is the city's largest department store, selling everything from fashion to designer furniture. You'll find the women's section on the corner of Elizabeth and Market streets, and the men's section on the corner of Castlereagh and Market streets. The food section here is the best in Australia by far.

Myer (☎ 02/9238 9111), formally Grace Brothers, is similar to David Jones, but the building is newer and flashier. It's on the corner of George and Market streets.

Duty-free shops

Sydney has several duty-free shops selling goods at a discount. To take advantage of the bargains, you need a passport and a flight ticket, and you must export what you buy. The duty-free shop with the best buys is **Downtown Duty Free,** which has two city outlets, one in the Strand Arcade, off Pitt Street Mall (☎ 02/9233 3166), and one at 105 Pitt St. (☎ 02/9221 4444). Five more stores are at Sydney International Airport and are open from the first to the last flight of the day.

Fashion

The best places to shop for fashion are the **QVB** and the **Sydney Central Plaza** (on the ground floor of the mall next to the Myer department store on Pitt Street Mall). Fashion-statement stores featuring the best of

Australian design at the QVB include Oroton, Country Road, and the fabulous woman's clothing designer Lisa Ho. In the **Strand Arcade,** off Pitt Street Mall, find Third Millennium, Allanah Hill, and Wayne Cooper. The major Pitt Street Mall outlets will also keep you up to date.

Other fashion shopping meccas in or close to Pitt Street Mall include the Glasshouse and the MLC Centre, which are linked to one another via a covered overpass. Farther down toward Circular Quay is Chifley Plaza, home to a selection of the world's most famous and stylish international brands. For really trendy clothing, walk up Oxford Street to **Paddington,** and for alternative clothes, go to **Newtown.**

Australian Outback clothing

Moleskin trousers may not be the height of fashion at the moment, but you never know. R. M. Williams boots are famous for being both tough and fashionable. You'll find Akubra hats, Driza-bone coats, and kangaroo-skin belts at **R. M. Williams,** 389 George St. (between Town Hall and Central CityRail stations; ☎ **02/9262 2228**).

Located between Town Hall and Central CityRail stations is **Thomas Cook Boot & Clothing Company,** 790 George St., Haymarket (☎ **02/9212 6616**), which specializes in Australian boots, Driza-bone coats, and Akubra hats. There's another shop at 129 Pitt St., near Martin Place (☎ **02/9232 3334**).

Men's fashion

Not-so-cheap but colorful clothes come from designer store **Esprit Mens,** Shop 10G, Sydney Central Plaza, 450 George St. (☎ **02/9233 7349**).

Quality clothing with a yachting influence is at **Outdoor Heritage,** Shop 13G, Sydney Central Plaza, 450 George St. (☎ **02/9235 1560**), a good-looking store specializing in casual, colorful gear.

Women's fashion

In addition to the places listed below, head to **Oxford Street** (particularly Paddington) for more avant-garde designers.

Internationally lauded and locally adored, few have left such an indelible watermark on the Australian fashion pages as **Akira Isagawa,** 12A Queen St., Woollahra (☎ **02/9361 5221**). Those who love shoes can't go past the cute little **Belinda,** 39 William St., Paddington (☎ **02/9380 8728**), just off Oxford Street. Meanwhile, movie sirens, pop royalty, and the world's most glamorous women all appreciate the seriously sexy designs at **Collette Dinnigan,** 33 William St., Paddington (☎ **02/9360 6691**).

Food

The goodies you'll find in the food section of **David Jones** department store on Castlereagh Street are enough to tempt anyone. The store sells the best local and imported products to the rich and famous (and the

rest of us). One of the few supermarkets in the city center is **Coles,**
Wynyard Station, Castlereagh Street, Wynyard (☎ **02/9299 4769**); it's
open daily from 6 a.m. to midnight.

Darrell Lea Chocolates, at the corner of King and George streets (☎ **02/
9232 2899**), is the oldest location of Australia's most famous chocolate
shop. Pick up some wonderful handmade chocolates as well as other
unusual candies, including the best licorice this side of the Casbah.

At **Sydney Fishmarkets,** at the corner of Bank Street and Pyrmont Bridge
Road, Pyrmont (☎ **02/9004 1100**), you can see and buy the catch of the
day. It's open daily from 7 a.m. to 4 p.m. Also here is a Doyles restaurant
and a sushi bar, a couple of cheap seafood eateries, and a good deli.

Markets

Several markets operate across central Sydney and out in the nearby
suburbs, especially on weekends. Saturday markets include **Paddington
Bazaar,** in the grounds of St. Johns Church, Oxford Street, which specializes in everything from essential oils and designer clothes to New Age
jewelry and Mexican hammocks.

Sunday markets include **Bondi Markets,** on Campbell Parade, while the
Rocks Market is held in The Rocks every Saturday and Sunday. This
touristy market has more than 100 vendors selling everything from
crafts, housewares, and posters to jewelry and curios.

Living It Up after Dark

Australians are party animals when they're in the mood; whether it's a
few beers around the barbecue with friends or an all-night rave at a
trendy dance club, they're always on the lookout for the next event. The
best way to find out what's on is to get hold of the "Metro" section of the
Friday *Sydney Morning Herald* or the "Seven Days" pullout from the
Thursday *Daily Telegraph.*

The performing arts

If you have a chance to see a performance in the **Sydney Opera House,**
jump at it. The "House" is not that impressive inside, but the walk back
after the show toward the ferry terminals at Circular Quay, with the
Sydney Harbour Bridge lit up and the crowd all around you — well,
you'll want the moment to stay with you forever. Dress is smart casual.

The **Australian Chamber Orchestra** performs at various venues around
the city, from nightclubs to specialized music venues, including the
Concert Hall in the Sydney Opera House. **Opera Australia** performs at
the Sydney Opera House's Opera Theatre. The opera runs January
through March and June through November. The **Sydney Symphony
Orchestra** performs throughout the year in the Opera House's Concert

Hall. The main symphony season runs March through November, and there's a summer season in February.

Sydney's blessed with plenty of theaters — we list just a few here. Check the *Sydney Morning Herald,* especially the Friday edition, for information on what's currently in production.

- ✔ **The Belvoir Street Theatre,** 25 Belvoir St., Surry Hills (☎ 02/9699 3444), is home to **Company B,** which pumps out powerful local and international plays upstairs in a wonderfully moody main theater. Downstairs, a smaller venue generally shows more experimental productions, such as Aboriginal performances and dance.

- ✔ **The Capital Theatre,** 17 Campbell St., Haymarket, near Town Hall (☎ 02/9320 5000), is Sydney's grandest theater and plays host to major international and local productions like (cough) Australian singing superstar Kylie Minogue. It's also been the Sydney home of musicals such as *Miss Saigon* and *My Fair Lady.*

- ✔ **The Wharf Theatre,** Pier 4, Hickson Road, The Rocks (☎ 02/9250 1777; www.sydneytheatre.com.au), is on a wharf on the edge of Sydney Harbour. The long walk from the entrance of the pier to the theater along creaky wooden floorboards builds up excitement for the show. The Sydney Theatre Company is based here.

All that jazz and more

Jazz places, along with music venues in general, are few and far between in Sydney, partly because investors can make more money out of installing dozens of *pokies* (one-arm bandits).

- ✔ One of Australia's hottest jazz clubs is **The Basement,** 29 Reiby Place, Circular Quay (☎ 02/9251 2797; www.thebasement.com.au), which also manages to squeeze in plenty of blues, folk, and funk. Make reservations. Call for the schedule, pick up one at the club, or visit the Web site.

- ✔ A medium-size rock venue with space for 1,000, the **Metro,** 624 George St. (☎ 02/9264 2666), is the best place in Sydney to see local and international acts.

Dance clubs

Clubs come and go, and change names and music, so check the latest with a phone call. You can also check the "Metro" section in the Friday *Sydney Morning Herald;* free newspapers available in some bars along Oxford Street have info about the latest clubs. Nightclub entrance charges change regularly, but generally are A$15 to A$20 (US$12– US$16/£6–£8).

Sydney gay and lesbian Mardi Gras

Each March, Sydney lights up to the biggest carnival this side of Rio. Some 450,000 people pack into the city center, concentrated on Oxford Street, to watch as members of Sydney's GLBT communities pack a punch with colorful floats and frocks. The crowd is diverse, from kids to grannies, and those in the know bring a stepladder or milk crate to get a better view. Sydney's hotels are at their busiest during Mardi Gras, particularly anything with a view of the route. The post-parade party is an affair not for the faint-hearted! Sequins, tight pants, and anything outrageously glamorous goes. Some 19,000 revelers attend. For more information visit the official Mardi Gras Web site (www. mardigras.org.au).

✔ **Dragonfly,** Earl Street, Potts Point (☎ **02/9356 2666**), is a club tucked away in less then salubrious surroundings. It features a cocktail bar, dance floor, and booths flush with leather chairs. Dress trendy. There's rhythm and blues on weekdays and house music on weekends. Weekends attract a hip crowd in their 30s. It's open Wednesday, Friday, and Saturday from 9 p.m. to 5 a.m.

✔ Another favorite is **Home,** Cockle Bay Wharf, Darling Harbour (☎ **02/9267 0654**). It's cavelike in shape and feel, with a balcony to look down upon the throng. There's a "silver room" for serious ravers. Friday nights are big for trance and hip-hop, Saturdays for house music. It's open Friday through Saturday from 11 p.m. to dawn.

✔ If you're in town any night of the week, then the **Q Bar,** 44 Oxford St. (☎ **02/9360 1375**) will be open. It attracts a varied crowd from youngsters to wrinklies, and has everything from a dance floor to pool tables. It's open daily from 9 p.m. to 7 a.m.

Gay and lesbian clubs

Sydney has a huge gay community, so there's a very happening scene. The center of it all is Oxford Street, though Newtown has established itself as a major gay hangout, too. For information on events, pick up a copy of the *Sydney Star Observer* or *Lesbians on the Loose,* available at art-house cinemas, cafes, and stores around Oxford Street. Nightclub entrance charges generally range from A$10 to A$15 (US$8–US$12/£4–£6).

✔ Popular gay clubs include **Arq,** 16 Flinders St., Taylors Square, Darlinghurst (☎ **02/9380 8700;** Open: Thurs–Sun 9 p.m.–9 a.m.), a 24-hour club with an amazing light show and some of the best DJs in town; and **Taxi Club,** 40 Flinders St., Darlinghurst (near Taylor Square), Oxford Street (☎ **02/9331 4256;** Open: Mon–Thurs 10 a.m.–2 a.m., Fri–Sun 10 a.m.–6 a.m.), a Sydney institution good for old pop and new pop.

✔ Bars of note include **Civic,** at the corner of Pitt and Goulburn streets, Sydney (☎ **02/8267 3181;** Open: Sun–Thurs 10 a.m.–11 p.m., Fri 10 a.m.–2 a.m., Sat 10 a.m.–3 a.m.), an original Art Deco hotel that's been spruced up to accommodate three levels of entertainment; the **Columbian Hotel,** 117–123 Oxford St., Darlinghurst (☎ **02/9360 2152;** Open: Daily until at least 4 a.m.), an enormous heritage building with a music video bar topped by a nightclub.

✔ A good cocktail bar is **Gilligan's,** in the Oxford Hotel, 134 Oxford St., Darlinghurst, corner of Taylor Square (☎ **02/9331 3467;** Open: Wed–Sun 6 p.m. to midnight).

The bar scene

Most of Australia's drinking holes are known as *hotels,* after the tradition of providing room and board along with a good drink in the old days. Occasionally, you may hear them referred to as *pubs.* The term *bar* tends to apply in upscale hotels and trendy establishments. Bars close at various times, generally from midnight to around 3 a.m. Unless the listing says otherwise, these bars do not charge a cover:

✔ An institution is the **Bondi Hotel,** 178 Campbell Parade, Bondi Beach (☎ **02/9130 3271**), which is across the road from Bondi Beach. Another waterside wonder is the **Watson's Bay Hotel,** 1 Military Rd., Watsons Bay (☎ **02/9337 4299**), a casual place with a glorious beer garden overlooking the harbor.

✔ If you want to see Sydney at its sexiest and most sophisticated, then head to **The Establishment,** 252 George St., Wynyard (☎ **02/ 9240 3040**), a four-level venue where style is everything. For a bit of fun head to **The Friend in Hand,** 58 Cowper St., Glebe (☎ **02/ 9660 2326**), which hosts a Crab Racing Party every Wednesday at around 8 p.m.

✔ Historic bars include the **Lord Nelson Hotel,** Kent and Argyle streets, The Rocks (☎ **02/9251 4044**), one of the oldest pubs in Sydney. The drinks are sold English-style, in pints and half pints, and the landlord makes his own prizewinning beers. Of those, Three Sheets is the most popular. You can get decent pub grub here.

✔ The **Marble Bar,** in the Sydney Hilton, 259 Pitt St. (☎ **02/9266 2000**), is the only grand-cafe-style drinking hole in Australia. With oil paintings, marble columns, and brass everywhere, the Marble Bar is the picture of 15th-century Italian Renaissance architecture — despite being crafted in 1893.

Fast Facts: Sydney

American Express

The main office is at Level 3, 130 Pitt St., near Martin Place (☎ 02/9236 4200). It cashes traveler's checks and acts as a travel-booking service. It's open Monday through Friday from 8:30 a.m. to 5 p.m. and Saturday from 9 a.m. to noon. Another foreign exchange office is on the walkway leading up to the Sydney Opera House (☎ 02/9251 1970). If you've lost your traveler's checks, go to the head office, 175 Liverpool St. (☎ 02/9271 1111). It's a locked security building so you need to call ahead.

Baby Sitters

Dial an Angel (☎ 02/9416 7511 or 02/9362 4225) is a recommended service.

Currency Exchange

Most major bank branches offer currency exchange. Small foreign-currency exchange offices are at the airport and around Circular Quay and Kings Cross. Thomas Cook has offices at the airport; at 175 Pitt St. (☎ 02/9231 2877), open Monday through Friday from 6:45 a.m. to 5:15 p.m. and Saturday from 10 a.m. to 2 p.m.; and on the lower ground floor of the QVB (☎ 02/9264 1133), open Monday through Saturday from 9 a.m. to 6 p.m. (until 9 p.m. Fri) and Sunday from 11 a.m. to 5 p.m.

Dentist

Try the City Dental Practice, Level 2, 229 Macquarie St., near Martin Place (☎ 02/9221 3300). For dental problems after-hours, call Dental Emergency Information (☎ 02/9369 7050).

Doctor

The Park Medical Centre, Shop 4, 27 Park St. (☎ 02/9264 4488), near Town Hall, is open Monday through Friday from 8 a.m. to 6 p.m.; visits cost around A$40 (US$32/£16). The Kings Cross Travellers' Clinic, Suite 1, 13 Springfield Ave., Kings Cross, off Darlinghurst Road (☎ 1300/369 359 in Australia, or 02/9358 3066), is great for travel medicines and emergency contraception pills. Hotel visits in the Kings Cross area cost A$80 (US$64/£32); consultations cost A$40 (US$32/£16).

Embassies and Consulates

You'll find the following consulates in Sydney: Canada, Level 5, 111 Harrington St., The Rocks (☎ 02/9364 3000); New Zealand, 55 Hunter St. (☎ 02/9223 0144); United Kingdom, Level 16, Gateway Building, 1 Macquarie Place, Circular Quay (☎ 02/9247 7521); United States, Level 59, MLC Centre, 19–29 Martin Place (☎ 02/9373 9200).

Emergencies

Dial ☎ 000 to call police, the fire service, or an ambulance. Call the Emergency Prescription Service (☎ 02/9235 0333) for emergency drug prescriptions, and the NRMA (National Roads and Motorists Association) for car breakdowns (☎ 13 11 11).

Hospitals

Go to Sydney Hospital, Macquarie Street, at Martin Place (☎ 02/9382 7111 for emergencies). St. Vincent's Hospital is at Victoria and Burton streets in Darlinghurst, near Kings Cross (☎ 02/9339 1111).

Internet Access

Internet and e-mail centers are scattered around Kings Cross, Bondi, and Manly.

Lost Property

Contact the nearest police station if you've lost something. For items lost on trains, contact the Lost Property Office, 494 Pitt St., near Central Railway Station (☎ 02/9379 3000). The office is open Monday through Friday from 8:30 a.m. to 4:30 p.m. For items left on planes or at the airport, go to the Federal Airport Corporation's administration office on the top floor of the International Terminal at Sydney International Airport (☎ 02/9667 9583). For stuff left on buses or ferries, call ☎ 02/9245 5777.

Luggage Storage

You can leave your bags at the International Terminal at the airport. The storage room charges around A$8 (US$6.40/£3.20) per bag for up to six hours and A$11 (US$9/£4.50) for up to 24 hours. The room is open from 4:30 a.m. to the last flight of the day. Call ☎ 02/9667 0926 for information. Otherwise, leave luggage at the cloakroom at Central Station, near the front of the main building (☎ 02/9219 4395). Storage at the rail station costs A$5 (US$4/£2) per article per day. The Travelers Contact Point, 428 George St., 7th floor (☎ 02/9221 8744), stores luggage for A$15 (US$12/£6) per piece per month. It also operates a general delivery service and has Internet access, a travel agency, and a jobs board.

Newspapers

The *Sydney Morning Herald* is considered one of the world's best newspapers — by its management, at least. The *Australian* is available nationwide. The *Daily Telegraph* is a more casual read and publishes a couple of editions a day. The *International Herald Tribune, USA Today,* the British *Guardian Weekly,* and other international papers can be found at Circular Quay newspaper stands and most newsdealers.

Pharmacies

Most suburbs have pharmacies (known as *chemist shops* in Australia) that are open late. For after-hours referral, contact the Emergency Prescription Service (☎ 02/9235 0333).

Police

In an emergency, dial ☎ **000.** Make non-emergency inquiries through the Sydney Police Centre (☎ 02/9281 0000).

Post Office

The General Post Office (GPO) is at 130 Pitt St., near Martin Place (☎ 13 13 18 in Australia). It's open Monday through Friday from 8:30 a.m. to 5:30 p.m. and Saturday from 10 a.m. to 2 p.m. General-delivery letters can be sent c/o *Poste Restante,* G.P.O., Sydney, NSW 2000, Australia (☎ 02/9244 3733), and collected at 310 George St., on the third floor of the Hunter Connection shopping center. It's open Monday through Friday from 8:15 a.m. to 5:30 p.m. For directions to the nearest post office, call ☎ 1800/043 300.

Restrooms

You can find restrooms on the second floor of the QVB, at most department stores, at Central Station and Circular Quay, near the escalators by the Sydney Aquarium, and in the Harbourside Festival Marketplace in Darling Harbour.

Safety

Sydney is an extremely safe city, but as anywhere else, it's good to keep your wits about you and your wallet hidden. If you wear a money belt, keep it under your shirt. Be wary in Kings Cross and Redfern at all hours and around Central Station and the cinema strip on George Street near Town

Hall station in the evening — the latter is a hangout for local gangs. Other places of concern are the back lanes of Darlinghurst, around the naval base at Woolloomooloo, and along the Bondi restaurant strip when drunken tourists spill out after midnight. If traveling by train at night, travel in the carriages next to the guard's van, marked with a blue light on the outside.

Telephones

Sydney's public phone boxes take coins, and many also accept credit cards and A$10 (US$8/£4) phone cards available from newsdealers. Local calls cost A$0.40 (US$0.25/£0.15).

Transit Information

Call the Infoline (☎ 13 15 00 in Australia) daily from 6 a.m. to 10 p.m.

Weather

For the local forecast, call ☎ 1196.

Chapter 12

The Best of New South Wales

by Marc Llewellyn

. . . .

In This Chapter

▶ Discovering the Blue Mountains
▶ Exploring the Hunter Valley wine country
▶ Going underground in the New South Wales Outback

. . . .

*I*f you want to get away from Sydney for a couple of days, we're giving you three different destinations that provide quite a contrast from the big city: mountains, valley, and the Outback.

First we show you the Blue Mountains, part of the Great Dividing Range that separates the lush eastern coastal strip from the more arid interior. This is a World Heritage–listed area, so you can expect spectacular views, eucalyptus trees, dripping ferns, deep valleys, and craggy cliffs. Then, we show you what's on offer for wine lovers in the Hunter Valley, and then on to the classic Outback town of Broken Hill.

The Blue Mountains

The Blue Mountains derive their name from the ever-present blue haze that is caused by light striking the droplets of eucalyptus oil that evaporate from the leaves of the dense surrounding forest. The area offers breathtaking views, rugged tablelands, sheer cliffs, deep, inaccessible valleys, enormous chasms, colorful parrots, cascading waterfalls, historic villages, and stupendous walking trails.

The whole area is known for its spectacular scenery, particularly the cliff-top views into the valleys of gum trees and across to craggy outcrops that tower from the valley floor. It's colder up here than down on the plains, and clouds can sweep in and fill the canyons with mist in minutes, while waterfalls cascade down sheer drops, spraying the dripping fern trees that cling to the gullies.

The Blue Mountains

The Blue Mountains are one of Australia's best-known adventure playgrounds. Rock climbing, caving, *abseiling* (rappelling), bushwalking, biking, horseback riding, and canoeing are available here year-round.

Katoomba (pop. 11,200) is the largest town in the Blue Mountains and the focal point of the Blue Mountains National Park. It's about 114km (71 miles) west of Sydney.

Getting to Katoomba
By car
From Sydney, travel along Parramatta Road and turn off onto the M4 motorway. You reach Katoomba in about two hours. Another route is via the Harbour Bridge to North Sydney, along the Warringah Freeway (following signs to the M2). Take the M2 to the end and follow signs to the M4 and the Blue Mountains. This takes around one-and-a-half hours.

By rail

Trains leave almost hourly from Central Station; contact **CityRail** (☎ **13 15 00**) or **Countrylink** (☎ **13 22 32**; www.countrylink.info) for details. The train trip takes two hours, stopping at Katoomba, and then at Mount Victoria and Lithgow. An adult same-day round-trip ticket costs around A$15 (US$12/£6) off-peak, A$22 (US$18/£9) during commuter hours. A child's ticket costs A$3 (US$2.40/£1.20).

Guided tours from Sydney

Many private bus operators offer day trips from Sydney. Some offer a guided coach tour during which you just stretch your legs, while others let you get your circulation going with a couple of longish bushwalks.

- ✔ One highly recommended operator is **Oz Trek Adventure Tours** (☎ **1300/661 234** in Australia, or 02/9666 4262; www.oztrek.com.au). Its trips include tours of all the major Blue Mountain sites, and a one-and-a-half-hour bushwalk. It costs A$55 (US$44/£22) adults, A$44 (US$35/£18) kids. You can add overnight packages, horseback riding, and abseiling.

- ✔ **Sydney Tours-R-Us** (☎ **02/9498 4084**; www.sydneytoursrus.com) runs minicoaches to the Blue Mountains, stopping at the Telstra Stadium (where the Sydney Olympics were held) and Featherdale Wildlife Park. You see all the major sights in the mountains and come home via ferry from Parramatta to Circular Quay. The trip costs A$93 (US$74/£37) adults, A$65 (US$52/£26) kids. It's a ten-hour day.

- ✔ **Wonderbus** (☎ **1300/556 357** in Australia, or 02/9630 0529; www.wonderbus.com.au) offers an exceptional tour to the Blue Mountains for A$87 (US$70/£35) adults, A$65 (US$52/£26) kids, including all entry fees and lunch. You also come back by ferry.

Finding information on the Blue Mountains

You can pick up maps, walking guides, and other information and book accommodations at **Blue Mountains Tourism,** Echo Point Road, Katoomba, NSW 2780 (☎ **1300/653 408** in Australia, or 02/4739 6266). The information center is an attraction itself, with glass windows overlooking a gum forest, and cockatoos and lorikeets feeding on seed dispensers. It's open daily from 9 a.m. to 5 p.m.

The **National Park Shop,** Heritage Centre, end of Govetts Leap Road, Blackheath (☎ **02/4787 8877**; www.npws.nsw.gov.au) is run by the National Parks and Wildlife Service and offers detailed information about the Blue Mountains National Park. The staff can also arrange personalized guided tours of the mountains. It's open daily from 9 a.m. to 4:30 p.m.

Check the great Web site www.bluemts.com.au for more information on the area, including bushwalks.

Getting around the Blue Mountains

The best way to get around the Blue Mountains without your own transport is the **Blue Mountains Explorer Bus** (☎ 02/4782 4807; www.explorerbus.com.au). The double-decker bus leaves from outside Katoomba train station every hour from 9:30 a.m. until 4:30 p.m. and stops at 27 attractions, resorts, galleries, and tearooms in and around Katoomba and Leura. You can get on and off as often as you want. Tickets cost A$32 (US$26/£13) adults, A$16 (US$13/£6.50) children, A$75 (US$60/£30) families; prices include discounts on the Scenic Railway and the Skyway, as well as at some other attractions and restaurants.

The **Blue Mountains Explorer Link Ticket,** available from CityRail stations, includes same-day, round-trip train fare and Explorer Bus tickets and costs A$42 (US$34/£17) adults, A$17 (US$13/£6.50) children, A$65 (US$52/£26) families. A three-day ticket, allowing you to travel by CityRail train on two days and stay a whole day in the mountains, costs A$58 (US$46/£23) adults, A$24 (US$19/£9.50) kids. (No family ticket is offered.)

If you're staying a few days, consider the **Explorer Bus Pass,** which allows up to seven days' travel in the mountains. It costs an extra A$32 (US$26/£13) adults, A$16 (US$13/£6.50) kids, A$80 (US$64/£32) families.

Another option is **Trolley Tours** (☎ 1800/801 577 in Australia; www.trolleytours.com.au), which is a kind of tram on wheels with commentary. An all-day pass costs A$15 (US$12/£6) and includes stops at 29 various attractions around Katoomba and Leura, too. The trolley leaves Katoomba Station each hour, connecting with the trains from Sydney.

If you fancy a day in the caves over at Jenolan, team up with **Fantastic Aussie Tours** (☎ 02/4782 1866, or 1300/300 915 in Sydney; www.fantastic-aussie-tours.com.au).Their day tour departs Katoomba at 10:30 a.m. and returns at 5:15 p.m. It costs A$75 (US$60/£30) adults, A$38 (US$30/£15) children, A$200 (US$160/£80) families. The company also runs transfers to Jenolan from Katoomba, departing at 10:30 a.m. and leaving Jenolan at 3:45 p.m. daily. They cost A$85 (US$68/£34) adults, A$43 (US$34/£17) kids. The company can transfer you to Jenolan Caves for A$50 (US$40/£20) adults, A$25 (US$20/£10) kids. Ask about family fares.

Orienting yourself in the Blue Mountains

Leading out of Sydney, the Great Western Highway runs toward the blue smudges of hills in the distance. Then, suddenly, the road starts to climb. A string of small towns then pop up from behind a growing number of European trees. The first place of any note is Wentworth Falls, which is soon followed by Leura, Katoomba, Medlow Bath, Blackheath, Mount Victoria, and Hartley. On the western fringes of the mountains is the small settlement of Lithgow.

Introducing the neighbourhoods

We concentrate on the main places of interest here, with more information on Katoomba.

Blackheath

Blackheath is the highest town in the Blue Mountains at 1,049m (3,441 ft.). The **Three Brothers** at Blackheath are not as big or as famous as the Three Sisters in Katoomba, but you can climb two of them for fabulous views. Or you could try the **Cliff Walk** from **Evans Lookout** to **Govetts Leap** (named after a surveyor who mapped the region in the 1830s), where there are magnificent views over the **Grose Valley** and **Bridal Veil Falls.** The one-and-a-half-hour tramp passes through banksia, gum, and wattle forests, with spectacular views of peaks and valleys. Blackheath has some interesting tearooms and antiques shops.

Katoomba

You'll find several of the area's better hotels in Katoomba and some of the nicest scenic attractions, too. Katoomba itself has an interesting main street, with plenty of eateries and cafes and a couple of good antiques shops. Expect an interesting mix of hippies, dropouts, the economically challenged, tourists, and city escapees.

Jenolan Caves

Located 70km (43 miles) southwest of Katoomba are a series of limestone caves. Known to the local Aborigines as *Binoomea,* meaning "dark place," the caves are an impressive amalgamation of stalactites, stalagmites, and underground rivers and pools. You can tour them.

Leura

Leura is known for its gardens, attractive old buildings (many holiday homes for Sydneysiders), and cafes and restaurants. Just outside Leura is the **Sublime Point Lookout,** which has spectacular views of the Three Sisters in Katoomba. From the southern end of **Leura Mall,** a cliff drive takes you all the way back to Echo Point in Katoomba; along the way, you'll enjoy spectacular views across the Jamison Valley.

Wentworth Falls

This pretty town has numerous crafts and antiques shops, but the area is best known for its 281m (922-ft.) waterfall, in **Falls Reserve.** On the far side of the falls is the **National Pass Walk** — one of the best in the Blue Mountains. It's cut into a cliff face with overhanging rock faces on one side and sheer drops on the other. The views over the Jamison Valley are spectacular. The track takes you down to the base of the falls to the **Valley of the Waters.**

Staying in style

If you have the option, don't stay over in the Blue Mountains on a Friday or Saturday night, when prices go up significantly. Many hotels also have a minimum two-night stay requirement over the weekend. Parking is free at all hotels.

The Carrington Hotel
$$ **Katoomba**

Construction started on this grand Victorian hotel in 1880. The Carrington is a must-stay if you're into buildings of the British Raj style. Downstairs are a restaurant and breakfast room (once a ballroom), a couple of lounges with antiques, and a wood-paneled billiard room. All the rooms are delightful, with royal gold and blue carpets and drapes that would probably be gaudy if they didn't fit in with the overall style. Traditional rooms share bathrooms; colonial rooms come with a deep tub in the bathroom (with a noisy fan) and no view; deluxe colonial rooms have a balcony and mountain views; premier rooms have Jacuzzis and great views; the suites are fit for a duke and duchess. Dinner is A$100 (US$80/£40) per person, and breakfast is one of the best we've had.

15–47 Katoomba St. (P.O. Box 28), Katoomba, NSW 2780. ☎ *02/4782 1111. Fax: 02/4782 7033.* www.thecarrington.com.au. *Rack rates: Traditional double A$119 (US$95/ £48) Sun–Thurs, A$139 (US$111/£55) Fri–Sat; colonial double A$170 (US$136/£68) Sun–Thurs, A$190 (US$152/£76) Fri–Sat; deluxe colonial double A$205 (US$164/ £82) Sun–Thurs, A$225 (US$180/£90) Fri–Sat; premier double (no view) A$205 (US$164/£82) Sun–Thurs, A$225 (US$180/£90) Fri–Sat; premier double (with view) A$245 (US$196/£99) Sun–Thurs, A$265 (US$212/£106) Fri–Sat; suite A$315–A$445 (US$252–US$356/£126–£178) Sun–Thurs, A$335–A$465 (US$268–US$372/£134–£186) Fri–Sat. Rates include full breakfast. AE, DC, MC, V.*

Echoes Hotel & Restaurant, Blue Mountains
$$$$ **Katoomba**

Lilianfels (see later in this section) may be more expensive, but Echoes, across the road on a cliff overlooking the Jamison Valley, has superior views. Large windows, balconies, and a sizeable deck allow guests to soak up the fantastic scenery. Rooms are simply furnished; all have underfloor heating and are recommended if you're cashed up.

3 Lilianfels Ave., Katoomba, NSW 2780. ☎ *02/4782 1966.* www.echoeshotel.com.au. *Rack rates: A$833 (US$666/£333) 2-night weekend double. A$950 (US$760/£388) 2-night weekend suite; A$335 (US$268/£134) weekday double; A$385 (US$308/£154) weekday suite. Rates include breakfast. Ask about packages. AE, DC, MC, V.*

Jenolan Caves House
$$ **Jenolan**

This heritage-listed hotel built between 1888 and 1906 is one of the most outstanding structures in the state. The main part of the three-story building is made of sandstone and fashioned in Tudor-style black and white. Around it are cottages and former servants' quarters. Accommodations in the main house vary, from "traditional" rooms with shared bathrooms to "classic" rooms with private bathrooms. The rooms are old-world and cozy, with views over red-tile rooftops or steep slopes. Classic rooms have views of Jenolan Caves Valley and gardens; "grand classic" rooms have spectacular views across the hills and countryside. "Mountain lodge" rooms, in a building behind the main house, are more motel-like.

Jenolan Caves Village, NSW 2790. ☎ *02/6359 3322. Fax: 02/6359 3227.* www.jenolan caves.org.au. *Rack rates: A$190–A$250 (US$152–US$200/£76–£100) traditional double, A$280–A$380 (US$224–US$304/£112–£152) classic double, A$330–A$450 (US$264–US$360/£132–£180) grand classic double, A$370–A$450 (US$296–US$360/ £150–£180) classic suite, A$400–A$560 (US$320–US$448/£160–£224) grand classic suite, A$210–A$280 (US$168–US$224/£85–£112) mountain lodge double. Rates include dinner. AE, DC, MC, V.*

Lilianfels Blue Mountains
$$$$$ **Katoomba**

Just across a road from Echo Point, this Victorian country-house hotel — a member of the Small Luxury Hotels of the World — is a full-service yet cozy establishment. Rooms are spacious, expensive, and furnished with antiques. Most have king-size beds. Those with views are more expensive. The living areas are just as grand, with log fires and more antiques. Views are impressive, especially from the lounge, which overlooks the Jamison Valley. On the grounds is an 1889 cottage. Meant for two, it has a sitting room, a bedroom with a four-poster bed, a Jacuzzi, an intimate fireplace, and its own gardens. Among the other offerings at Lilianfels are a billiards room, a library and reading room, a small pool, and a health club. The restaurant **Darley's** serves great Contemporary food.

Lilianfels Avenue, Katoomba, NSW 2780. ☎ *1800/024 452 in Australia, or 02/4780 1200.* www.slh.com. *Rack rates: A$530–A$630 (US$448–US$504/£224–£252) double, A$635–A$870 (US$508–US$696/£252–£350) suite. Ask about off-season packages. AE, DC, MC, V.*

Mercure Grand Hydro Majestic Hotel
$$$ **Medlow Bath**

The most famous hotel in the Blue Mountains was built in 1904 by Mark Foy, a retail baron, world traveler, and hypochondriac. The long, white-washed building, with great bushland views, is reminiscent of the grand hotels of Queen Victoria's time. The property even has a croquet lawn and English lawn bowls. The standard Heritage rooms are furnished in Art Deco style and have views of the garden. The Gallery rooms have better views, some with valley glimpses. Cloister rooms, mostly in another wing, are decorated in both Art Deco and Edwardian and have valley views. Some of these have Jacuzzis. Rooms in the Delmonte Wing, decorated in French Provincial style, also have views. The suites are sumptuous. Higher rates in the ranges below apply on Friday and Saturday. Definitely check the Web site for deals; we recently found a rate of A$150 (US$120/£60) per night for a double.

Medlow Bath, NSW 2780. ☎ *02/4788 1002.* www.hydromajestic.com.au. *Rack rates: A$250–A$290 (US$200–US$232/£100–£116) Heritage double, A$290–A$330 (US$232–US$264/£116–£132) Gallery double, A$330–A$370 (US$264–US$296/£132– £150) Cloister double, A$370–A$410 (US$296–US$328/£150–£164) Cloister double with Jacuzzi, A$830–A$1,070 (US$664–US$856/£332–£428) suite. Rates include breakfast. Check Web site for specials. AE, MC, V.*

Dining out

Katoomba Street has many ethnic dining choices, whether you're hungry for Greek, Chinese, or Thai. Restaurants in the Blue Mountains are generally more expensive than equivalent places in Sydney. In addition to the restaurants we list in this section, try **The Elephant Bean,** 159 Katoomba Rd. (☎ **02/4782 4620**), for hearty soups, burgers, muffins, and good coffee. You may want to eat breakfast, or "brekkie," at a cafe rather than in your hotel. **The Stockmarket Café,** 179 The Mall, Leura (☎ **02/4784 3121**), is small and casual with good coffee ordered at the counter, and great soups, pies, and stews at lunchtime. **The Fresh Espresso and Food Bar,** 181 Katoomba St., Katoomba (☎ **02/4782 3602**), does good eggs and porridge with fresh ricotta, strawberries, honey, and cinnamon.

Chork Dee Thai Restaurant
$$ **Katoomba   THAI**

Loved by the locals, Chork Dee offers good Thai food in a pleasant but modest setting. It serves Thai fare, including satay, spring rolls, and fish cakes to start, followed by lots of curries, noodles, and sweet-and-sour dishes. Although vegetarians won't find any starters without meat or fish, plenty of veggie and tofu dishes are available as main courses. It's BYO.

216 Katoomba St., Katoomba. ☎ *02/4782 1913. Main courses: A$7.70–A$17 (US$6.15– US$14/£3–£7). AE, MC, V. Open: Sun–Thurs 5:30–9 p.m., Fri–Sat 5:30–10 p.m.*

Conservation Hut Café
$$ **Wentworth Falls   CAFE**

This pleasant cafe is in the national park on top of a cliff overlooking the Jamison Valley. It's a good place for lunch on the balcony after the Valley of the Waters walk, which leaves from outside. It serves good cafe fare — burgers, salads, and sandwiches, with vegetarian options. Breakfast is served as well. There's a nice log fire inside in winter.

At the end of Fletcher Street, Wentworth Falls. ☎ *02/4757 3827. Main courses: A$17– A$25 (US$14–US$20/£7–£10). AE, MC, V. Open: Daily 9 a.m.–5 p.m.*

Lindsay's
$$$ Katoomba MODERN AUSTRALIAN

Swiss chef Beat Ettlin has been making waves in Katoomba ever since he left some of the best European restaurants behind to try his hand at dishes such as pan-fried crocodile nibbles on pumpkin scones with ginger dipping sauce. The food is as glorious as its décor — Tiffany lamps, sketches by Australian artist Norman Lindsay, and booths lining the walls. The three-level restaurant is warmed by a cozy fire surrounded by an antique lounge stage and resounds every night to piano, classical music, or a jazz band. The menu is seasonal and changes every few weeks.

122 Katoomba St., Katoomba. ☎ *02/4782 2753. Reservations recommended. Main courses: A$14–A$24 (US$11–US$19/£5.50–£9.50). AE, MC, V. Open: Wed–Sun 6 p.m. to midnight.*

Paragon Café
$ Katoomba CAFE

The Paragon has been a Blue Mountains institution since it opened in 1916. Inside, it's decked out with dark-wood paneling, bas-relief figures guarding the booths, and chandeliers. The homemade soups are delicious. The cafe also serves pies, pastas, seafood, waffles, and a Devonshire tea.

65 Katoomba St., Katoomba. ☎ *02/4782 2928. Main courses: A$3–A$10 (US$2.40–US$8/£1.20–£4). AE, MC, V. Open: Tues–Fri 10 a.m.–3:30 p.m., Sat–Sun 10 a.m.–4 p.m.*

TrisElies
$$$ Katoomba GREEK

Perhaps it's the belly dancers, the plate-smashing, or the smell of moussaka, but as soon as you walk into this lively eatery you feel as if you've been transported to an Athenian taverna. The restaurant folds out onto three tiers of tables, all with a good view of the stage where Greek or international performances take place every night. The food is solid Greek fare — souvlaki, traditional dips, fried halloumi cheese, Greek salads, sausages in red wine. In winter, warm up beside one of the log fires.

287 Bathurst Rd., Katoomba. ☎ *02/4782 4026. Fax: 02/4782 1128.* www.triselies. com.au. *Reservations recommended. Main courses: A$17–A$26 (US$14–US$21/£7–£11). AE, DC, MC, V. Open: Sun–Thurs 5 p.m. to midnight, Fri–Sat 5 p.m.–3 a.m.*

Exploring the Blue Mountains
The top attractions

The reason you come to the Blue Mountains is for the views and the walks. There are so many walks of various lengths and challenges that you need to stop off at the Tourist Information Office for local advice.

Jenolan Caves

There are nine caves open for exploration. The first tour starts at 10 a.m. weekdays and 9:30 a.m. weekends and holidays. The final tour departs at 4:30 p.m. (5 p.m. in warmer months). Tours last one to two hours. The best all-around cave is **Lucas Cave; Imperial Cave** is best for seniors. Adventure Cave Tours, which include canyoning, last three hours to a full day. Guided tours are also offered by the **Jenolan Caves Reserves Trust** (☎ **02/6359 3311;** www.jenolancaves.org.au). The fees are A$16 to A$23 (US$13–US$18/£7.50–£9) adults, A$10 to A$15 (US$8–US$12/£4–£6) children under 15. Family rates and multiple cave packages are available.

The Three Sisters

These craggy red rock formations are the most photographed attractions in the Blue Mountains. The Aboriginal Dreamtime legend has it that three sisters — Meehni, Wimlah, and Gunnedoo — lived in the Jamison Valley as members of the Katoomba tribe. These beautiful young ladies had fallen in love with three brothers from the Nepean tribe, yet tribal law forbade them to marry. The brothers decided to use force to capture the three sisters, which caused a major tribal battle. Because the lives of the three sisters were seriously in danger, a witch doctor from the Katoomba tribe took it upon himself to turn the three sisters into stone to protect them. Although he had intended to reverse the spell when the battle was over, the witch doctor himself was killed. Because only he could reverse the spell to return the ladies to their former beauty, the sisters remain in their magnificent rock formation as a reminder of this battle. For the best vantage point, head to **Echo Point Road,** across from the Blue Mountains Tourism office. Or try Evans Lookout, Govetts Leap, and Hargreaves Lookout, all at Blackheath.

Scenic World

One thing you have to do in the Blue Mountains is ride Katoomba's **Scenic Railway,** the world's steepest. It consists of a carriage on rails lowered 415m (1,361 ft.) into the Jamison Valley at a maximum incline of 52 degrees. It's *very* steep and quite a thrill. Originally the rail line was used to transport coal from the mines below in the 1880s. The trip takes only a few minutes; at the bottom are some excellent walks through forests of ancient tree ferns. Another popular attraction is the **Skyway,** a cable car that travels 300m (984 ft.) above the Valley. The round-trip takes six minutes.

Ticket office: 1 Violet St., Katoomba (follow the signs). ☎ *02/4782 2699. Admission: For both the Scenic Railway and the Skyway A$16 (US$13/£6.50) round-trip adults, A$8 (US$6.40/£3.20) round-trip children, A$40 (US$32/£16) round-trip families. Open: Daily 9 a.m.–5 p.m. (last trip at 4:50 p.m.).*

More cool things to see and do

If you have some time to spend in the Blue Mountains, you could include the following things to do:

✔ There are 50 **walking trails,** ranging from routes you can cover in 15 minutes to the three-day **Six Foot Track** that starts outside Katoomba and finishes at Jenolan Caves. The staff at the tourist offices and national park office will be happy to point you in the right direction, whether for an hour's stroll or a day's hike.

✔ One of the best adventure operators in the area, **High 'n' Wild,** 3–5 Katoomba St., Katoomba, NSW 2780 (☎ 02/4782 6224; www.high-n-wild.com.au), offers a series of canyoning expeditions, taking in scenic rain forest gullies and caverns made up of dramatic rock formations and fern-lined walls. There's a bit of swimming and plenty of walking, wading, and squeezing through tight spaces.

✔ Other excellent adventure operators are the **Blue Mountains Adventure Company,** 84a Bathurst Rd. (P.O. Box 242), Katoomba, NSW 2780 (☎ 02/4782 1271; www.bmac.com.au), above the Summit Gear Shop; and the **Australian School of Mountaineering,** 166 Katoomba St., Katoomba, NSW 2780 (☎ 02/4782 2014). Both offer rock climbing, rappelling, and canyoning trips. The Adventure Company offers caving and biking, and the School of Mountaineering offers bushcraft and survival training.

The Hunter Valley: Wining and Dining

The Hunter Valley is the oldest commercial wine-producing area in Australia. Internationally acclaimed wines have poured out of the Hunter since the early 1800s. People come here to visit the vineyards' "cellar doors" for wine tastings, to enjoy the scenery, to sample the area's highly regarded cuisine, or to escape from the city.

In the **Lower Hunter,** centered on the towns of Cessnock and Pokolbin, are around 110 wineries and cellar doors, including well-known producers such as Tyrell, Rothbury, Lindemans, Draytons, McGuigans, and McWilliams. Many varieties of wine are produced here, including sémillon, Shiraz, chardonnay, cabernet sauvignon, and pinot noir.

The **Upper Hunter** represents the essence of Australian rural life, with its sheep and cattle farms, historic homesteads, more wineries, and bushland. The vineyards tend to be larger than those in the south, and produce more aromatic varieties, such as traminers and Rieslings. February through March is harvest time.

Getting to the Hunter Valley

By car

Leave Sydney by the Harbour Bridge or Harbour Tunnel and follow the signs for Newcastle. Just before Hornsby, turn off the highway and head up the National 1/F3 freeway. After around an hour, take the Cessnock exit and follow signs to the vineyards. The trip will take about two-and-a-half hours.

The Hunter Valley

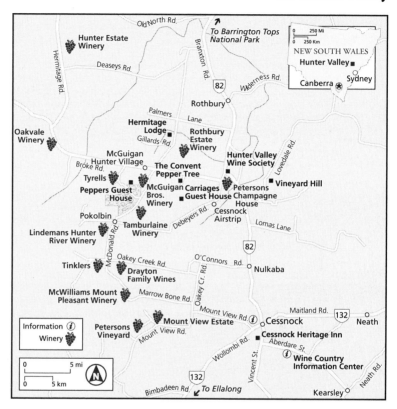

By bus

Several companies offer **day trips** to the Hunter Valley from Sydney.
Visitours (☎ **02/9909 0822;** www.visitours.com.au) takes small
groups to visit up to six wineries as well as cheese and fudge producers.
The trip costs A$85 (US$68/£34), A$95 (US$76/£38) with lunch. Meanwhile, **Grayline** (☎ **1300/858 687;** www.grayline.com.au) offers coach
trips to the vineyards every Tuesday, Wednesday, Friday, and Sunday
costing A$143 (US$114/£57) adults, A$72 (US$57/£29) kids; it visits three
wineries and includes lunch.

Finding information after you arrive

Wine Country Visitors Information Centre, Main Road, Pokolbin, NSW
2325 (☎ **02/4990 4477;** fax 02/4991 4518; www.winecountry.com.au), is
open Monday through Friday 9 a.m. to 5 p.m., Saturday 9:30 a.m. to
5 p.m., and Sunday 9:30 a.m. to 3:30 p.m.

Visiting the wineries

Most of the wineries in the region are open for tastings, and it's acceptable to turn up, taste a couple of wines or more, and then say your goodbyes without buying.

Many people start their journey through the Hunter by popping into the **Hunter Valley Wine Society,** 455 Wine Country Dr., Pokolbin (☎ **1300/ 303 307** in Australia, or 02/4941 3000). The club acts as a Hunter Valley wine clearinghouse, sending bottles and cases to members all over Australia, and some overseas. It's a good place to talk to experts about the area's wines, and taste a few. It's open daily 9 a.m. to 5 p.m.

You may also like to visit the **Small Winemakers Centre,** 426 McDonalds Rd., Pokolbin (☎ **02/4998 7668**). At any one time it represents six or so of the region's smaller producers.

Australia's drunk-driving laws are strict and rigidly enforced. Both easily identifiable and unmarked police cars patrol the vineyard regions. If you're interested in tasting some grapes in the Hunter Valley, choose a designated driver or take a guided tour.

Here are just a few of the popular wineries you can visit:

- ✓ **Lindemans Hunter River Winery,** McDonald Road, Pokolbin (☎ **02/4998 7684**): Open Monday through Friday from 9 a.m. to 4:30 p.m., Saturday and Sunday from 10 a.m. to 4:30 p.m., Lindemans offers an interesting sparkling red Shiraz.

- ✓ **McGuigan Brothers Cellars,** corner of Broke and McDonalds roads, Pokolbin (☎ **02/4998 7402**): Open daily from 9:30 a.m. to 5 p.m., with tours at noon, McGuigan Brothers also has a cheese factory and bakery on-site.

- ✓ **Rothbury Estate,** Broke Road, Pokolbin (☎ **02/4998 7555**): Open daily from 9:30 a.m. to 4:30 p.m., Rothbury is a friendly winery that produces magnificent Brokenback Shiraz and Mudgee Shiraz.

- ✓ **Tamburlaine Winery,** 358 McDonald Rd., Pokolbin (☎ **02/4998 7570**): Open daily from 9:30 a.m. to 5 p.m., Tamburlaine is a nice boutique winery and the winner of many wine and tourism awards.

- ✓ **Tinklers,** Pokolbin Mountains Road, Pokolbin (☎ **02/4998 7435**): Open daily from 10 a.m. to 4 p.m., Tinklers sells some 30 different varieties of grapes between December and March, and nectarines, plums, peaches, and vegetables at other times. It also offers wine tasting and free vineyard walks at 11 a.m. Saturday and Sunday.

Fun ways to see the wineries

If you don't have a car, you'll have to get around as part of a tour, because no public transport runs between the wineries.

✔ **Trekabout Tours** (☎ **02/4990 8277;** www.hunterweb.com.au/ trekabout) offers half-day and full-day winery tours for up to six people. Half-day tours cost A$35 (US$28/£14), with visits to five or six wineries; full-day tours cost A$45 (US$36/£18) and take in up to nine wineries. Trekabout can pick you up in Cessnock or Pokolbin.

✔ **Balloon Aloft,** in Cessnock (☎ **1800/028 568** in Australia, or 02/ 4938 1955; www.balloonaloft.com.au), offers year-round dawn balloon flights that include post-flight champagne and optional breakfast for A$16 (US$13/£6.50). Flights last about an hour and cost A$280 (US$224/£112) adults, A$170 (US$136/£68) kids ages 8 to 12.

✔ On **Grapemobile Bicycle and Walking Tours** (☎ **0500/804 039** in Australia, or ☎/fax 02/4991 2339), you're supplied with a mountain bike, helmet, guide, and support bus, and taken on a peaceful meander through the wineries. Tours cost A$98 (US$78/£39), including lunch in a restaurant. Grapemobile also rents bicycles — A$22 (US$18/£9) half-day, A$30 (US$24/£12) full day.

The top hotels

The Hunter Valley is far more expensive on weekends and holidays than on weekdays. Room prices jump significantly, and some properties insist on a two-night stay. It's worth checking out the information board in the Wine Country Visitors Information Centre for special deals, including self-contained accommodations, cottages, resorts, and guesthouses.

Bunking down in a caravan, man

Two trailer (caravan) parks offer comfortable accommodations in trailers and cabins. **Cessnock Cabins and Caravan Park** (☎ **02/4990 5819;** fax 02/4991 2944), Allandale/ Branxton Road, Nulkaba (2km/1¼ miles north of Cessnock), has four on-site vans for A$30 to A$40 (US$24–US$32/£12–£16), and a double and 12 cabins with shower for A$48 to A$69 (US$38–US$55/£19–£28) — the more expensive prices for weekends. There are also camping sites for A$14 (US$11/£5.50) and powered sites for A$16 (US$13/£6.50).

The **Valley Vineyard Tourist Park** (☎/fax **02/4990 2573**) on Mount View Road (on the way to the vineyards) has five trailers for A$35 (US$28/£14) and 12 cabins with shower for A$55 (US$44/£22). Two two-bedroom units are A$75 (US$60/£30). Powered sites cost A$16 to A$20 (US$13–US$16/£6.50–£8) and a camping site is A$12 (US$10/£5). A BYO restaurant, a campers' kitchen, and a swimming pool are all on-site.

Barrington Guest House
$$ Barrington Tops

Barrington Guest House is in a valley just outside the Barrington Tops National Park, 90 minutes from the main Hunter wine region. It retains an old-world charm and serves bacon and eggs for breakfast, scones and cream, and vegetables boiled soft enough for your dentures. The place has lace tablecloths in the dining room, a log fire beneath a higgledy-piggledy brick chimney, mahogany walls, high ceilings, and personalized service — despite the communal mealtimes and the lack of a menu. Rooms come with or without private bathroom; they're basic (no TV) but comfortable enough. The guesthouse grounds attract plenty of animals and act as a wildlife reserve for several rescued kangaroos. Activities include horseback riding, guided walks through the rain forest, "billy tea" tours, night spotting for *quolls* (native cats) and possums, bush dancing, tennis, film evenings, and skeet shooting. Several luxury rain forest cottages are also available. They sleep up to five people.

Salisbury (3½ hours from Sydney), NSW 2420. ☎ *02/4995 3212. Fax: 02/4995 3248. www.barringtonguesthouse.com.au. Rack rates: Weekend A$230 (US$184/£92) double for 2 nights without bathroom, A$260 (US$208/£104) double with bathroom; weekday A$95 (US$76/£38) double without bathroom, A$130 (US$104/£52) double with bathroom. Rates include all meals and activities. Minimum 2-night stay on weekends. Ask about packages and child rates. AE, DC, MC, V.*

Carriages Guest House
$$ Pokolbin

Tucked away on 15 hectares (37 acres) and off the main road, Carriages is a secluded retreat. A two-suite cottage is on a separate part of the grounds. In the main two-story house, a veranda circles downstairs rooms, which are furnished in antique country pine. Upstairs, the two lofty gable suites center on huge fireplaces. The Gatehouse suites offer incredible luxury; the stained-glass windows and rescued timber give them a rustic feel (these two Jacuzzi rooms share a lounge with a full kitchen and an open fire). There are open fires in six of the rooms. (The two standard doubles don't have them.) Breakfast is served in your room, and Robert's Restaurant is next door. There's a large heated outdoor pool.

Halls Road, Pokolbin, NSW 2321. ☎ *02/4998 7591. Fax: 02/4998 7839. www.thecarriages.com.au. Rack rates: A$150–A$195 (US$148–US$156/£75–£78) double, A$195–A$275 (US$156–US$220/£78–£110) suite, A$235–A$295 (US$188–US$236/£94–£118) Jacuzzi suite. Rates include breakfast. Minimum 2-night stay on weekends. AE, MC, V.*

Casuarina Restaurant and Country Inn
$$$ Pokolbin

Each of the different suites has a theme: the Moulin Rouge, the Oriental, the Bordello, Casanova's Loft, the Mariners Suite, British Empire, Out of Africa, and Romeo's Retreat. The most popular is the Bordello, with a pedestaled king-size bed, voluptuous pink curtains, and strategically placed mirrors. To get the full picture, it's worth roaming around the Web site before you book. The award-winning **Casuarina Restaurant** serves Mediterranean-style food. There's a large outdoor pool.

Hermitage Road, Pokolbin, NSW 2321. ☎ *02/4998 7888.* www.casuarinainn. com.au. *Rack rates: A$285–A$310 (US$212–US$248/£106–£124) weekday, A$310–A$350 (US$248–US$280/£124–£140) weekend. Minimum 2-night stay on weekends. AE, DC, MC, V.*

Peppers Convent Hunter Valley
$$$$ **Pokolbin**

Originally a convent in the early part of the 20th century, this building was transported some 600km (372 miles) from Coonamble in central New South Wales to its present location in 1990. Rooms are elegant and spacious, with baroque décor, including plaster frieze ceilings and thick, rich drapes. French doors open onto private verandas overlooking patches of bushland. King rooms are larger and have wicker lounge areas. There is an elegant sitting area where drinks are served, and a light and airy breakfast room serving the best breakfasts in the Hunter. The complex includes Pepper Tree Wines and the excellent Robert's Restaurant.

In the Pepper Tree Complex, Halls Road, Pokolbin, NSW 2320. ☎ *02/4998 7764.* www. peppers.com.au. *Rack rates: Weekend A$323–A$387 (US$258–US$309/£128–£155) double; weekday A$291–A$332 (US$233–US$265/£117–£133) double. Minimum 2-night stay on weekends. Ask about packages and check Web site for specials. AE, DC, MC, V.*

Peppers Guest House
$$$$ **Pokolbin**

This tranquil escape is set in beautiful bush gardens. The spot is so peaceful that kangaroos hop up to the veranda looking for treats. The "classic" rooms downstairs have French doors that you can fling open; upstairs rooms have a tad more old-fashioned charm and come with air-conditioning. All rooms have king-size beds and are furnished with colonial antiques. Guests don't come here for action; they come to relax. The Pampering Place offers massages and facials, and a gentle 30-minute trail winds through the bush. The restaurant, **Chez Pok,** is an upscale establishment with mismatched china and pretty good country food.

Ekerts Road, Pokolbin, NSW 2321. ☎ *02/4998 7596. Fax: 02/4998 7739.* www.peppers. com.au. *Rack rates: Weekend A$277 (US$221/£110) colonial double, A$303 (US$242/£121) classic double, A$315 (US$252/£126) vintage double, A$347 (US$277/£139) heritage suite; weekday A$273 (US$218/£109) colonial double, A$283 (US$226/£113) classic double, A$292 (US$233/£117) vintage double, A$327 (US$261/£131) heritage suite. Minimum 2-night stay on weekends. Weekday rates include buffet breakfast. AE, DC, MC, V.*

The best places to eat

Most hotels have their own restaurants, as do many of the vineyards. The three restaurants in the Hunter with the best reputations are

Robert's Restaurant, Chez Pok, and **Casuarina Restaurant.** Another good offering is **Beltree@Margan,** 266 Hermitage Rd., Pokolbin (☎ 02/ 6574 7216), which serves Mediterranean-influenced food either out on a courtyard or in front of a fireplace. It's open for a lingering lunch daily from 10 a.m. to 5 p.m.

For good coffee see **Bliss Coffee Roasters,** Shop 2, Hunter Valley Gardens Shopping Centre, Broke Road, Pokolbin (☎ 02/4998 6700).

Café Enzo
$$ Pokolbin   MODERN AUSTRALIAN

This charming cafe offers a nice ambience and good cuisine. Pastas, pizzettas, antipasti, and steaks dominate the menu. The pizzetta with char-grilled baby octopus, squid, king prawns, Kalamata olives, fresh chile, onion, and freshly shaved Parmesan is particularly nice. Cakes and cheese plates are a specialty.

At the corner of Broke and Ekerts roads (adjacent to Peppers Creek Antiques, near Peppers Guest House), Pokolbin. ☎ *02/4998 7233. Main courses: A$10–A$18 (US$8– US$14/£4–£7), Devonshire tea A$7.50 (US$6/£3). AE, DC, MC, V. Open: Wed–Fri and Sun 10 a.m.–5 p.m., Sat 10 a.m.–10 p.m.*

Robert's at Peppertree
$$$$ Pokolbin   EUROPEAN

Chef and owner Robert Molines is a legend in Hunter Valley gourmet circles for coming up with great dishes that complement the region's wines. His restaurant is known for its eclectic mix of antiques and his country-style dishes, such as rabbit with olives and vegetables, and the signature dish, twice-roasted duckling with braised savoy cabbage and pear glaze. Other nice dishes could include the lamb rack Provençal, and venison steaks on a beetroot and baby onion confit, with muscat sauce.

In the Pepper Tree complex, Halls Road, Pokolbin. ☎ *02/4998 7330.* www.roberts restaurant.com. *Reservations required. Main courses: A$38–A$42 (US$30– US$34/£15–£17); A$5 (US$4/£2) per-person surcharge weekends and public holidays. AE, DC, MC, V. Open: Daily noon to 5 p.m. and 7 p.m. to midnight.*

Outback New South Wales: Broken Hill

The Outback is a powerful Australian image. Hot, dusty, and prone to flies, it can also be a place where wedge-tailed eagles float in the shimmering heat as you spin in a circle, tracing the unbroken horizon. If you drive out here, you have to be constantly on the lookout for emus, large flightless birds that dart across roads open-beaked and wide-eyed.

Broken Hill (1,157km/717 miles west of Sydney) — or "Silver City," as it's been nicknamed — is still a hard working, hard-drinking mining town. Its beginnings date to 1883, when a rider named Charles Rasp noticed something odd about the craggy rock outcrops at a place called the Broken Hill. He thought he saw deposits of tin, but they turned out to be silver and lead. Today, the city's main drag, Argent Street, bristles with colonial mansions, heritage homes, and public buildings.

Getting to Broken Hill

By car

Take the Great Western Highway from Sydney to Dubbo, then the Mitchell Highway to the Barrier Highway, to Broken Hill.

By train

The *Indian Pacific* stops here on its way from Sydney to Perth twice a week. It takes nearly 16 hours, leaving Sydney at 2:55 p.m. on Saturday and Wednesday and arriving in Broken Hill at 6:40 a.m. the next day. The fare from Sydney is A$564 (US$451/£226) adults and A$473 (US$378/£180) children in a first-class sleeper, A$375 (US$300/£150) adults and A$283 (US$226/£113) children in an economy sleeper, and A$225 (US$180/£90) adults and A$120 (US$96/£48) children in an economy seat. Contact **Great Southern Railways** (☎ **08/8213 4530;** www.gsr.com.au).

By bus

Greyhound Australia (☎ **13 14 99** in Australia, or 07/4690 9950; www.greyhound.com.au) runs buses from Adelaide for around A$60 (US$48/£24); the trip takes seven hours. The 16-hour trip from Sydney costs from A$96 (US$77/£38).

Getting information after you arrive

You can find the **Broken Hill Visitors Information Centre** at the corner of Blende and Bromide streets (☎ **08/8087 6077;** www.visitbrokenhill.com.au). It's open daily from 8:30 a.m. to 5 p.m.

The area code in Broken Hill is **08,** the same as the South Australia code, not 02, the New South Wales code.

Getting around Broken Hill

Free, volunteer-led tours lead off from the Visitor's Centre at 10 a.m. on Monday, Wednesday, and Friday from March to October.

Silver City Tours, 380 Argent St. (☎ **08/8087 3144**), conducts tours of the city and Outback. City tours take around four hours and cost A$45 (US$36/£18) adults, A$20 (US$16/£8) children. The company also offers a range of other tours of the area.

Another good operator is **Tri State Safaris** (☎ **08/8088 2389;** www.tristate.com.au), which runs multiday tours into the Outback.

Cool things to see and do

Broken Hill has more places per capita to see **art** than anywhere else in Australia. The **Broken Hill Regional Art Gallery,** Chloride Street, between Blende and Beryl streets (☎ 08/8088 5491), houses an extensive collection of Australian colonial and Impressionist works. The gallery is open Monday through Friday from 10 a.m. to 5 p.m., and Saturday and Sunday from 1 to 5 p.m. Admission is A$3 (US$2.40/£1.20) adults, A$2 (US$1.60/£0.80) children, A$6 (US$4.80/£2.40) families.

Other galleries worth visiting include **Absalom's Gallery,** 638 Chapple St. (☎ 08/8087 5881), and the **Pro Hart Gallery,** 108 Wyman St. (☎ 08/8087 2441). Both are open daily. In Pro Hart's gallery, you'll find his own works: pieces based on incidents and scenes of Broken Hill as well as everything from a bas-relief of Salvador Dalí to a landscape by Claude Monet.

Join the **Bush Mail Run** (☎ 08/8087 2164, or 0411/102 339 mobile), an Outback mail delivery service that operates every Wednesday and Saturday. The day starts at 7 a.m. and you cover roughly 500km (310 miles). You stop at various homesteads. The run costs A$120 (US$96/£48).

Around Broken Hill

At least 44 movies have been filmed in the Wild West town of **Silverton** (pop. 50), 23km (14 miles) northwest of Broken Hill. It's the Wild West Australian-style, though, with camels instead of horses sometimes placed in front of the **Silverton Pub,** worth a visit for its kitschy appeal. Silverton once had a population of 3,000, following the discovery of silver in 1882, but within seven years almost everyone had left. There are some good galleries here, as well as a restored jail and hotel.

   ✔ **Mutawintji National Park:** Also known by its old name, Mootwingee (130km/81 miles northeast of Broken Hill), this place was one of the most important spiritual meeting places for Aborigines. The ancient, weathered fireplaces are still here, laid out like a giant map to show where each group came from. Hundreds of ocher outlines of hands and animal paws, some up to 30,000 years old, are stenciled on rock overhangs. The two-hour Outback trip from Broken Hill to Mootwingee is along red-dirt tracks not suitable for two-wheel-drives. It should not be attempted after a heavy rain.

   ✔ **Mootwingee Heritage Tours** (☎ 08/8088 7000) leads inspections of the historical sites every Wednesday and Saturday at 10:30 a.m. Broken Hill time (11 a.m. Mootwingee time). The tours may be canceled in very hot weather. The **NPWS office** in Broken Hill (☎ 08/8088 5933) also has details.

✔ **Living Desert Nature Park:** Twelve sandstone obelisks, up to 3m (10 ft.) high and carved totemlike by artists from as far away as Georgia, Syria, Mexico, and the Tiwi Islands, make up the Sculpture Symposium. Surrounding them on all sides is mulga scrub. It's fantastic at sunset.

Staying in Broken Hill

One option is to rent a local cottage from **Broken Hill Historic Cottages** (☎ 08/8087 9966) for A$80 (US$64/£32) a night.

Mario the Palace Hotel
$ **Broken Hill**

With its high painted walls, a mural of Botticelli's *Birth of Venus* on the ceiling two flights up, and an office crammed with stuffed animal heads and crabs, the Palace Hotel is an intriguing sanctuary. The owners have put a lot of work into restoring the place. The more expensive doubles are larger and come with a small lounge area, but all are comfortable and cool. Ten double rooms come with an attached shower. The Priscilla Suite is famous because that's where the transvestites stayed in *The Adventures of Priscilla, Queen of the Desert.*

227 Argent St., Broken Hill, NSW 2880. ☎ *08/8088 1699. Fax: 08/8087 6240. E-mail:* mariospalace@bigpond.com. *Rack rates: A$44 (US$35/£18) double without bathroom, A$53–A$70 (US$42–US$56/£21–£28) double with bathroom, A$90 (US$72/£36) Priscilla suite for 2. AE, MC, V.*

Underground Motel
$ **White Cliffs**

We love this place; it's worth making the trip out to White Cliffs to stay here. All but two of the rooms are underground; they're reached by a maze of tunnels dug out of the rock and sealed with epoxy resin. The temperature below ground is a constant 72°F (22°C), which is decidedly cooler than a summer day outside. Rooms are comfortable though basic, with shared toilets and showers. Turn off the light, and it's dark as a cave. Every night guests sit around large tables and dig into the roast of the day. (Vegetarians have options, too.)

Smiths Hill, White Cliffs (P.O. Box 427), NSW 2836. ☎ *1800/021 154 in Australia, or 08/8091 6677. Fax: 08/8091 6654.* www.undergroundmotel.com.au. *Rack rates: A$83 (US$66/£33) double; extra person A$24 (US$19/£10). MC, V.*

Dining locally

The best place for a meal Aussie-style is a local club. You'll find one of the best bistros at the **Barrier Social & Democratic Club,** 218 Argent St. (☎ 08/8088 4477). It serves breakfast, lunch, and dinner. Another good one is at the **Southern Cross Hotel,** 357 Cobalt St. (☎ 08/8088 4122). Interestingly, the fresh fish is a standout. Locals go for steaks at the **Sturt Club,** 321 Blende St. (☎ 02/8087 4541).

Chapter 13

Melbourne

by Lee Mylne

In This Chapter

▶ Getting around Melbourne: Tram-tastic!
▶ Eating, sleeping, and sightseeing in Melbourne
▶ Enjoying Melbourne's nightlife
▶ Parading with penguins on Phillip Island

*R*attling trams, twisting cobblestone laneways hiding trendy bars and restaurants, stately European architecture, parklands, galleries galore, and a diverse population that's passionate about their hometown — you'll find all this and more in Australia's largest city. Victoria's capital, Melbourne (pronounced *mel*-bun) is a cultural melting pot.

Melbourne is at the head of the pack in Australia when it comes to shopping, restaurants, fashion, music, nightlife, and cafe culture.

Melbourne was founded in the 1850s, when gold was found in the surrounding hills. British settlers prided themselves on coming freely to the city, rather than in chains. The city grew wealthy and remained a conservative bastion until World War II, when another wave of immigration, from southern Europe, made it a more relaxed place.

Getting There

By plane

Qantas (☎ 13 13 13 in Australia; www.qantas.com.au) and **Virgin Blue** (☎ 13 67 89 in Australia; www.virginblue.com.au) both fly to Melbourne from all state capitals. Qantas's discount arm, **Jetstar** (☎ 13 15 38 in Australia, or 03/8341 4901; www.jetstar.com.au) flies to and from Darwin, Townsville, Hamilton Island, the Sunshine Coast and Gold Coast, and Hobart. Jetstar also flies between Avalon Airport, about a 50-minute drive outside Melbourne's city center, and Sydney, Brisbane, Perth, and Adelaide. With a rapidly expanding network more flights are likely to have been added by the time you arrive.

Melbourne Airport's international and domestic terminals (www.melair.com.au) are all under one roof at Tullamarine, 22km (14 miles) northwest of the city center (often referred to as Tullamarine Airport). A travelers' information desk is on the ground floor of the international terminal and is open from 6 a.m. until the last flight. The international terminal has snack bars, a restaurant, currency-exchange facilities, and duty-free shops. ATMs are available at both terminals. Showers are on the first floor of the international area. Baggage carts are free in the international baggage claim hall but cost A$3 (US$2.40/£1.20) in the parking lot, departure lounge, or domestic terminal. Baggage storage is available in the international terminal and costs from A$10 to A$20 (US$8–US$16/£4–£8) per day, depending on size. The storage desk is open from 5 a.m. to 12:30 a.m. daily, and you need photo ID. The **Hilton Melbourne Airport** (☎ 03/8336 2000) and **Holiday Inn Melbourne Airport** (☎ 1300/724 944 in Australia) are both within a five-minute walk of the terminals.

Getting from the airport to your hotel

The Tullamarine freeway from the airport joins with the CityLink, a toll road. Drivers need a CityLink pass. A 24-hour pass costs A$11 (US$8.80/£4.40). Check with your car rental company.

The red **Skybus** (☎ 03/9335 2811; www.skybus.com.au) runs between the airport and Melbourne's Southern Cross Station in Spencer Street every 10 to 15 minutes throughout the day and every 30 to 60 minutes overnight 24 hours a day, daily. Buy tickets from Skybus desks outside the baggage claim areas or at the Travellers Information Desk in the international terminal. A free Skybus hotel shuttle will pick you up at your hotel to connect with the airport-bound bus at Southern Cross, but you must book this. It operates from 6 a.m. to 10 p.m. weekdays and 7:30 a.m. to 6:30 p.m. weekends. Tickets for adults cost A$15 (US$12/£6) one-way, A$24 (US$19/£9.60) round-trip. Kids cost A$5 (US$4/£2) each way. A family ticket for up to six people costs A$30 (US$24/£12) one-way, A$50 (US$40/£20) round-trip. The trip takes about 20 minutes from the airport to Southern Cross station, but allow longer for your return journey.

Sunbus (☎ 03/9689 6888; www.sunbusaustralia.com.au) meets all flights and runs back to the airport from 167 Franklin St. and Southern Cross Station, and operates a transfer service to Avalon Airport for Jetstar flights. One-way tickets from Melbourne airport cost A$21 (US$17/£8.40) adults, A$15 (US$12/£6) children 4 to 14, A$122 (US$98/£49) families of four. Round-trip fares are double. One-way fares from Avalon Airport are A$19 (US$15/£7.60) adults, A$9.50 (US$7.60/£3.80) children to Southern Cross station, more to other Central Business District (CBD) locations and other suburbs.

A **taxi** to the city center takes about 30 minutes and costs around A$45 (US$36/£18).

Avis, Budget, Europcar, Hertz, and Thrifty have **car rental** desks at the airport.

By train

Interstate trains arrive at **Southern Cross Railway Station,** Spencer and Little Collins streets (5 blocks from Swanston Street in the city center). After a multimillion-dollar face-lift completed in 2006, the station was renamed Southern Cross, but you'll still hear locals refer to it as "Spencer Street Station." Taxis and buses connect with the city.

The **Sydney-Melbourne** *XPT* travels between Australia's two largest cities daily (trip time: 11 hours). The adult fare is A$75 (US$60/£30) economy class, A$105 (US$84/£42) first class. A first-class sleeper costs A$193 (US$154/£77). For more information, contact **Countrylink** (☎ **13 22 32** in Australia; www.countrylink.info).

The *Overland* train, overhauled in 2007, provides service between Melbourne and Adelaide (trip time: 11 hours) three times a week. The adult one-way fare is A$89 (US$71/£36) economy class, A$139 (US$111/£56) first class. For more information, contact **Great Southern Railways** (☎ **13 21 47** in Australia; www.gsr.com.au).

V/Line services also connect Melbourne with Adelaide. This trip is by train from Melbourne to Bendigo, and by bus from Bendigo to Adelaide. Total trip time is around 11 hours, and the fare is A$65 (US$52/£26) adults, A$33 (US$26/£13) children. The **Canberra Link** connects Melbourne with the nation's capital; it's a train journey from Melbourne to Bairnsdale, and then a bus from there to Canberra. The journey takes about ten hours and costs A$63 (US$50/£25) adults, A$33 (US$26/£13) kids. For information, contact **V/Line** (☎ **13 61 96** in Australia; www.vline.com.au).

By bus

Several bus companies connect Melbourne with other capitals and regional areas of Victoria. Among the biggest is **Greyhound Australia** (☎ **1300/473 946** in Australia, or 07/4690 9950; www.greyhound.com.au). Coaches serve Melbourne's Transit Centre, 58 Franklin St., 2 blocks north of the Southern Cross Railway Station on Spencer Street. Trams and taxis serve the station; V/Line buses (☎ **13 61 96** in Australia; www.vline.com.au), which travel all over Victoria, depart from the Spencer Street Bus Terminal.

By car

You can drive from Sydney to Melbourne along the Hume Highway (trip time: nine-and-a-half hours), via Goulburn in New South Wales (good for supplies), and Wangaratta in Victoria (where you can detour into the Victorian Alps). Another route is along the coastal Princes Highway, for which you need a minimum of two days, with stops. For information on road travel in Victoria, contact the **Royal Automotive Club of Victoria** (☎ **13 13 29** in Australia, or 03/9790 2211; www.racv.com.au).

Orienting Yourself in Melbourne

Melbourne is on the Yarra River and stretches inland from Port Philip Bay, which lies to its south. On a map, you'll see a distinct central oblong area surrounded by Flinders Street to the south, Latrobe Street to the north, Spring Street to the east, and Spencer Street to the west. Cutting north–south through its center are the two main shopping thoroughfares, Swanston Street and Elizabeth Street. Cross streets between these major thoroughfares include Bourke Street Mall, a pedestrian-only shopping promenade. If you continue south along Swanston Street and over the river, it turns into St. Kilda Road, which runs to the coast. Melbourne's various urban "villages," including South Yarra, Richmond, Carlton, and Fitzroy, surround the city center. The seaside suburb of St. Kilda is known for its diverse restaurants.

Introducing the Neighbourhoods

City Center

Bordered by Flinders, Latrobe, Spring, and Spencer streets, the city center has good shopping and cafes, and in recent years an active nightlife has sprung up with the opening of funky bars and restaurants playing live and recorded music to suit all ages. The city center's landmark is the ornate Flinders Street Station, with its dome and clock tower, flanked by the modern Federation Square precinct.

Chinatown

Centered on Little Bourke Street, between Swanston and Exhibition streets, this is Australia's oldest permanent Chinese settlement, dating from the 1850s, when boardinghouses catered to Chinese prospectors lured by gold rushes. Plenty of cheap restaurants crowd its alleyways.

Carlton

Carlton's fame stems from the many Italian restaurants that line Lygon Street (although the quality of the food varies). It's the home of the University of Melbourne, so there's a strong student population. From Bourke Street Mall, it's about a 15-minute walk to the restaurant strip.

Fitzroy

Bohemian and a funky, Fitzroy is about 2km (1¼ miles) north of the city center. Students and artists hang out here, with Brunswick Street's cheap restaurants, busy cafes, late-night bookshops, art galleries, and pubs as the hub. Johnston Street is a growing Spanish quarter with tapas bars, flamenco restaurants, and Spanish clubs.

Richmond

One of Melbourne's earliest settlements, Richmond is noted for its multi-cultural quarter, historic streets, and back lanes. Victoria Street is "little Vietnam," and Bridge Road is a discount-fashion precinct.

Southgate and Southbank

This flashy entertainment district on the banks of the Yarra River opposite Flinders Street Station (linked by several pedestrian bridges) is home to the Crown Casino, Australia's largest gaming venue. Southbank has restaurants, bars, cafes, nightclubs, cinemas, and designer shops galore. On the city side of the river is the Melbourne Aquarium. All are a ten-minute stroll from Flinders Street Station.

Docklands

Not far from the city center, this former industrial area has become the biggest development in Melbourne. NewQuay, on the waterfront, has a range of restaurants, shops, and cinemas. Next door is the 52,000-seat Telstra Dome stadium, home to Australian-rules football.

St. Kilda

Hip, bohemian, and shabby-chic, this bayside suburb (6km/3¾ miles south of the city center) has Melbourne's highest concentration of restaurants, ranging from glitzy to cheap, as well as some superb cake shops and delis. The Esplanade hugs a slim beach, lined by palm trees, with a historic pier and is the scene of a lively arts-and-crafts market on Sundays. Acland Street is home to many restaurants and cake shops. Check out Luna Park, one of the world's oldest fun parks, built in 1912, and ride the historic wooden roller coaster.

South Yarra/Prahan

This posh part of town abounds with boutiques, cinemas, nightclubs, and galleries. Chapel Street is famous for its fashion houses, while Commercial Road is popular with the gay and lesbian community. Off Chapel Street in Prahan is Greville Street, an enclave of retro boutiques and music outlets. Every Sunday from noon to 5 p.m. the Greville Street Market offers arts, crafts, old clothes, and jewelry.

South Melbourne

One of the city's oldest working-class districts, South Melbourne is known for its historic buildings, pubs, hotels, and markets.

The River District

The Yarra River runs southeast past the Royal Botanic Gardens and near other attractions such as the Victorian Arts Centre, the National Gallery of Victoria, and the Melbourne Cricket Ground. Birrarung Marr is the first new major parkland in Melbourne in over 100 years.

Williamstown

This outer waterfront suburb has a rich architectural heritage, which centers on Ferguson Street and Nelson Place. On the Strand overlooking the sea is a line of bistros and restaurants, and a World War II warship museum. Take the ferry from Southgate or St. Kilda Pier.

Finding Information after You Arrive

The first stop on any visitor's itinerary should be the **Melbourne Visitor Centre,** Federation Square, Swanston and Flinders streets (☎ **03/9658 9658;** www.thatsmelbourne.com.au). The center serves as a one-stop shop for tourism information, accommodations and tour bookings, event ticketing, public transport information, and ticket sales. Also here are an ATM, Internet terminals, and interactive multimedia providing information on Melbourne and Victoria. The center is open daily from 9 a.m. to 6 p.m. (except Good Friday and Dec 25). The **Melbourne Greeter Service** also operates from the Melbourne Visitor Centre. This service is available in 15 languages and connects visitors to local volunteers who offer free one-on-one, half-day orientation tours of the city. Book at least three days in advance (☎ **03/9658 9658**) if you can. The Melbourne Visitor Centre also operates staffed information booths in Bourke Street Mall, between Swanston and Elizabeth streets.

✔ You'll also find information services at **Information Victoria,** 356 Collins St. (☎ **1300/366 356** in Australia).

✔ In the central city area, also look for Melbourne's **City Ambassadors** — people, usually volunteers, who give tourist information and directions. They'll be wearing bright red shirts and caps.

✔ Good Web sites about the city include **CitySearch Melbourne** (http://melbourne.citysearch.com.au), as well as the official City of Melbourne site (www.melbourne.vic.gov.au) and the official tourism site for the city (www.visitmelbourne.com). Also worth a look are locally run sites www.onlymelbourne.com.au and www.thatsmelbourne.com.au.

Getting Around Melbourne

By tram

Melbourne has the oldest tram network in the world. Trams are an essential part of the city, and a cultural icon. Several hundred trams run over 325km (202 miles) of track. Instead of phasing out this non-smoggy method of transport, Melbourne is expanding the network.

The cheapest tram travel within the city center is with a **City Saver ticket,** which costs A$2.30 (US$1.85/£0.90) adults, A$1.30 (US$1.05/£0.50) children, for a single journey. Or you can buy a **2-Hour Metcard,** good for unlimited transport on buses or trams for up to two hours to all the attractions and suburbs listed in this book, for A$3.20 (US$2.55/£1.30) adults, A$1.90 (US$1.50/£0.75) children.

If you plan to pack in the sightseeing, try the **Zone 1 Metcard Daily ticket,** which allows travel on all transport (trams and trains) within the city and close surrounding suburbs mentioned in this chapter from 5:30 a.m. to midnight (when transportation stops). It costs A$6.10 (US$4.90/£2.45) adults, A$3.20 (US$2.55/£1.30) children.

Buy single-trip and two-hour tram tickets at ticket machines on trams, ticket offices (such as at the tram terminal on Elizabeth Street, near Flinders Street), at most newsdealers, and at Metcard vending machines at many railway stations. A Metcard must be validated by the Metcard Validator machine on the tram, on the station platform, or on the bus before each journey; the only exception to this is the 2-Hour Metcard purchased from a vending machine on a tram, which is automatically validated for that journey only. Vending machines on trams only accept coins — but give change — while larger vending machines at train stations accept coins and paper money and give change up to A$10 (US$8/£4).

You can pick up a **free route map** from the Melbourne Visitor Centre, Federation Square, or the Met Information Centre, 103 Elizabeth St., at the corner of Collins Street (☎ **13 16 38** in Australia; www.metlink melbourne.com.au), which is open Monday through Friday from 8:30 a.m. to 4:30 p.m., and Saturday from 9 a.m. to 1 p.m.

The **City Circle Tram** is the best way to get around the center of Melbourne — and it's free. The burgundy-and-cream trams travel a circular route between all the major central attractions, and past shopping malls and arcades. The trams run, in both directions, every 12 minutes between 10 a.m. and 6 p.m., except Good Friday (Fri before Easter) and December 25. The trams run along all the major thoroughfares including Flinders and Spencer streets. Burgundy signs mark City Circle Tram stops.

Normal trams stop at green-and-gold tram-stop signs, sometimes in the middle of the road (so beware of oncoming traffic!). To get off the tram, press the red button near handrails or pull the cord above your head.

By bus

The free **Melbourne City Tourist Shuttle** operates buses that pick up and drop off at 15 stops around the city, including the Melbourne Museum, Queen Victoria Market, Immigration Museum, Southbank Arts Precinct, the Shrine of Remembrance and Botanic Gardens, Chinatown, and Flinders Lane, among others. You can hop on and off during the day. The bus runs every 15 minutes from 10 a.m. until 4 p.m. daily, taking in many of Melbourne's attractions.

By taxi

Cabs are plentiful in the city, but hailing one may be difficult in the city center late on Friday and Saturday night. Taxi companies include **Silver Top** (☎ **13 10 08**), **Embassy** (☎ **13 17 55**), and **Yellow Cabs** (☎ **13 22 27**).

By car

Driving in Melbourne can be challenging. Roads can be confusing, there are trams everywhere, and there is a strange rule about turning right from the left lane at major intersections in the downtown center (which leaves the left-hand lane free for oncoming trams and through traffic). Here, you must wait for the lights to turn amber before turning. Also, you must always stop behind a tram if it stops, because passengers usually step directly into the road. Add to this the general lack of parking and expensive hotel valet parking, and you'll know why it's better to get on a tram instead. For road rules, pick up a copy of the Victorian Road Traffic handbook from bookshops or from a **Vic Roads** office (☎ **13 11 71** for the nearest office).

Major car rental companies, all with offices at Melbourne Airport, include **Avis,** 8 Franklin St. (☎ **03/9663 6366**); **Budget,** 398 Elizabeth St. (☎ **03/9203 4844**); **Hertz,** 10 Dorcas St., South Melbourne (☎ **13 30 39** or 03/9698 2444); and **Thrifty,** 390 Elizabeth St. (☎ **1300/367 227**). Expect to pay at least A$40 (US$32/£16) per day for a small car.

By boat

Melbourne River Cruises (☎ **03/8610 2600;** www.melbcruises.com.au) offers a range of boat trips up and down the Yarra River, taking about 75 minutes. It's an interesting way to get a feel for the city, and the tours include commentaries. Tours cost A$20 (US$16/£8) adults, A$11 (US$8.80/£4.40) kids, A$50 (US$40/£20) families of four. Or you can combine both up- and down-river tours for A$34 (US$27/£14) adults, A$19 (US$15/£7.60) kids, A$86 (US$69/£34) families. Call ahead to confirm cruise departure times, because they change. Pick up tickets from the blue Melbourne River Cruises kiosks at the Federation Square riverfront (opposite Flinders Street Station).

Secrets of the seasons

Melbourne's weather is notorious. "Four seasons in one day" is the stereotype, but it's not always true. Summers can be excruciatingly hot, and winter can bring snow to the suburbs. A day may start out sunny and mild and end with a hailstorm — or vice versa. That's the beauty of it, but you have to be prepared. Melbourne's residents love its changing seasons, with balmy summer days, spectacular autumn colors, and crisp winter days. With Victoria officially in drought, Melbourne may look dry and you may be surprised to find people rejoicing when (or if) it rains.

Staying in Style

Getting a room is generally easy on weekends in Melbourne, where many hotels are busy with business travelers on weekdays. But advance bookings are recommended for whenever Melbourne is hosting a major event, such as the Melbourne Cup, the Grand Prix, or the Australian Open tennis tournament. Hostels in bayside St. Kilda tend to fill up quickly in December and January as holidaymakers hit the sands.

To feel right in the heart of the action, stay in the city center, which buzzes day and night. Another option is the inner-city suburbs, which all have good street life, restaurants, and pubs — and are just a quick tram ride from the city center. If you arrive without booked accommodations, contact either of the **travelers' information desks (☎ 03/9297 1805)** in the international airport terminal, open daily from 6 a.m. to the last flight. Or try the **Best of Victoria** booking service, Federation Square (**☎ 1300/780 045** or 03/9928 0000), open weekdays from 9 a.m. to 6 p.m. and weekends from 9 a.m. to 5 p.m.

The top hotels

Adelphi Hotel
$$$–$$$$ City Centre

It may be worth staying in this designer boutique hotel, a minute's walk from the city center, for the experience of taking a dip in its top-floor 25m (82-ft.) lap pool, which juts out from the end of the building and overhangs the streets. The pool has a glass bottom, so you can watch pedestrians below. The 34 rooms are similarly modern, with colorful leather seating and lots of burnished metal. Deluxe rooms differ from the so-called Premier King rooms in that they come with a bathtub. Executive rooms come with a separate lounge. Within the hotel is **Ezard,** a well-regarded restaurant offering contemporary Australian fare.

See map p. 203. 187 Flinders Lane, Melbourne, VIC 3000. ☎ 1800/800 177 in Australia, or 03/9650 7555. Fax: 03/9650 2710. www.adelphi.com.au. *Rack rates: A$560 (US$448/£224) Premier King room, A$610 (US$488/£244) deluxe double, A$1,250 (US$1,000/£500) executive suite. Rates include breakfast. AE, DC, MC, V.*

Central Melbourne Hotels and Dining

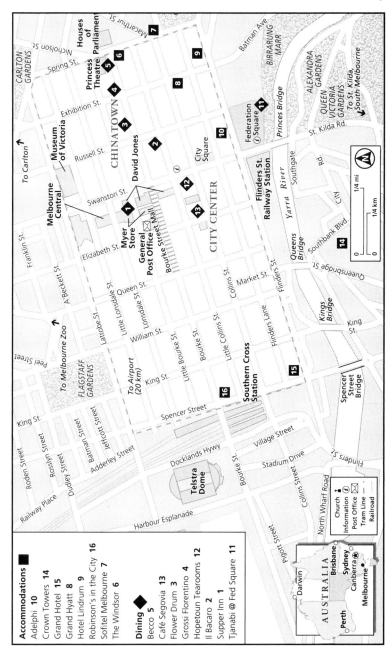

Accommodations ■
Adelphi **10**
Crown Towers **14**
Grand Hotel **15**
Grand Hyatt **8**
Hotel Lindrum **9**
Robinson's in the City **16**
Sofitel Melbourne **7**
The Windsor **6**

Dining ◆
Becco **5**
Café Segovia **13**
Flower Drum **3**
Grossi Florentino **4**
Hopetoun Tearooms **12**
Il Bacaro **2**
Supper Inn **1**
Tjanabi @ Fed Square **11**

The Como Melbourne
$$$–$$$$ **South Yarra**

The Como basks in its reputation for excellent service and great accommodations, which include studio rooms, open-plan suites (all with spa tubs, some with private offices and/or wet bars), one- or two-bedroom suites (some with an office), and penthouse and executive suites (split level, with oversize spa tubs). Rooms are large — at least 40 sq. m (431 sq. ft.) — and the bathrooms have a bath menu and a rubber duck for you to take home. Some suites have a private Japanese garden, and the Como Suite has a grand piano. The health club is brightly painted and the pool has a wonderful retractable roof.

630 Chapel St., South Yarra, VIC 3141. ☎ *1800/033 400 in Australia, or 03/9825 2222; 800-552-6844 in the U.S. and Canada; 0800/389 7791 in the U.K. Fax: 03/9824 1263.* www. mirvachotels.com.au. *Rack rates: A$295 (US$236/£118) studio, A$335 (US$268/ £134) open-plan suite, A$375 (US$300/£150) 1-bedroom suite; extra person A$30 (US$24/£12). AE, DC, MC, V.*

Crown Towers
$$$–$$$$ **Southbank**

Crown Towers is part of the Crown Casino complex, on the banks of the Yarra River. Entry to the 482-room hotel is through a glittering lobby, paved in black marble. The complex has an enormous collection of gambling machines (called *pokies* in Australia), as well as gaming tables. Upstairs in the hotel, standard guest rooms are cozy. Superior guest rooms occupy floors 5 to 15, and those above the tenth floor have spectacular city views. Deluxe rooms, which run up to the 28th floor, are similar, and all have great views. Rooms above the 28th floor are part of Crown's Crystal Club, which offers club lounge services. From the 32nd floor upward are the luxury villas. **Crown Casino** offers 24-hour gambling. The 900-seat Showroom features live entertainment nightly; a 14-screen cinema complex and three cabaret theaters provide additional activities. There are plenty of eateries and designer shops around here, too.

See map p. 203. 8 Whiteman St., Southbank, Melbourne, VIC 3006. ☎ *1800/811 653 in Australia, or 03/9292 6868. Fax: 03/9292 6299.* www.crowntowers.com.au. *Rack rates: A$335–A$455 (US$268–US$364/£134–£182) double, A$525–A$600 (US$420– US$480/£210–£240) double suite, A$1,200 (US$960/£480) 2-bedroom suite, from A$1,250 (US$1,000/£500) villa; extra person A$55 (US$44/£22). Children under 13 stay free in parent's room. AE, DC, MC, V.*

Grand Hotel
$$$–$$$$ **City Centre**

This heritage-listed building is striking for its remarkable scale and imposing Italianate facade. Building started on the six-story site in 1887, and additions were still being made in 1958. It became a hotel in 1997 and is now managed by Sofitel. Suites have plush red Pullman carpets and a full kitchen with a dishwasher; the one-bedroom loft suites have European-style espresso machines, CD player, a second TV in the bedroom, and great views over the new Docklands area beyond — though rooms are whisper quiet. All rooms are similar but vary in size; some have balconies. Many suites are split-level, with bedrooms on the second floor.

See map p. 203. 33 Spencer St., Melbourne, VIC 3000. ☎ *1300/361 455 in Australia, or 03/9611 4567. Fax: 03/9611 4655.* www.grandhotelsofitel.com.au. *Rack rates: A$215–A$459 (US$172–US$367/£86–£184) studio suite, A$235–A$479 (US$188–US$383/£94–£192) 1-bedroom suite, A$364–A$590 (US$291–US$472/£146–£236) 2-bedroom suite, A$800 (US$640/£320) 3-bedroom suite; extra person A$74 (US$59/£30). Children under 14 stay free in parent's room. AE, DC, MC, V.*

Grand Hyatt
$$$–$$$$ City Centre

The Grand Hyatt is a glamorous affair — the tower is infused with 24-carat gold — in the best part of town, a short walk from Swanston Street, Elizabeth Street, Chinatown, and public transport. The 548 rooms are large and luxurious, and come with a nice-size marble bathroom and all the details you'd expect from a five-star establishment. The hotel's three diplomatic suites feature floor to ceiling windows that overlook the Botanic Gardens and Yarra River. The suites' bathrooms boast sunken spa tubs, saunas, and rain showers. Prices vary with the view over the city, but the best values are the Grand Club rooms, for which the rate includes evening cocktails, canapés, afternoon tea, and full breakfast in the Grand Club lounge. The hotel's gymnasium and fitness center is Australia's largest hotel gym, and there's also a new day spa offering the usual treatments as well as therapeutic treatments to combat jet lag.

See map p. 203. 123 Collins St., Melbourne, VIC 3000. ☎ *13 12 34 in Australia, or 03/9657 1234; 800-492-8804 in the U.S. and Canada. Fax: 03/9650 3491.* www.melbourne. grand.hyatt.com. *Rack rates: A$280 (US$224/£112) Hyatt Guest double, A$350 (US$280/£140) Grand Club double, A$430 (US$344/£172) suite; extra person A$55 (US$44/£22). Children under 12 stay free in parent's room. AE, DC, MC, V.*

Hotel Lindrum
$$$–$$$$ City Centre

If you like your hotels stylish and contemporary, then the Hotel Lindrum is for you. It's typical of the new wave of modern hotels that emphasize trendy design and have features like broadband access in the rooms and Wi-Fi in the lobby. Standard rooms, if you can call them that, have a queen-size bed or two singles, lots of hardwood, soft lighting, and forest greens — and even a CD player. Superior rooms have king-size beds and lovely polished wood floorboards, and deluxe rooms have wonderful views across to the Botanic Gardens through large bay windows. The hotel boasts a smart restaurant, a billiard room, and a bar with an open fire.

See map p. 203. 26 Flinders St., Melbourne, VIC 3000. ☎ *03/9668 1111.* www.hotel lindrum.com.au. *Rack rates: A$410 (US$328/£164) standard double, A$450 (US$360/£180) superior room, A$460 (US$368/£184) deluxe room, A$500 (US$400/£200) suite. AE, DC, MC, V.*

Sofitel Melbourne
$$$–$$$$ **City Centre**

This luxury hotel, in the best area of Collins Street, is a short walk from the major shopping and business district. The hotel has a glass-topped atrium that allows natural light to flood in and a bar with wonderful city views on the 35th floor. Breakfasts in **Café La** are fabulous, and come with views. Rooms are large and pleasant. They come with a flat-screen TV, the latest high-tech gizmos, and comfortable king-size beds. A new executive lounge was opened in 2007. The service is impressive.

See map p. 203. 25 Collins St., Melbourne, VIC 3000. ☎ *03/9653 0000. Fax: 03/9650 4261.* www.sofitelmelbourne.com.au. *Rack rates: A$350 (US$280/£140) double, A$430 (US$344/£172) suite; extra person A$55 (US$44/£22). 1 child under 12 stays free in parent's room. AE, DC, MC, V.*

The Windsor
$$$–$$$$ **City Centre**

The Windsor is Australia's only surviving authentic "grand" hotel. It opened in 1883 and was restored to its original condition by Oberoi Hotels International. This upper-crust establishment oozes sophistication and has hosted such guests as Lauren Bacall, Muhammad Ali, and Omar Sharif. The lobby is luxuriously carpeted and the staff friendly and efficient. Standard rooms are comfortable, with high ceilings and tasteful furnishings. Each has a good-size bathroom. Deluxe rooms are twice as big, and many have views of Parliament House and the Melbourne Cathedral across the way. Suites are huge and furnished with antiques. Guests can choose from ten types of pillows, including an aromatherapy version filled with rose petals and herbs. You may want to take a traditional "high tea," in the 111 Spring St. restaurant on weekdays from 3:30 to 5:30 p.m.

See map p. 203. 103 Spring St., Melbourne, VIC 3000. ☎ *1800/033 100 in Australia, or 03/9633 6000. Fax: 03/9633 6001.* www.thewindsor.com.au. *Rack rates: A$205– A$295 (US$164–US$236/£82–£118) double, A$405–A$1,350 (US$324–US$1,080/£162– £540) double suite; extra person from A$55 (US$44/£22). AE, DC, MC, V.*

The runner-up hotels

Cotterville

$$ **Toorak**   Warm hosts, friendly dogs, elegant courtyard gardens, and a home filled with art and music. All this inside a beautifully restored terrace house. You'll likely go home fast friends with your hosts and their two schnauzer dogs. You can join them for "happy hour" drinks at 5 p.m. and for an extra A$40 (US$32/£16) per person (and advance notice), Howard will whip up a three-course gourmet dinner. There are only two guest rooms (with a shared bathroom), so book ahead. *204 Williams Rd., Toorak, Melbourne, VIC 3142.* ☎ *1300/301 630 in Australia, 03/9826 9105, or 0409/900 807 mobile.* www.cotterville.com. *Rack rates: A$ 130 (US$ 104/£52) single, A$ 160 (US$ 128/£64) double. Weekly rates available. Rates include breakfast. MC, V.*

Georgian Court Guest House

$$ **East Melbourne** The Georgian Court's appearance hasn't changed much since it was built in 1910; the sitting and dining rooms have high ceilings and an old-world atmosphere. The 31 guest rooms are simply furnished, some with en-suite bathrooms, others with private bathrooms in the hallway. One room has a queen-size bed and a Jacuzzi. The Georgian Court is set in a shady tree-lined street, a 15-minute stroll through the Fitzroy and Treasury Gardens from the city center. *21 George St., East Melbourne, VIC 3002.* ☎ *03/9419 6353.* Fax: 03/9416 0895. www.georgiancourt. com.au. *Rack rates: A$ 109 (US$ 87/£44) double without bathroom, A$ 129 (US$ 103/ £52) double with bathroom, A$ 159 (US$ 127/£64) queen spa room; A$ 10–A$ 20 (US$ 8–US$ 16/£4–£8) surcharge during busy periods; extra adult A$ 20 (US$ 16/£8); extra child under 14 A$ 12 (US$ 9.60/£4.80). Rates include breakfast. AE, DC, MC, V.*

The Hatton

$$–$$$ **South Yarra** This Italianate mansion, built as a hotel in 1902, has been restored and updated to become a sophisticated and contemporary boutique hotel. Many of the original features are still in place, and the 20 guest rooms have been fashioned from the original structure, making each an individual space. Clever combinations of old and new — antiques alongside modern art pieces specially commissioned — give it an unusual but welcoming atmosphere. *65 Park St., South Yarra, VIC 3141.* ☎ *03/9868 4800.* Fax: 03/9868 4899. www.hatton.com.au. *Rack rates: A$ 195– A$ 220 (US$ 156–US$ 176/£78–£88) double, A$ 300 (US$ 240/£120) suite; extra person or crib A$ 30 (US$ 24/£12). Rates include continental breakfast. AE, DC, MC, V.*

Dining Out

Melbourne's diverse population ensures a great selection of international cuisines. Chinatown offers Chinese, Malaysian, Thai, Indonesian, Japanese, and Vietnamese fare, often at bargain prices. Carlton has plenty of Italian cuisine, but the outdoor restaurants on Lygon Street aim at unsuspecting tourists and can be overpriced and disappointing. Richmond is crammed with Greek and Vietnamese restaurants, and Fitzroy has cheap Asian, Turkish, Mediterranean, and vegetarian food. To see and be seen, head to Chapel Street or Toorak Road in South Yarra, or to St. Kilda, where you can join the throng dining out along Fitzroy and Acland streets. Most of the cheaper places in Melbourne are BYO (bring your own wine or beer).

Smoking is banned by law in cafes and restaurants.

Becco
$$ **City Center** **MODERN ITALIAN**

Tucked away in a lane, this award-winning favorite of Melbournians is unlikely to disappoint. You find stylish service and customers, and food that mixes Italian favors with Australian flair — things like roast duck with muscatel and grappa sauce, tasty pasta dishes, or the specials, which your waiter will fill you in on. For lighter meals, there's a bar menu of equally tempting dishes from A$5.50 to A$16 (US$4.40–US$13/£2.20–£6.40). Upstairs is the cool late-night bar, Bellavista Social Club.

See map p. 203. 11–25 Crossley St. (near Bourke Street). ☎ *03/9663 3000. Main courses: A$26–A$40 (US$21–US$32/£10–£16). AE, DC, MC, V. Open: Mon–Sat noon to 3 p.m. and 6–11 p.m., Sun 5:30–10 p.m.*

Brunetti
$$$ **Carlton   TRATTORIA/PASTICCERIA**

There will be crowds around the cake counters — of that you can be sure. And you can also be assured that it'll be worth lining up and waiting. If you can get past the enormous mouthwatering array of excellent cakes on display, head to the a la carte restaurant section for some authentic Italian food, done very well. Or just pop in for coffee and cake, or a gelato. If you can't get to Carlton, cafe-style Brunetti City Square is on the corner of Swanston Street and Flinders Lane in the city.

198–204 Faraday St., Carlton. ☎ *03/9347 2801. Main courses: A$17–A$28 (US$14–US$22/£6.80–£11), with a minimum charge of A$18 (US$14/£7) per person. AE, DC, MC, V. Open: Mon–Fri 7 a.m.–10 p.m., Sat 8 a.m.–10 p.m., Sun 8 a.m.–1 p.m. Tram: 1, 15, 21, or 22 traveling north on Swanston Street.*

Café Segovia
$$–$$$ **City Center   CAFE**

Tucked into an atmospheric laneway in the heart of the city, Café Segovia has a winning combination of friendly staff, simple cafe food, and an attractive buzz. It has an intimate interior, and there's also seating outside in the arcade, but you have to come early at lunchtime to nab a chair. The food is light fare such as focaccias, cakes, and light meals (but the servings are generous). There's live music Thursday and Friday, and it's one of our favorite places to meet friends in the city.

See map p. 203. 33 Block Place. ☎ *03/9650 2373. Main courses: A$16–A$27 (US$13–US$22/£6.40–£11). AE, DC, MC, V. Open: Mon–Sat 8 a.m.–11 p.m., Sun 9 a.m.–5 p.m.*

Cicciolina
$$–$$$$ **St. Kilda   CONTEMPORARY**

We'd like to keep Cicciolina a secret, but it's too late. Because you can't make reservations, it's sometimes hard to get a table, but we'd be depriving you of a terrific night out or a wonderful lunch if we said that you shouldn't bother trying. If you're looking for somewhere intimate, crowded, well-run, that has superb but simple food, look no further. You may have to wait for your table (have a drink in the bar, and they'll call you), but it'll be worth the wait for delights such as yellowfin tuna carpaccio soused in lime-infused olive oil, or — a favorite — spaghettini tossed with spinach, chilies, and oil.

130 Acland St., St. Kilda. ☎ 03/9525 3333. Main courses: A$14–A$37 (US$11–US$30/ £5.60–£15). AE, DC, MC, V. Open: Daily noon to 11 p.m. (until 10 p.m. on Sun). Tram: 16 from Swanston Street, or 94 or 96 from Bourke Street.

Donovans
$$$$ St. Kilda   CONTEMPORARY

Watch the sun go down over St. Kilda Beach, with a glass in hand, from the veranda at Donovans, and you'll find it the perfect way to end the day. Gail and Kevin Donovan have transformed a 1920s bathing pavilion into a welcoming restaurant designed to make you feel as though you're in a private beach house. A log fire, book cases, scattered cushions, coffee-table books, a jazz soundtrack, and the sound of water on the beach complete the picture. The menu includes a mind-boggling array of dishes, many big enough for two. Chef Robert Castellani's trademarks include steamed mussels, linguine with seafood, and stuffed squid.

40 Jacka Blvd., St. Kilda. ☎ 03/9534 8221. Reservations recommended. Main courses: A$19–A$48 (US$15–US$38/£7.60–£19). AE, DC, MC, V. Open: Daily noon to 10:30 p.m. Tram: 12 from Collins Street, 16 from Swanston Street, or 94 or 96 from Bourke Street.

Flower Drum
$$$$ Chinatown   CANTONESE

Be prepared to splash out if you dine at this upscale restaurant just off Little Bourke Street in Chinatown. Take a slow elevator up to the restaurant, which has widely spaced tables for privacy. The chefs are extremely creative and use ingredients they find in the markets each day, and the best idea is to take your waiter's advice on what to order. The signature dish is Peking duck. King crab dumplings in soup are a great starter, and you can also order more unusual (and expensive) dishes, such as abalone. The atmosphere is clubby and a bit old-fashioned; the service is superb.

See map p. 203. 17 Market Lane. ☎ 03/9662 3655. Reservations required. Main courses: A$30–A$45 (US$24–US$36/£12–£18). AE, DC, MC, V. Open: Mon–Sat noon to 2:30 p.m. and 6–10 p.m., Sun 6–10:30 p.m.

Grossi Florentino
$$$$ City Center   ITALIAN

This is possibly the best Italian restaurant in Melbourne — and that's saying something. Owned and managed by the Grossi family, it has a casual bistro downstairs, next to the Cellar Bar (where you can pick up a bowl of pasta for less than A$20 (US$16/$8); upstairs is the fine-dining restaurant, with its chandeliers and murals reflecting the Florentine way of life. The signature dishes are wet-roasted suckling lamb and suckling pig, and you also find risotto, seafood, and steak dishes. Save some room for the chocolate soufflé.

See map p. 203. 80 Bourke St. ☎ *03/9662 1811. Fax: 03/9662 2518.* www.grossi florentino.com. *Reservations recommended. Main courses: A$35–A$65 (US$28–US$52/£14–£26). AE, DC, MC, V. Open: Mon–Fri noon to 3 p.m., Mon–Sat 6–11 p.m.*

Hopetoun Tearooms
$ City Center   CAFE

The first cup of coffee was poured in this Melbourne institution in 1892 — and they've just kept coming. It's prim and civilized, with green-and-white Regency wallpaper and marble tables. You're here for the tea (or coffee) and the excellent cakes. Scones, croissants, and grilled food are also available. A minimum charge of A$5 (US$4/£2) per person applies from noon to 2 p.m.

See map p. 203. Shops 1 and 2, Block Arcade, 280–282 Collins St. ☎ */fax 03/9650 2777. Main courses: A$4.50–A$9.50 (US$3.60–US$7.60/£1.80–£3.80), sandwiches A$4.50–A$6.50 (US$3.60–US$5.20/£2.90–£4.15), focaccias A$7–A$8.50 (US$5.60–US$6.80/£2.80–£3.40). AE, DC, MC, V. Open: Mon–Thurs 8:30 a.m.–5 p.m., Fri 8:30 a.m.–6 p.m., Sat 10 a.m.–3:30 p.m.*

Il Bacaro
$$$$ City Center   ITALIAN

At Il Bacaro, you'll feel as if you're in a corner of Venice. Dominated by a horseshoe-shaped bar, it's packed with small tables and waiters carrying dishes like organic baby chicken wrapped in prosciutto, filled with pumpkin and ricotta, served on an oyster mushroom ragu. The pasta dishes and the risotto of the day go down well, as do the salad side dishes, and there's an excellent wine list. Lunchtimes can be crowded with local businesspeople.

See map p. 203. 168–170 Little Collins St. ☎ *03/9654 6778. Reservations recommended. Main courses: A$19–A$39 (US$15–US$31/£7.60–£16). AE, DC, MC, V. Open: Mon–Sat noon to 3 p.m. and 6–11 p.m.*

Mecca Bah
$$$ Docklands   MIDDLE EASTERN

The best way to order in this excellent Middle Eastern restaurant is to go for several of the *meze,* small plates of tasty delicacies. In the newish waterside precinct of Docklands, not far from the city center, Mecca Bah will impress you with its interesting cuisine. Mezes may be things like pastry filled with Middle Eastern cheeses, silverbeet rolls filled with chickpeas, rice, and herbs, or spicy lamb and pine nut boureks. There's also an interesting range of Turkish pizzas, and main courses including lamb or chicken tagines. The wine list is good and not too expensive.

55 Newquay Promenade, Docklands. ☎ *03/9642 1300.* www.meccabah.com. *Reservations recommended. Main courses: A$18–A$21 (US$14–US$17/£7.20–£8.40), meze plates A$6–A$12 (US$4.80–US$9.60/£2.40–4.80). AE, DC, MC, V. Open: Daily 11 a.m.–11 p.m. Tram: 30 or 48 from Latrobe or Swanston streets.*

Lentil As Anything

Vegetarian restaurant **Lentil As Anything** has a menu without prices, and a policy where you pay whatever you feel the meal and service are worth. It's not surprising that it's a hit. The food is organic, with noodles and vegetables and things like tofu, curries, and stir-fries. Before you leave, you put your money in the box. There are four Lentil restaurants in Melbourne — at Abbotsford (☎ **03/9419 6444**), St. Kilda (☎ **03/9534 5833**), and Brunswick (☎ **03/9388 0222**), where there is also **Lentil Africa** (☎ **03/9387 4647**), run by a local African women's cooperative. They take cash only. Opening hours vary between the restaurants, so check the Web site (www.lentilas anything.com).

Supper Inn
$$ City Center   CANTONESE

This is the real thing when it comes to Chinese food, and the best place to head if you get the munchies late at night. It's a friendly place with a mixed crowd of locals and tourists chowing down on such dishes as steaming bowls of congee (rice-based porridge), barbecued suckling pig, mud crab, or stuffed scallops.

See map p. 203. 15 Celestial Ave. ☎/fax 03/9663 4759. Reservations recommended. Main courses: A$11–A$22 (US$8.80–US$18/£4.40–£8.80). AE, DC, MC, V. Open: Daily 5:30 p.m.–2:30 a.m.

Tjanabi @ Fed Square
$$–$$$$ City Center   INDIGENOUS AUSTRALIAN

For a taste of what Aboriginal Australians have been eating for thousands of years, stop in at Tjanabi (it means "to celebrate") at Federation Square. Native produce, including plants, fruits, and berries, matched with quality Australian game (kangaroo, wild boar, barramundi, and the like) and fresh steaks from regional Victoria are on the menu. You find tastes of things like native pepper, lemon myrtle, roasted wattle seed, and saltbush leaves used in the dishes. A casual bistro is outside, and the bar serves Victorian wines and boutique beers. Aboriginal elder Carolyn Briggs has adorned the walls of her restaurant with contemporary Aboriginal artwork, in changing exhibitions. You can also book a 90-minute guided walking tour of indigenous Melbourne, followed by dinner.

See map p. 203. Federation Square. ☎ 03/9662 2155. www.tjanabi.com.au. Reservations recommended. Main courses: A$9–A$20 (US$7.20–US$16/£3.60–£8) in the bistro, A$28–A$34 (US$22–US$27/£11–£14) in the restaurant. AE, DC, MC, V. Open: Daily 11 a.m.–11 p.m. Restaurant closed Mon.

Exploring Melbourne

The top attractions

Federation Square

When you're "in" Federation Square (www.federationsquare.com.au), you'll appreciate what a great space it is. This is a place that polarizes Melbournians — they either love it or hate it. We're big fans. Visit on the weekend and you can see that it really works as a gathering place, with lots of events held in the amphitheatre. Restaurants and attractions are clustered around the open piazza, which is cobbled with misshapen paving. The architecture is made up of geometrical designs, and there's also an impressive glass atrium. "Fed Square," as the locals call it, is home to the **National Gallery of Victoria: The Ian Potter Centre–Australian Art** (see later in this section) and the **Australian Centre for the Moving Image (ACMI).** The National Gallery building contains the largest collection of Australian art in the country, including Aboriginal and Torres Strait Islander art. The ACMI has two state-of-the-art cinemas and areas where visitors can view movies, videos, and digital media.

See map p. 213. Corner of Flinders Street and St. Kilda Road, opposite Flinders Street Railway Station. Outdoor spaces are open 24 hours. Admission: Free, but charges apply for some special events and exhibitions.

Melbourne Museum

This is Australia's largest museum and one of its most interesting. Highlights include a blue whale skeleton, an indoor rain forest, and a brilliant insect and butterfly collection. Kids love the exhibits, including cockroaches, ant colonies, and spiders, as well as the interactive stuff and science displays, the Children's Museum, and the mummified remains of Australia's most famous racehorse, Phar Lap. Bunjikata is an award-winning Aboriginal and Torres Strait Islander Centre. The complex also includes an IMAX movie theatre.

11 Nicholson St., Carlton. ☎ 13 11 02 in Victoria, or 03/8341 7777. Admission: A$6 (US$4.80/£2.40) adults, free for children under 16. Open: Daily 10 a.m.–5 p.m. (except Good Friday and Dec 25). Tram: 86 or 96 to the Museum and Royal Exhibition Building tram stop at the corner of Nicholson and Gertrude streets, or the free City Circle Tram to Carlton Gardens.

National Galley of Victoria, International

The NGV International is a showcase for Australia's finest collections of international art, including works by Gainsborough, Constable, Bonnard, Delacroix, Van Dyck, El Greco, Monet, Manet, Magritte, and Rembrandt. Architecturally, the building is a masterpiece, with high ceilings, fabulous lighting, and great open spaces.

See map p. 213. 180 St. Kilda Rd. ☎ 03/8620 2222. www.ngv.vic.gov.au. Admission: Free admission to general collection; fees for some temporary exhibitions. Open:

Central Melbourne Attractions

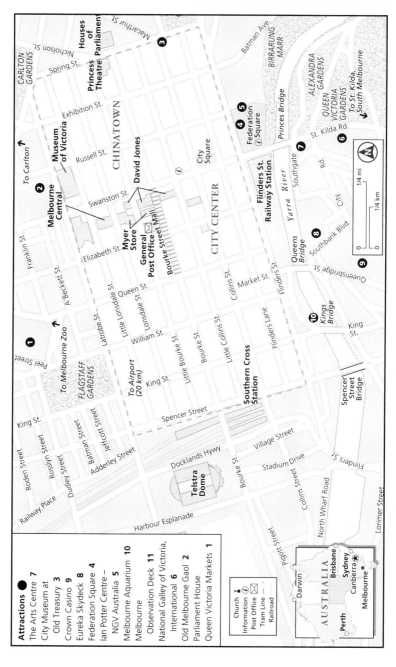

Attractions ●
The Arts Centre **7**
City Museum at
  Old Treasury **3**
Crown Casino **9**
Eureka Skydeck **8**
Federation Square **4**
Ian Potter Centre –
  NGV Australia **5**
Melbourne Aquarium **10**
Melbourne
  Observation Deck **11**
National Galley of Victoria,
  International **6**
Old Melbourne Gaol **2**
Parliament House
Queen Victoria Markets **1**

Church
Information ⓘ
Post Office ⊠
Tram Line —
Railroad —

Wed–Mon 10 a.m.–5 p.m. Closed Tues, Good Friday (Fri before Easter), Dec 25, and until 1 p.m. on Apr 25.

The Ian Potter Centre–NGV Australia

This fascinating gallery, featuring 20 rooms dedicated to Australian art, sits in the heart of Federation Square. Aboriginal art and colonial art collections are the centerpieces, but you find modern paintings here, too, and a constantly changing array of interesting exhibitions.

See map p. 213. Federation Square, Flinders Street. ☎ 03/8660 2222. www.ngv.vic. gov.au. *Admission: Free. Open: Tues–Sun 10 a.m.–5 p.m. Closed Mon (except public holidays), Good Friday (Fri before Easter), Dec 25, and until 1 p.m. on Apr 25.*

Old Melbourne Gaol

This historic old prison, with its tiny cells and collection of death masks and artifacts of 19th-century prison life, is one of our favorite places to take visitors. Some 135 hangings took place here, including that of notorious bushranger Ned Kelly, in 1880. The scaffold where he was hanged still stands, and his gun and a suit of armor used by a member of his gang are on display. Profiles of prisoners give a fascinating perspective of what it was like to be locked up here until the jail closed in 1929. Each Saturday, free performances of *The Real Ned Kelly Story — Such a Life* are held at 12:30 p.m. and 2 p.m. Chilling night tours run every Monday, Wednesday, Friday, and Saturday, where you can experience the jail by candlelight with a "hangman" who recounts tales from the jail, its inmates, and his infamous art. Not for the fainthearted or children under 12. Tickets for the tours, available from **Ticketek** (☎ **13 28 49;** www.ticketek.com.au), cost A$25 (US$20/£10) adults, A$17 (US$14/£6.80) children under 15. Allow one hour or more.

See map p. 213. Russell Street. ☎ 03/9663 7228. Admission: A$13 (US$10/£5.20) adults, A$7.50 (US$6/£3) children, A$34 (US$27/£14) families. Open: Daily 9:30 a.m.–5 p.m. Closed Good Friday (Fri before Easter) and Dec 25. Tram: City Circle tram to corner of Russell and Latrobe streets.

Queen Victoria Market

This Melbourne institution has hundreds of indoor and outdoor stalls, where you can find anything from pets to vintage clothes. It's a bit cramped, and there's a lot of junk, but you'll get a real taste of Melbourne. Look for the delicatessen section and cheap eateries, and allow at least an hour to rummage about. The two-hour **Foodies Tour** of the market explores its food and heritage. It runs Tuesday, Thursday, Friday, and Saturday at 10 a.m. and costs A$28 (US$22/£11) per person, including sampling. Top chefs give cooking classes, costing A$75–A$80 (US$60–US$64/£30–£32) per session. Call ☎ **03/9320 5835** for reservations. **Night markets** are held every Wednesday from 5:30 to 10 p.m. in summer (from late Nov to late Mar, except the last week of Dec).

See map p. 213. Between Peel, Victoria, Elizabeth, and Therry streets on the northern edge of the city center. ☎ 03/9320 5822. www.qvm.com.au. *Open: Tues and Thurs 6 a.m.–2 p.m., Fri 6 a.m.–6 p.m., Sat 6 a.m.–3 p.m., Sun 9 a.m.–4 p.m. Closed Mon, Wed, and public holidays. Food stalls closed Sun.*

View from the top

Once Melbourne's highest lookout, the **Melbourne Observation Deck** now has hot competition in the bid to claim the city's best views. The new **Eureka Skydeck 88,** the highest public vantage point in the Southern Hemisphere, is on the 88th floor of the Eureka Tower, Riverside Quay, Southbank (☎ **03/9685 0188;** www.eurekatower. com.au). The viewing deck gives a 360-degree view of the city below from 285m (935 ft.) above ground. But it's not for those who have vertigo. And there's more to get your adrenaline pumping than just the view. Only the brave will enter a huge moving glass cube called **The Edge,** essentially a 6-ton horizontal elevator that moves from inside the walls of Skydeck 88, carrying 12 passengers out over the tower's east side. As the opaque glass cube reaches its full extension, the 45mm-thick (1¾-inch) glass becomes clear, giving passengers uninterrupted — and incredibly scary — views below, above, and to three sides. All this is accompanied by recorded sounds of creaking chains and breaking glass. Ticket prices for adults are A$17 (US$14/£6.80) adults, A$9 (US$7.20/ £3.60) children, plus an extra A$12 (US$9.60/£4.80) adults and A$8 (US$6.40/£3.20) children for the four-minute-long ride on The Edge. It's open daily from 10 a.m. to 10 p.m.

By contrast, the **Melbourne Observation Deck** on the 55th floor — that's 253m (830 ft.) above the street — of the Rialto Building, 525 Collins St. (☎ **03/9629 8222;** www. melbournedeck.com.au), now seems a bit tame. Admission is A$15 (US$12/£6) adults, A$8 (US$6.40/£3.20) children 5 to 15, A$40 (US$32/£16) families of six. It's open daily from 10 a.m. to 11 p.m.

More cool things to see and do

- The **City Museum at Old Treasury** (☎ **03/9651 2233**) tells the story of Melbourne through several permanent exhibits and a variety of changing ones. *Making Melbourne* tells the city's history, while *Built on Gold* shows how Melbourne was built using the profits from the gold rushes. Built in 1857, the Old Treasury Building is an imposing neoclassical sandstone structure that once housed precious metal from the Ballarat and Bendigo gold rushes. The building is on Spring Street (at the top of Collins Street). Admission is A$8.50 (US$6.80/£3.40) adults, A$5 (US$4/£2) children, A$18 (US$14/£7.20) families. It's open Monday through Friday from 9 a.m. to 5 p.m., weekends and public holidays from 10 a.m. to 4 p.m. Closed Good Friday (Fri before Easter) and December 25 and 26.

- The **Melbourne Aquarium** (☎ **03/9620 0999;** www.melbourne aquarium.com.au) features a Barrier Reef–type exhibit, some interesting jellyfish displays, and an enormous walk-through tank with larger fish, sharks, and rays. It's on the corner of Queens Wharf Road and Kings Street. Admission is A$24 (US$19/£9.60) adults, A$14 (US$11/£5.60) children 3 to 15, A$65 (US$52/£26) families of five. It's open daily from 9:30 a.m. to 6 p.m. Tram: City Circle.

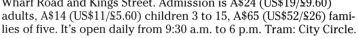

✔ **Melbourne Zoo** (☎ 03/9285 9300; www.zoo.org.au) was built in 1862 and is the oldest zoo in the world. There are 3,000 animals, including kangaroos, wallabies, echidnas, koalas, wombats, and platypuses. Most animals are in almost natural surroundings or well-tended gardens. Don't miss the butterfly house, with its thousands of colorful occupants; the free-flight aviary; the lowland gorilla exhibit; and the treetop orangutan exhibit. The zoo is on Elliott Avenue, Parkville, north of the city center. Admission is A$22 (US$18/£8.80) adults, A$11 (US$8.80/£4.40) children 4 to 15, A$52 (US$42/£21) families of four. It's open daily from 9 a.m. to 5 p.m. Free guided tours run daily from 10 a.m. to 3 p.m. Tram: 55 going north on William Street to stop 25; 19 from Elizabeth Street to stop 16 (then a short walk, following signs). Train: Royal Park Station.

Shopping the Local Stores

Australians regard Melbourne as the country's shopping capital — it has everything from fashion houses to major department stores and unusual souvenir shops. Start in the magnificent city arcades, such as the **Block Arcade** (between Collins and Little Collins streets), which has more than 30 shops, and the **Royal Arcade** (from Little Collins Street to the Bourke Street Mall). Then hit the courts and lanes around **Swanston Street** and the **Melbourne Central shopping complex** between Latrobe and Lonsdale streets. Next, fan out across the city, taking in **Chapel Street** in South Yarra, for its fashions, and **The Jam Factory,** 500 Chapel St., South Yarra (☎ 03/9860 8500), a series of buildings with a range of shops and food outlets, including a branch of Borders bookshop. Get there on tram no. 8 or 72 from Swanston Street. There's also **Toorak Road** in Toorak, for Gucci and other high-priced names; **Bridge Road** in Richmond, for budget fashions; **Lygon Street** in Carlton, for Italian fashion, footwear, and accessories; and **Brunswick Street** in Fitzroy, for a more alternative scene.

High-fashion boutiques line the eastern stretch of **Collins Street,** between the Grand Hyatt and the Hotel Sofitel, and **Chapel Street** in South Yarra. In addition, dozens of retail shops and factory outlets are around the city, many of them on **Bridge Road** near Punt Road and **Swan Street** near Church Street in Richmond. You find designer clothes at a fraction of the original price.

In the city, the hottest fashion center is the QV building, which takes up a block, bordered by Swanston, Russell, Lonsdale, and Little Lonsdale streets. Despite its size, it has a nice feel to it. This is where you find top Australian and international designers, tucked into QV's laneways. The premium fashion alley is Albert Coates Lane, where you find the likes of Christensen Copenhagen and Wayne Cooper.

Collins Street features most international labels as well as shoe heaven **Miss Louise,** 123 Collins St. (☎ 03/9654 7730). Nearby Flinders Lane has

earned style status with the likes of **Christine,** 181 Flinders Lane
(☎ **03/9654 2011**), where women faint over the accessories. Down
the road is **Little Collins Street,** another fashion-rat run. Look for local
labels **Bettina Liano** (☎ **03/9654 1912**), **Scanlan & Theodore**
(☎ **03/9650 6195**), and **Verve** (☎ **03/9639 5886**). **Alice Euphemia,**
37 Swanston St. (☎ **03/9650 4300**), also stocks upcoming Australian
and New Zealand designers.

For Aboriginal paintings and other indigenous arts and crafts, try the
Aboriginal Gallery of Dreamings, 73–77 Bourke St. Mall (☎ **03/9650
3277**), and **Original & Authentic Aboriginal Art,** 90 Bourke St.
(☎ **03/9663 5133;** www.authaboriginalart.com.au).

The Australian Geographic Shop has two city center stores, at Shop
253, Melbourne Central, 300 Lonsdale St. (☎ **03/8616 6725**), and in the
Galleria Shopping Plaza, Little Collins Street (☎ **03/9670 5813**). They
stock Australiana, including crafts, books, and various gadgets.

The city's two major department stores are **Myer** and **David Jones** (or
DJ's as it's known). Both span two city blocks and are separated into
men's and women's stores. David Jones, 310 Bourke St. Mall (☎ **03/9643
2222;** www.davidjones.com.au) has a fabulous food hall. Myer, 314
Bourke St. Mall (☎ **03/9661 1111;** www.myer.com.au), is the grande
dame of Melbourne's department stores, and has household goods, per-
fume, jewelry, and fashions, as well as a food section. It's a little less conservative than David Jones.

Serious shoppers may like to contact **Shopping Spree Tours**
(☎ **03/9596 6600;** www.shoppingspree.com.au), a company that
takes you to exclusive and alternative shopping venues, manufacturers,
and importers that you likely wouldn't find by yourself. Tours depart
Monday through Saturday (except holidays) at 8:30 a.m. and cost A$74
(US$59/£30) adults, A$35 (US$28/£14) children under 12. They'll pick
you up at hotels in the city center.

Living It Up after Dark

Finding out what's happening

The official government entertainment information site (www.melbourne.
vic.gov.au/events) shows "What's On" in the theater world for up to
two months in advance, as well as what's happening in dance, film,
comedy, music, exhibitions, sports, and tours. The best place to buy
tickets for everything from theater to major sporting events, and to
obtain details on schedules, is **Ticketmaster** (☎ **13 61 00** in Australia;
www.ticketmaster.com.au).

Raising the curtain on performing arts and music

Melbourne's performing-arts scene offers everything from offbeat productions to large-scale Broadway-style musicals. The city is also the home of prestigious festivals, with the annual **Melbourne Fringe Festival** (www.melbournefringe.com.au) and **Melbourne International Comedy Festival** (www.comedyfestival.com.au), attracting the best of Australian and international talent. Try to get tickets if you're in town during either festival, but keep in mind that hotels fill up fast at these times. Another good time to plan your visit is during late July to mid-August, when the **Melbourne International Film Festival** (www.melbournefilmfestival.com.au) is on. **The Arts Centre,** which you'll identify from the spire atop the Theatres Building, on the banks of the Yarra, is the city's leading performing arts complex, home to the State Theatre, the Playhouse, and the Fairfax Studio.

Buy half-price tickets for events including opera, dance, and drama, on the day of the performance from **Half-Tix** (www.halftixmelbourne.com) in the Melbourne Town Hall on Swanston Street. The booth is open Monday 10 a.m. to 2 p.m., Tuesday through Thursday 11 a.m. to 6 p.m., Friday 11 a.m. to 6:30 p.m., and Saturday 10 a.m. to 4 p.m. (also selling for Sun shows). Tickets must be purchased in person and in cash. Available shows are displayed on the booth door and on the Web site.

Theater

The Arts Centre, 100 St. Kilda Rd (☎ **1300/136 166** for tickets, or 03/9281 8000; www.theartscentre.net.au) is the focal point for most major theater events. The **State Theatre** seats 2,085 on three levels and hosts opera, ballet, musicals, and more. The **Playhouse** is a smaller venue that often books the Melbourne Theatre Company. The **Fairfax** is more intimate still, and is often used for experimental theater or cabaret. **Hamer Hall** is home of the Melbourne Symphony Orchestra and often host to visiting orchestras and many international stars. Guided tours of the complex are run at noon and 2:30 p.m. Monday through Saturday, and backstage tours are on Sundays at 12:15 p.m. Tours cost A$11 (US$8.80/£4.40) adults, A$28 (US$22/£11) families; A$14 (US$11/£5.60) per person on Sundays.

Buy tickets from the concierge in the foyer of the Theatres Building. Ticket prices vary depending on the event. The Box Office is open Monday through Saturday 9 a.m. to 9 p.m. in the Theatres Building.

Here are some of the other top venues in town:

- ✔ **The Comedy Club,** at the Athenaeum Theatre, 188 Collins St. (☎ **03/9650 6668**), is the place to see local and international comedy acts, musicals, and special shows. It offers a dinner and show Friday and Saturday for A$35 (US$28/£14). Discount ticket offers can bring the show-only price down to as low as A$7 (US$5.60/£2.80) sometimes, so ask what's on offer.

✔ **The Comedy Theatre,** 240 Exhibition St. (☎ **03/9299 4951**), seats more than 1,000 people, but with an ornate Spanish rococo interior, it still has an intimate feel. Plays and musicals usually fill the bill, but dance companies and comedians also appear.

✔ **The Forum Theatre,** 154 Flinders St. (☎ **03/9299 9700**), books well-known bands and international comedians. Seating is in cabaret-style booths, from which you can order drinks and meals.

✔ **Sidney Myer Music Bowl,** in King's Domain, off Alexandra Avenue, is a massive outdoor entertainment center, run by The Arts Centre. You'll come here in summer for opera, jazz, and ballet, and for ice-skating in the winter. Bookings are through Ticketmaster (☎ **1300/ 136 166**).

Checking out the club and bar scene

Some of Melbourne's best bars and clubs are hidden down atmospheric alleys. You'll find nightclubs of varying quality in the King Street area, but the city's best are unique, secluded bars and clubs. Sometimes you can follow the crowds and see what appeals to you; otherwise the following options are some of Melbourne's more enduring and appealing.

✔ **Young & Jackson,** at Flinders and Swanston streets (☎ **03/9650 3884;** www.youngandjacksons.com.au), is Melbourne's oldest pub. Whether you're stopping in for a drink or a meal in the stylish upstairs restaurant or bistro areas, head upstairs to see the nude *Chloe,* a famous painting brought to Melbourne from Paris for the Great Exhibition in 1880. The painting has a special place in the hearts of customers and Melbournians. The pub, built in 1853, started selling beer in 1861.

✔ For jazz fans, **Bennetts Lane Jazz Club,** 25 Bennetts Lane (☎ **03/9663 2856;** www.bennettslane.com) is one of the best in Australia. The back-lane location may be a little hard to find, but inside it's everything a jazz club should be. The best international players seek it out and the music is often exceptional and always varied. Open every night from 8:30 p.m. (music starts at 9:30 p.m.). The cover is A$12 (US$9.60/£4.80).

Crown Casino

Melbourne is home to Australia's largest casino, a plush affair that's open 24 hours. You'll find all the usual roulette and blackjack tables and so on, as well as an array of gaming machines. Crown Casino (or just "Crown"), Clarendon Street, Southbank (☎ **03/9292 6868;** www.crowncasino.com.au), is also a major venue for international headline acts, and there are around 25 restaurants and 11 bars on the premises, with more in the extended Southgate complex of which it's a part.

Bar Secrets

For an easy way of sorting out which bar may appeal to you, consult the cards. **Bar Secrets Melbourne** (www.bar-secrets.com) is a pack of 52 cards, each featuring one of the city's great drinking holes. The cards have pictures of, and information (including maps) on, the hippest and most unusual pubs and bars in town. Pick a few at random, and your night is quickly planned. The cards cost A$9.95 (US$7.95/£4) at bookshops and newsdealers. They're worth seeking out. You'll find yourself weaving up alleyways, climbing into lofts and down into basements, and ending up somewhere unique.

✔ The tiny but hugely atmospheric **Double Happiness,** 21 Liverpool St. (☎ **03/9650 4488**), has a retro-Asian theme that would make Chairman Mao proud. Rub shoulders with hip young business types and make sure you order a Gang of Four cocktail (mango, vodka, Cointreau, and lemon). Open Monday through Thursday 5 p.m. to 1 a.m. (until 3 a.m. on Thurs), Friday 4:30 p.m. to 3 a.m., Saturday 6 p.m. to 3 a.m., and Sunday 6 p.m. to 1 a.m.

✔ A younger crowd frequents the **Hi-Fi Bar & Ballroom,** 125 Swanson St. (☎ **03/9654 7617**; www.thehifi.com.au), which has lots of live music — mostly hard rock and contemporary. This cavernous underground venue features many visiting acts. Ticket prices vary and can be anywhere between A$15 and A$55 (US$12–US$44/ £6–£22).

A Day Trip from Melbourne: Phillip Island

Phillip Island's **penguin parade,** which happens every evening at dusk, is one of Australia's most popular animal attractions. Phillip Island also offers nice beaches, good bushwalking, fishing, and Seal Rocks.

Getting there

Most visitors come to Phillip Island on a day trip and arrive in time for the Penguin Parade and dinner. Several tour companies run day trips. Among them are **Gray Line** (☎ **03/9663 4455**; www.grayline.com), which operates penguin trips daily departing Melbourne at 1:30 p.m. and returning at around 11:30 p.m. Tours cost A$117 (US$94/£47) adults, A$59 (US$47/£24) children, and can be booked online before arrival.

If you're driving yourself, Phillip Island is an easy two-hour trip from Melbourne along the South Gippsland Highway and then the Bass Highway. A bridge connects the highway to the mainland.

Getting information after you arrive

The **Phillip Island Visitor Information Centre,** 895 Phillip Island Tourist Rd., Newhaven (☎ **1300/366 422** in Australia, or 03/5956 7447; www.visitphillipisland.com), is an attraction itself, with interactive computer displays, dioramas, and a small theater. It's open daily from 9 a.m. to 5 p.m. (to 6 p.m. in summer), and 1 to 5 p.m. on Good Friday (Fri before Easter) and December 25.

The top attraction

Phillip Island Penguin Reserve

The Penguin Parade takes place every night at dusk, when hundreds of penguins gather in the shallows, and waddle up the beach toward their burrows. They're the smallest of the world's 17 species of penguins, standing 33cm (13 in.) high, and they're the only penguins that breed on the Australian mainland. Flash photography is banned, as are smoking and touching the penguins. Wear a sweater or jacket, because it gets chilly after the sun goes down. Reservations for the Penguin Parade are essential during busy holiday periods such as Easter and summer. For a better experience, there are more exclusive small group tours which allow you a better view of the penguins. **Penguins Plus** allows you to watch the parade from an exclusive boardwalk in the company of rangers, while the **Penguin Sky Box** is an adults-only elevated viewing tower. The **Ultimate Penguin Tour** for groups of ten people (no children under 16), takes you to a secluded beach away from the main viewing area to see penguins coming ashore. Another option is a ranger-guided tour, a few hours before the penguins appear, to see behind-the-scenes research.

Summerland Beach, Phillip Island Tourist Road, Cowes. ☎ 1300/366 422 in Australia, or 03/5951 2800. www.penguins.org.au. *Admission: A$17 (US$14/£6.80) adults, A$8.70 (US$6.95/£3.50) children 4–15, A$44 (US$34/£18) families of 4; visitor center only A$4 (US$3.20/£1.60) adults, A$2 (US$1.60/£0.80) children 4–15, A$11 (US$8.80/£4.40) families of 4; Penguins Plus A$29 (US$23/£12) adults, A$15 (US$12/£6) children, A$72 (US$58/£29) families; Penguin Sky Box A$40 (US$32/£16); Ultimate Penguin Tour A$60 (US$48/£24); ranger-guided tour A$10 (US$8/£4) adults, A$5 (US$4/£2) children, A$25 (US$20/£10) families, in addition to visitor center entry. Open: Summer daily 9 a.m.–6 p.m., winter daily 9 a.m.–5 p.m.*

Fast Facts: Melbourne

Area Code

The area code for Melbourne and all of Victoria is **03.** Even within Victoria you need to use the code if you're calling outside the immediate area you're in.

American Express

The main office is at 233 Collins St. (☎ 1300/139 060 in Australia, or 03/9633 6333). It's open Monday through Friday from 9 a.m. to 5 p.m., and Saturday from 10 a.m. to 1 p.m.

ATMs

ATMs are widely available. You find some in the Bourke Street Mall and every few blocks in the city center.

Currency Exchange

Travelex has two branches in Melbourne's city center, at 261 Bourke St. (☎ 03/9654 4222) and at 136 Exhibition St. (☎ 03/9650 3222). Both are open 9 a.m. to 5 p.m. weekdays, 10 a.m. to 5 p.m. Saturdays (Exhibition Street until 3 p.m.) and 11 a.m. to 4 p.m. Sundays (Bourke Street only). There are also Travelex booths in the arrivals hall of Melbourne International Airport and in the Qantas domestic terminal.

Doctors

The Traveller's Medical & Vaccination Centre, 2nd Floor, 393 Little Bourke St. (☎ 03/9602 5788), offers full vaccination and travel medical services. It's open Monday and Thursday 9 a.m. to 8.30 p.m., Tuesday 9 a.m. to 8 p.m., Wednesday and Friday 9 a.m. to 5 p.m., and Saturday 9 a.m. to 1 p.m.

Embassies and Consulates

The United States consulate is at Level 6, 553 St. Kilda Rd. (☎ 03/9526 5900). Other consulates include the United Kingdom, Level 17, 90 Collins St. (☎ 03/9652 1600); New Zealand, Level 3, 350 Collins St. (☎ 03/9642 1279); Ireland, 295 Queen St. (☎ 03/9919 1802); and Canada, Level 50, 101 Collins St. (☎ 03/9653 9674).

Emergencies

Dial ☎ 000 for fire, ambulance, or police help. This is a free call from a private or public phone.

Hospitals

The Royal Melbourne Hospital is on Grattan Street, Parkville (☎ 03/9342 7000), just north of the city center.

Internet Access and Cybercafes

You can get free Internet access at the State Library of Victoria, 328 Swanston St. (☎ 03/8664 7000; www.slv.vic.gov.au). It's open Monday through Thursday 10 a.m. to 9 p.m., Friday through Sunday and public holidays 10 a.m. to 6 p.m. There are Internet cafes along Elizabeth Street, between Flinders and Latrobe streets, and also around Flinders Lane and Little Bourke Street in Chinatown. Most are open from early until well into the night. N2C at Shop 100, 200 Bourke St. (☎ 03/9639 3220) is open Monday through Thursday 10 a.m. to 2 a.m., Friday and Saturday 10 a.m. to 7:30 a.m. (the next day), and Sunday 10 a.m. to 2 a.m. Zone AdrenaLan Melbourne is upstairs at 387 Bourke St. (☎ 03/9600 0106) and is open Monday through Saturday 10 a.m. to 7 p.m. and Sunday from 11 a.m. until late. Global Gossip has a branch at 440 Elizabeth St. (☎ 03/9663 0511), open daily 8 a.m. until midnight.

Maps

The best place to get good local maps is at the visitor center at Federation Square or from the Royal Automobile Club of Victoria (RACV) shop at 438 Little Collins St. (☎ 13 72 28; www.racv.com.au). It's open weekdays 9 a.m. to 5 p.m., Saturday 10 a.m. to 1 p.m.

Newspapers and Magazines

Melbourne has two daily newspapers, the *Age* (www.theage.com.au) and the *Herald-Sun* (www.news.com.au/heraldsun). Both publish seven days a week.

Pharmacies

The Mulqueeny Pharmacy is on the corner of Swanston and Collins streets (☎ 03/9654 8569). It's open Monday through Friday 8 a.m. to 8 p.m., Saturday 9 a.m. to 6 p.m., and Sunday 11 a.m. to 6 p.m.

Police

Dial ☎ **000** in an emergency. For general enquiries, call Victoria Police Centre, 637 Flinders St. (☎ 03/9247 6666). It's open 24 hours.

Post Office

The General Post Office (GPO) at 250 Elizabeth St. (☎ 13 13 18 in Australia) is open Monday through Friday 8:30 a.m. to 5:30 p.m., Saturday 9 a.m. to 4 p.m., and Sunday 10 a.m. to 4 p.m.

Restrooms

There are lots of public toilets in Melbourne's Central Business District, many open 24 hours. During business hours, you'll find good clean toilets in the major department stores such as Myer and David Jones. Other 24-hour locations are in Collins Place, 24 Collins St., and at Flinders Street train station.

Safety

Use normal common sense and caution, especially at night. Some areas around the King Street nightclub precinct and parts of St. Kilda can be risky late at night, as can parks and gardens.

Smoking

In Victoria, smoking is banned in restaurants, cafes, shopping centers, gambling venues, and bars. It's prohibited outside (and inside) at underage music and dance events, and under covered areas of train station platforms and tram and bus shelters.

Weather

Two good Web sites are the Weather Channel (www.weatherchannel.com.au) and the Australian Bureau of Meteorology (www.bom.gov.au).

Chapter 14

The Best of Victoria

by Lee Mylne

*W*hen you've finished exploring Melbourne's cosmopolitan streets and laneways, it's time to head into the Victorian countryside. Diversity is the watchword here; as you travel around Australia's southernmost mainland state, you'll see landscapes of all kinds, from rain forests and mountain ranges to parched Outback desert and a rugged coast where waves crash dramatically onto sandstone outcrops.

Melbourne may be the heart of the state, but the Murray River, which separates Victoria from New South Wales, is its lifeblood, providing irrigation for vast areas of semidesert. As Australia's drought has worsened over recent years, the once-mighty Murray has been a focus of concern, which is likely to still be in the news when you visit.

In this chapter, we give you a few of the myriad possibilities for exploring Victoria, from one of the great scenic drives of the world to heading inland and upward and following the footsteps of Australia's most famous outlaw.

Driving the Great Ocean Road

The Great Ocean Road is one of Australia's most spectacular drives. It hugs the coast starting in Torquay, 94km (58 miles) southwest of Melbourne, and passes through attractive small towns — Anglesea, Lorne, Apollo Bay, Port Campbell, and Peterborough — until it reaches Warrnambool. The scenery along the 106km (66-mile) route includes huge cliffs, ocean vistas, beaches, rain forests, and incredible rock formations. The most spectacular is the 27km (17-mile) stretch between Princeton and Peterborough. The best way to travel along the Great Ocean Road is to drive yourself at a leisurely pace, stopping wherever

Victoria

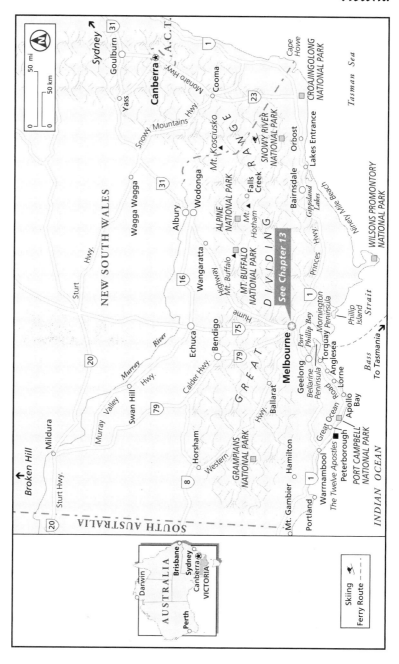

your fancy takes you. The main attractions are in the coastal Port Campbell National Park, so don't be surprised if you're not overly impressed until you get there.

Finding information along the way

Most towns along the Great Ocean Road have information centers. If you're coming from Melbourne, stop at the **Geelong & Great Ocean Road Visitors Centre,** Stead Park, Princess Highway, Corio, VIC 3214 (☎ **1800/620 888** in Australia or 03/5275 5797; www.greatoceanrd. org.au). You can book accommodations here, which you should do in advance, especially in summer. The useful Web site gives plenty of tour options. There's also a visitor center at the **National Wool Museum,** 26 Moorabool St. (at Brougham Street), Geelong (☎ **1800/620 888** in Australia, or 03/5222 2900).

Along the route, the **Port Campbell Visitor Information Centre,** 26 Morris Street, Port Campbell (☎ **03/5598 6089**), is a good place to pick up brochures. It has some interesting displays and an audiovisual show of the area; plus, it acts as a hotel-booking service.

Most information centers are open from 9 a.m. to 5 p.m. daily.

Staying along the Great Ocean Road

The **Great Ocean Road Accommodation Centre,** 136 Mountjoy Parade, Lorne, VIC 3232 (☎ **03/5289 4233;** www.gorac.com.au), rents cottages and units along the route.

Chris's Beacon Point Villas
$$ Apollo Bay

Perched high in the Otways, above the Great Ocean Road, these villas have wonderful views of the coast. Host Chris Talihmanidis has a passion for the food of southern Europe and runs an award-winning restaurant. There are two studios and six self-contained, two-bedroom villas, all with the same panoramic views. Villas have a queen-size bed and a double or two singles, while studios sleep two in a king-size bed.

280 Skenes Creek Rd., Apollo Bay, VIC 3233. ☎ 03/5237 6411. Fax: 03/5237 6930. Rack rates: A$160 (US$128/£64) double studio, A$220–A$290 (US$176–US$232/£88–£116) villa (sleeps 4). Rates include breakfast. AE, DC, MC, V.

Cumberland Lorne Conference & Leisure Resort
$$$–$$$$ Lorne

This large resort, which stands between the sea and the foothills of the Otway Ranges, is comfortable and luxurious. Every apartment has a queen-size bed and a sofa bed, plus a kitchen, a laundry, a Jacuzzi, a balcony, Internet access, free in-house movies, and a CD player. All units have large bathrooms with tub/shower combinations. More than half of the rooms have panoramic ocean views; the rest overlook gardens. Two-bedroom apartments have two extra single beds, and split-level penthouses have two Jacuzzis and two balconies. The resort has a restaurant, an indoor swimming pool, and sporting facilities, and it's across the road from the beach.

150–178 Mountjoy Parade, Lorne, VIC 3232. ☎ *1800/037 010 in Australia, or 03/5289 2400. Fax: 03/5289 2256.* www.cumberland.com.au. *Rack rates: Peak season (summer and Easter) A$315–A$375 (US$252–US$300/£126–£150) 1-bedroom apartment, A$400–A$460 (US$320–US$368/£160–£184) 2-bedroom apartment, A$525–A$545 (US$420–US$436/£210–£218) penthouse; off season A$250–A$315 (US$200–US$252/£100–£126) 1-bedroom apartment, A$335–A$400 (US$268–US$320/£134–£160) 2-bedroom apartment, A$430–A$460 (US$344–US$368/£172–£184) penthouse. AE, DC, MC, V.*

Great Ocean Road Cottages & Backpackers YHA
$–$$ **Lorne**

These cottages are popular with family groups especially in summer. The self-contained cottages, set away from each other in a quiet patch of bushland, are a five-minute walk from the town center. Each wooden cottage is two stories, with a double bed, twin beds, and a pullout mattress, as well as a full kitchen and bathroom. A two-night minimum stay applies on weekends, and a one-week minimum in high season (Dec 26–Jan 26).

10 Erskine Ave. (P.O. Box 60), Lorne, VIC 3232. ☎ *03/5289 1070. Fax: 03/5289 2508.* www.greatoceanroadcottages.com. *Rack rates: Weekdays A$150 (US$120/£60) double, weekends A$170 (US$136/£68) double; extra adult A$25 (US$20/£10), extra child A$10 (US$8/£4). AE, DC, MC, V.*

Macka's Farm Lodge
$$–$$$$ **Port Campbell**

This working farm, with pigs, cows, ducks, and chickens running around, sits inland from the Twelve Apostles rock formations. There are four self-contained lodges and a farmhouse. The lodges form the "homestead" complex and have views across the farm, across the bush, and to the ocean. Two of the lodges sleep three people. The third lodge has three bedrooms, with a queen-size bed, a king-size bed (interchangeable to two singles), and a bedroom with singles and bunks. The fourth lodge has two bedrooms, each with a queen-size bed. The farmhouse has four bedrooms, three with queen-size beds, one with four singles. All the lodges and the farmhouse have a TV, DVD player, and CD player — but you may not even turn them on.

RSD 2305 Princetown Rd., Princetown, VIC 3269. ☎ *03/5598 8261. Fax: 03/5598 8201.* www.mackasfarm.com.au. *Rack rates: A$165–A$360 (US$132–US$288/£66–£144), depending on the house and the season (check Web site for different price categories). MC, V.*

Dining along the Great Ocean Road

Marks Restaurant
$$–$$$ Lorne   CONTEMPORARY

Seaside chic, a friendly staff, and great food are a winning recipe for this favorite with the locals and travelers. Marks is stylish, simple, and smart, with an emphasis on seafood. Dishes may include fried calamari salad, spicy octopus, or char-grilled whole baby snapper. The restaurant has a good wine list, or you can BYO.

124 Mount Joy Parade, Lorne. ☎ *03/5289 2787. Main courses: A$18–A$25 (US$14–US$20/£7–£10). AE, MC, V. Open: Daily 6 p.m. to late. Closed Aug.*

The Victoria Hotel
$$–$$$ Port Fairy   CONTEMPORARY

Built in 1874, this historic bluestone pub in Port Fairy is a great place to recharge your batteries while driving the Great Ocean Road. By day, you can eat in the cafe overlooking the courtyard; by night, the café becomes an a la carte restaurant. In addition to traditional pub favorites, you're likely to find a menu that includes dishes such as lamb cutlets on a bed of olives, pine nut and spinach risotto, or homemade sweet potato and spinach gnocchi. Over summer (Dec–Mar) the restaurant becomes Simply Seafood. There's often live music on Friday or Saturday night.

42 Bank St., Port Fairy. ☎ *03/5568 2891. Main courses: Lunch A$15–A$21 (US$12–US$17/£6–£8.40), dinner A$20–A$30 (US$16–US$24/£8–£12). AE, DC, MC, V. Open: Tues–Sun noon to 2 p.m. and 6 p.m. to late.*

Exploring the Great Ocean Road

Your first stop along the coastal road is likely to be at the surfing town of **Torquay.** The main surf beach is much nicer than the one farther down the coast at Lorne. Check out **Surf World museum,** Surf City Plaza, Beach Road, West Torquay (☎ **03/5261 4606;** www.surfworld.org.au), which has interactive exhibits dealing with surfboard design and surfing history, and a video of the world's best surfers. Admission is A$8.50 (US$6.80/£3.40) for adults, A$6 (US$4.80/£2.40) for children, and A$19 (US$15/£7.60) for families. It's open daily from 9 a.m. to 5 p.m. (closed Dec 25). **Bells Beach,** just down the road, is world-famous in surfing circles for its perfect waves.

Lorne has some nice boutiques and is a good place to stop for lunch or to spend the night. The stretch from Lorne to Apollo Bay is one of the most spectacular sections of the Great Ocean Road; the road snakes along a cliff edge with the ocean on the other side. **Apollo Bay,** once a whaling station, is a pleasant, low-key town with sandy beaches. Next you come to the **Angahook-Lorne State Park,** which protects most of the coastal section of the Otway Ranges from Aireys Inlet, south of Anglesea, to Kennett River. It has many well-marked rain forest walks and picnic areas at Shelly Beach, Elliot River, and Blanket Bay. Plenty of wildlife is around.

About 13km (8 miles) past Apollo Bay, just off the main road, you can stroll on the **Maits Rest Rainforest Boardwalk.** A little farther along, an unpaved road leads north past Hopetoun Falls and Beauchamp Falls to **Beech Forest.** Seven kilometers (4⅓ miles) farther along the main road, another unpaved road heads south for 15km (9⅓ miles) to a windswept headland and the **Cape Otway Lightstation** (☎ **03/5237 9240;** www. lightstation.com), one of several lighthouses along the coast. Built by convicts in 1848, the 100m-tall (328-ft.) lighthouse is open to tourists. Admission is A$11 (US$8.80/£4.40) for adults and A$6 (US$4.80/£2.40) for children. It's open daily from 9 a.m. to 5 p.m. Free guided tours are run regularly.

Back on the main road, your route heads inland through an area known as **Horden Vale** before running to the sea at Glenaire — there's good surfing and camping at **Johanna,** 6km (3¾ miles) north. Then the Great Ocean Road heads north again to **Lavers Hill,** a former timber town. Five kilometers (3 miles) southwest of Lavers Hill is **Melba Gully State Park,** where you can spot glowworms at night and walk along routes of rain forest ferns. Check out one of the last giant gum trees that escaped the loggers — it's some 27m (88 ft.) in circumference and is estimated to be more than 300 years old.

The next place of note is **Moonlight Head,** which marks the start of the **Shipwreck Coast** — a 120km (74-mile) stretch running to Port Fairy that claimed more than 80 ships at the end of the 19th century and the beginning of the 20th.

 Just past Princetown, you're nearing the biggest attraction of the trip, **Port Campbell National Park.** With its sheer cliffs and coastal rock sculptures, it's one of the most recognizable natural images of Australia. You can't miss the **Twelve Apostles,** a series of rock pillars just offshore in the surf. Other attractions are the **Blowhole,** which throws up huge sprays of water; the **Grotto,** a rock formation carved by the waves; **London Bridge,** which looked quite like the real thing until the center of the bridge crashed into the sea in 1990; and the **Loch Ard Gorge. Port Fairy,** a lovely fishing town once called Belfast by Irish immigrants who settled here to escape the potato famine, is also on the Shipwreck Coast.

Taking a guided tour along the Great Ocean Road

Tours to the Great Ocean Road take around 12 hours (sometimes more), which makes for a big day out even when you aren't doing the driving. But if you *really* can't spare more time, several companies do day tours from Melbourne. The coach operator **AAT Kings** (☎ **03/9663 3377;** www. aatkings.com.au) runs daily trips that cost A$129 (US$103/£52) for adults, and A$65 (US$52/£26) for children. **Gray Line sightseeing tours** (☎ **1300/858 687** or 03/9663 4455; www.grayline.com) also has day trips for a similar price. A better option would be Gray Line's two-day

Great Ocean Road tour, which overnights in Lorne. It costs A$349 (US$279/£140) adults double (single supplement is A$61/US$49/£24) and A$120 (US$96/£48) for children.

Wild-Life Tours (☎ 1300/661 730 in Australia, or 03/9741 6333; www.wildlifetours.com.au) offers several well-priced, multiday, backpacker-style tours that take in the Great Ocean Road tour from Melbourne. A one-day tour costs A$90 (US$72/£36), and a two-day tour, which overnights at Hall's Gap and also takes in the Grampians, costs A$183 (US$146/£73), including accommodations.

Autopia Tours (☎ 1800/000 507 in Australia, or 03/9419 8878; www.autopiatours.com.au) offers a one-day tour from Melbourne taking in all the sights and including lunch and a bushwalk in Otway National Park. It costs A$95 (US$76/£38). The company does a more relaxed three-day tour for A$375 (US$300/£150), including most meals and dorm accommodations in hostels. Upgrades to double rooms are A$65 (US$52/£26) per person; to single rooms, A$150 (US$120/£60) per person.

The High Country

Victoria's High Country consists of the hills and mountains of the Great Dividing Range, which runs almost the length of eastern Australia, from Queensland in the north to the western part of Victoria. The highest peak in the Victoria segment of the range is **Mount Bogong,** at 1,988m (6,521 ft.). The main attractions of the High Country are its natural features, which include moorland and typical mountainous alpine scenery, and its wealth of outdoor activities, including skiing, hiking, canoeing, white-water rafting, mountain-biking, and rock climbing. The Victorian ski fields are based around Mount Buller, Mount Stirling, Falls Creek, Mount Buffalo, and Mount Hotham.

If you plan to go walking here, make sure you have plenty of water and sunscreen, and be aware that as in any alpine region, temperatures can plummet dramatically. In summer, the days can be hot and the nights can be very cold.

The townships of **Bright** (310km/193 miles northeast of Melbourne) and **Beechworth** (267km/166 miles northeast of Melbourne) are good bases for exploring the High Country. Set in a valley and surrounded by pine forests, Bright is known for its dramatic fall colors. There are nice walks, especially along the Ovens River, or you can hire bicycles and take off down a former railway track, now the **Rail Trail** (www.railtrail.com.au). The track stretches 94km (58 miles) from Bright to Wangaratta, but you can turn back whenever you want.

Historic **Beechworth,** one of Victoria's best-preserved gold rush towns, has more than 30 buildings listed by the National Trust, including pubs, churches, government offices, miners' cottages, and the jail where bushranger Ned Kelly was imprisoned (see the sidebar "The story of Ned Kelly" for more information).

Getting to the High Country

V/Line trains (www.vline.com.au) run daily between Melbourne and Bright, via Wangaratta. Return fares cost A$91 (US$73/£36), though if you travel in off-peak times, it's much cheaper. The trip takes about four hours, and from Wangaratta, you take the bus to Bright. However, getting around the area without your own transport is difficult.

The story of Ned Kelly

The story of bushranger **Ned Kelly** is legend. Kelly is a folk hero to many and a criminal to others. Opinion may be divided, but 125 years after the events that made him famous, he is still a presence in Australia. The area of Victoria he lived in is called Kelly Country, and, in 2005, to mark the anniversary of his death, the government created the **Ned Kelly Touring Route** (www.nedkellytouringroute.com.au), linking important sites in the story.

Ned was the eldest of eight children born to Irish parents in Victoria in 1854. When Ned was 12, his father died and the family moved to Greta, 240km (150 miles) northeast of Melbourne. Like many other poor families, the Kellys took up the government's offer of cheap land. As part of the deal, they had to clear the bushland, build a house, and plant crops. More often than not, the land parcels were too small and the soil was too poor for them to make a living. At 16, Ned was convicted of horse-rustling and sentenced to three years in jail. A few years later, his mother was imprisoned for allegedly attacking a police officer who was accused of attacking Ned's sister first. During the scuffle, Ned shot the officer through the wrist. Ned escaped — with a bounty on his head.

On October 26, 1878, together with friends Joe Byrne and Steve Hart, Ned and his brother Dan came across police camped at Stringy Bark Creek. Ned believed the police intended to kill him and his brother, so he called on them to surrender. Three officers resisted, and in the fight that followed, Ned Kelly shot them dead. In the years that followed, the Kelly Gang avoided capture with the help of sympathetic locals. During this time, they robbed two banks, and during each robbery Ned gave his hostages a letter, explaining to the government how he'd been persecuted by police.

In June 1880, police surrounded the Kelly Gang at the Glenrowan Hotel. Prepared for the fight, the four bushrangers put on homemade suits of armor. It was no use — Ned's body took 28 bullets, and the others were all killed. Ned was hanged in Old Melbourne Gaol (see Chapter 12) on November 11, 1880. He was 25 years old.

Glenrowan, a quiet town surrounded by wineries and orchards, pays homage to Ned with a 6m-high (18-ft.) outdoor statue of the bushranger in his homemade armor and helmet, with rifle in hand, as well as a couple of small museums full of Kelly memorabilia — and much more besides. Other towns on the route include Avenel, Benalla, Mansfield, and Jerilderie in southern New South Wales. You can pick up a touring route brochure from the **Old Melbourne Gaol** before setting out, or from information centers in the region.

Finding information along the way

The **Bright Visitors Centre,** 119 Gavan St., Bright (☎ **1800/500 117** or 03/5755 2275; www.brightescapes.com.au), is open daily from 8:30 a.m. to 5 p.m. The **Beechworth Visitor Information Centre** is in the Town Hall, 103 Ford St., Beechworth (☎ **1300/366 321,** or 03/5728 8065; www.beechworthonline.com.au), and is open daily from 9 a.m. to 5 p.m.

For information on the Snowy River National Park and Alpine National Park, drop into the **Buchan Caves Information Centre,** in the Buchan Caves complex (see "Buchan Caves," later in this chapter). It's open daily from 9 a.m. to 4 p.m. (closed Dec 25). Or call **Parks Victoria** (☎ **13 19 63** in Australia).

Where to stay in the High Country

Alpinelink (www.alpinelink.com.au) offers a comprehensive list of places to stay in Bright.

Alinga-Longa Holiday Units
$–$$ Bright

The six large two-bedroom units here are spacious, clean, and comfortable, and fine for a few days, especially if you're traveling as a family. The kitchen gives you the freedom to eat in. Plus, there's a barbecue area, a small outdoor swimming pool, a playground, bikes and toboggans, and Wi-Fi!

12 Gavan St. (Great Alpine Road), Bright 3741. ☎ *03/5755 1073.* www.alingalonga holidays.com.au. *Rack rates: A$90–A$120 (US$72–US$96/£36–£48) double. AE, DC, MC, V.*

Kinross
$$ Beechworth

This historic bungalow, set in an attractive garden, was built in 1858 as a manse for the Beechworth Presbyterian Church. It has five spacious rooms for bed-and-breakfast guests, each decorated in period style with high ceilings, fireplaces, chairs and sofas, and TVs and DVD players. Gail and Terry Walsh host their guests to drinks each evening. Enjoy the shady veranda and courtyard at the back. It's less than a five-minute walk from the main street of Beechworth.

34 Loch St., Beechworth. ☎ *03/5728 2351. Fax: 03/5728 3333.* www.innhouse.com.au/kinross.html. *Rack rates: A$155–A$180 (US$124–US$144/£62–£72) double. MC, V.*

Villa Gusto
$$$–$$$$ Buckland

At the foot of Mount Buffalo, about 6km (4 miles) from Bright, this luxurious, Italian-style villa caters to only 18 guests. The Great Room has a log fire and is furnished with antiques and leather sofas. You can enjoy the luxury of an in-house cinema and 2 acres of Tuscan-style gardens. The Grande Suite and three deluxe suites have Jacuzzis, and all have private terraces. There are also special touches like bathrobes, Bulgari toiletries, and fine linens. A five-course Italian degustation menu is available from the restaurant (open Wed–Sun nights only) for A$70 (US$56/£28) per person, but bookings are essential. Children under 10 are not accepted.

630 Buckland Valley Rd., Buckland, 3740. ☎ *03/5756 2000.* www.villagusto. com.au. *Rack Rates: A$285–A$325 (US$228–US$260/£114–£130) suite. Rates include breakfast. MC, V.*

Exploring the High Country
Alpine National Park

Victoria's largest national park covers 646,000 hectares (1.6 million acres) and connects the High Country areas of New South Wales and the Australian Capital Territory. The park's scenery is spectacular, encompassing most of the state's highest mountains, rivers, escarpments, forests, and high plains. It is easily accessed 330km (205 miles) northeast of Melbourne. The flora is diverse; in all, some 1,100 plant species have been recorded in the park, including 12 not found anywhere else. Walking is particularly good in spring and summer, when a carpet of wildflowers covers the Bogong High Plains. Other impressive trails include the 5.7km (3½-mile) route through Bryce Gorge to The Bluff, a 200m-high (356-ft.) escarpment with panoramic views. Of the other walking trails in the park, the best known is the Alpine Walking Track, which bisects the park for 400km (248 miles) from Walhalla to the township of Tom Groggin, on the New South Wales border.

Buchan Caves

The Buchan Caves are in a scenic valley that is lovely in autumn, when all the European trees are losing their leaves. Tourists can visit the Royal and Fairy caves (which are quite alike), with their fabulous stalactites and stalagmites. Several tours run daily: from the end of Easter to September at 11 a.m., 1 p.m., and 3 p.m.; from October to Easter at 10 a.m., 11:15 a.m., 1 p.m., 2:15 p.m., and 3:30 p.m. Entry to one cave costs A$13 (US$10/£5.20) for adults, A$6.50 (US$5.20/£2.60) for children 5 to 16, and A$32 (US$26/£13) for families of four. To reach the caves from the Princes Highway, turn off at Nowa Nowa (it's well marked). If you're coming south from Jindabyne, follow the Barry Way, which runs alongside the Snowy River.

Snowy River National Park

The Snowy River National Park, with its lovely river scenery and magnificent gorges, protects Victoria's largest forest wilderness areas. The Snowy River was once a torrent, but a series of dams for a hydroelectric scheme in the 1950s has reduced it to a trickle of its former self. And, of course, students of poetry will recognize it as the setting for Banjo Paterson's epic *The Man from Snowy River.*

The two main access roads into the Park are the Gelantipy Road from
Buchan and the Bonang Freeway from the logging township of Orbost.
MacKillop's Road (also known as Deddick River Road) runs across the
park's northern border from Bonang to a little south of Wulgulmerang.
The area around MacKillop's Bridge, along MacKillop's Road, has spectacular scenery and the park's best campgrounds, set beside some nice
swimming holes and sandy river beaches. The Barry Way leads through
the main township of Buchan (see the preceding section).

More cool things to see and do

✔ Keen walkers should pull on their boots and hit the trails. **Ecotrek**
(☎ **08/8383 4155;** www.ecotrek.com.au) offers an eight-day
Bogong Alpine Traverse trek, including four nights camping and
three nights in ski lodges. It's graded moderate/hard, and you carry
your own pack, but it's worth the effort for the stunning panoramic
views of peaks, plains, and forested valleys. The trek costs A$1,695
(US$1,356/£678), including round-trip transport from Melbourne.

✔ Horseback-riding treks are another great way to explore the High
Country. **Stoney's High Country** (www.stoneys.com.au) acts as a
one-stop shop for local tour operators offering trail rides. A two-
hour ride in the foothills costs around A$50 (US$40/£20); a day ride
to higher elevations, A$180 (US$144/£72); a weekend ride, around
A$400 (US$320/£160). Longer rides are also available — check the
Web site for details and phone numbers of operators. Stoney's
can also help you organize a custom ride, on dates of your choice.
Longer tours generally include camping, food, and just about everything else, though you should check whether you'll need a sleeping
bag.

✔ **Angling Expeditions** (☎ **03/5754 1466;** www.anglingvic.com.au)
is the best option for fly-fishing for trout in the alpine area during
spring, summer, and fall. Trips last from three hours to all day and
are suitable for everyone from beginners to experts. Overnight
trips are also available.

Chapter 15

Canberra/ACT

by Marc Llewellyn

. . . .

In This Chapter

▶ Getting to the Australian Capital Territory
▶ Getting oriented in Canberra
▶ Staying and eating in Canberra
▶ Exploring the Australian Capital Territory

. . . .

*I*f you've been to Washington, D.C., you've been to Canberra . . . *not!*
Both cities are federal capitals, and both were planned and laid out to
be what they are. And in the Land Down Under, Canberra (pop. 310,000)
offers gentle virtues and comforts: The roads are wide and well kept,
the buildings are modern, and the suburbs are pleasant and leafy.
Canberra is also the seat of government and the home of thousands
of civil servants — it's very much a company town.

There are lots of open spaces, parklands, and monuments, and you'll
find more than enough to keep you busy — from museum-going and
gallery-hopping to boating on Lake Burley Griffin.

Canberra was born after the Commonwealth of Australia was created in
1901. Melbourne and Sydney each bid to become the federal capital. In
the end, Australian leaders created a federal district and in 1908, they
chose an undeveloped area between the two cities.

Chicago landscape architect Walter Burley Griffin, a contemporary of
Frank Lloyd Wright, designed the city. The place he mapped out was
christened "Canberra" (a local Aboriginal word meaning "meeting
place"), and, by 1927, the first meeting of Parliament took place here.

Getting There

Canberra is between Sydney and Melbourne, and is easily accessible:
The drive is doable, it's only a short flight from the eastern cities, and
it's serviced well by trains, which means you have plenty of travel
options.

By air

Qantas (☎ **13 13 13** in Australia; www.qantas.com.au) runs frequent daily service to Canberra from all the major cities. The fun, discount airline **Virgin Blue** (☎ **13 67 89** in Australia; www.virginblue.com.au) offers discount daily flights to Canberra from Melbourne, Brisbane, and Adelaide, but not from Sydney.

Canberra Airport is about 15 minutes from the city center. By taxi it costs approximately A$20 (US$16/£8). In addition, the **Airliner Bus** (☎ **02/6299 3722;** www.deanesbuslines.com.au/queanbeyan) operates a shuttle between the central business district and the airport daily, leaving every half-hour on weekdays and hourly on weekends. The one-way fare is A$7 (US$5.60/£2.80) and a round-trip costs A$12 (US$9.60/£4.80).

By train

Countrylink (☎ **13 22 32** in Australia; www.countrylink.info) runs three **Canberra Xplorer** trains daily between Sydney and Canberra. The four-and-a-quarter-hour trip costs around A$70 (US$56/£28) in first class, A$50 (US$40/£20) in economy; children are half-price, and a round-trip costs double.

Many people book Countrylink transport-hotel packages, which can save you quite a bit. Depending on the accommodations in Canberra, prices range from A$90 to A$190 (US$72–US$152/£36–£76) a night for a couple, and if you book in advance, you can save up to 40 percent on the fare through a Rail Escape package. Call **Countrylink Holidays** (☎ **13 28 29**) for details. Countrylink has an office at Wynyard CityRail station in Sydney.

From Melbourne, the **Canberra Link,** run by **V/Line** (☎ **13 61 96** in Australia; www.vlinepassenger.com.au), involves a five-hour bus trip and a three-and-a-half-hour train trip. It costs A$55 (US$44/£22) adults, A$34 (US$27/£13) children and students. **Canberra Railway Station** (☎ **02/6239 6707**) is on Wentworth Avenue, Kingston, about 5km (3 miles) southeast of the city center. Coaches connect the railway station to the center.

By bus

Greyhound (☎ **13 14 99** in Australia, or 07/4690 9950; www.greyhound.com.au) does ten runs a day from Sydney to Canberra. The trip takes four to four-and-a-half hours and tickets cost around A$37 (US$30/£15) adults, A$33 (US$27/£13) pensioners and students, A$29 (US$23/£12) children 3 to 14. From Melbourne, tickets to Canberra cost A$62 (US$50/£25) adults, A$52 (US$42/£21) pensioners and students, A$46 (US$37/£18) children.

Advance-purchase fares can be as much as 35 percent lower.

Murrays Australia (☎ **13 22 51** in Australia; www.murrays.com.au) runs buses from Sydney to Canberra five times a day. The journey costs

A$36 (US$29/£15) adults, A$29 (US$23/£12) children. Several sightseeing companies in Sydney, including **AAT King's** and **Australia Pacific Tours,** offer day trips to Canberra.

Interstate buses arrive at **Jolimont Tourist Centre,** at the corner of Northbourne Avenue and Alinga Street, Canberra City.

By car

The Australian Capital Territory (ACT) is surrounded by New South Wales. Sydney is 306km (190 miles) northeast, and Melbourne is 651km (404 miles) southwest. From Sydney, you can use an extension to the M5 motorway that links with the Eastern Distributor highway near the Sydney airport. Veer left before you reach the airport, follow signs heading toward Canberra, and veer left onto the M5. The drive takes between three and three-and-a-half hours. From Melbourne, take the Hume Highway to Yass and switch to the Barton Highway; the trip takes about eight hours.

Orienting Yourself in Canberra

The first things that strike a visitor to Canberra are its parklike feel and wide, unclogged roads. The city's centerpiece is **Capital Hill,** where Parliament House stands. A dozen avenues radiate off from here and each of these broad, tree-shaded streets leads to a traffic circle, from which more streets emanate. Around each hub, the streets form a pattern of concentric circles.

Another of Canberra's most notable features is **Lake Burley Griffin,** created by damming the Molonglo River. The centerpiece of the lake is the **Captain Cook Memorial Jet,** a spire of water that reaches 147m (482 ft.) into the air.

Introducing the Neighbourhoods

- ✔ **Civic:** Canberra's main shopping district is centered on Northbourne Avenue, one of the city's main thoroughfares. Officially it's known as Canberra City.

- ✔ **Mount Ainslie:** Northeast of Civic is this hill, featuring spectacular views of the city and beyond from its summit. The Australian War Memorial is at its foot.

- ✔ **Parkes:** Wedged between Commonwealth Avenue and Kings Avenue is the National Triangle. Here you'll find many of the city's attractions, such as the National Gallery of Australia and Questacon (the National Science and Technology Centre).

- ✔ **Yarralumla:** Many embassies and consulates are in this leafy suburb east of Capital Hill.

Finding Information after You Arrive

The **Canberra Visitors' Centre,** 330 Northbourne Ave., Dickson
(☎ 02/6205 0044; www.visitcanberra.com.au), dispenses information and books hotels. The office is open Monday through Friday from
9 a.m. to 5:30 p.m., and Saturday and Sunday from 9 a.m. to 4 p.m.

Getting Around Canberra

✔ **By taxi:** Canberra's only taxi company is **Canberra Cabs** (☎ 13 22
27 in Australia). Taxis are scarce and you may be asked to share a
cab from the airport to the city with other passengers. For this you
get a discounted fare.

✔ **By bus:** ACTION (☎ 13 17 10 in Australia, or 02/6207 7611; www.
action.act.gov.au) runs Canberra's bus system. The central
bus terminal is on Alinga Street in Civic. Single tickets cost A$3
(US$2.40/£1.20) adults, A$1.50 (US$1.20/£0.60) children 5 to 15.
Daily tickets cost A$6.60 (US$5.30/£2.70) adults, A$3.30 (US$2.60/
£1.30) kids; weekly tickets cost A$24 (US$19/£10) adults, A$12
(US$9.60/£4.80) kids. You can purchase single tickets on the bus
and daily and weekly tickets from most newsdealers and ACTION
interchanges (transfer points).

Bus route maps are available at bus interchanges, newsdealers, and
the Canberra Visitors' Centre.

Canberra Day Tours (☎ 02/6298 3344; www.canberradaytours.
com.au) offers a hop-on/hop-off day tour by bus including stops at
Old Parliament House, the Australian War Memorial, Parliament
House, the Embassy region, Telstra Tower, and Lake Burley Griffin.
It costs A$35 (US$28/£14) adults, A$15 (US$12/£6) kids under 16.
The first bus leaves at 9:30 a.m. from the Canberra Visitors' Centre.

✔ **By bicycle:** Canberra is unique in Australia for its extensive system
of cycle tracks — some 120km (74 miles) of them — which makes
sightseeing on two wheels a pleasurable experience. Rent a bike
from **Mr. Spoke's Bike Hire,** Barrine Drive, near the ferry terminal,
Acton (☎ 02/6257 1188).

Staying in Style

Canberra's accommodations are generally cheaper than in other state
capitals. Many people stay here during the week, so you can often find
cheaper weekend rates. Always ask about deals and packages. You
should be able to do better than the rack rates, especially booking
through the hotel's Web site. The **Canberra Visitors' Centre**
(☎ 02/6205 0044) has information about other accommodations
options.

Canberra

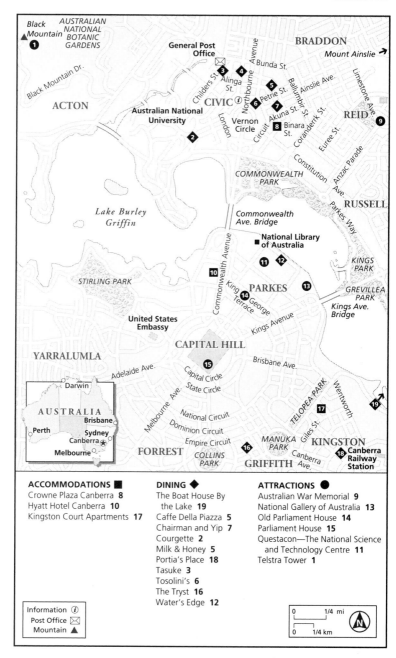

ACCOMMODATIONS ■
Crowne Plaza Canberra **8**
Hyatt Hotel Canberra **10**
Kingston Court Apartments **17**

DINING ◆
The Boat House By
  the Lake **19**
Caffe Della Piazza **5**
Chairman and Yip **7**
Courgette **2**
Milk & Honey **5**
Portia's Place **18**
Tasuke **3**
Tosolini's **6**
The Tryst **16**
Water's Edge **12**

ATTRACTIONS ●
Australian War Memorial **9**
National Gallery of Australia **13**
Old Parliament House **14**
Parliament House **15**
Questacon—The National Science
  and Technology Centre **11**
Telstra Tower **1**

Information ⓘ
Post Office ⊠
Mountain ▲

0		1/4 mi
0		1/4 km

The top hotels

Crowne Plaza Canberra
$$$ Civic

This hotel is next door to the National Convention Centre and Casino Canberra. Its car-oriented approach makes it inconvenient for pedestrians, but the gardens (Glebe Park) at the back are good for early-morning strolls. Rooms face onto internal balconies that look down to the restaurants below. Standard rooms are user-friendly and comfortable; most come with one queen-size bed or two doubles. Park-view doubles overlook the gardens. The hotel has a medium-size indoor pool and an adequate health club.

See map p. 239. 1 Binara St., Canberra, ACT 2601. ☎ *1300/363 300 in Australia, or 02/6247 8999. Fax: 02/6257 4903.* www.crowneplaza.com. *Free parking. Rack rates: A$300 (US$240/£120) standard double, A$315 (US$252/£126) park-view double, A$425–A$500 (US$340–US$400/£170–£200) suite. Weekend discounts available. AE, DC, MC, V.*

Hyatt Hotel Canberra
$$$$ Yarralumla

Visiting heads of state and pop stars make this their residence of choice in Canberra, and it's not hard to see why. It has a great location, a two-minute drive from the city center, in the shadow of Parliament House, and between Lake Burley Griffin and the Parliamentary Triangle. Originally the Hotel Canberra, it opened in 1924. For many years the Hyatt was an important part of Canberra's social and political life, with key decisions affecting all Australians being made over drinks in the bar. All staff members wear 1920s costumes to add to the atmosphere. Some 39 rooms are in the original two-story section. These have more historical appeal, but they're darker than their modern counterparts, which were added in the 1980s. Standard rooms have king-size beds and marble bathrooms. The hotel has a health club and spa, as well as a good indoor pool and a tennis court.

See map p. 239. Commonwealth Avenue, Yarralumla, ACT 2600. ☎ *13 12 34 in Australia, or 02/6270 1234; 800-233-1234 in the U.S. and Canada; 0181/335 1220 in London or 0845/758 1666 elsewhere in the U.K.; 0800/441 234 in New Zealand. Fax: 02/6281 5998.* www.canberra.park.hyatt.com. *Free parking. Rack rates: A$380 (US$304/£152) standard double, A$605 (US$484/£242) executive suite, A$1,200 (US$960/£480) diplomatic suite. Weekend packages and Internet deals available. AE, DC, MC, V.*

Kingston Court Apartments
$$ Kingston

About 1km (½ mile) from the Parliamentary Triangle and 6km (3¾ miles) from Civic, this apartment complex is a good option if you're looking for the comforts of home. All the one- and two-bedroom apartments are modern and spacious and come with a full kitchen, a washer and dryer, and a balcony or a private courtyard. A small outdoor heated pool and a half-size tennis court are on the grounds.

See map p. 239. 4 Tench St., Kingston, ACT 2604. ☎ *1800/655 754 in Australia, or 02/6295 2244. Fax: 02/6295 5300.* www.kingstonterrace.com.au. *Free parking. Rack rates: A$170 (US$136/£68) apartment for 1, A$190 (US$152/£76) apartment for 2. Internet and package rates available. AE, DC, MC, V.*

Dining Out

With so many politicians and bureaucrats with money to burn and time to spend it, it's no wonder that Canberra boasts a swag of top-class restaurants and ethnic eateries to appease the most refined of palates.

The Boat House by the Lake
$$$ Barton   MODERN AUSTRALIAN

On the shores of Lake Burley Griffin, the Boat House is a pleasant retreat with water views. The large dining room's floor-to-ceiling windows capture the view, and the terrace is a nice spot on a sunny day for lunch. To start, try Coffin Bay oysters, either natural with lemon, or topped with litchi, avocado, and chile salsa. The wine list features local vintages.

See map p. 239. Grevillea Park, Menindee Dr., ACT. ☎ *02/6273 5500.* www.boat housebythelake.com.au. *Reservations required. Main courses: A$32 (US$26/ £16) lunch, A$35 (US$28/£14) dinner. AE, DC, MC, V. Open: Mon–Fri noon to 3 p.m., Mon–Sat 6–10:30 p.m.*

Caffe Della Piazza
$ Civic   ITALIAN/CAFE

This place has won several awards for its Italian-inspired cooking, including the catering industries' award for the best restaurant in the state. The restaurant offers indoor and outdoor dining, and is a good place to pop in for a light meal and a coffee or for something more substantial. Pastas cost around A$12 (US$10/$8), and the bestseller is chicken breast strips in macchiato sauce. Book early for Friday or Saturday evening.

See map p. 239. 19 Garema Place, Civic. ☎ *02/6248 9711. Reservations recommended. Main courses: A$7.50–A$19 (US$6–US$15/£3–£8). AE, DC, MC, V. Open: Daily 10:30 a.m. to midnight.*

Chairman and Yip
$$$$ Civic   ASIAN AUSTRALIAN

This is one of Canberra's best restaurants. Upbeat and popular with political bigwigs, it has a reputation of being the place to see and be seen. The chairs are comfortable, the menus are tucked inside art magazines, and Mao-style pop art decorates the walls. A favorite is the prawns with homemade chile jam, served on vermicelli noodles with mango salsa. Abalone and lobster also find their way onto the menu. Chef William Suen keeps his regulars happy with his iconic Shanghai duck pancakes.

See map p. 239. 108 Bunda St., Civic. ☎ *02/6248 7109.* www.thechairmanandyip. com. *Reservations required. Main courses: A$27–A$40 (US$21–US$32/£10–£16). AE, DC, MC, V. Open: Sun–Fri noon to 3 p.m., daily 6–11 p. m.*

Courgette
$$$$ Civic   EUROPEAN/AUSTRALIAN

This plush dining room features hanging lamps and candlelight, cream velour chairs, theatrical drapes, and thick blue carpets. There are two dining areas: an intimate place behind the bar, and a larger, brighter space with floor-to-ceiling windows overlooking a pebbled garden. The food is French-influenced and features stand-out dishes such as roasted rabbit with muscatel grapes, glazed pearl onions, bacon, Brussels sprouts and butter puff pastry; or the caramelized suckling pig with cauliflower puree, cinnamon spiced apple, and aromatic jus. A good choice is the seven-course degustation menu for A$90 (US$72/£36) for food only and A$135 (US$108/£54) for food and wine. The wine list is very good.

See map p. 239. 54 Marcus Clarke St., Civic. ☎ *02/6247 4042.* www.courgette. com.au. *Reservations required. Main courses: A$32–A$36 (US$25–US$28/£13–£14). AE, DC, MC, V. Open: Mon–Fri noon to 3 p.m., Mon–Sat 6–11 p.m.*

Milk and Honey
$$ Civic   MODERN AUSTRALIAN/CAFE

There's a happy buzz of students and workers in this youthful joint. It offers everything from light snacks, smoothies, and milkshakes to full meals. The food is reasonably priced and contemporary, and the décor is 1970s retro. A great choice of alcoholic drinks and a range of freshly squeezed fruit juices are offered. Milk and Honey also does pasta well; its generous risotto stacked with seafood is recommended, too.

See map p. 239. Centre Cinema Building, 29 Garema Place, Civic. ☎ *02/6247 7722. Reservations recommended. Main courses: A$14–A$25 (US$11–US$20/£5.50–£10). AE, DC, MC, V. Open: Mon–Fri 7:30–10 p.m., Sat 8 a.m.–10 p.m., Sun 9 a.m.–3 p.m.*

Portia's Place
$ Kingston   CANTONESE/MALAYSIAN/PEKING

A small restaurant serving excellent traditional cookery, Portia's Place often fills up early and does a roaring lunchtime trade. The best things on the menu are lamb ribs in *shang tung* sauce, King Island filet steak in pepper sauce, flaming pork (brought to your table wrapped in foil and, yes, flaming), and Queensland trout stir-fried with snow peas.

See map p. 239. 11 Kennedy St., Kingston. ☎ *02/6239 7970. Main courses: A$9.80–A$19 (US$7.80–US$15/£4–£7.50). AE, DC, MC, V. Open: Daily noon to 2:30 p.m., Sun–Wed 5–10 p.m., Thurs–Sat 5–10:30 p.m.*

Ethnic eating

Canberra, like other Australian cities, has an interesting mix of people from all over the world. Canberra's best ethnic eateries include **Ottoman Cuisine,** 9 Broughton St., Barton (☎ **02/6273 6111**), which features fabulous Turkish food costing around A\$26 (US\$21/£11) for a main course. Another highlight is **Rama's,** Shop 6, Pearce Shopping Centre, on the corner of Mcfarland and Hodgson crescents, Pearce (☎ **02/6286 1964**), which specializes in Fijian Indian food with mains averaging A\$16 (US\$13/£7.50). For Ethiopian food (such as hot curries, cauliflower fritters, and lamb and rosemary kebabs), try **Fekerte's,** 74/2 Cape St., Dickson (☎ **02/6262 5799**), and call ahead to book; main courses here cost around A\$20 (US\$16/£8). Japanese-food addicts should head to tiny **Tasuke,** 122 Alinga St., Civic (☎ **02/6257 9711**); call ahead to book a table. Try the udon noodles, fish cakes, and deep-fried oysters; mains average around A\$20 (US\$16/£8).

Tosolini's
$$ Civic MODERN AUSTRALIAN/CAFE

Because it's next to the bus terminal and close to the major shopping areas, Tosolini's pulls in the passing crowd. You can sit on the sidewalk terrace and watch the world go by. Battered flathead and pan-fried broadbill (local fish) are tasty, but Tosolini's made its name with its pastas and focaccias. Try the popular spaghettini con granchio: succulent pieces of blue swimmer crab, fresh tomato, rocket leaves, chilli, garlic and extra virgin olive oil served on a bed of spaghettini. The tiramisu is a delight.

See map p. 239. Corner of London Circuit at East Row, Civic. ☎ *02/6247 4317. Main courses: A\$15–A\$18 (US\$12–US\$14/£6–£7). AE, DC, MC, V. Open: Sun–Mon 7:30 a.m.–5 p.m., Tues–Sat 7:30 a.m.–10:30 p.m.*

The Tryst
$$ Manuka MODERN AUSTRALIAN

The personal touches and service shine here, and the food is delicious. The restaurant is decorated in upscale cafe style, with the kitchen staff on show as they rustle up some of the capital's best tucker. It's relaxed, feeling more communal than intimate on busy nights. A favorite dish is Atlantic salmon served with beurre blanc sauce and potatoes. If you have room left for dessert, don't miss out on sticky date pudding with hot butterscotch sauce, pralines, and ice cream — it's as good as it sounds.

See map p. 239. Bougainville Street, Manuka. ☎ *02/6239 4422. Reservations recommended. Main courses: A\$15–A\$23 (US\$12–US\$18/£6–£9). AE, DC, MC, V. Open: Daily noon to 2:30 p.m., Mon–Sat 6–10 p.m.*

Waters Edge
$$$ **Parkes**   MODERN AUSTRALIAN

Minimalist décor, vaulted ceilings, crisp linen, and white leather chairs offset the striking architecture. Sweeping views across Lake Burley Griffin offer diners an outlook befitting the capital's most highly awarded restaurant. In keeping with the prime location, outstanding food, and carefully designed wine list, the polished service is non-intrusive but knowledgeable. Waters Edge has received several awards including Canberra's Restaurant of the Year 2006. Try the finely sliced cuttlefish on a bed of refried beans and cauliflower surrounded by crisply fried sweetbreads on a rich meat jus with a vinegar reduction.

See map p. 239. Commonwealth Place, Parkes. ☎ *02/6273 5066. Reservations required. Main courses: A$26–A$38 (US$21–US$31/£11–£16). AE, DC, MC, V. Open: Tues–Fri noon to 2:30 p.m., Tues–Sun 6:30–11 p.m.*

Exploring Canberra
The top attractions
Australian War Memorial

This monument to Australian troops who gave their lives for their country is truly moving. Artifacts and displays tell the story of Australia's conflicts abroad. You won't soon forget the exhibition on Gallipoli, the World War I battle in which so many Anzac (Australian and New Zealand Army Corps) servicemen were slaughtered. The Hall of Memory is the focus of the memorial, where the body of the Unknown Soldier lies entombed. The memorial also holds one of the largest collections of Australian art in the world.

See map p. 239. At the head of Anzac Parade on Limestone Avenue. ☎ *02/6243 4211. Free admission. Open: Daily 10 a.m.–5 p.m. (when the Last Post is played). Closed Dec 25. Guided tours at 10 a.m., 10:30 a.m., 11 a.m., 1:30 p.m., and 2 p.m.*

Canberra Deep Space Communication Complex

This information center, which stands beside huge tracking dishes, is a must for anyone interested in space. There are plenty of models, audiovisual recordings, and displays, including a spacesuit, space food, and archival footage of the Apollo moon landings. The complex is still active, tracking and recording results from space exploration projects, as well as providing a link with NASA spacecraft. There's no public bus service, but several tour companies offer programs that include the complex.

Tidbinbilla, 39km (24 miles) southwest of Civic. ☎ *02/6201 7880.* www.cdscc. nasa.gov. *Admission: Free. Open: Summer daily 9 a.m.–8 p.m., rest of year daily 9 a.m.–5 p.m.*

National Museum of Australia

Using state-of-the-art technology and hands-on exhibits, the museum concentrates on three main themes: Australian society and its history since 1788; the interaction of people with the Australian environment; and Aboriginal and Torres Strait Islander cultures and histories. It relies more on images and sound than on historical objects to tell the stories of Australia. Allow a couple of hours if it grabs you, and 30 minutes if it doesn't.

See map p. 239. Acton Peninsula (about 5km/3 miles from the city center). ☎ *1800/ 026 132 or 02/6208 5000.* www.nma.gov.au. *Admission: Free (but fees apply for special exhibitions). Open: Daily 9 a.m.–5 p.m.*

Parliament House

Conceived by architect Walter Burley Griffin in 1912, but not built until 1988, Canberra's focal point was designed to blend into its setting at the top of Capital Hill; only a national flag supported by a giant flagpole rises above the peak. In good weather, picnickers crowd the grass that covers the roof, where the view is spectacular. Inside are more than 3,000 works of Australian arts and crafts, and extensive areas of the building are open to the public. Just inside the main entrance, look for a mosaic by Michael Tjakamarra Nelson, *Meeting Place,* which represents a gathering of Aboriginal tribes. Free 50-minute guided tours run throughout the day.

See map p. 239. Capital Hill. ☎ *02/6277 5399. Admission: Free. Open: Daily 9 a.m.–5 p.m.*

Guided tours

Canberra Day Tours (☎ 02/6298 3344; www.canberradaytours.com.au) offers a hop-on/hop-off day tour by bus including stops at Old Parliament House, the Australian War Memorial, Parliament House, the Embassy region, Telstra Tower, and Lake Burley Griffin. The tour costs A$35 (US$28/£14) adults, A$15 (US$12/£6) kids under 16. The first bus leaves at 9:30 a.m. from the Canberra Visitors' Centre.

Living It Up after Dark

Of the pubs in town, the best are the British-style **Wig & Pen,** on the corner of Limestone and Alinga streets (☎ 02/6248 0171); popular **Moosehead's Pub,** 105 London Circuit (☎ 02/6257 6496); the **Phoenix,** 21 E. Row (☎ 02/6247 1606), which has live music (cover charge); and **P. J. O'Reileys** (☎ 02/6230 4752), on the corner of West Row and Alinga Street, an authentic Irish-style pub.

Fast Facts: Canberra

Area Code

The area code for the ACT is **02**.

American Express

Amex is located at Shop 1, Centerpoint, 185 City Walk (corner of Petrie Plaza), Civic (☎ 02/6247 2333). It's open Monday through Friday 9 a.m. to 5 p.m., Saturday 9 a.m. to noon.

Doctors

The Capital Medical Centre, 2 Mort St., Civic (☎ 02/6257 3766), is open Monday through Friday 8:30 a.m. to 4:30 p.m. The Travellers' Medical & Vaccination Centre, Level 5, 8–10 Hobart Place, Civic (☎ 02/6257 7154), offers vaccinations and travel medicines.

Embassies and Consulates

The U.S. Embassy is at Moonah Place, Yarralumla (☎ 02/6214 5600). The Canadian High Commission is at Commonwealth Avenue, Yarralumla (☎ 02/6270 4000). The British High Commission is on the tenth floor of the SAP Building, on the corner of Bunda and Akuna streets, Canberra City (☎ 02/6270 6666).

Emergencies

Call ☎ **000** for an ambulance, the police, or the fire department.

Hospitals

The most central hospital is Canberra Hospital, Yamba Drive, Garran (☎ 02/6244 2222), or call the Accident and Emergency Department (☎ 02/6244 2324).

Newspapers/Magazines

The *Canberra Times* is the local paper.

Pharmacies

A central drugstore is Develin's City Chemist, 3 Garema Place, Civic (☎ 02/6248 5250).

Police

City Station, 16/18 London Circuit, Civic (☎ 02/6256 7777).

Part IV
Brisbane, Queensland, and the Great Barrier Reef

The 5th Wave   By Rich Tennant

"As this is your first visit to Queensland, I suppose you're eager to see the Great Barrier Reef."

In this part . . .

*T*raveling the vast state of Queensland — known around Australia as the "Sunshine State" for its magnificent weather — is a vast undertaking in a territory with a huge coastline to match its massive Barrier Reef.

In Chapter 16, we take you to its capital, Brisbane, a river city with much to explore. Set your sightseeing dial to "relaxed" and enjoy the balmy subtropical delights of this laid-back city.

Brisbane is also the gateway to the beaches of the Gold Coast and the Sunshine Coast, to the south and north of the city, respectively. We cover these destinations — along with the rest of the coastline of Queensland — in Chapter 17.

This part is also where you find everything you need to know about planning a holiday on the Great Barrier Reef. We look at jumping-off points for the reef from Cairns, in the north, to the Whitsundays, farther south. Whether you're a first-time snorkeler or an experienced diver, we offer tips aplenty on how to get the most out of your time and ensure your visit is one that you'll remember forever.

In addition to the Reef, there's plenty more to explore along Queensland's coast. Head for the rain forest or the islands. Have close (but not too close) encounters with crocodiles, cassowaries, dolphins, butterflies, birds, and other wildlife. Go sea-kayaking, bungee-jumping, or white-water rafting. Stay in five-star luxury or a tent on a remote island.

Chapter 16

Brisbane

by Lee Mylne

In This Chapter

▶ Discovering sunny Brisbane, gateway to the Great Barrier Reef
▶ Sleeping, eating, and sightseeing in Brisbane
▶ Enjoying Brisbane's nightlife

*Q*ueensland's capital is rich in history and character; it's friendly, relaxed, and laid-back, befitting its subtropical climate. Set on the banks of the Brisbane River, this is a city that has evolved from a country town to an increasingly sophisticated place. The city is green and leafy: Moreton Bay fig trees give shade, and in summer, the purple haze of jacarandas competes with the scarlet blaze of poinciana trees.

Brisbane (pronounced *briz*-bun) is known for its timber *Queenslanders,* cottages and houses set high on stumps to catch the breeze, with wide verandas to keep out the sun.

In the city center, colonial sandstone buildings stand alongside modern glass towers. Wander in the city botanic gardens, in-line skate or bike along the riverfront pathways, have a drink in a pub beer garden, or get out on the river on a CityCat ferry, and you'll discover Brisbane's allure. Getting around is cheap and easy, good food — including fantastic seafood — is abundant, and accommodations are affordable, especially in some of the city's comfortable, elegant B&Bs.

Getting There

By plane

About 20 international airlines serve Brisbane from Europe, Asia, and New Zealand, including Qantas, Air New Zealand, Pacific Blue, Singapore Airlines, Thai International, Malaysia Airlines, and Cathay Pacific. From North America, you can fly direct from Los Angeles to Brisbane on Qantas, but from other places you'll likely fly to Sydney and connect on Qantas, or fly direct from Auckland, New Zealand.

Qantas (☎ **13 13 13** in Australia; www.qantas.com.au) and its sub-sidiary **Qantaslink** (book through Qantas) operate daily flights from state capitals, Cairns, Townsville, and several other regional towns. No-frills **Jetstar** (☎ **13 15 38** in Australia; www.jetstar.com.au) has daily service from Proserpine, Hamilton Island, Melbourne's Avalon airport, and Hobart and Launceston in Tasmania. **Virgin Blue** (☎ **13 67 89** in Australia; www.virginblue.com.au) offers direct services from all capi-tal cities as well as Cairns, Townsville, Hamilton Island and Proserpine in the Whitsundays, Mackay and Rockhampton in Queensland, and New-castle in New South Wales.

Getting oriented at the airport

Brisbane International Airport is 16km (10 miles) from the city, and the domestic terminal is 2km (1¼ miles) farther away. The arrivals floor, on Level 2, has an information desk that can help with flight inquiries, dis-pense tourist information, and make hotel bookings, and a check-in counter for passengers transferring to domestic flights.

Getting from the airport to your hotel

Coachtrans (☎ **07/3238 4700**; www.coachtrans.com.au) runs a shuttle between the airport and Roma Street Transit Centre every 30 minutes from 5 a.m. to 11 p.m. The one-way cost is A$9 (US$7.20/£3.60), A$11 (US$8.80/£4.40) for hotel drop-off. The round-trip fare is A$15 (US$12/£6), A$18 (US$14/£7) for hotel drop-off. One-way family tickets are A$24 (US$19/£9.60), A$29 (US$23/£12) for hotel drop-off. The trip takes about 40 minutes, and reservations are not needed. No public buses serve the airport. A **taxi** to the city costs around A$25 (US$20/£10) from the inter-national terminal and A$30 (US$24/£12) from the domestic terminal, plus A$2 (US$1.60/£0.80) for departing taxis.

Airtrain (☎ **07/3216 3308**; www.airtrain.com.au), a rail link between the city and the domestic and international airport terminals, runs every 15 minutes from around 6 a.m. to 7:30 p.m. daily. Fares from the airport to city stations are A$12 (US$9.60/£4.80) adults, A$6 (US$4.80/£2.40) chil-dren. The trip takes about 20 minutes. The Airtrain fare between the international and domestic terminals is A$4 (US$3.20/£1.60). A taxi between terminals costs about A$10 (US$8/£4).

By train

Queensland Rail (☎ **13 22 32** in Queensland; www.qr.com.au) operates several long-distance trains to Brisbane from Cairns. The high-speed Tilt Train takes about 25 hours and costs A$303 (US$242/£121) for business class. The *Sunlander* takes 32 hours and costs A$207 (US$166/£83) for a sitting berth, A$265 (US$212/£106) for an economy-class sleeper, A$409 (US$327/£164) for a first-class sleeper, or A$743 (US$594/£297) for the all-inclusive Queenslander class. **Countrylink** (☎ **13 22 32** in Australia; www.countrylink.info) runs two daily train services to Brisbane from Sydney. The 7:15 a.m. departure arrives in the town of Casino, south of the border, at 6:34 p.m., where passengers transfer to a bus for the rest of the trip to Brisbane, arriving at 10:20 p.m. The trip costs A$124 (US$99/£50) adults. The overnight train, which leaves Sydney at 4:20 p.m. and arrives in Brisbane at 6:30 a.m. the next day, costs A$175 (US$140/£70) for a seat, an extra A$88 (US$70/£35) for a sleeper. Ask about off-peak discounts, depending on the time of year.

All intercity and interstate trains pull into the city center's **Brisbane Transit Centre at Roma Street,** often called the Roma Street Transit Centre. From here, most city and Spring Hill hotels are a few blocks' walk or a quick cab ride away. The station has food outlets, showers, tourist information, and lockers.

Queensland Rail CityTrain (☎ 13 12 30 in Queensland) provides daily train service from the Sunshine Coast and the Gold Coast.

By bus

All intercity and interstate coaches pull into the **Brisbane Transit Centre** (see "By train," earlier). **Greyhound Australia** (☎ 13 14 99 in Australia, or 07/4690 9950; www.greyhound.com.au) serves the city several times daily. A one-way Cairns–Brisbane ticket costs A$234 (US$187/£94); the trip takes 29½ hours. The Sydney–Brisbane trip takes 16½ hours and costs A$116 (US$93/£46) one-way. Coachtrans provides daily service from the Gold Coast. Call **Transinfo** (☎ 13 12 30) for details.

By car

The Bruce Highway from Cairns enters the city from the north. The Pacific Highway enters Brisbane from the south.

Orienting Yourself in Brisbane

Central Brisbane is easy to navigate when you remember that the east–west streets are named after female British royalty, and the north–south streets are named after their male counterparts. The northernmost is Ann, followed by Adelaide, Queen, Elizabeth, Charlotte, Mary, Margaret, and Alice. From east to west, the streets are Edward, Albert, George, and William, which becomes North Quay, flanking the river's northeast bank. Queen Street, the main thoroughfare, is a pedestrian mall between Edward and George streets. Ann Street leads all the way east into Fortitude Valley. The main street in Fortitude Valley is Brunswick Street, which runs into New Farm.

The city center's office towers shimmer on the north bank of the Brisbane River. At the tip of the curve in the river are the Brisbane City Gardens (sometimes called the City Botanic Gardens). The 30m (98-ft.) sandstone cliffs of Kangaroo Point rise on the eastern side of the south bank; to the west are the South Bank Parklands and the Queensland Cultural Centre precinct, known as South Bank. The **Goodwill Bridge,** for pedestrians and bikes only, links South Bank with the City Gardens. To the west, 5km (3 miles), is Mount Coot-tha (pronounced *coo*-tha).

The **Brisbane Map,** free from Brisbane Visitor Information Centre or your concierge, shows the river and outlying suburbs, as well as the city. It's great for drivers because it shows parking lots and one-way streets on the city-center grid. It can also be downloaded from www.ourbrisbane. com. Rental cars usually come with street directories. Newsdealers and some bookstores sell this map; the state auto club, the **RACQ,** in the General Post Office, 261 Queen St. (☎ 13 19 05), is also a good source.

Introducing the Neighbourhoods

- ✔ **City Center:** This is where Brisbane people eat, shop, and socialize. The Queen Street Mall is the heart of the city center. The Eagle Street financial and legal precinct has great restaurants with river views and Sunday markets. Strollers, bike riders, and in-line skaters shake the heat in the green haven of the Brisbane City Gardens at the business district's southern end.

- ✔ **Fortitude Valley:** "The Valley" was once one of the sleazier parts of town, but today you'll find trendy pubs and cool cafes. The lanterns, food stores, and shopping mall of Chinatown are here, too.

- ✔ **New Farm:** Always appealing, New Farm is great for cafe-hopping. Merthyr Street is where the action is, especially on Friday and Saturday night.

- ✔ **Paddington:** This hilltop suburb is a couple miles northwest of the city. Brightly painted Queenslander cottages line the main street, Latrobe Terrace, as it winds west along a ridge top. Many of the houses have been turned into shops and cafes.

- ✔ **Milton & Rosalie:** Park Road, Milton, is distinguished by its replica Eiffel Tower above the cafes and shops. Italian restaurants line the street, buzzing with office workers. Sip a cappuccino, scout the interior design stores for a new objets d'art, or stock up on European designer rags.

- ✔ **West End:** This small inner-city enclave is alive with ethnic restaurants, cafes, and interesting stores. Most action centers on the intersection of Vulture and Boundary streets.

- ✔ **Bulimba:** One of the emerging suburbs, Bulimba has a long connection with the river through the boat-building industry. Take the CityCat, and walk to Oxford Street, lined with cafes and shops.

Finding information after you arrive

The **Brisbane Visitor Information Centre** (☎ 07/3006 6290) is in the Queen Street Mall, between Edward and Albert streets. It's open Monday through Thursday from 9 a.m. to 5:30 p.m., Friday 9 a.m. to 7 p.m. or later, Saturday 9 a.m. to 5 p.m., Sunday 9:30 a.m. to 4:30 p.m., and holidays 9 a.m. to 4:30 p.m. The official Web site (www.ourbrisbane.com) and the **Brisbane Transit Centre** (☎ 07/3236 2020) are other good sources of information.

Getting Around Brisbane

TransLink operates a network of buses, trains, and ferries. For timetables and route inquiries, call **TransInfo** (☎ 13 12 30; www.translink.com.au; open: Mon–Thurs 6 a.m.–9 p.m., and from 6 a.m. Fri to 9 p.m. Sun, although hours may vary on holidays). The easiest place to buy your tickets is on the buses or at the train stations. You can also buy tickets and pick up maps and timetables at the Queen Street bus station information center (in the Myer Centre, off Queen Street Mall) and the Brisbane Visitor Information Centre in the Queen Street Mall. Tickets are also sold at some inner-city newsdealers.

A trip in one zone on the bus, train, or ferry costs A$2.20 (US$1.75/£0.90). A ticket is good for up to two hours on a one-way trip on any combination of bus, train, or ferry. When traveling with a parent, kids under 5 travel free. Kids 5 to 14 and students pay half fare.

If you plan on using public transport a lot, a **ten-trip ticket** may be a good investment.

You probably won't need to travel farther than four zones on the transport system. This will cost you A$3.40 (US$2.70/£1.35) each way. A one-day ticket for four zones costs A$6.80 (US$5.45/£2.70).

On weekends and public holidays, it's cheaper to buy an off-peak ticket, which lets you travel all day for A$3.30 (US$2.65/£1.30) adults. The off-peak ticket is also available on weekdays but cannot be used before 9 a.m. or between 3:30 p.m. and 7 p.m.

By bus

Buses operate from around 5 a.m. to 11 p.m. weekdays, with less service on weekends. On Sunday, many routes stop around 5 p.m. Most buses depart from City Hall at King George Square, from Adelaide or Ann Street.

The **Downtown Loop** is a free bus service that circles the city center. The Loop's red buses run on two routes, stopping at convenient places including Central Station, Queen Street Mall, City Botanic Gardens, and King George Square. Look for the red bus stops. They run every ten minutes from 7 a.m. to 5:50 p.m. Monday through Friday.

Brisbane

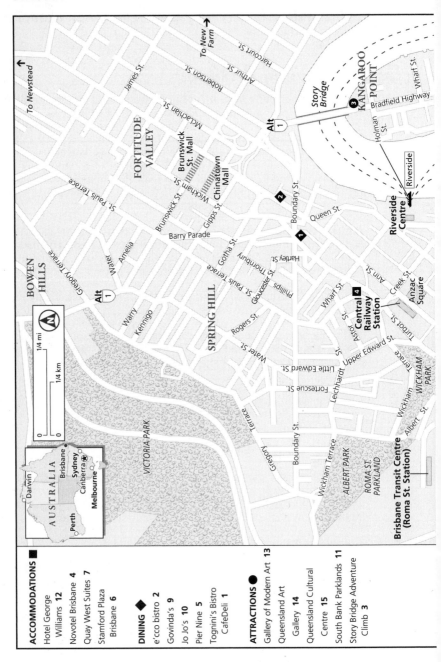

To Newstead

To New Farm →

Harcourt St.

Arthur St.

Robertson St.

James St.

McLachlan St.

Story Bridge

KANGAROO POINT

Bradfield Highway

Wharf St.

Holman St.

3

FORTITUDE VALLEY

Brunswick St. Mall

St. Pauls Terrace

Wickham St.

Brunswick St.

Chinatown Mall

Gipps St.

Barry Parade

Gotha St.

Boundary St.

Queen St.

2

Riverside

Riverside Centre

1

Alt 1

Amelia

Water St.

Gregory Terrace

Alt 1

BOWEN HILLS

Warry

Kennigo

St. Pauls Terrace

Thornbury St.

Phillips St.

Gloucester St.

Hartley St.

1

SPRING HILL

Rogers St.

Water St.

Wharf St.

Astor

Wharf St.

Ann St.

Creek St.

Anzac Square

Turbot St.

4 Central Railway Station

Leichhardt St.

Upper Edward St.

Little Edward St.

Fortescue St.

Boundary St.

Wickham Terrace

Gregory Terrace

Albert St.

Wickham Terrace

WICKHAM PARK

ALBERT PARK

ROMA ST. PARKLAND

Brisbane Transit Centre (Roma St. Station)

VICTORIA PARK

1/4 mi
1/4 km
0
0

AUSTRALIA

Darwin

Brisbane

Sydney

Canberra

Perth

Melbourne

ACCOMMODATIONS ■

Hotel George Williams **12**

Novotel Brisbane **4**

Quay West Suites **7**

Stamford Plaza Brisbane **6**

DINING ◆

e'cco bistro **2**

Govinda's **9**

Jo Jo's **10**

Pier Nine **5**

Tognini's Bistro CafeDeli **1**

ATTRACTIONS ●

Gallery of Modern Art **13**

Queensland Art Gallery **14**

Queensland Cultural Centre **15**

South Bank Parklands **11**

Story Bridge Adventure Climb **3**

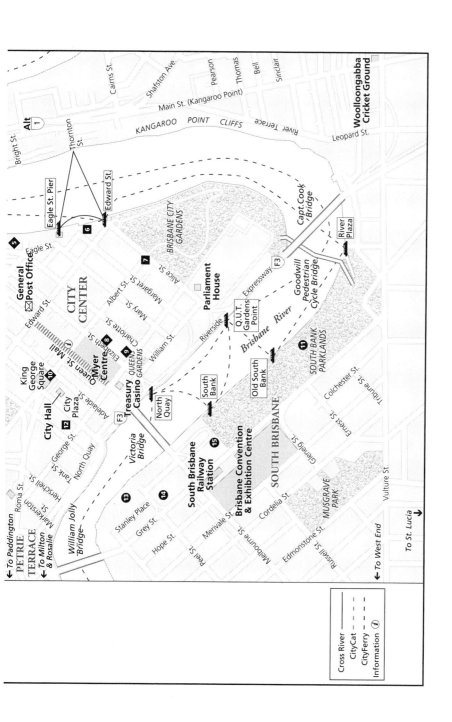

By ferry

The fast **CityCat** ferries run to many places, including South Bank and the Queensland Cultural Centre; the restaurants and Sunday markets at the Riverside Centre; and New Farm Park, not far from the cafes of Merthyr Street. They run every half-hour between Queensland University, approximately 9km (5½ miles) to the south, and Brett's Wharf, about 9km (5½ miles) to the north. Slower but more frequent CityFerry service (**Inner City** and **Cross River** ferries) stops at a few more points, including the south end of South Bank Parklands, Kangaroo Point, and Edward Street outside the Brisbane City Gardens. Ferries run from around 6 a.m. to 10:30 p.m. daily.

By train

Brisbane's suburban rail network is fast, safe, and clean. Trains run from around 5 a.m. to midnight (until about 11 p.m. on Sun). All trains leave Central Station, between Turbot and Ann streets at Edward Street.

By car

Brisbane's grid of one-way streets can be confusing, so plan your route before you set off. Brisbane's biggest car park is at the Myer Centre (enter from Elizabeth Street) and is open 24 hours (☎ **07/3229 1699**). Most hotels and motels have free parking for guests.

Avis (☎ **13 63 33** or 07/3221 2900), **Budget** (☎ **1300/362 848** in Australia, or 07/3220 0699), **Europcar** (☎ **13 13 90** in Australia, or 07/3006 7440), and **Hertz** (☎ **13 30 39** or 07/3221 6166) all have outlets in the city center. **Thrifty** (☎ **1300/367 227** in Australia) is at 49 Barry Parade, Fortitude Valley.

On foot

Because Brisbane is leafy, warm, and full of colonial-era Queenslander architecture, it's a great city for walking — except in summer, when it can become uncomfortably hot and humid. Pick up one of the free **Heritage Trail Maps** from the Brisbane Visitor Information Centre (see "Finding information after you arrive," earlier in this chapter). The map books include a history of the area and detailed information of historic buildings and other sights along the way.

A "floating" **River Walk** connects over 20km (13 miles) of pathways, roads, bridges, and parks along the Brisbane River. You can stroll along River Walk on the north bank of the river between the University of Queensland at St. Lucia and Teneriffe, and on the south bank from the West End ferry terminal at Orleigh Park to Dockside at Kangaroo Point.

 The Brisbane City Council's **Gonewalking** program (☎ **07/3403 8888**) runs about 80 free guided walks each week, exploring all kinds of territory, from bushland to heritage buildings to riverscapes to cemeteries. The walks are aimed at locals, not tourists, so you'll get to explore

Brisbane and meet the locals at the same time. Each walk has a flexible distance option and usually lasts about an hour.

 The **Brisbane Mobility Map** outlines wheelchair access to buildings in the city center and includes a detailed guide to the Queen Street Mall and a map of the Brisbane Botanic Gardens Mount Coot-tha. The council's disability-services unit also has a range of publications, including a Braille Trail and an access guide to parks, available from council customer service centers (☎ **07/3403 8888**).

Staying in Style

The top hotels

 ### Hotel George Williams
$–$$ City Center

It's hard to believe that this smart hotel is a YMCA. Accommodations have vivid bedcovers, chrome chairs, and Wi-Fi access. The rooms are small but some can sleep up to four adults. Facilities include a 24-hour front desk, safe-deposit boxes, and a cybercafe and bar. Guests have free access to the City Y health club, the largest hotel gym in Australia. Four rooms are designed for guests with disabilities.

See map p. 254. 317–325 George St. (between Turbot and Ann streets), Brisbane, QLD 4000. ☎ *1800/064 858 in Australia, or 07/3308 0700. Fax: 07/3308 0733.* www.hgw. com.au. *Rack rates: A$95–A$175 (US$76–US$140/£38–£70) double; extra person A$25 (US$20/£10). Children under 4 stay free in parent's room. AE, DC, MC, V.*

 ### Novotel Brisbane
$$$ City Center

Contemporary and well-appointed, this hotel is a short walk from Brisbane's main shopping areas, and is popular with families and business travelers. The modern, stylish rooms and suites are spacious and have superb views, as does the inviting lap pool. Kids' meals are offered in both the swish **Cilantro** restaurant or the more casual **Loose Goose** cafe.

See map p. 254. 200 Creek St., Brisbane, QLD 4000. ☎ *1300/656 565 in Australia, or 07/3309 3309; 800-221-4542 in the U.S. and Canada; 0870/609 0961 in the U.K.; 0800/44 4422 in New Zealand. Fax: 07/3309 3308.* www.accorhotels.com.au. *Rack rates: A$226–A$246 (US$181–US$197/£90–£98) double. Children under 16 stay free in parent's room with existing bedding. AE, DC, MC, V.*

Quay West Suites
$$$–$$$$ City Center

This all-suite hotel, 4 blocks from Queen Street Mall, offers great package deals, particularly on weekends. A one-bedroom suite will sleep four, using the sofa bed. The suites have all the amenities of a five-star hotel — daily servicing, concierge, a bar and restaurant with an outdoor terrace — and their own laundries, dining areas, separate bedrooms, and fully equipped kitchens. Pamper yourself in the plunge pool or Jacuzzi; then back in your room get into your bathrobe, order up room-service (24 hours), gaze over the Botanic Gardens, turn on the CD player, or watch one of the two TVs.

See map p. 254. 132 Alice St. (between Albert and George streets), Brisbane, QLD 4000. ☎ *1800/672 726 in Australia, or 07/3853 6000. Fax: 07/3853 6060.* www.mirvac hotels.com.au. *Rack rates: A$295 (US$236/£118) 1-bedroom apartment, A$405 (US$324/£162) 2-bedroom apartment; extra person A$35 (US$28/£14). AE, DC, MC, V.*

Stamford Plaza Brisbane
$$$$–$$$$$ City Center

The Stamford is one of Brisbane's most luxurious hotels. It has river views from every room — especially stunning from the southern rooms at night, when the Story Bridge is illuminated. The guest rooms are not enormous, but all fit a king-size bed or two twins. In what must be the biggest bathrooms in Brisbane, you'll find small TVs. A riverside boardwalk leads from the hotel to the Eagle Street Pier restaurants.

See map p. 254. Edward and Margaret streets (adjacent to the Brisbane City Gardens), Brisbane, QLD 4000. ☎ *1800/773 700 in Australia, or 07/3221 1999. Fax: 07/3221 6895.* www.stamford.com.au. *Rack rates: A$300–A$650 (US$240–US$520/ £120–£260) double, A$690–A$3,500 (US$552–US$2,800/£276–£1,400) suite; extra person A$40 (US$32/£16). Children under 12 stay free in parent's room with existing bedding. AE, DC, MC, V.*

A great B&B

Eton
$$ City Center

This heritage-listed cottage, not far from the Brisbane Transit Centre, has five rooms and an attic suite all with en-suite bathrooms. The attic suite is a self-contained apartment with its own entrance and kitchen. We recommend room no. 1, at the front of the house, because of its claw-foot bathtub and king-size bed. The B&B also has Wi-Fi. Out the back is a garden courtyard, where you can have breakfast among the palms, ferns, and frangipani trees.

436 Upper Roma St., Brisbane, QLD 4000. ☎ *07/3236 0115.* www.babs.com. au/eton. *Rack rates: A$110–A$130 (US$88–US$104/£44–£52) double, A$490 (US$392/£196) apartment weekly. Rates include breakfast (except apartment). AE, MC, V.*

Dining Out

Stylish bistros and cafes line Merthyr Street in New Farm; cute cafes are plentiful in Paddington; Asian eateries are a good choice around the intersection of Vulture and Boundary streets in West End; and in

Fortitude Valley ("the Valley" for short), you find Chinatown. A street full of upscale but laid-back restaurants, many with a Mediterranean flavor, sits under the kitsch replica Eiffel Tower on Park Road in Milton. The intersection of Albert and Charlotte streets buzzes with inexpensive, good-quality cafes.

Breakfast Creek Hotel
$ Albion   CONTEMPORARY/STEAK

Built in 1889 and listed by the National Trust, this French Renaissance-style pub is known as the Brekky Creek — or simply "the Creek." It is a Brisbane icon, famed for its gigantic steaks, and for serving beer "off the wood" (from the keg). The Spanish Garden restaurant and the beer garden are always popular, and an outdoor dining area overlooks Breakfast Creek. The Substation No. 41 bar, created in the shell of a derelict electricity sub-station next door, makes the most of its exposed brick walls and soaring ceilings.

12 Kingsford Smith Dr. (at Breakfast Creek Road), Albion. ☎ *07/3262 5988.* www.breakfastcreekhotel.com. *Main courses: A$17–A$25 (US$14–US$20/£7–£10). AE, DC, MC, V. Open: Daily 11:30 a.m.–2:30 p.m., Mon–Fri 5:30–9:30 p.m., Sat 5– 9:30 p.m., Sun 5–8:30 p.m.; pub Sun–Thurs 10 a.m.–10 p.m., Fri–Sat 10 a.m.–11 p.m; Substation No. 41 daily noon to late, breakfast Sunday 8–10:30 a.m.*

e'cco bistro
$$$$ Brisbane City   CONTEMPORARY

Simple food, done exceptionally well and with passion. That's the winning philosophy behind the food at e'cco, one of Australia's top restaurants. Housed in a former tea warehouse, the bistro has large windows, bold colors, and modern furniture. Dishes include such delights as duck breast with Peking duck consommé, wombok, broccolini, chilli and ginger; or grilled white fish with a cassoulet of white beans, clams, mussels, parsley, and peppers. The price structure is simple — each course's offerings are all the same price — and there's an extensive wine list.

See map p. 254. 100 Boundary St. (at Adelaide Street). ☎ *07/3831 8344. Fax: 07/3831 8460.* www.eccobistro.com. *Reservations required. Main courses: A$37 (US$30/£15). AE, DC, MC, V. Open: Tues–Fri noon to 2:30 p.m., Tues–Sat 6–10 p.m.*

Govinda's
$ Brisbane City   VEGETARIAN

Vegetarians, travelers on a budget, or those who love cheap and good food, should seek out the Hare Krishnas' chain of Govinda restaurants. This one serves vegetable casserole, samosas, and other tasty stuff with a north Indian influence. The atmosphere is spartan, but the food is satisfying. Don't expect wine (or tea or coffee) — the only drinks you're likely to get will be something like homemade ginger and mint lemonade. On Sunday nights, the meal comes with lectures and dancing.

See map p. 254. 99 Elizabeth St. (opposite Myer Centre), 2nd floor. ☎ 07/3210 0255. Main courses: A$9 (US$7.20/£3.60) all-you-can-eat, A$8 (US$6.40/£3.20) concessions, A$6 (US$4.80/£2.40) students (2–3 p.m. only). No credit cards. Open: Mon–Thurs 11 a.m.–3 p.m. (takeout 4:30–6:30 p.m.), Fri 11 a.m.–8:30 p.m., Sat 11 a.m.–2:30 p.m., Sun Feast from 5 p.m. (A$5/US$4/£2).

Green Papaya
$$$ Woolloongabba   NORTH VIETNAMESE

Clean, fresh, and simple dishes are the hallmark of this popular restaurant. After 12 years in operation, it changed ownership in 2007, but Chef Thang is still at the helm, so the quality remains. There are two cheerful rooms, usually crowded with a faithful clientele. The staff will give advice if you don't know your *bo xao cay ngot* (spicy beef) from your *nom du du* (green papaya salad). The restaurant is licensed, but you can bring your own wine for a corkage charge of A$3 (US$2.40/£1.20) per person.

898 Stanley St. E. (at Potts Street, 1 block from Woolloongabba Cricket Ground), East Brisbane. ☎ 07/3217 3599. www.greenpapaya.com.au. Reservations recommended. Main courses: A$25–A$36 (US$20–US$29/£10–£14), banquet menus (for minimum of 4 people) A$50–A$60 (US$40–US$48/£20–£24). Minimum charge A$30 (US$24/£12) per person. AE, DC, MC, V. Open: Tues–Sun 5:30–10 p.m., Thurs–Fri lunch by reservation only. Closed Good Friday (Fri before Easter) and Dec 25 to early Jan.

Jo Jo's
$–$$ Brisbane City   INTERNATIONAL

This smart but casual spot offers four menus — char grill, Thai, pizza, and Mediterranean — and the locals have been dropping in here for years for a pit stop or a post-cinema meal. The food is well-priced and good, and there is a huge wine list. Order your meals at the bar and they'll be delivered to the table (try to get one on the balcony overlooking the Queen Street Mall). Among the options are steaks and seafood from the grill; curries and stir-fries from the Thai menu; Mediterranean pastas, antipasto, and designer sandwiches; and gourmet toppings on wood-fired-oven pizzas.

See map p. 254. 1st floor, Queen Street Mall at Albert Street. ☎ 07/3221 2113. www.jojos.com.au. Main courses: A$10–A$30 (US$8–US$24/£4–£12). AE, DC, MC, V. Open: Daily 9:30 a.m. to midnight, happy hour daily 4:30–6 p.m.

Pier Nine
$$$ Riverside   CONTEMPORARY/SEAFOOD

Ask the locals to recommend the best seafood joint in town, and you'll find yourself in this light-filled restaurant overlooking the river and Story Bridge. The menu changes daily; specialties include oysters shucked to order and served several ways or au naturel. There are plenty of options for meat-lovers and vegetarians, but the emphasis here is on fresh seafood. Try the shredded omelette with sand crab, shrimp, and fine egg noodles.

It's always busy, but if you show up without a reservation you can cool your heels at the oyster bar.

See map p. 254. Eagle Street Pier, 1 Eagle St. ☎ 07/3226 2100. Reservations recommended. Main courses: A$21–A$48 (US$17–US$38/£8.40–£19). AE, DC, MC, V. Open: Mon–Fri 11:30 a.m.–10 p.m., Sat 5–10 p.m. Closed Sun and public holidays.

The Summit
$–$$$ Mount Coot-tha   CONTEMPORARY

For food-with-a-view, head to the top of Mount Coot-tha. A teahouse of some kind has been on this mountaintop for more than a century. Today's restaurant is part Queenslander house and part modern extension, with wraparound decks giving sweeping views of the city and Moreton Bay. A changing menu features local produce teamed with Australian wines. Try saltwater barramundi (fish) filet. The early-bird special — A$30 (US$24/£12) for three courses — is served between 5 and 7 p.m. There's a kids' menu for under A$15 (US$12/£6). And when you've finished dining, spend some time on the observation deck — at night, the city lights provide a glittering panorama.

Mount Coot-tha Lookout, Sir Samuel Griffith Drive, Mount Coot-tha. ☎ 07/3369 9922. Fax: 07/3369 8937. www.brisbanelookout.com. *Reservations recommended Fri–Sat night. Main courses: A$29–A$38 (US$23–US$30/£12–£15). AE, DC, MC, V. Open: Daily 11:30 a.m. to midnight, Sun brunch 8–10:30 a.m. Closed for lunch Jan 1, Good Friday (Fri before Easter), Dec 26; closed for dinner Dec 25.*

Tognini's BistroCafeDeli
$–$$ Spring Hill   CONTEMPORARY

There are three Tognini's to choose from in Brisbane — the others are at Baroona Road in Milton and in the State Library building at South Bank. This one is ideal for inner-city dwellers, especially if you're staying in an apartment hotel and don't feel like cooking. Mark and Narelle Tognini's relaxed modern bistro incorporates an extensive deli and walk-in cheese room. If you're eating in, sit at one of the communal tables and try salmon and sweet potato fish cakes with Asian noodle salad. Don't pass up the vanilla *panna cotta* for dessert — it's divine.

See map p. 254. Turbot and Boundary streets, Spring Hill. ☎ 07/3831 5300. Fax: 07/3831 5311. www.togninis.com. *Reservations not accepted. Main courses: A$15–A$23 (US$12–US$18/£6–£9). AE, DC, MC, V. Open: Mon–Fri 7 a.m.–6 p.m., Sat–Sun 8 a.m.–4 p.m. Closed Easter and Dec 25.*

Watt Modern Dining
$$$–$$$$ New Farm   CONTEMPORARY

With a menu of modern fare with Asian, Middle Eastern, and European influences, and a terrific wine list, Watt is one of our favorite places in Brisbane — because of the riverside setting, and the great food. Dishes include interesting things like blackened duck breast with sea scallops, pickled cucumber and star anise broth. Come for a leisurely weekend breakfast, lunch, or dinner before a show at the Brisbane Powerhouse. The Park Lounge is great for pre-theater drinks and light meals.

Brisbane Powerhouse, 119 Lamington St. (near the river), New Farm. ☎ *07/3358 5464.* www.watt.net.au. *Reservations recommended. Main courses: A$25–A$37 (US$20–US$30/£10–£15). AE, DC, MC, V. Open: Tues–Fri 10 a.m. to late, Sat–Sun 8 a.m. to late.*

Exploring Brisbane

The top attractions

Lone Pine Koala Sanctuary

Banned in New South Wales and Victoria, koala cuddling is allowed in Queensland under strict conditions. When it opened in 1927, Lone Pine had only two koalas, Jack and Jill; it is now home to more than 130. You can have a photo taken holding one for A$15 (US$12/£6). Lone Pine is also home to kangaroos and wallabies and lots of other native wildlife including emus, snakes, baby crocs, parrots, wombats, Tasmanian devils, skinks, lace monitors, frogs, bats, turtles, and possums. The nicest way to get to Lone Pine is a cruise down the Brisbane River aboard M.V. *Mirimar* (☎ **1300/729 742** in Australia), which leaves the Queensland Cultural Centre at South Bank Parklands at 10 a.m. The 19km (12-mile) trip to Lone Pine takes 90 minutes and includes commentary. You have two hours to explore before returning, arriving in the city at 2:45 p.m. The fare is A$48 (US$38/£19) adults, A$27 (US$22/£11) children 3 to 13, A$135 (US$108/£54) families of five, including entry to Lone Pine. Cruises run daily except April 25 (Anzac Day) and December 25.

Jesmond Road, Fig Tree Pocket. ☎ *07/3378 1366. Fax: 07/3878 1770.* www.koala. net. *By car (20 minutes from the city center), take Milton Road to the roundabout at Toowong Cemetery, then Western Freeway toward Ipswich. Signs point to Fig Tree Pocket and Lone Pine. Bus: No. 430 from the city center hourly 8:45 a.m.–3:40 p.m. weekdays, 8:30 a.m.–3:30 p.m. weekends and public holidays; no. 445 at 8:45 a.m. and 3:45 p.m., and hourly from 9:10 a.m.–2:10 p.m. weekdays, 7:55 a.m.–2:55 p.m. Sat. Ample free parking. Bus fare A$2.90 (US$2.30/£1.15) adults, A$1.50 (US$1.20/£0.60) children. Taxi from the city center about A$24 (US$19/£9.60). Admission: A$20 (US$16/£8) adults, A$15 (US$12/£6) children 3–13, A$52 (US$42/£21) families of 5. AE, DC, MC, V. Open: Daily 8:30 a.m.–5 p.m., 1:30–5 p.m. Apr 25 (Anzac Day), 8:30 a.m.– 4:30 p.m. Dec 25.*

Queensland Art Gallery

One of Australia's most attractive galleries, the Queensland Art Gallery (QAG) has vast, light-filled spaces and interesting water features inside and out. It is a major player in the Australian art world, attracting international exhibitions and showcasing modern Australian painters, sculptors, and other artists. It also has an impressive collection of Aboriginal art. The adjacent Queensland Gallery of Modern Art, provides more space for the collections of modern and contemporary Australian, indigenous

Australian, Asian, and Pacific art. The Australian Cinémathèque has two cinemas in which it presents films as well as a gallery of film-related exhibitions.

See map p. 254. Grey Street, South Brisbane. ☎ *07/3840 7303.* www.qag.qld.gov.au. *Admission: Free. Open: Mon–Fri 10 a.m.–5 p.m., weekends 9 a.m.–5 p.m. Closed Good Friday (Fri before Easter), and until noon on April 25 (Anzac Day).*

South Bank Parklands

Spend some time at this delightful 16-hectare (40-acre) complex of parks, restaurants, shops, playgrounds, and weekend markets and you're sure to meet the locals. There's a man-made beach, lined with palm trees, with real waves and sand, where you can swim, stroll, and cycle the meandering pathways. Or sit over a cafe latte in one of the cafes and enjoy the city views. From the parklands it's an easy stroll to the museum, art gallery, and other parts of the adjacent Queensland Cultural Centre.

See map p. 254. South Bank. ☎ *07/3867 2051.* www.south-bank.net.au. *Admission: Free. From the Queen Street Mall, cross the Victoria Bridge to South Bank or walk across Goodwill Bridge from Gardens Point Road entrance to Brisbane City Gardens. Plentiful underground parking in Queensland Cultural Centre. Train: South Brisbane. Ferry: South Bank (CityCat or Cross River Ferry). Bus: Numerous routes from Adelaide Street (near Albert Street), including nos. 100, 111, 115, and 120, stop at the Queensland Cultural Centre; walk through the Centre to South Bank Parklands. Open: Park daily 24 hours, Visitor Information Centre daily 9 a.m.–5 p.m.*

Story Bridge Adventure Climb
Kangaroo Point

If you're over 12 years old and at least 130 centimeters (just over 4'3") tall, you can "climb" Brisbane's Story Bridge. The Story Bridge Adventure Climb peaks at a viewing platform 44m (143 ft.) above the roadway and 80m (262 ft.) above the Brisbane River. If you brave the height, you'll be rewarded with magnificent 360-degree views of the city, river, and Moreton Bay and its islands.

See map p. 254. 170 Main St. (at Wharf Street), Kangaroo Point. ☎ *1300/254 627 in Australia, or 07/3514 6900.* www.storybridgeadventureclimb.com.au. *Rates: Day climbs weekdays A$110 (US$88/£44) adults, A$83 (US$66/£33) children 12–16; day climbs weekends A$130 (US$104/£52), A$98 (US$78/£39) children; twilight climbs A$130 (US$104/£52) adults, A$98 (US$78/£39) children; night climbs weekdays A$120 (US$96/£48) adults, A$90 (US$72/£36) children; night climbs weekends A$130 (US$104/£52), A$98 (US$78/£39); dawn climbs (Sat–Sun only) A$130 (US$104/£52) adults, A$98 (US$78/£39) children. Children must be accompanied by an adult. Climbs operate Wed–Sun only.*

Guided tours

For a good introduction to Brisbane, take a **City Sights** bus tour run by Brisbane City Council (☎ **13 12 30** in Australia). The blue-and-yellow buses stop at 19 points of interest in a continuous loop around the city center, Spring Hill, Milton, South Bank, and Fortitude Valley. The driver gives a commentary, and it's hop on/hop off as you want.

The tour is a good value as your ticket also gives unlimited access to buses, ferries, and CityCats for the day, as well as discounts to some attractions. The bus departs every 45 minutes from 9 a.m. to 3:45 p.m. daily except Good Friday (Fri before Easter), April 25 (Anzac Day), and December 25. The whole trip takes 90 minutes. Tickets cost A$22 (US$18/£8.80) adults, A$16 (US$13/£6.40) children 5 to 14. Buy your ticket on board. You can join anywhere along the route, but the most central stop is City Hall, stop 2, on Adelaide Street at Albert Street.

Shopping the Local Stores

Brisbane's major shopping precinct is the **Queen Street Mall,** which has around 500 stores. Fronting the mall at 171–209 Queen St., under the Hilton, is the three-level **Wintergarden** shopping complex (☎ 07/3229 9755; www.wgarden.com.au), housing upscale jewelers and Aussie fashion designers.

Farther up the mall at 91 Queen St. (at Albert Street) is the **Myer Centre** (☎ 07/3223 6900), which has Brisbane's biggest department store and five levels of moderately priced stores, mostly fashion. The delightful, atmospheric **Brisbane Arcade,** 160 Queen St. Mall (☎ 07/3221 5977), abounds with the boutiques of Queensland designers. Just down the mall from it is the **Broadway on the Mall** arcade (☎ 07/3229 5233; www.broadwayonthemall.com.au), which stocks fashion, gifts, and accessories on two levels. Across from the Edward Street end of the mall is a new fashion and lifestyle shopping precinct, **MacArthur Central** (☎ 07/3007 2300; www.macarthurcentral.com), on the block between Queen and Elizabeth streets. This is where you'll find designer labels, Swiss watches, galleries, and accessory shops.

Retro '50s and '60s fashion, offbeat stuff like old LPs, secondhand crafts, fashion by up-and-coming young designers, and all kinds of trash and treasure are for sale at the **Valley Markets,** Brunswick Street and Chinatown malls, Fortitude Valley (☎ 07/3854 0860). It's open Saturday and Sunday from 8 a.m. to 4 p.m.

On Friday nights, the buzz is outdoors at the **South Bank Lifestyle Markets,** Stanley Street Plaza, South Bank Parklands. The market is open Friday from 5 to 10 p.m., Saturday and Sunday from 10 a.m. to 5 p.m.

One of the best places in Queensland to find Aboriginal art is the renowned **Fire-Works Gallery**, upstairs at 11 Stratton St., Newstead (☎ 07/3216 1250; www.fireworksgallery.com.au). You may blanch at some of the prices, but this is where you'll find art by established and emerging Aboriginal artists from all over Australia. They also ship your acquisition home for you. Open Tuesday to Friday 11 a.m. to 5 p.m., Saturday 11 a.m. to 4 p.m., or by appointment.

Living It Up after Dark

Finding out what's happening

You can find out about festivals, concerts, and events, and book tickets through **Ticketek** (☎ **13 28 49** in Queensland; www.ticketek.com). You can book in person at Ticketek agencies, the most convenient of which are on Level E at the Myer Centre, 91 Queen St. Mall, and in the Visitor Information Centre at South Bank Parklands. Or try **Ticketmaster** (☎ **13 61 00;** www.ticketmaster7.com).

QTIX (☎ **13 62 46** in Australia; www.qtix.com.au) is a major booking agent for performing arts, including all events at the Queensland Performing Arts Complex (QPAC). There is a A$2.75 (US$2.20/£1.10) fee per ticket. You can book in person at the box office at QPAC between 8:30 a.m. and 9 p.m. Monday through Saturday, and at the South Bank Parklands Visitor Information Centre.

The free weekly *Brisbane News* lists performing arts, music performances, art exhibitions, concerts, and events. The free weekly *TimeOff,* published on Wednesdays and available in bars and cafes, is a good guide to live music, as is Thursday's *Courier-Mail* newspaper.

Raising the curtain on performing arts and music

Many of Brisbane's performing arts events are at the Queensland Performing Arts Centre (QPAC) in the Queensland Cultural Centre. The city also has a lively theater scene. To find out what's playing and to book tickets, contact QTIX (see the preceding section).

Theater

✔ **Queensland Theatre Company (☎ 07/3010 7600** for information; www.qldtheatreco.com.au) is the state theater company, offering eight or nine productions a year, from the classics to new Australian works. Most performances are at the Playhouse or Cremorne Theatre at the Queensland Performing Arts Centre (QPAC), South Bank. Tickets cost from A$26 (US$21/£10) — if you're under 25 — to A$68 (US$54/£27).

✔ **Brisbane Powerhouse–Centre for the Live Arts,** 119 Lamington St., New Farm (☎ **07/3358 8600;** www.brisbanepowerhouse.org), is a venue for innovative and fringe contemporary works. A former electricity powerhouse, the massive brick factory is a dynamic space for exhibitions, contemporary performance, and live art. It's a short walk from the New Farm ferry terminal along the riverfront through New Farm Park.

Checking out the club and pub scene

Brisbane's many pubs have wide, shady verandas and beer gardens, which make them a very attractive place to be on a sunny afternoon or on a steamy summer's night.

The best known is the **Breakfast Creek Hotel,** 2 Kingsford Smith Dr., Breakfast Creek (☎ 07/3262 5988). Built in 1889, the hotel is a Brisbane institution and for many people, a visit to the city isn't complete without a steak and beer "off the wood" at the Brekky Creek.

Another landmark is the riverside **Regatta Hotel,** 543 Coronation Dr., Toowong (☎ 07/3871 9595; www.regattahotel.com.au), with its pretty iron balconies. Their newish **Boatshed restaurant** (☎ 07/3871 9533) is popular but not inexpensive.

In Red Hill, on the city fringe, is the **Normanby Hotel,** 1 Musgrave Rd. (☎ 07/3831 3353; www.thenormanby.com.au), built in 1872 and recently stylishly revamped. Features are the giant Moreton Bay fig tree in the beer garden and the biggest outdoor TV screen in town.

One of the most popular nightclub complexes is **Friday's,** 123 Eagle St. (☎ 07/3832 2122), which overlooks the Brisbane River and is a haunt for lovely young things. Gather on the large outdoor terrace with its huge island bar, or head for the restaurant, supper club, or dance floor. Wednesday through Saturday nights see some kind of happy-hour deal, cocktail club, or drinks special; the dance action starts pumping around 9 p.m. on Friday and Saturday. Cover charge is A$7 to A$10 (US$5.60–US$8/£2.80–£4).

For greater sophistication, head to **Zenbar,** on the park level at Post Office Square, 215 Adelaide St. (☎ 07/3211 2333), a minimalist bar with an 8m-high (26-ft.) glass wall overlooking a bamboo garden. There are about 40 wines by the glass, but in this kind of place you should be drinking a margarita or martini. The music ranges from '70s under-ground jazz and lounge to ultramodern funk house on Friday; on Saturday, the mood changes to easy background music.

Brisbane's **Treasury Casino,** on Queen Street between George and William streets (☎ 07/3306 8888), is in a heritage building — once the state's Treasury offices — and is open 24 hours. Three levels of 100 gaming tables offer roulette, blackjack, baccarat, craps, sic-bo, and Aussie two-up. There are over 1,000 slot machines, five restaurants, and seven bars. Live bands appear nightly in the Livewire Bar. You must be 18 to enter and there's a dress code (no beachwear or thongs). Closed Good Friday (Fri before Easter), December 25, and until 1 p.m. on April 25 (Anzac Day).

Cool spots for jazz and blues

At 1 Annie St., Kangaroo Point, almost right under the Story Bridge, the **Brisbane Jazz Club** (☎ **07/3391 2006;** www.brisbanejazzclub. com.au) is the only Australian jazz club featuring big band dance music (every Sun night). Watch out for the slightly sloping dance floor — it was once a boat ramp! Traditional and mainstream jazz is featured on Saturday nights. Open Fridays 6:30 to 11:30 p.m., Saturday 7 to 11:30 p.m., and Sunday 5:30 to 8:30 p.m. On Thursdays from 6:30 to 9 p.m., there's a casual jazz appreciation session. Reservations are necessary for some events. The cover is usually A$15 (US$12/£6), higher for some guest acts.

Exposed brick walls, wooden booths and a courtyard set the scene for **The Bowery** (☎ **07/3252 0202**), an intimate and sophisticated jazz venue. This atmospheric bar at 676 Ann St., Fortitude Valley, was modeled on Prohibition-era speakeasies. It has live jazz during the week and on Sunday from around 8 or 8:30 p.m. and DJs on Friday and Saturday from 9 p.m. Open Tuesday through Sunday 5 p.m. to 3 a.m.

Fast Facts: Brisbane

Area Code

The area code for Brisbane, and the rest of Queensland, is **07**. You need to use the code if you're calling other places in Queensland outside Brisbane.

American Express

The office at 131 Elizabeth St. (☎ 1300/139 060) cashes traveler's checks, exchanges currency, and replaces lost traveler's checks. It's open Monday through Friday 9 a.m. to 5 p.m., Saturday 9 a.m. to noon.

ATMs

ATMs are widely available. You'll find several in the Queen Street Mall.

Currency Exchange

Travelex, in the Myer Centre, Queen Street Mall (☎ 07/3210 6325; www.travelex. com.au), is open Monday through Thursday 9 a.m. to 5:30 p.m., Friday 9 a.m. to 8 p.m., Saturday 9 a.m. to 5 p.m., and Sunday 10 a.m. to 4 p.m. Locations at the

airport are open whenever flights are arriving.

Doctors

The Travellers Medical & Vaccination Centre (☎ 07/3221 9066; www.the traveldoctor.com.au) is on Level 5 of the Qantas building, 247 Adelaide St., between Creek and Edward streets. It's open Monday and Friday 8 a.m. to 5 p.m., Tuesday 8 a.m. to 7 p.m., Wednesday 8 a.m. to 9 p.m., Thursday 8 a.m. to 4:30 p.m., and Saturday 8:30 a.m. to 2 p.m. For after-hours emergencies, call ☎ 0408/199 166.

Emergencies

Dial ☎ **000** for fire, ambulance, or police help. This is a free call from a private or public phone.

Hospitals

The Royal Brisbane Hospital is about a 15-minute drive from the city at Herston Road, Herston (☎ 07/3636 8111).

Information

The Brisbane Visitor Information Centre (☎ 07/3006 6290) is in the Queen Street Mall, between Edward and Albert streets. It's open Monday through Thursday from 9 a.m. to 5:30 p.m., Friday 9 a.m. to 7 p.m. or later, Saturday 9 a.m. to 5 p.m., Sunday 9:30 a.m. to 4:30 p.m., and public holidays 9 a.m. to 4:30 p.m. The official Web site (www.ourbrisbane.com) and the Brisbane Transit Centre (☎ 07/3236 2020) are also good sources.

Internet Access and Cybercafes

The South Bank Visitor Information Centre, Stanley Street Plaza, South Bank Parklands, offers Internet access daily from 9 a.m. to 4:30 p.m. and charges A$1 (US$0.80/£0.40) for ten minutes. There are several Internet cafes on Adelaide Street, including the Cyber Room, 25 Adelaide St. (☎ 07/3012 9331), and Netparadise, 198 Adelaide St. (☎ 07/3211 8218).

Newspapers/Magazines

The *Courier-Mail* (Mon–Sat) and the *Sunday Mail* are Brisbane's daily papers. Another news source is the online *Brisbane Times* (www.brisbanetimes.com.au). The free weekly *Brisbane News* magazine is a good guide to dining, entertainment, and shopping.

Pharmacies

The T & G Corner Day & Night Pharmacy, 141 Queen St. Mall (☎ 07/3221 4585), is open Monday through Thursday 7 a.m. to 9 p.m., Friday 7 a.m. to 9:30 p.m., Saturday 8 a.m. to 9 p.m., Sunday 8:30 a.m. to 5:30 p.m., and public holidays 9 a.m. to 7:30 p.m.

Police

Dial ☎ 000 in an emergency, or ☎ 07/3364 6464 for police headquarters. Police are stationed 24 hours a day at 65–69 Adelaide St. (☎ 07/3224 4444) in the city.

Post Office

The GPO is at 261 Queen St. (☎ 13 13 18). It's open Monday through Friday 9 a.m. to 5 p.m.

Restrooms

There are public toilets in most major inner-city shopping centers, such as the Myer Centre and Wintergarden in the Queen Street Mall. The toilets at Central Station and Roma Street Station are open from very early until midnight or later.

Smoking

Queensland has some of Australia's toughest nonsmoking laws. You can't smoke in any pub, club, restaurant, or workplace, or in outdoor public places including patrolled beaches, playgrounds, stadiums, or within 4m (12 ft.) of nonresidential building entrances.

Taxis

Call Yellow Cabs (☎ 13 19 24 in Australia) or Black and White Taxis (☎ 13 10 08 in Australia). There are taxi stands at each end of Queen Street Mall, on Edward Street and on George Street (outside the Treasury Casino).

Time Zone

The time in Brisbane is Greenwich mean time plus ten hours. Brisbane does not observe daylight saving time, which means it's on the same time as Sydney and Melbourne in winter, and one hour behind those cities October through March. For the exact local time, call ☎ 1194.

Weather

Call ☎ 1196 for the southeast Queensland weather forecast. Two good Web sites are the Weather Channel (www.weatherchannel.com.au) and the Australian Bureau of Meteorology (www.bom.gov.au).

Chapter 17

Queensland and the Best of the Great Barrier Reef

by Lee Mylne

In This Chapter

▷ Diving into activities on the Great Barrier Reef
▷ Settling into Cairns, Port Douglas, and other Reef towns
▷ Finding the best of the rest of the Reef
▷ Beaching yourself on the Sunshine Coast and Gold Coast

*W*hite sandy beaches fringe the coastline of Queensland, and a string of tantalizing islands and coral atolls making up one of the great natural wonders of the world — the Great Barrier Reef — dangles offshore. In the north, the rain forest teems with flora and fauna. At the southern end, Gold Coast beaches and theme parks keep tourist hordes happy. With rain forest hills and village to explore, and a harbor full of boats waiting to take you to the Reef, the city of Cairns is a good base, although some prefer the smaller, beachfront village of Port Douglas.

You'll be tempted by one tropical island after another until you hit the cluster of 74 that makes up the Whitsundays. The islands are on the same latitude as Tahiti and, in our opinion, are equally lovely. We also spend some time on another special island: Heron Island.

North of Brisbane lies the aptly named Sunshine Coast — more white sandy beaches, crystal-clear waters, and rolling mountains dotted with villages. Then there's the Gold Coast with its 35km (22 miles) of rolling surf and sandy beaches and family-focused theme parks.

Getting to and Around Queensland

By plane

Qantas (☎ 13 13 13 in Australia; www.qantas.com.au) and its subsidiaries **QantasLink** and the no-frills **Jetstar** (☎ 13 15 38 in Australia;

www.jetstar.com.au) serve most coastal towns from Brisbane, and a few from Cairns. **Virgin Blue** (☎ **13 67 89** in Australia; www.virgin blue.com.au) services Brisbane, Cairns, Townsville, Mackay, Proserpine and Hamilton Island in the Whitsundays, Rockhampton, Hervey Bay, the Gold Coast, and Maroochydore on the Sunshine Coast.

Remember, you can't fly for 24 hours after scuba diving!

By train

Queensland Rail's **Traveltrain** (☎ **1300/131 722** in Australia; www.traveltrain.com.au) operates two long-distance trains along the Brisbane–Cairns route, a 32-hour trip aboard the ***Sunlander*** or about 8 hours less on the high-speed **Tilt Train.**

By car

The Bruce Highway goes along the coast from Brisbane to Cairns. It's mostly a narrow two-lane highway, and the scenery is fairly unexciting.

Tourism Queensland publishes regional motoring guides. All you're likely to need, however, is a state map from the **Royal Automobile Club of Queensland** (RACQ), 300 St. Pauls Terrace, Fortitude Valley, Brisbane, QLD 4006 (☎ **13 19 05** in Australia). In Brisbane, you can get maps and advice from the RACQ office in the General Post Office (GPO), 261 Queen St. For recorded road condition reports, call ☎ **1800/629 501.** The **Department of Natural Resources** (☎ **07/3896 3216**) publishes excellent **Sunmaps** that highlight tourist attractions, national parks, and so on, although they're of limited use as road maps. You can get them at newsdealers and gas stations throughout the state.

Secrets of the Seasons

Winter (June–Aug) is high season in Queensland. At this time, Australians think the water is chilly, but its temperature rarely drops below 22°C (72°F). August through January is peak visibility time for divers. Summer is hot and sticky across the state. In North Queensland (Mission Beach, Cairns, and Port Douglas), the monsoonal Wet season is from November or December through March or April. It brings heavy rains, high temperatures, extreme humidity, and cyclones. It's no problem to visit then, but if the Wet turns you off, consider the beautiful Whitsundays, which are generally beyond the reach of the rains and the worst humidity (but not of cyclones).

Discovering the Great Barrier Reef

The Great Barrier Reef is a World Heritage Site and is the biggest marine park in the world. More than 2,000km (1,240 miles) long, stretching from Lady Elliot Island off Bundaberg to just south of Papua New Guinea, it is home to 1,500 kinds of fish, 400 species of coral, 4,000 kinds of clams and snails, and countless sponges, starfish, sea urchins, and other forms of marine life.

Apart from the impressive fish life around the corals, the Reef is home to numbers of green and loggerhead turtles, one of the biggest dugong (manatee) populations in the world, sharks, giant manta rays, and sea snakes. In winter (June–Aug), humpback whales gather in the warm waters around Hervey Bay and the Whitsunday Islands to calve.

For most people, the Great Barrier Reef means the Outer Reef, the network of platform and ribbon reefs that lie an average of 65km (40 miles) off the coast (about 60–90 minutes by boat from the mainland). To see the Reef, you can snorkel, dive, fish, or fly over it. You can also explore the fringing reef around islands closer to the mainland.

Learning about the Reef before you hit the water

Learning about the Reef before you get there will enhance your visit. **Reef Teach** (☎ 07/4031 7794) is a multimedia presentation by a team of experienced marine biologists, conservationists, and researchers. You'll learn everything you need to know about the Reef, from how it was formed and how coral grows, to what creatures to avoid and how to take underwater photos. The presentation takes place throughout the year at 14 Spence St., Cairns, Monday through Saturday 6:30 to 8:30 p.m., and costs A$13 (US$10/£5.20) adults and A$7 (US$5.60/£2.80) children under 14.

Townsville is the headquarters of the **Great Barrier Reef Marine Park Authority** (☎ 07/4750 0700; fax 07/4772 6093; www.gbrmpa.gov.au or www.reefhq.com.au) and a visit to **Reef HQ** (see "The top attractions" in the "Exploring Townville" section, later in this chapter), is a superb introduction. The star attraction at this aquarium is a re-created living-reef ecosystem in a massive viewing tank.

Ways to see the Reef

Snorkeling

Snorkeling the Reef can reveal green and purple clams, pink sponges, red starfish, purple sea urchins, and fish from electric blue to neon yellow to lime. The rich colors of the coral only survive with lots of light, so the nearer the surface, the brighter and richer the marine life. That means snorkelers see it at its best.

If your Reef cruise offers a guided snorkel tour or "snorkel safari," take it. Some include it as part of the price, but even if you pay an extra A$30 (US$24/£12) or so, it's worth it. Most safaris are suitable for both beginners and advanced snorkelers, and are led by marine biologists who tell you about the fascinating sea creatures you're seeing. Snorkeling is easy to master, and crews on cruise boats are always happy to tutor you.

Queensland

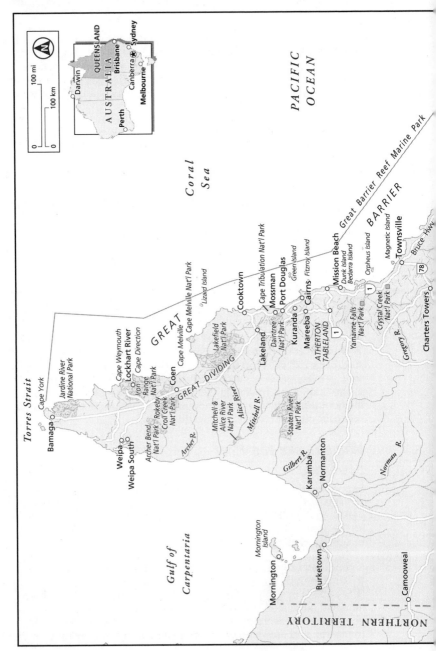

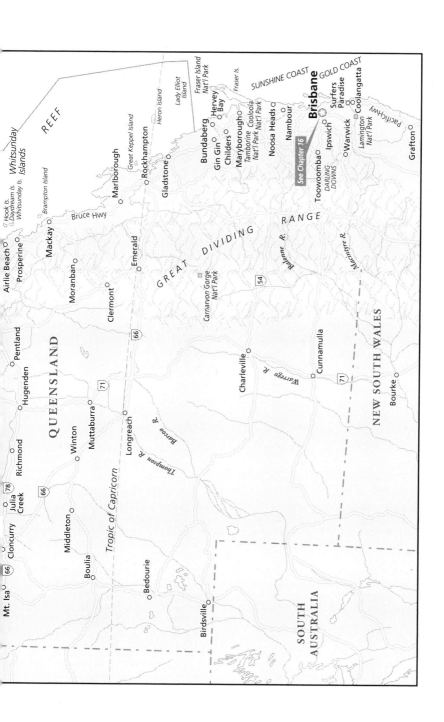

See Chapter 16

Scuba diving

A day trip to the Reef also offers a great opportunity to go scuba diving — even if you've never dived before. Every major cruise boat and many dedicated dive boats offer introductory dives that allow you to dive without certification to a depth of 6m (20 ft.) in the company of an instructor. You'll need to complete a medical questionnaire and undergo a 30-minute briefing on the boat.

Intro dives are also called "resort dives."

Deciding where to base yourself

Cairns and **Port Douglas** are good places from which to visit the Reef — but the quality of the coral is just as good off any town along the coast between Gladstone and Cairns. The Reef is pretty much equidistant from any point on the coast — about 90 minutes away by high-speed catamaran. An exception is **Townsville,** where the Reef is about two-and-a-half hours away. The main gateways, north to south, are **Port Douglas, Cairns, Mission Beach, Townsville,** the **Whitsunday Islands, Gladstone** (for Heron Island), and **Bundaberg.** The Whitsundays have the added attractions of islands to sail among; resorts offering a wealth of water-sports and other activities; and a large array of diving, fishing, and day cruises. Most important, you can snorkel every day off your island or join a sailing or cruise day trip to a number of magnificent inner reefs much nearer than the main Outer Reef. Many people stay in Cairns simply because of its easy international airport access.

If you're not a swimmer, choose a reef cruise that visits a coral cay, because a cay slopes gradually into shallow water and the surrounding coral. The Low Isles at Port Douglas; Green Island, Michaelmas Cay, or Upolu Cay off Cairns; Beaver Cay off Mission Beach; and Heron Island are all good locations.

Making day trips to the Reef

The most common way to get to the Reef is on one of the motorized catamarans that carry up to 300 passengers each from Cairns, Port Douglas, Townsville, Mission Beach, and the Whitsunday mainland and islands. Each of the boats is air-conditioned and has a bar, videos, and educational material, as well as a marine biologist who gives a talk on the Reef's ecology en route. The boats tie up at their own private permanent pontoons anchored to a platform reef. The pontoons have glass-bottom boats for passengers who don't want to get wet, dry underwater viewing platforms, usually a bar, sun decks, shaded seats, and often showers.

An alternative to traveling on a big tour boat is to go on one of the many smaller boats. These typically visit two or three Reef sites rather than just one. There are usually no more than 20 passengers, so you get more personal attention, and you get to know the other passengers. Another advantage is that you'll have the coral pretty much all to yourself. The drawbacks of a small boat are that you have only the cramped deck to sit on when you get out of the water, and your traveling time to the Reef may be longer. If you're a nervous snorkeler, you may feel safer on a boat where you'll be swimming with 300 other people.

Most day-trip fares include snorkel gear — fins, mask, and snorkel (plus wet suits in winter, although you rarely need them) — free use of the underwater viewing chambers and glass-bottom-boat rides, a plentiful buffet or barbecue lunch, and morning and afternoon refreshments. Diving is an optional activity for which you pay extra.

The big boats post snorkeling scouts to keep a lookout for anyone in trouble and to count heads periodically. If you wear glasses, ask whether your boat offers prescription masks — this could make a big difference to the quality of your experience! Don't forget, you can travel as a snorkel-only passenger on most dive boats, too.

If you get seasick, come prepared with medication. Some boats sell a ginger-based anti-seasickness pill, but it doesn't always work!

Major reef sites to visit
From Cairns

About 20 reefs lie within a one-and-a-half- to two-hour boat ride from Cairns. These are the reefs most commonly visited by snorkelers and divers on day trips, because they're so close and so pretty. Some reefs are small coral "bommies," or outcrops, that you can swim around in a matter of minutes, whereas others are miles wide. Some reefs have more than one good dive site; Norman Reef, for example, has at least four.

✔ Three of the most popular reefs with both snorkelers and divers are **Hastings, Saxon,** and **Norman,** which are all within a short boat ride of one another. Each has a wonderful array of coral; big, colorful reef fish; schools of pretty rainbow-hued small reef fish; and the odd giant clam. Green sea turtles and white-tip reef sharks are common, especially at Saxon, though you won't necessarily spot one every day. Divers may see a moray eel and a grouper or two, barracuda, reef sharks, eagle and blue-spotted rays, and octopus. Norman is an especially lovely reef with several nice sites. South Norman has lovely sloping coral shelves. If you're an experienced diver and like swim-throughs, the Caves at Norman is a good spot; it has boulder and plate corals.

✔ Some of the best diving anywhere on the Great Barrier Reef is on the **Ribbon Reefs** on the outer Reef edge, which fringes the continental shelf off Cairns and Port Douglas. Glorious coral walls, abundant fish, and pinnacles make these a rich, colorful dive area with lots of variety. The currents can be stronger here, because the reefs are the last stop between the open sea, so drift dives are a possibility. The Ribbon Reefs are beyond the reach of day boats, but are commonly visited by live-aboard boats.

✔ For divers, experts recommend **Steve's Bommie** and **Dynamite Pass.** Steve's Bommie is a coral outcrop in 30m (98 ft.) of water, topped with barracudas, and covered in colorful coral and small marine life. You can swim through a tunnel here amid crowds of fish. Dynamite Pass is a channel where barracuda, trevally, grouper, mackerel, and tuna gather to feed in the current. Black coral trees and sea whips grow on the walls, patrolled by eagle rays and reef sharks.

✔ The most famous dive site in Cairns is **Cod Hole,** where you can hand-feed giant potato cod as big as you are, or bigger. The site also has Maori wrasse, moray eels, and coral trout. Cod Hole is about 20km (13 miles) off Lizard Island, 240km (149 miles) north of Cairns, so it isn't a day trip unless you're staying at exclusive Lizard Island. However, it's a popular stop with just about every live-aboard vessel, often combined in a trip to the Ribbon Reefs lasting about four days, or in a trip to the Coral Sea lasting between four and seven days. Either itinerary makes an excellent dive vacation.

✔ Divers looking for adventure in far-flung latitudes can visit the **Far Northern** region of the Great Barrier Reef, much farther north than most dive boats venture. Up in this large region you'll find a wide choice of good sites, little explored by the average diver. Visibility is always clear. **Silvertip City** on Mantis Reef has sharks, pelagics, potato cod, and beautiful lion fish that patrol a wall up to 46m (150 ft.) deep. Another goodie is the **Magic Cave** swim-through adorned with lots of colorful fans, soft corals, and small reef fish. Sleeping turtles are often spotted in caves on the reefs off **Raine Island,** the world's biggest green turtle rookery. Visibility averages 24m (80 ft.) at Rainbow Wall, a colorful wall that makes a nice gentle drift dive with the incoming tide.

✔ Some 100km to 200km (63–126 miles) east of Cairns, out in the **Coral Sea,** isolated mountains covered in reefs rise more than a kilometer (½ mile) from the ocean floor to make excellent diving. Although not within the Great Barrier Reef Marine Park, the Coral Sea is often combined into an extended live-aboard trip that also takes in Cod Hole and the Ribbon Reefs. The whole trip usually takes four to seven days. The most popular site is **Osprey Reef,** a 100-sq.-km (39-sq.-mile) reef with 1,000m (3,300-ft.) drop-offs, renowned for its year-round visibility of up to 70m (230 ft.). The highlight of most Osprey Reef itineraries is a **shark feeding** session. White-tip reef sharks are common, but the area is also home to gray reef sharks, silvertips, and hammerheads. Green turtles, tuna, barracuda, potato cod, mantas, and grouper are also common.

✔ Closer to shore, Cairns has several coral cays and reef-fringed islands within the **Great Barrier Reef Marine Park.** Less than an hour from the city, **Green Island** is a 15-hectare (37-acre) coral cay with snorkeling equal to that on the Great Barrier Reef. It's also a popular diving spot. You can visit it in half a day.

✔ The **Frankland Islands** are a pristine group of uninhabited rain-forested isles edged with sandy beaches, reefs, and fish 45km (28 miles) south of Cairns. The islands are a rookery for **green sea turtles,** which snorkelers and divers often spot in the water. In February and March, you may even see dozens of baby turtles hatching in the sand. **Michaelmas Cay** and **Upolu Cay** are two pretty coral sand blips in the ocean, 30km (19 miles) and 25km (16 miles) off Cairns, surrounded by reefs. Michaelmas is vegetated and is home to 27,000 seabirds; you may spot dugongs (manatees) off Upolu.

From Port Douglas

The waters off Port Douglas are just as close to shore and just as colorful and varied as those off Cairns.

✔ Some of the most visited reefs off Port Douglas are **Tongue, Opal,** and **St. Crispin Reefs.**

✔ The **Agincourt** complex of reefs also has many excellent dive sites; experts recommend the double-figure-eight swim-through at the Three Sisters, where baby gray whale sharks gather, and the coral walls of Castle Rock, where stingrays often hide in the sand. **Nursery Bommie** is a 24m (79-ft.) pinnacle that is a popular haunt with big fish like barracudas, rays, sharks, and moray eels; under the big plate corals of Light Reef, giant grouper hide out. Other popular sites are the staghorn coral garden at the Playground; one of the region's biggest swim-throughs at **The Maze,** where parrot fish and an enormous Maori wrasse hang out; the Stepping Stones, home of the exquisitely pretty clownfish (like Nemo!); **Turtle Bommie,** where hawksbill turtles are frequently sighted; and **Harry's Bommie,** where divers see the occasional manta ray. Among the 15-plus dive sites visited by *Poseidon* (see "From Port Douglas" section below) are Turtle Bay, where you may meet Killer, a friendly Maori wrasse; the Cathedrals, a collection of coral pinnacles and swim-throughs; and Barracuda Pass, home to coral gardens, giant clams, and schooling barracudas.

✔ The closest Reef site off Port Douglas, the **Low Isles,** lies 15km (9 miles) northeast. Coral sand and 22 hectares (55 acres) of coral surround these two tiny coral cays, which are covered in lush vegetation and are home to many seabirds. The coral is not quite as dazzling as the outer Reef's, but the fish life is rich, and you may spot sea turtles. Because you can wade out to the coral right from the beach, the Low Isles are a good choice for nervous snorkelers. A half-day or day trip to the Low Isles makes for a more relaxing day than a visit to outer Reef sites. If you visit the Low Isles, wear old shoes, because the coral sand can be rough underfoot.

From Mission Beach

Mission Beach is the closest point on the mainland to the Reef, an hour by boat.

The main site visited is **Beaver Cay,** a sandy coral cay surrounded by marine life. The waters are shallow, making the cay ideal both for snorkelers eager to see the coral's vibrant colors and for novice divers still getting a feel for the sport.

From Townsville

Townsville's waters boast hundreds of large patch reefs, some miles long, and many almost never visited by anyone. Here you can find excellent coral and fish life, including mantas, rays, turtles, and sharks, and sometimes canyons and swim-throughs in generally good visibility.

✔ One of the best reef complexes is **Flinders Reef,** which is in the Coral Sea, beyond the Great Barrier Reef Marine Park boundaries, but still included on many dive trips because it has 30m (100-ft.) visibility, plenty of coral, and big walls and pinnacles with big fish to match, like whaler shark and barracuda.

✔ What draws most divers to Townsville, though, is one of Australia's best wreck dives, **S.S. *Yongala.*** Still largely intact, the sunken remains of this steamer lie 90km (56 miles) from Townsville, 16km (10 miles) off the coast, in 15m to 30m (50–98 ft.) of water with visibility of 9m to 18m (30–60 ft.). A cyclone sent the *Yongala* and its 49 passengers and 72-member crew to the bottom of the sea in 1911. Today it's surrounded by a mass of coral and marine life, including barracuda, enormous grouper, rays, sea snakes, turtles, moray eels, shark, cod, and reef fish. You can even enter the ship and swim its length, with care. The boat is usually visited on a live-aboard trip of at least two days, but some companies run day trips.

The *Yongala* is not for beginners — the wreck is deep, and there is a strong current. Most companies require their customers to have advanced certification or to have logged a minimum of 15 dives with open-water certification.

From the Whitsundays

Visitors to the Whitsundays have the best of both worlds; they can visit the outer Reef and enjoy some good dive and snorkel sites in and around the islands. Many islands have rarely visited fringing reefs, which you can explore in a rented dinghy. The reef here is just as good as it is off Cairns, with many drop-offs and drift dives, a dazzling range of corals, and a rich array of marine life, including whales, mantas, shark, reef fish, morays, turtles, and pelagics. Visibility is usually around 15m to 23m (49–75 ft.).

✔ The Stepping Stones on 800-hectare (1,976-acre) **Bait Reef** is one of the most popular sites on the Outer Reef. It is made up of a series of pinnacles that abound with fish life and offer caverns, swim-throughs, and channels.

✔ A family of grouper often greets divers at Grouper Grotto on **Net Reef,** and a pod of dolphins hang around Net Reef's southeast wall.

- ✔ **Oublier Reef** has plate corals over 2m (7-ft.) wide in its lovely coral gardens.

- ✔ Among the island sites, one of the most popular is **Blue Pearl Bay** off Hayman Island, for both snorkeling and diving. It has loads of corals and some gorgonian fans in its gullies, and heaps of reef fish, including Maori wrasse and even manta rays. It's a good place to make an introductory dive, walking right in off the beach.

- ✔ **Mantaray Bay** on Hook Island is renowned for its range of marine life, from small reef fish and nudibranches to bigger pelagics farther out. Mantas hang around here in November.

- ✔ Another good snorkel and dive spot is **Black Reef,** commonly called **Bali Hai Island,** between Hayman and Hook islands. You'll see soft shelf and wall coral; tame Maori wrasse; octopus; turtles; reef shark; various kinds of rays, including mantas, eagles, and cowtails; plus loads of fish. Divers may even see hammerhead shark.

From Bundaberg

The southern reefs of the Great Barrier Reef are just as prolific, varied, and colorful as the reefs off Cairns. However, because this part of the coast is less populated, fewer snorkel and dive boats visit them.

- ✔ **Lady Musgrave Island** is one of the Bunker Group of islands and reefs, which lie approximately 80km (50 miles) due north of Bundaberg. They are closer to Gladstone, but no boats visit them from there. Little explored by divers, these vividly colored reefs are some of the most pristine on the Great Barrier Reef.

- ✔ Although it lies outside the borders of the Great Barrier Reef Marine Park, Bundaberg's **Woongarra Marine Park** is a popular destination. It hugs the town's coastline, and has loads of soft and hard corals, nudibranches, wobbegongs, epaulette sharks, sea snakes, some 60 fish species, and frequent sightings of green and loggerhead turtles. Most of this is in water less than 9m (30 ft.) deep, and you can walk right into it off the beach.

Diving the Reef

Divers have a big choice of dive boats that make day trips to the Outer Reef and live-aboard dive boats making excursions that last up to a week. On a typical five-hour day trip to the Reef, you'll fit in about two dives. The companies listed give you an idea of the kinds of trips available and how much you'll be paying. Prices quoted here include full gear rental, but you can expect to pay about A$20 (US$16/£8) less if you have your own gear.

Many dive companies in Queensland offer dive courses. To take a course, you'll need to have a medical exam done by a Queensland doctor. Your dive school can arrange it, and it costs about A$55 (US$40/£20). You'll also need two passport photos for your certificate, and you must be able to swim!

Staying on the Reef

Down Under Dive (☎ **1800/079 099** in Australia, or 07/4052 8300; fax 07/4031 1373; www.downunderdive.com.au) in Cairns offers a chance to "sleep on the Reef" aboard the (120-ft.) *Spirit of Freedom,* a modern motor yacht with electronic stabilizers, TV/DVD, lounge areas, sun decks, and 11 luxury double or quad share cabins, each with an en suite bathroom. There are three-, four- and seven-day cruises to choose from.

You'll visit Cod Hole and Ribbon Reef and, on the four- and seven-day trips, venture into the Coral Sea. A three-day, three-night trip costs from A$1,100 to A$1,750 (US$880–US$1,400/£440–£700), depending on your choice of cabin, and ends with a 193km (120-mile), one-way, low-level flight from Lizard Island back to Cairns. The four-day, four-night cruise begins with the flight and then cruises from Lizard Island back to Cairns. It costs between A$1,375 and A$2,100 (US$1,100–US$1,680/£550–£840) and includes up to 16 dives. A seven-day cruise, priced from A$2,325 to A$3,700 (US$1,860–US$2,960/£930–£1,480), is a combination of both shorter trips. On a three-day trip, you'll fit in up to 11 dives; on the seven-day trip, up to 27. Prices include all meals and pickup from your Cairns accommodations. Allow around A$100 (US$80/£40) extra for equipment rental.

Courses usually begin every day or every week. Some courses take as little as three days, but five days is generally regarded as the best. Open-water certification usually requires two days of theory in a pool, followed by two or three days out on the Reef, where you make four to nine dives. Prices vary considerably but are generally around A$600 (US$480/£240) for a five-day open-water certification course, or A$500 (US$400/£200) for the same course over four nights.

From Cairns

✔ **Tusa Dive Charters** (☎ **07/4040 6464;** www.tusadive.com) runs two 24m (72-ft.) dive boats daily to two dive sites from a choice of 21 locations on the Outer Reef. The day costs A$190 (US$152/£76) for divers and A$130 (US$104/£52) adult or A$80 (US$64/£32) child ages 4 to 14 for snorkelers, with wet suits, guided snorkel tours, lunch, and transfers from your Cairns or northern beaches hotel.

If you want to be shown the best spots under the water, you can take a guided dive for an extra A$20 (US$16/£8). Day trips for introductory divers cost A$195 (US$156/£78) for one dive or A$240 (US$192/£96) for two. The groups are kept to a maximum of 28 people, so you get personal attention. The company is the Nitrox and Rebreather facility for north Queensland, and certified divers can take two introductory dives on Nitrox/Safe Air in one day for A$220 (US$176/£88).

✔ **Deep Sea Divers Den** (☎ **07/4046 7333;** fax 07/4031 1210; www.divers-den.com) runs a five-day open-water diving course that involves two days of theory in the pool in Cairns, and three days and two nights on a live-aboard boat. The course costs A$690 (US$552/£276) per person, including all meals on the boat, nine dives (one a guided night dive), all your gear, a wet suit, and transfers from your hotel. The same course over four nights, with one night on the boat and five dives, costs A$555 (US$444/£222). New courses begin every day.

From Port Douglas

The waters off Port Douglas are home to dramatic coral spires and swim-throughs at the Cathedrals; giant clams at Barracuda Pass; a village of parrot fish, anemone fish, unicorn fish, and two moray eels at the soaring pinnacle of Nursery Bommie; fan corals at Split-Bommie; and many other wonderful sites.

Poseidon (☎ **1800/085 674** in Australia, or 07/4099 4772; www.poseidon-cruises.com.au) is a fast 24m (79-ft.) vessel that visits three Outer Reef sites. The day-trip price of A$155 (US$124/£62) for adults, A$120 (US$96/£48) for kids 3 to 12, includes snorkel gear, a marine biology talk, snorkel safaris, lunch, and pickups from Port Douglas hotels. Certified divers pay A$40 (US$32/£16) extra for two dives or A$55 (US$44/£22) extra for three, plus A$20 (US$16/£8) gear rental. Guides will accompany you, free of charge, to show you great locations. Introductory divers pay A$50 (US$40/£20) extra for one dive, and A$40 (US$32/£16) each for the second and third. The vessel carries no more than 48 passengers, less than half its capacity, and gets you to the Reef in just over an hour, giving you five hours on the coral. The boat departs Marina Mirage daily at 8:30 a.m. Transfers from Cairns and the northern beaches cost an extra A$15 (US$12/£6) per adult, A$10 (US$8/£4) per child.

From Townsville

Off Townsville, you can dive not only the Reef but also a wreck, the *Yongala,* off the coast in 30m (98 ft.) of water with good visibility.

Adrenalin Dive (☎ **07/4724 0600;** www.adrenalindive.com.au) runs day trips in which you can do two dives on the *Yongala.* The cost is A$199 (US$159/£80), plus A$35 (US$28/£14) for gear hire and A$30 (US$24/£12) per dive for a guide if you've logged less than 15 dives.

From the Whitsundays

In and around the Whitsunday Islands, you can visit the Outer Reef and explore the many excellent dive sites close to shore.

H20 Sportz (☎ **07/4946 9888;** www.h2osportz.com.au), based at Hamilton Island marina, runs day tours to Bait Reef, one of the best known locations on the Great Barrier Reef. Tours are limited to 30 passengers, leave at 9:30 a.m., and return at 5 p.m. That gives you three-and-a-half hours at the reef, allowing plenty of time for one snorkel or two dives. The cost is A$161 (US$129/£64) adults, A$81 (US$65/£32) kids aged 4 to 13.

One child 13 years and under travels free when accompanied by two adults. The cost includes lunch, snacks, snorkel equipment, and wet suit.

Welcome to Cairns

This part of Queensland is the only place in the world where two World Heritage–listed sites — the Great Barrier Reef and the Wet Tropics rain forests — lie side by side. In parts of the far north, the rain forest touches the Reef, reaching right down to sandy beaches from which you can snorkel the Reef. Cairns is the gateway to these natural attractions, as well as man-made tourist destinations such as the Skyrail Rainforest Cableway. It's also a steppingstone to islands of the Great Barrier Reef and the grasslands of the Gulf Savannah.

When international tourism to the Great Barrier Reef boomed, the small sugar-farming town of Cairns boomed along with it. The town now boasts outstanding hotels, offshore island resorts, big Reef-cruise catamarans in the harbor, and too many souvenir shops. The only beach in town is a man-made 4,000-sq.-m (43,000-sq.-ft.) saltwater lagoon and artificial beach on the Esplanade.

The 110-million-year-old rain forest, the **Daintree,** where plants that are fossils elsewhere in the world exist in living color, is a couple of hours north. The Daintree is part of the Wet Tropics, a World Heritage–listed area that stretches from north of Townsville to south of Cooktown, and houses half of Australia's animal and plant species.

If you're spending more than a day or two in the area, consider basing yourself on the city's pretty northern beaches, in Kuranda, or in Port Douglas (see "Port Douglas, Daintree, and the Cape Tribulation Area," later in this chapter). Although prices will be higher in the peak season (Australian winter and early spring, July–Oct), affordable accommodations are available year-round.

Getting to Cairns
By plane
Qantas (☎ 13 13 13 in Australia; www.quantas.com) has direct flights throughout the day to Cairns from Sydney and Brisbane, and at least one flight a day from Darwin, Uluru (Ayers Rock), and Perth. From Melbourne you can sometimes fly direct, but most flights connect through Sydney or Brisbane. **QantasLink** flies from Townsville, Hamilton Island in the Whitsundays, and Alice Springs. **Virgin Blue** (☎ 13 67 89 in Australia) flies to Cairns from Brisbane, Sydney, and Melbourne. **Jetstar** (☎ 13 15 38 in Australia) flies from Brisbane, Sydney, Adelaide, and Melbourne. **Australian Airlines** (☎ 1300/799 798 in Australia) links Cairns with Sydney, and several international carriers serve Cairns from various Asian cities and New Zealand.

Cairns

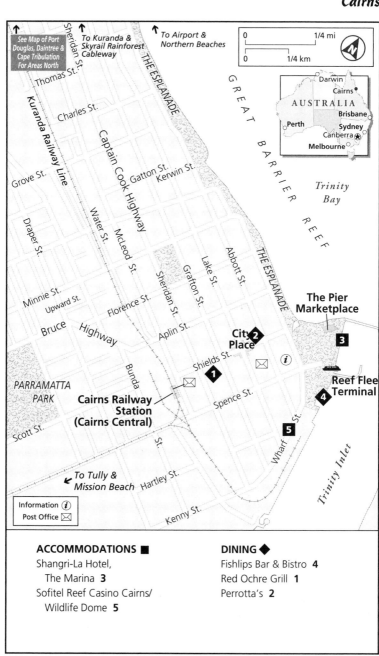

ACCOMMODATIONS ■
Shangri-La Hotel,
   The Marina **3**
Sofitel Reef Casino Cairns/
   Wildlife Dome **5**

DINING ◆
Fishlips Bar & Bistro **4**
Red Ochre Grill **1**
Perrotta's **2**

Getting oriented at the airport

Cairns Airport is 8km (5 miles) north of downtown. The domestic and international terminals are linked by a covered walkway — it takes about five minutes to walk between the two.

Getting from the airport to your hotel

Airport Connections (☎ **07/4099 5950;** www.tnqshuttle.com) will meet all flights at both terminals. Transfers to the city cost A$11 (US$8.80/£4.40) adults and A$5.50 (US$4.40/£2.20) children 4 to 14. It also runs transfers to as far as Cape Tribulation, Mission Beach, and Dunk Island.

Sun Palm Express Coaches (☎ **07/4084 2626;** www.sunpalmtransport.com) provides transfers from the airport to the city and northern beaches. The one-way fare is A$10 (US$8/£4) adults and A$5 (US$4/£2) children 2 to 12 to the city, and A$16 (US$13/£6.40) adults and A$8 (US$6.40/£3.20) children to Palm Cove.

A **taxi** from the airport costs around A$15 (US$12/£6) to the city, A$30 (US$24/£12) to Trinity Beach, and A$40 (US$32/£16) to Palm Cove. Call **Black & White Taxis** (☎ **13 10 08** in Australia).

By train

Long-distance trains operated by **Traveltrain** (☎ **1300/131 722** in Queensland; www.traveltrain.com.au) run from Brisbane several times a week. The 160kmph (100-mph) Tilt Train takes about 25 hours and costs A$295 (US$236/£118) for business class. Northbound trains leave Brisbane at 6:25 p.m. on Monday and Friday; southbound runs depart Cairns at 8:15 a.m. on Wednesday and Sunday. The train features luxury business-class seating, with an entertainment system for each seat, including multiple movie and audio channels.

The *Sunlander,* which runs four times a week between Brisbane and Cairns, takes 32 hours and costs A$207 (US$166/£83) for a sitting berth, A$265 (US$212/£106) for an economy-class sleeper, A$409 (US$327/£166) for a first-class sleeper, or A$725 (US$580/£290) for all-inclusive Queenslander class (only available twice a week). Trains pull into the Cairns **Central terminal** (☎ **1300/131 722** in Australia for reservations, or 07/4036 9250 for the terminal) on Bunda Street in the center of town.

By bus

Greyhound Australia (☎ **13 14 99** in Australia, or 07/4690 9950) buses pull into **Trinity Wharf Centre** on Wharf Street in the center of town. Buses travel from the south via all towns and cities on the Bruce Highway, and from the west from Alice Springs and Darwin via Tennant Creek on the Stuart Highway and the Outback mining town of Mount Isa to Townsville, where they join the Bruce Highway and head north. The 46-hour Sydney–Cairns trip costs A$350 (US$280/£140); the 30-hour trip from Brisbane is A\$234 (US\$187/£94); and from Darwin, the journey takes about 38 hours and costs A\$517 (US\$414/£207).

By car

From Brisbane and all major towns in the south, you'll enter Cairns on the Bruce Highway. To reach the northern beaches or Port Douglas from Cairns, take Sheridan Street in the city center, which becomes the Captain Cook Highway.

Orienting yourself in Cairns

Downtown Cairns is on a grid 5 blocks deep, bounded on the east by the Esplanade on the water and on the west by McLeod Street, where the train station and the Cairns Central shopping mall are. In between are shops, offices, and restaurants. The focal point of the Esplanade is a 4,000-sq.-m (43,000-sq.-ft.) saltwater swimming lagoon with a wide sandy beach and surrounding parkland with public artworks and picnic areas. A walkway links the Esplanade to the Reef Fleet Terminal, the departure point for Great Barrier Reef boats.

Heading 15 minutes north from the city along the Captain Cook Highway, you come to the **northern beaches:** Holloway's Beach, Yorkey's Knob, Trinity Beach, Kewarra Beach, Clifton Beach, Palm Cove, and Ellis Beach.

Finding information after you arrive

Tourism Tropical North Queensland's **Gateway Discovery Centre,** 51 The Esplanade, Cairns, QLD 4870 (☎ 07/4051 3588; fax 07/4051 2509; www.tropicalaustralia.com), has information on Cairns and its environs, Mission Beach, Port Douglas, the Daintree Rainforest, Cape York, and Outback Queensland. It's open daily from 8:30 a.m. to 6:30 p.m. (10 a.m.–6 p.m. on public holidays). It's closed December 25, New Year's Day, and Good Friday (the Fri before Easter).

Getting around Cairns

By bus

Sunbus (☎ 07/4057 7411) buses depart City Place Mall at the intersection of Lake and Shields streets. Buy all tickets and passes onboard, and try to have correct change. You can hail buses anywhere it's convenient for the driver to stop. Bus nos. 1X, 2, and 2A travel to Trinity Beach and Palm Cove. The N route is an express bus that runs between the city and Palm Cove on Friday and Saturday nights only. Routes and timetables change, so check with the driver. Most buses run from early morning until almost midnight.

By car

Avis (☎ 07/4051 5911), **Budget** (☎ 07/4051 9222), **Hertz** (☎ 07/4051 6399), and **Thrifty** (☎ 1300/367 227 in Australia) have offices in Cairns city and at the airport. One long-established local outfit, **Sugarland Car**

Rentals (☎ **07/4052 1300**), has reasonable rates. **Britz Campervan Rentals** (☎ **1800/331 454** in Australia, or 07/4032 2611) and **Maui Rentals** (☎ **1300/363 800** in Australia, or 07/4032 2065) rent motor homes. Britz and most major car rental companies rent four-wheel-drive vehicles.

Staying in Cairns and the northern beaches

There are loads of options for staying in and around Cairns. The city has a good supply of affordable accommodations, but you can also stay at any of the northern beaches, or in the rain forest village of Kuranda, or get away from it all at an island resort.

Don't think you have to stay in Cairns if you don't have a car: Most tour and cruise operators will pick you up and drop you off in Cairns, or on the northern beaches, a string of white sandy beaches, which starts 15 minutes north of the city center.

Trinity Beach is secluded, elegant, and scenic. The most upscale is **Palm Cove,** where colorful shops and smart apartment blocks nestle among giant Paperbarks and palms across from a perfect curve of beach.

High season in Cairns includes two weeks at Easter, the period from early July to early October (when it isn't so hot), and the Christmas holiday through January. Book ahead in those periods. In the off season (Nov–June), many hotels offer discounts.

The top hotels

Outrigger Beach Club & Spa
$$$$$ Palm Cove

Set behind a grove of melaluca trees across the street from the beach, the rooms and apartments in this resort complex have touches of Queensland colonial style. Hotel rooms are small but have Jacuzzis and timber outdoor furniture on the decks. Eight penthouses have private rooftop terraces and pools, but there's no elevator. The large lagoon-style pool has a sandy beach and swim-up bar. Coconut palms with white-painted trunks surround the lagoon, which is lit by torches at night. A "resort within the resort," the Serenity Wing, has 42 suites and a private rain forest pool. The suites are secluded, with kitchens, gas barbecues, washers and dryers, and state-of-the-art entertainment units, including DVDs and flat-screen TVs. Pamper yourself at the **Sanctum Spa**. If you're staying five nights or more at full rates and want to arrive in style, order the free limousine or Rolls Royce transfers from Cairns Airport to Palm Cove. For guests staying three nights or more, the rate includes coach transfers to the airport.

123 Williams Esplanade, Palm Cove, Cairns, QLD 4879. ☎ ***800-688-7444** in the U.S., 1800/134 444 in Australia, or 07/4059 9200. Fax: 07/4059 9222.* www.outrigger. com. *Rack rates: A$295–A$360 (US$236–US$288/£118–£144) double with Jacuzzi, A$371–A$460 (US$297–US$368/£149–£184) double 1-bedroom suite, A$469–A$502 (US$375–US$402/£188–£201) double 1-bedroom suite with Jacuzzi, A$533–A$656 (US$426–US$525/£213–£262) 2-bedroom suite with Jacuzzi for up to 4, A$1,056*

(US$845/£422) 2-bedroom penthouse suite for up to 4 with plunge pool; extra person A$35 (US$28/£14). Minimum 3-night stay at Easter and Christmas to mid-Jan. AE, DC, MC, V.

Reef Retreat
$$–$$$　Palm Cove

A low-rise collection of contemporary studios and suites built around a saltwater swimming pool in a grove of palms and silver Paperbarks, Reef Retreat has 36 units (including studios, which are much larger than the average hotel room and offer terrific value). Some suites have two rooms; others have a Jacuzzi and a kitchenette outside on the balcony. There are also two-bedroom villas and a two-bedroom town house, each of which sleeps up to six people. Units are serviced once for every five-day stay. Extra cleanings A$20 to A$30 (US$16–US$24/£8–£12).

10–14 Harpa St., Palm Cove, Cairns, QLD 4879. ☎ 07/4059 1744. Fax: 07/4059 1745. www.reefretreat.com.au. *Rack rates: A$170 (US$136/£68) studio double, A$185 (US$148/£74) suite, A$195 (US$156/£78) suite with Jacuzzi, A$295 (US$236/£118) 2-bedroom villa for up to 4, A$230 (US$184/£92) town house for up to 4; extra person A$25 (US$20/£10); children under 3 stay free in parent's room with existing bedding; crib A$25 (US$20/£10). AE, MC, V.*

Sebel Reef House
$$$$$　Palm Cove

Drop-dead gorgeous. That's the only way to describe this period piece from the colonial era. This is one of the most romantic hotels in Australia. The white walls are swathed in bougainvillea; the beds, with mosquito netting. Airy interiors feature rustic handmade artifacts and white wicker furniture. The Verandah Spa rooms, which have a Jacuzzi on the balcony, overlook the pool, waterfalls, and lush gardens. They have extra touches such as bathrobes and CD players, as well as balconies within earshot of the ocean. The beachfront restaurant, on a large covered wooden deck beneath towering Paperbarks, is a favorite with locals and tourists alike for its ocean views, gentle breezes, and unpretentious food.

99 Williams Esplanade, Palm Cove, Cairns, QLD 4879. ☎ 1800/079 052 in Australia, or 07/4055 3633. Fax: 07/4055 3305. www.reefhouse.com.au. *Rack rates: A$405–A$573 (US$324–US$458/£162–£229) double, A$520–A$730 (US$416–US$584/ £208–£292) suite. AE, DC, MC, V.*

Shangri-La Hotel, The Marina
$$$$$　Reef Fleet Terminal

Modern and sophisticated, as its name suggests, this hotel overlooks the marina. The 256 rooms include 36 that are part of the Horizon Club. All have broadband and wireless Internet connectivity. Rooms are contemporary in style and some are quite spacious — more than 56 sq. m (603 sq. ft.), with 3.3m (11-ft.) ceilings. Bathrooms have ocean views, and the rooms have terraces looking to the moored yachts and the mountains. The hotel adjoins the Pier Shopping Centre and the Esplanade lagoon, and is not far from the Reef Fleet Terminal, making it convenient to everything.

See map, p. 283. Pierpoint Road, Cairns, QLD 4870. ☎ *800-942-5050 in the U.S. and Canada, 1800/222 448 in Australia, 0800/442 179 in New Zealand, 020/8747 8485 in the U.K., or 07/4031 1411. Fax: 07/4031 3226.* www.shangri-la.com. *Rack rates: A$397–A$444 (US$318–US$355/£159–£178) double, A$601–A$1,133 (US$481–US$906/ £240–£453) suite; children under 18 stay free in parent's room with existing bedding. AE, DC, MC, V.*

Sofitel Reef Casino Cairns
$$$$–$$$$$ The Esplanade

This is probably the most stylish property in Cairns, a block from the water, with partial harbor views from some rooms, and city/hinterland outlooks from others. All rooms have lots of natural light, high-quality amenities, Jacuzzis, bathrobes, and balconies with smart timber furniture. The hotel is attached to the Reef Casino and has four restaurants and lots of great amenities such as a rooftop pool, health club, and 24-hour room service.

See map p. 283. 35–41 Wharf St., Cairns, QLD 4870. ☎ *1800/808 883 in Australia, 800-221-4542 in the U.S. and Canada, 020/8283 4500 in the U.K., 0800/44 4422 in New Zealand, or 07/4030 8888. Fax: 07/4030 8777.* www.accorhotels.com. *Rack rates: A$370–A$395 (US$296–US$316/£148–£158) double, A$480–A$585 (US$384–US$468/ £192–£234) suite, A$1,865 (US$1,492/£746) presidential suite. AE, DC, MC, V.*

Dining in Cairns

Cairns has a number of good restaurants, many of them along the seafront Esplanade, where you'll also find plenty of cheap cafes, pizzerias, fish-and-chips places, and ice cream parlors.

Fishlips Bar & Bistro
$ Cairns   SEAFOOD

This Cairns institution, inside the Cairns Yacht Club, with a view over the Cairns Inlet, serves up innovative seafood dishes that have kept the locals coming here for years. Chef Ian Candy has devised a huge menu featuring everything from burgers to lobster, and creates up to 15 specials daily. Try local "barra" (barramundi), in spring rolls with chile plum sauce, beer-battered, or pan-fried with meuniere on potato mash. Don't worry if you're not a fish fan — all sorts of other dishes, including steak, are on the menu. Finish off with homemade ice cream; the flavors change each week. Enjoy live jazz on Thursday nights and a singer/guitarist on Friday nights.

See map p. 283. 4 Wharf St. ☎ *07/4031 2750.* www.fishlips.com.au. *Reservations recommended. Main courses: A$12–A$27 (US$9.60–US$22/£4.80–£11). AE, DC, MC, V. Open: Daily 11:30 a.m.–2:30 p.m. and 5:30 p.m. to late (Yacht Club open until midnight).*

Perrotta's
$ Cairns CONTEMPORARY/CAFE

Locals flock here for weekend brunch and lunch, and it's a handy spot to rest after a visit to the Cairns Regional Art. Breakfast offerings include such delights as smoked salmon and sweet-potato hash browns with sour cream and avocado. For lunch, there's a choice of bruschettas, focaccia, or panini; pasta; or more individual dishes, such as barbecued Cajun Spanish mackerel with tomato and basil salad. At dinner, try wild barramundi or lamb shanks. Remember to check the daily specials board.

See map p. 283. Abbott and Shields streets. ☎ 07/4031 5899. Reservations recommended. Main courses: Breakfast A$2.50–A$8 (US$2–US$6.40/£1–£3.20), lunch A$6.50–A$12 (US$5.20–US$9.60/£2.60–£4.80), dinner A$13–A$24 (US$10–US$19/£5.20–£9.60). MC, V. Open: Daily 8:30 a.m. to late.

Red Ochre Grill
$ Cairns INDIGENOUS/CONTEMPORARY

If the food wasn't so good, you might think this was a gimmick. Daily specials are big on fresh local seafood, and the regular menu — which changes often — lets you try Aussie wildlife (even the national coat of arms) in several different ways. Try char-grilled kangaroo sirloin with a quandong chile glaze, sweet potato fritter, and bok choy, or maybe ostrich filet with refried kipfler potatoes, crisp pancetta, and green beans.

See map p. 283. 43 Shields St. ☎ 07/4051 0100. www.redochregrill.com.au. Reservations recommended. Main courses: Lunch A$16–A$33 (US$13–US$26/£6.40–£13), dinner A$21–A$33 (US$17–US$26/£8.40–£13); Australian game platter A$45 (US$36/£18) per person; seafood platter A$66 (US$53/£26) per person; Tastes of Australia 4-course set menu A$60 (US$48/£24) per person (minimum 2 people). AE, DC, MC, V. Open: Daily noon to midnight (public holidays 6 p.m. to midnight). Closed Dec 25.

Exploring Cairns
The top attractions

Hartley's Crocodile Adventures
Port Douglas

Hartley's is the original Australian croc show and the best we've seen. What makes it different from others is the natural setting — a 2-hectare (5-acre) lagoon surrounded by melaluca (Paperbark) and bloodwood trees and home to 23 estuarine crocs. The best time to visit is for the 3 p.m. Crocodile Attack Show, when you can witness the crocodile "death roll" during the 45-minute performance. At 11 a.m. you can see them get hand-fed or hear an informative talk on the less aggressive freshwater crocodiles. Tours of the croc farm are at 10 a.m. and 1:30 p.m., a snake show is at 2 p.m., and 4:30 p.m. is koala feeding time. Cassowaries are fed at 9:30 a.m. and 4:15 p.m. Hartley's is a good place to stop en route to Port Douglas.

Capt. Cook Highway (40km/24 miles north of Cairns; 25km/16 miles south of Port Douglas). ☎ *07/4055 3576. Fax: 07/4059 1017.* www.crocodileadventures.com. *Transfers from Cairns available through Down Under Tours (☎ 07/4035 5566) or from Cairns and Port Douglas through Wildlife Discovery Tours (☎ 07/4099 6612). Admission: A$29 (US$23/£12) adults, A$15 (US$12/£6) children 4–15, A$73 (US$58/£29) families. Open: Daily 8:30 a.m.–5 p.m. Closed Dec 25.*

Kuranda Scenic Railway
Cairns/Kuranda

This 34km (21-mile) ride is one of the most scenic rail journeys in the world. The train snakes through the magnificent vistas of the Barron Gorge National Park, past gorges and waterfalls on the 90-minute trip to Kuranda. It rises 328m (1,076 ft.) and goes through 15 tunnels before emerging at Kuranda station, adorned by ferns in hanging baskets. Built by hand over 5 years in the 1880s, the railway track is a monument to the 1,500 men who toiled to link the two towns. Most people prefer to do the journey one way by train and the other by Skyrail. Packages are available.

☎ *07/4036 9333.* www.kurandascenicrailway.com.au. *Tickets: One-way A$37 (US$30/£15) adults, A$19 (US$15/£7.60) children 4–14, A$93 (US$42/£21) families of 4. AE, DC, MC, V. Train departs Cairns Central at 8:30 a.m. and 9:30 a.m. daily and leaves Kuranda at 2 p.m. and 3:30 p.m. Closed Dec 25.*

Skyway Rainforest Cableway
Smithfield

Skyrail is a magnificent feat of engineering. About 114 six-person gondolas leave every few seconds for the 7.5km (4½-mile) journey to the rain forest village of Kuranda. The view of the coast is breathtaking. As you rise over the foothills of the coastal range, the lush green of the rain forest takes over beneath you, and you're rewarded with spectacular views over Cairns and north toward Trinity Bay. There are two stops during the 90-minute trip. After about 10 minutes, you reach Red Peak, 545m (1,788 ft.) above sea level, where kauri pines dominate the view. You must change gondolas at each station, so take the time to stroll around the boardwalks. Guided walks start every 20 minutes. The second stop is at Barron Falls station, built on the site of an old construction camp for workers on the first hydroelectric power station on the Barron River in the 1930s. There is a rain forest information center and boardwalks to the lookouts for views of the Barron Gorge and Falls. From here, the gondola travels over the rain forest and you can spot ferns and orchids and the blue Ulysses butterflies. Near the end of the trip, the gondola passes over the Barron River and across the Kuranda railway line into the station. And don't worry if it rains on the day you go — one of the best trips we've made on Skyrail was in a misty rain.

Capt. Cook Highway (at Kamernga Road), Caravonica Lakes, Smithfield (about 15km/9.5 miles north of Cairns city center). ☎ *07/4038 1555.* www.skyrail. com.au. *Admission: One-way A$37 (US$30/£15) adults, A$19 (US$15/£7.60) children 4–14, A$93 (US$74/£37) families of 4; round-trip, including transfers from Cairns or* *northern beaches hotels, A$73 (US$58/£29) adults, A$37 (US$30/£15) children, A$183 (US$146/£73) for families; round-trip from Port Douglas A$88 (US$70/£35) adults, A$44 (US$35/£18) children, A$220 (US$176/£88) families. AE, DC, MC, V. Open: Daily 8:30 a.m.–5:30 p.m.; last boarding in Cairns at 4:15 p.m. Closed Dec 25.*

Tjapukai Aboriginal Cultural Park
Smithfield

The Tjapukai (pronounced jab-*oo*-guy) Aboriginal Cultural Park is one of the best chances you have in Queensland to discover the history and culture of the Aborigines. Perhaps because it was founded by American theater director Don Freeman and his French-Canadian dancer wife, Judy — working with the local Aborigines who now own 51 percent of the business — Tjapukai is more of a theme park than an authentic cultural experience. Despite this, the park has won numerous international awards since it opened 20 years ago, and it's worth a look. Start in the Creation Theatre, where performers use illusion, theatrics, and special effects to tell the story of the creation of the world according to the spiritual beliefs of Tjapukai people. Actors work with holographic images to illustrate the legends, and the production is performed in the Tjapukai language, translated through headsets. Move through the museum and gallery section of the complex to the theater, where a 20-minute film relates the history of the Tjapukai people since the coming of white settlers. Outside, there's a village where you can try boomerang and spear throwing, fire making and didgeridoo playing, and learn about bush foods and medicines. Shows and demonstrations are planned so visitors can move from one to another easily. **Tjapukai by Night** tours run daily from 7:30 to 10 p.m. They include a Creation Show performance, and an outdoor Serpent Circle — an interactive show featuring tap sticks, a join-in *corroboree* (an Aboriginal dance), and a ceremony involving fire and water. Following are a buffet dinner and dance show, and the chance to meet the Tjapukai dancers.

Captain Cook Highway (beside the Skyrail terminal), Smithfield. ☎ 07/4042 9900. Fax: 07/4042 9990. www.tjapukai.com.au. *Park is 15 minutes north of Cairns and 15 minutes south of Palm Cove. One-way shuttle transfers from Cairns hotels through the park A$11 (US$8.80/£4.40 adults), A$5.40 (US$4.30/£2.15) children. Admission: A$30 (US$24/£12) adults, A$16 (US$13/£6.40) children 4–14, A$78 (US$62/£31) families. AE, DC, MC, V. Ask about packages that include transfers, lunch, and a guided Magic Space tour, or Skyrail and/or Scenic Rail travel to and from Kuranda. Tjapukai by Night costs A$103 (US$82/£41) adults, A$52 (US$42/£21) children, or A$258 (US$206/£53) for a family of 4, including transfers to and from Cairns. Open: Daily 9 a.m.–5 p.m. Closed Jan 1 and Dec 25.*

More cool things to see and do

✔ **Cairns Wildlife Dome** (☎ 07/4031 7250; www.cairnsdome.com.au) makes exploring the rain forest and its wildlife as easy as taking an elevator to the top of the Sofitel hotel, where 200 animals — including a huge saltwater crocodile called Goliath — are housed in a 20m-high (66-ft.) glass dome on the rooftop. There are also koalas, lizards, kookaburras, frogs, pademelons, turtles, and snakes. Wildlife presentations and free guided tours are run throughout the day. Admission is A$22 (US$18/£8.80) adults, A$11 (US$8.80/£4.40) children 4–14, A$55 (US$44/£22) for a family of 4. Open: Daily 8 a.m.–6 p.m. Closed Dec 25.

✔ **RnR Rafting** (☎ 07/4041 9444) is one of several companies offering exciting **white-water-rafting** trips from Cairns on the Class III to IV Tully River (90 minutes south of Cairns), the Class III Barron River (in the hills behind the city), and the Class IV to V rapids of the Johnstone River (inland). The gentler Barron River is a good choice for the timid, with a half-day trip costing A$98 (US$78/£39) from Cairns or A$116 (US$93/£46) from Port Douglas, including pickup from your accommodations and two hours of rafting. Prices do not include a A$25 (US$20/£10) levy for national park and other fees. One-day trips on the Tully are the most popular. The trip costs A$155 (US$124/£62) from Cairns or the northern beaches, including transfers.

Going Beyond Cairns

A day trip to Kuranda

Getting there

Although undeniably touristy, the mountain village of Kuranda, 34km (21 miles) northwest of Cairns is worth a day trip, if only for the journey itself. There's cool mountain air, mist-wrapped rain forest, and a handful of cafes and restaurants. The town is easy to negotiate on foot; pick up a visitors' guide and map at the Skyrail gondola station or train station — because that's almost certainly where you'll arrive.

Getting to Kuranda is part of the fun. Some people drive up the winding 25km (16-mile) mountain road, but the most popular approaches are to steam up the mountainside in a scenic train, or to glide silently over the rain forest in the world's longest gondola cableway, the Skyrail Rainforest Cableway (see "The top attractions," earlier this chapter). The most popular round-trip is one-way on the Skyrail and the other way on the train. A package combining one-way travel on the Skyrail and a trip back on the Scenic Railway is A$74 (US$59/£30) adults, A$37 (US$30/£15) children; with round-trip transfers from Cairns or the northern beaches, it's A$93 (US$74/£37) adults, A$47 (US$38/£19) kids. Skyrail runs a shuttle bus from most Cairns hotels. An option including the Skyrail, Scenic Railway, and Kuranda attraction Rainforestation (see "Seeing the sights," later in this section), including transfers from Cairns, is A$148 (US$118/£59) adults, A$74 (US$59/£30) kids, A$369 (US$295/£148) families of four. All packages can upgrade to Gold Class service on the train for an extra A$43 (US$34/£17) per person. Book packages through Skyrail or Queensland Rail.

For those on a budget, **Whitecar Coaches** (☎ 07/4091 1855) operates a bus to Kuranda from Cairns. The fare is A$4 (US$3.20/£1.60) per person. Catch it at Stop D in the city mall, Cairns.

Taking a rain forest tour

If you want to learn about the rain forest, explore it with a former crocodile hunter. Brian Clarke of **Kuranda Riverboat Tours** (☎ 07/4093 7476 or 0412/159 212), has lived in the rain forest for more than 30 years. Brian's informative 45-minute river cruises depart hourly from 10:30 a.m. to 2:30 p.m. from the riverside landing across the railway footbridge near the train station. The cost is A$14 (US$11/£5.60) adults, A$7 (US$5.60/£2.80) children 5 to 15, and A$35 (US$28/£14) families of four. Buy your tickets on board.

Seeing the sights

Kuranda is known for its markets — the small "original" markets at 7 Therwine St., behind Kuranda Market Arcade (open Wed–Fri and Sun 8 a.m.–3 p.m.), which mainly sell cheap imports, and the 90-stall Heritage Market (open daily 9 a.m.–3 p.m.), which offers a wider variety of goods including arts and crafts, fresh produce, boomerangs, T-shirts, and jewelry.

Now there's the New Kuranda Markets, in an undercover complex in Coondoo St., which has a range of stalls and shops including an Aboriginal art gallery. About 50 local artisans sell their work in the **Kuranda Arts Co-Operative**, Shop 6, 43 Rob Veivers Dr. (☎ 07/4093 9026), next to the Butterfly Sanctuary. It's open from 10 a.m. to 4 p.m. daily.

Kuranda has several wildlife attractions:

✔ At the **Australian Butterfly Sanctuary** (☎ 07/4093 7575; www.australianbutterflies.com), a colorful array of 1,500 tropical butterflies, including the electric-blue Ulysses and Australia's largest species, the Cairns bird wing, flutters in a lush walk-through enclosure. The butterflies will land on you if you wear pink, red, and other bright colors. Admission A$15 (US$12/£6) adults, A$7.50 (US$6/£3) children 4 to 15, A$38 (US$30/£15) families of four. Open daily 9:45 a.m. to 4 p.m. Free guided tours every 15 minutes from 10 a.m. to 3:15 p.m. Closed December 25.

✔ **Birdworld** (☎ 07/4093 9188), behind the Heritage markets off Rob Veivers Drive, has eye-catching macaws, a pair of cassowaries, and Australia's largest collection of free-flying birds. It's open daily from 9 a.m. to 4 p.m. (closed Dec 25); admission is A$12 (US$9.60/£4.80) adults, A$5 (US$4/£2) children 4 to 14, A$29 (US$23/£12) families.

✔ **Kuranda Koala Gardens** (☎ 07/4093 9953; www.koalagardens.com) is a small wildlife park at the Heritage Markets. You can be photographed cuddling a koala and see other animals. You can take a stroll through the snake enclosure, while they slither around your feet. The Gardens is open daily from 9 a.m. to 4 p.m., and costs A$15 (US$12/£6) adults and A$7.50 (US$6/£3) children 4 to 15.

The Kuranda Koala Gardens is packaged with Birdworld and the Australian Butterfly Sanctuary as the **Kuranda Wildlife Experience,** and you can buy a pass to all three on arrival at any one for A$36 (US$29/£14) adults and A$18 (US$14/£7.20) children.

✔ **Rainforestation Nature Park** (☎ **07/4085 5008;** www.rainforest. com.au) is a 40-hectare (99-acre) nature and cultural complex on the Kennedy Highway, a five-minute drive from the center of Kuranda. You can take a 45-minute ride into the rain forest in a World War II amphibious Army Duck, with a commentary on rain forest flora and fauna. You can also see a performance by Aboriginal dancers; learn about Aboriginal legends and throw a boomerang on the Dreamtime Walk; or have your photo taken cuddling a koala. You can do any of these activities separately, or do them all (except cuddle a koala) for one price. Koala photos are A$12 (US$9.60/£4.80). The Army Duck runs on the hour beginning at 10 a.m.; the Aboriginal dancers perform at 10:30 a.m., noon, and 2 p.m.; and the 30-minute Dreamtime Walk leaves at 10 a.m., 11 a.m., 11:30 a.m., 12:30 p.m., 1:30 p.m., and 2:30 p.m. Admission is A$36 (US$29/£14) adults, A$18 (US$14/£7.20) kids 4 to 14, A$90 (US$72/£36) families of four. Open daily 8:30 a.m. to 4 p.m. Closed December 25.

A shuttle runs from the Australian Butterfly Sanctuary, Rob Veivers Drive, every 30 minutes from 10:45 a.m. to 2:45 p.m. for A$7 (US$5.60/£2.80) adults, A$3.50 (US$2.80/£1.40) children, A$18 (US$14/£7.20) families, round-trip.

Port Douglas, Daintree, and Cape Tribulation

The village of Port Douglas is where the rain forest meets the Reef. Just over an hour's drive from Cairns, through rain forest and along the sea, Port Douglas has stylish shops and seriously trendy restaurants. Beautiful Four Mile Beach is not to be missed. "Port," as the locals call it, is a favorite spot with celebrities big and small — you may find yourself dining next to anyone from Bill Clinton to Kylie Minogue, Sean Penn to rock bands or minor soap stars.

The lovely and uncrowded beach, the rural surroundings and limited (so far) development make this an attractive alternative to staying in Cairns. And you won't be out of the action, as many Reef and rain forest tours originate in Port Douglas, and many tours pick up from Port Douglas as well as Cairns. Daintree National Park lies just north of Port Douglas, and just north of that is Cape Tribulation National Park, another wild tract of rain forest and hilly headlands sweeping down to the sea. Exploring these two national parks is easy on a four-wheel-drive day safari from Port Douglas.

Port Douglas, Daintree, and Cape Tribulation

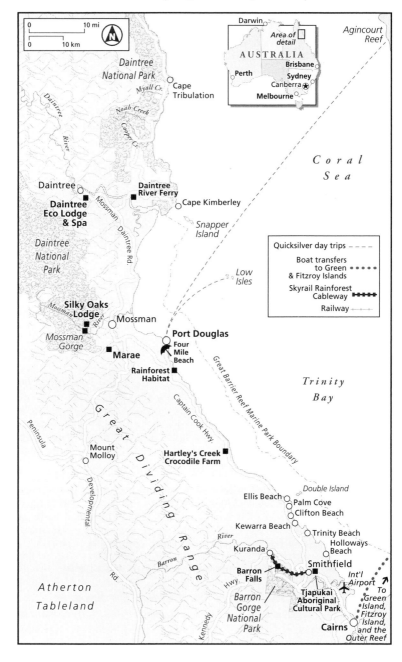

0 10 mi
0 10 km

Darwin

Area of detail

AUSTRALIA

Perth

Brisbane
Sydney
Canberra
Melbourne

Agincourt Reef

Daintree National Park

Myall Cr.

Noah Creek

Cooper Cr.

Cape Tribulation

Daintree River

Coral Sea

Daintree

Daintree
River Ferry

Cape Kimberley

Daintree Eco Lodge & Spa

Daintree National Park

Mossman Daintree Rd.

Snapper Island

Low Isles

Quicksilver day trips
Boat transfers to Green & Fitzroy Islands
Skyrail Rainforest Cableway
Railway

Silky Oaks Lodge

Mossman River

Mossman

Mossman Gorge

Marae

Rainforest Habitat

Port Douglas
Four Mile Beach

Great Barrier Reef Marine Park Boundary

Trinity Bay

Great Dividing Range

Captain Cook Hwy.

Peninsula

Mount Molloy

Hartley's Creek Crocodile Farm

Developmental

Double Island

Ellis Beach
Palm Cove
Clifton Beach
Kewarra Beach
Trinity Beach
Holloways Beach

River

Kuranda

Barron Falls

Smithfield

Barron
Barron Gorge National Park

Tjapukai Aboriginal Cultural Park

Int'l Airport

To Green Island, Fitzroy Island, and the Outer Reef

Atherton Tableland

Rd.

Hwy.

Kennedy

Cairns

Getting to Port Douglas

By car

Port Douglas is a scenic 65-minute drive from Cairns, in part along a narrow winding road that skirts the coast. Take Sheridan Street north out of the city as it becomes the Captain Cook Highway; follow the signs to Mossman and Mareeba until you reach the Port Douglas turnoff.

By bus

A one-way ticket aboard **Sun Palm Express Coaches** (☎ 07/4084 2626) to Port Douglas hotels is A$30 (US$24/£12) from the Cairns airport. Fares for children 2 to 12 are half-price. If you're staying in Cairns but taking a **Quicksilver** (☎ 07/4087 2100) cruise to the Great Barrier Reef for the day, you can take a bus transfer to Port Douglas for A$16 (US$13/£6.40) adults, half-price for kids.

By taxi

A **taxi** from Cairns runs around A$100 (US$80/£40); call **Black & White Taxis** (☎ 13 10 08 in Cairns).

Finding information after you arrive

The best sources of information in Port Douglas are the private tour information and booking centers. One of the biggest and most centrally located is the **Port Douglas Tourist Information Centre,** 23 Macrossan St. (☎ 07/4099 5599), open from 7:30 a.m. to 6 p.m. daily. There is no official visitor information office in town.

Getting around Port Douglas

A good way to get around the town's flat streets is by **bike. Holiday Bike Hire,** 40 Macrossan St. (☎ 07/4099 6144), is open daily from 8 a.m. to 6 p.m. or later and rents a large range of good mountain bikes; prices start at A$11 (US$8.80/£4.40) for a half-day, A$17 (US$14/£6.80) for a full day. **Port Douglas Bike Hire,** at Warner and Wharf streets (☎ 07/4099 5799), rents bikes for A$10 (US$8/£4) for a half-day, A$14 (US$11/£5.60) for a full day. It's open 9 a.m. to 5 p.m. daily.

If you feel like you need a car to get around, **Avis** (☎ 07/4099 4331), **Budget** (☎ 07/4099 5702), and **Thrifty** (☎ 07/4069 9977) have offices in Port Douglas. A good local company is **Port Douglas Car Rental** (☎ 07/ 4099 4988). All rent regular vehicles as well as four-wheel-drives, which you need if you plan to drive to Cape Tribulation.

For a **taxi,** call **Port Douglas Taxis** (☎ 07/4084 2650).

Where to stay in Port Douglas and the Daintree

Port Douglas Accommodation Holiday Rentals (☎ 1800/645 566 in Australia, or 07/4099 4488; www.portdouglasaccom.com.au) has a wide range of apartments and homes for rent.

High season in Port Douglas is from around June 1 through October 31.

Archipelago Studio Apartments
$$–$$$ **Port Douglas**

You won't find a friendlier or more convenient place to stay in Port Douglas than these 21 apartments, across from the beach and less than a ten-minute walk from town. Hosts Wolfgang Klein and Christel Bader are eager to help with tour bookings and to give advice — and they also speak fluent German, conversational French, and some Spanish. The apartments are on the small side (most suit only three people, at the most), but are well cared for. You can opt for a tiny Garden apartment with a patio; Balcony and Seaview apartments are larger and have private balconies. A saltwater pool is on-site. General housekeeping services cost A$20 (US$16/£8) extra. The apartments have no elevator and no porter, so you have to carry your luggage upstairs. No children under 6.

72 Macrossan St., Port Douglas, QLD 4877. ☎ *07/4099 5387. Fax: 07/4099 4847.* www. archipelago.com.au. *Rack rates: High season (June–Oct) A$133–A$235 (US$106–A$188/£53–£94) double; off season A$113–A$190 (US$90–US$152/£45–£76) double; additional person A$20 (US$16/UK£8). Minimum 3-night stay. MC, V.*

Daintree Eco Lodge & Spa
$$$$$ **Daintree**

Make no mistake, what you're here for is the spa. There's a large range of treatments, including the two-hour, A$280 (US$224/£112) Walbul-Walbul body treatment, in which you're wrapped in mud as you recline on a carved timber "wet bed," and the Yiri Jalaymba rain therapy treatment. This lodge in the primeval forest has 15 rooms, each with marble floors, timber and bamboo furniture, and tiled bathrooms with robes. Five have Jacuzzis on their screened balconies. You can join a yoga or Ki-Aikido (based on Japanese aikido) session, laze by the solar-heated pool, follow rain forest trails, join members of the local Aboriginal Kuku tribe on a bush tucker and native medicine walk, or take a four-wheel-drive day trip to modern-day Aboriginal communities. The **Julaymba Restaurant** overlooks a lily pond and serves food with a gourmet bush-tucker slant. The lodge is 98km (61 miles) north of Cairns and 40km (25 miles) north of Port Douglas, and the road is paved all the way. No children under 7.

20 Daintree Rd. (4km/2½ miles south of Daintree village), Daintree, QLD 4873. ☎ *1800/ 808 010 in Australia, or 07/4098 6100. Fax: 07/4098 6200.* www.daintree-ecolodge. com.au. *Rack rates: A$530–A$580 (US$424–US$464/£212–£232) double; extra person A$55 (US$44/£22). Rates include full breakfast. AE, DC, MC, V. Once-a-day scheduled minibus service to or from Mossman A$25 (US$20/£10), to or from Port Douglas hotels A$60 (US$48/£24), to or from Cairns hotels or Cairns airport A$80 (US$64/£32) per person, one-way. On-call transfers A$160 (US$128/£64) per car from Port Douglas, A$210 (US$168/£84) per car (maximum 2 passengers) from Cairns, one-way. Take Captain Cook Highway north to Mossman, where it becomes the Mossman-Daintree Road; follow to lodge.*

Marae
$$$ Shannonvale

John and Pam Burden's stunning timber home, on a hillside 15km (9½ miles) north of Port Douglas, is a restful luxurious retreat. The three rustic-meets-sleek contemporary bedrooms have mosquito nets and smart linens on king-size beds, and elegant bathrooms. The garden room opens onto a plunge pool overlooking the valley, and there is also a lap pool. Wallabies and bandicoots feed in the garden, kingfishers and honeyeaters use the pools, and butterflies are everywhere. A delicious tropical breakfast is served on the west deck in the company of a flock of red-browed finches and doves, and the rain forest trails of Mossman Gorge are just a few miles away. Children under 13 not accepted.

Lot 1, Chook's Ridge, Shannonvale (P.O. Box 133, Port Douglas, QLD 4877). ☎ *07/4098 4900. Fax: 07/4098 4099.* www.marae.com.au. *Rack rates: A$180 (US$144/£72) double. 2-night minimum. Rates include full breakfast. MC, V. From Port Douglas, take Captain Cook Highway toward Mossman for 10km (6¼ miles), go left onto Mount Molloy turnoff for 1km (½ mile), then right onto Ponzo Road for 2km (1¼ miles). Chook's Ridge is on your left.*

Port Douglas Peninsula Boutique Hotel
$$$$–$$$$$ Port Douglas

This intimate studio apartment hotel fronting Four Mile Beach is one of the nicest places in town. Each of the apartments has an open-plan living room/bedroom, a contemporary kitchenette (with microwave and dishwasher), and a bathroom boasting a giant double tub (or Jacuzzi, in some units). Corner apartments are a little bigger. There are extra touches like a CD player and Twining's teas, and most units have beach views from the roomy balcony or patio. A few look onto the complex of Art Deco–style pools, waterfalls, Jacuzzis, and sun deck on several levels. A two-minute walk brings you to the main street. No children under 15.

9–13 The Esplanade, Port Douglas, QLD 4877. ☎ *1800/676 674 in Australia, or 07/4099 9100. Fax: 07/4099 5440.* www.peninsulahotel.com.au. *Rack rates: A$340–A$460 (US$272–US$368/£136–£184) double. Rates include full breakfast and round-trip transfers from Cairns airport. AE, DC, MC, V.*

Port Douglas Retreat
$–$$ Port Douglas

This well-kept Queenslander-style studio-apartment complex is a good value. Some of the ritzier places in town don't boast its lagoonlike saltwater pool, surrounded by dense jungle and wrapped by a shady sun deck. The apartments are not enormous, but they're fashionably furnished, with terra-cotta tile floors, wrought-iron beds, cane seating, and colorful bedcovers. All have large balconies or patios looking into tropical gardens; some on the ground floor open onto the common-area boardwalk, so you may want to ask for a second-story unit for a bit more privacy. The town and beach are a five-minute walk away.

31–33 Mowbray St. (at Mudlo Street), Port Douglas, QLD 4877. ☎ *07/4099 5053. Fax: 07/4099 5033.* www.portdouglasretreat.com.au. *Rack rates: High season (June–Oct) A$145–A$169 (US$116–A$135/£58–£68) double; low season (Nov–May) A$79–A$110 (US$63–US$88/£32–£44) double; crib A$5.50 (US$4.40/£2.20) per night. Minimum 3-night stay. AE, MC, V.*

Port O'Call Lodge
$-$$ Port Douglas

A mixed clientele of backpackers, families, and travelers on a budget give a communal feeling to this modest motel a ten-minute walk from town. The rooms are light and cool, with tile floors, loads of luggage space, and small patios. There are 28 rooms, in double and quad configurations. Half the double rooms have king-size beds, and all have air-conditioning, a TV, hairdryer, and other amenities. Hostel rooms have private bathrooms and no more than five beds in each. A 24-bed bunkhouse has facilities for travelers with disabilities. At night the poolside bistro is the place to be. Other features include free board games, Internet access, and a kiosk selling refreshments. A free once-daily shuttle operates to and from Cairns and the airport Monday through Saturday, and there's a bus stop at the front door.

Port Street at Craven Close, Port Douglas, QLD 4877. ☎ *1800/892 800 in Australia, or 07/4099 5422. Fax: 07/4099 5495.* www.portocall.com.au. *Rack rates: A$69–A$119 (US$55–US$95/£28–£48) double; extra person A$15 (US$12/£6). Hostel quad rooms A$29 (US$23/£12) YHA/Hostelling International members, A$30 (US$24/£12) nonmembers; bunkhouse A$24 (US$19/£9.60) YHA/Hostelling International members, A$25 (US$20/£10) nonmembers. Children under 3 stay free in parent's room. MC, V.*

Sheraton Mirage
$$$$$ Port Douglas

This large low-rise resort has 2 hectares (5 acres) of saltwater pools and a championship Peter Thomson–designed 18-hole golf course. It is a bit too far from Port's main street by foot, but a free shuttle runs from 9 a.m. to 6 p.m. to the country club and health center, to Marina Mirage shopping center, and into town. All rooms are large and light-filled, and have excellent extras like mini stereo systems, PlayStations, and Internet access. You may want to upgrade to a Mirage room with a corner Jacuzzi and king-size beds, but we think the standard rooms are fine. The Sheraton also handles rental of 101 privately owned two-, three-, and four-bedroom luxury villas with golf course, garden, or sea views; the décor varies, but each has a kitchenette, a Jacuzzi, and two bathrooms.

Davidson Street (off Port Douglas Road), Port Douglas, QLD 4877. ☎ *1800/073 535 in Australia, or 07/4099 5888; 800-325-3535 in the U.S. and Canada; 00800/325 3535 in the U.K., Ireland, and New Zealand. Fax: 07/4099 4424, or Starwood Hotels reservation fax 07/4099 5398.* www.sheraton-mirage.com.au. *Rack rates: A$619–A$830 (US$495–US$664/£248–£332) double, A$2,500 (US$2,000/£1,000) suite, A$950–A$1,150 (US$760–US$920/£280–£460) 2-, 3-, or 4-bedroom villa; extra person A$92 (US$74/£37). Children under 17 stay free in parent's room with existing bedding. AE, DC, MC, V.*

Silky Oaks Lodge & Healing Waters Spa
$$$$$ Mossman

From the veranda of your room, you will hear the gushing waters of the Mossman River. Stroll down for a swim (there are no crocs) or admire it from afar. Despite its popularity, this luxury resort at the edge of cane fields exudes a restful feeling. Treehouses are scattered through the rain forest and gardens, each in its own private part of the gardens and rain forest; the five Riverhouses overlook the river frontage, and all have Jacuzzis. Each of the 50 units has timber floors, attractive furnishings, a king-size bed, bathrobes, a CD player — but no TV — and a double hammock. Make sure you head to the **Healing Waters Day Spa** (book ahead, it's popular). Rates include guided nature walks, tennis, mountain bikes, and kayaking or snorkeling in the Mossman River, and there is a daily activities program. Children under 15 not accepted.

Finlayvale Road, Mossman, 7km (4½ miles) west of Mossman Township; 27km (17 miles) from Port Douglas (c/o Voyages, G.P.O. Box 3589, Sydney, NSW 2001). ☎ *1300/134 044 in Australia, 02/8296 8010 (Sydney reservations office), or 07/4098 1666 (lodge). Fax: 02/9299 2103 (Sydney reservations office) or 07/4098 1983 (lodge).* www.voyages.com.au. *Rack rates: A$590–A$780 (US$472–US$624/£236–£312) double; extra person A$58 (US$46/£23). Rates include full breakfast and a morning and afternoon shuttle from Port Douglas. AE, DC, MC, V. Town-car transfers A$145 (US$116/£58) per car one-way from Cairns city or airport; stretch limousine transfers A$250 (US$200/£100). Take Captain Cook Highway to Mossman, where it becomes the Mossman-Daintree Road; continue approximately 3.5km (2¼ miles) past Mossman and turn left onto Finlayvale Road.*

Thala Beach Lodge
$$$$$ Port Douglas

This luxury hideaway in the rain forest will delight you from the moment you arrive in the open-air lobby. From the elevated restaurant, the impact is even greater, with views from the Daintree to Cape Grafton, south of Cairns. Thala (pronounced *ta*-la) Beach is on a 59-hectare (146-acre) private peninsula, bordered on three sides by private beaches and coves. When designing it, owners Rob and Oonagh Prettejohn took their inspiration from the flora and fauna of the World Heritage area that surrounds it. The 85 secluded bungalows are spacious and comfortable, with timber-paneled walls and your choice of king-size or twin beds. All are built on high poles in the trees, where lorikeets and red-faced flying foxes feed on blossoms and hang from the branches. The 16 Coral Sea bungalows overlook the ocean; the rest have forest and mountain views. Some of the bungalows are a bit of a walk from the public areas and swimming pools, but it's a small price to pay for the privacy and the rain forest setting.

16km (10 miles) south of Port Douglas (P.O. Box 199, Smithfield, Cairns, QLD 4878). ☎ *1800/251 958 in Australia (Small Luxury Hotels of the World) or 07/4098 5700 (lodge). Fax: 07/4098 5837.* www.slh.com/thala. *Rack rates: A$440–A$680 (US$352–US$544/£176–£272) double. AE, DC, MC, V. Transfers from Cairns A$26 (US$21/£10) per person.*

Dining in Port Douglas

Port O'Call Bistro
$ CAFE FARE

Locals mix with guests at this poolside bistro and bar because it offers good, simple food like lamb shanks and steaks in hearty portions at painless prices. The atmosphere is fun and friendly. The restaurant serves pasta and curry dishes, as well as burgers, chicken, and Asian stir-fries. Every night you can try one of the chef's blackboard surprises, including local seafood. Kids' meals are A$9 (US$7.20/£3.60).

In the Port O'Call Lodge, Port Street at Craven Close. ☎ *07/4099 5422. Main courses: A$14–A$20 (US$11–US$16/£5.60–£8). MC, V. Open: Daily 6 p.m. to midnight.*

Salsa Bar & Grill
$ CONTEMPORARY/TROPICAL

This popular restaurant, in a lovely timber Queenslander with wraparound verandas, has terrific food, great prices, and lively, fun service. There are no pretensions here. Choose simple fare such as gnocchi, Caesar salad, or fantastic Thai chicken spring rolls with banana mayo and Asian greens, or a sumac-crusted lamb loin with cannellini bean and potato galette. Don't resist dessert: The *panna cotta* is to-die-for.

26 Wharf Street (at Warner Street). ☎ *07/4099 4922.* www.salsa-port-douglas. com.au. *Reservations required. Main courses: A$15–A$35 (US$12–US$28/£6–£14). AE, DC, MC, V. Open: Mon–Sat 10 a.m. to midnight, Sun 8 a.m. to midnight.*

Getting to the Reef from Port Douglas

The most glamorous large vessels visiting the Outer Reef are the ultra-sleek **Quicksilver Wavepiercers** (☎ **07/4087 2100**). These high-speed, air-conditioned 37m (121-ft.) and 46m (151-ft.) catamarans carry 300 or 440 passengers, respectively, from Port Douglas to Agincourt Reef, 39 nautical miles (72km/45 miles) from shore on the outer edge of the Reef. After the 90-minute trip, you tie up at a two-story pontoon, where you spend three-and-a-half hours.

Quicksilver departs Marina Mirage at 10 a.m. daily except December 25. The cost for the day is A$186 (US$149/£74) adults, A$93 (US$74/£37) kids 4 to 14. Guided snorkel safaris cost A$58 (US$46/£23) per person, and introductory dives cost A$134 (US$107/£54) per person. Qualified divers can make one dive for A$92 (US$74/£37) or two dives for A$134 (US$107/£54) per person, all gear included. Because Quicksilver carries so many passengers, it pays to book snorkel safaris and dives in advance.

The dive boat *Poseidon* welcomes snorkelers. You'll hear a Reef ecology talk en route and a guided snorkel safari is included. The price of A$155 (US$124/£62) for adults and A$120 (US$96/£48) for children 3 to 12 includes lunch and transfers from Port Douglas hotels.

Snorkeling specialist boat *Wavelength* (☎ 07/4099 5031; www. wavelength.com.au) does a full-day trip to the Outer Reef for A$160 (US$128/£64) for adults, A$110 (US$88/£44) for children 2 to 12, A$485 (US$388/£194) for a family of four. The trip visits three different snorkel sites and incorporates a guided snorkel tour and a reef presentation by a marine biologist. It carries up to 30 passengers and includes snorkel gear, sunsuits, lunch, and transfers from your hotel. It departs daily at 8:15 a.m. from the Wavelength jetty, Wharf Street.

Another way to spend a pleasant day on the Great Barrier Reef, closer to shore, is to visit the **Low Isles,** 15km (9½ miles) northeast of Port Douglas. The isles are 1.5-hectare (3¾-acre) coral-cay specks of lush vegetation surrounded by white sand and 22 hectares (54 acres) of coral — which is what makes them so appealing.

The trip aboard the 30m (98-ft.) luxury sailing catamaran *Wavedancer* (☎ 07/4087 2100), operated by Quicksilver, is A$132 (US$106/£53) adults, A$66 (US$53/£26) kids 4 to 14, A$330 (US$264/£132) families. You have the option of making an introductory scuba dive for an extra A$112 (US$90/£45) per person. Coach transfers are available through Quicksilver from Cairns and Palm Cove for A$16 (US$13/£6.40) adults, half-price for children.

Discovering the national parks

The Daintree and Cape Tribulation rain forests are two separate national parks, but the forests merge into one. The World Heritage–listed **Daintree Rainforest,** largely unchanged over the past 110 million years, is home to rare plants that provide key links in the evolution story. In the 56,000-hectare (138,320-acre) **Daintree National Park,** you'll find cycads, dinosaur trees, fan palms, giant strangler figs, and epiphytes like the basket fern, staghorn, and elkhorn. Nighttime croc-spotting tours on the Daintree River vie for popularity with early-morning cruises to see the rich bird life. Pythons, lizards, frogs, and electric-blue Ulysses butterflies attract photographers, and sport fishermen come here in pursuit of barramundi.

The best way to learn the most about the rain forest is to take a guided, four-wheel-drive day trip. Most tour operators in the area cover the same basic territory and sights, including a one-hour Daintree River cruise to spot crocs, a visit to the Marrdja Botanical Walk, a stroll along an isolated beach, lunch in the forest, and a visit to Mossman Gorge. Some also go to Bloomfield Falls in Cape Tribulation National Park. Expect to pay about A$140 (US$112/£56) per adult and about A$95 (US$76/£38) per child. Trips that include Bloomfield Falls cost more.

A company that provides an excellent, gently adventurous alternative is Pete Baxendell's **Heritage & Interpretive Tours** (☎ 07/4098 7897; www.nqhit.com.au). On a daylong bushwalk into a tract of privately owned rain forest with Pete, a naturalist and professional tour guide, you taste green ants (not nasty at all!) and other native "bush tucker,"

discover how to rustle up a toothbrush from a shrub, learn about bush medicine and the wildlife around you, and clamber up a stream to a waterfall. Pete takes a maximum of six people at a time. Lunch and Port Douglas pickups are included in the price of A$130 (US$104/£52) per person. Pickups from Cairns and the northern beaches can be organized through **BTS Tours** (☎ **07/4099 5665**) for an extra cost. Walks run Tuesday and Saturday, leaving Port at 8:30 a.m. You can charter Pete and his four-wheel-drive on other days for day bushwalks for A$185 (US$148/£74) per person (minimum of two). A longer "go anywhere" adventure costs A$650 (US$520/£260) per day, including Cairns and northern beaches pickups. The charter prices compare favorably to a regular Daintree four-wheel-drive tour if there are three or more of you — and you get a tailored itinerary, Pete's knowledge, and the vehicle all to yourself. He often takes charter customers inland to Outback gold mining ghost towns, or north to tiny Cooktown, which boasts an excellent museum devoted to Australia's "discoverer," Captain James Cook. If you have two days, he can take you farther west to see Aboriginal rock art and stay at a permanent safari camp, or to the amazing Undara Lava Tubes.

Other established operators are **Trek North Safaris** (☎ **07/4033 2600**) and **BTS Tours** (☎ **07/4099 5665**). As is the case in most tourist hot spots, some tour operators battle fiercely to pay tour desks the highest commission to recommend their tours, even though those tours may not necessarily be the best for your needs. Take tour desks' recommendations with a grain of salt, and ask other travelers for their recommendations. You may not see too much wildlife — rain forest animals are shy, camouflaged, nocturnal, or all three! Most four-wheel-drive tours will pick you up in Port Douglas at no charge; there is usually a fee from Cairns and the northern beaches. Floods and swollen creeks can quash your plans to explore the Daintree in the Wet season (Dec–Mar or Apr), so keep your plans flexible.

If your chosen safari does not visit **Mossman Gorge,** 21km (13 miles) northwest of Port Douglas near the sugar town of Mossman, try to get there under your own steam. The river tumbling over boulders, and the short forest walks are magical. Don't climb on the rocks or enter the river, because strong currents are extremely dangerous and have claimed at least one life in recent years.

More cool things to see and do

🖊 **Dan Irby's Mangrove Adventures** (☎ **07/4090 7017;** www. mangroveadventures.com.au) will take you out on the Daintree River in a small open boat, which can get up intriguing side creeks the bigger boats can't. Originally from Tonkawa, Oklahoma, Dan has been in Australia for 35 years and is extremely knowledgeable about the wildlife and habitat. He takes no more than ten people at a time on two- to four-hour cruises. Making advance reservations with Dan (at least 24 hours ahead, if possible) is very important. A two-hour trip costs A$45 (US$36/£18). The early morning sunrise tours and night tours leave from Daintree Eco Lodge, 20 Mossman

Daintree Rd., 4km (2½ miles) south of Daintree village; day tours leave from the public jetty next to the Daintree River ferry crossing. You can combine both, taking an afternoon tour, followed by a 45-minute break for a snack at Daintree Eco Lodge, and then the night tour. Chances are, you'll spot lots of fascinating wildlife on his two-hour night cruise, but even if you don't, it's worth it just to see the stars.

Take the Captain Cook Highway north to Mossman, where it becomes the Mossman Daintree Road, and follow it for 24km (15 miles) to the signposted turnoff for the ferry on your right. The ferry is 5km (3 miles) from the turnoff. You'll need a car to get there; transfers are not available.

✔ **Fine Feather Tours** (☎ 07/4094 1199; www.finefeathertours. com.au) has a full-day bird-watching safari through the Daintree and Cape Tribulation national parks to the edge of the Outback for A$225 (US$180/£90). It also offers an afternoon cruise on the Daintree River for A$165 (US$132/£66) and other tours.

✔ **KuKu-Yalanji Dreamtime Walks** (☎ 07/4098 2595; www.yalanji. com.au) offers a guided walk by members of the native KuKu-Yalanji tribe through the rain forest to see cave paintings and visit "special sites"; the tour is followed by a dreamtime story and didgeridoo performance over billy tea and damper in a bark *warun* (shelter). Walks run for 90 minutes and leave Monday through Friday at 9 a.m., 11 a.m., 1 p.m. and 3 p.m. from the KuKu-Yalanji community, on the road to Mossman Gorge (1km/½ mile before you reach the gorge parking lot). Tours cost A$25 (US$20/£10) adults, A$15 (US$12/£6) children under 12, A$65 (US$52/£26) families of four.

✔ **Extra Action Water Sports** (☎ 07/4099 3175) offers parasailing, jet-skiing, and tube rides on Four Mile Beach, Port Douglas. A half-hour on a jet ski or parafly costs A$70 (US$56/£28) solo, A$90 (US$72/£36) tandem. The booking office is at the end of the jetty on the Port Douglas slipway.

Mission Beach and Islands

For years, the lovely coastal town of Mission Beach, between Cairns and Townsville, was a well-kept secret. Today, it's a small, prosperous, pretty rain forest town with one of Australia's most beautiful beaches, a long white strip fringed with the only surviving lowlands rain forest in the Australian tropics. It's also one of the least crowded and least spoiled.

Tucked away off the Bruce Highway, 140km (87 miles) south of Cairns, Mission Beach is on what's called the Cassowary Coast. Signs on the way into town warn you to watch out for cassowaries emerging from the bush to cross the road. Dense rain forest hides the town from view until you round a corner and discover appealing hotels, neat shops, and smart little restaurants. Mission Beach is actually a conglomeration of four beachfront towns: South Mission Beach, Wongaling Beach, Mission Beach proper, and Bingil Bay. Most activity centers on the small nucleus of shops and businesses at Mission Beach proper.

The nearby Tully River is white-water-rafting heaven for thrill-seekers, who can also bungee-jump and tandem sky-dive if the mood takes them. From Mission Beach it's a short ferry ride to Dunk Island, a large resort island that welcomes day-trippers (or you can get there by sea kayak from the mainland, if you're feeling energetic). Mission Beach is closer to the Great Barrier Reef than any other point along the coast — just an hour — and cruise boats depart daily from the jetty, stopping en route at Dunk Island.

Getting to Mission Beach

By car

From Cairns, follow the Bruce Highway south. The Mission Beach turnoff is at the tiny town of El Arish, about 15km (9½ miles) north of Tully. Mission Beach is 25km (16 miles) off the highway. It's a 90-minute trip from Cairns. If you're coming from Townsville, a turnoff just north of Tully leads 18km (11 miles) to South Mission Beach.

By bus

Mission Beach Connections (☎ **07/4059 2709**) operates door-to-door shuttles three times a day from Cairns and Cairns Airport for A$38 (US$30/£15) adults and A$19 (US$15/£7.60) children, and from the northern beaches for A$49 (US$39/£20) adults and A$25 (US$20/£10) children.

Greyhound Australia (☎ **13 14 99** in Australia) coaches stop in Mission Beach proper (not South Mission Beach) several times daily. The fare is A$29 (US$23/£12) from Cairns, A$227 (US$182/£91) for the 26-hour-plus trip from Brisbane.

By train

Five trains a week on the Cairns–Brisbane–Cairns route serve the nearest station, Tully, about 20km (13 miles) away. One-way travel from Cairns on the Tilt Train costs A$46 (US$37/£18) for the just-under-three-hour journey. From Brisbane, fares range from A$179 (US$143/£72) in an economy seat to A$367 (US$294/£147) for a first-class sleeper on the *Sunlander* or A$661 (US$529/£264) for Queenslander class. For more information, call Queensland Rail's long-distance division, **Traveltrain** (☎ **1300/131 722** in Australia, or 07/3235 1133; www.traveltrain. com.au). A taxi from Tully to Mission Beach with **Supreme Taxis** (☎ **07/4068 3937**) is about A$40 (US$32/£16).

Finding information after you arrive

The **Mission Beach Visitor Information Centre,** Porters Promenade, Mission Beach, QLD 4852 (☎ **07/4068 7099;** fax 07/4068 7066;

www.missionbeachtourism.com), is at the northern end of town. It's open daily from 9 a.m. to 5 p.m. (except Dec 25).

Getting around Mission Beach

A **Trans North Bus & Coach** (☎ **07/4068 7400**) provides bus service linking the beach communities from Bingal Bay to South Mission Beach. Just flag the bus down outside your accommodations or wherever you see it. **Sugarland Car Rentals** (☎ **07/4068 8272**) is the only car rental company in town. For Mission Beach taxi service, call ☎ **0429/689 366.**

Staying in Mission Beach

The Horizon
$$$–$$$$

Perched on a steep hillside, a minute or two down the rain forest track to the beach, this resort is comfortable and beautiful. With wonderful views to Dunk Island, a rain forest setting, and spacious rooms, you'll find it easy to relax. Even the least expensive of the 55 rooms are spacious and have luxurious bathrooms; all but a handful have a sea view. There are three restaurants, a large saltwater pool, and tennis courts.

Explorer Drive, South Mission Beach, QLD 4852. ☎ *1800/079 090 in Australia, or 07/4068 8154. Fax: 07/4068 8596.* www.thehorizon.com.au. *Rack rates: A$220–A$420 (US$176–US$336/£88–£168) double, A$260 (US$208/£104) suite, A$290–A$350 (US$232–US$280/£116–£140) family room (sleeps 5); extra child 4–14 A$15 (US$12/£6). Rates may be higher Dec 22–Jan 2. AE, DC, MC, V.*

Mackays
$–$$

This well-kept, family-run motel is one of the best deals in town. It's 80m (262 ft.) from the beach and 400m (¼ mile) from the heart of Mission Beach. All 22 rooms are pleasant and spacious, with white-tiled floors, cane sofas, colorful bedcovers, and clean bathrooms. Some have views of the granite-lined pool and gardens. Rooms in the older wing have garden views from a communal patio. Apartments have kitchenettes but only have air-conditioning in the main bedrooms. Ask about special packages; they can be good deals and may include extras like rafting on the Tully River and day trips to the Reef and Dunk Island.

7 Porter Promenade, Mission Beach, QLD 4852. ☎ *07/4068 7212. Fax: 07/4068 7095.* www.mackaysmissionbeach.com. *Rack rates: A$95–A$110 (US$76–US$88/£38–£44) double, A$110–A$155 (US$88–US$124/£44–£62) 1- and 2-bedroom apartment; extra adult A$20 (US$16/£8), extra child under 14 A$10 (US$8/£4). AE, DC, MC, V.*

Exploring the Reef and rain forest from Mission Beach

Mission Beach is the closest point on the mainland to the Reef, just one hour by the high-speed **Quick Cat Cruises** catamaran (☎ **07/4068 7289**). The trip starts with an hour at Dunk Island, 20 minutes offshore, where you can walk rain forest trails, play on the beach, or parasail or jet-ski for an extra fee. Then it's a one-hour trip to sandy Beaver Cay on the Outer Reef, where you have three hours to snorkel or to check out the coral from a glass-bottom boat.

There's no shade on the cay, so come prepared with a hat and sunscreen.

The trip departs daily from **Clump Point Jetty** at 9:30 a.m. It costs A$144 (US$115/£58) adults, A$72 (US$58/£29) children 4 to 14. An introductory scuba dive costs A$80 (US$64/£32) for the first dive, A$35 (US$28/£14) for the second. Be sure to prebook your introductory scuba dive to ensure a place. Qualified divers pay A$60 (US$48/£24) for the first dive, A$35 (US$28/£14) for the second, with all gear included for both dives. Free pickups from Mission Beach are included. You can also join this trip from Cairns; coach connections from your Cairns or northern beaches hotel will cost extra.

Hiking trails abound through national parks, in rain forests, through fan palm groves, and along the beach. The 8km (5-mile) **Licuala Fan Palm** track starts at the parking lot on the Mission Beach–Tully Road about 1.5km (1 mile) west of the turnoff to South Mission Beach. The track leads through dense forest and over creeks, and comes out on the El Arish–Mission Beach Road about 7km (4½ miles) north of the post office. Then you can cross the road and keep going on the 1km (⅔-mile) Lacey Creek loop in the Tam O'Shanter State Forest. A shorter Rainforest Circuit option leads from the parking lot at the start of the Licuala Fan Palm track and makes a 1km (⅔-mile) loop incorporating a fan palm boardwalk. There's also a ten-minute fun children's walk, which starts in the parking lot and follows "cassowary footprints."

For a walk with ocean views, take the 7km (4½-mile) **Edmund Kennedy track,** which starts below the Horizon resort at the southern end of the Kennedy Esplanade in South Mission Beach. You get views of the sea and the rain forest on this trail. The Mission Beach Visitor Centre has free trail maps.

More cool things to see and do

Coral Sea Kayaking (☎ **07/4068 9154** or 0419/782 453; www.coralsea kayaking.com) offers a range of sea-kayaking expeditions that interpret the rich environment around you. Groups are usually between five and eight people, so you get personal attention and time to ask questions. The half-day sea-kayak trip (A$60/US$48/£24 per person) follows the coast near South Mission Beach. Between mid-May and mid-November, owners David Tofler and Atalanta Willy also run a three-day sea-kayak camping trip to the nearby Family Islands. This costs A$570 (US$456/£228), including pickup from your accommodations, all meals, and equipment including snorkeling gear. Extended five- and seven-day paddles are also available.

Townsville and More Islands

Townsville, 346km (215 miles) south of Cairns, is Australia's largest tropical city. Because of its size, and an economy based on mining, manufacturing, education, and tourism, it is often — unjustly, we think — discounted as a good holiday destination. The people are friendly, the city is pleasant, and there's plenty to do. The town sits by the sea below the pink face of Castle Rock, which looms 300m (1,000 ft.) directly above.

Townsville's major attraction is the world-class Museum of Tropical Queensland, where a full-size replica of H.M.S. *Pandora* is the centerpiece. Next door is the Reef HQ aquarium.

The Great Barrier Reef is about two-and-a-half hours away, and just 8km (5 miles) offshore is Magnetic Island, a popular place for watersports, hiking, and spotting koalas in the wild.

Getting to Townsville

By plane

Qantas (☎ **13 13 13** in Australia; www.qantas.com.au) flies direct from Brisbane. **QantasLink** flies from Cairns, Brisbane, Hamilton Island in the Whitsundays, and Mackay. **Jetstar** (☎ **13 15 38** in Australia) flies from Brisbane, Sydney, and Melbourne's Tullamarine airport. **Virgin Blue** (☎ **13 67 89** in Australia) flies direct to Townsville from Brisbane and Sydney daily.

Abacus Charters & Tours (☎ **07/4775 5544**) runs a door-to-door airport shuttle. It meets all flights from Brisbane, and from Cairns or elsewhere if you book in advance. A trip into town is A$8 (US$6.40/£3.20) one-way. A **taxi** from the airport to most central hotels costs about A$15 (US$12/£6).

By car

Townsville is on the Bruce Highway, a three-hour drive north of Airlie Beach and four-and-a-half hours south of Cairns. The Bruce Highway breaks temporarily in the city. From the south, take Bruce Highway Alternate 1 route into the city. From the north, the highway leads into the city. The drive from Cairns to Townsville through sugar-cane fields, cloud-topped hills, and lush bushland is a pretty one — one of the most picturesque stretches in Queensland.

By bus

Greyhound Australia (☎ **13 14 99** in Australia) coaches stop at Townsville many times a day on their Cairns–Brisbane–Cairns routes. The fare from Cairns is A$62 (US$50/£25); trip time is six hours. The fare from Brisbane is A$200 (US$160/£80); trip time is 23 hours.

By train

Seven **Queensland Rail** (☎ **1300/131 722** in Queensland, or 07/3235 1122; www.traveltrain.com.au) long-distance trains stop at Townsville each week. The 19-hour Tilt Train journey from Brisbane costs A$263 (US$210/£105). The 24-hour *Sunlander* journey costs A$179 (US$143/£72) economy seat, A$237–A$367 (US$190–US$294/£95–£147) sleeper, A$661 (US$529/£264) luxury Queenslander class.

Finding information after you arrive

Townsville Enterprise Limited (☎ **07/4726 2728**; www.townsville online.com.au) has two information centers. One is in the heart of town on Flinders Mall (☎ **1800/801 902** in Australia, or 07/4721 3660); it's open Monday through Friday from 9 a.m. to 5 p.m., and weekends from 9 a.m. to 1 p.m. The other information center is on the Bruce Highway 10km (6¼ miles) south of the city (☎ **07/4778 3555**); it's open daily from 9 a.m. to 5 p.m. For information on Magnetic Island, also check www.magnetic-island.com.au or www.magneticisland.info.

Getting around Townsville

Sunbus (☎ **07/4725 8482**) buses depart Flinders Mall.

Car rental chains include **Avis** (☎ **07/4721 2688**), **Budget** (☎ **07/4725 2344**), **Hertz** (☎ **07/4775 4821**), and **Thrifty** (☎ **07/4725 4600**).

Detours Coaches (☎ **07/4771 3986**) runs tours to most attractions in and around Townsville.

For a **taxi**, call ☎ **13 10 08.**

Staying in Townsville

Holiday Inn Townsville
$$

You'll understand why this hotel — one of Townsville's favorites — is nick-named "the Sugar Shaker." Centrally located on Flinders Mall, it's a stroll from Reef HQ, Museum of Tropical Queensland, and Magnetic Island ferries. The 230 rooms are fitted out in sleek blond wood, and because the 20-story building is circular, every one of them faces the city, the bay, or Castle Hill. Suites have kitchenettes, and a restaurant is on-site. The hotel has a rooftop pool and sun deck with barbecues.

334 Flinders Mall, Townsville, QLD 4810. ☎ *1800/079 903 in Australia, or 07/4729 2000; 800-835-7742 in the U.S. and Canada; 0345/581 666 in the U.K. or 020/8335 1304 in London; 0800/801 111 in New Zealand. Fax: 07/4721 1263.* www.ichotelsgroup. com. *Rack rates: A$140–A$165 (US$112–US$132/£56–£66) double, A$170–A$180 (US$136–US$144/£68–£72) suite; extra person A$40 (US$32/£16). Children stay free in parent's room with existing bedding. AE, DC, MC, V.*

Seagulls Resort
$$

This popular resort, a five-minute drive from the city, is built around an inviting free-form saltwater pool in 1.2 hectares (3 acres) of tropical gardens. Despite the Esplanade location, the 70 motel-style rooms do not have water views, but they are comfortable and a good size. The larger deluxe rooms have painted brick walls, a sofa, dining furniture, and a kitchen sink. Studios and family rooms have kitchenettes; executive suites have Jacuzzis. Apartments have a main bedroom and a bunk bedroom (sleeps 3), a kitchenette, dining furniture, and a roomy balcony. The whole resort is wheelchair accessible. The accommodations wings surround the pool area and its open-sided restaurant, which is popular with locals. It's a ten-minute walk to The Strand, the bus to the city costs A$3 (US$2.40/£1.20), and most tour companies pick up at the door.

74 The Esplanade, Belgian Gardens, QLD 4810. ☎ *1800/079 929 in Australia, or 07/ 4721 3111. Fax: 07/4721 3133.* www.seagulls.com.au. *Rack rates: A$110–A$140 (US$88–US$112/£44–£56) double, A$150 (US$120/£60) 2-bedroom apartment, A$170 (US$136/£68) executive suite; extra adult A$20 (US$16/£8), extra child under 14 A$10 (US$8/£4). AE, DC, MC, V. Bus: 7.*

Dining in Townsville

You'll find lots of restaurants and cafes on Palmer Street, an easy stroll across the river from Flinders Mall, on Flinders Street East, and on The Strand.

Michel's Café and Bar
$$–$$$ CONTEMPORARY

This large, spacious restaurant is popular with Townsville's "in" crowd. Choose a table on the sidewalk, or opt for air-conditioning inside. Head chefs and owners Michel Flores and Jason Makara work in the open kitchen where they can keep an eye on the excellent waitstaff. The menu may include such dishes as vanilla-scented slow-cooked duck legs with caramelized sweet potato, steamed broccolini, and orange marmalade; roasted sweet pork cutlet with braised red cabbage, hazelnuts, and spiced apple chutney; or stylish pastas, seafood, or warm salads.

7 Palmer St. ☎ *07/4724 1460. Reservations recommended. Main courses: A$20–A$33 (US$16–US$26/£8–£13). AE, DC, MC, V. Open: Tues–Fri 11:30 a.m.–2:30 p.m., Tues–Sat 5:30–10 p.m.*

Exploring the Reef

Barrier Reef Dive, Cruise & Travel (☎ 1800/636 778 in Australia, or 07/4772 5800; www.divecruisetravel.com) runs day trips to Wheeler Reef and John Brewer Reef. It takes only one-and-a-half hours to reach John Brewer Reef, where you can make introductory dives for A$229 (US$183/£92) for the first dive and A$274 (US$219/£110) for two dives, and certified divers can make two dives for A$244 (US$195/£98); all gear is included. The cruise costs A$139 (US$111/£56) adults, A$125 (US$100/£50) seniors, A$84 (US$67/£34) children 5 to 15, A$357 (US$287/£143) families of four. The price includes lunch and morning and afternoon tea. There are freshwater showers on board. Cruises depart Townsville at 8:30 a.m., with a pickup at Magnetic Island en route, and returns by about 5 p.m.

Several other operators, including **Adrenalin Dive** (☎ **07/4724 0600;** www.adrenalindive.com.au), have trips to the *Yongala* wreck, the Coral Sea, and the Reef, but most boats visiting the Reef from Townsville are live-aboard vessels that make trips of two or more days, designed for serious divers.

Exploring Townsville
The top attractions

Museum of Tropical Queensland

With a stunning curved roof, like a ship in full sail, this A$22-million (US$17.6-million/£8.8-million) museum, is easy to spot. The centerpiece of the museum is the exhibition of relics salvaged from the wreck of H.M.S. *Pandora,* which lies 33m (108 ft.) underwater on the edge of the Great Barrier Reef, 120km (74 miles) east of Cape York. The exhibit includes a full-scale replica of a section of *Pandora*'s bow and her 17m-high (56-ft.) foremast. Standing three stories high, the replica and its copper-clad keel were crafted by local shipwrights. *Pandora* sank in 1791, but the wreck was not discovered until 1977. The exhibition traces the ship's voyage and the retrieval of the sunken treasure. The museum has six galleries, including a hands-on science center, and a natural history display that looks at life in tropical Queensland — above and below the water. Another is dedicated to north Queensland's indigenous heritage, with items from Torres Strait and the South Sea Islands as well as stories from people of different cultures about the settlement and labor of north Queensland. Exhibitions change every three months.

70–102 Flinders St. ☎ *07/4726 0600, or 07/4726 0606 info line.* www.mtq.qld.gov.au. *Admission: A$12 (US$9.60/£4.80) adults, A$8 (US$6.40/£3.20) seniors and students, A$7 (US$5.60/£2.80) children 4–16, A$30 (US$24/£12) families of 5. MC, V. Open: Daily 9:30 a.m.–5 p.m. Closed Good Friday (Fri before Easter), Dec 25, and until 1 p.m. Apr 25 (Anzac Day).*

Reef HQ

Reef HQ is the largest living coral reef aquarium in the world. The highlight of your visit may be walking through a 20m-long (66-ft.) transparent tunnel, gazing into a giant predator tank where sharks cruise silently. The wreck of S.S. *Yongala* provides an eerie backdrop for blacktip and whitetip reef sharks, leopard sharks, and nurse sharks, sharing their 750,000-liter (195,000-gallon) home with stingrays, trevally, and a green turtle. Watching them feed is quite a spectacle. The tunnel also reveals the 2.5-million-liter (650,000-gallon) coral reef exhibit, with its hard and soft corals providing a home for thousands of fish, giant clams, sea cucumbers, sea stars, and other creatures. Other highlights include the shark-feeding scuba-dive show, a marine creature touch tank, a wild sea-turtle rehabilitation center, plus interactive activities. Reef HQ is an easy walk from the city center.

2–68 Flinders St. ☎ *07/4750 0800.* www.reefhq.com.au. *Admission: A$22 (US$18/ £8.80) adults, A$17 (US$14/£7) seniors and students, A$11 (US$8.80/£4.40) children 4–16, A$54 (US$43/£22) families of 5. AE, DC, MC, V. Open: Daily 9:30 a.m.–5 p.m. Closed Dec 25. Bus: 1, 1A, or 1B (stop 3-minute walk away).*

More cool things to see and do

The Strand is a 2.5km (1½-mile) strip where you can stroll along the promenade or relax at one of the many cafes, restaurants, and bars while you gaze across the Coral Sea to Magnetic Island. There are safe swimming beaches, a fitness circuit, a water park for kids, and plenty of picnic areas and free gas barbecues, as well as areas to in-line skate, cycle, walk, or fish. Four rocky headlands and a jetty adjacent to Strand Park provide good fishing spots, and there are two surf lifesaving clubs to service the three swimming areas. During summer (Nov–Mar), three swimming enclosures operate to keep swimmers safe from marine stingers. If watersports are on your agenda, try a jet ski, hire a canoe, or take to the latest in pedal skis.

The Whitsundays

A day's drive or a one-hour flight south of Cairns brings you to the dazzling collection of 74 islands known as the Whitsundays. No more than 3 nautical miles (5.6km/3½ miles) separate most of the islands, and altogether they represent countless bays, beaches, dazzling coral reefs, and fishing spots that make up one fabulous Great Barrier Reef playground. Sharing the same latitude as Rio de Janeiro and Hawaii, the water is at least 72°F (22°C) year-round, the sun shines most of the year, and in winter you'll require only a light jacket at night.

All the islands consist of rainforested national park land, mostly uninhabited. The surrounding waters belong to the Great Barrier Reef Marine Park. Don't expect palm trees and coconuts — these islands are covered with pine and eucalyptus forests full of dense undergrowth, and rocky coral coves far outnumber the sandy beaches. More than half a dozen islands have resorts that offer just about all the activities you could ever want — snorkeling, scuba diving, sailing, reef fishing, water-skiing, jet-skiing, parasailing, sea kayaking, hiking, rides over the coral in semi-submersibles, fish feeding, putt-putting around in dinghies to secluded beaches, playing tennis or squash, and taking aqua-aerobics classes. Accommodations range from small, low-key wilderness retreats to midrange family havens to Australia's most luxurious resort, Hayman.

The village of **Airlie Beach** is the center of the action on the mainland. The town is only a few blocks long, but you'll find a good choice of accommodations, some good restaurants and bars, a boutique or two,

The Whitsunday Region

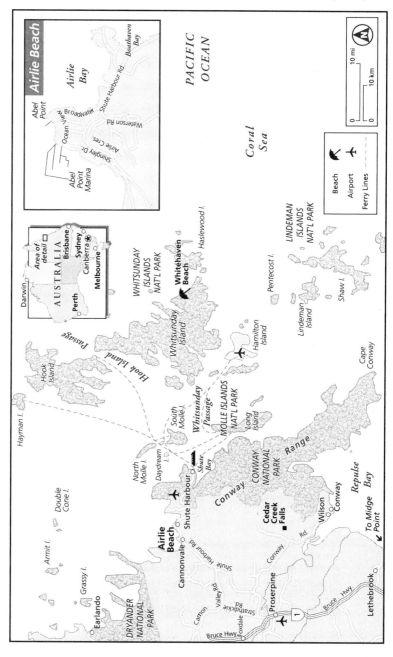

banks, and a supermarket. Airlie Beach has a massive beachfront artificial lagoon, with sandy beaches and landscaped parkland, which solves the problem of where to swim in stinger season. The lagoon is the size of about six full-size Olympic swimming pools, set in 4 hectares (10 acres) of botanic gardens, with a children's pool, plenty of shade, barbecues, picnic shelters, toilets, showers, and parking.

The Whitsundays are just as good a steppingstone to the outer Great Barrier Reef as Cairns, and some people consider them better, because you don't have to make the 90-minute trip to the Reef before you hit coral. Just about any Whitsunday island has fringing reef around its shores, and there are good snorkeling reefs between the islands, a quick boat ride away from your island or mainland accommodations. Cruises and yachts depart from Shute Harbour, a ten-minute drive south on Shute Harbour Road, and Abel Point Marina, a ten-minute walk west along the foreshore or a quick drive over the hill on Shute Harbour Road.

Although they haven't been sighted at Airlie Beach for several years, deadly marine stingers may frequent the shorelines from October through April. The best place to swim is in the beachfront Airlie Beach lagoon. The rivers in these parts are home to dangerous saltwater crocodiles (which mostly live in fresh water, contrary to their name), so don't swim in streams, rivers, and water holes.

Getting to the Whitsunday region
By plane
There are two air routes into the Whitsundays: **Hamilton Island Airport**, and **Whitsunday Coast Airport** at Proserpine on the mainland. **Qantas-Link** (☎ 13 13 13 in Australia) flies direct to Hamilton Island from Cairns and Townsville. **Virgin Blue** (☎ 13 67 89 in Australia) flies to Proserpine direct from Brisbane and Sydney, and with connections from Canberra, Melbourne, Adelaide, Perth, Hobart, and Launceston, and direct from Brisbane to Hamilton Island. **Jetstar** (☎ 13 15 38 in Australia) flies from Brisbane and Sydney to Proserpine and from Adelaide, Brisbane, Melbourne, and Sydney to Hamilton Island. If you stay on an island, the resort may book your launch transfers automatically. These may appear on your airline ticket, in which case your luggage will be checked through to the island.

By boat
Fantasea Cruises' Blue Ferries (☎ 1800/650 851 in Australia, or 07/4946 5111) makes ferry transfers from Hamilton Island Airport to Shute Harbour, Daydream Island, Long Island, and, for guests only, to Lindeman Island. The one-way fare is A$37 (US$30/£15) adults, A$20 (US$16/£8) children, or A$2 (US$1.60/£0.80) extra to Lindeman Island.

By train

Several **Queensland Rail** (☎ **1300/131 722** in Australia; www.travel train.com.au) long-distance trains stop at Proserpine every week. The one-way fare from Cairns on the Tilt Train is A$144 (US$115/£58). There is a bus link to Airlie Beach. Brisbane fares range from A$233 (US$186/ £93) on the Tilt Train to A$336 (US$269/£134) for a first-class sleeper on the *Sunlander* or A$606 (US$485/£242) for the all-inclusive Queenslander class service.

By bus

Greyhound Australia (☎ **13 14 99** in Australia) operates plentiful daily services to Airlie Beach from Brisbane (trip time: around 19 hours) and Cairns (trip time: 10 hours). The fare is A$173 (US$138/£69) from Brisbane and A$108 (US$86/£43) from Cairns.

Whitsunday Transit (☎ **07/4946 1800**) meets all flights and trains at Proserpine and provides door-to-door transfers to Airlie Beach hotels or to Shute Harbour. The fare from the airport is A$17 (US$14/£7) adults, A$9 (US$7.20/£3.60) children to Airlie Beach or Shute Harbour. From the train station, it's A$8.20 (US$6.55/£3.30) adults, A$4.20 (US$3.35/£1.70) children to Airlie Beach; A$11 (US$8.80/£4.40) adults, A$5.50 (US$4.40/£2.20) children to Shute Harbour.

By car

The Bruce Highway leads south from Cairns or north from Brisbane to Proserpine, 26km (16 miles) inland from Airlie Beach. Take the Whitsunday turnoff to reach Airlie Beach and Shute Harbour. Allow a good eight hours to drive from Cairns. There are several car storage facilities at Shute Harbour. **Whitsunday Car Security** (☎ **07/4946 9955**) will collect your car anywhere in the Whitsunday area and store it in locked covered parking for A$10(US$8/£4) per day or A$15 (US$12/£6) overnight.

Finding information after you arrive

The **Whitsundays Information Center** (☎ **1800/801 252** in Australia, or 07/4945 3711; www.whitsundaytourism.com) is in Proserpine, on the Bruce Highway in the town's south. It's open Monday through Friday from 8:30 a.m. to 5 p.m. and weekends and public holidays (except Good Friday and Dec 25) from 9 a.m. to 3 p.m. If you're staying in Airlie Beach, picking up information from the private booking agents lining the main street is easier. All stock a vast range of cruise, tour, and hotel information, and they make bookings free of charge. They all have pretty much the same stuff, but because some represent certain boats exclusively, and because prices can vary a little from one to the next, shop around. Another useful Web site is www.whitsunday.net.au.

Getting around the mainland and islands

By bus

Whitsunday Transit (☎ 07/4946 1800) runs half-hourly buses between Airlie Beach and Shute Harbour to meet all ferries. The fare is A$4.65 (US$3.70/£1.85). A **Ten Trip Ticket,** valid for one month and able to be used by more than one person, can be used to travel between Shute Harbour, Airlie Beach, Cannonvale, and Proserpine. It costs A$23 (US$18/£9.20) adults and A$12 (US$9.60/£4.80) children, which means A$2.25 (US$1.80/£0.90) per trip. An Explorer Pass, good for unlimited travel between Shute Harbour, Airlie Beach, Cannonvale, and Proserpine from 6 a.m. to 10:30 p.m. on the date of issue, costs A$8.50 (US$6.80/£3.40) for adults, half-price for children.

By car

Avis (☎ 07/4946 6318), Hertz (☎ 07/4946 4687), and Thrifty (☎ 07/4946 7727) have outlets in Airlie Beach and at Proserpine Airport (telephone numbers serve both locations).

By ferry

Fantasea Cruises (☎ 1800/650 851 in Australia, or 07/4946 5111) makes ferry transfers from Shute Harbour to the islands and between the islands. A one-way transfer from the mainland to Long and Daydream islands costs A$26 (US$21/£10) adults, A$17 (US$14/£6.80) children 4 to 14; to Hamilton Island, A$39 (US$31/£16) adults, A$21 (US$17/£8.40) children 4 to 14. Reservations are not necessary, but do book your arrival and departure ferry so that you don't miss your connections. Most islands receive a boat only every two to four hours, so it's a long wait if you miss your boat.

Island ferries and Great Barrier Reef cruises leave from Shute Harbour, a ten-minute drive south of Airlie Beach on Shute Harbour Road. Most other tour-boat operators and bareboat charters anchor at Abel Point Marina, a 15-minute walk west from Airlie Beach.

Staying on the Whitsunday Coast and Islands

There are pros and cons to staying on the mainland — which really means Airlie Beach — or at an island resort. If you stay on the mainland, accommodations are cheaper, you have a greater a choice of restaurants, and you're free to visit a different island each day. The mainland has jet-skiing, kayaking, parasailing, catamaran rental, and windsurfing.

On an island, swimming, snorkeling, bushwalking, and a huge range of watersports, many of them free, are right on your doorstep. The deadly stingers that can infest mainland shores do not — except in rare cases — make it to the islands, so swimming in the islands is safe year-round. You won't be isolated if you stay on an island, because most Great Barrier Reef cruise boats, sail-and-snorkel yacht excursions, Whitehaven Beach cruises, dive boats, fishing tour vessels, and so on stop at the island resorts. One major disadvantage of an island is that you're "captive" to high food and drink prices. You can choose from about ten island resorts, ranging from positively plush to comfortably midrange to downright old-fashioned.

High season in the Whitsundays coincides with school vacations, which occur in January, in mid-April, from late June to early July, from late September to early October, and in late December. The Aussie winter (June–Aug) is popular, too. You have to book months ahead to secure high-season accommodations, but at any other time you can get some very good deals indeed.

The top hotels and resorts

Coral Sea Resort
$$$–$$$$$ Airlie Beach

This is one of the best places to stay on the Whitsunday mainland, with a superb location on the edge of Airlie Beach's Paradise Point and 280-degree views of the ocean. The wide range of great accommodations styles suits everyone from families to honeymooners; although it's relatively big and sprawling, it's so well designed that you can easily feel you're alone. All 78 rooms have a nautical feel. The Coral Sea suites are divine, complete with a Jacuzzi and double hammock on the balcony. There are four styles of suites, apartments, and family units, and other amenities include a great restaurant overlooking the pool and the Coral Sea. A three-minute walk along the waterfront brings you to Airlie Beach village.

25 Oceanview Ave., Airlie Beach, QLD 4802. ☎ *1800/075 061 in Australia, or 07/4946 6458. Fax: 07/4946 6516.* www.coralsearesort.com.au. *Rack rates: A$220–A$260 (US$176–US$208/£88–£104) double, A$300–A$360 (US$240–US$288/£120–£144) double suite, A$320 (US$256/£128) double 1-bedroom apartment, A$335–A$365 (US$268–US$292/£134–£146) 2-bedroom beach house apartment, A$500 (US$400/£200) 3-bedroom beach house apartment, A$320 (US$256/£128) family unit for up to 5, A$375 (US$300/£150) 1-bedroom penthouse, A$510 (US$408/£204) double 2-bedroom penthouse, A$715 (US$572/£286) double 3-bedroom penthouse; extra person A$40 (US$32/£16). Minimum 3-night stay at Easter and Dec 26–Jan 5. AE, DC, MC, V.*

Hamilton Island
$$$–$$$$$

Hamilton has the widest range of activities, accommodations styles, and restaurants of any Reef island resort. Accommodations choices are extra-large rooms and suites in the high-rise hotel; high-rise one-bedroom apartments; Polynesian-style bungalows in tropical gardens; and glamorous rooms in the two-story, adults-only Beach Club (with minimalist décor, a personal "host," and private restaurant, lounge, and pool for exclusive use of Beach Club guests); as well as one-, two-, three-, and four-bedroom apartments and villas. The ultraluxury **Qualia** (www.qualiaresort.com.au) resort-within-the-resort opened at the end of September 2007 (but not in time to review before we went to press). The best sea views are from the second-floor Beach Club rooms, from floors 5 to 18 of the Reef View Hotel, and from most apartments and villas. The hotel and Beach Club have concierge service.

A marina village has cafes, restaurants, shops, and a yacht club, and near the accommodations are a large free-form pool and swim-up bar and the curve of Catseye Beach. Hamilton offers a huge range of watersports; fishing trips; cruises; speedboat rides; go-karts; a Wire Flyer flying fox hang glider; a pistol and clay-target rifle range; mini golf; an aquatic driving range; beach barbecue safaris; hiking trails; a wildlife sanctuary where you can cuddle a koala or hold a baby crocodile; and an extensive daily activities program. Because a steep hill splits the resort, the best way to get around is on the free bus service, which operates on three different loops around the island from 7 a.m. to 11 p.m., or by golf buggy (A$40/US$32/£16 per hour or A$80/US$64/£32 for 24 hours). To get away from the main area, hit the beach or the hiking trails — most of the 750-hectare (1,853-acre) island is virgin bushland. The biggest drawback is that just about every activity costs.

Hamilton Island (16km/10 miles southeast of Shute Harbour), Whitsunday Islands, QLD 4803. ☎ 13 73 33 in Australia, 02/9433 3333 (Sydney reservations office), or 07/4946 9999 (the island). Fax: 02/9433 0488 (Sydney reservations office) or 07/4946 8888 (the island). www.hamiltonisland.com.au. Rack rates: A$299–A$365 (US$239–US$292/£120–£146) Palm Bungalow or Palm Terrace, A$277–A$458 (US$222–US$366/£111–£183) hotel double, A$378–A$458 (US$302–US$366/£151–£183) suite, A$655–A$740 (US$524–US$592/£328–£296) Beach Club double, A$570–A$645 (US$456–US$516/£228–£258) Whitsunday Holiday Apartments. Standard self-catering accommodations (4-night minimum): A$493 (US$394/£197) 1 bedroom, A$573 (US$458/£229) 2 bedrooms, A$625 (US$500/£250) 3 bedrooms. Superior self-catering accommodations: A$578 (US$462/£231) 1 bedroom, A$658 (US$526/£263) 2 bedrooms, A$737 (US$590/£295) 3 bedrooms, A$669–A$817 (US$535–US$654/£268–£327) 4-bedroom. Deluxe self-catering accommodations: A$597–A$743 (US$478–US$594/£239–£297) 2 bedrooms, A$675–A$822 (US$540–US$658/£270–£329) 3 bedrooms, A$762–A$923 (US$610–US$738/£305–£369) 4 bedrooms. Luxury self-catering accommodations: A$1,221–A$1,576 (US$977–US$1,261/£489–£631) 3 bedrooms. Minimum 4 night stay for all self-catering accommodations. Children 14 years and under stay free in parent's room using existing bedding and eat free from kids' menu at some restaurants before 7 p.m. (not applicable to Hamilton Island Holiday Properties guests). Rates include airport transfers. AE, DC, MC, V.

Hayman
$$$$$ **Hayman Island**

This resort is the most luxurious and glamorous one in Australia. Check-in is done over a glass of bubbly aboard the resort's sleek launch as you travel from Hamilton Island Airport. On arrival, you'll find your way through the open-air sandstone lanais, cascading ponds, and tropical foliage to the hexagonal complex of swimming pools by the sea. Despite the luxury, Hayman is relaxed. Dress is beachwear by day, smart casual at night. An impressive lineup of activities is available, and it's fair to say the staff at Hayman can organize almost anything. Although Hayman is renowned for the antiques, artworks, and objets d'art gracing its public areas, the accommodations are welcoming. Every room, suite, villa, and penthouse has a balcony or terrace, bathrobes, and valet service (and butler service in the penthouses). Pool Wing rooms with marble floors and bathrooms and elegant furnishings have views over the pool and, from the third and fourth floors, to the sea. Lagoon Wing rooms have sea views from the third floor. Retreat Rooms have a private veranda, open patio, and outdoor rinse shower. The Beach Villa has a private Balinese-style courtyard, walled gardens, a private infinity plunge pool, and personalized concierge service. Head to **Spa Chakra Hayman** for the ultimate in pampering.

Hayman Island (33km/20 miles from Shute Harbour), Great Barrier Reef, QLD 4801. ☎ *1800/075 175 in Australia, 02/8272 7070 (Sydney sales office), or 07/4940 1234 (the island); 800-745-8883 in the U.S. and Canada, 0800/1010-1111 in the U.K. and Ireland, 0800/44 1016 in New Zealand (Leading Hotels of the World). Fax: 02/8272 7010 (Sydney sales office) or 07/4940 1567 (the island).* www.hayman.com.au. *Rack rates: A$665–A$1,150 (US$532–US$920/£266–£460) double, A$2,200 (US$1,760/£880) suite, A$2,800–A$4,500 (US$2,240–US$3,600/£1,120–£1,800) penthouse, A$3,600 (US$2,880/£1,440) Beach Villa. Minimum 2-night stay and 10 percent surcharge Dec 24–Jan 7. Children under 13 stay free in parent's room; A$140 (US$112/£56) child over 13 sharing parent's room; 50 percent of room rate for child under 13 in adjoining room. Dining for children 5–12 half price. AE, DC, MC, V. Resort launch meets all flights at Hamilton Island Airport for the 55-minute transfer. Helicopter and seaplane transfers available.*

Peppers Palm Bay
$$$$$ **Long Island**

This is a private, romantic hideaway, with no phone, radio, or television in your room, and no air-conditioning. But you can catch the breeze from the hammock on the veranda of your Balinese-style beachfront *bure* (hut). The dining and bar area overlooks the pool, which is surrounded by timber decking. When it all gets too much, check in to the spa. For even greater privacy, there is Platinum House, a two-bedroom house on the hill behind the bures. Each bedroom has its own entry and bathroom, and features a lounge with large plasma TVs and stereo. A wraparound deck has views of the Whitsunday Passage. For those who want to be active, there is a tennis court and non-motorized watersports such as kayaks are available.

Palm Bay, Long Island (16km/10 miles southeast of Shute Harbour), Whitsunday Islands (P.M.B. 28, Mackay, QLD 4741). ☎ *1800/095 025 in Australia, or 07/4946 9233. Fax: 07/4946 9309.* www.peppers.com.au. *Rack rates: A$460 (US$368/£184) double cabin, A$658 (US$526/£263) double bure, A$777 (US$622/£311) 2-bedroom bungalow, A$1,199 (US$959/£480) house; extra person (age 13 and over) A$100 (US$80/£40) per night. Rates include breakfast. AE, DC, MC, V. Fantasea Cruises (☎ 1800/650 851 in Australia, or 07/4946 5111) launches transfers from Hamilton Island Airport; water taxi transfers available from Shute Harbour.*

ReefSleep

Fancy having the Reef all to yourself? **Fantasea Cruises** (☎ **07/4946 5111**; www. fantasea.com.au) offers a two-day, one-night ReefSleep, where you overnight on its pontoon. This gives you a fabulous chance to see the reef at night when the coral is luminescent in the moonlight and nocturnal sea creatures are active. The trip includes a presentation by a marine biologist, two scuba dives, night snorkeling, all meals — including dinner under the stars with wine. Accommodations are in a clean, comfortable bunkroom for four for A$395 (US$316/£158) per person, or in the double cabin, which has a king-size bed, for A$495 (US$396/£198) per person.

Dining in Airlie Beach

Mangrove Jack's Café Bar
$–$$ PIZZA/CAFE FARE

Sailors, sugar farmers, Sydney yuppies, and European backpackers all flock to this big, open-fronted sports bar and restaurant. The mood is upbeat and casual, the surroundings are spick-and-span, and the food passes muster. Wood-fired pizza with trendy toppings is the specialty. There is no table service; place your order at the bar and collect your food when your number is called. Kids' meals are available for A$8.50 (US$6.80/ £3.40). More than 50 wines come by the glass.

Shute Harbour Road (behind the Airlie Beach Hotel). ☎ *07/4946 6233. Reservations recommended. Main courses: A$12–A$26 (US$9.60–US$21/£4.80–£10), pizzas A$19– A$24 (US$15–US$19/£7.60–£9.60). AE, DC, MC, V. Open: Mon–Fri 11:30 a.m.–2:30 p.m. and 5:30–9:30 p.m. (until 10 p.m. on Fri), Sat 11 a.m.–10 p.m., Sun 11 a.m.–9:30 p.m.*

OnAquA Restaurant & Bar
$$ CONTEMPORARY

With ocean views and fantastic food, this is a great place for an intimate dinner. A 200m (660-ft.) walk from the main street will bring you to one of Airlie Beach's best restaurants, run by one of the region's best chefs, Damien Orth. Using seasonal produce, Damien whips up such delights as Tasmanian salmon filet on local mud-crab-infused mash with wilted baby spinach, green beans, and a champagne brie cream. Save room for a "summer berry orgy" — that's a wild berry *fonde suisse* with caramel shards and a basil-infused orange.

Shute Harbour Road, Airlie Beach. ☎ *07/4948 2782. Reservations recommended. Main courses: A$29–A$35 (US$23–US$28/£12–£14). AE, DC, MC, V. Open: Wed–Sun dinner.*

Exploring the Whitsundays
Cruising to the Reef

Fantasea Cruises (☎ 07/4946 5111; www.fantasea.com.au) makes a daily trip to **Hardy Reef** from Shute Harbour, near Airlie Beach, in a high-speed, air-conditioned catamaran, with a marine ecology talk en route. You anchor at the massive Fantasea Reefworld pontoon, which holds up to 600 people, and spend up to three-and-a-half hours on the Reef. The day trip costs A$176 (US$141/£70) adults, A$150 (US$120/£60) seniors and students, A$30 (US$24/£12) children 4 to 14. Up to five children may travel with each full paying adult. Guided snorkel safaris cost A$25 (US$20/£10) extra or A$75 (US$60/£30) for a family of four. Cruise-dive packages are available for A$89 (US$71/£36) extra for both introductory and certified dives, or you can book one on board for A$95 (US$76/£38) for first-time divers, A$80 (US$64/£32) for certified divers. Cruises depart at 8 a.m. and pick up passengers at Daydream and Hamilton island resorts. Passengers from Long Island can connect by water taxi.

Bareboat sailing

Bareboating means you're sailing the boat yourself. Don't worry if you have limited (or no) sailing experience, thousands of people manage to do it every year. Most yacht-charter companies in the islands will want one person on the boat to have a little experience, but you don't need a license and sailing is easy in these uncrowded waters, where the channels are deep and hazard-free and the seas are protected from big swells by the Great Barrier Reef.

The 74 islands of the Whitsundays are so close to each other that one is always in sight, and safe anchorages are easy to find. If you have no boating experience, the company may require you to take a skipper along for the first day at an extra cost of around A$200 (US$160/£80) a day or A$275 (US$220/£110) overnight. If you think you know what you're doing but want extra reassurance, you can take a skipper along for the first couple of hours for A$60 (US$48/£24). Before departure you will have a two- to three-hour briefing and will be given easy-to-read maps marking channels, anchorage points, and the few dangerous reefs. Your charter company will radio in once or twice a day to check that you're still okay, and you can contact the company anytime for advice.

Most yachts are fitted for two to eight passengers and have a galley kitchen, a barbecue mounted to the stern, hot showers, a toilet, linens, a radio or stereo (or both), a motorized dinghy, and snorkeling equipment. You can buy your own provisions or have the charter company stock the boat at an extra cost of about A$40 (US$32/£16) per person per day.

In peak season you may have to charter the boat for a week. At other times, most companies impose a minimum of five days, but many will rent for three nights rather than let a vessel sit idle. In peak season, expect to pay A$615 to A$790 (US$492–US$632/£246–£316) per night for a four- to six-berth yacht. Rates in the off season, and even in the

Whitsundays' busiest time (June–Aug), will be anywhere from A$100 to A$200 (US$80–US$160/£40–£80) less. Advance bookings can sometimes reduce the price even further. You'll be asked to post a credit card bond of around A$2,000 (US$1,600/£800). Mooring fees apply if you want to stop at one of the island resorts overnight. Some charter companies offer "sail 'n' stay" packages that combine a few days of sailing with a few days at an island resort.

Well-known operators include **Whitsunday Rent-A-Yacht** (☎ **1800/075 000** in Australia, or 07/4946 9232; www.rentayacht.com.au); **Queensland Yacht Charters** (☎ **1800/075 013** in Australia, or 07/4946 7400; www.yachtcharters.com.au); **Sail Whitsunday** (☎ **07/4946 7070;** fax 07/4946 7044; www.sailwhitsunday.com.au); and **The Moorings** (☎ **888-952-8420** in the U.S., or 07/4948 9509 in Australia; www.moorings.com). Tourism Whitsunday (www.tourismwhitsunday.com) can furnish you with a complete list of operators.

Sailing and snorkeling trips around the Whitsundays

Numerous yachts offer three-day/two-night sailing adventures around the islands. Most boats carry a maximum of 12 passengers, so the atmosphere is always friendly and fun. The food is good, the showers are usually hot, and you sleep in comfortable but small berths. Some have small private twin or double cabins. You can get involved with sailing the boat as much or as little as you want, snorkel to your heart's content, explore national park trails, stop at secluded bays, swim, sunbathe, and generally have a relaxing time. A few companies offer introductory and qualified scuba diving for an extra cost. Prices usually include all meals, marine park entrance fees, snorkel gear, and transfers to the departure point (Abel Point Marina or Shute Harbour). In the off season, competition is fierce and you'll be able to get great standby deals.

Among the better-known operators are *Ragamuffin* (☎ **07/4946 7777**), a 17m (56-ft.) oceangoing yacht; and **Prosail** (☎ **1800/810 116** in Australia, or 07/4946 5433; www.prosail.com.au), which runs trips on a fleet of 28 yachts. Prosail's two-day/two-night guided sailing trips cost A$340 (US$272/£136) plus A$30 (US$24/£12) in marine park fees. The company also offers three- and six-day packages. Contact Tourism Whitsunday (www.tourismwhitsunday.com) for a complete list of operators.

Island-hopping in the Whitsundays

Day-trippers to Hamilton, Daydream, South Molle, Club Crocodile's Long Island, and Hook Island resorts can rent the hotels' watersports equipment, laze by the beaches and pools, scuba-dive, join the resorts' activities programs, hike their trails, and eat at some or all of their restaurants. Club Crocodile's Long Island Resort is rather noisy but unpretentious, with plentiful watersports, picturesque hiking trails, wild wallabies, and a large beach–cum–tidal flat where you can relax on sun lounges. You can get to the islands on your own by ferry (see "Getting around the mainland and islands," earlier in this chapter), or take an organized day trip that visits one, two, or even three islands in a day. **Fantasea Cruises** (☎ **1800/650 851** in Australia, or 07/4946 5111; www.fantasea.com.au) and **Whitsunday Island Adventure Cruises** (☎ **07/4946 5255** for the booking agent) all offer them, as do several yachts.

More cool things to see and do

✔ Humpback whales migrate to the Whitsundays July through September to give birth. **Fantasea Adventure Cruising** (☎ **07/4946 5111;** www.fantasea.com.au) runs whale-watching cruises in season; trips feature an onboard talk and videos. The cost is about A$100 (US$80/£40) per adult. If you don't see whales, you can go free another day, or choose another of Fantasea's cruises as an alternative.

✔ **Proserpine River Eco Tours** (book through Fantasea Cruises, ☎ **07/ 4946 5111**) will show you another side of the Whitsundays — away from the sea and islands — with a day tour that combines an open-air wagon ride through the pristine Goorganga wetlands and a boat trip on the river to learn more about one of Queensland's major crocodile-breeding grounds. This is the only place to see crocs in safety in the wild south of the Daintree. Bus pickups operate from Airlie Beach, Cannonvale, and Proserpine for the tours, which run about four hours, depending on tides, and cost A$89 (US$71/ £36) adults, A$57 (US$46/£23) kids 4 to 14, A$235 (US$188/£94) families of four. Back on land, you'll enjoy billy tea, the best damper (Outback-style food) we've ever tasted, and a talk on native wildlife over a barbecue lunch.

✔ The championship **Turtle Point golf course** at Laguna Whitsundays Resort, Kunapipi Springs Road, Midge Point (☎ **07/4947 7777**), a 45-minute drive south of Airlie Beach, is one of Australia's best resort courses. An 18-hole round dodging wallabies, goannas, and kookaburras on the difficult fairways will set you back around A$95 (US$76/£38), plus A$25 (US$20/£10) for club hire.

The Capricorn Coast and Heron Island

The small towns and rural country south of the Whitsundays may not seem very exciting at first, but closer inspection will reveal plenty to see and do. For a start, this is where you find the most spectacular of the Great Barrier Reef islands, **Heron Island,** off the coast from Gladstone. Heron's reefs are beloved by divers and snorkelers; its waters boast 21 fabulous dive sites. In summer giant turtles nest on its beaches, and in winter humpback whales cruise by.

The sugar town of **Bundaberg** is the closest to the southernmost point of the Great Barrier Reef. If you visit the area between November and March, allow an evening to visit the Mon Repos Turtle Rookery. Divers may want to take in some of Australia's best shore diving right off Bundaberg's beaches.

Getting to the Capricorn Coast
By plane
QantasLink (☎ 13 13 13 in Australia) has flights to Rockhampton from Brisbane, Mackay, and Gladstone. **Virgin Blue** (☎ 13 67 89 in Australia) flies direct from Brisbane and Sydney. **Jetstar** (☎ 13 15 38 in Australia) flies from Brisbane to Rockhampton. QantasLink also has daily flights to Gladstone from Brisbane (trip time: 75 minutes), Rockhampton, and Mackay, and to Bundaberg from Brisbane daily and from Gladstone three times a week.

Helicopter transfers can be arranged to Heron Island for A$291 (US$233/£116) per adult or A$145 (US$116/£58) per child one-way. Book through Heron Island Resort (see "Finding information after you arrive," later in this section).

By train
Queensland Rail (☎ 1300/131 722 in Queensland; www.traveltrain.com.au) trains stop in Bundaberg, Gladstone, and Rockhampton every day en route between Brisbane and Cairns. You can travel either on the high-speed Tilt Train — which has both economy- and business-class seats — or on the *Sunlander,* which offers sleeping berths in the luxury Queenslander class. If you're traveling south from Cairns, be warned that the trip is long — 20 hours to Gladstone and 25 hours to Bundaberg.

By bus
Greyhound Australia (☎ 13 14 99 in Australia; www.greyhound.com.au) stops at Bundaberg, Rockhampton, and Gladstone many times a day on runs between Brisbane and Cairns. The bus from Brisbane takes 6½ hours to Bundaberg, 10 hours to Gladstone, and 12 hours to Rockhampton. From Cairns, trip time is 18 hours to Rockhampton, 22 hours to Bundaberg, and 20 hours to Gladstone.

By car
Rockhampton is on the Bruce Highway, 1,055km (654 miles) south of Cairns and 638km (396 miles) north of Brisbane. Gladstone is on the coast 21km (13 miles) off the Bruce Highway. Bundaberg is on the Isis Highway, about 50km (31 miles) off the Bruce Highway from Gin Gin in the north and 53km (33 miles) off the Bruce Highway from just north of Childers in the south. **Avis, Budget, Hertz,** and **Thrifty** have offices in all three towns.

By ferry
Heron Island transfers are by launch from Gladstone Marina. A courtesy coach meets flights from Brisbane (with connections from other cities) at Gladstone airport at 10:30 a.m. to take guests to Gladstone Marina; the launch departs 11 a.m. daily (except Dec 25). Round-trip transfers aboard the 130-seater catamaran *Heron Spirit* cost A$200 (US$160/£80)

Central Queensland Coast

for adults, half-price for kids 3 to 14. Trip time is around two to two-and-a-half hours.

Finding information after you arrive

The **Capricorn Tourism** information center is at Rockhampton's southern entrance on Gladstone Road at the Capricorn Spire (☎ **1800/676 701** in Australia, or 07/4927 2055; www.capricorntourism.com.au). It's open daily from 9 a.m. to 5 p.m. You can also find information about Great Keppel Island there.

The **Gladstone Visitor Information Centre** is in the ferry terminal at Gladstone Marina, Bryan Jordan Drive, Gladstone (☎ **07/4972 9000;** www.gladstonholidays.info). It's open from 8:30 a.m. to 5 p.m. Monday through Friday, and 9 a.m. to 5 p.m. Saturday and Sunday.

The **Bundaberg City Visitor Information Centre,** 186 Bourbong St., Bundaberg (☎ **1800/308 888** in Australia, or 07/4153 8888; www. bundabergregion.org), is open Monday through Friday from 9 a.m. to 5 p.m. and Saturday and Sunday from 9 a.m. to noon. Closed public holidays. There is another information center at 271 Bourbong St. (at Mulgrave Street), Bundaberg West.

Staying on the Capricorn Coast and Islands

Country Plaza International
$$ Gladstone

Although this hotel — Gladstone's largest and best — caters mostly to business travelers, everyone will like its spacious rooms with balconies, seafood restaurant, pool, sun deck, and 24-hour room service. Most rooms have views over the port or the city. There are six three-bedroom apartments and a two-bedroom apartment. A free shuttle runs to the wharf for guests bound for Heron Island.

100 Goondoon St., Gladstone, QLD 4680. ☎ *07/4972 4499. Fax: 07/4972 4921.* www. plazahotels.com.au/gladstone.htm. *Rack rates: A$140 (US$112/£56) double, A$150–A$160 (US$120–US$128/£60–£64) apartment. Rates include transfers from airport, coach terminal, marina, and train station. AE, DC, MC, V.*

Heron Island Resort
$$$$–$$$$$

The brilliant colors of the island's surrounding water and Reef are reflected in the interiors of this lovely low-key resort, and everything is light-filled and breezy. Heron's central complex is equal parts grand Queenslander home and sophisticated beach house, with bar and lounge areas open to ocean views and sunsets. Duplex-style Turtle rooms are designed for couples or families, with casual living areas and verandas, or you can go for greater luxury in the suites or the private beach house. The property has a lounge with a TV, public phones (only the four Point suites and the Beach House have private phones), and Internet access. The **Aqua Soul Spa** offers double treatment rooms, therapies designed for two, and the usual spa treatments. The spa is in a secluded spot on the edge of the island's pisonia forests, removed from the main resort. Families will love it for the activities and the Heron Kids Junior Rangers program for ages 7 to 12 during school vacations.

Heron Island, off Gladstone, QLD 4680 (Voyages, G.P.O. Box 3589, Sydney, NSW 2001). ☎ *1300/134 044 in Australia, or 02/8296 8010 (Sydney reservations office). Fax: 02/9299 2103 (Sydney reservations office).* www.voyages.com.au. *Rack rates: A$370 (US$296/£148) Turtle room double; A$440 (US$352/£176) Reef suite double; A$590 (US$472/£236) Heron Beachside suite double; A$830 (US$664/£332) Point suite, Wistari suite, or Beach House double. Extra adult A$58 (US$46/£23). Children 3–12 stay free if sharing with 2 adults. Rates include all meals and many activities. AE, DC, MC, V. No children allowed in Point and Wistari suites or Beach House.*

Rydges Capricorn Resort
$$$$–$$$$$ Yeppoon

Popular with large and sometimes noisy conference groups, this resort is not a quiet getaway, but it offers lots to do and the location makes it a good place to break your coastal drive. About 20km (13 miles) of unbroken beach fronts the resort, the only one of any size or style in this region. It's about 9km (5½ miles) from the seaside town of Yeppoon, about 45km (28 miles) north of the Rockhampton airport. It was built by Japanese businessman Yohachiro Iwasaki, and you may still hear the locals refer to it as the "Iwasaki Resort" despite its several changes of name over the years. The best of the accommodations is the Palms, with views over the beach and out to Great Keppel Island. The main resort block is dominated by one of the largest freshwater swimming pools in the Southern Hemisphere, popular with visiting local families, especially on weekends. There are four restaurants and two 18-hole golf courses as well as a free daytime kids' club (you pay in the evenings). Accommodations vary: Some suites and all apartments have kitchenettes, hotel rooms have minibars, and two-bedroom apartments and Capricorn suites with kitchens have washing machines and dryers. Set in 8,910 hectares (22,000 acres) of bushland, the resort has extensive wetlands teeming with bird life. Wetlands tours are available for a fee, as are horseback riding, fishing, canoeing, and WaveRunners. Rates include most watersports.

Farnborough Road (P.O. Box 350), Yeppoon, QLD 4703. ☎ *1300/857 922 in Australia, or 07/4925 2525.* www.rydges.com. *Rack rates: A$320 (US$256/£128) double, A$370 (US$296/£148) junior suite, A$395 (US$316/£158) junior suite with kitchenette, A$445 (US$356/£178) Capricorn suite, A$470 (US$376/£188) Capricorn suite with kitchenette, A$440 (US$352/£176) 1-bedroom apartment, A$490 (US$392/£196) 2-bedroom apartment. Transfers from airport or train station A$20 (US$16/£8) adults, A$10 (US$8/£4) children 2–12. AE, DC, MC, V.*

Sun City Motel
$ Bundaberg

This neat and tidy motel is a short stroll across the river from the town center. The rooms are clean and well kept, and each has a ceiling fan, toaster, and tea- and coffee-making facilities. Two family rooms have a double bed and twin bunks. Home-cooked meals can be delivered or you can use the barbecue and outdoor dining area. The motel has a saltwater swimming pool, too. Hosts Sue and Steve will pick you up from the bus or train station or from the airport.

11a Hinkler Ave., North Bundaberg, QLD 4670. ☎ *1800/308 888 in Australia, or 07/4152 1099. Fax: 07/4153 1510.* www.suncitymotel.com.au. *Rack rates: A$70 (US$56/£28) double, A$85 (US$68/£34) family room (sleeps 4); extra adult A$12 (US$9.60/£4.80), extra child under 12 A$10 (US$8/£4). AE, DC, MC, V.*

Exploring the Capricorn Coast and Islands

✔ The **Capricorn Caves** (☎ 07/4934 2883; wwwcapricorncaves. com.au), 23km (14 miles) north of Rockhampton at Olsen's Caves Road, off the Bruce Highway, have been a popular attraction in this part of the world ever since Norwegian pioneer John Olsen stumbled upon them in 1882. The limestone caves originated in an ancient coral reef (380 million years old) and today are a maze of small tunnels and larger chambers. The one-hour tour, which winds through large caverns with stalactite and stalagmite formations before entering the 20m-high (66-ft.) Cathedral Cave, is A$20 (US$16/£8) adults, A$10 (US$8/£4) children 5 to 15. It departs daily (except Dec 25) on the hour from 9 a.m. to 4 p.m. (closing time is 5 p.m.).

Spelunkers over age 16 can squeeze through tunnels and chimneys and rock-climb on a three-hour adventure tour that costs A$65 (US$52/£26); minimum of two people required. Book 24 hours ahead for this.

From December 1 to January 10, you can catch the Summer Solstice light cave on a tour departing every morning at 11 a.m. On the longest day of the year, the sun moves slowly over the Tropic of Capricorn, and a ray of pure light pours through a hole in the limestone caves. The caves are also home to thousands of small insectivorous bats, which leave the cave at sunset to feed. Plan enough time here to walk the 30-minute dry rain forest trail, watch the video on bats in the interpretive center, and feed the wild kangaroos. If you like it so much you want to stay, a motor-home park and campground are attached. Bus tours operate from Rockhampton; contact the Capricorn Caves for details.

✔ At least once a month, on a Saturday night, at the **Great Western Hotel,** Stanley and Denison streets (☎ 07/4922 3888), you can see bull-riding cowboys take to the rodeo ring to test their skills against local Brahman bulls.

The best of Heron Island

When you're on **Heron Island,** you're already on the Reef. Entering magnificent fields of coral is as easy as stepping off the beach and into the water. The life forms that abound are accessible to everyone through diving, snorkeling, or reef walks at low tide, or aboard a semisubmersible vessel.

There has been a resort on Heron since 1932, and in 1943 the island became a national park. It is a haven for wildlife and people, and an experience of a lifetime is almost guaranteed at any time of year. Heron is a rookery for giant green and loggerhead turtles who nest and lay eggs from late November to February. Hatchlings emerge and scuttle down the sand to the water from February to mid-April. Humpback whales pass through from June through September.

Turtle time on Heron and Mon Repos

The egg-laying ritual of the turtles is central to a trip to Heron Island in Australia's summer months. At night and in the early morning, you can head to the beaches to witness the turtles lumber up the beach, dig holes in the sand, and lay their eggs. They are not easily disturbed, and you can get very close. Every night during the season, volunteer guides from the University of Queensland research station based on the island are on hand, tagging and measuring the turtles before they return to the water. The laying season runs December through February, and this could be one of the most memorable parts of your visit to Australia: the sight of a giant green turtle, tears rolling from her eyes as she lays a clutch of about 120 eggs in a pear-shaped chamber dug from the sand.

You can also see turtles nesting on the mainland, at **Mon Repos Beach,** outside Bundaberg. Mon Repos Conservation Park is one of the two largest loggerhead-turtle rookeries in the South Pacific. The visitor center by the beach has a great display on the turtle life cycle and shows films at approximately 7:30 p.m. daily in summer. There is a strict booking system for turtle-watching tours, to help cope with the crowds. Access to the beach is by ticket only, and during the turtle season you must book your visit to Mon Repos.

Tickets are sold through the **Bundaberg City Visitor Information Centre (☎ 07/4153 8888)** at 189 Bourbong St., Bundaberg. Tours start at 7 p.m. and you'll be given a time for your tour, which saves waiting around in a long queue of people. Nesting happens around high tide; hatching usually occurs between 8 p.m. and midnight. Take a flashlight if you can, and a sweater, because it can get quite cool. The Mon Repos Turtle Rookery (**☎ 07/4159 1652** for the visitor center) is 14km (8¾ miles) east of Bundaberg's town center. Follow Bourbong Street out of town toward Burnett Heads as it becomes Bundaberg-Bargara Road. Take the Port Road to the left and look for the Mon Repos signs to the right.

During turtle nesting season (November to late March) the park and information center is open 24 hours a day. Public access to the beach is closed from 6 p.m. to 6 a.m. Turtle viewing tours run from 7 p.m. until 1 a.m. daily (except for Dec 24, 25, and 31). From April to early November (when there are no turtles around), the information center is open Monday through Thursday from 7:30 a.m. to 4 p.m. and Friday from 7:30 a.m. to noon. The park is open 24 hours. Admission to the visitor center is free from April through November, but when the turtles start nesting, the cost is A$8.70 (US$6.95/£3.50) adults, A$4.60 (US$3.70/£1.85) children ages 5 to 17, A$21 (US$17/£8.40) families.

Three days on Heron gives you plenty of time to see everything, and the island is so small that you can walk around it in about half an hour. One of the first things to do is to take advantage of the organized activities that operate several times a day and that are designed so guests can plan their own days. Diving, snorkeling, and reef walking are major occupations for visitors. The island is home to 21 stunning dive sites. Guided walks provide another way to explore the island; they include a visit to the island's research station.

As for the reef walk, just borrow a pair of sand shoes, a balance pole, and a viewing bucket, and head off with a guide at low tide. The walk can take up to 90 minutes, but there's no need to stay; if it gets too hot, you can head to the sanctuary of your room or the shady bar area.

The Sunshine Coast

No prizes for guessing how this stretch of coastline got its name. Warm weather, miles of sandy beaches, trendy restaurants, and a relaxed lifestyle attract Aussies vacationers to the Sunshine Coast in droves. Despite some rather unsightly commercial development in recent years, the Sunshine Coast is still a great spot to unwind.

The Sunshine Coast starts at **Caloundra,** 83km (51 miles) north of Brisbane, and runs to **Rainbow Beach,** 40km (25 miles) north of **Noosa Heads,** where the fashionable crowd goes. Most of Noosa's dining, shopping, and socializing takes place on Hastings Street, in Noosa Heads; for sunbathing and swimming head to the adjacent Main Beach. The commercial strip of **Noosa Junction** is a one-minute drive away; a three-minute drive west along the river takes you to the low-key town of **Noosaville,** which has a huge range of holiday apartments. Giving Noosa a run for its money in recent years is newly spruced-up **Mooloolaba,** about 30km (19 miles) south, which has a better beach and about 90 restaurants.

Getting to the Sunshine Coast
By plane
Virgin Blue (☎ **13 67 89** in Australia) flies direct to **Maroochydore** from Melbourne and Sydney. **Jetstar** (☎ **13 15 38** in Australia) flies direct from Sydney, Adelaide, and Melbourne airports.

Henry's Airport Bus Service (☎ **07/5474 0199;** www.henrys.com.au) meets all flights; one-way door-to-door transfers to Noosa Heads are A$20 (US$16/£8) adults, A$10 (US$8/£4) kids 4 to 14, A$50 (US$40/£20) families of four. Bookings are essential, and should be made 24 hours ahead if possible. A **taxi** from the airport will cost around A$15 (US$12/£6) to Maroochydore or A$45 (US$36/£18) to Noosa.

By train
The nearest **train** station to Noosa Heads is in **Cooroy,** 25km (16 miles) away. **Queensland Rail** (☎ **13 16 17** in Queensland; www.qr.com.au) serves Cooroy once daily from Brisbane on its **CityTrain** (☎ **07/3606 5555;** www.citytrain.com.au) network. The trip takes about two-and-a-half hours, and the fare is A$17 (US$14/£6.80). Other trains will take you there via Nambour or Caboolture, but you'll still have to then get a bus connection to get to Noosa Heads. Queensland Rail's long-distance trains from Brisbane pick up but do not drop off passengers in Cooroy, with the exception of the high-speed **Tilt Train** (which runs Sun–Fri).

The fare is A$28 (US$22/£11). The *Sunlander* makes several trips from Cairns each week; the fare is A$183 (US$146/£73) for a seat, A$345 (US$276/£138) for a first-class sleeper.

Local bus company **Sunbus** (☎ **13 12 30** in Australia, or 07/5450 7888) meets most trains at Cooroy station and travels to Noosa Heads; take bus no. 631.

By bus

Several **coach** companies have service to Noosa Heads from Brisbane, including **Suncoast Pacific** (☎ **07/5443 1011**). **Greyhound Australia** (☎ **13 14 99** in Australia) has many daily services from all major towns along the Bruce Highway between Brisbane and Cairns. Trip time to Noosa Heads is 2½ hours from Brisbane, and just over 27 hours from Cairns. The fare is A$25 (US$20/£10) from Brisbane and A$228 (US$182/£91) from Cairns.

By car

If you're driving from Brisbane, take the Bruce Highway north to the Aussie World theme park at Palmview, then exit onto the Sunshine Motorway to Mooloolaba, Maroochydore, or Noosa Heads. The trip takes about two hours.

Finding information after you arrive

Tourism Sunshine Coast, Level 1, The Wharf Complex, Mooloolaba, QLD 4557 (☎ **07/5452 2501**; www.sunshinecoast.org) has several information centers at major towns. In Noosa, drop into the **Noosa Visitor Information Centre**, at the eastern roundabout on Hastings Street where it intersects Noosa Drive (☎ **07/5447 4988;** fax 07/5474 9494; www.tourismnoosa.com.au). It's open daily from 9 a.m. to 5 p.m.

Other tourist information centers are: **Maroochy Tourism,** Sunshine Coast Airport (☎ **07/5479 1566**), and Sixth Avenue and Melrose Parade, Maroochydore (☎ **07/5479 1566**); and **Caloundra Visitor Information Centre,** 7 Caloundra Rd., Caloundra (☎ **07/5420 6240**).

Getting around the Sunshine Coast

By bus

The local bus is **Sunbus** (☎ **13 12 30** in Australia, or 07/5450 7888).

By car

Major car rental companies on the Sunshine Coast are **Avis** (☎ **07/5443 5055** Sunshine Coast Airport, or 07/5447 4933 Noosa Heads), **Budget** (☎ **07/5448 7455** airport, or 07/5474 2820 Noosa Heads), **Hertz** (☎ **07/5448 9731** airport, or 07/5447 2253 Noosa Heads), and **Thrifty** (☎ **1300/367 227**). Many local companies rent cars and four-wheel-drives, including **Trusty** (☎ **07/5491 2444**).

Staying on the Sunshine Coast

Room rates on the Sunshine Coast are mostly moderate, but they jump sharply in the Christmas period (Dec 26–Jan 26), during school holidays, and in the week following Easter. Book well ahead at these times. Weekends are often busy, too, as Brisbane people head north to the beaches.

Avocado Grove Bed & Breakfast
$$ Flaxton

Joy Barron and Brian Baxter's red-cedar Queenslander home is in a peaceful setting in the middle of an avocado grove just off the ridge-top road. The cozy, comfortable rooms have country-style furniture, full-length windows opening onto private verandas, and oil heaters for cool mountain nights. The big suite downstairs has a TV and kitchen facilities. Colorful parrots and other birds are a common sight. Guests are welcome to picnic on the sloping lawns, which have wonderful views west to Obi Obi Gorge in the Connondale Ranges. You'll also find a tour desk, and you can book a massage in your room.

10 Carramar Court, Flaxton via Montville, QLD 4560. ☎ */fax **07/5445 7585**.* www. avocadogrove.com.au. *4 units, 3 with bathroom with shower only, 1 with private adjacent bathroom. Rack rates: A$110–A$130 (US$88–US$104/£44–£52) double, A$130–A$150 (US$104–US$120/£52–£60) suite. Rates include full breakfast. Ask about weekend and midweek packages. MC, V. Turn right off ridge-top road onto Ensbey Road; Carramar Court is the first left.*

Hyatt Regency Coolum
$$$–$$$$$ Coolum

The Village Square is the heart of this sprawling bushland resort. It has everything you need — shops, restaurants, bars, and takeout joints — so if you want, you never have to leave the grounds. The accommodations are spread out, but you can rent a bike to get around, wait for the two free resort shuttles, or get into the swing of things and walk. Accommodations all have contemporary décor and come as "suites" (one room divided into living and sleeping quarters); two-bedroom President's Villas with a kitchenette; villas in the Ambassador Club, which has its own concierge, pool, tennis court, and lounge; and two-story, three-bedroom Ambassador Club residences with rooftop terraces and Jacuzzis. Then, of course, you can head to the **Sun Spa** or the 18-hole Robert Trent Jones, Jr.–designed golf course. The Sun Spa does 130 treatments in all and has massage rooms, aqua-aerobics, yoga, and a 25m (82-ft.) lap pool. The golf course has been rated as one of the top five resort courses in Australia. Or you can play tennis, express yourself in the Creative Arts Center, take the twice-daily free shuttle into Noosa to shop, or surf at the resort's private beach.

Warran Road, off David Low Way (approximately 2km/1¼ miles south of town), Coolum Beach, QLD 4573. ☎ *13 12 34 in Australia, or 07/5446 1234; 800-633-7313 in the U.S. and Canada; 0845/758 1666 in the U.K. or 020/8335 1220 in London; 0800/44 1234 in New Zealand. Fax: 07/5446 2957.* www.coolum.regency.hyatt.com.

Rack rates: A$240–A$285 (US$192–US$228/£96–£114) double, A$385–A$1,480 (US$308–US$1,184/£154–£592) villa, A$1,025–A$1,305 (US$820–US$1,044/£410–£522) Ambassador Residence; extra person A$45 (US$36/£18). Rates include continental breakfast. Children under 13 stay free in parent's room with existing bedding. AE, MC, V. Resort shuttle (A$18/US$14/£7.20 per person, one-way) meets all flights at Sunshine Coast Airport. Town-car transfers from Brisbane Airport A$79 (US$63/£32) per person, one-way. Limousine transfers available.

Noosa Village Motel
$$–$$$ **Noosa Heads**

Owners John and Mary Skelton work hard to keep this bright motel in the heart of Hastings Street fresh and up-to-date, and the effort pays off. The pleasant rooms are spacious, with a cheerful atmosphere, and all have ceiling fans. And at these rates, it's one of Hastings Street's best values.

10 Hastings St., Noosa Heads, QLD 4567. ☎ *07/5447 5800. Fax: 07/5474 9282.* www.noosavillage.com.au. *Rack rates: A$115–A$125 (US$92–US$100/£46–£50) double, A$155–A$165 (US$124–US$132/£62–£66) suite (sleeps 4), A$230–A$240 (US$184–US$192/£92–£96) 2-bedroom unit (sleeps 6); extra person A$10–A$15 (US$8–US$12/£4–£6). Rates may be higher in peak season. MC, V.*

Sheraton Noosa Resort & Spa
$$$–$$$$$ **Noosa Heads**

A great place to enjoy a spa by the sea is Noosa's first AAA-rated five-star resort. In the heart of Hastings Street, the Sheraton has a prime spot among the chic boutiques and restaurants. There are several styles of rooms, but the ones we like best are those with views away from the beach looking down the Noosa River to the mountains. Sit on the balcony at sunset and drink it in. All rooms are extra-large, and all have Jacuzzis. You'll pay more for two-level poolside villas, which have private access to the pool area but no view. Some rooms have ocean (but not beach) views. The **Aqua Day Spa** has a Roman-bathhouse feel and offers a wide range of treatments. The restaurant, **Cato's** — named for the late Australian novelist Nancy Cato, who lived in Noosa — fronts Hastings Street and is a great place to watch the world go by.

Hastings Street, Noosa Heads, QLD 4567. ☎ *1800/073 535 in Australia, or 07/5449 4888; 888-625-5144 in the U.S. Fax: 07/5449 2230.* www.sheraton.com. *Rack rates: A$295–A$490 (US$236–US$392/£118–£196) double; extra adult A$50 (US$40/£20). AE, DC, MC, V.*

Dining on the Sunshine Coast

Noosa's Hastings Street is the place to see and be seen. This is where the action is at night, as vacationers wine and dine at restaurants as sophisticated as those in any big city. Make sure you make reservations in high season.

The best breakfast in town is at **Bistro C,** one of the few restaurants offering beachfront dining, but **Café Le Monde** at the southern end of

Hastings Street (opposite the back of the Surf Club), is a Noosa institution and you'll find a crowd there. Noosa Junction is a less attractive place to eat, but the prices are cheaper. There are also about 90 restaurants at Mooloolaba.

Madame Fu's
$$–$$$$ Noosa Heads   MODERN ASIAN

Madame Fu's is the only Asian restaurant on the Hastings Street strip. The food is interesting, the staff friendly, and the décor stylish. House specialties include such dishes as chili-salted squid with dry fired onion, slated duck egg and mustard green sauce, and caramelized beef cheek with lemon, cucumber, radish, and watercress. There are plenty of noodle dishes and the restaurant also does takeout.

8 Hastings St., Noosa Heads. ☎ *07/5447 2433. Reservations recommended. Main courses: A$17–A$35 (US$14–US$28/£7–£14). AE, DC, MC, V. Open: Daily 11:30 a.m.–3 p.m. and 5:30 p.m. until late.*

Season
$$–$$$ Noosa Heads   CONTEMPORARY

Chef Gary Skelton has one of the few beachfront restaurant locations in Noosa, and his popularity has been boosted by the following he brought with him from vacationing Sydneysiders. So make sure to reserve a table, especially for dinner. Some of the locals balk at the A$10 (US$8/£4) corkage fee for BYO wine, but there's no quibbling about the quality of the food. Breakfast dishes can be as simple as muffins, or you can indulge with buttermilk-and-banana pancakes (with palm sugar butter and maple syrup). The dinner menu includes dishes such as pan-fried snapper with honey-roasted pumpkin, green beans, chèvre, and a cabernet dressing.

25 Hastings St., Noosa Heads. ☎ *07/5447 3747. Reservations essential for dinner; accepted same day only. Main courses: A$22–A$33 (US$18–US$26/£9–£13), breakfast items A$5–A$15 (US$4–US$12/£2–£6). AE, DC, MC, V. Open: Daily 8 a.m.–10 p.m.*

Spirit House
$$$–$$$$ Yandina   ASIAN

Walk along the jungle paths to the hidden building, and you'll get an idea of what's in store at this amazing restaurant, hidden in Yandina, a less fashionable part of the Sunshine Coast. Tables are set around a lagoon and among the trees, with statues and other artworks scattered throughout. At night the effect is enhanced by torches and lighting. It won't prepare you for the flavors that come out of this kitchen — mainly Thai but with other Asian influences. Dishes like crispy fish with tamarind and chili sauce, palm sugar and lime poached schnappers, or Penang chicken curry with snake beans and caramelized pumpkin with coconut, Thai basil, and peanuts. Before you leave, buy the cookbook or sign up for cooking classes. This is a restaurant you'll be thinking and talking about for a long time.

20 Ninderry Rd., Yandina. ☎ *07/5446 8994.* www.spirithouse.com.au. *Reservations essential. Main courses: A$27–A$34 (US$22–US$27/£11–£14). AE, DC, MC, V. Open: Daily lunch from noon, Wed–Sat dinner from 6 p.m.*

Exploring the Sunshine Coast
The top attractions

Australia Zoo
Beerwah

The Animal Planet Crocoseum, a 5,000-seat stadium in which daily croc feedings are held at noon is the highlight of the late "Crocodile Hunter" Steve Irwin's zoo. Irwin's widow Terri has ensured that little has changed in the day-to-day running of the zoo, and this is a world-class attraction. Covering 100 hectares (251 acres), the zoo has much to see. Demonstrations and feedings are held throughout the day, and you can also hand-feed 'roos, pat a koala, check out foxes and camels, and watch and hold (if you're braver than we are) venomous snakes and pythons. You can tour the Koala and Wildlife Hospital next door to see how sick and injured animals are cared for. There are lots of exotic animals — check out the Tiger Temple, home to five tigers and four cheetahs. The Irwin family has made November 15 Steve Irwin Day at the zoo, so for fans this may be the time to visit.

Glass House Mountains Tourist Drive, Beerwah (off the Bruce Highway). ☎ *07/5436 2000.* www.australiazoo.com.au. *Courtesy buses operate daily from 8.30 a.m. with pickups at Noosa and other spots around the Sunshine Coast, arriving at the zoo at 10:20 a.m. The return transfer leaves the zoo at 4 p.m. The courtesy bus will also pick up train passengers at Beerwah train station. Bookings are essential, so call ahead to the zoo. Sunbus (*☎ *07/5450 7888, or 13 12 30 in Australia) services run to Australia Zoo from Maroochydore's Sunshine Plaza shopping center, Mooloolaba, and Landsborough train station. Take bus no. 615. Admission: A$49 (US$39/£20) adults, A$38 (US$30/£15) seniors and students, A$29 (US$23/£12) kids 3 to 14, A$147 (US$118/£59) families of 4. Open: Daily 9 a.m.–4:30 p.m. Closed Dec 25.*

Underwater World
Mooloolaba

A transparent tunnel with an 80m (262-ft.) moving walkway that takes you through a tank filled with sharks, stingrays, groupers, eels, and coral is the highlight here. Kids can pick up starfish and sea cucumbers in the touch pool, and there are displays on whales and sharks, shark breeding, freshwater crocodile talks, an otter enclosure, and a 30-minute seal show. You can swim with the seals (A$76/US$61/£30) or dive with the sharks (A$99/US$79/£40 for certified divers, including gear, or A$165/US$132/£66 for non-divers). Age restrictions apply for these activities.

The Wharf, Parkyn Parade, Mooloolaba. ☎ *07/5458 6222.* www.underwater world.com.au. *Admission: A$26 (US$21/£10) adults, A$18 (US$14/£7.20) seniors and* *students, A$15 (US$12/£6) children 3–15, A$69 (US$55/£28) families of 5. Open: Daily 9 a.m.–6 p.m. (last entry 5 p.m.). Closed Dec 25.*

More cool things to see and do

- ✔ The **Big Pineapple** (☎ **07/5442 1333**) is 6km (3¾ miles) south of Nambour on the Nambour Connection Road in Woombye. You won't miss it — this 16m-tall (52-ft.) monument to pineapple growers stands out on the side of the road. You can take a train ride through a working pineapple plantation, ride through a rain forest and a macadamia farm in a macadamia-nut-shaped carriage, and visit a baby animal farm. Entry is free, but you pay for tours. The train ride costs A$12 (US$9.60/£4.80) adults, A$9.50 (US$7.60/£3.80) children 4 to 14; the macadamia tour costs A$7.50 (US$6/£3) adults, A$5.50 (US$4.40/£2.20) children. The best option is a family pass, which costs A$55 (US$44/£22) for two adults and up to four children. Open: Daily from 9 a.m. to 5 p.m. (rides start at 10 a.m.); it opens later on April 25 (Anzac Day) and December 25 (call for exact time).

- ✔ **Learn to surf** with two-time Australian and World Pro-Am champion Merrick Davis (☎ **0418/787 577** mobile; www.learntosurf. com.au), who's been teaching here since 1992. Merrick and his team run two-hour lessons on Main Beach daily for A$55 (US$44/£22), three-day certificate courses for A$150 (US$120/£60), and five-day courses for A$220 (US$176/£88). They'll pick you up and drop you off at your accommodations. They also rent surfboards, body boards, and sea kayaks.

- ✔ The **Eumundi Markets,** in the historic village of Eumundi, 13km (8 miles) west of Noosa along the Eumundi Road, are held on Saturdays from 6:30 a.m. to 2 p.m. and Wednesdays from 8 a.m. to 1:30 p.m. Locals and visitors wander under the huge trees among dozens of stalls selling locally grown organic lemonade, fruit, hats, teddy bears, antique linen, homemade soaps, handcrafted furniture — even live emu chicks! Get your face painted, your palm read, or your feet massaged. Listen to some didgeridoo music or bush poetry. When shopping's done, pop into one of the cafes on Eumundi's main street.

The Gold Coast

The Gold Coast is one of Australia's icons, and since the 1950s it has been the favored holiday playground for families. Its icons are bronzed lifeguards, bikini-clad meter maids, overly tanned tourists draped with gold jewelry, and high-rise apartment towers that cast long shadows over parts of the beach. The white sands stretch uninterrupted for 70km (43 miles), making up for the long strips of neon-lit motels and cheap souvenir shops. Despite the crowds and the development, you can still find yourself a quiet strip of beach.

The Gold Coast

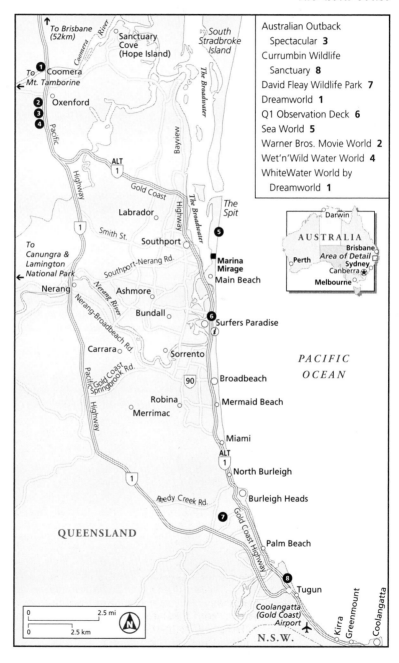

Australian Outback
   Spectacular **3**
Currumbin Wildlife
   Sanctuary **8**
David Fleay Wildlife Park **7**
Dreamworld **1**
Q1 Observation Deck **6**
Sea World **5**
Warner Bros. Movie World **2**
Wet'n'Wild Water World **4**
WhiteWater World by
   Dreamworld **1**

To Brisbane
(52km)

Sanctuary
Cove
(Hope Island)

South
Stradbroke
Island

The Broadwater

1 To Coomera
Mt. Tamborine

2 Oxenford
3
4

Pacific

Coomera River

Bayview

ALT
1

Gold Coast
Highway

Highway

Labrador

The
Spit

The Broadwater

5

1

Smith St.

Southport

To
Canungra &
Lamington
National Park

Southport-Nerang Rd.

Marina
Mirage

Nerang

Nerang River

Ashmore

Main Beach

Nerang-Broadbeach Rd.

Bundall

6 Surfers Paradise
i

PACIFIC
OCEAN

Carrara

Sorrento

Pacific Highway

Gold Coast Springbrook Rd.

90

Broadbeach

Robina

Mermaid Beach

Merrimac

Miami

ALT
1

North Burleigh

1

Reedy Creek Rd.

Burleigh Heads

7

Gold Coast Highway

QUEENSLAND

Palm Beach

8 Tugun

0   2.5 mi

0   2.5 km

Coolangatta
(Gold Coast)
Airport

Kirra

Greenmount

Coolangatta

N.S.W.

AUSTRALIA

Darwin

Brisbane
Area of Detail
Sydney
Canberra

Perth

Melbourne

The Gold Coast's **theme parks** are not as large or as sophisticated as Disneyland, but they're fun all the same. There are three major parks — Dreamworld, Warner Bros. Movie World, and Sea World — as well as two water parks. If theme parks aren't your thing, there are also 40 golf courses, dinner cruises, and loads of adrenaline-fueled outdoor activities, from bungee jumping to jet-skiing. The best activity on the Gold Coast, though, is the natural kind, and it doesn't cost a cent — hitting the surf and lazing on the beach.

Getting to the Gold Coast

By plane

Domestic flights land at Gold Coast Airport, Coolangatta, 25km (16 miles) south of Surfers Paradise. **Qantas** (☎ 13 13 13) operates direct flights from Sydney. **Virgin Blue** (☎ 13 67 89) flies direct from Sydney, Melbourne, and Adelaide. **Jetstar** (☎ 13 15 38 in Australia) flies from Melbourne, Newcastle, and Adelaide. The nearest international gateway is **Brisbane International Airport.**

The **Gold Coast Tourist Shuttle** (☎ 13 12 30 in Australia) meets every flight at Coolangatta and will transfer you to your accommodations. The fare is A$18 (US$14/£7.20) one-way, A$33 (US$26/£13) round-trip adults; A$9 (US$7.20/£3.60) one-way, A$17 (US$14/£6.80) round-trip kids ages 4 to 13; A$45 (US$36/£18) one-way, A$83 (US$66/£33) round-trip families of four. A better deal if you're going to use buses a lot is to buy a Freedom Pass (see "Getting around the Gold Coast," later in this chapter), which includes your airport transfers. A taxi from the airport to Surfers Paradise is about A$30 (US$24/£12) but may be higher if traffic is heavy.

The **Coachtrans Airporter** bus meets most flights at Brisbane Airport and makes about 20 trips a day from the domestic and international terminals to Gold Coast accommodations for A$35 (US$28/£14) adults, A$18 (US$14/£7.20) children 4 to 13, A$89 (US$71/£36) families of four. The trip takes about 90 minutes to Surfers Paradise. You don't need to book in advance unless you're on an evening flight; if you are, call ☎ **1300/ 664 700** in Queensland, or 07/3358 9700.

AirtrainConnect links Brisbane Airport and the Gold Coast by train and bus for A$37 (US$30/£15) adults, A$19 (US$15/£7.60) children 5 to 14, A$93 (US$74/£37) groups/families of four. Take Airtrain to the Gold Coast, and then an air-conditioned coach to any accommodations between Southport Spit at the northern end of the Gold Coast and Burleigh Heads to the south.

A three-day **Airtrain SmartPass** costs A$112 (US$90/£45) adults, A$56 (US$45/£22) children, A$280 (US$224/£112) families of four; it covers AirtrainConnect transfers, as well as unlimited door-to-door theme park transfers on the Gold Coast Tourist Shuttle and use of the Surfside bus network. Passes are also available for 5, 7, 10, and 14 days.

By train

Suburban trains (call **Queensland Rail Citytrain; ☎ 07/3235 5555**) depart Brisbane Central and Roma Street stations every 30 minutes for the 70-minute trip to the Gold Coast suburb of Nerang. The fare is A$23 (US$18/£9.20) adults, A$12 (US$9.60/£4.80) children 5 to 14. Numerous local buses meet the trains to take passengers to Surfers Paradise.

If you come by train to Surfers Paradise from Sydney or other southern cities, service is on **Countrylink (☎ 1300/131 722** in Australia; www. countrylink.nsw.gov.au), and you'll need to transfer to a connecting coach in Casino or Murwillumbah, just south of the Queensland border. The trip from Sydney takes 14 to 15 hours and the fare is A$96 (US$77/£38) for a first-class seat.

By bus

Coachtrans (☎ 13 12 30 in Queensland, or 07/3238 4700) runs between Brisbane and Gold Coast hotels. The fare is A$26 (US$21/£10) adults one-way, A$15 (US$12/£6) children 4 to 13, A$67 (US$54/£27) families of four.

Greyhound Australia (☎ 13 14 99) makes daily stops at Surfers Paradise from Sydney and Brisbane. The trip from Sydney takes 14 to 15 hours, and the fare is A$112 (US$90/£45). Trip time from Brisbane is 90 minutes, and the fare is A$24 (US$19/£9.60).

By car

Access to the Gold Coast Highway, which runs the length of the coast, is off the Pacific Highway from Sydney or Brisbane. The drive takes about 80 minutes from Brisbane. From Sydney, it's an 11-hour trip, sometimes longer, on the crowded, run-down Pacific Highway.

Finding information after you arrive

Gold Coast Tourism (☎ 1300/309 440 in Australia, or 07/5538 4419; www.verygc.com) has an information kiosk on Cavill Avenue, Surfers Paradise. It is open Monday through Friday from 8:30 a.m. to 5:30 p.m., Saturday 8:30 a.m. to 5 p.m., and Sunday and holidays from 9 a.m. to 4 p.m. A second information booth is at the corner of Griffith and Warner streets in Coolangatta. It is open from 8:30 a.m. to 5:30 p.m. weekdays, from 8 a.m. to 2 p.m. weekends and public holidays.

Getting around the Gold Coast

By bus

Surfside Buslines (☎ 13 12 30 in Australia, or 07/5571 6555) is the local bus company. Its best deal is the **Freedom Pass,** which allows you to hop on and off the buses anytime you like. The three-day pass costs A$58 (US$46/£23) adults, A$29 (US$23/£12) children, A$145 (US$116/£58) families of four; 5-, 7-, 10-, and 14-day passes are also available. The pass gives you door-to-door return Gold Coast Airport transfers, unlimited door-to-door transfers to Dreamworld, Warner Bros. Movie World, Sea World, Wet'n'Wild Water World and Currumbin Wildlife Sanctuary, as well as unlimited use of the Surfside bus network, 24 hours a day.

By car

Most major hotels, including all those listed here, are within walking distance of the beach, shops, and restaurants. Many tour companies pick up at hotels, and you can reach the theme parks by bus, so a car isn't essential. It is, however, handy for a day trip to the hinterland, and to get around to restaurants and golf courses. Parking is cheap and plentiful in numerous lots and on the side streets between the Gold Coast Highway and The Esplanade.

Avis (☎ **07/5539 9388**), **Budget** (☎ **07/5538 5470**), **Hertz** (☎ **07/5538 5366**), and **Thrifty** (☎ **07/5570 9999**) have outlets in Surfers Paradise and at Gold Coast Airport. Endless local outfits rent cars at cheap rates.

Staying on the Gold Coast

School holidays, especially the Christmas vacation from mid-December to the end of January, are peak season on the Gold Coast. Accommodations are booked months in advance at these times. The rest of the year, occupancy levels plummet — and so do rates! Packages and deals abound in the off season, so make sure you ask.

Most accommodations require a one-week minimum stay during school holiday periods and a four-day minimum stay at Easter. When the Gold Coast Indy car race takes over the town for four days in October, hotel rates skyrocket and most hostelries demand a minimum stay of three or four nights. Don't leave accommodations bookings to the last minute!

The **Gold Coast Booking Centre** (☎ **1300/737 111;** www.gcbc.com.au) is a centralized booking service that offers great deals at more than 1,200 apartments in Surfers Paradise and Broadbeach. Apartments make good sense for families and for any traveler who wants to self-cater to save money.

Because the Gold Coast has a dramatic oversupply of apartments that stand empty except during school vacations, you can get a spacious modern unit with ocean views for the cost of a midrange hotel. Apartment-block developers got in quick to snag the best beachfront spots when the Gold Coast boomed in the 1970s, so apartment buildings, not hotels, have the best ocean views.

The top hotels

Palazzo Versace
$$$$$ Main Beach

In the unlikely location of the Gold Coast, fashion designer Donatella Versace has created a tribute to her late brother, Gianni, in the form of an opulent resort furnished exclusively with Versace gear. It's over the top and not for everyone, but we kinda like it. Everyone has his own — usually strong — opinion of this place. Everything was imported from Italy, from the river stones that pave the porte-cochere to the antique chandelier that dominates the vast, marbled lobby. Vaulted ceilings are hand-detailed in gold, and marble columns dominate. Guest rooms are in four colors (red, blue, gold, and orange) and are a bit more muted than the eye-catching public areas. Everything in them — furniture, cutlery, crockery, toiletries — is Versace (either from the home wares collection or created for the hotel). Many rooms overlook the huge pool, the Broadwater (a stretch of ocean), and the marina. Everything is beautifully appointed, and the corridors are lined with Gianni's artwork and designs. You can choose from eight room types (Donatella stays in the A$3,500/US$2,800/£1,400 Imperial Suite) or from a pool of 72 two- and three-bedroom condominiums. All rooms and suites have Jacuzzis; condos have kitchens. A spa and health club are in the basement. Plus, the resort has 28 swimming pools and a Versace boutique.

94 Sea World Dr., Main Beach, QLD 4217. ☎ *1800/098 000 in Australia, or 07/5509 8000. Fax: 07/5509 8888.* www.palazzoversace.com. *Rack rates: A$410–A$725 (US$328–US$580/£164–£290) double superior room, A$475–A$790 (US$380–US$632/ £190–£316) double superior suite, A$495–A$810 (US$396–US$648/£198–£324) double lagoon room, A$615–A$930 (US$492–US$744/£246–£372) deluxe suite, A$775–A$1,090 (US$620–US$872/£310–£436) Broadwater suite, A$2,500–A$3,500 (US$2,000–US$2,800/ £1,000–£1,400) Imperial suite. AE, DC, MC, V.*

Paradise Resort Gold Coast
$$$ Surfers Paradise

If keeping the kids amused is a priority — as well as having some time without them — this place is for you. This resort has a licensed child-care center for little ones as young as 6 weeks and up to 5 years old. For 5- to 12-year-olds, there's the **Zone 4 Kids,** complete with pedal minicars, the Leonardo painting room, and an underwater-themed pirate adventure world. Or you can laze around the leafy pool area — there are four pools — and watch the kids play on the water slide. The child-care center charges moderate fees, and the Zone 4 Kids is free; both operate daily year-round. Rooms are comfortable and have views of the pool or the gardens. Family quarters sleep up to five in two separate rooms, and some (the family studios) have kitchenettes. Each Junior Bunkhouse room has a queen-size bed in the main room and brightly painted bunks in a separate kids' area, with its own TV, PlayStation, chalkboard, and desk. The resort also rents a wide range of stuff such as strollers, bottle warmers, car seats, and PlayStations, and it has a minisupermarket and takeout meal service as well as two restaurants. The range of activities makes this a great value for families, and the center of Surfers Paradise and the patrolled beach are a few blocks across the highway. Some rooms are near the highway, so ask for a quiet spot.

122 Ferny Ave., Surfers Paradise, QLD 4217. ☎ *1800/074 111 in Australia, or 07/5579 4444. Fax: 07/5579 4492.* www.paradiseresort.com.au. *Rack rates: A$138–A$178*

(US$110–US$142/£55–£71) resort room for up to 4, A$218 (US$174/£87) Junior Bunkhouse room (sleeps 4), A$238 (US$190/£95) resort family room for up to 5, A$268 (US$214/£107) interconnecting room (sleeps 6). AE, DC, MC, V.

Q1
$$$$–$$$$$ **Surfers Paradise**

This is absolutely the best view in town! Q1 opened in 2005 as the world's tallest residential tower — it reaches 322.5 meters (1,058 ft). From your room, you can look down on everyone else on the Gold Coast, especially if you're staying at level 46 or higher, which dwarfs all other buildings in sight. From inside, or on your glass-enclosed balcony, you can see much of the expanse of the coast or hinterland. For the complete 360-degree experience, head to the 77th floor for the **Observation Deck** (see "The top attractions," later in this section). Each apartment has a luxury kitchen, dining, and lounge area, and is given a daily miniclean service (which consists of making the beds, replacing towels, and replenishing toilet paper and kitchen supplies). It's all glass, granite, and stainless steel, but there are nice personal touches (the bathroom drawer in our room had old-fashioned hair curlers in it). Each apartment has laundry facilities and two- and three-bedroom apartments have two bathrooms. The hotel also has an in-house cinema, as well as two lagoon pools and an indoor heated lap-pool.

See map p. 337. Hamilton Avenue (at Northcliffe Terrace), Surfers Paradise, QLD 4217. ☎ *1300/792 008 in Australia, or 07/5630 4500. Fax: 07/5630 4555.* www.q1.com.au. *Rack rates: A$240–A$380 (US$192–US$304/£96–£152) 1-bedroom apartment, A$325–A$490 (US$260–US$392/£130–£196) 2-bedroom apartment, A$425–A$550 (US$340–US$440/£170–£220) 3-bedroom apartment; extra person A$35 (US$28/£14). Crib A$40 (US$32/£16) per week. Minimum 3-night stay (5 nights in high season, mid-Dec to mid-Jan). AE, DC, MC, V.*

Dining on the Gold Coast
You don't have to look hard to find good restaurants on the Gold Coast. There are many stylish restaurants and cafes, most reasonably priced, around **Surf Parade** and **Victoria Avenue** in Broadbeach, as well as in the nearby **Oasis shopping mall.** Other trendy spots are the stylish **Marina Mirage** shopping center, opposite the Sheraton on Sea World Drive in Main Beach, and the hip **Tedder Avenue** cafes in Main Beach.

Elephant Rock Café
$$–$$$ **Currumbin**   **CONTEMPORARY**

This chic pavilion overlooking Currumbin Beach has mesmerizing views of the surf, and food that's among the best on the Gold Coast. Whether you're after breakfast, lunch, or dinner you'll not be disappointed with food that includes gourmet vegetarian choices as well as something for those who like more traditional fare. Lunch and dinner menus change seasonally, and many of the wines are from small boutique wineries. The cakes and biscuits are all hand-made at the cafe, and there are burgers, bagels, and more. There's also a kids' menu for A$7 to A$8 (US$5.60–US$6.40/£2.80–£3.20).

776 Pacific Parade, Currumbin. ☎ ***07/5598 2133.*** *Breakfast A$4.20–A$14 (US$3.35–US$11/£1.70–£5.60). Main courses: Lunch A$14–A$23 (US$11–US$18/£5.60–£9.20), dinner A$20–A$26 (US$16–US$21/£8–£10). AE, DC, MC, V. Open: Daily 7 a.m.–10 p.m.*

Ristorante Fellini
$$$–$$$$ **Main Beach   ITALIAN**

Diners flock to this family-owned restaurant for the flavors of Naples and Tuscany — as well as views of the marina and Broadwater. On warm days, the windows are opened to let in the sea breeze, and the split-level design means every table gets a great view. In a stylish place like this, you may expect the prices to be high and the staff to be superior, but they're not. The service is friendly and welcoming but snappy. On the menu, you'll find plenty of pasta dishes such as ravioli filled with roasted duck and vegetables cooked in a light sauce of butter, sage, and parmesan topped with poppy seeds, and a range of chicken, beef, and seafood dishes.

Level 1, Marina Mirage, Sea World Dr., Main Beach. ☎ ***07/5531 0300.*** *Main courses: A$31–A$36 (US$25–US$29/£12–£14). AE, DC, MC, V. Open: Daily noon to 10:30 p.m.*

Exploring the Gold Coast

Thirty-five white sandy beaches are the top attraction on the Gold Coast. These patrolled beaches stretch almost uninterrupted from the Spit north of Surfers Paradise to Rainbow Bay, south of Coolangatta. In fact, the Gold Coast is just one long fabulous beach. The most popular beaches are **Main Beach, Surfers North, Elkhorn Avenue, Surfers Paradise, Mermaid Beach, Burleigh Heads, Coolangatta,** and **Greenmount.** All are patrolled 365 days a year.

Away from the beach, the Gold Coast's major attractions are theme parks. The big three — **Dreamworld, Sea World,** and **Warner Bros. Movie World** — are joined by two water parks and by an Aussie-themed outback show, **Australian Outback Spectacular.** Sea World is the only major theme park in the center of town. The others are in northern bushland on the Pacific Highway, about 15 to 20 minutes away from Surfers Paradise. You can ride to the theme parks on the **Gold Coast Tourist Shuttle** or on Surfside Buslines. Take bus no. TX1 or TX2 to Dreamworld, Movie World, and Wet'n'Wild; bus no. 750 from Surfers Paradise or 9 from Southport to get to Sea World.

Trains (☎ **13 12 30**) run to Coomera and Helensvale on the Brisbane–Gold Coast line. Queensland Rail Citytrain sells tickets to the theme parks at attended stations, including Brisbane Central, which saves the time of standing in line to get in, rather than any money.

The top attractions

Australian Outback Spectacular
Oxenford

Wild horses, stampeding cattle, and even a helicopter are all part of a A$23-million (US$18-million/£9.2-million) extravaganza that's part theme park, part dinner show. Aimed at introducing visitors to the "spirit of the Outback," the 90-minute show is staged while you're tucking in to a three-course Aussie barbecue-style meal. With seating for 1,000, part of the show is built around the competitive spirit of Australians. The audience is split into two groups after receiving free stockmen's hats whose headbands depict their respective station for which they are encouraged to cheer. The "station muster" is billed as the most breathtaking part of the show, high-lighting the skills of both horse and rider.

See map p. 337 Pacific Highway, Oxenford (21km/13 miles north of Surfers Paradise).
☎ *13 33 86 in Australia or 07/5519 6200.* www.outbackspectacular.com.au. *Admission: A$95 (US$76/£38) adults, A$65 (US$52/£26) children 4–13. Bookings essential. AE, DC, MC, V. Open: Tues–Sun doors open 6:15 p.m., entertainment starts 6:45 p.m. Closed Dec 25. Coach transfers (☎ 13 33 86) from Gold Coast accommodations cost A$15 (US$12/£6) per person round-trip. Free parking.*

Currumbin Wildlife Sanctuary
Currumbin

Currumbin Wildlife Sanctuary is celebrating 60 years in business and is one of the Gold Coast's best-loved attractions. It began life as a bird sanctuary and is almost synonymous with the wild rainbow lorikeets, with their vivid green backs, blue heads, and red-and-yellow chests, that flock here by the hundreds twice a day for feeding. The chattering birds descend onto visitors holding trays of food. Photographers go crazy, and tourists love it. Feeding times are 8 a.m. and 4 p.m., and feedings last about 90 minutes. You can also have your photo taken cuddling a koala, feed kangaroos, take a miniature steam-train ride through the park, and attend animal talks and feeding demonstrations. An Aboriginal song-and-dance show takes place daily. The park's 27 hectares (67 acres) are home to 1,400 native birds and animals, including two saltwater crocodiles, and the wetlands on the grounds attract lots of native birds. A highlight is the free-flight birds show at 11 a.m. and 2 p.m. Wildnight Tours are run daily at 7:15 p.m., and last for around two-and-a-half hours. They cost A$49 (US$39/£20) adults, A$27 (US$22/£11) children 4 to 13.

See map p. 337. 28 Tomewin St., Currumbin (18km/11 miles south of Surfers Paradise).
☎ *07/5534 1266.* www.currumbin-sanctuary.org.au. *Admission: A$30 (US$24/£12) adults, A$20 (US$16/£8) children 4–13. AE, DC, MC, V. Open: Daily 8 a.m.– 5 p.m. Closed Dec 25 and until 1 p.m. Apr 25 (Anzac Day). Ample free parking. Take bus no. 700, 760, or 765 (stop 15m/49 ft. from entrance).*

David Fleay Wildlife Park
West Burleigh

This is one of Australia's premier wildlife parks, named for naturalist David Fleay, who established it in 1952 and lived here until his death in 1993. Platypus, saltwater, and freshwater crocodiles; wallabies; kangaroos; glider possums; dingoes; wombats; and the rare Lumholtz's tree kangaroo are all to be seen here. There's also a large range of Australian birds, including emus, cassowaries, wedge-tailed eagles, black swans, and lorikeets. A series of boardwalks leads through mangrove, rain forest, and eucalyptus habitats, where most of the animals roam free. The nocturnal house, open from 11 a.m. to 5 p.m. daily, is where you'll see many of the most elusive animals. Talks and demonstrations throughout the day include a reptile show and saltwater-croc feeding — usually only October through April, when the crocs are hungry. Aboriginal rangers give talks about weaponry, bush medicine, and their links with this region. Free guided tours are run throughout the day. The Queensland National Parks and Wildlife Service (QNPWS) has run the park since 1983; because it frowns on handling animals, you can't cuddle a koala here.

See map p. 337. Kabool Road, West Burleigh (17km/11 miles south of Surfers Paradise). ☎ **07/5576 2411.** *Admission: A$15 (US$12/£6) adults, A$10 (US$8/£4) seniors and students, A$7.20 (US$5.75/£2.90) children 4–17, A$39 (US$31/£16) families of 6. MC, V. Open: Daily 9 a.m.–5 p.m. Closed Dec 25. Free parking.*

Dreamworld
Coomera

Adrenaline-junkies will love the action rides, such as the **Giant Drop,** in which you free-fall 39 stories in five seconds; the **Tower of Terror,** which propels you forward and upward at 4.5 Gs before you fall backward 38 stories in seven seconds; the hair-raising **Cyclone** roller coaster, with its 360-degree loop; and the **Wipeout,** which spins, twists, and tumbles you upside down at 2.5 Gs. Dreamworld is a Disney-style/Aussie-style family fun park, where giant koalas called Kenny and Belinda roam the streets. Other activities include an IMAX theater, Nick Central (the only Nickelodeon cartoon attraction outside the U.S.), a native wildlife park where you can cuddle a koala and hand-feed kangaroos, river cruises livened by a bushranger shootout, and a carousel and other rides for young kids. You can also watch trainers swim, wrestle, and play with Bengal tigers on Tiger Island. Souvenir stores, restaurants, and ice cream shops abound. There's a water-slide park, so bring your swimsuit.

See map p. 337. Pacific Highway, Coomera (25km/16 miles north of Surfers Paradise). ☎ **1800/073 300** *in Australia, 07/5588 1111, or 07/5588 1122 (24-hour info line).* www. dreamworld.com.au. *Admission: A$64 (US$51/£26) adults, A$42 (US$34/£17) children 4–13. AE, MC, V. Open: Daily 10 a.m.–5 p.m.; Main St., Plaza Restaurant, and Koala Country open at 9 a.m. Closed Dec 25 and until 1:30 p.m. Apr 25 (Anzac Day). Extended hours during Easter and Dec–Jan. Free parking.*

Q1 Observation Deck
Surfers Paradise

The Gold Coast's newest, tallest building is Q1, a gleaming steel-and-glass tower. At the top of this stunning piece of architecture is the Q1 Observation Deck. From here, 230 meters (690 ft.) above the ground on levels 77 and 78 of the building, you can gaze down on all the Gold Coast has to offer. A small theater in the Skyline Room shows a short film on the history of the Gold Coast, or you can stop at the cafe for a piece of Q1-shaped cake and a coffee. Head to Skybar for a cocktail just before sunset.

See map p. 337. Surfers Paradise Boulevard, Surfers Paradise. ☎ *07/5630 4700.* www.q1observationdeck.com.au. *Admission: A$18 (US$14/£7.20) adults, A$13 (US$10/£5) seniors and students, A$10 (US$8/£4) children 5–14, A$45 (US$36/£18) families of 4 (extra children A$8.50/US$6.80/£3.40 each). All admissions are A$10 (US$8/£4) after 8 p.m. Fri–Sat. Last tickets are sold 45 minutes before closing time. AE, MC, V. Open: Sun–Thurs 9 a.m.–9 p.m., until midnight Fri–Sat.*

Sea World
Main Beach

Four polar bears — Lia and Lutik, and Canadian orphan cubs Hudson and Nelson — are the star attractions at this marine park, where you can see them frolic, dive, and hunt for fish in a large pool. The cubs are usually out in the morning, and the adult bears in the afternoon. Sea World may not be as sophisticated as similar parks in the United States, but it has all the things you'd expect to see — performing dolphins and sea lions, ski shows, an aquarium, shark feeding, and an array of rides. At Shark Bay, you can see some of the larger and more dangerous species, such as tiger sharks. You can snorkel with the sharks for A$60 (US$48/£24) per person (age 10 and over) or dive with them if you're a certified diver for A$90 (US$72/£36). Adults (age 14 and over) can participate in several hands-on "animal adventures," which include interactions with some of the park's residents (such as seals and dolphins) for prices ranging from A$135 to A$165 (US$108–US$132/£54–£66), which includes a souvenir photo. An hour-long **Dolphin Dive Encounter** uses "ocean-walker" technology to allow guests without dive qualifications to have a divelike encounter with dolphins. It costs A$250 (US$200/£100) per person (you must be 14 or over). Younger kids can attend a 30-minute dolphin talk, pat one, and have their photo taken with one for A$90 (US$72/£36). A monorail makes getting around the park easy, and there's a free water-slide playground.

See map p. 337. Sea World Drive (3km/1¾ miles north of Surfers Paradise), The Spit, Main Beach. ☎ *07/5588 2222, or 07/5588 2205 (24-hour info line). Fax: 07/5591 1056.* www.seaworld.com.au. *Admission: A$64 (US$51/£26) adults, A$42 (US$34/£17) children 4–13. MC, V. Open: Daily 10 a.m.–5:30 p.m.; opens 1:30 p.m. Anzac Day (Apr 25). Closed Dec 25.*

Wet'n'Wild Water World
Oxenford

If hurtling down a seven-story piece of fiberglass at 70kmph (43 mph) into the water is your idea of fun, then this water park with rides that have names like Double Screamer, Mammoth Falls, the Twister, Terror Canyon, and White Water Mountain, is the thing for you. And if you just want to cool off in a Queensland summer without the adrenaline boost, you can stick to the four white-water flumes, float gently past palm-studded "islands" at Calypso Beach, swim in the artificial breakers in the Wave Pool or in the regular pool, or soak in a spa at Whirlpool Springs. There's also a water playground for young kids, and all pools are heated from April to September. Every night in January, and every Saturday night from September through April, is **Dive-In Movie** night, during which film fans can recline on a rubber tube in the pool while watching the flick on a giant screen.

See map p. 337. Pacific Highway, Oxenford (21km/13 miles north of Surfers Paradise). ☎ *07/5556 1610, or 07/5573 2255 for 24-hour recorded info.* www.wetnwild.com.au. *Admission: A$42 (US$34/£17) adults, A$28 (US$22/£11) children 4–13; half-price "afternoon rate" applies after 2 p.m. or 3 p.m. for the final 2 hours of operation each day, or after 5 p.m. on Dive-In Movie nights. MC, V. Open: Daily 10 a.m.–5 p.m.; Apr 25 (Anzac Day) 1:30–6:30 p.m. Closes at 4 p.m. May–Aug. Open until 9 p.m. Dec 27–Jan 25 and on Dive-In Movie nights. Closed Dec 25. Free parking.*

WhiteWater World by Dreamworld
Coomera

This $60-million (US$48-million/£24-million) water park opened in late 2006. You won't miss it as you drive the Pacific Highway. Themed around Australian surf culture, it also has some of the most modern waterslides and thrill rides in the world. The Super Tubes HydroCoaster is a "roller coaster on water" and is one of two in the world; the Blue Ringed Octopus (BRO) is the world's only eight-lane Octopus Racer. For families, there's Nickelodeon's Pipeline Plunge, a playground for kids ages 5 to 12. The water is heated April to September, there are lifeguards, and you can rent towels and lockers, and use hot showers.

See map p. 337. Pacific Highway, Coomera (next to Dreamworld). ☎ *1800/073 300 in Australia, or 07/5588 1111.* www.whitewaterworld.com.au. *Admission: A$42 (US$34/£17) adults, A$28 (US$22/£11) children 4–13. AE, MC, V. Open: Daily 10:30 a.m.–4:30 p.m. (but may be extended during summer). Closed Dec 25 and the morning of Apr 25 (Anzac Day).*

Part V
The Red Centre and the Top End

"Uluru must be just ahead."

In this part . . .

*U*luru (Ayers Rock) is one of the iconic sights of Australia, and in Chapter 18, we tell you how to get there and how to best see it. We also fill you in on the other stark natural wonders in the Red Centre of Australia, as well as the small town at its heart, Alice Springs. This area is where you find many Aboriginal people, share their Dreamtime stories, and learn about their traditional way of life.

The Top End is a vast sweep of sparsely inhabited country, where you find some of Australia's most rugged, wild, and unforgettable landscapes. In Chapter 19, we introduce you to Darwin, the capital of the territory. Tall tales (usually true) abound, and you'll hear more than one great croc story. Then it's on to the outback town of Katherine and the wonders of Kakadu National Park.

Chapter 18

The Best of the Red Centre

by Marc Llewellyn

In This Chapter

▶ Finding your way to and around the Red Centre
▶ Making your base in Alice Springs
▶ Choosing the best tours
▶ Exploring Kings Canyon, Uluru (Ayers Rock), and other natural wonders

*T*he Red Centre is at the southernmost part of the Northern Territory (see Chapter 19), though Alice Springs is 1,491km (921 miles) south of the Northern Territory capital of Darwin. It also borders on South Australia (see Chapter 20), but Alice is 1,544km (957 miles) north of Adelaide.

In the middle of the Red Centre is the third of the "Big Three" sites: **Uluru** (Ayers Rock), thrusting up from the barren Outback, drawing the eye, as it has for thousands of years.

Uluru is why people come to the Red Centre, and we certainly think you should see the iconic formation. You should also see the other amazing natural wonders of the interior, like **Kings Canyon** and **Kata Tjuta** (the Olgas), and visit in the Outback town of **Alice Springs,** perhaps spend some time with the Aboriginal people who are caretakers of these mysterious places.

Getting to the Red Centre

The gateway to the Red Centre is **Alice Springs,** the only large town in central Australia. Alice Springs is 462km (286 miles) from Uluru. You can see Uluru in a day from Alice Springs, but it's an effort. We recommend you spend a few days in Alice or at one of the Red Centre resorts.

By air

The only major airline that flies to the airports at Ayers Rock/Uluru Airport and Alice Springs is **Qantas** (☎ **13 13 13** in Australia; www. qantas.com.au).

There are daily flights from most state capitals to Alice Springs. You can fly daily to Ayers Rock Airport from Perth, Sydney, Cairns, and Alice Springs. Direct flights operate twice a week from Melbourne. Flights from Darwin and Brisbane connect through Alice Springs to Ayers Rock Airport. The flying time to Ayers Rock Airport from both Sydney and Melbourne is three hours.

Ayers Rock Airport is just 6km (4 miles) from Voyages Ayers Rock Resort. Coach transfers from Ayers Rock Airport to Voyages Ayers Rock Resort are free and meet every scheduled flight.

In Alice Springs, the **Alice Springs Airport Shuttle,** Gregory Terrace (☎ **08/8953 0310**), meets all major flights. Transfers to your hotel cost A$12 (US$9.60/£4.80) one-way, A$20 (US$16/£8) round-trip. A taxi from the airport to town, a distance of 15km (9⅓ miles), is around A$25 (US$20/£10).

By train

The *Ghan* train, named after Afghan camel-train drivers who carried supplies in the Red Centre in the 19th century, makes the trip from Adelaide to Alice every week, continuing to Darwin. The Adelaide–Alice service (leaving Adelaide Sun and Wed at 12:20 p.m. and Alice Springs Thurs and Sat) takes roughly 24 hours.

The *Ghan* departs Alice Springs for Darwin on Monday and Thursday at 6 p.m., arriving in Katherine on Tuesday and Friday mornings, and Darwin in the afternoon. The service from Darwin departs on Wednesday and Saturday. Stopovers in Katherine last at least four hours. The route is often treeless and empty, if fascinatingly so; don't be concerned that you'll miss it by overnighting on the train. The train has sleeper berths.

For fares and schedules, contact **Great Southern Railway** (☎ **13 21 47** in Australia, or 08/8213 4592; www.gsr.com.au), or see Chapter 2, for its booking agencies abroad.

The **Airport Shuttle** (☎ **08/8953 0310**) runs between the train station and Alice Springs town center for A$5 (US$4/£2) one-way, A$8 (US$6.40/£3.20) round-trip. A taxi costs about A$7 (US$5.60/£2.70) for the same trip.

By bus

It's a long journey, but you could go to Alice Springs by bus from either Adelaide or Darwin. **Greyhound** (☎ **13 14 99** in Australia, or 07/4690 9950; www.greyhound.com.au) runs a 21-hour trip from Adelaide. The fare is around A$220 (US$176/£88). The 21-hour trip from Darwin costs about A$240 (US$192/£96). A daily five-and-three-quarter-hour run connects with Uluru (Ayers Rock); the fare is around A$75 (US$60/£30).

The Red Centre

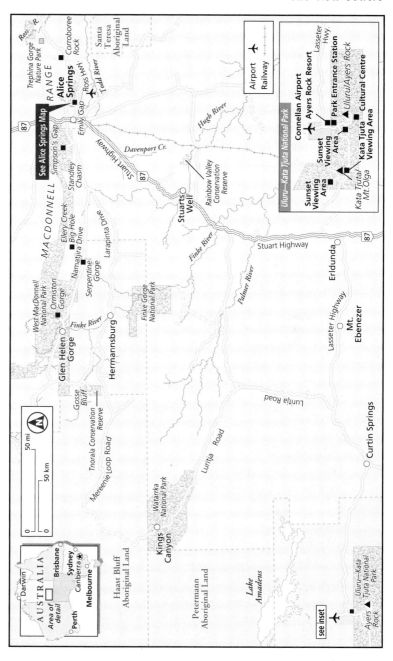

Taking a tour of the Red Centre

Numerous coach, minicoach, and four-wheel-drive tour operators run tours that take in Alice Springs, Kings Canyon, and Uluru. They depart from Alice Springs or Uluru, offering accommodations ranging from spiffy resorts, comfortable motels, and basic cabins to shared bunkhouses, tents, or swags (sleeping bags) under the stars. Most pack the highlights into a two- or three-day trip, though leisurely trips of six days or more are available. Among the reputable companies are the following:

- **AAT Kings** (☎ **1800/334 009** in Australia, or 03/9274 7422 for the Melbourne central reservations office; www.aatkings.com), which specializes in big-bus coach tours but also has four-wheel-drive camping itineraries

- **Aboriginal Desert Discovery Tours** (☎ **08/8952 3408**; www.aboriginal art.com.au), which is owned by Alice Springs Aboriginal people and teams up its Aboriginal guides with Alice-based companies to offer tours with an Aboriginal slant

- **Alice Springs Holidays** (☎ **08/8953 1411**; www.alicesprings holidays.com.au), which does upscale soft-adventure tours for groups

- **Connections** (☎ **08/8252 5000**; www.connections.travel), which conducts camping safaris in small groups for all ages

- **Discovery Ecotours** (☎ **08/8956 2563**; www.ecotours.com.au), which specializes in ecotours for groups

- **VIP Travel Australia** (☎ **1800/806 412** in Australia, or 08/8956 2388; www.vipaustralia.com.au), which offers luxury tours in limos, minicoaches, and four-wheel-drives, with desert barbecues and champagne dinners

By car

Only a handful of highways and arterial roads in the Northern Territory are paved. A two-wheel-drive car will get you to 95 percent of what you want to see, but consider renting a four-wheel-drive for complete freedom. All the big chains have them. Some attractions are on unpaved roads good enough for a two-wheel-drive car, but your car rental company will not insure a two-wheel-drive for driving on them.

Outside settled areas, the territory has no speed limit, but before you hit the gas, consider the risk of hitting the wildlife: camels, kangaroos, and other protected native species. Locals stick to a comfortable 120kmph (75 mph) or less. Avoid driving at night, early morning, and late afternoon, when 'roos feed; beware of cattle lying down on the warm bitumen at night. A white road sign bearing a black circle outline crossed by a diagonal black line indicates the point when speed restrictions no longer apply. Make sure you have a full tank of gas before setting out.

The **Automobile Association of the Northern Territory,** 79–81 Smith St., Darwin, NT 0800 (☎ **08/8981 3837**), offers emergency breakdown service to members of affiliated automobile associations and gives maps and advice. It has no office in the Red Centre, though you can call the main office for emergency breakdown service in the Red Centre. For a recorded report of road conditions, call ☎ **1800/246 199** in Australia.

Surviving the Red Centre

Secrets of the seasons

April, May, September, and October have sunny days (coolish in May, hot in Oct). Winter (June–Aug) means mild temperatures with cold nights. Summer (Nov–Mar) is extremely hot and best avoided. In summer, limit your physical exertions to early and late in the day, and choose air-conditioned accommodations. Rain is rare but can come at any time of year.

Permits

If you plan to "go bush" in remote regions not covered by this guide, you may need a **permit** from the relevant Aboriginal lands council to cross Aboriginal land. This can be a drawn-out bureaucratic affair that takes weeks, so plan ahead. The **Northern Territory Tourist Commission,** Tourism House, 43 Mitchell St., Darwin, NT 0800 (☎ **13 61 10** in Australia, or 08/8999 3900; www.ntholidays.com), can put you in touch with the appropriate council. All good road maps mark Aboriginal lands clearly.

Water

Always carry drinking water. When hiking, carry 4 liters (about a gallon) per person per day in winter, and a liter (¼ gallon) per person per hour in summer.

Clothes

Wear a broad-brimmed hat, high-SPF sunscreen, and insect repellent. Evenings can get cool, even in summer.

Alice Springs

"The Alice," as Australians fondly dub it, is the unofficial capital of Outback Australia. In the 1870s, a handful of telegraph-station workers struggled north from Adelaide to settle by a small spring in what must have seemed like the ends of the earth. Alice Springs, as the place was called, was just a few huts around a repeater station on the telegraph line that was to link Adelaide with Darwin and the rest of the world.

Today Alice Springs is a city of 27,000 people, with supermarkets, banks, and the odd nightclub. It's a friendly, rambling, unsophisticated place. Many tourists visit Alice only to get to Uluru, but Alice has charms of its own. The red folds of the **MacDonnell Ranges** hide lovely gorges with shady picnic grounds. The area has an old gold-rush town to poke around in, quirky museums, wildlife parks, a couple of cattle stations (ranches) that welcome visitors, a couple of nice day trips to the surrounding area, and one of the world's top ten desert golf courses. You could easily fill two or three days.

This is the heart of the Aboriginal Arrernte people's country, and Alice is a rich source of tours, shops, and galleries for those interested in Aboriginal culture, art, or souvenirs. There is a sad side to this story: Not every Aborigine succeeds in splicing his ancient civilization with the 21st century, and the result is dislocated communities living in the riverbed with only alcohol for company.

Orienting yourself in Alice Springs

The main street is called **Todd Mall.** Most shops, businesses, and restaurants are here or within a few blocks. Most hotels, the casino, the golf course, and many attractions are a few kilometers outside of town. The dry Todd River "flows" through the city east of Todd Mall.

Finding information after you arrive

The **Central Australian Tourism Industry Association (CATIA) Visitor Information Centre,** 60 Gregory Terrace, Alice Springs, NT 0870 (☎ 08/8952 5800; www.centralaustraliantourism.com), is the official one-stop shop for bookings and touring information for the Red Centre, including Alice Springs, Kings Canyon, and Uluru–Kata Tjuta National Park (Ayers Rock). It also acts as the visitor center for the Parks & Wildlife Commission of the Northern Territory. It's open Monday through Friday from 8:30 a.m. to 5:30 p.m. and weekends and public holidays from 9 a.m. to 4 p.m. It also has a desk at the airport.

Getting around Alice Springs

✔ **By taxi:** Taxis tend to congregate at Todd Street and Gregory Terrace. Or call **Alice Springs Taxis (☎ 08/8952 1877).** Taxi fares tend to be quite high, so try to use other means to get around.

✔ **By bus:** Asbus (☎ 08/8950 0500) operates public buses departing from the Yeperenye shopping center on Hartley Street. Bus no. 3 passes the School of the Air, several hotels, and caravan parks along Gap Road and Palm Circuit.

The **Alice Wanderer** bus (☎ 1800/722 111 in Australia, or 08/8952 2111; www.alicewanderer.com.au) does a running loop of 12 town attractions every 70 minutes starting at 9 a.m., with the last departure at 4 p.m. Hop on and off as you please, and enjoy the commentary from the driver. The bus departs daily from the south

Alice Springs

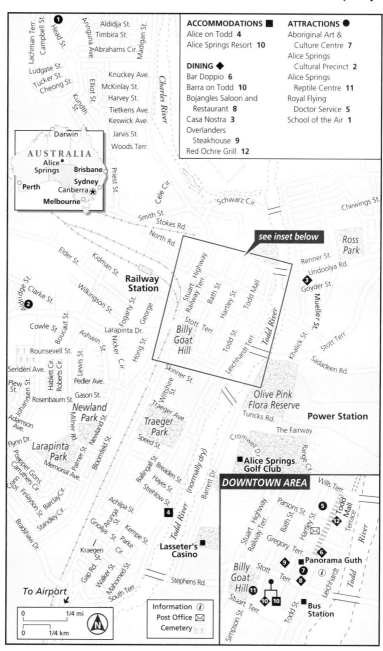

ACCOMMODATIONS ■
Alice on Todd **4**
Alice Springs Resort **10**

DINING ◆
Bar Doppio **6**
Barra on Todd **10**
Bojangles Saloon and
   Restaurant **8**
Casa Nostra **3**
Overlanders
   Steakhouse **9**
Red Ochre Grill **12**

ATTRACTIONS ●
Aboriginal Art &
   Culture Centre **7**
Alice Springs
   Cultural Precinct **2**
Alice Springs
   Reptile Centre **11**
Royal Flying
   Doctor Service **5**
School of the Air **1**

end of Todd Mall. Tickets are sold on board and cost A$40 (US$32/£16) adults, A$30 (US$24/£12) kids 4 to 14. Call for free pickup from your hotel. The ticket lasts for two days and you can use it on nonconsecutive days.

Organized tours

The **Alice Wanderer** bus (see the preceding section) also runs full-day tours to outlying areas, including to the West MacDonnell Ranges, a stark but picturesque semidesert area with red gorges and occasional swimming holes. It also goes to Santa Teresa Aboriginal Community, where you can meet local Aborigines and view and purchase their artwork.

Many Alice-based companies offer minicoach or four-wheel-drive day trips and extended tours of Alice and of outlying areas including the East and West Macs, Hermannsburg, and Finke Gorge National Park.

Among the well-regarded ones are: **Discovery Ecotours** (☎ 08/8956 2563; www.ecotours.com.au) and **Alice Springs Holidays** (☎ 1800/ 801 401 in Australia, or 08/8953 1411; www.alicespringsholidays. com.au).

The **Aboriginal Art & Culture Centre,** 6 Todd St., Alice Springs (www. aboriginalart.com.au), runs half-day tours with Aboriginal guides.

Staying in style

Alice's hotel stock is not grand. Many properties have dated rooms and modest facilities; they're no match for the gleaming standard of **Ayers Rock Resort** (see later in this chapter). You may pay lower rates than those listed in the summer off season (Dec–Mar), and even as late as June. Peak season typically runs from July through October or November. Parking is free everywhere.

The top hotels

Alice on Todd
$$ **Town Centre**

A new addition to the Alice accommodations scene, Alice on Todd has nice one- and two-bedroom apartments. It's a good option, particularly if you have kids (those under 4 years old stay free). The hotel overlooks the Todd River and is just a short stroll from town. Each of the two luxury two-bedroom apartments has an extra sofa bed. There's a small outdoor pool, too.

See map, p. 357. Strehlow Street and South Terrace (P.O. Box 8454), Alice Springs, NT 0870. ☎ 08/8953 8033. www.aliceontodd.com. Rack rates: A$105 (US$84/£42) studio apartment, A$130 (US$104/£52) 1-bedroom apartment, A$160 (US$128/£64) 2-bedroom apartment, A$180 (US$144/£72) luxury 2-bedroom apartment. AE, MC, V.

Alice Springs Resort
$$ **Town Centre**

This friendly, well-run, low-rise property is a three-minute walk from town over the Todd River. Standard rooms are pleasant, while deluxe rooms are plusher and have views across the Todd River or the gardens. In summer, it's nice to head to the pool under a couple of palms after a hot day's sightseeing. A fire glows in the **Gumtree Lounge** bar on winter evenings.

See map p. 357. 34 Stott Terrace, Alice Springs, NT 0870. ☎ *800-225-9849 in the U.S.; 1300/134 044 in Australia, or 08/8951 4545. Fax: 08/8953 0995.* www.alicesprings resort.com.au. *Rack rates: A$150–A$240 (US$120–US$192/£60–£96) double. Ask about packages with Ayers Rock Resort and Kings Canyon Resort. AE, DC, MC, V.*

Bond Springs Outback Retreat
$$$ **Outback**

This working 1,515-sq.-km (585-sq.-mile) cattle ranch is a great place to get a taste of Outback life with a real Aussie family. It's 25km (16 miles) north of Alice Springs, but in these parts that's a short drive. Expect country dinners with the family and a choice of two cottages. The first is Corkwood Cottage, which was built for the station's head stockman and his family. The main bedroom features a queen-size bed and each of the two other bedrooms has twin beds and a single bed. There's a comfortable lounge and dining room, a fully equipped kitchen, and an outdoor BBQ. The second cottage has a main bedroom with a queen-size bed and a second bedroom with twin beds. There's a lounge and dining room, which includes a kitchenette. Gourmet breakfasts are delivered to both cottages. The owners run a good range of day trips, overnight bush camps, and tours throughout the Red Centre, making this a good base for exploring.

P.O. Box 4, Alice Springs, NT 0870. ☎ *08/8952 9888. Fax: 08/8953 0963.* www.outback retreat.com.au. *Rack rate: A$277 (US$221/£111) Corkwood Cottage, A$231 (US$185/£93) Wurlie Cottage. Rates include full breakfast. Dinner A$55 (US$44/£22) per person. MC, V. Transfers from Alice Springs A$40 (US$32/£16) from town, A$80 (US$64/£32) from airport, one-way, per vehicle.*

Dining out
You can get some inexpensive meals with a bit of character in Alice!

Bar Doppio
$ **Town Centre   EAST/WEST CAFE FARE**

If you're in need of a dose of cool — style, as well as air-conditioning — this arcade cafe is the place to chill over good coffee and feast on cheap, wholesome food. Sacks of coffee beans are stacked all over, Gypsy music plays, no tables and chairs match, and the staff doesn't care if you sit here all day. It's largely vegetarian, but fish and meat figure on the blackboard menu. Hot and cold breakfast choices are served until 11 a.m.

See map p. 357. 2 and 3 Fan Arcade (off the south end of Todd Mall). ☎ *08/8952 6525. Main courses: A$7–A$16 (US$5.60–US$13/£2.80–£6.50), sandwiches A$6 (US$4.80/ £2.40). No credit cards. Open: Mon–Fri 7:30 a.m.–5:30 p.m., Sat 7:30 a.m.–4:30 p.m., Sun 10 a.m.–4:30 p.m., Fri–Sat 6–9 p.m. Closed holidays and Dec 25–Jan 1.*

Barra On Todd
$$ Town Centre   MODERN AUSTRALIAN

Ask the locals for the best chow in town, and this is where they'll send you. There are usually two or three barramundi dishes on the menu, as well as steak, prawns, and roasted chicken dishes. It does a good breakfast menu and all-day-dining by the pool. Live piano music plays nightly.

See map p. 357. At the Alice Springs Resort, 34 Stott Terrace. ☎ *08/8951 4545. Reservations recommended at dinner. Main courses: A$18–A$28 (US$14–US$22/£7– £11). AE, DC, MC, V. Open: Daily 6 a.m.–9:30 p.m.*

Bojangles Saloon and Restaurant
$ Town Centre   BURGERS/MODERN AUSTRALIAN

Swing open the saloon doors and enter a world of cowhide seats, wooden tables, Western knickknacks, American Civil War guns, and so on. The front bar is friendly and serves good beers by the bottle or schooner, and food such as burgers, salads, and fish and chips. The restaurant out back has more gourmet offerings, but it's a great atmosphere. Aussie-style country and folk singers strum away in the evenings, and the staff is terrific.

See map p. 357. 80 Todd St. ☎ *08/8952 2873. Main courses: A$7–A$18 (US$5.60– US$15/£2.70–£7.50) front bar, A$12–A$25 (US$9.60–US$20/£4.80–£10) restaurant. AE, DC, MC, V. Open: Daily noon to 3 p.m. and 6–10 p.m.*

Casa Nostra
$$ Town Centre   ITALIAN

The only difference between this cheery family eatery and every other Italian restaurant is that this one has autographed photos of Tom Selleck pinned to the wall. Judging by his scrawled praise, Tom loved eating here (when filming *Quigley Down Under*) as much as the locals do. You've seen the red-checked tablecloths and the basket-clad chianti bottles before, but the food is surprisingly good. A long list of pastas, pizzas, and chicken and veal dishes are the main offerings. It's BYO wine.

See map p. 357. Corner of Undoolya Road and Sturt Terrace. ☎ *08/8952 6749. Reservations recommended. Main courses: A$13–A$22 (US$10–US$18/£5–£9). MC, V. Open: Mon–Sat 5–10 p.m. Closed Dec 25–Jan 1.*

Overlanders Steakhouse
$$$ Town Centre   STEAK/AUSSIE TUCKER

This landmark on the dining scene is famous for its "Drover's Blowout" menu, which assaults the mega-hungry with soup and damper, then a platter of crocodile *vol-au-vents,* camel and kangaroo filet, and emu medallions — these are just the *appetizers* — followed by Scotch filet, or barramundi (freshwater fish), and dessert. There's a regular menu with a 700-gram (1-lb., 10-oz.) steak, plus lots of lighter fare. The barnlike interior is Outback all through, from the rustic bar to the saddlebags hanging from the roof beams. An "Overlanders' Table" seats solo diners together.

See map p. 357. 72 Hartley St. ☎ 08/8952 2159. Reservations required in peak season. Main courses: A$23–A$35 (US$18–US$28/£9–£14), Drover's Blowout A$45 (US$36/ £18). AE, DC, MC, V. Open: Daily 6–10 p.m.

Red Ochre Grill
$$ **Town Centre** **GOURMET BUSH TUCKER**

If you've never tried wallaby mignons on a bed of native pasta and polenta cake with native berry and red-wine cream sauce, or barramundi (fish) baked in Paperbark with wild lime and coriander butter, here's your chance. The chef at this upscale chain fuses native Aussie ingredients with dishes from around the world. And the food is mouthwatering. Dine in the contemporary interior fronting Todd Mall, or in the courtyard.

See map p. 357. Todd Mall. ☎ 08/8952 9614. www.redochrealice.com.au. *Reservations recommended at dinner. Main courses: A$9–A$21 (US$7.20–US$17/ £3.60–£8.50) lunch, A$15–A$23 (US$12–US$19/£6–£16) dinner, A$13–A$16 (US$11– US$13/£5.50–£6.50) buffet breakfast. AE, DC, MC, V. Open: Daily 6:30 a.m.–9:30 p.m.*

Exploring Alice Springs
The top attractions
Alice Springs Cultural Precinct
At least one or two attractions here will pique your interest. All of them are within walking distance of each another.

Some impressive Aboriginal and contemporary Aussie art is on display at the **Araluen Centre (☎ 08/8951 1122)**, the town's performing arts hub; check out the "Honey Ant Dreaming" stained-glass window in its foyer. One of Australia's best-known indigenous artists is Albert Namatjira, who painted the MacDonnell Ranges with startling accuracy. A collection of his work can be viewed at the Albert Namatjira Gallery.

Aviation nuts may want to browse the old radios, aircraft, and wreckage in the **Aviation Museum,** which preserves the territory's aerial history.

You can buy stylish crafts, and sometimes catch artists at work, in the **Territory Craft** gallery. You may want to amble among the outdoor sculptures, including the 15m (49-ft.) *Yeperenye Dreamtime Caterpillar,* or among the gravestones in the cemetery, where "Afghani" camel herders (from what is now Pakistan) are buried facing Mecca.

See map p. 357. Larapinta Drive, 2km (1¼ miles) south of town. ☎ 08/8951 1120. Admission: A$9 (US$7.30/£3.70) adults, A$6 (US$4.80/£2.40) children 5–16, A$23 (US$18/£9) families. Open: Mon–Fri 10 a.m.–4 p.m., Sat–Sun 11 a.m.–4 p.m.

Hiking the Larapinta Trail

The 223km (138-mile) **Larapinta Trail** winds west from Alice through the sparse red ranges, picturesque semidesert scenery, and rich bird life of the West MacDonnell National Park. This long-distance walking track is divided into 12 sections, each a one- to two-day walk. Sections range from easy to hard. The shortest is 8km (5 miles), ranging up to several 23km to 29km (14- to 18-mile) stretches. The Larapinta Trail begins at the old Alice Springs Telegraph Station. Each section is accessible to vehicles (some by high clearance four-wheel-drive only), so you can join or leave the trail at any of the trailheads.

Camping out under a sea of stars in the outback is a highlight of the experience. Although they vary, most campsites offer picnic tables and tent sites; all trailheads have a water supply and some have free gas barbecues. The **Parks & Wildlife Commission of the Northern Territory** office in Alice Springs (☎ **08/8951 8211**) and the **CATIA Visitor Information Centre** dispense trail maps and information. Check www.nt.gov.au/nreta/parks/walks/larapinta for information on the trail and maps. *Warning:* Always carry drinking water. The trail may close in extremely hot summer periods.

Alice Springs Reptile Centre

Kids can walk around with pythons or bearded dragons on their shoulders, at this Aussie reptile park. The easygoing proprietor lifts up the cages' glass fronts for better photos and lets kids hand-feed bugs to the animals at feeding time. Some 30 species are on display, including the world's deadliest land snake — the taipan — and big goannas. Also here are brown snakes, death adders, and mulga, otherwise known as king brown snakes. Do not miss the saltwater crocodile exhibit featuring underwater viewing.

See map p. 357. 9 Stuart Terrace (opposite the Royal Flying Doctor Service). ☎ *08/8952 8900.* www.reptilecentre.com.au. *Admission: A$8 (US$6.40/£3.20) adults, A$4 (US$3.20/£1.60) children under 17, A$20 (US$16/£8) families. Open: Daily 9 a.m.–5 p.m.*

Alice Springs Telegraph Station Historical Reserve

Alice Springs began life in 1872 as this telegraph repeater station, set by a water hole amid red hills, gum trees full of parrots, and green lawns. An oasis in the harsh landscape, it's a place tourists often overlook. You can wander around the stationmaster's residence; the telegraph office, with its Morse code machine tap-tapping away; the shoeing yard packed with blacksmith's equipment; and the stables, housing vintage buggies and saddlery. May through October, "kitchen maids" in period dress serve scones (biscuits) and damper (campfire bread) from the original wood-fired ovens. There are several hiking trails leading from the extensive grounds.

Stuart Highway, 4km (2½ miles) north of town (beyond the School of the Air turnoff). ☎ *08/8952 3993*. Admission: Free to picnic grounds and trails; station A$7 (US$5.60/ £3.30) adults, A$3.75 (US$3/£1.50) children 5–15. Open: Daily 8 a.m.–5 p.m. (picnic grounds and trails until 9 p.m.).

Royal Flying Doctor Service

Alice is a major base for this airborne medical service that treats people living and traveling in the vast Outback. An interesting 20-minute tour runs every half-hour, featuring a video and a talk in the communications room. Some of the recorded conversations between doctors and patients are intriguing. There is a nice garden cafe and a gift shop.

See map p. 357. 8–10 Stuart Terrace (at the end of Hartley Street). ☎ *08/8952 1129.* www.flyingdoctor.net. Admission: A$6.50 (US$5.20/£2.60) adults, A$3 (US$2.40/ £1.20) children 6–15. Open: Mon–Sat 9 a.m.–5 p.m. (last tour 4 p.m.); Sun and public holidays 1–5 p.m.

School of the Air

Sitting in on classes may not be your idea of a vacation, but this school is different — it broadcasts to a 1.3-million-sq.-km (507,000-sq.-mile) "school-room" of 140 children on Outback stations. Visitors watch and listen in when classes are in session; outside class hours, you may hear taped classes. You can browse the kids' artwork, videos, and other displays in the well-organized gallery. Free 30-minute tours run throughout the day.

See map p. 357. 80 Head St. (2.5km/1½ miles from town). ☎ *08/8951 6834.* Admission: A$6.50 (US$5.20/£2.60) adults, A$4 (US$3.20/£1.60) children 5–16, A$16 (US$13/£6.50) families. Open: Mon–Sat and public holidays 8:30 a.m.–4:30 p.m., Sun 1:30–4:30 p.m.

More cool things to see and do

Here are a few recommendations for things to see and do in town and a little farther out:

✔ Worth a look is the **Aboriginal Art & Culture Centre,** 86 Todd St. (☎ **08/8952 3408**), set up by the Southern Arrernte Aboriginal people. It houses a small, intriguing museum with exhibits on Aboriginal life and displays a timeline of the Aboriginal view of history since "contact" (the arrival of Europeans). Admission is free, and it's open daily from 8 a.m. to 5 p.m.

✔ You may not associate camels with Australia, but the camel's ability to get by without water was key to opening the arid inland parts of the country to European settlement in the 1800s. With the advent of cars, they were released into the wild, and today more than 200,000 camels roam central Australia. Australia even exports them to the Middle East! **Frontier Camel Tours** (☎ **08/8950 3030;** http://cameltours.ananguwaai.com.au) runs camel rides daily, including sunset tours, with pickup from your hotel.

Fast Facts: Alice Springs

Area Code
The area code for the Red Centre and the rest of the Northern Territory is **08**.

Doctor
There are two clinics on Todd Street, the Central Clinic, 76 Todd St. (☎ 08/8952 1088), and the Mall Medical Centre, 1/51 Todd St. (☎ 08/8952 2741).

Emergencies
Call ☎ **000** for an ambulance, the police, or the fire department.

Hospitals
The Alice Springs Hospital is on Gap Road (☎ 08/8951 7777).

Newspapers
The Northern Territory's largest independent newspaper is the *Alice Springs Times.*

Pharmacies
There are several pharmacies around town including Alice Springs Pharmacy, 45 Hartley St. (☎ 08/8952 1554).

Police
Alice Springs Police Station is on Parsons Street (☎ 08/8951 8888).

Post Offices
The post office is at 31–33 Hartley St. It's open Monday through Friday from 8:15 a.m. to 5 p.m., Saturday 9 a.m. to noon.

Public Toilets
Restrooms are located inside Alice Plaza Shopping Centre on Todd Mall and Alice Springs Shopping Centre on the corner of Bath Street and Gregory Terrace.

Kings Canyon

Anyone who saw the movie *The Adventures of Priscilla, Queen of the Desert* will remember the stony plateau that the transvestites climb to gaze over the plain below. You can stand on that same spot (wearing sequined underpants is optional) at **Kings Canyon** in **Watarrka National Park** (☎ **08/8956 7460** for park headquarters).

As the crow flies, it is 320km (198 miles) southwest of Alice Springs. The sandstone walls of the canyon drop about 100m (330 ft.) to rock pools and gum trees. There is little to do except walk the dramatic canyon rim for a sense of the peaceful emptiness of the Australian Outback.

Getting there
The best way is to drive. Numerous **four-wheel-drive** tour outfits head to Kings Canyon from Alice Springs or Uluru (Ayers Rock), with time allowed for the rim walk.

With a four-wheel-drive, you can get to Kings Canyon from Alice Springs on the unpaved **Mereenie Loop Road.** The regular route is the 480km (349-mile) trip from Alice Springs south on the Stuart Highway, then west onto the Lasseter Highway, then north and west on the Luritja Road. All three roads are paved.

Uluru (Ayers Rock) is 306km (190 miles) to the south; from Yulara, take the Lasseter Highway east for 125km (78 miles), then turn left onto Luritja Road and go 168km (104 miles) to Kings Canyon Resort. The resort sells leaded and unleaded gasoline and diesel fuel.

Taking an organized tour

AAT Kings (☎ **1800/334 009** in Australia, or 08/8956 2171; www.aat kings.com) offers a one-day tour to Kings Canyon from the Ayers Rock Resort for A$103 (US$82/£41) per person. You can book through AAT Kings or the resort.

Exploring the park

The way to explore the canyon is on the 6km (3¾-mile) **walk** up the side (short but steep!) and around the rim. Even if you're in good shape, it's a strenuous three- to four-hour hike. It leads through a maze of rounded sandstone formations called the Lost City, across a bridge to a fern-fringed pocket of water holes called the Garden of Eden, and back along the other side through more sandstone rocks.

If you're not up to making the rim walk, take the shady 2.6km (1½-mile) round-trip trail along the mostly dry **Kings Creek bed** on the canyon floor. It takes about an hour. Wear sturdy boots, because the ground can be rocky. This walk is all right for young kids and travelers in wheelchairs for the first kilometer (½ mile).

Both walks are signposted. Avoid the rim walk in the middle of the day between September and May, when it's too hot.

Professional Helicopter Services (☎ **08/8956 7873;** www.phs.com.au) makes 15-minute flights over the canyon for A$115 (US$92/£46) per person.

Staying in style

Apart from campgrounds, the only place to stay in Watarrka National Park is at Kings Canyon Resort.

Kings Canyon Resort
$$$$ **Kings Canyon**

This attractive, low-slung complex 7km (4⅓ miles) from Kings Canyon blends into its surroundings. All but four of the larger deluxe rooms have desert views from glass-enclosed Jacuzzis. The remaining rooms are typical accommodations, comfortable enough, with range views from the balcony. The double/twin, shared quad, and family lodge rooms are adequate low-budget choices, with a communal kitchen and bathroom facilities. The resort has a minimart where you can buy meat for the barbecues. There are two pools. The resort runs and books several tours.

Luritja Road, Watarrka National Park, NT 0872. ☎ *1800/817 622 in Australia, or 08/8956 7442. Fax: 08/8956 7426.* www.voyages.com.au *or* www.kingscanyon resort.com.au. *Rack rates: Hotel July–Nov A$330–A$397 (US$264–US$317/£132– £158) double, Dec–June A$277–A$343 (US$221–US$275/£110–£138) double; lodge July–Nov A$100 (US$80/£40) double, A$168 (US$135/£68) quad, A$185 (US$148/£74) families (up to 5 people); lodge Dec–June A$98 (US$78/£39) double, A$163 (US$130/ £65) quad, A$178 (US$142/£71) families. Tent site A$28 (US$22/£11), powered site A$32 (US$26/£13) double. Children under 16 dine free at restaurant breakfast and dinner buffets with an adult. Ask about packages with Ayers Rock Resort and Alice Springs Resort. AE, DC, MC, V.*

Uluru–Kata Tjuta National Park (Ayers Rock/The Olgas)

Uluru (Ayers Rock) is the Australia tourism industry's pinup icon, a glamorous red stone that has been splashed on more posters than Cindy Crawford has been on magazine covers. You can put its popularity down to the faint shiver up the spine and the indescribable sense of place it evokes in anyone who looks at it. Even Aussie bushmen reckon it's "got somethin' spiritual about it."

This famous rock is in the middle of nowhere. The nearest town is Alice Springs, some 462 km (286 miles) away. It's 1,934km (1,199 miles) south of Darwin, 1,571km (974 miles) north of Adelaide, and 2,841km (1,761 miles) northwest of Sydney.

In 1985, the park was returned to its Aboriginal owners, the Pitjantjatjara and Yankunytjatjara people, known as the **Anangu,** who manage the property with the Australian government. People used to speculate that the Rock was a meteorite, but we now know it was formed by sediments laid down 600 million to 700 million years ago in an inland sea and thrust up above ground 348m (1,141 ft.) by geological forces.

With a circumference of 9.4km (6 miles), the Rock is no pebble, especially because two-thirds of it is thought to be underground. On photos it looks like a big smooth blob. In the flesh, it's more interesting — dappled with holes and overhangs, with curtains of stone draping its sides, creating coves hiding water holes and Aboriginal rock art. It also changes color from pink to a deep red, depending on the slant of the sun.

Don't think a visit to Uluru is just about snapping a few photos and going home. You can walk around the Rock, climb it (although the local Aborigines prefer you don't), fly over it, ride a camel to it, circle it on a Harley-Davidson, trek through the Olgas, eat in an outdoor restaurant, tour the night sky, and join Aboriginal people on guided walks.

The peak time to catch the Rock's beauty is sunset, when oranges, peaches, pinks, reds, and then indigo and deep violet creep across its face as if it were a giant opal. Some days it's fiery; other days the colors are muted. At sunrise the colors are less dramatic, but many folks enjoy the spectacle of the Rock unveiled by the dawn to birdsong.

Although not everyone has heard of **Mount Olga** (or "the Olgas"), a sister monolith an easy 50km (31-mile) drive west of Uluru, many folks say it's lovelier and more mysterious. Known to the Aborigines as *Kata Tjuta,* or "many heads," the Olgas' 36 red domes bulge out of the earth like turned clay on a potter's wheel. The tallest is 200m (656 ft.) higher than Uluru.

Getting there

By air

Qantas (☎ **13 13 13** in Australia) flies to Ayers Rock (Connellan) Airport direct from Sydney, Alice Springs, Perth, and Cairns. Flights from other ports go via Alice Springs. The airport is 6km (3¾ miles) from Ayers Rock Resort. Expect to pay around A$320 (US$256/£128) one-way. A free shuttle ferries all resort guests, including campers, to their door.

By car

Take the Stuart Highway south from Alice Springs 199km (123 miles), turn right onto the Lasseter Highway, and go 244km (151 miles) to Ayers Rock Resort. The Rock is 18km (11 miles) farther on. (Everyone mistakes the mesa they see en route for Uluru; it's Mount Conner.)

Avis (☎ 13 63 33 or 08/8956-2266; www.avis.com.au), **Hertz** (☎ 13 30 39 or 08/8956-2244; www.hertzcom.au), and **Thrifty** (☎ 1300/367 227 or 08/8956-2030; www.thrifty.com.au) have Uluru depots, both at the airport and in town. Thrifty charges around A$110 (US$88/£44) a day for bookings under three days; Hertz charges A$137 (US$109/£55) a day for bookings under seven days; and Avis charges A$137 (US$109/£55) a day for bookings of two days or fewer. If you want to rent a car in Alice Springs and drop it at Uluru, brace yourself for a one-way penalty.

Visitor information

For information before you leave, contact the **Central Australian Tourism Industry Association (CATIA),** 60 Gregory Terrace, Alice Springs (☎ **08/8952 5800;** www.centralaustraliantourism.com), or drop into its **Visitor Information Centre** in Alice Springs. One of the best online sources is Ayers Rock Resort's site (www.voyages.com.au).

The **Ayers Rock Resort Visitor Centre,** next to the Desert Gardens Hotel (☎ **08/8957 7377**), has displays on the area's geology, wildlife, and Aboriginal heritage, and a store. It's open daily from 8:30 a.m. to 7:30 p.m. You can book tours at every hotel at the resort.

Another option is the **Ayers Rock Resort Tour & Information Centre** (☎ **08/8957 7324**) at the shopping center in the resort complex. It's open daily from 7:30 a.m. to 8:30 p.m.

One kilometer (½ mile) from the base of the Rock is the **Uluru–Kata Tjuta Cultural Centre** (☎ **08/8956 3138**), owned and run by the Anangu, the Aboriginal owners of Uluru. It uses eye-catching wall displays, frescoes, interactive recordings, and videos to tell about Aboriginal Dreamtime myths and laws. A National Park desk has information on ranger-guided activities and animal, plant, and bird-watching checklists. It's open daily from early in the morning to after sundown; exact hours vary from month to month.

Park entrance fees

Entry to the Uluru–Kata Tjuta National Park is A$25 (US$20/£10) per adult, free for children under 16, valid for three days. The cost of many organized tours includes the entry fee.

Getting around

Getting around the park is expensive. Ayers Rock Resort runs a **free shuttle** every 15 minutes or so around the resort complex from 10:30 a.m. to after midnight, but to get to the Rock or Kata Tjuta (the Olgas), you need to take transfers, join a tour, or have your own wheels. The shuttle also meets all flights.

By camel

Legend has it that a soul travels at the same pace as a camel; going by camel is certainly a peaceful way to see the Rock. **Anangu Tours** (☎ **08/8950 3030;** www.anangutours.com.au) makes daily forays aboard "ships of the desert" to view Uluru. The one-hour rides depart Ayers Rock Resort an hour before sunrise or one-and-a-half hours before sunset, and cost A$95 (US$76/£38) per person, including transfers from your hotel. All tours leave from the Camel Depot at the Ayers Rock Resort.

By car

If you're traveling with another person, the easiest and cheapest way to get around is likely to be a rental car. All roads in the area are paved, so a four-wheel-drive is unnecessary. Expect to pay around A$70 to A$95 (US$56–US$76/£28–£38) per day for a medium-size car. Rates drop a little in the off season. **Avis** (☎ **08/8956 2266**), **Hertz** (☎ **08/8956 2244**), and **Thrifty** (☎ **08/8956 2030**) book four-wheel-drives through their Darwin offices. All rent regular cars and four-wheel-drives.

On foot

A paved road runs around the Rock. The 9.4km (6-mile) **Base Walk** circumnavigating Uluru takes about two hours, but allow time to linger around the water holes, caves, folds, and overhangs. A shorter walk is the easy 1km (½-mile) round-trip trail from the **Mutitjulu** parking lot to the pretty water hole near the Rock's base, where there is some rock art. The **Liru Track** is another easy trail; it runs 2km (1¼ miles) from the Cultural Centre to Uluru, where it links with the Base Walk.

Make time for the free daily 2km (1¼-mile) **Mala Walk,** where the ranger, often an Aborigine, explains the Dreamtime myths, talks about Aboriginal lifestyles and hunting techniques, and explains the significance of the rock art and other sites you see. The 90-minute trip leaves the Mala Walk sign at the base of the Uluru climb at 10 a.m. May through September, and at a cooler 8 a.m. October through April.

 Before setting off on any walk, arm yourself with the self-guided walking notes available from the Cultural Centre.

By helicopter

A top-class way to see the rock is from the air. **Professional Helicopter Services (☎ 08/8956 2003;** www.phs.com.au) operates 15-minute flights over Uluru for A$115 (US$92/£46) per adult. A 30-minute flight includes the Olgas, and costs A$220 (US$176/£88). Kids under 13 usually pay half-price (depending more on their weight than on their age).

By motorbike

Harley-Davidson tours are available as sunrise or sunset rides, laps of the Rock, and other Rock and Kata Tjuta (Olgas) tours with time for the Olgas walks. A blast out to the Rock at sunset with **Uluru Motorcycle Tours (☎ 08/8956 2019)** will set you back A$145 (US$116/£58), which includes a glass of champagne. The guide drives the bike; you sit behind and hang on. Self-ride tours are available, too, at a hefty price. You can rent a Harley for a half-day for around A$365 (US$292/£146).

By shuttle

Uluru Express (☎ 08/8956 2152; www.uluruexpress.com.au) provides a minibus shuttle from Ayers Rock Resort to and from the Rock about every 50 minutes from before sunrise to sundown, and several trips per day to the Olgas. The basic shuttle costs A$35 (US$28/£14) adults, A$20 (US$16/£8) kids (including to see the sunset); a sunrise trip costs A$60 (US$48/£24) adults, A$30 (US$24/£12) kids.

To the Olgas, it costs A$55 (US$44/£22) adults, A$25 (US$20/£10) kids. A three-day pass covering as many trips as you like to both sites costs A$150 (US$120/£60) adults, A$60 (US$48/£24) kids. A combined Uluru and Olgas trip costs A$60 (US$48/£24) adults, A$30 (US$24/£12) kids. All fares are round-trip.

Guided tours

Several tour companies run a range of sunrise and sunset viewings, circumnavigations of the Rock by coach or on foot, guided walks, camel rides, observatory evenings, visits to the Uluru–Kata Tjuta Cultural Centre, and innumerable permutations and combinations thereof.

One of the best is **Discovery Ecotours** (☎ **1800/803 174;** www.discovery ecotours.com.au), which runs a five-hour base tour at sunset. The tour costs A$115 (US$92/£46) adults, A$87 (US$70/£35) children 6 to 15. *Note:* The tour is not suitable for kids under 10. The company runs a four-hour sunset trip to the Olgas for A$84 (US$67/£34) adults, A$62 (US$50/£25) kids.

Another great option is a tour with **Anangu Tours** (☎ **08/8950 3030;** www.anangutours.com.au). It's owned and run by the Rock's Aboriginal owners, and the tours give you an insight into Aboriginal culture. Tours are in the Anangu language and translated by an interpreter. They aren't cheap, but if you're going to spend money on just one tour, this group is a good choice.

The company does a **Kuniya** walk during which you visit the Uluru–Kata Tjuta Cultural Centre and the Mutitjulu water hole at the base of the Rock, learn about bush foods, and see rock paintings, before watching the sunset. It departs daily March through October at 2:30 p.m., November through February at 3:30 p.m. With hotel pickup, the tour costs A$99 (US$80/£40) adults, A$55 (US$44/£22) children.

There's also a four-and-a-half-hour breakfast tour for A$119 (US$95/£48) adults, A$79 (US$63/£32) children. It includes a base tour and demonstrations of bush skills and spear-throwing. A standard tour during the day costs A$75 (US$60/£30) adults, A$49 (US$39/£20) kids. Dot-painting workshops at the Uluru Cultural Centre cost A$79 (US$63/£32) adults, A$56 (US$45/£23) kids.

Staying in style

Not only is **Ayers Rock Resort** *in* the township of Yulara — it *is* the township of Yulara. Located about 30km (19 miles) from the Rock, outside the national park boundary, it's the only place to stay. The resort is an impressive, contemporary complex, built to a high standard, efficiently run, and attractive — all things you can end up paying an arm and a leg for. Because everyone either is a tourist or lives and works here, it has a village atmosphere — with a supermarket; a bank; a post office; a news-dealer; baby-sitting services; a medical center; a beauty salon; several gift, clothing, and souvenir shops; a place to buy beer; and a gas station.

You have a choice of seven places to stay, from hotel rooms and apartments to luxury and basic campsites. In keeping with this village feel, no matter where you stay, even in the campground, you're free to use all the pools, restaurants, and facilities of every hostelry, except the glamorous Sails in the Desert pool, which is reserved for Sails guests.

Money-saving Ayers Rock Resort tips

✔ Prices tend to work out cheaper if you stay for more than one night.

✔ Compare prices both on the Internet and with travel agencies. In my experience, people staying here have a paid wide range of prices for similar packages.

✔ High season is July through November. Book well ahead.

✔ If you like wine, bring some with you, because it's expensive here.

Voyages Hotels & Resorts manages Ayers Rock Resort, Alice Springs Resort, and Kings Canyon Resort. You can book accommodations for all three properties through the central reservations office in Sydney (☎ **1300/139 889** in Australia, or 02/9339 1040; Fax: 02/9332 4555; www. voyages.com.au).

Ayers Rock Campground
$

Instead of red dust you get green lawns at this campground, which has barbecues, a playground, Internet access, a general store, and clean communal bathrooms and kitchen. If you don't want to camp but want to travel cheap, consider the cabins. They're a great value; each has air-conditioning, a TV, a kitchenette with fridge, a double bed, and four bunks. They book up quickly in winter.

Yulara Drive, Yulara, NT 0872. ☎ **08/8956 2055.** *Fax: 08/8956 2260. Rack rates: A$150 (US$120/£60) cabin for up to 6, A$29 (US$23/£12) double tent site, A$34 (US$27/£14) powered motor-home site. AE, DC, MC, V.*

Desert Gardens Hotel
$$$$$

This is the only hotel with views of the Rock (albeit distant ones), from some of the deluxe rooms. The accommodations are not as lavish as Sails in the Desert, but they're comfortable and have elegant furnishings. The **White Gums** restaurant serves a la carte flame grill and buffet meals.

Yulara Drive, Yulara, NT 0872. ☎ **08/8957 7888.** *Fax: 08/8957 7716. Rack rates: A$448–A$520 (US$358–US$416/£179–£208) double, off season A$354–A$412 (US$283–US$330/£142–£165) double. AE, DC, MC, V.*

Emu Walk Apartments
$$$$$

These bright, contemporary apartments have full kitchens, separate bedrooms, and roomy living areas, plus daily maid service. There's no restaurant or pool, but Gecko's Café and the market are close, and you can cool off in the Desert Gardens Hotel pool next door.

Yulara Drive, Yulara, NT 0872. ☎ *08/8957 7888. Fax: 08/8957 7742. Rack rates: High season A$436 (US$349/£175) 1-bedroom apartment, A$540 (US$432/£216) 2-bedroom apartment for 4; off season A$354 (US$283/£142) 1-bedroom apartment, A$448 (US$358/£179) 2-bedroom apartment for 4. AE, DC, MC, V.*

Longitude 131
$$$$$

You can find this African-style luxury safari camp, with perfect views of Uluru, in the sand dunes a mile or two from the main complex. It offers 15 top-class air-conditioned tents, each with a private bathroom and a balcony overlooking the rock. The resort is promoting them as "six star." Whatever — A$9 million (US$7.2 million/£3.6 million) on 15 tents makes them pretty expensive. A central facility, **Dune House,** holds a restaurant (with superb food), bar, library, and shop.

Yulara Drive, Yulara, NT 0872. ☎ *08/8957 7888. Fax: 08/8957 7474. Rack rate: A$1,980 (US$1,584/£792) tent for 2. Rates include walking and bus tours around the area, meals, selected drinks. Minimum 2-night stay. AE, DC, MC, V.*

The Lost Camel
$$$$

This AAA-rated 3½-star hotel opened its doors in late 2002 on the site of the resort's demolished Spinifex Lodge, which once offered the best budget deals outside the campgrounds. It's aimed at young urbanites and is as bright, crisp, and modern as something you might find in Sydney's Darlinghurst. (Don't you just love that urban feel in the red dirt? You could forget you're in the Outback altogether.) The Red Camel offers lush courtyards and a generous swimming pool. Bang goes that budget, though.

Yulara Drive, Yulara, NT 0872. ☎ *08/8957 7888. Fax: 08/8957 7474. Rack rates: High season A$404 (US$323/£162) double, off season A$296 (US$237/£119) double. AE, DC, MC, V.*

Outback Pioneer Hotel and Lodge
$$–$$$$

A happy all-ages crowd congregates at this midrange collection of hotel rooms, budget rooms, shared bunkrooms, and dorms. Standard rooms come with a queen-size bed and a single; these have TVs with pay movies, a fridge, a minibar, and a phone. Some budget rooms have a TV and a fridge; 24 of the budget rooms come with two bunk beds and have private bathrooms. A dozen budget rooms have a double bed and a bunk; these share bathrooms. Each quad bunkroom holds two sets of bunk beds; these are coed and share bathrooms. Children under 16 aren't allowed in bunkrooms unless you book the entire room. Plenty of lounge chairs sit by the pool, and there's also an Internet lounge. The **Bough House Restaurant** offers buffets, and a kiosk sells burger-style fare. What seems like the entire resort gathers nightly at the **Outback Pioneer Barbeque.** This barn with big tables, lots of beer, and live music is the place to join the throngs throwing a kangaroo steak or emu sausage on the cook-it-yourself barbie.

Yulara Drive, Yulara, NT 0872. ☎ *08/8957 7888. Fax: 08/8957 7615. Rack rates: High season A\$404 (US\$323/£162) double, A\$206 (US\$165/£83) budget room with bathroom, A\$180 (US\$144/£72) budget room without bathroom; off season A\$296 (US\$127/£64) double, A\$192 (US\$154/£77) budget room with bathroom, A\$170 (US\$136/£68) budget room without bathroom; bunkroom bed A\$40 (US\$32/£16), dorm bed A\$32 (US\$26/£13), year-round. AE, DC, MC, V.*

Sails in the Desert
\$\$\$\$\$ **Ayers Rock Resort**

This top-of-the-range hotel offers expensive, contemporary-style rooms, many overlooking the pool and six with Jacuzzis (though watch your head on the glass doors leading to the private balcony, if you have one). You can't see the Rock from your room, but most guests are too busy sipping cocktails by the pool to care. The pool area is shaded by white "sails" and surrounded by sun lounges. The lobby art gallery has artists in residence. The **Kuniya** restaurant serves elegant a la carte fine-dining fare with bush tucker ingredients; **Winkiku** is a smart a la carte and buffet venue; and the lively **Rockpool** (open seasonally) serves Thai fare poolside.

Yulara Drive, Yulara, NT 0872. ☎ *08/8957 7888. Fax: 08/8957 7474. Rack rates: High season A\$548–A\$640 (US\$438–US\$512/£219–£256) double, A\$894 (US\$715/£358) suite; off season A\$442–A\$514 (US\$354–US\$411/£178–£206) double, A\$880 (US\$704/£352) suite. AE, DC, MC, V.*

Chapter 19

The Best of the Top End

by Lee Mylne

- -

In This Chapter

▶ Heading up top to Darwin
▶ Discovering "the Wet" and "the Dry"
▶ Experiencing Kakadu National Park

- -

Darwin is the capital of the Northern Territory (NT); it's a frontier town; small, rich, modern, and tropical. Bombed to bits during World War II and comprehensively flattened by Cyclone Tracy on Christmas Eve in 1974, Darwin is a hardy town — and so, often, are the people who call it home. It's a little bit edgy, a little bit wild.

Darwin is a laid-back, casual place where you'll almost never need to dress up. Shorts and sandals are de rigueur, and you'll soon learn that even the fanciest events require *Territory rig,* which means the men must wear long pants and a shirt with a collar (but open-necked and usually with short sleeves; no ties, please).

The population is around 100,000, with 80,000 living in the city and the rest in the surrounding area. In fact, around half the population of the whole Northern Territory lives within a 40km (25-mile) radius of Darwin.

Darwin is the gateway to Kakadu National Park. But allow a couple of days to look around the city, visit its wildlife parks, and maybe do some barramundi fishing. It's also a good place to pick up authentic Aboriginal art and South Sea pearls.

 Stay away from the water. Crocodiles inhabit almost all waterways including Darwin Harbour. You won't outrun them, and the consequences of a face-to-face with a croc don't bear thinking about.

Getting There

Flying is the best way of getting to Darwin from almost anywhere else in Australia. It's at the end of the Stuart Highway, at least two, and probably three, long days' drive from Alice Springs in the south. Train and bus are other options, depending on where you're coming from.

The Northern Territory

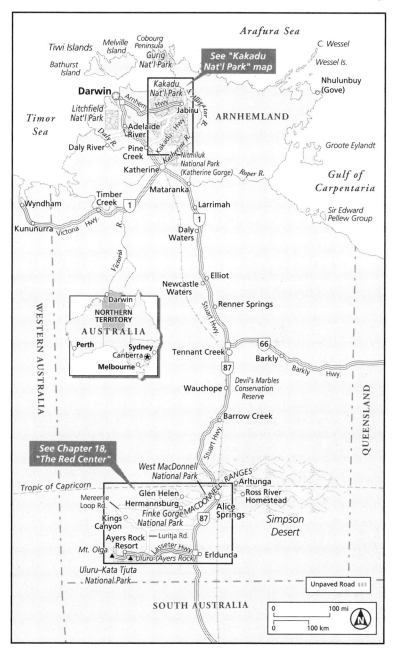

Arafura Sea

Tiwi Islands
Melville Island
Bathurst Island
Cobourg Peninsula
Gurig Nat'l Park

C. Wessel
Wessel Is.

Nhulunbuy (Gove)

See "Kakadu Nat'l Park" map

Darwin
Kakadu Nat'l Park
Jabiru

ARNHEMLAND

Litchfield Nat'l Park

Timor Sea

Adelaide River

Daly River

Pine Creek

Nitmiluk National Park (Katherine Gorge)

Katherine

Groote Eylandt

Roper R.

Gulf of Carpentaria

Mataranka

Timber Creek

Wyndham

1

Larrimah

Sir Edward Pellew Group

Kununurra

Victoria Hwy.

1

Daly Waters

Elliot

Newcastle Waters

Renner Springs

NORTHERN TERRITORY

Darwin

AUSTRALIA

Perth

Sydney
Canberra
Melbourne

Stuart Hwy.

66

Tennant Creek

Barkly

87

Barkly Hwy.

Devil's Marbles Conservation Reserve

Wauchope

Barrow Creek

See Chapter 18, "The Red Center"

West MacDonnell National Park

MACDONNELL RANGES

Arltunga

Ross River Homestead

Glen Helen

Hermannsburg

Finke Gorge National Park

Alice Springs

87

Mereenie Loop Rd.

Tropic of Capricorn

Kings Canyon

Luritja Rd.

Ayers Rock Resort

Lasseter Hwy.

Mt. Olga

Uluru (Ayers Rock)

Erldunda

Uluru–Kata Tjuta National Park

Simpson Desert

SOUTH AUSTRALIA

WESTERN AUSTRALIA

QUEENSLAND

Victoria R.

Daly R.

Katherine R.

Arnhem Hwy.

Alligator R.

Kakadu Hwy.

Unpaved Road

0   100 mi
0   100 km

N

By plane

Qantas (☎ **13 13 13** in Australia; www.qantas.com) serves Darwin daily from most state capitals and from Cairns; flights are direct or connect in Alice Springs. **Virgin Blue** (☎ **13 67 89** in Australia; www.virginblue. com) flies direct to Darwin from Brisbane, Newcastle, and Melbourne, with connections from Sydney, Cairns, Canberra, the Gold Coast, Adelaide, Perth, and Tasmania, as well as other regional centers. **Airnorth** (☎ **1800/627 474** in Australia, or 08/8920 4001; www.airnorth.com.au) flies from Broome and Kununurra in Western Australia. There are also direct flights to Darwin from Asia.

Getting oriented at the airport

Darwin Airport is about 13km (8 miles) from town. It's a small, easily navigated terminal, with ATMs on the ground and first floors. Baggage trolleys are free. A tourist information desk is on the ground floor, and there are showers in both the domestic and international areas of the terminal. The viewing deck on the first floor has smoking areas.

Getting from the airport to your hotel

A cab to the city is around A$25 (US$20/£10). **Darwin Airport Shuttle Services** (☎ **1800/358 945** in the NT, or 08/8981 5066) meets every flight and delivers to any hotel between the airport and city for A$8.50 (US$6.80/£3.40) one-way, A$15 (US$12/£6) round-trip. Children 6 to 13 pay A$4.50 (US$3.60/£1.80), A$8 (US$6.40/£3.20) round-trip. **Avis** (☎ 13 63 33; www.avis.com.au), **Budget** (☎ 1300/362 848; www.budgetrentacar.com), **Europcar** (☎ 1300/13 13 90; www.europcar.com.au), **Hertz** (☎ 13 30 39; www.hertzcom.au), and **Thrifty** (☎ 1300/367 227; www.thrifty.com.au) have airport desks.

By train

Great Southern Railway's *Ghan* (☎ **13 21 47** in Australia; www.trainways.com.au) runs a twice-weekly round-trip between Alice Springs and Darwin, leaving Alice on Mondays and Saturdays, arriving in Darwin about 24 hours later. The return trip leaves Darwin on Wednesdays and Mondays. The adult one-way fare is A$355 (US$284/£142) for a "daynighter" seat, A$705 (US$564/£226) for a sleeper, A$1,095 (US$876/£438) for a first-class sleeper.

By bus

Greyhound Australia (☎ **13 14 99** in Australia; www.greyhound.com.au) makes a daily coach run from Alice Springs. The trip takes around 20 hours, and the fare is A$278 (US$222/£111). Greyhound also has a daily service from Broome via Kununurra and Katherine; this takes around 24 hours and costs A$353 (US$282/£141). Buses also run from Cairns via Townsville and Tennant Creek, a 40-hour trip costing A$517 (US$414/£166).

Orienting Yourself in Darwin

Darwin is a small city. The city heart is the **Smith Street pedestrian mall.** One street over is the **Mitchell Street Tourist Precinct,** with backpacker lodges, cheap eateries, and souvenir stores. Two streets away is the harborfront **Esplanade.** In the **Wharf Precinct,** a short walk from town, are a couple of attractions, a jetty popular with fishermen, and a working dock. **Cullen Bay Marina** is a hub for restaurants, cafes, and expensive boats; it's about a 25-minute walk northwest of town. Northwest of town is **Fannie Bay,** where you'll find the Botanic Gardens, sailing club, golf course, museum and art gallery, and casino.

After you arrive, you can pick up information from **Tourism Top End,** which runs the official visitor center, on Knuckey Street at Mitchell Street, Darwin, NT 0800 (☎ **08/8936 2499;** www.tourismtopend.com.au). It can provide maps, bookings, national park notes, and information on Darwin and other regions throughout the Northern Territory, including Arnhemland, Katherine, and Kakadu and Litchfield national parks. It's open Monday through Friday from 8:30 a.m. to 5:45 p.m., Saturday from 9 a.m. to 2:45 p.m., and Sunday and public holidays from 10 a.m. to 1:45 p.m.

Getting Around Darwin

By bus

Darwinbus (☎ **08/8924 7666**) is the local bus company. Unlimited travel for three hours costs A$2 (US$1.60/£0.80) adults, A$0.50 (US$0.40/£0.20) children. A **Show&Go ticket** gives unlimited bus travel for one day for A$5 (US$4/£2); one week (valid Mon–Sun) for A$15 (US$12/£6). The city terminus is on Harry Chan Place (off Smith Street, near State Square). Get timetables there, or from the Tourism Top End visitor center.

The **Tour Tub bus** (☎ **08/8985 6322**) does a loop of most city attractions and major hotels between 9 a.m. and 4 p.m. daily. Hop on and off as you like all day for A$25 (US$20/£10) adults, A$15 (US$12/£6) children 4 to 12. It departs the Knuckey Street end of Smith Street Mall, opposite Woolworths, every hour.

By taxi

Call **Darwin Radio Taxis** (☎ **13 10 08**). Taxi stands are at the Knuckey Street and Bennett Street ends of Smith Street Mall.

By car

You don't really need a car to get around Darwin, but if you'd like to travel on your own outside the city, for car and four-wheel-drive rentals, call **Avis** (☎ 08/8981 9922), **Budget** (☎ 08/8981 9800), **EuropCar** (☎ 08/8941 0300), **Hertz** (☎ 08/8941 0944), or **Thrifty** (☎ 08/8924 0000).

On foot

Darwin's parks, harbor, and tropical climate make it lovely for strolling during the Dry. The tourist office has a free map showing a Historical Stroll of 17 points of interest around town. The **Esplanade** makes a short and shady saunter, and the 42-hectare (104-acre) **George Brown Darwin Botanic Gardens** on Gardens Road 2km (1¼ miles) from town, has paths through palms, orchids, baobabs, and mangroves. Entry is free. Take bus no. 4 or 6; the buses drop you at the Gardens Road entrance, but you may want to walk to the visitor center (open 8:30 a.m.–4 p.m. daily) near the Geranium Street entrance (open 24 hours) to pick up self-guiding maps to the Aboriginal plant-use trails.

The 5km (3-mile) trail along **Fannie Bay** from the SKYCITY Darwin hotel and casino to the East Point Military Museum is also worth doing. Keep a lookout for wallabies on the east side of the road near the museum.

Secrets of the Seasons

The Top End — which includes the Darwin, Kakadu, and Katherine regions — starts and ends the year with tropical thunderstorms and monsoonal rains. This is called *the Wet.* Many Australians choose not to visit during the Wet (Oct–Mar), when the humidity can be murderous, with afternoon downpours the norm. The upside to this is that Darwin is less crowded with tourists, and the pace is slower. The temperatures can hit nearly 104°F (40°C), and cyclones may hit the coast, with the same savagery and frequency as hurricanes hit Florida. Many people find the buildup to the Wet, in October and November, when clouds gather but don't break, to be the toughest time.

Despite that, many people love traveling in the Wet. Waterfalls become torrents, lightning storms crackle, the flooded land turns vivid green, and there's an eerie beauty to it all. If you plan to travel at this time, keep your plans flexible to account for floods, take it slowly in the heat, and carry lots of drinking water. Sleep in air-conditioned accommodations, and call ahead for tours, because some operators close.

Tropical thunderstorms from October to December can be memorable, as can the rainfalls in January and February. For some, it's not-to-be-missed, so don't discount traveling to the Territory at this time of year.

Towards mid-year (late Apr to Oct), the humidity levels drop and the days are warm and sunny and nights are cool. This is called *the Dry.* Cloudless skies and more comfortable temperatures are usual. This is peak season, so book your hotels and tours in advance.

Staying in Style

Darwin has plenty of overnight options, from cheap hostels to modern hotels with all the amenities. Hotels usually have their lowest rates from November through March during the Wet. April through October is the peak Dry.

The top hotels

Saville Park Suites Darwin
$$$–$$$$ **The Esplanade**

This apartment hotel, a block from Smith Street Mall and overlooking the Esplanade, is comfortable and elegant. Rich, dark cane lobby armchairs and sofas are welcoming and the rooms feature contemporary-style spacious studios and one- and two-bedroom apartments. Apartments have balconies with great views. Premium Harbour View apartments have an eclectic blend of Asian-style teak, mahogany, and wicker furniture. The kitchens feature granite bench tops and stainless steel appliances and the two penthouses include 104cm (40-in.) plasma screens with digital surround sound. A pantry-stocking service does grocery shopping. Premium apartments have CD players and all apartments have dataports.

See map p. 381. 88 The Esplanade, Darwin, NT 0800. ☎ *1300/881 686 in Australia, or 08/8943 4333. Fax: 08/8943 4388.* www.savillesuites.com.au. *Rack rates: A$255–A$280 (US$204–US224/£102–£112) double, A$270 (US$216/£108) studio apartment, A$280–A$315 (US$224–US$252/£112–£126) 1-bedroom apartment, A$485–A$520 (US$388–US$416/£194–£208) 2-bedroom apartment, A$650–A$660 (US$520–US$528/£260–£264) 3-bedroom apartment. Children under 15 stay free in parent's room with existing bedding. AE, DC, MC, V.*

SKYCITY Darwin
$$$–$$$$ **Mindil Beach**

Part of the complex that includes Darwin's casino, this tropical palace has recently had a A$10-million (US$8-million/£4-million) facelift, including the addition of ten five-star Superior Rooms and an infinity-edged lagoon-style swimming pool. The rooms are a cocktail of European-style, contemporary Spanish furniture, and tropical elegance. All have balconies. Superior Rooms feature luxurious spa tubs and marble bathrooms. Full-length glass windows provide views over a private balcony terrace to tropical gardens and Mindil Beach. A free shuttle runs four times a day to and from the city.

See map p. 381. Gilruth Avenue, Mindil Beach, Darwin, NT 0800. ☎ *1800/891 118 in Australia, or 08/8943 8888. Fax: 08/8943 8999.* www.skycitydarwin.com.au. *Rack rates: A$220 (US$176/£88) double, A$330 (US$264/£132) suite; extra person A$50 (US$40/£20). Children under 14 stay free in parent's room with existing bedding. AE, DC, MC, V.*

Travelodge Mirambeena Resort
$$–$$$ City Center

A stone's throw from the city center, this modern hotel complex has two swimming pools and a restaurant, shaded by a sprawling strangler fig tree, giving it a castaway-island feel. Each of the decent-sized rooms has a garden or pool view. Loft apartments with kitchenettes are good for families (if you can handle sharing the compact bathroom with your kids) and sleep up to five. All rooms have broadband Internet access.

See map p. 381. 64 Cavenagh St., Darwin, NT 0800. ☎ 1800/891 100 in Australia, or 08/8946 0111. Fax: 08/8981 5116. www.travelodge.com.au. *Rack rates: A$185–A$245 (US$148–US$196/£74–£98) double, A$275 (US$220/£110) loft apartment for up to 3; extra person A$30 (US$24/£12). Children under 12 stay free in parent's room. AE, DC, MC, V.*

Value Inn
$ City Centre

The cheerful rooms at this neat hotel in the Mitchell Street Tourist Precinct are small but tidy, with colorful modern fittings. Each room is big enough to hold both a queen-size and a single bed, and a writing table. The views aren't much, and there's no phone — but there is a pay phone on each floor. Smith Street Mall and the Esplanade walking path are 2 blocks away. There are vending machines and an iron on each floor, microwave ovens on the first and second floors, and a small swimming pool.

See map p. 381. 50 Mitchell St., Darwin, NT 0800. ☎ 08/8981 4733. Fax: 08/8981 4730. www.valueinn.com.au. *Rack rates: A$69–A$115 (US$55–US$92/£28–£46) double. AE, MC, V.*

Dining Out

For a remote and relatively small town, Darwin has some very good restaurants. The food often has an Asian style to it, adapted by local chefs, and you'll also find "bush tucker" drawing on Aboriginal foods in some more upmarket restaurants.

Cullen Bay Marina, a 25-minute walk or a short cab ride from town, is packed with trendy restaurants and cafes.

If it's Thursday, head to the **Mindil Beach Sunset Market,** where for just a few dollars you can eat your fill from around 60 stalls offering Asian, Greek, Italian, and Aussie food. There's also live music, almost 200 arts-and-crafts stalls, masseurs, tarot card readers, and street performers, or you can just sit and watch the sun set into the sea. The action runs from 5 to 10 p.m. in the Dry (approximately May–Oct). A smaller market of about 50 stalls runs Sunday from 4 to 9 p.m. The markets' season changes from year to year, so if you're visiting Darwin on the seasonal cusp, in April or September, check with your hotel, call ☎ 08/8981 3454, or go to www.mindil.com.au. The beach is about a A$10 (US$8/£4) cab ride from

Darwin

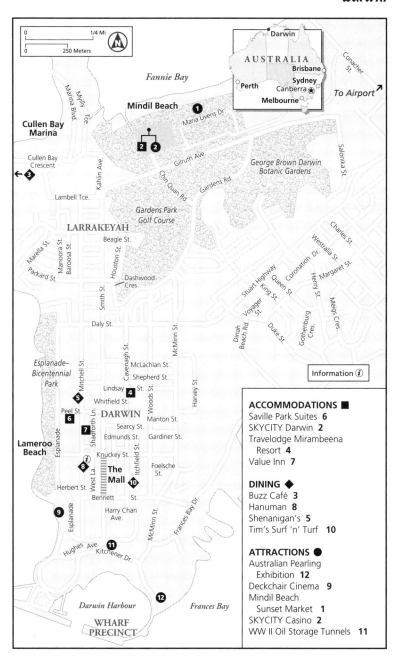

0   1/4 Mi
0   250 Meters

Darwin

AUSTRALIA
Brisbane
Perth   Sydney
      Canberra
      Melbourne

To Airport

Fannie Bay

Mindil Beach **1**

Cullen Bay
Marina

Cullen Bay
Crescent

3

Lambell Tce.

Maria Livens Dr.

Gilruth Ave.

Chin Quan Rd.

Gardens Rd.

George Brown Darwin
Botanic Gardens

Salonika St.

Conacher St.

Kahlin Ave.

Myilly Tce.

Marina Blvd.

*Gardens Park
Golf Course*

LARRAKEYAH

Beagle St.

Marella St.
Manoora St.
Baroosa St.
Packard St.

Houston St.

Dashwood
Cres.

Smith St.

Charles St.
Westralia St.
Margaret St.
Coronation Dr.
Henry St.
Queen St.
King St.
Voyager St.
Stuart Highway
Dinah Beach Rd.
Duke St.
Gothenburg Cres.
Meigs Cres.

Daly St.

McMinn St.

*Esplanade–
Bicentennial
Park*

Cavenagh St.

McLachlan St.

Shepherd St.

Lindsay St. **4**

Whitfield St.

5

Peel St.

6

DARWIN

Searcy St.

Manton St.

7

Edmunds St.

Gardiner St.

*Lameroo
Beach*

Knuckey St.

Foelsche
St.

8

**The
Mall** **10**

Herbert St.

Bennett   St.

9

Harry Chan
Ave.

11

Hughes Ave.

Kitchener Dr.

12

Darwin Harbour

Frances Bay

**WHARF
PRECINCT**

Mitchell St.

Shadforth Ln.

Esplanade

West La.

Litchfield St.

Woods St.

Harvey St.

McMinn St.

Frances Bay Dr.

Information ⓘ

ACCOMMODATIONS ■
Saville Park Suites **6**
SKYCITY Darwin **2**
Travelodge Mirambeena
    Resort **4**
Value Inn **7**

DINING ◆
Buzz Café **3**
Hanuman **8**
Shenanigan's **5**
Tim's Surf 'n' Turf **10**

ATTRACTIONS ●
Australian Pearling
    Exhibition **12**
Deckchair Cinema **9**
Mindil Beach
    Sunset Market **1**
SKYCITY Casino **2**
WW II Oil Storage Tunnels **11**

town, or take bus no. 4. The Tour Tub's last run of the day, at 4 p.m. (see "Getting Around," earlier in this chapter), goes by the markets.

On Saturdays mornings, head to the **Parap Markets,** which transform a small street into a corner of Asia. The focus is on food, with a sprinkling of arts and crafts, and it's a favorite place for locals to have brunch, choosing from the Southeast Asian soups, noodle dishes, and satays, washed down with fresh-squeezed fruit drinks. The stalls cover about a block, on Parap Road in Parap (**☎ 0438/882 373** mobile).

Buzz Café
$$ Cullen Bay   CONTEMPORARY

This smart waterfront cafe is as well known for its "loo with a view" as it is for its terrific food and relaxed atmosphere. The food is flavorsome East-meets-West fare like jungle curry of chicken with snake beans and green peppercorns, and pan-fried barramundi on potato mash in lemon-butter sauce; the lamb shanks are so huge almost no one can finish them. Wash it down with a cocktail, and then check out the men's bathroom! Don't be shy, ladies — everyone does it, just make sure you get a man to take you in there. It nudges out the women's for interest value.

See map p. 381. Marina Boulevard, Cullen Bay. ☎ *08/8941 1141. Reservations recommended May–Oct. Bus: 4 or 6. Main courses: A$17–A$30 (US$14–US$24/£7–£12). AE, DC, MC, V. Open: Mon–Fri noon to 2 a.m., Sat–Sun 10:30 a.m.–2 a.m. (brunch until 11:30 a.m.).*

Hanuman
$$ Darwin   THAI/NONYA/TANDOORI

Black walls and an Eastern atmosphere make this restaurant popular as a business venue by day and as a rendezvous for couples, families, and more business folk by night. You can rely on it for interesting dishes such as roasted duck in a red curry of coconut, litchis, kaffir lime, and sweet basil. There is a separate tandoori menu. Service is prompt and friendly.

See map p. 381. 28 Mitchell St. ☎ *08/8941 3500. Reservations recommended. Main courses: A$20–A$30 (US$16–US$24/£8–£12). AE, DC, MC, V. Open: Mon–Fri noon to 2:30 p.m., daily 6:30–11 p.m.*

Pee Wee's at The Point
$$ East Point   CONTEMPORARY

Surrounded on three sides by forest, this gleaming venue has views of Fannie Bay from just about every table, inside, out on the deck, or on the lawn. The owners — two chefs and a sommelier — offer an extensive wine list and the food emphasizes local produce with an Asian twist. An example: miso-baked, locally caught, crisp-skin, saltwater barramundi fillet on wok-charred choy sum, with kaffir lime and ginger fish cakes and a Thai-style coleslaw with mango chutney. Get there in time to watch the sun set.

Alec Fong Lim Dr., East Point Reserve (4km/2½ miles from town). ☎ *08/8981 6868. Reservations recommended, especially in the Dry (May–Oct). Main courses: A$25–A$46 (US$20–US$37/£10–£19). AE, DC, MC, V. Open: Daily 6 p.m. to late. Closed Dec 26.*

Shenanigan's
$$ Darwin IRISH PUB FARE

Hearty Irish stews and braised beef-and-Guinness pies, washed down with the odd pint of Guinness, get everyone in the mood for eating, talking, and dancing at this convivial bar and restaurant. A friendly mix of solo travelers, families, seniors, and backpackers eat and drink in atmospheric wooden booths, standing up at bar tables, or by the fire. Besides hearty meat dishes, there is lighter stuff including vegetarian dishes and a good smattering of local produce. Try the "Taste of the Territory." There are daily specials and entertainment every night — bands, a quiz, or karaoke.

See map p. 381. 69 Mitchell St. (at Peel Street). ☎ *08/8981 2100. Reservations recommended. Main courses: A$15–A$28 (US$12–US$22/£6–£11). AE, DC, MC, V. Open: Daily 10:30 a.m.–2 a.m.*

Tim's Surf 'n' Turf
$$ Darwin STEAK/SEAFOOD

In this Darwin favorite, diners can choose the air-conditioned open plan dining and bar area, its walls hung with Top End Aboriginal artworks, or head outside to sit under the palms. The lunch menu offers a range of A$10 (US$8/£4) specials, including salads, baguettes and rolls, or hot dishes such as crocodile schnitzels, Malay curries, crumbed barramundi, and salmon fettuccine. At dinner, the menu offers steaks, seafood platters, oysters, and vegetarian dishes, along with a range of salads, chicken, and pasta dishes. The wine list features mostly Australian wines, with around half offered by the glass.

See map p. 381. 10 Litchfield St. ☎ *08/8981 1024. Main courses: A$14–A$21 (US$11–US$17/£5.60–£8.40). AE, DC, MC, V. Open: Mon–Fri noon to 2 p.m., daily for dinner.*

Exploring Darwin

The top attractions

Crocodylus Park
Berrimah

As well as having a small crocodile museum, this park doubles as Darwin's zoo, with exotic species including lions, Bengal tigers, leopards, and monkeys on display. Croc-feeding sessions and free hour-long guided tours run at 10 a.m., noon, and 2 p.m.

815 McMillan's Rd., Berrimah (opposite the police station). ☎ *08/8922 4500.* www.wmi.com.au/crocpark/crocpark.html. *Bus: 5 (Mon–Fri only) from Darwin (drops you about a 5-minute walk from the park entrance, or it's a 15-minute drive from town). Admission: A$25 (US$20/£10) adults, A$20 (US$16/£8) seniors, A$13 (US$10/£5) children 3–15, A$65 (US$52/£26) families. Open: Daily 9 a.m.–5 p.m. Closed Dec 25.*

East Point Military Museum
East Point

Darwin was bombed 64 times during World War II, and 12 ships were sunk in the harbor. The city was an Allied supply base, and many American airmen were based here. The museum is in a World War II gun command post. You can watch a film of the 1942 and 1943 Japanese bombings, and check out the small but fine displays of photos, memorabilia, artillery, armored vehicles, weaponry (old and new), and gun emplacements.

East Point Road, East Point. ☎ *08/8981 9702. Admission: A$10 (US$8/£4) adults, A$9 (US$7.20/£3.60) seniors, A$5 (US$4/£2) children, A$28 (US$22/£11) families. Open: Daily 9:30 a.m.–5 p.m. Closed Good Friday (Fri before Easter) and Dec 25.*

Museum and Art Gallery of the Northern Territory
Bullocky Point

The preserved body of Sweetheart, a 5m (16-ft.) man-eating saltwater croc captured in Kakadu National Park takes pride of place here. This is a great place to learn about Darwin in Australia's modern history, with sections on Aboriginal, Southeast Asian, and Pacific art and culture. A highlight is the Cyclone Tracy gallery, where you can stand in a small, dark room as the sound of the cyclone rages. We find it fascinating to wander in the maritime gallery, which has a pearling lugger and other boats that have sailed into Darwin from Indonesia and other northern parts.

Conacher Street, Bullocky Point. ☎ *08/8999 8264. Take bus no. 4 or 6. Admission: Free. Open: Mon–Fri 9 a.m.–5 p.m., Sat–Sun and public holidays 10 a.m.–5 p.m. Closed Jan 1, Good Friday (Fri before Easter), and December 25–26.*

Territory Wildlife Park
Berry Springs

Take a free shuttle or walk 6km (4 miles) of bush trails to see native wildlife in re-created natural habitats, including monsoon rain forest boardwalks, lagoons with *hides* (shelters for watching birds), a walk-through aviary, a walk-through aquarium housing stingrays and sawfish, and a nocturnal house with marsupials. Bats, birds, spiders, crocs, frill-neck lizards, kangaroos, and other creatures (but not koalas) also make their homes here. A program of talks runs throughout the day. The best is the birds of prey show, at 10 a.m. and 3 p.m. Go first thing to see the animals at their liveliest. It takes about 45 minutes to get here from Darwin.

Cox Peninsula Road, Berry Springs, 61km (38 miles) south of Darwin. ☎ *08/8988 7200.* www.territorywildlifepark.com.au. *Take the Stuart Highway for 50km (31 miles) and turn right onto the Cox Peninsula Road for another 11km (7 miles). Admission: A$20 (US$16/£8) adults, A$10 (US$8/£4) children 5–16, A$55 (US$44/£22) families of 6. Open: Daily 8:30 a.m.–6 p.m. Closed Dec 25.*

More cool things to see and do

✔ **Deckchair Cinema,** Kitchener Drive (☎ 08/8981 0700; www.deckchaircinema.com), is the place to lie back in a canvas chair under the stars and watch Aussie hits, foreign films, and cult classics. Set on the edge of Darwin Harbour (opposite Parliament House on the Esplanade), this outdoor cinema is run by the Darwin Film Society. Take a picnic dinner and get there early to soak up the scene. There are 250 deck chairs as well as about 100 straight-backed seats, and they even supply cushions and insect repellent if you need it. Tickets are A$13 (US$10/£5.20) adults, A$6 (US$4.80/£2.40) children, A$30 (US$24/£12) families of four; double features cost A$20 (US$16/£8) adults, A$9 (US$7.20/£3.60) children, A$45 (US$36/£18) families. The box office and kiosk open at 6:30 p.m. and movies start at 7:30 p.m. daily in the Dry (Apr–Nov), with double features on Friday and Saturday. In the Wet, the movies screen indoors. Entry is by a walkway from the Esplanade, or by car off Kitchener Drive, where there's a parking lot.

✔ The **Australian Pearling Exhibition** (☎ 08/8999 6573), on Kitchener Drive near the Wharf Precinct, has displays following the pearling industry from the days of the lugger and hard-hat diving to modern farming and culture techniques. Tickets cost A$6.60 (US$5.30/£2.65) adults, A$3.30 (US$2.65/£1.30) children, A$17 (US$14/£7) families of five. It's open daily from 10 a.m. to 5 p.m.; closed January 1, Good Friday (Fri before Easter), and December 25 and 26.

✔ The **Australian Aviation Heritage Centre,** 557 Stuart Hwy., Winnellie (☎ 08/8947 2145), has a B-52 bomber on loan from the United States as its most prized exhibit, but also boasts a B-25 Mitchell bomber, Mirage and Sabre jet fighters, and rare Japanese Zero fighter wreckage. Admission is A$11 (US$8.80/£4.40) adults, A$8 (US$6.40/£3.20) seniors and students, A$6 (US$4.80/£2.40) children 6 to 12, A$28 (US$22/£11) families. It's open daily from 9 a.m. to 5 p.m.; closed Good Friday (Fri before Easter) and December 25. Guided tours begin at 10 a.m., 2 p.m., and 4 p.m. It's ten minutes from town; take the no. 5 or 8 bus.

✔ **World War II oil storage tunnels** (☎ 08/8985 6333), on Kitchener Drive, house a collection of black-and-white photographs of the war in Darwin, each lit up in the dark. It's simple, but haunting. Admission is A$5 (US$4/£2) adults, A$3 (US$2.40/£1.20) children. It's open May through September daily from 9 a.m. to 4 p.m., October through April Tuesday through Sunday (and public holidays) from 9 a.m. to 1 p.m.; closed December and February.

Fishing heaven

The Top End is **fishing** heaven. The big prey is barramundi, or *barra,* as the locals call it. Loads of charter boats conduct jaunts of up to ten days in the river and wetland systems around Darwin, Kakadu National Park, and into remote Arnhemland. The **Northern Territory Fishing Office** (☎ **1800/632 225** in Australia, or 08/8985 6333; www.ntfishing office.com.au) is a booking agent for charter boats offering fishing day trips of almost infinite variety — barramundi fishing, extended wetland safaris, reef fishing, light tackle sportfishing, fly-fishing, and estuary fishing. A day's barra fishing on wetlands near Darwin costs around A$300 (US$240/£120) per person; for an extended barra safari, budget about A$1,440 (US$1,152/£576) per person for a three-day trip.

If you simply want to cast a line in Darwin Harbour for trevally, queenfish, and barra, the company will take you out for A$90 (US$72/£36) per adult (A$70/US$56/£28 for kids under 12) for a half-day, or A$165 (US$132/£66) per adult (A$145/US$116/£58 kids under 12) for a full day. It also rents skipper-yourself fishing boats and tackle. Also check out the fishing section at www.travelnt.com for detailed information on fishing tours, guides, and everything you need to know to make your arms ache from reelin' 'em in!

Guided tours

Many companies run guided day-tours of Darwin. A half-day or one-day tour is all you need, just to get your bearings and see the highlights, depending on how much time you're planning to spend in Darwin. Reputable tour company **AAT Kings** (☎ **1300/556 100** in Australia, or 08/8923 6555; www.aatkings.com) runs an afternoon sightseeing tour of Darwin, which takes in the city's historic sites, the Botanic Gardens, East Point Military Museum, Stokes Hill Wharf, and the Museum and Art Gallery of the Northern Territory.

Shopping the Local Stores

The main shopping area in Darwin is the **Smith Street Mall** and the streets surrounding it.

Casuarina Square, a bit out of town, is the largest shopping center in the Territory, with around 180 stores. A free bus from the city to Casuarina Square is available, with hourly pickups from all major hotels. Check with your hotel for details. Most stores are open Monday through Saturday from 9 a.m. to 5 p.m.

Darwin's best buys are Aboriginal art, pearls, opals, and diamonds.

Aboriginal art

⊯ For a good range of Aboriginal artworks and artifacts at reasonable prices, check out **Raintree Aboriginal Fine Arts Gallery,** Shop 5, 20 Knuckey St. (☎ 08/8941 2732).

⊯ For collectors looking for works by internationally sought-after artists, visit the Aboriginal-owned **Aboriginal Fine Arts Gallery,** on the second floor at the corner of Knuckey and Mitchell streets (☎ 08/8981 1315; www.aaia.com.au). Its Web site is a useful guide to art and artists.

⊯ **Maningrida Arts & Culture,** 32 Mitchell St. (☎ 08/8981 4122; www.maningrida.com), features works from one of Australia's largest Aboriginal artist's cooperatives, based in Arnhemland. It concentrates on traditional and contemporary arts, including bark paintings, wooden sculpture, fiber craft, and prints.

⊯ **Karen Brown Gallery,** in N.T. House, 22 Mitchell St. (☎ 08/8981 9985; www.karenbrowngallery.com), is also worth checking out.

South Sea pearls and jewels

The world's best South Sea pearls are farmed in the Top End seas.

⊯ Drool in the window, or go in for a closer look and to buy, at **Paspaley Pearls,** off Smith Street Mall on Bennett Street (☎ 08/8982 5515).

⊯ **The World of Opal,** 52 Mitchell St. (☎ 08/8981 8981), has a re-creation of an opal mine in the showroom.

⊯ If you fancy a pink diamond — the world's rarest — you can get them at **Creative Jewellers,** 27 Smith St. Mall (☎ 08/8941 1233), which buys directly from the mine. It also stocks the champagne diamonds for which Argyle is renowned and other Argyle diamond colors, as well as South Sea pearls and opals.

Crocodile styles

For your own croc-skin fashion statement, head to **di Croco,** in the Paspaley Pearls building in Smith Street Mall (☎ 08/8941 4470). You'll find bags, purses, wallets, card holders, belts, pens, and other accessories, all made from saltwater croc skins farmed locally. And suddenly the jokes about "snapping handbags" may make sense.

Living It Up after Dark

With a young population and lots of backpackers, Darwin's city center, around **Mitchell Street,** is the place to find nightlife. Cover charge for most places is around A$5 (US$4/£2).

The gaming tables at the **SKYCITY Darwin casino,** Gilruth Avenue, Mindil Beach (☎ 08/8943 8888), are in play Sunday through Thursday from noon until 4 a.m., Friday and Saturday until 6 a.m. Slot machines operate 24 hours. The dress code allows neat jeans, shorts, and sneakers, but men's shirts must have a collar.

A good spot to catch Darwin's amazing sunsets is the super-casual **Darwin Sailing Club,** Atkins Drive on Fannie Bay (☎ 08/8981 1700). You have to be signed in by a member, but the staff will happily do that. Dine on affordable meals outdoors while a family of *goannas* (monitor lizards) picks around your feet looking for scraps. The bar is open Sunday through Thursday from 10 a.m. until midnight, Friday and Saturday until 2 a.m.

The cafes and restaurants of **Cullen Bay Marina** are a good place to be day or night, but especially for Dry season sunsets. And if it's Thursday, you should be nowhere except the **Mindil Beach Sunset Market.**

Fast Facts: Darwin

Area Code

The area code for Darwin, and the whole Northern Territory, is **08.** Within the territory, you need to use the code if you're calling outside the immediate area.

American Express

There is an American Express foreign exchange desk inside the Westpac bank branch at 24 Smith St., Darwin.

ATMs

ATMs are widely available in Darwin. You find several in the Smith Street Mall, on Mitchell Street, on Knuckey Street, and at Stokes Hill Wharf.

Currency Exchange

Travelex has two branches in Darwin — in the arrivals hall at the international airport terminal (☎ 08/8945 2966) and in the Smith Street Mall (☎ 08/8981 6182).

Doctors

The Travellers Medical & Vaccination Centre is on level 1 of the Cavanagh Centre, 43 Cavanagh St. (☎ 08/8981 7492). It's open

Monday through Friday 8:30 a.m. to noon and 1:30 to 5 p.m. (after hours by arrangement). Bookings are necessary. The Cavanagh Medical Centre (☎ 08/8981 8566) is at 50 Woods St., and is open Monday through Friday 8 a.m. to 5 p.m., Saturday 9 a.m. to noon (closed Sun).

Emergencies

Dial ☎ **000** for fire, ambulance, or police help. This is a free call from a private or public phone.

Hospitals

The Royal Darwin Hospital (☎ 08/8922 8888), along with Darwin Private Hospital, is located on Rocklands Drive, Tiwi, on the northern side of Darwin.

Information

Tourism Top End runs the visitor center on Knuckey Street (at Mitchell Street), Darwin, NT 0800 (☎ 08/8936 2499; www.tourism topend.com.au). It's the place to go for maps, bookings, national park notes, and information on Darwin and other regions in the Northern Territory, including

Arnhemland, Katherine, and Kakadu and Litchfield national parks. It's open Monday through Friday 8:30 a.m. to 5:45 p.m., Saturday 9 a.m. to 2:45 p.m., and Sunday and holidays 10 a.m. to 1:45 p.m.

Internet Access and Cybercafes

It isn't hard to find an Internet cafe in Darwin. Global Gossip, 44 Mitchell St. (☎ 08/8942 3044; www.globalgossip.com.au), is open Monday through Friday 8 a.m. to midnight, Saturday and Sunday 9 a.m. to midnight. SauS IT, Shop 10, Paspalis Centrepoint Arcade in the Smith Street Mall (☎ 08/8941 0622; www.sausit.com.au), is open Monday through Friday 9 a.m. to 5:30 p.m., Saturday 9:30 a.m. to 3 p.m., Sunday 10 a.m. to 3 p.m. in the Dry (Apr–Oct) and shorter hours during the Wet (Nov–Mar); it's closed on Saturdays from November through January, as well as on Sundays and public holidays for the whole of the Wet. Didjworld Internet, in the Harry Chan Arcade, 60 Smith St. (☎ 08/8981 3510; www.didjworld.com), is open Monday through Saturday 9 a.m. to 10 p.m., Sunday 10 a.m. to 8 p.m.

Maps

The best places to get good local maps are at the visitor center on Knuckey Street (see "Information," earlier) or from the Automobile Association of the Northern Territory (AANT), 79–81 Smith St. (☎ 08/8981 3837; www.aant.com.au). See also the Northern Territory Tourist Commission's site (www.travelnt.com), which has sections designed specifically for those setting out on a driving holiday.

Newspapers/Magazines

The local daily newspaper is the *Northern Territory News,* which on Sundays becomes the *Sunday Territorian.*

Pharmacies

There are several seven-day pharmacies (also called *chemists* in Australia) in the CBD. Bardens Pharmacies in the Woolworths CBD Plaza, Cavanagh Street (☎ 08/8981 8522), is open Monday through Friday 8 a.m. to 8 p.m., Saturday 9 a.m. to 5 p.m., Sunday 9 a.m. to 3 p.m.

Police

Dial ☎ 000 in an emergency, or 13 14 44 for non-urgent police matters (24 hours). For general enquiries, call Darwin Police Station (☎ 08/8999 5511). Police headquarters is on Mitchell Street, Darwin.

Post Office

The General Post Office is at 48 Cavanagh St. (☎ 13 13 18). It's open Monday through Friday 9 a.m. to 5 p.m., Saturday 9 a.m. to 12:30 p.m.

Restrooms

There are public toilets in Austin Lane, 1 block behind the Smith Street Mall, open 24 hours, and on the Esplanade, near the end of Peel Street, just inside the park.

Smoking

In the Northern Territory, you can still smoke in most outdoor areas, including outdoor dining areas, such as a courtyard, footpath, or balcony, depending on the policy of individual restaurateurs. Smoking is also permitted in certain areas of bars, clubs, hotels, roadhouses, and casinos — and in this, the Top End is alone in Australia, where other states ban it. Smoking in most public areas, such as museums, cinemas, and theaters, is restricted or banned.

Weather

Two good Web sites are the Weather Channel (www.weatherchannel.com.au) and the Australian Bureau of Meteorology (www.bom.gov.au).

Heading to Kakadu

Kakadu National Park is an ecological jewel, a sometimes lush, some-times barren natural masterpiece. Kakadu, a World Heritage area, is Australia's largest national park, covering 1.7 million hectares (4.3 mil-lion acres). You won't see it all, but you should still plan to savor as much as you can, spending at least one night in the area.

Cruising the lily-clad wetlands to spot crocodiles, plunging into natural swimming holes, hiking through spear grass and cycads, fishing for bar-ramundi, soaring in a light aircraft over torrential waterfalls during the Wet season, photographing thousands of birds flying over the eerie red sandstone escarpment that juts 200m (650 ft.) above the flood plain, and admiring some of Australia's most superb Aboriginal rock-art sites — these are the things that draw people to Kakadu.

Some 275 species of birds and 75 species of reptiles inhabit the park, making it one of the richest wildlife habitats in the country. But be aware that the vast distances between points of interest, and the sometimes monotonous outback landscape can detract from Kakadu's appeal for some. Wildlife spotting is not the breathtaking equivalent of an African game park, where herds roam the plains — which is why even Australians get excited when they spot a kangaroo in the wild.

Kakadu is derived from **Gagudju,** the group of languages spoken by Aborigines in the northern part of the park, where they and their ances-tors are believed to have lived for 50,000 years. Today, Aborigines manage the park as its owners with the Australian government. This is one of the few places in Australia where some Aborigines stick to a tradi-tional lifestyle of hunting and living off the land. You won't see them, because they keep away from prying eyes, but their culture is on display at a cultural center and at rock-art sites. Kakadu and the vast wilds of Arnhemland to the east are the birthplace of the "X-ray" style of art.

The best time for **wildlife viewing** is the late Dry season, around September and October, when crocs and birds gather around shrinking water holes. Wildlife viewing is not particularly good in the Wet, when birds disperse widely and you may not see a croc at all.

Getting to Kakadu

Follow the Stuart Highway 34km (21 miles) south of Darwin, and turn left onto the Arnhem Highway to the park's northern entrance station. The trip takes two-and-a-half to three hours. If you're coming from the south, turn off the Stuart Highway at Pine Creek onto the Kakadu Highway, and follow the Kakadu Highway for 79km (49 miles) to the park's southern entrance.

Seeing the sights en route to Kakadu

Stop at the **Fogg Dam Conservation Reserve** (☎ **08/8988 8009**), 25km (16 miles) down the Arnhem Highway and 7km (4½ miles) off the highway.

Kakadu National Park

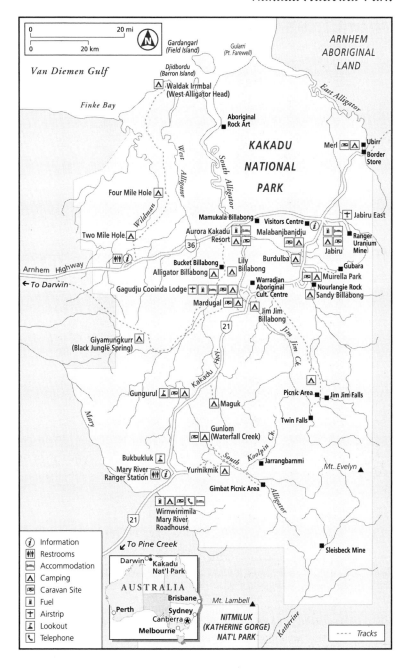

You'll get a close-up look at geese, finches, ibis, brolgas, and other wetland birds from lookouts over ponds of giant lilies, or by walking through monsoon forests to viewing blinds. There are two lookouts on the road and three walks, two of 2.2km (1½ miles) round-trip and one of 3.6km (2¼ miles) round-trip. Entry is free. This is crocodile territory, so don't swim, and keep well away from the water's edge. To take a ranger-guided walk, you must book by calling ☎ 08/8999 4555.

Four kilometers (2½ miles) down the Arnhem Highway at Beatrice Hill, you may want to stop at the **Window on the Wetlands Visitor Centre** (☎ 08/8988 8188), a hilltop center with views across the Adelaide River flood plain and displays and touch-screen information on the wetlands' ecology. It's free and open daily from 8 a.m. to 7 p.m.

Just past Beatrice Hill on the highway at the Adelaide River Bridge (look out for the statue of a grinning croc), **Adelaide River Queen Cruises** (☎ 1800/888 542 in Australia, or 08/8988 8144) runs the original **jumping crocodiles cruise.** From the relative safety of a paddle steamer or a smaller boat, you can watch wild crocodiles leap out of the water for hunks of meat dangled by the boat crew — but don't lean out too far! It's an unabashed tourist trap, with a souvenir shop that sells all things croc, including crocodile toilet seat covers. It may not be very tasteful, but because crocs typically move fast only when they attack, it may be your only chance to witness their immense power and speed. The cruises depart April through October at 9 a.m., 11 a.m., 1:30 p.m., and 3 p.m., and November through March at 9 a.m., 11 a.m., and 3 p.m. (closed Dec 24–25). The cost is from A$30 (US$24/£12) adults, A$20 (US$16/£8) children 5 to 15, depending on which cruise and which vessel. Children aged 4 or under are not permitted on the tour. If you need transport, **Darwin Day Tours** (☎ 08/8924 1111) and **Goanna Eco Tours** (☎ 1800/003 880 in Australia) both run tours from Darwin that include the cruise.

Finding information after you arrive

Both the park entrances — the northern station on the Arnhem Highway used by visitors from Darwin, and the southern station on the Kakadu Highway for visitors from Katherine — hand out free visitor guides with maps. In the Dry, they also issue a timetable of free ranger-guided bushwalks, art-site talks, and slide shows taking place that week. Entry to the park is free.

You can get a lot of information at the **Bowali Visitor Centre** (☎ 08/8938 1120), on the Kakadu Highway, 5km (3 miles) from Jabiru, 100km (62 miles) from the northern entry station, and 131km (81 miles) from the southern entry station. The attractive, environmentally friendly, Outback-style center shows a program of one-hour videos on the park's natural history and Aboriginal culture, stocks maps and park notes, has a library and displays, and has a gift shop and a cafe. Information officers are on hand to help you plan your visit (they provide tour times, costs, and telephone numbers, but do not make bookings). It's open daily from 8 a.m. to 5 p.m. You can also book tours and get information

at **Kakadu Tours and Travel,** Shop 6, Tasman Plaza, Jabiru, NT 0886
(☎ 08/8979 2548).

Before you arrive, you can find information on Kakadu and book tours at
the Tourism Top End visitor information center in Darwin. You can also
contact the rangers at **Kakadu National Park** (☎ 08/8938 1100; www.
environment.gov.au/parks/kakadu).

Where to stay and dine in Kakadu

Rates at Kakadu hotels are usually lowest from November through March
during the Wet. High season is usually from April 1 to late October or early
November, the Dry.

A campground near Jim Jim Falls and Twin Falls has sites for 200 people.
Garnamarr Campground (named for the red-tailed black cockatoo commonly found in Kakadu) doesn't accept reservations, so check at the
Bowali Visitor Centre (☎ 08/8938 1121) before driving there, to see if
it's full. The campground manager collects the fee of A$5.40 (US$4.30/
£2.15) per person per night (cash only). A gate at the campground controls access to Jim Jim and Twin Falls and is locked between 8:30 p.m.
and 6:30 a.m.

Aurora Kakadu
$–$$ **Kakadu**

Green lawns and gardens with wandering peacocks and goannas and
native birds make this a restful haven. This property is near the northern
entrance to the park, which makes it the farthest accommodations from
attractions like Yellow Waters and Nourlangie, but many tour operators
pick up here. Don't dive into the lily-filled lagoon down the back — like
every other waterway in Kakadu, it's home to saltwater crocs! A 3.6km (2-
mile) nature trail winds from the hotel through monsoon forest and past
a billabong. All but the end rooms of these motel-style accommodations
have pitched timber ceilings, and all have views from a balcony or patio.
Budget rooms have two sets of bunks. All rooms are nonsmoking. There
are also 60 unpowered campsites.

*Arnhem Highway, South Alligator (41km/25 miles west of Bowali Visitor Centre),
Kakadu National Park, NT 0886.* ☎ *1800/818 845 in Australia, or 08/8979 0166. Fax:
08/8979 0147.* www.auroraresorts.com.au. *Rack rates: A$157 (US$126/£63)
double, extra person A$42 (US$34/£17); budget rooms A$104 (US$83/£42) for private
use, A$26 (US$21/£10) per person for 4-share by gender; family rooms double rate
plus A$84 (US$67/£34). Children under 14 free when sharing with 2 adults. Free crib.
AE, DC, MC, V.*

Bamurru Plains
$$$$$ **Swim Creek Station**

The best way to get to this safari camp is by light plane, a 20-minute flight
from Darwin. If you drive to this working buffalo station, you'll have to

leave your car at the gate, and a staff member will pick you up. Bamurru Plains, on the edge of the Mary River floodplains, between the coast and the western boundary of Kakadu National Park, is about a three-hour drive from Darwin. The nine luxury tents have timber floors, fine linens on the beds, and high-pressure showers in the individual bathrooms, but no phones or TVs. You can lie in bed and look through the screen walls to the floodplains. Meals are served at the main lodge and feature crocodile, emu, and other local delicacies. Activities include guided walks, river cruises, fishing, four-wheel-drive safaris to view wildlife (*Bamurru* is the Aboriginal name for magpie geese), and day trips to Kakadu and Arnhemland by light plane to see Aboriginal rock art.

Swim Creek Station, Harold Knowles Road (P.O. Box 1020, Humpty Doo, NT 0836). ☎ *1300/790 561 in Australia, or 02/9571 6399.* www.bamurruplains.com. *Rack rates: A$850 (US$340/£170) double, A$425 (US$340/£170) children under 16 sharing with adults, A$765 (US$612/£306) children under 16 sharing a separate room. No children under 12. Minimum 2-night stay. Closed Nov 1–Jan 31. Rates include all meals, drinks, and activities. AE, DC, MC, V.*

Gagudju Crocodile Holiday Inn
$$–$$$ Jabiru

Built in the shape of a giant crocodile, this hotel is either grossly kitsch or fabulously creative, depending on your viewpoint. The owners, the Gagudju Aborigines, have designed the hotel in the form of their spirit ancestor, a croc called Ginga. The building's entrance is the "jaws," the two floors of 110 rooms are in the "belly," the circular parking lot clusters are "eggs," and so on. The best way to make out the shape is from the air. This hotel is one of the best places to stay near Kakdu, with basic but comfortable rooms and a range of amenities including a restaurant, two bars, and a small swimming pool. Guests can use the town's 9-hole golf course, tennis courts, and Olympic-size swimming pool a few blocks away. The lobby doubles as an art gallery selling the works of local Aborigines.

1 Flinders St. (5km/3 miles east of Bowali Visitor Centre), Jabiru, NT 0886. ☎ *1800/007 697 in Australia, 800-465-4329 in the U.S. and Canada, 0800/405060 in the U.K. Fax: 08/8979 2707. Rack rates: A$155–A$250 (US$124–US$200/£62–£100) double. Discounts often available in the Wet. Children under 20 stay free in parent's room with existing bedding. Free crib. AE, DC, MC, V.*

Gagudju Lodge Cooinda
$–$$ Cooinda

These modest but pleasant accommodations are set among tropical gardens at the departure point for Yellow Water Billabong cruises. The simply furnished tile-floor bungalows are big and comfortable, and there are four family rooms, which sleep up to four. Another 24 budget rooms are twin or triple share (4 have double beds) in an air-conditioned corrugated iron portable cabin with shared bathrooms. The lodge is something of a town center, with a general store, gift shop, currency exchange, post office, fuel, and other facilities. Cook up a steak at the do-it-yourself barbecue in the rustic and ultracasual **Barra Bistro and Bar,** or go for the bush tucker meals at lunch or dinner at **Mimi's,** which has a nice ambience. The Barra Bistro serves a buffet breakfast and an all-day snack menu, with live entertainment in the Dry. Dining options can be limited between December and March. Scenic flights take off from the lodge's airstrip, and the Warradjan Aboriginal Cultural Centre is a 15-minute walk away. There are also powered and unpowered campsites.

Kakadu Highway (50km/31 miles south of Bowali Visitor Centre), Jim Jim, NT 0886.
☎ *1800/500 401 in Australia, or 08/8979 0145; 800-835-7742 in the U.S. and Canada; 0800/897 121 in the U.K.; 1800/553 155 in Ireland; 0800/801 111 in New Zealand. Fax: 08/8979 0148.* www.gagudjulodgecooinda.com.au. *48 bungalows, all with shower only; 24 budget rooms, none with bathroom; 80 powered and 300 unpowered campsites. Rack rates: Lodge A$155–A$250 (US$124–US$200/£62–£100) double; budget rooms A$70 (US$56/£28) double, A$31 (US$25/£12) per person for twin or triple share; campsites A$30–A$35 (US$24–US$28/£12–£14) for powered sites, A$15 (US$12/£6) unpowered. Children under 14 stay free in campsites. Bungalow and budget room discounts often available in Wet season. AE, DC, MC, V.*

Exploring Kakadu

The only town of any size near Kakadu is **Jabiru** (pop. 1,455), a mining community where you can find banking facilities and a few shops. The only other real "settlements" are the park's accommodations houses.

Kakadu is a big place — about 200km (124 miles) long by 100km (62 miles) wide — so plan to spend at least a night. Day trips are available from Darwin, but it's too far and too big to see much in a day.

Most major attractions are accessible in a two-wheel-drive vehicle on paved roads, but a four-wheel-drive vehicle allows you to get to more falls, water holes, and campsites.

Car rental companies will not permit you to take two-wheel-drive vehicles on unpaved roads.

You can rent cars at the Gagudju Crocodile Holiday Inn, Flinders Street, Jabiru; otherwise, rent a car in Darwin. If you rent a four-wheel-drive in the Wet season (Nov–Apr), always check floodwater levels on all roads at the **Bowali Visitor Centre** (☎ **08/8938 1120**). The Centre, and attractions such as Nourlangie, Yellow Water Billabong, Jabiru, and Cooinda usually stay above the floodwaters year-round.

The top attractions

Yellow Water Billabong
Cooindah

This lake, 50km (31 miles) south of the Bowali Visitor Centre, is one of Kakadu's biggest attractions and one of the best places to spot saltwater crocs. It's rich with mangroves, Paperbarks, pandanus palms, water lilies, and masses of birds gathering to drink — sea eagles, magpie geese, kites, china-blue kingfishers, and jaçanas (called *Jesus birds,* because they seem to walk on water as they step across the lily pads). Cruises in canopied boats with running commentary depart near Gagudju Lodge, Cooinda, six times a day starting at 6:45 a.m. in the Dry (Apr–Nov) and four times a day starting at 8:30 a.m. in the Wet (Dec–Mar). A 90-minute cruise costs A$43 (US$34/£17) adults, A$22 (US$18/£9) children 2 to 14. A two-hour cruise (available in the Dry only) costs A$50 (US$40/£20) adults, A$25 (US$20/£10) children. Book through Gagudju Lodge Cooinda (☎ **1800/500 401** in Australia).

 In the Wet, when the Billabong floods and joins up with Jim Jim Creek and the South Alligator River, the bird life spreads far and wide over the park and the crocs head upriver to breed, so don't expect wildlife viewing to be spectacular.

Ubirr Rock and Nourlangie Rock

These are two of the best of the 5,000 or so Aboriginal rock art sites throughout the park, though for cultural reasons the traditional owners make only a few accessible to visitors. Some paintings may be 50,000 years old. Nourlangie, 31km (19 miles) southeast of the Bowali Visitor Centre, features "X-ray"-style paintings of animals; a vivid, energetic striped Dreamtime figure of Namarrgon, the "Lightning Man"; and depictions of a man in boots, a rifle, and a sailing ship. You'll also find rock paintings at Nanguluwur, on the other side of Nourlangie Rock.

Ubirr Rock is a steep 250m (820-ft.) climb, for art sites higher up the cliff and for the views of the flood plain. It can be cut off in the Wet, but the views of afternoon lightning storms from the top are breathtaking. Unlike most sites in Kakadu, Ubirr is not open 24 hours — it opens at 8:30 a.m. April through November and at 2 p.m. December through March, and it closes at sunset year-round.

There is a 1.5km (1-mile) trail past Nourlangie's paintings (short trails to the art sites shoot off it), an easy 1.7km (1-mile) trail from the parking lot into Nanguluwur, and a 1km (½-mile) circuit at Ubirr. Access is free.

More cool things to see and do

- ✔ **Guluyambi East Alligator River Cruise** (☎ **1800/089 113** in Australia, or 08/8979 2411) focuses on Aboriginal myths, bush tucker, and hunting techniques. The East Alligator River forms the border between Kakadu and isolated Arnhemland. The cruise lasts about 1 hour and 45 minutes, starting at 9 a.m., 11 a.m., 1 p.m., and 3 p.m. daily May through October. A free shuttle will take you from the Border Store, at Manbiyarra just before the river, to the boat ramp. It costs A$40 (US$32/£16) adults, A$20 (US$16/£8) children 4 to 14.

- ✔ **Kakadu Fishing Tours** (☎ **08/8987 2025** or book through Gagudju Lodge Cooinda) takes you fishing in a 5m (17-ft.) sportfishing boat. Tours depart from Jabiru, 5km (3 miles) east of the Bowali Visitor Centre, and cost A$144 (US$115/£58) per person for five hours, A$260 (US$208/£104) per person for a full day.

✔ **Warradjan Aboriginal Cultural Centre (☎ 08/8979 0145)** at Cooinda, has displays and videos about bush tucker, Dreamtime creation myths, and lifestyles of the local Bininj Aborigines. The building is in the shape of a pig-nose turtle, and has a gift shop selling items like didgeridoos, bark paintings, and baskets woven from pandanus fronds. The center is open daily from 9 a.m. to 5 p.m. Admission is free. A 1km-long (½-mile) trail connects it to Gagudju Lodge Cooinda and the Yellow Water Billabong.

Guided tours

A big range of coach, minibus, and four-wheel-drive tours and camping safaris, usually lasting one, two, or three days, depart from Darwin daily. These are a good idea, because many of Kakadu's geological, ecological, and Aboriginal attractions come to life only with a guide. The best water holes, lookouts, and wildlife-viewing spots change dramatically from month to month — even from day to day.

Reputable companies include **AAT Kings (☎ 1300/556 100** in Australia, or 08/8923 6555; www.aatkings.com), **Odyssey Safaris (☎ 1800/891 190** in Australia, or 08/8984 3504; www.odysaf.com.au), **Sahara Adventures (☎ 1800/806 240** in Australia, or 08/8252 5333; www.sahara adventures.com.au), **Adventure Tours (☎ 1300/654 604** in Australia, or 08/8132 8230; www.adventuretours.com.au), and **Billy Can Tours (☎ 1800/813 484** in Australia, or 08/8947 1877; www.billycan.com.au).

✔ **Far Out Adventures (☎ 0427/152 288** mobile; www.farout.com. au) does tailor-made four-wheel-drive safaris into Kakadu, Katherine, and more Top End regions. Proprietor-guide Mike Keighley will create a private adventure to suit your interests, budget, and time restrictions. Accommodations can range from luxury hotels to "under the stars" in Aussie bush swags. Touring with Mike can involve hiking, fishing, meeting or camping with his Aboriginal mates, canoeing, exploring seldom-seen Aboriginal rock art, taking extras like scenic flights, and swimming under (croc-free) waterfalls. Fun and personal, his trips are accompanied by good wine (sometimes in locations like a bird-filled lagoon at sunset) and "bush gourmet" meals.

✔ **Lord's Kakadu & Arnhemland Safaris (☎ 08/8948 2200;** www. lords-safaris.com) operates charter tours throughout Kakadu. Owner Sab Lord was born on a buffalo station in Kakadu before it was a national park, and has a strong rapport with local Aborigines. His small-group four-wheel-drive tours, which can be tailor-made, visit the Injalak Hill rock-art sites in Arnhemland and the arts center at Oenpelli and have exclusive access to the Minkinj Valley. Day tours to Arnhemland cost A$189 (US$151/£76) adults, A$149 (US$119/£60) children under 14. They operate May to November. The company also runs tours to Jim Jim and Twin Falls.

Kakadu from the air

They may be expensive, but scenic flights over the flood plains and the surprising rain-forest-filled ravines of the escarpment are well worth taking. They're much more interesting in the Wet than in the Dry, because the flood plains spread and Jim Jim Falls and Twin Falls swell from their Dry season trickle to a roaring flood. Viewing it from the air is also the best way to appreciate the clever crocodile shape of the Gagudju Crocodile Holiday Inn. **North Australian Helicopters (☎ 1800/898 977** in Australia, or 08/8972 2444) operates flights from Jabiru from A$170 (US$136/£68) per person, but to see Jim Jim and Twin Falls, you must take the flight costing A$420 (US$336/£168) per person. **Kakadu Air Services (☎ 1800/089 113** in Australia, or 08/8979 2411) runs 30-minute fixed-wing flights from Jabiru and Cooinda for A$110 (US$88/£44) per person, as well as heli flights.

Part VI
The South and West

"The rocks themselves were shaped by the wind, rain, and sea. But Ranger Cody can tell you more about them. He's been out here nearly as long as the rocks have."

In this part . . .

Adelaide, the capital of South Australia, is also a great place to base yourself if you're up for a winery tour. In Chapter 20, we introduce you to a city originally settled by Englishmen who hadn't been transported as convicts, and where early German immigrants planted the first vineyards. South Australia is now world famous for its wines, and the Barossa wine region.

In the far west, you'll find lovely Perth and nearby Fremantle, a lovely harbor town. In Chapter 21, we introduce you to the remote-yet-cosmopolitan city of Perth, and then head out into the best of the West, where you can see thousands of acres of wildflowers in bloom, and enjoy another world-class winery region.

Chapter 20

Adelaide and the Best of South Australia

by Marc Llewellyn

- -

In This Chapter

▶ Getting to Adelaide and South Australia
▶ Eating, sleeping, and sightseeing in Adelaide
▶ Wining and dining in the Barossa
▶ Meeting marsupials on Kangaroo Island

- -

"The City of Churches" as Adelaide, the capital city of South Australia, is affectionately known, is a place of numerous parks and gardens; wide, tree-lined streets; the River Torrens, which runs through its center; sidewalk cafes; colonial architecture; and, of course, churches. It's a pleasant, open city, perfect for strolling or bicycling.

Though the immigrant population has added a cosmopolitan flair to the restaurant scene, Adelaide still has a feeling of old England about it. Adelaide was the only capital settled by English free settlers rather than by convicts, and it attracted more of them after World War II, when Brits flocked here to work in the city's car and appliance factories.

But it was earlier immigrants, from Germany, who gave Adelaide and the surrounding area a romantic twist. Arriving in the 1830s, German immigrants brought winemaking skills and established wineries. Today, more than one-third of all Australian wine — including some of the world's best — comes from areas within about an hour's drive from Adelaide. As a result, Adelaidians are more versed in wine than even the French, regularly comparing vintages and winemaking trends.

Any season is a good time to visit Adelaide, though May through August can be chilly and January and February can be hot.

Getting There

By air

Qantas (☎ **13 13 13** in Australia, or ☎ 800-227-4500 in the U.S. and Canada; www.qantas.com.au) flies to Adelaide from the other major state capitals. Discount carrier **Virgin Blue** (☎ **13 67 89** in Australia, or 07/3295 2296; www.virginblue.com.au) flies from Melbourne, with connections from other state capitals and some major towns. Check the airlines' Web sites for cheap deals.

Adelaide International Airport is 5km (3 miles) west of the city center. Major car rental companies (Avis, Budget, Hertz, and Thrifty) have desks in both the international and domestic terminals.

Connecting the airport with the city is **SkyLink** (☎ **08/8332 0528;** www.coachaust.com.au). One-way tickets cost A$7.50 (US$6/£3) for adults, A$2.50 (US$2/£1) for children each way; round-trip tickets cost A$13 (US$10/£5) for adults. On weekdays, buses leave the terminals at 30-minute intervals from 5:30 a.m. to 9:30 p.m., and on weekends and public holidays hourly (on the half-hour).

By train

The *Overland* train operates four weekly round-trips between Adelaide and Melbourne. It offers a daylight service from Adelaide to Melbourne and an overnight service from Melbourne to Adelaide (trip time: 12 hours). One-way first-class tickets cost A$139 (US$111/£56) for adults, A$98 (US$78/£39) for children; one-way economy-class tickets cost A$89 (US$71/£36) for adults, A$55 (US$44/£22) for children. The train leaves Adelaide every Monday, Wednesday, and Friday, and Melbourne every Tuesday, Thursday, and Saturday.

One of the great trains of Australia, the *Indian Pacific* transports passengers from Sydney to Adelaide (trip time: 28 hours) every Saturday and Wednesday at 2:55 p.m., and from Perth to Adelaide (trip time: 36 hours) on Wednesday and Sunday at 11:55 a.m. The other legendary Australian train is the *Ghan,* which runs from Adelaide to Alice Springs (trip time: 25 hours) and from Alice Springs to Darwin (trip time: 20 hours) on Sunday and Wednesday at 2:20 p.m. Prices vary depending on which of the three classes you travel in on both the *Indian Pacific* and the *Ghan.* Contact **Great Southern Railways** (☎ **13 21 47** in Australia, or 08/8213 4530; www.gsr.com.au) for information.

The **Keswick Interstate Rail Passenger Terminal,** 2km (1¼ miles) west of the city center, is Adelaide's main railway station. The terminal has a small snack bar and a cafe.

South Australia

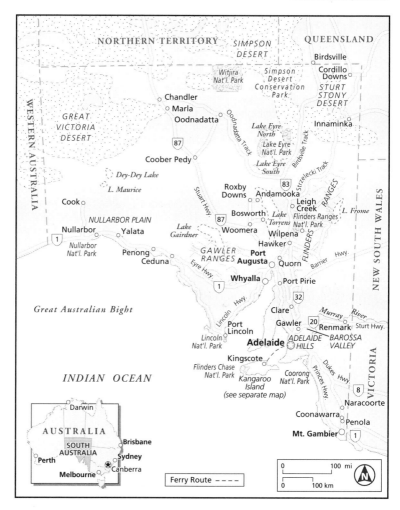

By bus

Greyhound Australia (☎ **13 14 99** in Australia, or 07/4690 9950;
www.greyhound.com.au) runs buses between Adelaide and all other
major cities. The trip from Melbourne takes 11 hours and costs A$60
(US$48/£24); from Sydney, 25 hours and A$138 (US$110/£55); and from
Alice Springs, 21 hours and A$258 (US$206/£103).

Intercity coaches leave and arrive at the **central bus station,** 101
Franklin St. (☎ **08/8415 5533**).

Orienting Yourself in Adelaide

Adelaide is easy to navigate because of its gridlike pattern, planned down to each wide street and airy square by Colonel William Light in 1836. The city's official center is **Victoria Square,** where you'll find the Town Hall. Bisecting the city from south to north is **King William Street.** Streets running perpendicular to King William Street change their names on either side; Franklin Street, for example, changes into Flinders Street.

Of these cross streets, the most interesting are the restaurant strips of **Gouger Street** and **Rundle Street,** the latter running into the pedestrian-only shopping precinct of Rundle Mall. Another is **Hindley Street,** with inexpensive restaurants and nightlife.

On the banks of the River Torrens north of the city center, you'll find the **Riverbank Precinct,** the home of the Festival Centre, the Convention Centre, and the SKYCITY Adelaide casino. Bordering the city center on the north and south are **North Terrace,** which is lined with galleries and museums and leads to the Botanic Gardens, and **South Terrace.**

Introducing the Neighbourhoods

- ✔ **Glenelg:** A trendy beach-side suburb south of the city center.

- ✔ **North Adelaide:** An area crammed with Victorian and Edwardian architecture. The main avenues, O'Connell and Melbourne streets, are lined with restaurants, cafes, and bistros that offer the tastes of a multicultural city.

- ✔ **Port Adelaide:** A seaport, and the historic maritime heart of South Australia. It's home to some of the finest colonial buildings in the state, as well as good pubs and restaurants.

Finding Information after You Arrive

Go to the **South Australia Visitor & Travel Centre,** 18 King William St. (☎ **1300/655 276** in Australia, or 08/8303 2033), for maps, travel advice, and hotel and tour bookings. It's open weekdays from 8:30 a.m. to 5 p.m., weekends from 9 a.m. to 2 p.m. The info booth on Rundle Mall (☎ **08/ 8203 7611**) is open daily from 10 a.m. to 5 p.m.

Getting Around Adelaide

By bus

Adelaide's public bus network covers three zones, and fares are calculated according to the number of zones traveled. The city center is in Zone 1. The fare in Zone 1 is A$2.20 (US$1.75/£88) weekdays from 9 a.m.

to 3 p.m. and A$3.80 (US$3/£1.50) at most other times. Kids travel for half-price. You can buy tickets on board or at kiosks around the city.

You can get timetable and destination information over the phone or in person from the **Passenger Transport Board Information Centre** (☎ 08/ 8210 1000; www.adelaidemetro.com.au), on the corner of Currie and King William streets. It's open Monday through Saturday from 8 a.m. to 6 p.m. and Sunday from 10:30 a.m. to 5:30 p.m.

 The free **CityLoop bus** (no. 99C) operates every 15 minutes (Mon–Thurs 8 a.m.–6 p.m., Fri 8 a.m.–9 p.m., Sat 8 a.m.–5 p.m.) around the city center, along North Terrace, East Terrace, Grenfell Street, Pulteney Street, Wakefield Street, Grote Street, Morphett Street, Light Square, Hindley Street, and West Terrace.

 Another free bus, the **Bee Line** (no. 99B), runs along North Terrace, down King William Street to Victoria Square. Routes are well signposted. All free city buses are wheelchair accessible.

The **Adelaide Explorer bus** (☎ 08/8293 2966; www.adelaideexplorer. com.au; A$30/US$24/£12 adults, A$19/US$15/£7.50 kids 6 to 16, A$70/ US$56/£28 family) stops at 26 sights around town, including Glenelg. You can buy tickets on the bus. The loop takes a leisurely three hours, with commentary, and you can hop on or hop off as you want. The first bus departs from 38 King William St., on the corner of Rundle Mall, at 9 a.m. The company will pick you up from your hotel between 8 a.m. and 8:30 a.m. if you call ahead, and will drop you off at the airport (with your luggage) as part of the fare. Call or e-mail in advance. The last loop starts at 1:30 p.m., ending at 4:30 p.m.

By tram
The **Glenelg Tram** runs between Victoria Square and the beachside suburb of Glenelg from 9 a.m. to 3 p.m. Tickets cost A$3.60 (US$2.90/ £1.45) for adults and A$1.60 (US$1.30/£0.65) for children 5 to 14. The journey takes 29 minutes.

By taxi
The major cab companies are **Yellow Cabs** (☎ 13 22 27 in South Australia), **Suburban** (☎ 08/8211 8888), and **Amalgamated** (☎ 08/ 8223 3333). **Access Cabs** (☎ 1300/360 940 in South Australia) offers wheelchair taxis.

By car
Major car rental companies are **Avis,** 136 N. Terrace (☎ 08/8410 5727); **Budget,** 274 N. Terrace (☎ 08/8223 1400); **Hertz,** 233 Morphett St. (☎ 08/8231 2856); and **Thrifty,** 296 Hindley St. (☎ 08/8211 8788).

The **Royal Automobile Association (RAA) of South Australia,** 41 Hindmarsh Sq. (☎ 13 11 11 in South Australia, or 08/8202 4500; www. raa.net), has maps and provides emergency breakdown services.

Staying in Style

Most of Adelaide's hotels are central, though if you fancy a bit of a sea change then you may want to head over to Glenelg. The journey to the city center by car or tram takes less than 30 minutes, and the airport is less than 10 minutes away. Add to this the sea, the lovely beach, the amusement park, the great shops, the good pub, and the nice accommodations, and you have a perfect place to relax on your holiday.

The **South Australia Visitor & Travel Centre** can supply information on B&Bs and homestays around the state. Satellite and cable TV are rare in South Australian hotels, though some provide pay-per-view movies.

The top hotels

Hilton Adelaide
$$$$ City Centre

The Hilton is a luxurious establishment around the corner from a host of restaurants on Gouger Street and right next to the Adelaide Central Markets. The lobby is polished marble with a cascading fountain and piano music tinkling throughout. Guest rooms are pleasant, with all you might expect from a classy establishment. The hotel has a good swimming pool and a nice health club. In a pinch, we'd probably choose the Hyatt for the extensive views, but there's not much difference between them.

See map p. 407. 233 Victoria Sq., Adelaide, SA 5000. ☎ *1800/222 255 in Australia, or 08/8217 2000. Fax 08/8217 2001.* www.hilton.com. *Parking: A$16 (US$13/£6.50). Rack rates: A$325–A$335 (US$260–US$270/£130–£135) double, A$440 (US$352/£220) executive floor, A$650 (US$520/£260) suite. AE, DC, MC, V.*

Hyatt Regency Adelaide
$$$$ City Centre

The 20-story Hyatt Regency is in the heart of the city, part of the complex that includes the Adelaide Festival Centre, the casino, and the Convention Centre. The property overlooks the River Torrens and nearby parklands, and there are wonderful views from the higher floors. Guests staying in club-level Regency rooms get a good complimentary breakfast and free evening drinks and canapés. Afternoon tea is served in the Atrium Lounge, which gets surprisingly full as the night wears on.

See map p. 407. North Terrace, Adelaide, SA 5000. ☎ *13 12 34 in Australia, 800-233-1234 in the U.S. and Canada, or 08/8231 1234. Fax: 08/8231 1120.* www.hyatt.com. *Parking: A$18 (US$14/£7). Rack rates: A$250–A$300 (US$200–US$240/£100–£120) double, A$300–A$340 (US$240–US$272/£120–£136) Regency Club City View, A$320–A$360 (US$256–US$288/£178–£144) Club River Park View, A$390 (US$312/£156) executive suite, A$840 (US$672/£336) deluxe suite. Ask about packages and weekend discounts. AE, DC, MC, V.*

Hotels, Dining, and Sightseeing in Adelaide

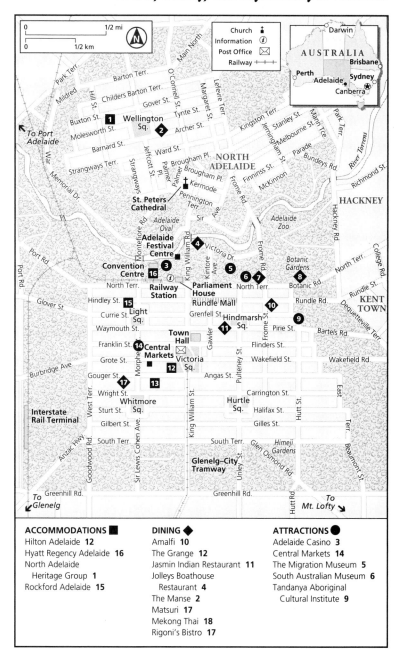

ACCOMMODATIONS ■
Hilton Adelaide **12**
Hyatt Regency Adelaide **16**
North Adelaide
  Heritage Group **1**
Rockford Adelaide **15**

DINING ◆
Amalfi **10**
The Grange **12**
Jasmin Indian Restaurant **11**
Jolleys Boathouse
  Restaurant **4**
The Manse **2**
Matsuri **17**
Mekong Thai **18**
Rigoni's Bistro **17**

ATTRACTIONS ●
Adelaide Casino **3**
Central Markets **14**
The Migration Museum **5**
South Australian Museum **6**
Tandanya Aboriginal
  Cultural Institute **9**

North Adelaide Heritage Group
$$–$$$ North Adelaide

It's worth coming all the way to Adelaide for the experience of staying in one of these out-of-this-world apartments, cottages, or suites. Each of the 21 properties in North Adelaide and Eastwood are fabulous. We recommend the former Friendly Meeting Chapel Hall, once the headquarters of the mouthwatering Albert Lodge No. 6 of the Independent Order of Oddfellows, Manchester Unity Friendly Society, and the Court Huntsman's Pride No. 2478 of the Ancient Order of Foresters Friendly Society. The structure — a small, simple, gabled hall of bluestone rubble trimmed with brick — resembles a small church. Built in 1878, it's stocked with period pieces and antiques and rounded off with a modern, fully stocked kitchen; a huge Jacuzzi; a queen-size bed; and a CD player and TV.

Another standout is the George Lowe Esquire unit. The 19th-century apartment is decorated with antiques and has a four-poster bed, a lounge, and a full kitchen. Guests also have use of nice gardens. Owners Rodney and Regina Twiss have added touches that make you feel at home, from magazines piled everywhere to bacon and eggs in the fridge. The company offers three apartments in the old North Adelaide Fire Station; the ground-floor apartment comes with a full-size, bright red, fire engine. All properties are within walking distance of the main attractions in the area.

See map p. 407. Main office (contact for reservations): 109 Glen Osmond Rd., Eastwood, SA 5063. ☎ *08/8272 1355. Fax: 08/8272 1355.* www.adelaideheritage.com. *Parking: Free. Rack rates: A$155–A$345 (US$124–US$276/£62–£138) double; extra person A$60–A$85 (US$48–US$68/£24–£34). AE, DC, MC, V.*

Stamford Grand Adelaide
$$$$ Glenelg

A classic Adelaide photo is of trams awaiting passengers in front of the Stamford Grand. Right on the beach, this classy hotel offers nice rooms with modern furnishings; many overlook the beach, the ocean, and the pier. This is a nice hotel, with a good indoor pool and health club. The Pier and Pines is a popular bar with youngish crowds most nights; for a mellower scene, Horizons piano bar delivers.

Moseley Square (P.O. Box 600), Glenelg, SA 5045. ☎ *1800/882 777 in Australia, or 08/8376 1222. Fax: 08/8376 1111. Parking: A$10 (US$8/£4). Rack rates: A$322 (US$257/£129) double, A$349–A$546 (US$279–US$437/£140–£219) suite. AE, DC, MC, V.*

Runner-up hotels

Atlantic Tower Motor Inn
$$ Glenelg   This is the place for relatively inexpensive accommodations near the beach. You can't miss the tubular building, with its revolving restaurant on the 12th floor. Rooms are simple but bright, and have park views through large windows. Each has a double bed and a single bed.

Deluxe rooms come with bathrooms rather than just showers. Suites have two rooms and excellent views; the most expensive have Jacuzzis. The gently turning Rock Lobster Cafe upstairs is open for lunch on Thursday, Friday, and Sunday, and dinner every evening. *760 Anzac Hwy., Glenelg, SA 5045.* ☎ *08/8294 1011. Fax: 08/8376 0964.* www.atlantictowermotorinn.com. *Parking: Free. Rack rates: A$ 101 (US$ 80/£40) double, A$ 120 (US$ 96/£48) deluxe double, A$ 170 (US$ 136/£68) suite. AE, DC, MC, V.*

Rockford Adelaide (The Townhouse)

$$ **City Centre** This contemporary boutique hotel is five minutes from the casino and near the nightclub and red-light district. Nice spa rooms are available, each with a large LCD TV. All rooms are spacious, comfortable, and modern; riverside rooms have balconies. Many of the rooms were refurbished in 2007. The hotel has an alfresco dining area, and you can eat some good seafood and char-grilled meats in the restaurant. *See map p. 407. 164 Hindley St., Adelaide, SA 5000.* ☎ *1800/606 562 in Australia, or 08/8211 8255. Fax: 08/8231 1179.* www.rockfordhotels.com.au. *Rack rates: A$ 140 (US$ 112/£66) standard double, A$ 180 (US$ 144/£72) business double, A$ 190 (US$ 152/£76) executive double, A$ 205 (US$ 164/£82) spa suite. Look for specials listed on Web site. AE, DC, MC, V.*

Dining Out

With more than 600 restaurants, pubs, and cafes, Adelaide boasts more dining spots per capita than anywhere else in Australia. Many cluster in areas such as Rundle Street, Gouger Street, and North Adelaide — where you'll find almost every style of cuisine. For cheap noodles, laksas, sushi, and cakes, head to Adelaide's **Central Markets** (☎ **08/8203 7494**), behind the Hilton Adelaide between Gouger and Grote streets.

Glenelg has a host of nice cafes, including **Café Zest,** 2A Sussex St. (☎ **08/8295 3599**), which serves nice baguettes and bagels; and **Café Blu,** Ramada Pier Hotel, 16 Holdfast Promenade (☎ **08/8350 6688**), which has good pizzas.

Amalfi
$$ **City Centre   ITALIAN**

Come here for good cooking at reasonable prices in a lively atmosphere. The pizzas are the best in Adelaide — though a little expensive — and good veal and pasta dishes are always on the menu. Be sure to check out the daily specials, where you can pick a very good fish dish or two.

See map p. 407. 29 Frome St. (just off Rundle Street). ☎ *08/8223 1948. Reservations recommended. Main courses: A$14–A$17 (US$11–US$14/£5.50–£7). AE, DC, MC, V. Open: Mon–Fri 11:30 a.m.–3 p.m. and 5:30–11 p.m. (until midnight Fri), Sat 5:30 p.m. to midnight.*

The Grange
$$$$ City Centre   MODERN AUSTRALIAN

The Grange is an open-plan restaurant specializing in Contemporary food by Adelaide's most influential chef, Cheong Liew. Liew offers an innovative fusion of Western and Asian ingredients, as well as an extensive wine list. The menu begins with a choice of two starters, one of them Liew's signature dish, "the four dances of the sea" — an antipasto of fish, octopus in garlic sauce, prawn sushi, raw cuttlefish, and black noodles. For the next course, you might choose baby abalone, lobster baked with bourbon and lime, or Japanese quail with chestnuts and Chinese mushrooms.

See map p. 407. In the Hilton Adelaide, 233 Victoria Sq. ☎ 08/8217 2000. Reservations required. Main courses: 3-course dinner A$81 (US$65/£38), 4-course dinner A$97 (US$78/£39). AE, DC, MC, V. Open: Tues–Sat 7–10:30 p.m.

Jasmin Indian Restaurant
$$ City Centre   NORTH INDIAN

This is a seriously good Indian restaurant. Prices have crept up as this place has gotten more popular, but this family-run Adelaide institution is still a good value. Indian artifacts and signed cricket bats from visiting Indian teams decorate the walls. The atmosphere is comfortable yet busy, and the service is professional. The special is very hot beef vindaloo, but all the old favorites, such as butter chicken (a big seller), lamb korma, and Malabari beef with coconut cream, ginger, and garlic are here, too. Mop it all up with nan bread, and cool your palate with a side dish of raita. The *suji halwa* (semolina pudding with nuts) is the best we've tasted.

See map p. 407. 31 Hindmarsh Sq. ☎ 08/8223 7837. www.jasmine.com.au. Reservations recommended. Main courses: A$22–A$24 (US$18–US$19/£9–£9.50). AE, DC, MC, V. Open: Thurs–Fri noon to 2:30 p.m., Tues–Sat 5:30–10:30 p.m.

Jolleys Boathouse Restaurant
$$$ City Centre   MODERN AUSTRALIAN

Jolleys is on the banks of the River Torrens, with views of boats, ducks, and black swans. Businesspeople and ladies who lunch, rush for the three outside tables, but if you miss out, the bright, airy interior, with its cream-colored tablecloths and directors' chairs, isn't much of a letdown. You might start with miso-crusted venison with grilled mushroom, mizuna salad, and Japanese mustard sauce. Moving on, you could tuck into the crisp-fried, tea-smoked duck, with Chinese spinach, and blood plum and tamarind sauce. (Ignore the peaceful quacking out on the river if you can.)

See map p. 407. Jolleys Lane. ☎ 08/8223 2891. www.jolleysboathouse.com. Reservations recommended. Main courses: A$25–A$38 (US$20–US$31/£10–£16). AE, DC, MC, V. Open: Sun–Fri noon to 2:30 p.m., Mon–Sat 6–8:30 p.m.

The Manse
$$$ North Adelaide   FRENCH

This restaurant gives some of the best restaurants in Sydney and Melbourne a run for their money. The place is a mix of stately elegance and contemporary cool, with blacks and whites predominating. The food is superb, particularly the duck and rabbit. Try the rabbit cooked three ways — roasted loin, a small rabbit and mushroom pie, and braised rabbit leg in a prune and almanac sauce. The starter of roasted pork belly is a must. Book a table outside in the courtyard on a nice day. On Friday and Saturday evenings, a minimum order of two courses per person applies.

See map p. 407. 142 Tynte St., North Adelaide. ☎ *08/8267 4636.* www.themanse restaurant.com.au. *Reservations recommended. Main courses: A$29–A$38 (US$23–US$31/£12–£16). AE, DC, MC, V. Open: Fri noon to 3 p.m. (set menu), Mon–Sat 6:30–10 p.m.*

Matsuri
$$ City Centre   JAPANESE

We like the atmosphere in this very good restaurant on the Gouger Street restaurant strip. Takaomi Kitamura, world-famous ice sculptor and sushi master, prepares the sushi and sashimi dishes that are some of the best in Australia. Other popular dishes include vegetarian and seafood tempura, *yose nobe* (a hot pot of vegetables, seafood, and chicken), and *chawan mushi* (a steamed custard dish). The service is friendly and considerate.

See map p. 407. 167 Gouger St. ☎ *08/8231 3494. Reservations recommended. Main courses: A$8.60–A$28 (US$6.90–US$22/£3.50–£11). AE, DC, MC, V. Open: Fri noon to 2 p.m., Wed–Mon 5:30–10 p.m.*

Mekong Thai
$ City Centre   THAI/MALAYSIAN/HALAL

Though this place is not much to look at — with simple tables and chairs, some outside in a portico — it has a fiery reputation for good food among in-the-know locals. The food is spicy and authentic, and the portions are filling. It's also a vegetarian's paradise, with at least 16 meat-free mains on the varied menu. It's Adelaide's only halal restaurant.

See map p. 407. 68 Hindley St. ☎ *08/8231 2914. Main courses: A$11–A$13 (US$8.80–US$10/£4.40–£5). AE, DC, MC, V. Open: Daily 5:15–10:30 p.m. or later.*

Rigoni's Bistro
$ City Centre   ITALIAN

On a narrow lane west of King William Street, this Italian trattoria is often packed at lunch and less frantic in the evening. It's big and bright, with high ceilings and russet quarry tiles. A long bar runs through the middle of the dining room; brass plates mark the stools of regular diners. The food is very traditional and quite good. The chalkboard menu often changes, but you're likely to find lasagna, veal in white wine, marinated fish, and various pasta dishes. It's a good place for a nice pasta lunch.

See map p. 407. 27 Leigh St. ☎ *08/8231 5160. Reservations recommended. Main courses: A$28–A$32 (US$22–US$26/£11–£13), pastas A$20–A$25 (US$16–US$20/ £8–£10). AE, DC, MC, V. Open: Mon–Fri noon to 2:30 p.m. and 6:30–10 p.m., Sat 6:30– 10 p.m.*

Exploring Adelaide

Adelaide is a laid-back city. It's not jammed with tourist-oriented attractions like some of the larger state capitals. The best way to enjoy it is to take things nice and easy. Walk beside the River Torrens, ride the tram to the beachside suburb of Glenelg, and spend the evenings sipping wine and sampling some of the country's best alfresco dining.

The top attractions

Adelaide's Central Markets
City Centre

This is the largest produce market in the Southern Hemisphere. It's a fabulous place to shop for vegetables, fruit, meat, fish, and the like, although the markets are worth popping into even if you're not looking for picnic fixings. It's all a bit shabby, but fascinating.

See map p. 407. Behind the Adelaide Hilton Hotel between Gouger and Grote streets. ☎ *08/8203 7494. Admission: Free. Open: Tues 7 a.m.–5:30 p.m., Thurs 9 a.m.–5:30 p.m., Fri 7 a.m.–9 p.m., Sat 7 a.m.–3 p.m.*

Art Gallery of South Australia
City Centre

Adelaide's premier public art gallery has a good range of local and overseas works and a fine Asian ceramics collection. Of particular interest are Charles Hall's *Proclamation of South Australia;* Nicholas Chevalier's painting of the departure of explorers Burke and Wills from Melbourne; several works by Australian painters Sidney Nolan, Albert Tucker, and Arthur Boyd; and some excellent contemporary art. For an introduction, take a free guided tour.

North Terrace. ☎ *08/8207 7000. Admission: Free. Open: Daily 10 a.m.–5 p.m.; guided tours Mon–Fri 11 a.m. and 2 p.m., Sat–Sun 11 a.m. and 3 p.m.*

The Migration Museum
City Centre

This tiny museum, dedicated to immigration and multiculturalism, is one of the most important and fascinating in Australia. With touching personal displays, it tells the story of the immigrants who have helped shape this society, from the boatloads of convicts who came here in 1788 to the ethnic groups who have trickled in over the past two centuries.

See map p. 407. 82 Kintore Ave. ☎ 08/8207 7580. Admission: By donation. Open: Mon–Fri 10 a.m.–5 p.m., Sat–Sun and public holidays 1–5 p.m.

South Australian Museum
City Centre

The star attraction of this museum is the Australian Aboriginal Cultures Gallery. On display is an extensive collection of utensils, spears, tools, bush medicine, food, photographs, and the like. Also in the museum is a sorry-looking collection of stuffed animals (sadly including a few extinct marsupials, such as the Tasmanian tiger), a good collection of Papua New Guinea artifacts, and excellent mineral and butterfly collections. If you're interested in learning more about the exhibits, take a **Behind-the-Scenes Tour.** The tours take place after museum hours and cost A$12 (US$9.60/ £4.80) for adults. Allow two hours to see the museum.

See map p. 407. North Terrace, between State Library and Art Gallery of South Australia. ☎ 08/8207 7500. Admission: Free. Open: Daily 10 a.m.–5 p.m.

Tandanya Aboriginal Cultural Institute
City Centre

This place offers a great opportunity to experience Aboriginal life through Aboriginal eyes. Exhibits change regularly, but all give insight into Aboriginal art and cultural activities. At noon every day there's a didgeridoo performance. A shop sells Aboriginal art and books on Aboriginal culture, and a cafe on the premises serves several bush tucker (native food) items.

See map p. 407. 253 Grenfell St. ☎ 08/8224 3200. www.tandanya.com.au. *Admission: A$4 (US$3.20/£1.60) adults, A$3 (US$2.40/£1.20) children under 14, A$10 (US$8/£4) families. Open: Daily 10 a.m.–5 p.m.*

More cool things to see and do

✔ You'll stroll through the huddles of office workers having picnic lunches on the lawns at the **Botanic Gardens,** North Terrace (☎ 08/8222 9311; admission: free; open: Mon–Fri 8 a.m. to sundown; Sat–Sun 9 a.m. to sundown). Highlights include a broad avenue of Moreton Bay figs, duck ponds, giant water lilies, an Italianate garden, a palm house, and the Bicentennial Conservatory — a glass dome full of rain forest species. You may want to have lunch surrounded by bird song and lush vegetation in the **Botanic Gardens Restaurant** (☎ 08/8223 3526), in the center of the park; it's open daily from 10 a.m. to 5 p.m.

✔ Train buffs will enjoy the **National Railway Museum,** Lipton Street, North Adelaide (☎ 08/8341 1690; admission: A$9/US$7.20/£3.60 adults, A$3.50/US$2.80/£1.40 children, A$20/US$16/£8 families; open: daily 10 a.m.–5 p.m.). This former Port Adelaide railway yard houses Australia's largest and finest collection of locomotive engines and rolling stock. Among the most impressive trains are the gigantic Mountain-class engines and the Tea and Sugar trains that once ran between railway camps in remote parts of the desert. Entrance includes a train ride.

Living It Up after Dark

Adelaide's nightlife ranges from twiddling your thumbs to getting nude lap dances. For adult entertainment (clubs with the word *strip* in the name) head to **Hindley Street,** where you'll find a few pubs (though none that we recommend). For information on gay and lesbian options, pick up the *Adelaide Gay Times.*

Most pubs are open from 11 a.m. to midnight. For all-age pubs, locals point you toward **The Austral,** 205 Rundle St. (☎ **08/8223 4660**); **The Exeter,** 246 Rundle St. (☎ **08/8223 2623**); **The Lion,** at the corner of Melbourne and Jerningham streets (☎ **08/8367 0222**); and **The British Hotel,** 58 Finniss St. (☎ **08/8267 2188**), in North Adelaide, where you can cook your own steak on the courtyard barbecue.

Also popular with visitors and locals alike is the **Earl of Aberdeen,** 316 Pulteney St., at Carrington Street (☎ **08/8223 6433**), a colonial-style pub. **The Port Dock,** 10 Todd St., Port Adelaide (☎ **08/8240 0187**), was licensed as a pub in 1864; it brews four of its own beers and pumps them directly to its three bars with old English beer engines.

Fast Facts: Adelaide

Area Code

Adelaide's area code is **08.**

American Express

The office, Shop 32, Rundle Mall (☎ 1300/ 139 060), is open Monday through Friday 9 a.m. to 5 p.m., Saturday 9 a.m. to noon.

Doctors

The Travellers' Medical & Vaccination Centre, 29 Gilbert Place (☎ 08/8212 7522), offers vaccinations and travel-related medicines.

Emergencies

Call ☎ **000** for an ambulance, the police, or the fire department.

Hospitals

Contact the Royal Adelaide Hospital, North Terrace (☎ 08/8222 4000).

Internet Access

Zone Internet Café, 238 Rundle St. (☎ 08/ 8223 1947), is open daily from 9:30 a.m. to 11 p.m. Talking Cents, 53 Hindley St. (☎ 08/8212 1266), and Café Boulevard, 13 Hindley St. (☎ 08/8231 5734), are other options.

Newspapers/Magazines

The *Advertiser* is the local newspaper.

Pharmacies

Burden Chemists, Shop 11, Southern Cross Arcade, King William Street (☎ 08/8231 4701), is open Monday through Thursday 8 a.m. to 6 p.m., Friday 8 a.m. to 8 p.m., and Saturday 9 a.m. to 1 p.m.

Post Offices

The General Post Office (GPO), 141 King William St., Adelaide, SA 5000 (☎ 08/8216 2222), is open Monday through Friday 8 a.m. to 6 p.m., Saturday 8:30 a.m. to noon. General delivery mail can be collected Monday through Friday 8 a.m. to 5 p.m., Saturday 8:30 a.m. to noon.

Restrooms

Public restrooms are at Central Market Arcade, between Grote and Gouger streets, in Hindmarsh and Victoria squares, and at James Place (off Rundle Mall).

Wining and Dining in the Barossa

More than a quarter of Australia's wines, and many of its top labels, originate in the Barossa and Eden valleys — known collectively as the **Barossa.** Beginning just 45km (28 miles) northeast of Adelaide and easily accessible, the area has had an enormous influence on the city's culture.

Adelaidians of all socioeconomic levels partake in more wine talk than the French. German settlers from Silesia, who came to escape religious persecution, first settled the area. They brought their culture, their food, and their vines. Today, there are over 50 wineries in an area that retains its German flavor.

The focal points of the area are **Angaston,** farthest from Adelaide; **Nuriootpa;** and **Tanunda,** the nearest town to the city. Each has interesting architecture, crafts and antiques shops, and specialty food outlets. If you're adventurous, you may want to rent a bike in Adelaide, take it on the train to **Gawler,** and cycle through the Barossa. Other options are exploring the area by hot air balloon, motorcycle, or limousine.

The best times to visit the South Australian wine regions are in the spring (Sept–Oct), when it's not too hot and there are plenty of flowering trees and shrubs, and in the fall (Apr–May), when the leaves turn red. The main wine harvest is in late summer and early autumn (Feb–Apr). The least crowded time is winter (June–Aug). Hotel prices can be more expensive on the weekend.

Getting there

By car

Having your own wheels is by far the most flexible way of getting to the Barossa. It takes around 75 minutes to drive from Adelaide to Nuriootpa via the Sturt Highway. From Adelaide to Angaston, it's around 90 minutes via Springton.

By bus

Public buses run infrequently to the major centers from Adelaide. There are no buses between wineries.

Various companies run limited sightseeing tours by coach or mini bus. **Adelaide Sightseeing** (☎ 08/8413 6199; www.adelaidesightseeing. com.au) offers a day trip from Adelaide, stopping off at three wineries. It costs A$105 (US$84/£42) for adults and A$55 (US$44/£22) for children, including lunch.

Getting information in the Barossa

The **Barossa Wine and Visitor Information Centre,** 66–68 Murray St., Tanunda, SA 5352 (☎ 08/8563 0600; www.barossa-region.org), is open Monday through Friday from 9 a.m. to 5 p.m., and weekends from 10 a.m. to 4 p.m. Also check out www.barossa.com.

Touring the wineries

With some 50 wineries offering free cellar-door tastings, daily tours charting the winemaking process, or both, you won't be stuck for places to visit. All wineries are well signposted. Here are a few of our favorite places, but don't be shy about stopping whenever you come across a winery that tickles your fancy.

- **Orlando and Jacobs Creek,** Barossa Highway, Rowland Flat (☎ 08/8521 3000; open: daily 10 a.m.–5 p.m.), was established in 1847. It's the home of many award-winning brands, including Jacobs Creek, now sold worldwide. Premium wines include the Lawson Shiraz and the Jacaranda Ridge Cabernet; new vintages of either will set you back at least A$45 (US$36/£18) a bottle. The winery has a restaurant and a picnic area with barbecues.

- **Penfolds,** Nuriootpa (☎ 08/8568 9290; open: Mon–Fri 10 a.m.– 5 p.m., Sat–Sun 11 a.m.–5 p.m.), is Australia's biggest wine producer. It churns out some 23 million liters (5.8 million gallons) from this winery every year. The winery makes the famous Penfolds Grange, arguably Australia's greatest wine.

- **Saltram Wines,** Nuriootpa Road, Angaston (☎ 08/8564 3355; www. saltramwines.com.au), produces some nice wines and also has a great eatery, Salter's Kitchen, which is open for lunch daily and for dinner on Friday and Saturday evenings. When you taste the wine here, compliment the experience with a tasting platter of good local meats, wild olives, and dips. It's open Monday to Friday from 9 a.m. to 5 p.m., and weekends and holidays from 10 a.m. to 5 p.m.

- **Seppelts,** Seppeltsfield (☎ 08/8568 6200; open: daily 10:30 a.m.– 5 p.m.), is located in a National Trust–listed property founded in 1857 by Joseph Seppelt, an immigrant from Silesia. On a nearby slope, check out the family's Romanesque mausoleum, skirted by planted roadside palms, built during the 1930s recession to keep winery

The Barossa

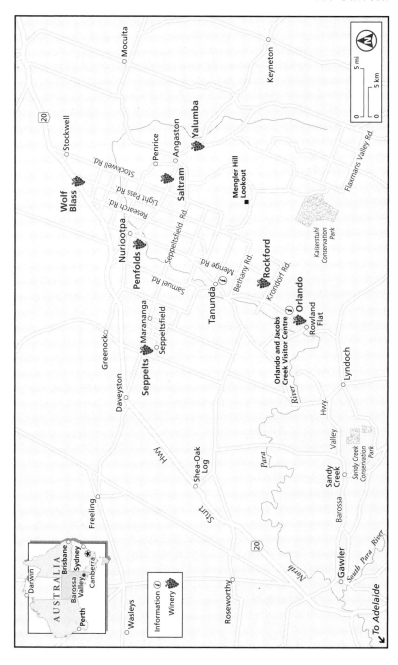

workers employed. Tours run daily at 11:30 a.m., 1:30 p.m., and 3:30 p.m.; the cost is A$10 (US$8/£4) for adults (children 5–16 free).

✔ **Yalumba,** Eden Valley Road, Angaston (☎ **08/8561 3200;** www.yalumba.com.au; open: Mon–Fri 8:30 a.m.–5 p.m., Sat 10 a.m.–5 p.m., Sun noon to 5 p.m.), came into being in 1849, making it the oldest family-owned winemaking business in Australia. It's also huge. Keep an eye out for the sad-looking Himalayan bear in the corner of the large tasting room; its sad look can be attributed to a run-in with a hunting rifle, and it's been Yalumba's advertising symbol ever since.

Staying in style

Plenty of standard motels and lots of interesting B&Bs are located throughout the Barossa, some with rooms for as little as A$60 (US$48/£24). Weekends often find lodgings sold out and prices higher than on weekdays.

Collingrove Homestead
$$$ **Angaston**

In our opinion, Collingrove is the best country-house experience not just in the Barossa but in Australia. Built in 1856, it was originally the home of John Howard Angas, one of the initial settlers of South Australia. Additions were made as Angas's sheep business prospered. The hallway is festooned with spears, artillery shells, rifles, oil portraits, and the mounted heads of stags and tigers. English oak paneling and creaky floorboards add a certain nuance, and the cedar kitchen, library, dining room, and other places burst with antiques and knickknacks. What the individually decorated guest rooms lack in modern amenities (phones and TVs) they make up for in charm. The modern communal Jacuzzi is in the old stables; there's also a flagstone-floored tennis court.

Eden Valley Road, Angaston, SA 5353. ☎ *08/8564 2061. Fax: 08/8564 3600.* www.collingrovehomestead.com.au. *Rack rates: A$220 (US$176/£88) luxury double, A$250 (US$200/£100) deluxe double. Rates include breakfast. AE, DC, MC, V.*

Marble Lodge
$$$$ **Angaston**

Wake up and smell the roses — there are plenty in the gardens surrounding this historic property. Away from the main house is a lodge made of local marble that holds two suites. The larger has two rooms and an open fireplace. Both have access to the shared Jacuzzi (in 2007, this was temporarily closed because of the drought) and are tastefully furnished in antiques. Fresh fruit, homemade biscuits, and chocolates are always available in the room, and it's a five-minute walk to local restaurants. A double room in the homestead, with shared bathroom, is sometimes available.

21 Dean St., Angaston, SA 5351. ☎ *08/8564 2478. Fax: 08/8564 2941.* www.marblelodge.com.au. *Rack rates: A$250 (US$200/£100) double. Rates include breakfast. MC, V.*

Blending your own wine at Penfolds

The Penfolds cellar door, in the heart of the Barossa, recently opened the country's first Make Your Own Blend tour.

When we took the tour, each of us was given a bottle of Grenache, Shiraz, and Mourvedre to play with. According to Jenny, our wine instructor, the Grenache adds a fruity character to a blend, the Shiraz gives depth and weight across the mid-palate, and the Mourvedre grapes add complexity.

Blending the three varieties will, with any luck, result in a medium-bodied, well-balanced wine with personality and structure. Or, most likely, it could end up being swamped and overbalanced. But still, because we were given such good ingredients, it should be drinkable.

Jenny gave us the rundown of the previous year's blend, so we could get an idea of a successful mix of each grape variety, and then warned us that each year's vintage is crafted differently. One of the beakers in front of us contained a sample of the 2006 vintage. We sniffed and tasted, and were then set loose.

Pouring from each bottle, we measured the amounts from each grape variety with care. We noted our percentages on the score sheet and tasted the result. It was nothing like the vintage we were trying to emulate, but it tasted okay, so we gulped down the lot.

Our second attempt was more successful, and we ended up drinking that, too. By then, we were all pretty animated and, like mad scientists, we cackled to ourselves and churned out greater quantities to share around.

By the third attempt, everything tasted good. One of us drank straight from her test tube, having run out of glasses, and the others joined in with glee.

In the end, our score sheets looked as messy as an artist's palette, and our once-white coats were splattered with red. Perhaps winemaking really is art rather than science.

We decanted our favorite blend into a half-size wine bottle and, once capped, were given a Penfolds label that bears our names and the title "assistant winemaker."

The Penfolds Make Your Own Blend tour costs A$55 (US$44/£22) per person. Bookings, made at least 24 hours in advance, are essential. Call ☎ **08/8568 9408** or visit www.penfolds.com.au for details.

Peppers the Louise
$$$$ **Marananga**

This luxury vineyard retreat is very classy. The rooms are large and luxurious, with all the latest gadgets, including a plasma TV, and a king-size bed featuring the very best linens and pillows. We loved the outdoor shower, in our own private courtyard, created from hand-carved limestone blocks. The hotel has a small swimming pool and a spa and sauna. The restaurant is a credit to executive chef Mark McNamara. Try the

Appellation Signature Tasting Menu, with wine matched to each of the nine courses. As part of an inspired cross-promotion, Peppers will create a special course to be paired with the wine you created at the Penfolds Make Your Own Blend tour. Our dish was roasted breast of local pigeon with mushrooms and barley, served with a reduction of peppered juniper.

Seppeltsfield Road, Marananga. ☎ *08/8562 2722.* www.thelouise.com.au. *Rack rates: Packages range from A$381 to A$651 (US$305–US$521/£153–£261), depending on room type, additional meals, and so on; check the Web site for more info. Closed July. AE, MC, V.*

Dining in the Barossa

The Barossa prides itself on its cuisine as well as its wine, so you'll find plenty of places of note, many serving traditional German food:

✔ A hot spot for lunch or dinner is **Vintner's Bar & Grill,** Nuriootpa Road, Angaston (☎ **08/8564 2488**); the wine list is six pages long! Main courses cost A$22 to A$27 (US$18–US$22/£9–£11). It's open daily for lunch and Monday through Saturday for dinner.

✔ Another choice is **Salters,** Satram Winery, Nuriootpa Road, Angaston (☎ **08/8564 3344**), where local produce is the specialty, with main courses such as slow-roasted baby pork, milk-fed lamb, and crisp-based pizzas. Main courses are A$20 to A$26 (US$16–US$21/£8–£11). It's open daily for lunch and Wednesday through Saturday for dinner from 6 p.m.

✔ Perhaps the best German-style bakery in the valley is the **Lyndoch Bakery,** on the Barossa Highway, Lyndoch (☎ **08/8524 4422**).

✔ In Angaston, stop off at **The Seasons of the Valley,** 6 Washington St. (☎ **08/8564 3688**). The 1840 homestead house has cottage gardens and a veranda, as well as delicious meals for A$15 to A$18 (US$12–US$14/£6–£7). It's open daily 10 a.m. to 5 p.m.

Hahndorf: Just Like the Old Country

This historic German-style village is one of South Australia's most popular tourist destinations. Lutherans fleeing religious persecution in eastern Prussia founded the town, 29km (18 miles) southeast of Adelaide, in 1839. They brought their winemaking skills, foods, and architectural inheritance, and put it all together. Hahndorf still resembles a small German town and is included on the World Heritage List as a Historical German Settlement. Walking around, you'll see **St. Paul's Lutheran Church,** erected in 1890. **The Wool Factory, L'Unique Fine Arts & Craft,** and **Bamfurlong Fine Crafts** are worth checking out and are within walking distance of Main Street.

Staying in style

The Hahndorf Resort

This large resort has a variety of accommodations as well as a number of trailer and tent sites. Lodgings include air-conditioned cabins, and motel-style rooms with queen-size beds and showers. The chalets look as if they're straight out of Bavaria; each can accommodate two to five people in one or two bedrooms. Each has a full kitchen and an attached bathroom with shower; some of them overlook a small lake. The larger spa chalets come with Jacuzzis. An on-site animal sanctuary has a few emus, kangaroos, and horses. The resort has an outdoor pool, too.

145A Main St., Hahndorf, SA 5245. ☎ *08/8388 7921. Fax: 08/8388 7282.* www.hahndorf resort.com.au. *Rack rates: A$68 (US$46/£23) cabin, A$99 (US$80/£40) motel room, A$125–A$159 (US$100–US$127/£50–£64) chalet; extra adult A$12 (US$9.20/£4.60), extra child A$5.50 (US$4.40/£2.20). AE, DC, MC, V.*

Dining out

If you want a treat, head to the **Bridgewater Mill,** Mt. Barker Road, Bridgewater (☎ **08/8339 3422;** www.bridgewatermill.com.au). In an impressive 1860s stone building with a terrace near a water wheel, this place serves some of the best-regarded food in the country. Try duck with braised cherries. Main courses cost A$33 (US$26/£13); a three-course menu, served Sunday only, is A$85 (US$68/£34). It's open Thursday through Monday for lunch.

Meeting Marsupials on Kangaroo Island

You won't find anyplace better than Kangaroo Island to see Australian marsupials in the wild. Spend a few days with the right guide and you can walk along a beach past a colony of sea lions; spot hundreds of New Zealand fur seals playing; creep through the bush on the trail of wallabies or kangaroos; spot sea eagles, black swans, sacred ibis, pelicans, little penguins, the rare glossy black cockatoo, and other birds; come across goannas; pick out bunches of koalas hanging sleepily in the trees above your head; and, if you're lucky, see platypus, echidna, bandicoots, and reclusive pygmy possums — the list goes on.

The secrets to Kangaroo Island's success are its perfect conditions, the most important of which is the fact that there are no introduced foxes or rabbits to prey on the native inhabitants or their environment. The island was also never colonized by the *dingo* (Australia's "native" dog), which is believed to have been introduced from Asia some 4,000 years ago. Today, about one-third of the island is national park.

Although the animals are what most people come to see, no one goes away without being impressed by the scenery. Kangaroo Island has low mallee scrubland, dense eucalyptus forests, rugged coastal scenery,

Kangaroo Island

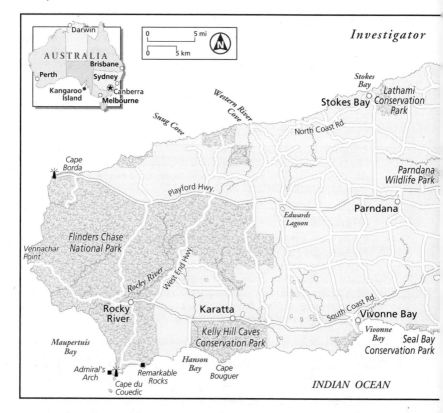

beaches, caves, lagoons, and blackwater swamps. The effect of 150 years of European colonization has taken its toll. In South Australia as a whole, some 27 mammal, 5 bird, 1 reptile, and 30 plant species have become extinct since British explorer Matthew Flinders arrived in 1802.

The best time to visit Kangaroo Island is between November and March (though you'll have difficulty finding accommodations over the Christmas holiday period). July and August tend to be rainy, and winter can be cold (though often milder than on the mainland around Adelaide).

 Many companies offer day trips to Kangaroo Island from Adelaide, but we recommend tailoring your holiday to spend at least two days here — three or even five days would be better. The island really does have a lot to see, and you won't regret spending the extra time.

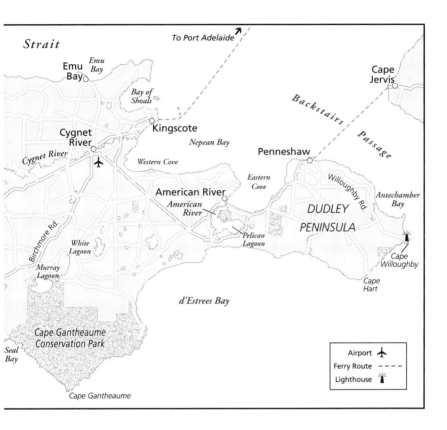

Getting there

By air

Regional Express (☎ **13 17 13** in Australia, or 08/8553 2938; www.regionalexpress.com.au) flies to Kangaroo Island. Flights leave from the General Aviation Terminal, Kel Barclay Avenue, Adelaide. The General Aviation Terminal is about a 20-minute walk (or shorter taxi ride) from the main airport terminal. The flight from Adelaide to Kangaroo Island usually takes about 25 minutes.

Air South (☎ **08/8234 4988;** www.airsouth.com.au) also flies to Kingscote from Adelaide's General Aviation Terminal, four times daily.

By ferry

If you prefer to go by sea, **Kangaroo Island SeaLink** (☎ **13 13 01** in Australia, or 08/8202 8688; www.sealink.com.au) operates two ferries three times daily at 9 a.m., 10 a.m., and 6 p.m. (and on the hour from

9 a.m. to 7 p.m. in peak periods) from Cape Jervis on the tip of the Fleurieu Peninsula on the mainland to Penneshaw on Kangaroo Island.

The trip takes 40 minutes and costs A$80 (US$64/£32) round-trip for adults, A$44 (US$35/£18) for children 3 to 14, and A$162 (US$129/£65) for cars. Connecting bus service from Adelaide to Cape Jervis costs an extra A$36 (US$29/£15) for adults, A$18 (US$14/£7) for children, round-trip. Off-peak prices may be cheaper; check when booking. Count on three hours for the trip from Adelaide if you take the bus. Reservations are essential.

SeaLink also runs a range of island tours, including the two-day, one-night KI Coast to Coast, which costs from A$389 (US$311/£156) per person sharing a double room. SeaLink also offers a wide range of accommodations, day tours, and adventure activities and offers Adelaide hotel pickups for selected tours.

Visitor information

Tourism Kangaroo Island, Gateway Information Centre, Howard Drive (P.O. Box 336), Penneshaw, Kangaroo Island, SA 5222 (☎ **08/8553 1185;** www.tourkangarooisland.com.au), has plenty of maps and can assist with accommodations and tour information.

For more information on the island's national parks, contact **National Parks and Wildlife South Australia** (NP&WSA), 39 Dauncey St., P.O. Box 39, Kingscote, SA 5223 (☎ **08/8553 2381**). It's open Monday through Friday from 9 a.m. to 5 p.m.

Island layout

Kangaroo Island is 156km (97 miles) long and 57km (35 miles) wide at its widest point. The distance across the narrowest point is 2km (1¼ miles). Approximately 3,900 people live there. More than half live on the northeast coast in the three main towns: **Kingscote** (pop. 1,800), **Penneshaw** (pop. 250), and **American River** (pop. 200).

- ✔ **American River:** Popular with fishermen, American River is 37km (23 miles) from Kingscote. It lacks a beach but offers black swans on Pelican Lagoon. Wild wallabies abound, and egrets, magpies, and cockatoos offer early wake-up calls.

- ✔ **Kingscote:** On the shores of the beautiful Nepean Bay, Kingscote is the commercial and business hub of the island. You'll find banks, ATMs, shops, and a boat-studded harbor.

- ✔ **Penneshaw:** On the northeast coast of the island, the pretty seaside village of Penneshaw acts as the port for SeaLink ferries. Plenty of accommodations options are here.

- ✔ **Parndana:** Developed by soldier settlers after World War II, Parndana is a rural service center 25 minutes by car from Seal Bay and Stokes Bay. It's just around the corner from Parndana Wildlife Park, which has more than 50 aviaries with collections of native and other birds, some of them rare and protected.

Getting around Kangaroo Island

Kangaroo Island is a big place, and apart from twice-daily SeaLink bus service, which connects Kingscote, Penneshaw, and American River, there is no public transport. Although you can get a lot out of the tours, we recommend renting a car.

By shuttle bus

The **Airport Shuttle Service (☎ 1800/750 850** in Australia) meets all flights to Kangaroo Island and takes passengers to Kingscote, Emu Bay, and American River. Book the return trip from your accommodations to the airport in advance.

By car

Major roads between Penneshaw, American River, Kingscote, and Parndana are paved, as are the road to Seal Bay and all major roads within Flinders Chase National Park. Most other roads are made of iron-stone gravel, and can be slippery if you take the corners too quickly. All roads are accessible by two-wheel-drive vehicles. If you're in a rental car from the mainland, make sure your policy allows you to drive on Kangaroo Island. Avoid driving at night — animals are all about.

Car rental agencies on the island include **Budget (☎ 08/8553 3133;** www.budgetki.com), **Hertz & Kangaroo Island Rental Cars (☎ 1800/ 088 296** in Australia, or 08/8553 2390; www.hertz.com.au), and **Wheels over Kangaroo Island (☎ 1800/750 850** in Australia, or 08/8553 3030; www.kangarooislandholidays.com). You can pick up cars at the airport or ferry terminals.

Organized tours

If you want to keep expenses down, you can't go wrong with one of the tours organized by **Kangaroo Island Ferry Connections (☎ 08/8202 8688;** www.sealink.com.au). The most popular includes afternoon pickup from the main bus station in Adelaide, coach and ferry to the island, a penguin tour that evening, and dorm accommodations (you can upgrade to a double room or a hotel). The next day involves ten hours of touring, taking in most of the main attractions. That evening you return to Adelaide. The tour costs A$302 (US$242/£121).

If you make your own way to the island, you can join one of several day tours, departing Penneshaw or American River Thursday, Saturday, Sunday, Monday, and Wednesday, also stopping off at many of the main attractions. The tour costs A$119 (US$95/£48) for adults and A$86 (US$69/£35) for children 3 to 14 years old.

More expensive options include **Kangaroo Island Wilderness Tours** (☎ 08/8559 5033; www.wildernesstours.com.au), which operates from the island with several small four-wheel-drive vehicles (maximum six people). Three different day trips cost A$334 to A$365 (US$267–US$292/£134–£146) per person, including transfers, an excellent lunch with wine, and park entry fees. Two-, three-, and four-day trips, including all meals and accommodations, cost A$829 (US$663/£332), A$1,323 (US$1,058/£524), and A$1,818 (US$1,454/£727) per person, respectively.

Another excellent operator on the island is **Adventure Charters of Kangaroo Island** (☎ 08/8553 9119; www.adventurecharters.com.au). Day trips cost A$340 (US$272/£136) with a big lunch, or A$648 (US$518/£260) for a one-day safari including flights from and to Adelaide. A two-day and one night safari including accommodations and flights costs A$1,230 (US$984/£492).

Another option is **Wayward Bus** (☎ 08/8410 8833; www.waywardbus.com.au) from Adelaide. Two-day trips depart daily between December and March, with fewer departures at other times, and cost A$380 (US$304/£152) in a hostel bunk or A$410 (US$328/£164) twin/double in a shared room.

Staying in style

The island has a wide variety of places, from B&Bs to campgrounds:

- ✔ If you feel like sleeping in one of 40 cottages or coastal lodgings, contact **Kangaroo Island Remote and Coastal Farm Accommodation** (☎ 08/8553 1233). Prices range from A$65 to A$100 (US$52–US$80/£26–£40). The staff can also arrange lodgings in local farms, homes, and B&Bs for A$60 to A$110 (US$48–US$88/£24–£44) for a double with breakfast.

- ✔ The NP&WSA also rents basic but comfortable lodgings, including relatively isolated **lighthouse cottages** (☎ 08 8559 7235; kiparksaccom@saugov.sa.gov.au) at Cape Willoughby, Cape Borda, Rocky River, and Cape du Couedic. The price is A$95 to A$140 (US$76–US$112/£38–£56) per night.

- ✔ If you're on a tight budget, head to the **Penneshaw Youth Hostel,** 43 North Terrace, Penneshaw, Kangaroo Island, SA 5222 (☎ 08/8553 1284; fax 08/8553 1295), with dorm beds for A$22 (US$18/£9) and doubles for A$72 (US$57/£29). It costs a few dollars less for YHA/Hostelling International members.

- ✔ Camping is allowed at designated sites and in national parks. There are many beach, river, and bush camping spots. Call ☎ 08 8559 7235 to book. Camping costs A$8 to A$19 (US$6.40–US$15/£3.20–£7.50) per car and A$4 to A$5.50 (US$3.20–US$4.40/£1.60–£2.20) per person.

The top hotels

Casuarina Coastal Units
$ **American River**

These simple, country-style accommodations offer a cozy budget option. Each comes with a double bed, two singles, and an attached shower. The property has a playground and fish-cleaning facilities.

9 Ryberg Rd., American River, SA 5221. ☎/fax **08/8553 7020.** www.casuarinaonki. com. *Rack rates: A$85 (US$68/£34) double, A$75 (US$60/£30) double for more than 1 night. MC, V.*

Hanson Bay Cabins
$$ **Southwest Coast**

On the southwest coast of the island, this property is a row of six log cabins perched above a beach. Each cabin has a picture window facing the ocean, a full kitchen, a bathroom, two bedrooms (including a double bed and three singles in all), and a wood stove. Bring your own food and supplies. The ocean can get wild and dramatic, with strong offshore winds whipping up the sand and spray. The cottages are near most of the major attractions, so they make a good base.

Hanson Bay Company, P.O. Box 614, Kingscote, SA 5225. ☎ **08/8853 2603.** *Fax: 08/8853 2673.* www.hansonbay,com.au. *Rack rates: A$170 (US$136/£68) double; extra adult A$30 (US$24/£12), extra child A$20 (US$16/£8). AE, DC, MC, V.*

Kangaroo Island Lodge
$$$ **American River**

Though Kangaroo Island Lodge was built in 1801, it has been so overhauled that you'd be hard pressed to find anything rustic remaining. It's a nicely appointed property with pleasant, quiet, motel-style rooms; a good pool; a Jacuzzi; a sauna; and a restaurant and bar (entrees average A$20/US$16/£8). Some units contain kitchens. The lodge looks over Pelican Lagoon (famous for its, well, pelicans), but the lagoon is a little too far away to make the water-view rooms worthwhile. Packages (which require a minimum two-night stay) include the ferry connection to Cape Jervis, and breakfast each day.

Scenic Road, American River, SA 5221. ☎ **08/8553 7053.** *Fax: 08/8553 7030.* www. kilodge.com.au. *Rack rates: A$295 (US$236/£118) double (for 2-night stays), A$363 (US$290/£145) double (for 3-night stays); extra person A$24 (US$19/£9.50). AE, DC, MC, V.*

Dining locally

Most accommodations on Kangaroo Island provide meals for guests (usually at an additional cost). You'll find a few takeout booths around the island at the popular tourist spots. For lunch, you can get sandwiches at Roger's Deli on Dauncey Street, in Kingscote.

Dudley Wines Cellar Door and Café
$$ Cape Willoughby LOCAL PRODUCE

This restaurant perches on a cliff on the eastern tip of the island, next to Cape Willoughby Lighthouse, about 30km (19 miles) from Penneshaw. One wall is all glass, and the veranda affords ocean views. The restaurant serves as a way to sell the local wine, by the bottle or the glass, but some good food is available, including a plastic bucket full of ice and cooked prawns, cheese plates, dips, and a Mediterranean platter of nibbles.

Cape Willoughby. ☎ 08/8553 1333. Reservations required for lunch. Main courses: A$15–A$20 (US$12–US$16/£6–£8). MC, V. Open: Daily 10a.m.–4 p.m. for coffee and cakes, 12:30–2:30 p.m. for lunch.

The top attractions
Cape du Couedic

Millions of years of crashing ocean have created curious structures, like the hollowed-out limestone promontory called Admiral's Arch and the Remarkable Rocks, where you'll see huge boulders balancing on top of a massive granite dome. Admiral's Arch is home to a colony of some 4,000 New Zealand fur seals.

A paved road leads from Rocky River Park Headquarters to Admiral's Arch and Remarkable Rocks, where a parking lot and a loop trail are located. There's a road, parking lot, and trail system around the Cape du Couedic heritage lighthouse district.

Flinders Chase National Park

After years of lobbying, politicians finally agreed to preserve this region of the island in 1919. Today, it makes up around 17 percent of the island and is home to true wilderness, coastal scenery, two old lighthouses, and plenty of animals. Birders have recorded at least 243 species here. Koalas are so common that they're almost falling out of the trees.

The **Platypus Waterholes walk** is a two-hour stroll that's great for all ages. It begins at the Flinders Chase Visitors Centre and has a shorter option that's suitable for wheelchairs. This walk offers the best opportunity to see the elusive platypus. Kangaroos, wallabies, and brush-tailed possums, on the other hand, are so tame and numerous that the authorities were forced to erect a barrier around the Rocky River Campground to stop them from carrying away picnickers' sandwiches!

Lathami Conservation Park

This park is a wonderful place to see **wallabies** in the wild. Just dip under the low canopy of casuarina pines and walk silently, keeping your eyes peeled. You're almost certain to spot them.

Penneshaw Penguin Centre

If you want to see little **penguins** — tiny animals that stand just 33cm (13 in.) tall — you can see them in a natural environment coming home to roost in their burrows at dusk. The Penneshaw Penguin Centre, Lloyd Collins Reserve, Penneshaw (☎ **08/8553 1103**), supports the largest penguin colony on the island. Tours depart between 7:30 p.m. and 8:30 p.m. in winter, and 8:30 p.m. to 9:30 p.m. in summer.

Seal Bay Conservation Park

You shouldn't miss out on the experience of walking through a colony of Australian sea lions. Some 100,000 people visit Seal Bay Conservation Park each year. Boardwalks through the dunes reduce the impact of so many feet. The colony consists of about 500 animals, but at any one time you may see up to 100 basking with their pups. Guided tours are given daily every 15 to 30 minutes from 9 a.m. to 4:15 p.m. for A$14 (US$11/ £5.50) for adults and A$8 (US$6.40/£3.20) for children. For information, call ☎ **08/8559 4207**.

More cool things to see and do

✔ Kangaroo Island is renowned for its fresh food, and across the island you'll see signs beckoning to you to have a taste of cheese, honey, wine, or the like. Worth a stop is **Clifford's Honey Farm** (☎ **08/8553 8295**; open: daily 9 a.m. to 5 p.m.). The farm is the home of the Ligurian honeybee, found nowhere else on earth.

✔ **Island Pure Sheep Dairy** (☎ **08/8553 9110**) is another worthwhile stop. Tours and tastings are conducted at milking time (1–5 p.m.). It's a great chance to sample delicious sheep's milk, yogurt, and mouthwatering haloumi cheese.

✔ For fabulous (though pricey) **fishing** for everything from King George whiting, trevally, and snapper, to mullet and mackerel, contact **Kangaroo Island Fishing Charters** (☎ **08/8552 7000**; www.kifishchart.com.au). A full day starts at A$125 (US$100/ £50), including lunch; a half-day trip starts at A$90 (US$72/£36). Kangaroo Island Fishing Charters also runs coastal wilderness tours, looking for birds, seals, and whales in season.

Chapter 21

Perth and the Best of Western Australia

by Marc Llewellyn

. . . .

In This Chapter

▶ Finding your way to Western Australia

▶ Enjoying Perth and Fremantle

▶ Touring the Margaret wineries

. . . .

*S*un, adventure, and an awesome natural environment is what you can expect from Western Australia, also known as WA. WA covers one-third of Australia at over 2.5 million sq. km (1 million sq. miles) but only 2.1 million inhabitants live in Perth. Perth is the most remote large city on Earth — Adelaide is 2,700km (1,700 miles) east.

The **Southwest** corner is the prettiest part. Vineyards and pastures sit between stands of karri and jarrah trees, the surf is world-class, there are limestone caverns, and the coastline is rugged.

We're a bit disappointed that we can only touch on the high points of this huge, diverse state, but we've selected the most accessible areas for this chapter — and we'll see if we can get some more in the next edition!

We start out with Perth, the most outdoorsy of all Aussie cities. Perth's brilliant setting along both the Swan River and the Indian Ocean, and the abundance of parkland mean that it's almost obligatory to get outside and enjoy the sun and fresh air. Its climate is pleasant throughout the year. Most visitors focus on the summer months of December through March, with lots of sun, sea, and sand, though the sea breeze can get (annoyingly) strong.

Fremantle, or "Freo" as it's known, is a working port and Perth's second city heart. It's a favorite weekend spot to eat, drink, shop, and sail. Fremantle is 19km (12 miles) downriver, at the mouth of the Swan.

After spending some time in Perth and Freo, we take a quick swing through the Margaret River to enjoy some of Australia's finest wines.

Getting to Western Australia

By air

Qantas, or its subsidiary **Qantaslink** (☎ 13 13 13 in Australia; www. qantas.com.au), flies at least once a day from all mainland capitals as well as Broome, Alice Springs, and Uluru (Ayers Rock). **Virgin Blue** (☎ 13 67 89 in Australia; www.virginblue.com.au) flies direct from Sydney, Melbourne, Adelaide, Brisbane, the Gold Coast, and Broome, with connections from other cities. **Jetstar** (☎ 13 15 38 in Australia; www.jetstar. com) has a daily flight from Melbourne, with connections from other eastern cities. **Skywest** (☎ 1300/660 088 in WA; www.skywest.com.au) connects Perth to all significant towns in WA and to Darwin.

Perth Airport is 12km (7½ miles) northeast of the city. At the international terminal, look out for volunteer Customer Service Officers called "Gold Coats," mostly in departures, and "WOWs" (West Oz Welcomers) wearing ocher jackets and Akubra hats in arrivals. The domestic and international terminals are a bit of a distance from each other, so if you're transferring from one to the other, you'll have to take a shuttle or taxi.

Getting to Perth and Fremantle from the airport

The **Airport City Shuttle** (☎ 08/9277 7958) aims to meet all flights within 30 to 45 minutes of Customs clearance, or luggage collection for domestic flights. There is no need to book ahead. City transfers from the international terminal cost A$15 (US$12/£6.15) one-way, A$25 (US$20/£10) round-trip; from the domestic terminal, A$12 (US$9.60/£4.90) one-way, A$22 (US$18/£9) round-trip.

The **Fremantle Airport Shuttle** (☎ 1300/668 687 in Australia, or 08/9335 1614) operates regular services each day from both airport terminals to hotels or anywhere else in Fremantle. You must reserve for the return trip. The fare is A$30 (US$24/£12) per person and gets cheaper the bigger your group is — down to A$10 (US$8/£4.10) per person for five or more people.

Transfers between terminals run regularly from 5 a.m. to 5 p.m. daily, with limited service until 9:30 p.m. Qantas/One World interflight transfers are free, otherwise it costs you A$8 (US$6.40/£3.30); taxis between the terminals are about A$24 (US$19/£7.75).

Public **bus** no. 37 runs to the city from the domestic terminal. No buses run from the international terminal. A **taxi** to the city is about A$40 (US$32/£16) from the international terminal and A$32 (US$26/£13) from the domestic terminal, including a A$2 (US$1.60/£0.80) fee for picking up a taxi at the airport.

Avis (☎ 08/9277 1177 domestic terminal, 08/9477 1302 international terminal), **Budget** (☎ 08/9277 9277), **Europcar** (☎ 08/9237 4320), **Hertz** (☎ 08/9479 4788), and **Thrifty** (☎ 08/9464 7333) have desks at both terminals.

By train

The three-day journey to Perth from Sydney via Broken Hill, Adelaide, and Kalgoorlie aboard the *Indian Pacific,* operated by Great Southern Railway (☎ **13 21 47** in Australia; www.trainways.com.au), is a great experience. It has the world's longest straight stretch of rail (over 483km/300 miles) along the Nullarbor Plain. The train runs twice a week in each direction, and can carry your vehicle. The one-way fare ranges from A$1,790 (US$1,432/£731) in first class with meals and en-suite bathroom, to A$1,320 (US$1,056/£539) in comfy, but cramped if you're large or tall, second class (meals cost extra, and bathrooms are shared), down to A$680 (US$544/£278) for sit-up-all-the-way coach class (not a good idea). Connections are available from Melbourne on the *Overland* train.

All long-distance trains pull into the **East Perth Terminal,** Summers Street off Lord Street, East Perth. A taxi to the city center from there costs about A$17 (US$14/£6.95).

Introducing the Neighbourhoods

- **The City Center:** The central business district (CBD) is home to offices, shops, and department stores. It has a modest collection of 19th-century heritage buildings, especially convict-built Government House and Town Hall. Four long avenues run east–west between riverside parkland and the railway reserve. **St. Georges Terrace** (it becomes Adelaide Terrace at Victoria Avenue) is the main thoroughfare and commercial and banking address, while **Hay Street** and **Murray Street** are the major retail avenues with pedestrian malls in the central blocks. Arcades link all three, plus Wellington Street, which has Perth's suburban railway station.

- **Northbridge:** Most of Perth's nightclubs, and a good many of its cool restaurants, bars, and cafes, are in this 5-block precinct north of the railway line. It's within easy walking distance of the city center, or take the free Blue CAT buses. Its boundaries are William, James, Aberdeen, and Parker streets. The Cultural Center is here, with the Western Australian Museum, Art Gallery of Western Australia, State Library, and Perth Institute of Contemporary Arts.

- **Subiaco:** This well-heeled inner suburb is on the other side of Kings Park. Take a stroll through "Subi's" villagelike concoction of restaurants, cafes, markets, boutiques, antiques shops, pubs, and galleries. Most of the action is near the intersection of Hay Street and Rokeby (pronounced *rock*-er-bee) Road, with the Subiaco Hotel and Art Deco Regal Theatre on opposing corners.

- **Burswood/East Perth:** These two areas are on opposite sides of the Swan River upstream of Perth city. Both are on land reclaimed from earlier industrial use, and show enlightened development with parkland, pathways, and artworks. Burswood has major entertainment complexes, a public golf course, and superb gardens. East Perth is mostly modern housing, parks, galleries, and restaurants, based around a river inlet with walkways.

Getting Around Perth

On foot
Perth is a good walking city, so bring comfortable shoes.

By bus
Transperth (www.transperth.wa.gov.au) runs Perth's buses, trains, and ferries. For information, call ☎ **13 62 13** in Western Australia, or drop into the **Transperth InfoCenters** at the Plaza Arcade off Hay Street Mall, the Perth Train Station, the Wellington Street Bus Station, or the Perth Esplanade Busport on Mounts Bay Road.

You can transfer between bus, ferry, and train services for up to two hours (zones 1–4) or three hours (zones 5–8). Travel costs A$2.10 (US$1.70/£0.85) in one zone (to Subiaco, for instance), and A$3.20 (US$2.55/£1) in two, which gets you most places, including Fremantle, with discounts for kids ages 5 to 14.

The **Wellington Street Bus Station** (close to Perth Train Station) and the **Perth Esplanade Busport** on Mounts Bay Road are the two main arrival and departure points. The vast majority of buses travel along St. Georges Terrace. You must hail the bus to ensure that it stops. Buy tickets from the driver. Buses run from about 5:30 a.m. until about 10:30 p.m. or 11:30 p.m., depending on the route.

By tram
The **Perth Tram Co.** (☎ **08/9322 2006;** www.perthtram.com.au) makes a daily loop of the city, the casino, and Kings Park in replica 1899 wooden trams; hop on and off as you want. Tickets, which you buy on board, cost A$24 (US$19/£9.80) adults, A$10(US$8/£4.10) children 4 to 14, A$48 (US$38/£20) families (up to six). City-to-casino or Kings Park single legs are also available. The tram starts at 565 Hay St. at 8:30 a.m. and makes nine 90-minute narrated loops per day, every day.

By bike
You're allowed, even encouraged, to take your bicycle on Perth's suburban trains and ferries. The only limitations are to avoid the Monday through Friday peak services — toward the city between 7 a.m. and 9 a.m., and away from the city between 4:30 p.m. and 6:30 p.m. — and not have your bike at Perth Train Station during either of these times.

By car
Perth's signposting is reasonably good for helping drivers find their way around. The major car rental companies are **Avis** (☎ 08/9325 7677), **Budget** (☎ 08/9480 3111), **Europcar** (☎ 08/9277 9144), **Hertz** (☎ 08/9321 7777), and **Thrifty** (☎ 08/9464 7444). All except Hertz also have outlets in Fremantle.

Take a free ride

A welcome freebie in Perth is free public transport within the city center and nearby areas. In the **Free Transit Zone (FTZ),** you can travel free on all buses within this zone any hour, day or night. The FTZ is bounded by Kings Park Road, Fraser Avenue, Thomas Street, and Loftus Street on the west; Newcastle Street on the north; and the river on the south and east. Basically, this means you can travel to Kings Park, Northbridge, and anywhere in the city center for free. Signs mark the FTZ boundaries; just ask the driver if you're not sure. FTZ boundaries for trains are City West station on the Fremantle line and Claisebrook on the Midland and Armadale lines.

You can buy a **DayRider** ticket and get one day of unlimited travel after 9 a.m. on weekdays and all day on weekends and public holidays for A$7.70 (US$6.15/£3.15). A **FamilyRider** pass is valid for unlimited all-day travel to any destination and back, for a group of up to seven people with a maximum of two adults, but only on weekends and public holidays, also for A$7.70 (US$6.15/£3.15).

By train

Trains are fast, clean, and safe. They start at about 5:30 a.m. and run every 15 minutes or more often during the day, and every half-hour at night until midnight. All trains depart from Perth Train Station opposite Forrest Place on Wellington Street. Buy your ticket before you board, at the vending machines on the platform. There are five lines: north to Joondalup; northeast to Midland; southeast to Armadale; southwest to Fremantle; and south to the resort town of Mandurah.

By ferry

You can use ferries to visit South Perth and Perth Zoo. They run every half-hour or so, more often in peak hours, daily from 6:50 a.m. weekdays and 7:50 a.m. weekends and holidays, until 7:24 p.m. (or until 9:15 p.m. Fri–Sat in summer, Sept–Apr) from the Barrack Street Jetty to Mends Street in South Perth. Buy tickets before you board from vending machine on the wharf. The trip takes approximately seven minutes.

By taxi

Perth's two biggest taxi companies are **Swan Taxis** (☎ **13 13 30** in Australia) and **Black & White Taxis** (☎ **13 10 08** in Australia). *Ranks* (stands) are at Perth Railway Station and at the Barrack Street end of Hay Street Mall.

Perth

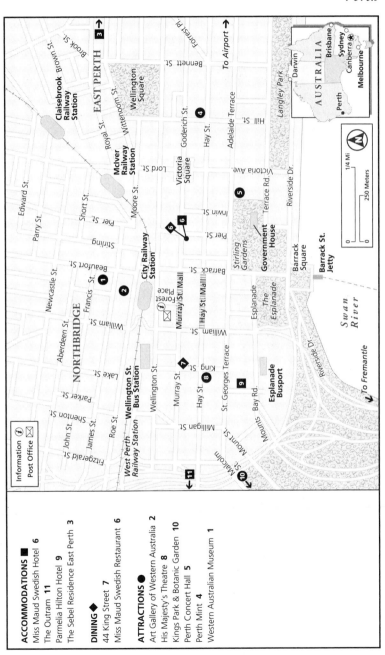

AUSTRALIA
Darwin
Brisbane
Sydney
Canberra
Melbourne
Perth

1/4 Mi
250 Meters

To Airport →

To Fremantle →

Swan River

Information ⓘ
Post Office ⊠

EAST PERTH

Claisebrook Railway Station

Brook St.
Brown St.
Bennett St.
Wellington Square
Wittenoom St.
Royal St.
Goderich St.
Hay St.
Adelaide Terrace
Hill St.
Langley Park
Forrest Pl.

McIver Railway Station

Lord St.
Moore St.
Short St.
Pier St.
Stirling St.
Edward St.
Parry St.
Beaufort St.
Francis St.
Newcastle St.
Aberdeen St.
William St.
NORTHBRIDGE
Lake St.
Parker St.
Shenton St.
John St.
James St.
Roe St.
Fitzgerald St.

City Railway Station
Wellington St. Bus Station
West Perth Railway Station

Victoria Square
Irwin St.
Terrace Rd.
Victoria Ave.
Riverside Dr.

Government House
Stirling Gardens
Barrack Square
Barrack St. Jetty

The Esplanade
Esplanade
Esplanade Busport

Forrest Place
Murray St. Mall
Hay St. Mall
Barrack St.
Wellington St.
Murray St.
Hay St.
King St.
St. Georges Terrace
Bay Rd.
Milligan St.
Mounts Bay Rd.
Malcolm St.

Riverside Dr.

ACCOMMODATIONS ■
Miss Maud Swedish Hotel **6**
The Outram **11**
Parmelia Hilton Hotel **9**
The Sebel Residence East Perth **3**

DINING ◆
44 King Street **7**
Miss Maud Swedish Restaurant **6**

ATTRACTIONS ●
Art Gallery of Western Australia **2**
His Majesty's Theatre **8**
Kings Park & Botanic Garden **10**
Perth Concert Hall **5**
Perth Mint **4**
Western Australian Museum **1**

Staying in Style in Perth

The city center has loads of hotels. That means competition can be high, especially on weekends when the business travelers go home, so ask about lower rates. You may strike a deal on a weeknight if business is slow. Many hotels throw breakfast or some other feature into weekend packages. Most hotels have rooms for travelers with disabilities.

The top hotels

Esplanade Hotel Fremantle
$$$$ Fremantle

Freo's best hotel is this low-rise 1897 colonial building wrapped by two verandas, now modernized and extended, and centered on the original glass and iron four-story atrium. It's opposite a park close to the Fishing Harbour, and within walking distance of all Freo's cafes, shops, and attractions. The rooms are all of reasonable size, with the suites especially spacious and having large balconies. Some studio units have Jacuzzis. Eleven rooms are designed for wheelchair access. The larger pool in the courtyard is a good place to chill out without getting buffeted by the pesky local sea breeze, the so-called Fremantle Doctor.

Marine Terrace at Essex Street, Fremantle, WA 6160. ☎ *1800/998 201 in Australia, or 08/9432 4000. Fax: 08/9430 4539.* www.esplanadehotelfremantle.com.au. *Parking: A$25 (US$15/£10). Rack rates: A$330–A$370 (US$234–US$260/£135–£151) double, A$400–A$419 (US$270–US$335/£163–171) studio, A$445–A$619 (US$356–US$495/£182–£253) suite. Several 1- and 2-night packages, and attractive Internet rates, are available. AE, DC, MC, V.*

Fothergills of Fremantle
$$ Fremantle

One of Perth's best B&Bs, it's in two restored 1890s limestone mansions. Fremantle with all its charms is a ten-minute walk, and Fremantle Prison is a block away. The houses have been extensively and tastefully modernized, and owner David Cooke has spread his art collection throughout, bringing color, light, and life. The upstairs balconies have views over the roofs of Fremantle to the Indian Ocean, ideal for evening sundowners. Most rooms have queen-size beds, while the O'Connor suite has a king-size and double foldout bed. The courtyards are quiet, restful havens.

18–20 Ord St., Fremantle, WA 6160. ☎ *08/9335 6784. Fax: 08/9430 7789.* www.babs.com.au/fothergills. *Parking: on street. Rack rates: A$140–A$200 (US$112–US$160/£57–£82) double. Minimum 2-night stay. Full breakfast included. Week-stay package available. MC, V.*

InterContinental Burswood Hotel
$$$–$$$$$ **Burswood**

It's the setting that first grabs your attention, the distinctively tiered building set within parkland next to the Swan River, overlooking the city. Then you walk into the glass-ceilinged atrium, set about with high-flying triangular sails. Glass-sided elevators ascend one wall. The hotel is part of an entertainment complex that includes Perth's casino, a theater, another hotel (Holiday Inn), and an 18-hole golf course. Being outside the city center, the main focus is on tourists not corporate travelers. The real stars are the spacious suites with large balconies, facing straight downriver; otherwise ask for river-view rooms.

1 Bolton Ave. (off Great Eastern Highway by the Causeway), Burswood, WA 6100. ☎ *13 83 88 (reservations) in Australia, or 08/9362 8888.* www.burswood.com.au/hotels. *Parking: A$20 (US$16/£8.15). Rack rates: A$184–A$335 (US$147–US$268/£75–£137) standard room, A$724–A$905 (US$579–US$724/£296–£369) suite. AE, DC, MC, V.*

Miss Maud Swedish Hotel
$$ **City Center**

This hotel offers a European *pensione*-style presence in the heart of the city. It's a 1911 building, and a bit of a rabbit warren. The whole place has been refurbished over the last five years, but it still retains its Swedish ambience. It has a comfortable "feel," with wallpaper used throughout. Miss Maud is real — Maud Edmiston who started the hotel and restaurant 35 years ago. Many of the staff members have been with her for years and there's a loyal customer base. Single women find it a safe and comfortable place to stay. There are six single rooms. Two principal aims are to provide sleeping comfort and a good breakfast, so large beds are provided — and there's a fabulous buffet in **Miss Maud Swedish Restaurant** (see "Dining in Perth," later in this chapter).

See map p. 435. 97 Murray St. (at Pier Street), Perth, WA 6000. ☎ *1800/998 022 in Australia, or 08/9325 3900. Fax: 08/9221 3225.* www.missmaud.com.au. *Parking: A$12 (US$9.60/£4.90) 1 block away. Rack rates: A$159 (US$127/£65) standard room double, A$139 (US$111/£57) standard room single, A$219 (US$175/£89) standard room triple, A$179 (US$143/£73) superior double, A$159 (US$127/£65) superior single. Rates include smorgasbord breakfast. Lots of packages available. AE, DC, MC, V.*

The Outram
$$$$ **West Perth**

Discreet and intimate are the key words for this small but elegant hotel, which also offers friendly service. It's Perth's only member of the Small Luxury Hotels of the World group. In West Perth, it's 2 blocks from Kings Park and within easy reach of the city center. Privacy is paramount, with full key-card access control. The rooms are large but not opulent, with king-size beds, open-plan bathrooms, "his and her" basins, a walk-through shower, and balcony. Most rooms have double spas. The foyer-level Club Room (with terrace extension) serves complimentary breakfasts, coffee and cake, and evening hors d'oeuvres with drinks. It's a smoke-free property.

*See map p. 435. 32 Outram St., West Perth, WA 6005. ☎ **1800/251 958** in Australia, or 08/9322 4888. Fax: 08/9322 1138. Parking: A$15 (US$12/£6.15). Rack rates: A$395 (US$316/ £161) double; A$365 (US$292/£149) single. Rates include breakfast. AE, DC, MC, V.*

Parmelia Hilton Hotel
$$$ City Center

This is Perth's first Hilton five-star hotel and still one of the best. It's steps from the Perth Convention Center, with the Swan River not far away. The marble foyer has a brass plaque commemorating the S.S. *Parmelia,* which brought 150 of the first settlers to these shores. The river views have mostly been built out, so ask for rooms from the seventh floor upward (no extra charge). The hotel has subtly striped wallpaper throughout, the spacious standard rooms and deluxe rooms are decorated in cool relaxing shades, while the suites boast separate living, working, and dining areas. The **Globe Restaurant** has one of Perth's most innovative menus, and hosts regular fashion and winemaker events.

*See map p. 435. 14 Mill St. (just off St. Georges Terrace), Perth, WA 6000. ☎ **1300/445 866** in Australia, or 08/9215 2000. Fax: 08/9215 2001.* www1.hilton.com/ en_US/hi/hotel/PERHITW-Parmelia-Hilton-Perth-hotel/index.do. *Parking: A$30 (US$24/£9.80). Rack rates: A$225–A$295 (US$180–US$236/£92–£120) double, A$345–A$520 (US$276–US$416/£141–£212) suite. Ask about packages and specials, especially on weekends. AE, DC, MC, V.*

The Sebel Residence East Perth
$$ East Perth

This four-year-old hotel is in a great location minutes from the city. It's quiet, and has views across Claisebrook (a broad pool, lined with artworks and upmarket housing) and down to the Swan River. Galleries, restaurants, parks, and walkways are a few steps away. A barbecue area and 25m (82-ft.) lap pool are outside. There is no restaurant but the corner cafe will deliver breakfast, and it and other local restaurants, and a wine shop, also deliver to the hotel, and you can charge it to your room. Each one-bedroom apartment has a full kitchen with microwave, washer and dryer, and balcony. Studios have kitchenette and shower only. You can combine a studio and a one-bedroom to make a two-bedroom apartment.

*See map p. 435. 60 Royal St. (at Plain Street), East Perth, WA 6004. ☎ **1800/010 559** in Australia, or 08/9223 2500. Fax: 08/9223 2590.* www.mirvachotels.com.au. *Free covered parking. Rack rates: A$195–A$215 (US$156–US$172/£80–£88) studio, A$245–A$265 (US$196–US$212/£100–£108) 1-bedroom apartment double, A$310 (US$248/£127) 2-bedroom apartment. AE, DC, MC, V. Train: Claisebrook. Bus: Yellow CAT stops 5 and 32.*

Dining in Perth

An array of upscale choices plus terrific cheap ethnic spots make Perth's restaurant scene as sophisticated as Sydney's and Melbourne's — which is to say, excellent. You'll find a great range in "restaurant city," Northbridge. Friday and Saturday nights tend to be very busy. Midweek is less busy, quieter, and generally more pleasant.

Many outlets emphasize the use of fresh local produce. You'll find seasonal berry, stone, citrus, and tropical fruit; lamb, beef, veal, and goat; seafood such as rock lobster, abalone, and prawns; freshwater crustaceans such as marron and yabbies; and superb fish including snapper, red emperor, and cobbler.

For inexpensive pasta, a Turkish bread sandwich, or excellent coffee and cake, you can't beat Perth's homegrown **DOME** chain of cafes. Look for the dark green logo at Trinity Arcade between Hay Street Mall and St. Georges Terrace (☎ **08/9226 0210**); at 149 James St., Northbridge (☎ **08/9328 8094**); among other places.

The Capri
$$ Fremantle   ITALIAN

A Fremantle institution, this place has been owned by the Pizzale family for 50 years, and the décor probably hasn't changed in that time. This is dining as it once was — no fussy furnishings, just good honest Italian grub. Free bread and water are served immediately, and complimentary soup with main courses. It's unlicensed so BYO. Here you'll find standard Italian fare, such as spaghetti marinara and scaloppine, available in small or large servings. It's right in the middle of the Cappuccino Strip.

21 South Terrace, Fremantle. ☎ *08/9335 1399. Main courses: A$20–A$25 (US$16–US$20/£8.15–£10). AE, DC, MC, V. Open: Daily noon to 2 p.m. and 5–10 p.m.*

Cicirello's
$$ Fremantle   SEAFOOD

On Fremantle's Fishing Boat Harbour, this is one of several places offering freshly cooked, tasty fish and chips — and other seafood. It's a functional, volume restaurant but still has character. Large fish tanks (for show) are the decorative feature, and floor-to-ceiling glass doors lead out to the broad timber balcony, also with seating, directly above the water. Fishing boats are moored next door. The food comes battered and fried, or grilled, but the essential meal is fish and chips. There's a kid's menu.

44 Mews Rd. (Fishermans Wharf), Fremantle. ☎ *08/9335 1911. Main courses: A$10–A$25 (US$8–US$20/£4.10–£10). AE, DC, MC, V. Open: Daily 9 a.m.–9 p.m.*

The Essex
$$$ Fremantle MODERN AUSTRALIAN

For a quiet, elegant, romantic night out, the Essex is hard to beat. Located just off Fremantle's Cappuccino Strip, and up the road from the Esplanade Hotel, it's in a restored 120-year-old limestone cottage, with the dining areas spread among several rooms. The service is discreet but can leave you unattended at times. Try the Balmain bugs (a curiously flattened, but tasty, crustacean) and ravioli, or the beef Gabrielle filled with scallops.

20 Essex St., Fremantle. ☎ 08/9335 5725. Reservations recommended. Main courses: A$30–A$52 (US$24–US$42/£12–£21); lunch A$32 (US$26/£13) 2 courses, A$39 (US$31/£13) 3 courses. AE, DC, MC, V. Open: Daily 6 p.m. to late, lunch Wed–Fri and Sun from noon.

44 King Street
$$$ City Center BISTRO

Socialites, hip corporate types, and casuals adorn this sophisticated hangout — for a meal, a snack, or good coffee, roasted on-site. The interior is a mix of industrial design and European cafe, with dark timber tables, exposed air ducts, and windows onto the street. The open kitchen produces all its own bread and pastries, and has a changing menu with some weird and wonderful choices — such as fennel-roasted duck with paella of Valencia, or Cajun pink snapper with sweet-potato frites and avocado sour cream. The menu helpfully lists wine suggestions for each dish, and offers over 70 wines by the glass from around A$8 (US$6.40/£3.30), and taster glasses, too. There's also a good beer selection.

See map p. 435. 44 King St. ☎ 08/9321 4476. Reservations not accepted. Main courses: A$18–A$38 (US$14–US$30/£7.35–£16); 10 percent surcharge weekends and public holidays. AE, DC, MC, V. Open: Daily 7 a.m. to late.

Fraser's
$$$ Kings Park MODERN AUSTRALIAN

You look past spiky grass trees and towering lemon-scented gums to Perth's panoply of skyscrapers and the Swan River. Even better, the victuals match the vista. Executive chef Chris Taylor changes the menu daily to focus on the latest fresh produce, with seafood especially prominent. This place was awarded a national title for "Best Informal Dining in Australia" in 2006. Fraser's Three Taste brings together beef, lobster, and salmon in a starter, while crisp fried soft-shell crabs married with turmeric and pumpkin curry comes as a starter or entree, and whitebait fritters are served with a tamarind sauce. Ask for a seat on the terrace.

Fraser Avenue (near the Information Kiosk), Kings Park. ☎ 08/9481 7100. Reservations required. Main courses: A$30–A$55 (US$24–US$44/£12–£22); 10 percent Sun surcharge. AE, DC, MC, V. Breakfast weekends and public holidays from 8 a.m. Open: Daily noon to late.

Jackson's
$$$$ **Highgate   MODERN AUSTRALIAN/INTERNATIONAL**

Understated contemporary design and ambience help to emphasize the quality of the food here. Chef Neil Jackson has a loyal clientele, and a host of awards for his ability to bring out the best in local produce, with some quirky touches. This place is a short distance out of town but worth the trip. The menu changes seasonally but with a reputation for duck dishes and soufflés, both sweet and savory. His degustation menu, called "the dego," offers nine courses, with suggested matching wines. Friday and Saturday are booked out weeks ahead, and diners are warned, "This food may contain traces of nuts, love, quality produce, and passion!"

483 Beaufort St., Highgate. ☎ *08/9328 1177. Reservations essential. Main courses: A$38 (US$30/£16); "the dego" A$95 (US$76/£39), A$150 (US$120/£61) with wines. AE, DC, MC, V. Open: Mon–Sat 7 p.m. to late.*

Lamont's East Perth
$$$$ **East Perth   MODERN AUSTRALIAN**

Kate Lamont has a well-deserved reputation for the flavor-driven food she produces at her three restaurants, in Margaret River, Swan Valley, and here. The menu changes depending on the availability of seasonal produce. Marron (a local crustacean) is a specialty, presented in various manners, including a poached version with pea risotto. Desserts are tapas-style, encouraging shared tastings. Weekend breakfast features a triple layer pyramid of various ingredients; more of a brunch offering. The modern glass-fronted restaurant faces directly on to Claisebrook Inlet, with the Swan River 50m (164 ft.) away, and the Holmes à Court Gallery is next door. There's an extensive wine list, with the option to take away the Lamont family wines, at cellar door prices.

11 Brown St., East Perth. ☎ *08/9202 1566. Reservations essential. Main courses: A$36–A$42 (US$29–US$34/£15–£17). AE, DC, MC, V. Open: Tues 10 a.m.–5 p.m., Wed–Fri 10 a.m. to late, Sat 9 a.m. to late, Sun 9 a.m.–5 p.m. Closed public holidays.*

Must Wine Bar
$$ **Highgate   BISTRO**

This place has one of Australia's finest wine lists, and there's some pretty good food, too. Check out the cool contemporary design, with suspended wine rack separating bar from restaurant. It's a trendy hangout especially on Friday and Saturday nights. There are 600 wines in stock, with some 50 available by the glass. Food is contemporary French, with a charcuterie plate (shared appetizer) and beef cheek ravioli specialties.

519 Beaufort St., Highgate (close to Jackson's). ☎ *08/9328 8255. Reservations recommended on weekends. Main courses: A$24–A$38 (US$19–US$30/£9.80–£16). AE, DC, MC, V. Open: Daily noon to late. Closed public holidays.*

Miss Maud Swedish Restaurant
$$ City Center   INTERNATIONAL

"Good food and plenty of it" is the motto at Miss Maud's homey establishment, and the crowds prove it works. Most diners skip the a la carte menu and go straight for the smorgasbord. At breakfast, that means 50 dishes, including pancakes made to order. At lunch and dinner you can tuck into soup, ten salads, a range of seafood (including oysters at dinner), cold meats, roasts, vegetables, pasta, cheeses, European-style breads, tortes, fruit, and ice cream — 65 dishes in all. Service is fast and polite.

See map p. 435. 97 Murray St. (at Pier Street), below the Miss Maud Swedish Hotel. ☎ *08/9325 3900. Reservations recommended. Main courses, sandwiches, and light meals: A$8–A$30 (US$6.40–US$24/£3.30–£12). AE, DC, MC, V. Open: Daily 6:45–10 a.m. (until 11 a.m. on Sun and holidays), noon to 2:30 p.m. (until 3 p.m. on Sun and holidays), and 5 p.m. to late.*

Star Anise
$$$$ Subiaco   ASIAN-INFLUENCED AUSTRALIAN

In ten years, chef/owner David Coomer has taken this restaurant on a suburban street to become one of the best in Perth. The converted house features several dining areas including a courtyard, and the décor is clean and subtle with Asian influences and contemporary art. The innovative menu is done daily and features a Signature Menu of six fixed courses (with suggested wines). The a la carte section is kept simple with five courses listed in each of the appetizer, main, and dessert sections. Among David's creations are crispy aromatic duck, seared scallops, and licorice ice cream. Tuesday is an optional BYO (bring your own alcohol) night.

225 Onslow Rd., Shenton Park (next to Subiaco). ☎ *08/9381 9811. Reservations recommended. Main courses: A$39–A$58 (US$31–US$46/£16–£24); Signature Menu A$110 (US$88/£45) food only, A$160 (US$128/£65) with wine. AE, DC, MC, V. Open: Tues–Sat 6:30–10:30 p.m.*

Witch's Cauldron
$$$ Subiaco   MODERN AUSTRALIAN

Australia's best garlic prawns arrive preceded by a cloud of sizzling garlic. The Cauldron has twice been voted Perth's favorite restaurant. Started in a single room in 1971, its owners Geoff and Tanis Gosling have expanded it into a double-story establishment without compromising style or standards. They've even bought some street-side parking bays, effectively extending the restaurant across the sidewalk. Numerous witches, including political cartoons, adorn the walls and ceilings. One feature is a series of circular banquettes for cozy dining for groups of four to six. Service is brisk, friendly, and efficient. Besides the garlic prawns there's an emphasis on simple cooking of quality fish and steak.

89 Rokeby Rd. (near Hay Street), Subiaco ☎ *08/9381 2508. Reservations recommended, especially when major events at nearby Subiaco Oval. Main courses: A$27–A$48 (US$22–US$38/£11–£20); lunch includes set menus, A$30 (US$24/£12) 2 courses, A$42 (US$34/£17) 3 courses. AE, DC, MC, V. Open: Daily 7:30–11 a.m., noon to 5 p.m., and 6 p.m. to late.*

The Top Attractions

AQWA *(Aquarium of Western Australia)*
City Center

There are no performing dolphins, but there's plenty to see, including Australia's largest walk-through aquarium, where you're surrounded by 4m (13-ft.) sharks, rays, turtles, and hundreds of colorful fish. AQWA specializes in the ocean ecosystems around WA, and has a touch pool, a great attraction for small (and bigger) kids; a lagoon full of stingrays; and the Seal Island underwater viewing area to watch sea lions at play. You can come face to fin with pretty leafy sea dragons, and observe some of the ocean's deadliest such as blue-ringed octopus and stonelike stonefish. Keepers feed the sharks and the touch-pool creatures daily, and a program of talks and movies on marine creatures runs throughout the day. For A$125 (US$100/£51) plus A$20 (US$16/£8.15) for snorkel gear or A$40 (US$32/£16) for dive gear (diving qualifications required), you can **swim with the sharks** (daily 1–3 p.m.). Advance bookings essential. Allow half a day here.

Sorrento Quay at Hillarys Boat Harbour, 91 Southside Dr., Hillarys. ☎ *08/9447 7500.* www.aqwa.com.au. *Admission: A$25 (US$20/£10) adults, A$14 (US$11/£5.70) children 4–15, A$65 (US$52/£27) families of 4. Open: Daily 10 a.m.–5 p.m., sometimes later in Jan.*

Kings Park & Botanic Garden
Kings Park

Overlooking the city and Swan River is this 406-hectare (1,000-acre) hilltop jewel of parkland, botanical gardens, and bush. The main entry, along Fraser Avenue, is lined with lemon-scented gums. You can inspect Western Australian flora; experience the solitude of the bush; and bike, stroll, or drive an extensive network of roads and trails. A walk through the Botanic Garden showcases many of the state's plant species, including banksias and baobabs, and leads to the Federation Walkway, a glass arched bridge that soars through the treetops. Visiting the spring **wildflower displays** (which peak Aug–Oct) is a highlight for many, with an excellent Wildflower Festival in September. Pick up self-guiding maps from the Visitor Information Centre, or take a free guided walk leaving from opposite the Centre. Walks depart daily at 10 a.m. and 2 p.m. and take one-and-a-half hours, or two or three hours for bushwalks (May–Oct only).

See map p. 435. Fraser Avenue off Kings Park Road. ☎ *08/9480 3634 information center, 08/9480 3600 administration.* www.bgpa.wa.gov.au. *Admission: Free. Open: Park daily 24 hours, information centre daily 9:30 a.m.–4 p.m.*

Perth Mint

This lovely historic building — built in the 1890s to refine gold and mint currency from the Kalgoorlie gold rush — is one of the world's oldest mints operating from its original premises. It now produces legal-tender precious metal coins and commemorative medallions for collectors, and bullion is still traded here. The "Gold Exhibition" allows visitors to see Australia's biggest collection of nuggets, watch gold coins being minted, handle a 400-ounce gold bar, and engrave their own medallion. Tours start with a guided walk on the half-hour, and lead on to the molten gold pouring demonstration (on the hour 10 a.m.–4p.m. weekdays, and 10 a.m. to noon weekends and holidays). The shop sells gold coins and nugget jewelry, and the Tea Garden provides a quiet spot to relax.

See map p. 435. 310 Hay St. (at Hill St.), East Perth. ☎ *08/9421 7223.* www.perth mint.com.au. *Admission to the Gold Exhibition A$15 (US$12/£6.15) adults, A$5 (US$4/£1.65) school-age children. Open: Mon–Fri 9 a.m.–5 p.m.; Sat–Sun and holidays 9 a.m.–1pm.*

Perth Zoo
South Perth

This is an excellent modern zoo — with re-created natural habitats and no cages in sight. It has several successful breeding programs, including one for orangutans. Others cover white rhinos, African painted dogs, and a number of West Australian fauna, including the numbat, which is WA's animal emblem. This is a good place to see a range of Australian wildlife such as kangaroos, koalas, wombats, quokkas, emus, echidnas, and penguins, and there's a walk-through aviary. Exotic animals include apes, Rothschild's giraffes, lions, tigers, meerkats, and elephants. Feeding demonstrations and talks run throughout the day. Volunteer guides are always around to provide information, and conduct free daily walking tours at 11 a.m. and 1:30 p.m. (Sept–Apr). You can do a behind-the-scenes **Close Encounters Tour** (with 3 weeks notice), and bring home a unique souvenir: paintings by the zoo's elephants.

20 Labouchere Rd., South Perth. ☎ *08/9474 3551 for recorded information, 08/9474 0444 administration.* www.perthzoo.wa.gov.au. *Admission: A$17 (US$14/£6.95) adults, A$8.50 (US$6.80/£3.50) children 4–15, A$45 (US$36/£16) families of 4. Open: Daily 9 a.m.–5 p.m.*

Swan River
City Center

The river is a great natural and free asset. Perth Water, immediately below the CBD, is a superb foreground and mirror to the city — best seen from South Perth, and stunning at and just after sunset. The South Perth ferry (see "Getting Around Perth" earlier in this chapter) is the easiest way of getting there. Perth Water is shallow, so ideal for "messing about in boats," and small catamarans can be hired on the South Perth foreshore. Past the Narrow Bridge, the river widens out and becomes home to several yacht clubs. Biking along riverside pathways is a great way to enjoy the city, the river, and the weather. You can rent both boats and bikes.

Surfcat hire: South Perth foreshore. ☎ *0408/926 003 in Australia.* www.funcats. com.au. *Bike rental: Corner of Riverside Drive and Plain Street.* ☎ *08/9221 2665.* www.aboutbikehire.com.au.

Western Australian Museum
Northbridge

Kids will like the dinosaur gallery, the drawers full of insects, the blue whale skeleton on the well-stocked aquatic zoology floor, the "megamouth" shark preserved in a tank in the ground in the courtyard, and assorted other examples of Australia's weird natural creatures. The main attraction for grown-ups is one of Australia's best displays of Aboriginal culture and heritage ("Listen to our stories"), and rare photographs, many housed in the Old Gaol (1856). Allow 90 minutes to see most highlights.

See map p. 435. Off James Street Mall, Cultural Center, Northbridge. ☎ *08/9212 3700. Enter by gold coin donation. Open: Daily 9:30 a.m.–5 p.m.*

Yanchep National Park
Yanchep

This is the best place in Perth to see traditional Aboriginal culture, with presentations three times a day on Saturdays and Sundays. The park is 51km (32 miles) north of the city, in glorious natural woodland, around a reed-fringed lake. You can follow a boardwalk through the koala enclosure, hire a rowboat, take a limestone cavern tour, have a coffee and snack (or beer) at the historic Tudor-style **Yanchep Inn,** or admire the wildlife. Kangaroos abound, there are resident (and noisy) black cockatoos, and other birds include swans, pelicans, wrens, parrots, and kookaburras.

Off Wanneroo Road, Yanchep. ☎ *08/9561 1004. Admission: A$10 (US$8/£4.10) per vehicle; tours, including the Aboriginal presentation, A$6.50 (US$5.20/£2.65) adults, A$3.50 (US$2.80/£1.45) children, A$16 (US$12/@bp6.55) families (2 adults, 2 children). Open: Daily 9:15 a.m.–4:30 p.m., Aboriginal tours Sat–Sun 1 p.m., 2 p.m., and 3 p.m.*

More cool things to see and do

✔ **His Majesty's Theatre and King Street:** A lovely old wedding cake of an Edwardian theater, the venue was rescued and revamped in 1979. It's Perth's major venue for the WA Ballet and Opera companies and visiting theater productions, including those for the Perth International Arts Festival. Friends (volunteers) of His Majesty's are on hand Monday through Friday 10 a.m. to 4 p.m., to provide information and tours of the theater (unless it's in use) and public areas for a donation. Downstairs houses the Museum of Performing Arts with an engrossing collection of costumes and other memorabilia. It's at the corner of Hay and King streets (☎ 08/9265 0900; www. hismajestystheatre.com.au). It's open Monday through Friday from 10 a.m. to 4 p.m., with gold coin donation.

✔ **Holmes à Court Gallery**: This small riverside gallery offers rotating exhibitions from one of the country's most outstanding private art collections, that of Janet Holmes à Court, Australia's richest woman. Many of the works are Aboriginal or by well-known Australian artists such as Sidney Nolan. It's at 11 Brown St., East Perth (☎ 08/9218 4540). Admission is free and it's open Wednesday through Sunday noon to 5 p.m. Closed public holidays.

Hitting the Beaches

Perth has great beaches right in the city — in an almost continuous line from Cottesloe in the south to Quinns Rocks in the north, including a section called the Sunset Coast. Mornings are usually best for the beach, because the sea breeze can make the afternoons unpleasant in summer. Evenings and sunsets are lovely on quiet days. Always swim between the red and yellow flags, which denote a safe swimming zone.

Bus nos. 400 and 408 run to Scarborough Beach every 15 minutes daily, while no. 102 goes to Cottesloe every 30 minutes. Bus no. 458 operates a summer timetable along the northern beaches from Scarborough to Hillarys, half-hourly on weekends and holidays and hourly on weekdays, in both directions. Surfboards under 1.2m (4 ft.) can be carried on nos. 400, 408, and 458. Bus no. 381 operates a weekday service between Fremantle and Warwick, with stops at both Cottesloe and Scarborough.

Here are some of the best beaches around town:

- **Cottesloe:** This pretty crescent, graced by the Edwardian-style Indiana Tea House, is Perth's most fashionable beach. It has grassed slopes overlooking the beach, safe swimming, and a small surf break. Train: Cottesloe, then walk several hundred meters (between a quarter- and a half-mile). Bus: 102.

- **Scarborough:** Scarborough's white sands stretch for miles. Swimming is generally safe, and surfers are guaranteed a wave, although inexperienced swimmers should take a rain check when the surf is rough. The Australian Surf Life Saving Championships will be held here in late March 2008 and 2009. Bus: 400.

- **Trigg:** Surfers like Trigg best for its consistent swells, but it can have dangerous rips. Stay within the flags. Bus: 400 to Scarborough, then walk; or 458 (summer).

The Fremantle Doctor is in . . .

In the summer, Perth gets an easterly offshore breeze in the morning then, as the land heats up, it switches to be a southwesterly onshore wind. This is called the **Fremantle Doctor** because it blows up the river from Fremantle and provides relief on hot summer days. The timing and strength of the breeze varies and it can be almost gale force, whipping up the sand on exposed beaches. Check the daily weather forecast for likely wind strength. The three most popular beaches are Cottesloe, Scarborough, and Trigg.

The Shopping Scene

Most major shops are downtown on the **Hay Street** and **Murray Street malls,** and in the network of arcades running off them, such as the Plaza, City, Carillon, and Tudor-style **London Court** arcades. Off Murray Street Mall on Forrest Place is the **Forrest Chase shopping complex,** housing the Myer department store and boutiques on two levels. The other major department store, David Jones, opens onto both malls. Add to your collection of designer brands on **King Street,** in the west end. **Harbourtown,** at the western edge of the city, is a large complex housing "factory outlets" of numerous retail chains.

If you want to avoid the chains, spend half a day in **Subiaco** or "Subi," where Hay Street and Rokeby Road are lined with boutiques, galleries, cafes, antiques shops, and markets. The Colonnade shopping center at 388 Hay St. showcases some groovy young Aussie fashion designers.

Shops are open until 9 p.m. on Friday in the city, and until 9 p.m. on Thursday in Subiaco and Fremantle.

Art and crafts

Two shops showcase contemporary ceramic, textile, glass, and jewelry products: **FORM** at 357 Murray St. just round the corner from King Street; and **Aspects of Kings Park,** behind the visitor center.

Aboriginal arts and crafts

- ✔ **Creative Native,** 32 King St. (☎ **08/9321 5470**), stocks Perth's widest range of Aboriginal arts and crafts. Upstairs is a gallery selling original works by some renowned Aboriginal artists. There's another branch at 65 High St., Fremantle (☎ **08/9335 7438**).

- ✔ **Indigenart,** 115 Hay St., Subiaco (☎ **08/9388 2899**), and 82 High St., Fremantle (☎ **08/9335 2911**), stocks works on canvas, paper, and bark, as well as artifacts, textiles, pottery, didgeridoos, boomerangs, and sculpture, by Aboriginal artists from all over Australia.

- ✔ **Japingka Gallery,** 47 High St., Fremantle (☎ **08/9335 8265**), is dedicated to encouraging and exhibiting Aboriginal art. It has a large stock of certificated art covering a cross section of areas and styles. There's an ongoing exhibition program, which usually involves having the artist present for discussion. The gallery is based over two floors in a historic building in central High Street.

Jewelry

Western Australia is renowned for farming the world's best **South Sea pearls** off Broome, for Argyle **diamonds** mined in the Kimberley, and for being one of the world's biggest **gold** producers.

- ✔ **Artisans of the Sea,** corner of Marine Terrace and Collie Street, Fremantle (☎ 08/9336 3633), sells elegant South Sea pearls and gold jewelry.

- ✔ Some of Perth's other leading jewelers, where you can buy opals, Argyle diamonds, and Broome pearls, are **Costello's,** Shop 5–6, London Court (☎ 08/9325 8588), and **Linneys,** 37 Rokeby Rd., Subiaco (☎ 08/9382 4077).

- ✔ For opals to suit all budgets, head to the Perth outlet of **Quilpie Opals,** Shop 6, Piccadilly Arcade off Hay Street Mall (☎ 08/9321 8687).

Perth after Dark

Scoop magazine is a good source of information on festivals and concerts, theater, classical music, exhibitions, and the like. Your best guide to clubs, concerts, and art-house cinemas is the free weekly *X-press* magazine, available at pubs, cafes, and music venues every Thursday. The *West Australian* (especially the Sat edition) and *Sunday Times* newspapers publish entertainment information, including cinema guides.

Two ticket agencies handle most of the city's major performing arts, entertainment, and sporting events: the performing-arts-oriented **BOCS** (☎ 1800/193 300 in Australia, or 08/9484 1133; www.bocsticketing. com.au) and the sports-and-family-entertainment-oriented **Ticketmaster** (☎ 13 61 00; www.ticketmaster.com.au). Book opera, ballet, the orchestra, and the Black Swan Theatre Company (see the following section) through BOCS.

The performing arts

The **West Australian Opera** (☎ 08/9278 8999) and **West Australian Ballet** (☎ 08/9481 0707) usually perform at **His Majesty's Theatre,** 825 Hay St. Perth's leading theater company, the **Black Swan Theatre Company** (☎ 08/6389 0311), plays at theaters around town. The **West Australian Symphony Orchestra** (☎ 08/9326 0000) usually performs at the **Perth Concert Hall,** 5 St. Georges Terrace, with other performances in **Kings Park** (open-air summer concerts) and the **Art Gallery.**

Hitting the pubs and nightclubs

Northbridge houses most of the city's lively pubs and dance clubs. Don't forget that Fremantle has good pubs, too.

- ✔ **The Brass Monkey,** 209 William St. at James Street, Northbridge (☎ 08/9227 9596), has several downstairs bars, including a wine bar serving gourmet pizzas, and a beer garden. Wednesday through Saturday, head upstairs to the Glasshouse for live entertainment, including the Laugh Resort comedy club at 8 p.m. Wednesday for a A$10 (US$8/$4.10) cover.

✔ **The Subiaco Hotel**, or "Subi,"465 Hay St. at Rokeby Road, Subiaco (☎ **08/9381 3069**), is a popular historic pub with a stylish cafe, great cocktails, and live jazz on Wednesday and Saturday nights.

✔ **Metro City,** 146 Roe St., Northbridge (☎ **08/9228 0500;** www.metro city.com.au), is the biggest and swingiest place on the nightclub scene, with ten bars over three levels. It opens every Saturday from 10 p.m. with its "Super Club," featuring R&B music. The cover of A$10 (US$8/£5) increases to A$15 (US$12/£7.50) after 11 p.m. It opens frequently on other nights, with varying cover charge, for events with visiting bands and artists.

Fast Facts: Perth

Area Code

For Perth and Western Australia, it's **08.**

American Express

The office at 645 Hay St. Mall (☎ 1300/139 060) is open Monday through Friday 9 a.m. to 5 p.m., Saturday 9 a.m. to noon.

Dentist

LifeCare Dental (☎ 08/9221 2777 or 08/9383 1620 after-hours) is on the Upper Walkway Level, Forrest Chase shopping complex, 425 Wellington St., opposite Perth Railway Station. It's open daily from 8 a.m. to 8 p.m.

Doctor

Central City Medical Center is on the Perth Railway Station concourse, 420 Wellington St. (☎ 08/9221 4747). It's open daily from 8 a.m. to 6 p.m.

Embassies and Consulates

The United States Consulate-General is at 16 St. Georges Terrace (☎ 08/9202 1224). The Canadian Consulate is at 267 St. Georges Terrace (☎ 08/9322 7930). The British Consular Agency is at 77 St. Georges Terrace (☎ 08/9224 4700).

Emergencies

Dial ☎ **000** for fire, ambulance, or police in an emergency. This is a free call; no coins are needed from a public phone.

Hospitals

Royal Perth Hospital in the city center has a public emergency/casualty ward (☎ 08/9224 2244). Enter from Victoria Square, which is off Murray Street.

Pharmacies

Forrest Chase Pharmacy (☎ 08/9221 1691), on the upper level of the Forrest Chase shopping center, 425 Wellington St., is open Monday through Thursday 8 a.m. to 7 p.m. (and until 9 p.m. Fri), Saturday 8:30 a.m. to 6 p.m., Sunday 10 a.m. to 6 p.m.

Police

Dial ☎ **000** in an emergency, or ☎ 13 14 44 to be connected to the nearest station. Perth Police Station, 60 Beaufort St. (☎ 08/9223 3715), and Fremantle Police Station, 45 Henderson St. (☎ 08/9430 1222), are open 24 hours.

Safety

Perth is safe, but steer clear of the back streets of Northbridge and the city center malls late at night — where groups of teenagers tend to congregate.

Visitor Information

The Western Australian Visitor Center, Albert Facey House, 469 Wellington St. at Forrest Place, Perth (☎ 1300/361 351 in Australia; www.westernaustralia. com), is the official visitor information source for Perth and the state. It's open Monday through Thursday 8:30 a.m. to 6 p.m. (to 5:30 p.m. in winter, May–Aug), Friday 8:30 a.m. to 7 p.m. (to 6 p.m. in winter), Saturday 9:30 a.m. to 4:30 p.m., and Sunday noon to 4:30 p.m. year-round.

The City of Perth's i-City Information Kiosk, in the Murray Street Mall near Forrest Place, is open Monday through Thursday and Saturday 9:30 a.m. to 4:30 p.m., Friday 9:30 a.m. to 8 p.m., and Sunday noon to 4:30 p.m. (closed public holidays).

Volunteers lead free 90-minute guided tours around the city, Monday through Friday at 11 a.m. and 2 p.m., Saturday at 11 a.m., Sunday at 2 p.m. The morning and Sunday sessions are general city orientation tours, while the other afternoon tours are more heritage-oriented. There's no need to book. Another source of information and maps (plus a free booking service) is Perth Tourist Lounge, Level 2, Carillon Arcade off 207 Murray St. Mall (☎ 08/9481 4400; www. perthtourist.com.au), open Monday through Saturday 9:30 a.m. to 4:30 p.m. (closed Sun, holidays).

Time Zone

Western Australian time (WST) is Greenwich mean time plus eight hours and is on a three-year trial of daylight saving, so GMT plus nine hours October through March. It is two hours behind Sydney and Melbourne. Call ☎ 1194 for the exact local time.

Weather

Call ☎ 1196 for a recorded local weather forecast.

A Day Out in Fremantle

The heritage port precinct of **Fremantle,** is 19km (12 miles) from downtown Perth on the mouth of the Swan River. In the lead-up to the Americas Cup in the 1980s, the city embarked on a major restoration of its gracious warehouses and Victorian buildings.

Today "Freo" is a bustling district of 150 National Trust buildings, alfresco cafes, museums, galleries, pubs, markets, and shops in a masterfully preserved historical atmosphere. It's still a working port, so you can see fishing boats unloading on one side, and yachts and container ships gliding in and out of the main commercial river-mouth harbor on the other. Weekends are best, with a wonderful hubbub of buzzing shoppers, merchants, coffee drinkers, locals, tourists, and fishermen. Allow a full day to take in even half the sights — and don't forget to knock back a beer or two on the veranda of one of the gorgeous old pubs.

Parking is plentiful, but driving is frustrating in the maze of one-way streets. Most attractions are within walking distance (or accessible on the free CAT bus), so take the train to Fremantle and explore on foot.

Getting around Fremantle

The orange Fremantle CAT bus makes a comprehensive running loop of local attractions every ten minutes Monday through Friday from 7:30 a.m. to 6:30 p.m., and on weekends and holidays from 10 a.m. to 6:30 p.m., except Good Friday (Fri before Easter) and December 25 and 26. It is free and departs from the train station.

Fremantle Trams (☎ **08/9339 8719;** www.fremantletrams.com) — an old tram carriage on wheels — conducts hop-on/hop-off commentated tours around the main sights. The tours depart from Fremantle Town Hall ten times a day starting at 9:45 a.m., with the last tour leaving at 2:45 p.m. Tickets cost A$20 (US$16/£8.15) adults, A$15 (US$12/£6.15) students and seniors, A$5 (US$4/£2.05) children, A$45 (US$36/£18) families of four; discount entry to the prison is included.

Finding information after you arrive

The **Fremantle Visitors Center** is in Town Hall, Kings Square (at High Street), Fremantle, WA 6160 (☎ **08/9431 7878;** www.fremantlewa.com.au). It's open Monday through Friday from 9 a.m. to 5 p.m., Saturday 10 a.m. to 3 p.m., Sunday 11:30 a.m. to 2:30 p.m.; closed public holidays. The best Web site is that of the Fremantle Council (www.fremantle.wa.gov.au).

Seeing the sights in Fremantle

You'll want to explore some of Freo's museums and other attractions, but don't forget to stroll the streets and admire the 19th-century offices and warehouses, many painted in rich, historically accurate colors. Take time to wander down to the docks — either Victoria Quay in the main shipping harbor, where sailing and pleasure craft dodge between tugs and container ships, or Fishing Boat Harbour, off Mews Road, where the catches are brought in — and get a breath of salt air.

Fremantle Arts Center

Housed in a neo-Gothic 1860s building built by convicts, this center contains one of Western Australia's best contemporary arts-and-crafts galleries, with a constantly changing array of works. A shop sells crafts from Western Australia, a bookstore stocks Australian art books and literature, and the leafy courtyard cafe is the perfect place to hang out. Free concerts play on the lawn every Sunday and public holiday from October to April, from 2 to 4 p.m. Also here is the Fremantle History Museum (see the following listing).

1 Finnerty St. at Ord Street. ☎ 08/9432 9555. Admission: Free. Open: Daily 10 a.m.–5 p.m.

Fremantle History Museum

Housed in a convict-built former lunatic asylum, this small but densely packed museum uses lots of old photographs and personal possessions to paint a realistic picture of what life was like for Fremantle's first settlers, the Aborigines they displaced, and later generations up to the present day, especially the post–World War II immigration boom.

In the Fremantle Arts Center (see preceding listing), 1 Finnerty St. at Ord Street. ☎ *08/9430 7966. Admission: Gold coin donation. Open: Mon–Fri 10 a.m.–4:30 p.m., Sat and public holidays 1–5 p.m., Sun 10:30 a.m.–4:30 p.m.*

Fremantle Prison

Even jails boasted attractive architecture in the 1850s. This limestone jail, built to house 1,000 inmates by convicts who no doubt ended up inside it, was Perth's maximum-security prison until 1991. Take the 75-minute main tour "Doing Time" to see cells re-created in the style of past periods of the jail's history, bushranger (highwayman) Joe Moondyne's "escape-proof" cell, the gallows, workshops, chapel, jailers' houses, and cell walls featuring artwork by the former inmates. The ticket price includes an additional 45-minute tour (the precinct tour) that visits other areas, including the women's prison and commissariat, hourly after the main tour. You must book ahead for the 90-minute **torchlight tours** on Wednesday and Friday only, and the 2½ hour **tunnel tour,** which takes you by foot and boat through limestone tunnels 20m (66 ft.) down.

1 The Terrace. ☎ *08/9336 9200.* www.fremantleprison.com. *Admission: Free to prison gatehouse and visitor center; day tours A$16 (US$13/£6.55) adults, A$8 (US$6.40/£3.25) children 4–15, A$42 (US$34/£17) families; torchlight tour A$20 (US$16/£8.15) adults, A$11 (US$8.40/£4.50) children, A$50 (US$40/£20) families; tunnel tour A$55 (US$44/£22) adults, A$38 (US$30/£16) children 12–15. Open: Daily 10 a.m.– 5 p.m.; main tours every 30 minutes, precinct tours every hour 11:30 a.m.–4:30 p.m., torchlight tours Wed and Fri every 20 minutes from sunset, daily tunnel tours hourly 9 a.m.–3:20 p.m.*

The Roundhouse

This 12-sided jail is the oldest public building in the state (built in 1831). It's worth a visit for history's sake, and for the one o'clock gun. The time cannon (a replica of a gun salvaged from an 1878 wreck) is fired and a **time ball** dropped at 1 p.m. daily, just as it was in the early 1900s, from a deck overlooking the ocean. You may be that day's honorary gunner chosen from the crowd! Volunteer guides are on hand to explain it all.

10 Arthur Head (enter over the railway line from High Street). ☎ *08/9336 6897. Admission: Gold coin donation. Open: Daily 10:30 a.m.–3:30 p.m.*

Shipwreck Galleries

The remnant hulk of the Dutch ship *Batavia,* wrecked north of Perth in 1629, will stop you in your tracks as you enter this fascinating museum, in a lovely old 1850s limestone building. The *Batavia*'s story is of survival and betrayal; most of the survivors of the wreck were massacred by a handful of mutineers. The mutiny and massacre have been the subject of films and an opera. You'll love the tales of old wrecks and displays of pieces of eight, glassware, cannon, and other deep-sea treasure recovered off the Western Australian coast. Displays date from the 1600s, when the Dutch became the first Europeans to visit Australia. The museum is world-renowned for its work in maritime archaeology and preservation.

Cliff Street at Marine Terrace. ☎ *08/9431 8444. Admission: Donation (suggested A$1/US$0.80/£0.40 or A$2/US$1.60/£0.80). Open: Daily 9:30 a.m.–5 p.m.*

Western Australian Maritime Museum

This museum at the western end of Fremantle's main harbor faces straight out through tall glass panels to the Indian Ocean. The museum looks at Fremantle's history and operations as a port, shipping in the Indian Ocean and Swan River, signaling and piloting, current sailing technology, naval defense, and Aboriginal maritime heritage. It also features historic boats, including *Australia II* (the Aussie yacht that won the America's Cup in 1983). You can tour HMAS *Ovens,* an Oberon-class submarine, every half-hour from 10 a.m. to 4:30 p.m. You can buy a ticket just for the sub, or a joint one for the museum and sub, at a discount.

Victoria Quay. ☎ *08/9431 8444. Admission: A$10 (US$8/£4.10) adults, A$3 (US$2.40/ £1.20) children 5–15, A$22 (US$18/£9) families; free 2nd Tues of each month. Admission to submarine only: A$8 (US$6.40/£3.30) adults, A$3 (US$2.40/£1.20) children 5–15, A$22 (US$18/£9) families. Open: Daily 9:30 a.m.–5 p.m.*

Wining and Dining in Margaret River

For most Australians, the words *Margaret River* (277km/173 miles south of Perth) are synonymous with great wine. The area has over 80 wineries and, although they produce only about 1 percent of Australia's wine output, they turn out around 10 percent of the country's top "premium" wines.

There's a selection of quality lodges and B&Bs, galleries, gourmet food outlets, and restaurants. Many crafts people have set up here, with producers of venison, cheese, chocolate, and olive oil. Statuesque forests of gracious karri trees create beautiful dappled drives; the west coast has spectacular surf breaks and cliffs perfect for *abseiling* (rappelling) and rock climbing; the northern coast has wonderfully peaceful safe beaches; and there's a honeycomb of limestone caves filled with stalagmites and stalactites.

Whales pass by June through December, wildflowers line the roads August through October, and wild birds, kangaroos, and shingle-backed lizards are everywhere.

The Margaret River region isn't large, so is easy to get around. It reaches 120km (75 miles) from Cape Naturaliste in the north to Cape Leeuwin on the southwest tip of Australia, both with attendant lighthouses. If you like hiking, pack your boots, because there are plenty of trails, from a 15-minute stroll around Margaret River township, or an hour's stroll

Taking a dip with Flipper

Just two hours' drive south of Perth, en route to Margaret River, is a place where you can **swim** with these creatures.

At the **Dolphin Discovery Centre**, Koombana Drive, Bunbury (☎ **08/9791 3088**; http:// dolphins.mysouthwest.com.au), bottlenose dolphins come into shore in Koombana Bay. You can "float" with them free in the waist-deep "interaction zone" on the beach, under the eye of volunteer guides. The dolphins don't show up about a third of the time (the best chance of seeing them is 8 a.m. to noon). Reservations are not necessary.

From November to April (weather dependent), the center runs two-hour **Swim on the Wild Side** tours where, accompanied by a marine biologist, you can snorkel with some of the bay's 100-plus dolphins in deeper water for A$125 (US$100/£51) including equipment; you must be over 8 years old to participate.

Naturaliste Charters (☎ **08/9755 2276**; www.whales-australia.com) runs excellent 90-minute **dolphin watch cruises** twice daily (except Dec 25 or in bad weather) from the center at 11 a.m. and 2 p.m.; they cost A$37 (US$30/£15) adults, A$24 (US$19/£9.80) kids 4 to 12, A$28 (US$22/£11) kids 13 to 17, A$109 (US$87/£44) families (two adults, two children).

along the Dunsborough beaches, to a 6-day Cape-to-Cape trek along the sea cliffs.

The main settlements are **Dunsborough** in the north, **Margaret River township** in the center, and **Augusta** in the south. **Busselton** is the gateway to the region, though not really part of it.

Getting to Margaret River
By car
It's a three-hour drive to Margaret River from Perth; take the inland South Western Highway or the more scenic Old Coast Road to Bunbury, and pick up the Bussell Highway to Busselton, the gateway to the region.

By bus
Southwest Coachlines (☎ **08/9324 2333**) runs a daily service to Margaret River from Perth for about A$31 (US$25/£13). The **Public Transport Authority** (PTA; ☎ **1300/602 205** in Western Australia, or 08/9326 2600; www.transwa.wa.gov.au) also runs a coach service from Perth. The services take four-and-a-half to five-and-a-half hours, so we don't recommend them.

Margaret River Region

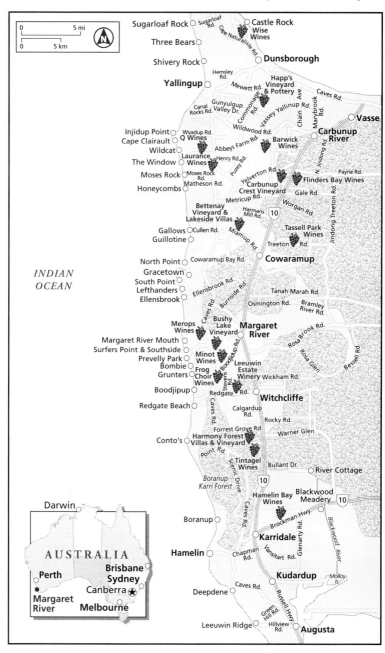

0 5 mi
0 5 km

Sugarloaf Rock ○ Sugarloaf Rd.
Castle Rock ○
Wise Wines
Cape Naturaliste Rd.
Three Bears ○
Shivery Rock ○
Dunsborough ○
Hemsley Rd.
Yallingup ○
Happ's Vineyard & Pottery
Mewett Rd.
Caves Rd.
Commonage Rd.
Canal Rocks Rd.
Gunyulgup Valley Dr.
Vasse Yallinup Rd.
Chain Ave
Marybrook Rd.
Vasse ○
Wildwood Rd.
Injidup Point ○ Wadup Rd.
Carbunup River
Cape Clairault ○ Q Wines
Barwick Wines
Wildcat ○
Abbeys Farm Rd.
N Jindong Rd.
The Window ○ Laurance Wines
Henry Rd.
Puzey Rd.
Payne Rd.
Moses Rock ○ Moses Rock Rd.
Yelverton Rd.
Flinders Bay Wines
Honeycombs ○ Matheson Rd.
Carbunup Crest Vineyard
Gale Rd.
Metricup Rd.
Jindong Treeton Rd.
Bettenay Vineyard & Lakeside Villas
Harmans Mill Rd.
Worgan Rd.
10
Gallows ○ Cullen Rd.
Tassell Park Wines
Guillotine ○
Miamup Rd.
Treeton Rd.
North Point ○ Cowaramup Bay Rd.
Cowaramup
INDIAN OCEAN
Gracetown ○
South Point ○
Ellensbrook Rd.
Tanah Marah Rd.
Lefthanders ○
Ellensbrook ○
Burnside Rd.
Osmington Rd.
Bramley River Rd.
Caves Rd.
Bushy Lake Vineyard
Merops Wines
Margaret River
Rosa Brook Rd.
Margaret River Mouth ○
Boodjidup Rd.
Bessell Rd.
Surfers Point & Southside ○
Minot Wines
Rosa Glen
Prevelly Park ○
Leeuwin Estate Winery
Bombie ○ Frog Choir Wines
Wickham Rd.
Grunters ○
Steeves Rd.
Boodjipup ○
Redgate Rd.
Witchcliffe
Redgate Beach ○
Calgardup Rd.
Caves Rd.
Rocky Rd.
Forrest Grove Rd.
Warner Glen
Conto's ○ Harmony Forest Villas & Vineyard
Point Rd.
Tintagel Wines
Bullant Dr.
River Cottage ○
Boranup Karri Forest
10
Hamelin Bay Wines
Blackwood Meadery
10
Scenic Drive
Brockman Hwy.
Blackwood River
Boranup ○
Caves Rd.
Karridale
Darwin
Hamelin ○
Chapman Rd.
Vansitart Rd.
Glenarty Rd.
AUSTRALIA
Brisbane
Kudardup
Molloy Is.
Perth
Sydney
Caves Rd.
Canberra
Margaret River
Melbourne
Deepdene ○
Russell Hwy.
Green Hill Rd.
Leeuwin Ridge ○ Hillview Rd.
Augusta

Getting information after you arrive

The **Margaret River Visitor Centre** is one of the best and most useful in the country. It's at 100 Bussell Hwy. (at Tunbridge Street), Margaret River, WA 6285 (☎ **08/9757 2911;** www.margaretriverwa.com). Pick up a winery guide, a guide to the artisans of the region, and maps. It's open daily from 9 a.m. to 5 p.m.

Getting around Margaret River

Two north–south roads service the area, **Bussell Highway** and the slower, winding **Caves Road.** Numerous smaller roads connect the two, or loop down to bayside settlements renowned for their surfing opportunities. The **Bussell Highway** turns due south 9km (5½ miles) past Busselton, and runs down the middle of the region, through Margaret River town to Augusta and windswept Cape Leeuwin. **Caves Road** runs past Dunsborough then swirls southward, closer to the coast, past limestone caves and karri forests toward Augusta.

A car is close to essential. **Hertz** (☎ **13 30 39** in Australia, or 08/9758 8331) has an office in Margaret River, or call **Avis** (☎ **1800/679 880** in Australia for reservations in the Southwest). For a taxi, call **Margaret River Taxi Service** (☎ **13 10 08** or 08/9757 3444).

Several companies run sightseeing and winery tours from Margaret River or Perth. One operator is **Taste the South** (☎ 04/3821 0373; www.tastethesouth.com.au), which offers half-day tours in minibuses in groups of about a dozen that take in five wineries running A$70 (US$56/£28), as well as individual tours, and several overnight tours, which can also include other Margaret River attractions. You can look at offerings from other companies, and find one that suits your needs at the **Margaret River Visitor Centre** Web site (www.margaretriver.com/tours).

The wines of Margaret River

Fans of premium wines will have a field day. Cabernet sauvignon and merlot are the star red varieties, with most wineries making a straight cabernet and/or cabernet/merlot blend. Shiraz is also popular and Cape Mentelle makes a powerful zinfandel. Chardonnay is the standard single-variety white wine, while fresh vibrant sémillon/sauvignon blanc blends have become synonymous with the region. A few wineries make (Australian-style) Rieslings. Most wineries offer free tastings from 10 a.m. to 4:30 p.m. daily. There are two main clusters of vineyards; the biggest grouping is in the northern half in the Willyabrup area, with a smaller number, including several big names, around Margaret River township.

Wine-buying tips

Most wineries don't deliver internationally, and the wine you like may not be exported to your country, so use the services of the **Margaret River Regional Wine Centre,** 9 Bussell Hwy., Cowaramup (☎ **08/9755 5501;** www.mrwines.com). It stocks about every local wine; does daily tastings of select vintages; and sells maps, visitor guides, and winery guides. The expert staff will help you make your choices, and even tailor your day's foray. It is open Monday through Saturday from 10 a.m. to 8 p.m., and Sunday from noon to 6 p.m. (closed Good Friday, Dec 25, and sometimes Jan 1). You can also order through the Web site.

The region's best known winery, and one of the very best, is **Leeuwin Estate,** Stevens Road, Margaret River (☎ **08/9430 4099**). It has a towering reputation, with its Art Series chardonnay often rated Australia's finest. Winery tours run three times a day.

A relative newcomer, **Voyager Estate,** Stevens Road, Margaret River (☎ **08/9757 6354**), has exquisite rose gardens and a South African Cape Dutch–style cellar and restaurant.

Three pioneer vineyards that date from the late 1960s, Moss Wood, Vasse Felix, and Cullen's, are all still rated very highly. Other labels to look for are Cape Mentelle, Devil's Lair, Madfish (Howard Park Wines), Lenton Brae, Pierro, Woodlands, and Cape Grace Wines. Ashbrook takes a very serious approach to style and quality, and makes one of the best WA Rieslings.

A food journey in Margaret River

Food-based attractions are opening up in the area all the time.

✔ You can pick your own kiwi, raspberries, and other fruit at the **Berry Farm,** 222 Bessell Rd., outside Margaret River (☎ **08/9757 5054;** www.berryfarm.com.au), or buy them ready-made as attractively packaged (fruit-based) wines, jams, and vinegars. It's open daily from 10 a.m. to 4 p.m. (4:30 p.m. for the "cellar door" wine shop). There's also a restaurant at the farm, called "The Cottage," which serves locally grown, seasonal food.

✔ At the **Margaret River Chocolate Company,** Harman's Mill Road, Metricup (☎ **08/9755 6555;** www.chocolatefactory.com.au), you can participate in free tastings, watch the candy-making through a window, and, of course, buy up the sweet stuff and coffees. It's open daily 9 a.m.–5 p.m.

✔ **Olio Bello,** corner of Armstrong Road and Cowaramup Bay Road, Cowaramup (☎ **08/9755 9771**), was the 2006 Australian Olive Grower of the Year. You can buy a range of olive oils, soaps, and body creams, dips, and tapenades. Olio Bello also has macadamias, fruit trees, and native shrubs so the place is full of birds. It's open daily from 10 a.m. to 4:30 p.m.

~ **Margaret River Venison,** Caves Road, just south of Olio Bello
(☎ **08/9755 5028**), is a family-run enterprise, selling products
derived from deer raised on the property. It's open daily from
9 a.m. to 6 p.m. The **Margaret River Dairy Company,** Bussell
Highway, Cowaramup, just north of the village (☎ **08/9755 7588;**
www.margaretriverdairy.com.au), uses local milk to make a
range of cheeses and yogurts. It's open daily 9:30 a.m. to 5 p.m.

Staying in Margaret River

You find an amazing selection of places to stay in **Margaret River** town
and **Dunsborough,** and around the vineyards.

A couple of medium-size hotels can be found near Dunsborough on the
edge of Geographe Bay, otherwise there are B&B establishments, self-
catering villas and cottages, campground chalets, and a range of excellent lodges. Some places may require a minimum two-night stay on
weekends.

Cape Lodge
$$$$ **Yallingup**

Cape Lodge has been voted one of the world's top 100 hotels. A member
of the Small Luxury Hotels of the World, it's set on 16 hectares (40 acres)
of vineyards and forest, with lakes, rolling lawns, and rose beds. The
impression is of space and tranquility, accompanied by birdsong. A
number of small blocks, or wings, are located so there are uninterrupted
views and you're not really aware of other people. The rooms are large and
elegantly furnished with king-size beds, and balcony or courtyard. The
Lodge Suite, in the original homestead, has a comfortable lounge and two
en-suite bathrooms. The restaurant, incorporating a guest lounge, has a
glass wall and decking on the edge of the main lake. It has won several
awards and opens for breakfast and dinner, with limited evening space for
nonguests.

Caves Road (between Abbey Farm and Johnson roads), Yallingup, WA 6282. ☎ *08/
9755 6311. Fax: 08/9755 6322.* www.capelodge.com.au. *Rack rates: A$365–A$425
(US$292–US$340/£149–£173) garden suite, A$495–A$595 (US$396–US$476/£202–£243)
superior and forest suites, A$650 (US$520/£265) lodge suite. Minimum 2-night stay
on weekends. Inclusive packages at Christmas, Easter, and for special events. Rates
include gourmet breakfast. AE, DC, MC, V.*

Heritage Trail Lodge
$$$ **Margaret River**

Although it's on the highway "in" Margaret River (within walking distance
of restaurants), this row of salmon-pink cabin-style rooms sits in a serene
karri forest, out of sight of town. Each spacious unit (including one for trav-
elers with disabilities) has a veranda and king-size double or king-size twin
beds, and a double Jacuzzi, from which you can see the forest. The rooms
back onto a number of bushwalk trails.

31 Bussell Hwy. (almost 0.5km/¼-mile north of town), Margaret River, WA 6285.
☎ *08/9757 9595. Fax: 08/9757 9596.* www.heritage-trail-lodge.com.au.
Rack rates: A$229–A$329 (US$183–US$263/£93–£134) double. Rates include gourmet continental breakfast. Children under 16 not accepted. Ask about midweek and romantic packages. AE, DC, MC, V.

Redgate Beach Escape
$$$ **Margaret River**

Four contemporary cottages sit on a hill, looking out across native bush to an expanse of ocean. There is no noise, just the breeze, birdsong, and the sound of the sea, with an occasional eagle floating past. The furnished cottages have a Balinese theme, full-height doors and windows facing the ocean, and are self-catering. Hosts Roger and Mim Budd built with a philosophy of uncluttered lines and sustainability. All services are underground including a rainwater tank which supplies the cottages.

Lot 14 Redgate Rd., off Caves Road (12km/7½ miles southwest of) Margaret River, WA 6285. ☎ *08/9757 6677, or 0437/770 107 mobile.* www.redgatebeachescape.com.au. *Rack rates: A$200–A$300 (US$160–US$240/£82–£122) double; A$20 (US$16/£8.15) per extra person. Reduced rates for over 2 nights. AE, DC, MC, V.*

Dining in Margaret River
Some of WA's finest dining is to be found here, with quality chefs attracted by the opportunities, the produce, and the lifestyle. Many of the better wineries have restaurants, but most are not open in the evening.

Cullen Wines
$$$ **Cowaramup   MODERN AUSTRALIAN/ORGANIC**

Owner and winemaker Vanya Cullen operates in a holistic manner, aiming for simplicity, integrity, and sustainability, using organic principles. Both vineyard and kitchen garden are certified biodynamic. The granite-and-timber restaurant is unpretentious but comfortable, with a shady outdoor option, and offers casual, relaxed dining, using fresh biodynamic and organic local produce. All dishes are labeled as organic, biodynamic, gluten-free, vegetarian, or free range. Cullen's produces an excellent sémillon/sauvignon blanc blend, and its Diane Madeleine cabernet/merlot is perhaps the best in Margaret River.

Caves Road, just north of Harmans South Road, Cowaramup. ☎ *08/9755 565. Reservations recommended, especially on weekends. Main courses: A$28–A$40 (US$22–US$32/£11–£16) lunch only. AE, DC, MC, V. Open: Daily 10 a.m.–4 p.m.*

Newtown House
$$$ **Vasse   MODERN FRENCH/AUSTRALIAN**

Folks come from far and wide to savor owner/chef Stephen Reagan's dishes, such as rare local venison with roast pears, beets, and red-wine glaze. Desserts are no letdown — caramel soufflé with lavender ice cream and hot caramel sauce is typical. The menu changes seasonally. In a historic 1851 veranda-ed homestead, the restaurant consists of two intimate rooms with contemporary, boldly colored walls. Log fires burn in winter and in summer there's the choice to eat outside, and it's BYO. It's been voted Best Country Restaurant in WA five times.

737 Bussell Hwy. (9km/5½ miles past Busselton), Vasse. ☎ *08/9755 4485. Reservations recommended, especially for dinner. Main courses: A$34 (US$27/£14). AE, DC, MC, V. Open: Tues–Sat lunch from 10 a.m. and dinner from 6:30 p.m.*

Vat 107
$$$ Margaret River   MODERN AUSTRALIAN

Touted by many locals as "one of the best restaurants in Australia," Vat 107 serves very good food. It's a slick, smart, city-bistro type place which puts it slightly at odds with the Margaret River laid-back style, but it's attractive and appealing. Dishes include seared duck breast with herb spaetzle and warm cherry purée, and slow-cooked salmon with truffled orzo and roasted forest mushroom and, for dessert, a chocolate trio.

107 Bussell Hwy., Margaret River. ☎ *08/9758 8877. Reservations recommended. Main courses: A$28–A$37 (US$22–US$30/£11–£15). AE, MC, V. Open: Daily 11 a.m. to late.*

Voyager Estate
$$$ Margaret River   MODERN AUSTRALIAN

Palatial white gates lead into spotless grounds, lined with rose gardens, and with what surely is the tallest flagpole in WA. In one corner, tucked behind a Cape-style garden, is the white Cape Dutch cellar and restaurant. The restaurant is in a long timber-vaulted room strung with chandeliers, and the menu is imaginative and varies seasonally, and comes with recommended wines (available by the glass). Try the Taste Plate or Seafood Assiette, and leave room for the specially selected range of cheeses.

Stevens Road, just south of Margaret River. ☎ *08/9757 6354. Reservations recommended, especially at weekends. Main courses: A$27–A$42 (US$22–US$34/£11–£17) lunch only. AE, DC, MC, V. Open: Daily 10 a.m.–4 p.m.*

Part VII
Tasmania

The 5th Wave   By Rich Tennant

THE TASMANIAN DEVIL ANNUAL BEST OF SHOW COMPETITION

In this part . . .

We head off the southeast coast of the Australian continent to the small island-state of Tasmania. In Chapter 22, we show you how much diversity can exist on a small (well, compared to the continent above, it's small!) island, starting off in Tasmania's main town, Hobart.

We explore the rest of the island, too, including the memorably beautiful Freycinet National Park in Chapter 23, and stop off in Launceston, as well as pay a visit to the sobering remains of Australia's prison heritage in Port Arthur.

Chapter 22

Tasmania

by Marc Llewellyn

In This Chapter

▶ Finding your way to and around Tasmania
▶ Getting the best deals for lodging
▶ Discovering the best places to eat
▶ Exploring Hobart and its environs

*T*here are a few really exotic-sounding places in the world — like the Galapagos, Patagonia, Madagascar . . . and Tasmania. All conjure up visions of remoteness, strange animals, and unexplored wilderness. Australia's largest offshore island has everything you might expect from such a place: vast tracts of rain forest roamed by creatures like the Tasmanian devil, wild coastline battered by ferocious winds, historic towns built by 19th-century convicts, mountain peaks, alpine meadows, lakes, eucalyptus stands, and fertile farmland.

Europeans arrived in Tasmania (or Van Diemen's Land, as it was once known) in 1642, when the sailor Abel Tasman set anchor off its south-west coast. It wasn't identified as an island until 1798. Tasmania made its mark as a dumping ground for convicts, who were more often than not transported for petty crimes in their homeland. The brutal system of control spilled over into persecution of the native population. The last full-blooded Tasmanian Aborigine died in 1876, 15 years after the last convict transportation.

Getting There

Tasmania is easily accessible by air from Sydney and other state capitals. Airfares are very competitive, with several companies trying to outdo each other for the cheapest fares. If you think that getting there is half the fun, then opt for a ferry trip from Melbourne.

By air

Qantas (☎ **13 13 13** in Australia; www.qantas.com.au) runs frequent daily service to both Hobart and Launceston from most major mainland cities. **Virgin Blue** (☎ **13 67 89** in Australia; www.virginblue.com.au) offers discount daily flights to Hobart and Launceston, with connections from other state capitals. **Jetstar** (☎ **13 15 38** in Australia; www.jetstar. com.au), a Qantas offshoot, also flies to Hobart and Launceston. **Regional Express** (☎ **13 17 13** in Australia; www.regionalexpress.com.au) flies from Melbourne to Devonport and Burnie in the state's north. A newcomer to the market is Singapore-based **Tiger Airways** (☎ **03/9335-3033;** www.tigerairways.com), which, started offering cut-price tickets between Melbourne and Launceston in 2007.

Hobart Airport is about 15 minutes from the city center. By taxi it costs approximately A$20 (US$16/£8). The **Airporter Shuttle Bus** (☎ **0419/ 382 240** mobile) meets planes and delivers passengers to hotels in the city and farther afield for A$12 (US$9.60/£4.80) adults one-way (A$20/ US$16/£8 adults round-trip), A$6 (US$4.80/£2.40) one-way for kids. If you're departing Hobart on an early flight (6 a.m., 6:30 a.m., or 7:25 a.m.), you need to make a booking by 8 p.m. the previous evening.

In Launceston, the **Airport Shuttle** (☎ **03/6343 6677**) provides transportation between city hotels and the airport from 8:45 a.m. to 5 p.m. daily for A$11 (US$8/£4) adults one-way, A$5 (US$4/£2) children 4 to 16.

By ferry

Two high-speed ferry services connect Melbourne and Tasmania. The *Spirit of Tasmania I* and *II* can each carry 1,400 passengers as well as cars. They make the crossing from Melbourne's Station Pier to Tasmania's Devonport (on the north coast) in around ten hours. The ferries leave both Melbourne and Devonport at 9 p.m. and arrive at around 7 a.m. From roughly December 20 to April 27, day service is available on weekends, leaving both ports at 9 a.m. and arriving at 7 p.m. Prices are based on shoulder and peak times: The shoulder seasons run from roughly August 31 to December 6, and from January 27 to April 27. A one-way seat costs A$114 to A$168 (US$91–US$134/£46–£67) adults, A$102 to A$131 (US$82–US$105/£41–£53) children; prices vary depending on the season. Three- to four-berth cabins cost A$212 to A$272 (US$170–US$218/ £85–£109) adults, A$118 to A$146 (US$94–US$117/£47–£58) kids; prices vary depending on the season and on whether you have a porthole. Twin cabins cost A$236 to A$302 (US$189–US$242/£95–£121) adults, A$128 to A$162 (US$102–US$130/£51–£65) children, depending on the season. Deluxe cabins cost A$326 to A$418 (US$261–US$334/£131–£167) adults and kids, depending on the season. Transporting a standard-size car costs A$79 to A$121 (US$63–US$97/£32–£48), depending on size, year-round.

Make reservations for any of the ferries through **TT-Line** (☎ **1800/634 906** in Australia, or 03/9206 6211; www.spiritoftasmania.com.au). Special offers are regularly available. **Tasmanian Redline** coaches (☎ **03/6336 1446;** www.redlinecoaches.com.au) connect with each ferry and transfer passengers to Launceston and Hobart.

Tasmania

Orienting Yourself in Hobart

Tasmania's capital (pop. 126,000) is second in age only to Sydney among Australia's cities. Its main features are its harbor and the colonial cottages that line the narrow lanes of Battery Point. As in Sydney, Hobart's harbor is the city's focal point, attracting yachts from all over the world. Down by the waterfront, Salamanca Place bursts with galleries, pubs, cafes, and an excellent market on Saturdays. Europeans settled in Hobart in 1804. Hobart, the southernmost Australian state capital, is closer to the Antarctic coast than it is to Perth in Western Australia; navigators, whalers, and explorers have long regarded it as the gateway to the south.

Introducing Hobart's Neighbourhoods

- **Battery Point:** This area was named after a battery of guns (long since removed) overlooking the Derwent River in 1818. In colonial times the sandstone buildings were occupied by sailors, fishermen, whalers, coopers, merchants, shipwrights, and master mariners.

- **Central Business District (CBD):** Located on the west side of the water, the CBD has main thoroughfares — Campbell, Argyle, Elizabeth, Murray, and Harrington streets — sloping down to the busy harbor.

- **Mount Wellington:** Mount Wellington is a 1,270m-high (4,000-ft.) mountain just a 20-minute drive from the city center. The drive to the summit takes you through temperate rain forest and up to sub-alpine flora and glacial rock formations. You can take in panoramic views of Hobart, Bruny Island, and the Tasman Peninsula from its peak.

- **North Hobart:** A northern suburb, North Hobart features a separate town center with good eateries and surrounding historic bed-and-breakfast properties.

- **Salamanca Place:** Hobart's historic waterfront includes this long row of stylish 1830s sandstone warehouses. The buildings house boutiques, bars, bookshops, restaurants, cafes, galleries, and jewelers. Each Saturday, the Salamanca Square, within Salamanca Place, hosts the Salamanca Markets, where you can buy anything from handmade toys to fruits and vegetables. Behind Salamanca Place is Salamanca Square, where you can sit by a fountain and listen to the street musicians.

Finding Information after You Arrive

The **Tasmanian Travel and Information Centre** (☎ **03/6230 8233;** tasbookings@tasvisinfo.com.au) is at 20 Davey Street. It's open Monday through Friday from 8:30 a.m. to 5:15 p.m., Saturday and public holidays from 9 a.m. to 4 p.m., and Sunday from 9 a.m. to 1 p.m. (Dec–Apr 9 a.m.–4 p.m. daily).

Hobart

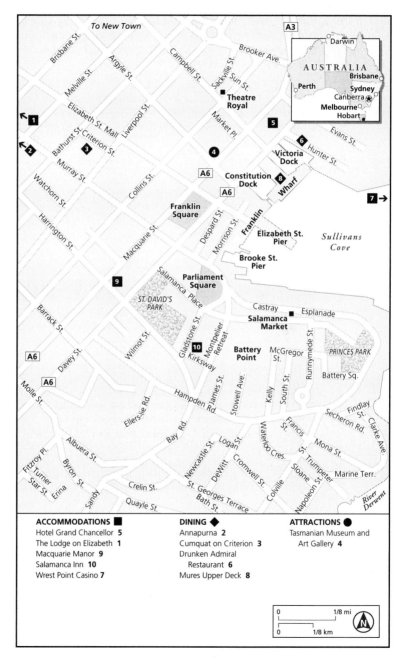

ACCOMMODATIONS ■
Hotel Grand Chancellor **5**
The Lodge on Elizabeth **1**
Macquarie Manor **9**
Salamanca Inn **10**
Wrest Point Casino **7**

DINING ◆
Annapurna **2**
Cumquat on Criterion **3**
Drunken Admiral
  Restaurant **6**
Mures Upper Deck **8**

ATTRACTIONS ●
Tasmanian Museum and
  Art Gallery **4**

Getting Around and Touring Hobart

✔ **By taxi:** Several cab companies operate in and around Hobart, though the city is so small you most likely won't use them. Try **City Cabs** (☎ **13 10 08** in Australia) or **Taxi Combined Services** (☎ **13 22 27** in Australia).

✔ **By bus: Metro Tasmania** (☎ **13 22 01** or 03/6233 4232; www.metro tas.com.au) operates public buses throughout the city and suburban areas. Single tickets cost A$1.90 to A$4.30 (US$1.50–US$3.40/£0.75–£1.70) depending on how far you're going. Day Rover tickets are good between 9 a.m. and 4:30 p.m. and after 6 p.m. during the week and all day on weekends; they cost A$4.60 (US$3.70/£1.85). A family day ticket costs A$13 (US$10/£5). Buy tickets from the bus driver. If you plan on busing about, stop at the Metro Shop, in the General Post Office building on the corner of Elizabeth and Macquarie streets, and pick up a timetable, brochures, and sightseeing information.

Tassielink (☎ **1300/300 520** in Australia, or 03/6230 8900; www.tassielink.com.au) offers half-day sightseeing tours of Hobart and Mount Wellington by coach. The tours leave at 2 p.m. Tuesday and Thursday afternoons and 9 a.m. on Sunday morning from the Hobart Bus terminal, 64 Brisbane St. Tickets cost A$55 (US$44/£22) adults, A$33 (US$26/£13) kids.

✔ **On foot: Hobart Historic Tours** (☎ **03/6230 8233** or 03/6278 3338; www.hobarthistorictours.com.au) runs a fascinating two-hour walking tour of Hobart every day between October 1 and April 30. It departs at 10 a.m. from outside the Tasmanian Travel and Information Centre. A Historic Pub Tour, departing the same place at 5 p.m. in the same months, takes you to three waterfront pubs and will enthrall you with stories of alcohol-sodden shenanigans. You even get to meet some shady actor-characters. The price includes two tastings. Both tours cost A$25 (US$20/£10) adults, A$13 (US$10/£5) children 8 to 16. Kids under 8 are free. It also runs a Battery Point Walk looking at the small artisans' cottages and grand houses. It departs at 3:30 p.m. daily and costs A$23 (US$18/£9), A$12 (US$9.60/£4.80) for children ages 8 to 16.

Staying in Style in Hobart

Hobart isn't an expensive city for lodgings, though you should expect prices to go up if you have water views. For something different, you could stay with a Tasmanian family in town or at a farm in the country, or arrange accommodations in one of the many boutique B&Bs throughout Tasmania. Contact **Heritage Tasmania Pty Ltd.,** P.O. Box 780, Sandy Bay, TAS 7005 (☎ **03/6233 5511;** fax 03/6233 5510). Nightly B&B rates range from A$60 to A$160 (US$48–US$128/£24–£64) for a double.

The top hotels

Hotel Grand Chancellor
$$$ CBD

If you prefer standard hotel accommodations to one of Hobart's many stately old homesteads, then book a room at this property overlooking the yachts and fishing boats in Victoria Dock. Standard rooms are spacious and comfortable, with large polished granite bathrooms. More than half the rooms have water views. Eight are equipped for travelers with disabilities. The lobby is an impressive marble-and-granite construction with a big curved window to catch the action on the docks. The hotel also has a first-class restaurant specializing in innovative Tasmanian cuisine. A heated indoor pool and a health club come as standard.

See map p. 467. 1 Davey St., Hobart, TAS 7000. ☎ 1800/753 379 in Australia, or 03/6235 4535. Fax: 03/6223 8175. www.ghihotels.com/hgc. *Free parking. Rack rates: A$260 (US$208/£104) double, A$365 (US$292/£146) executive suite; extra person A$30 (US$24/£12). Children under 15 stay free in parent's room. Very good deals are available on the Web site. AE, DC, MC, V.*

Macquarie Manor
$$ City Centre

Macquarie Manor is a classic colonial-style manor, built in 1875 as a doctor's surgery and residence. Extra rooms were added in 1950. Thick carpets and double-glazed windows keep the place quiet, even though it's on the main road, 2 blocks from the bus terminal. Rooms, which vary enormously, are comfortable and elegantly furnished. One room is suitable for people with disabilities. The staff is friendly and will be happy to escort you around the premises. Check out the delightful dining room and the drawing room complete with old couches and a grand piano.

See map p. 467. 172 Macquarie St., Hobart, TAS 7000. ☎ 1800/243 044 in Australia, or 03/6224 4999. Fax: 03/6224 4333. www.macmanor.com.au. *Free parking. Rack rates: A$190 (US$152/£76) double, A$250 (US$200/£100) Heritage suite, A$275 (US$220/£110) Macquarie suite; extra adult A$40 (US$32/£16), extra child A$20 (US$16/£8). Rates include full breakfast. AE, DC, MC, V.*

Wrest Point Casino
$$$–$$$$ Wrest Point

Beside the Derwent River, 3km (2 miles) from the city center, this hotel/casino complex looks out across the harbor and the city and up to Mount Wellington. All rooms feature Tasmanian oak furniture and plush carpets, and more expensive units have exceptional views. Although it may not be as convenient to the city center as the Hotel Grand Chancellor (though it's certainly walkable), the views make it a class above. Wrest Point Casino has several bars and restaurants, as well as a large outdoor pool, a health club, and a nine-hole putting course. Taxis from Wrest Point to the city cost around A$10 (US$8/£4), and the Busy Bee bus nos. 54 and 55 operates to and from the city every 15 minutes.

See map p. 467. 410 Sandy Bay Rd., Sandy Bay, TAS 7005. ☎ *1800/703 006 in Australia, or 03/6211 1750. Fax: 03/6225 3744.* www.wrestpoint.com.au. *Free parking. Rack rates: A$242–A$264 (US$193–US$211/£97–£106) double, A$330 (US$264/£132) suite with Jacuzzi; extra adult A$33 (US$26/£13). Check the Web site for deals. AE, DC, MC, V.*

Runner-up hotels

The Lodge on Elizabeth

$$ City Centre   The Lodge on Elizabeth is in the second-oldest building in Tasmania, some parts of which date to 1810. Originally a gentleman's residence, it later became the first private boys' school in Tasmania. It's well situated just a 12-minute walk from Salamanca Place and is surrounded by restaurants. All rooms are decorated with antiques; many are quite romantic, with four-poster beds. Standard rooms have just a shower, whereas deluxe rooms come with more antiques and a large granite bathroom with a Jacuzzi. The Convict's Cottage is a cute self-contained spa cottage, just for two, in the grounds.

See map p. 467. 249 Elizabeth St., Hobart, TAS 7000. ☎ *03/6231 3830. Fax: 03/6234 2566.* www.thelodge.com.au. *Free parking. Rack rates: A$ 120 (US$ 96/£48) small double with bathroom, A$ 140 (US$ 112/£56) large double with bathroom, A$ 160 (US$ 128/£65) Convict's Cottage; extra person A$ 30 (US$ 24/£12). Rates include breakfast. AE, DC, MC, V.*

Salamanca Inn

$$ City Centre   Conveniently located on the edge of the central business district and toward the waterfront near Battery Point, Salamanca Inn features modern and pleasant apartments. The place features queen-size beds, leather couches, Tasmanian oak furniture, galley-style kitchens, and spacious living areas. The more expensive suites are a bit plusher.

See map p. 467. 10 Gladstone St., Hobart, TAS 7000. ☎ *03/6223 3300. Fax: 03/6223 7167.* www.salamancainn.com.au. *Free parking. Rack rates: A$ 198 (US$ 158/£78) 1-bedroom apartment, A$ 220 (US$ 176/£88) 2-bedroom suite, A$ 260 (US$ 208/£104) 2-bedroom deluxe suite; extra adult A$ 25 (US$ 20/£10), extra child 3–14 A$ 15 (US$ 12/ £6). Ask about weekend and long-stay packages. AE, DC, MC, V.*

Dining Out

Hobart specializes in seafood, so make sure you take the opportunity to taste some of the local catch.

amulet
$$$ North Hobart   MODERN AUSTRALIAN

North Hobart has a reputation for happening restaurants, and the eatery of the moment is amulet, which prides itself on seasonal produce and local ingredients. Inside, it's light and lovely during the day and moody at night.

This restaurant is a wonderful place for breakfast and a weekend brunch — the extensive menus are inspiring. As for dinner, try the eggplant *cordon bleu* stuffed with smoked soy on hummus and pine nuts, or the spice-crusted lamb on pumpkin mash with sour cherry sauce.

333 Elizabeth St., North Hobart. ☎ *03/6234 8113.* www.northhobart.com/amulet. *Reservations recommended. Main courses: A$26–A$28 (US$21–US$22/£11). AE, MC, V. Open: Daily 10 a.m.–3 p.m. and 6–10 p.m.*

Annapurna
$$ North Hobart   INDIAN

This is a fabulous Indian restaurant, with rich red walls and even richer food. All your usual Indian fare is on the menu, plus some unusual dishes, such as the Calcutta chicken, a Goan prawn curry, and a goat curry. Top of the lot is the *masala dosa,* a south Indian crepe filled with curried potato. Plenty of vegetarian options are available.

See map p. 467. 305 Elizabeth St., North Hobart. ☎ *03/6236 9500.* www.north hobart.com/annapurna. *Reservations recommended. Main courses: A$12–A$17 (US$9.50–US$14/£4.80–£7). AE, MC, V. Open: Mon–Fri noon to 3 p.m., daily 5:30–10 p.m.*

Cumquat on Criterion
$ City Centre   ASIAN/AUSTRALIAN

This cafe is an excellent breakfast venue, offering everything from egg on toast to traditional porridge with brown sugar. On the menu for lunch and dinner you may find Thai beef curry, laksa, a daily risotto, and chermoula-marinated fish. The desserts can be great. Vegetarians, vegans, and those on a gluten-free diet are very well catered to, as are carnivores.

See map p. 467. 10 Criterion St., Hobart. ☎ *03/6234 5858. Reservations recommended. Main courses: A$7.50–A$15 (US$6–US$12/£3–£6). No credit cards. Open: Mon–Fri 8 a.m.–6 p.m.*

Drunken Admiral Restaurant
$$ City Centre   SEAFOOD

The Drunken Admiral, opposite the Hotel Grand Chancellor on the water-front, is a popular spot with tourists, and can get raucous on busy evenings. The main attraction to start the meal with is its famous seafood chowder, swimming with anything that was on sale at the docks that morning. The Yachties Seafood Grill (A$28/US$22/£11) is a full plate of squid, scallops, fish, mussels, and prawns, but plenty of simpler fish dishes are on the menu. We recommend the Tassie mussels steamed in white wine, tomatoes, and shallots with a hunk of bread.

See map p. 467. 17–19 Hunter St., Hobart. ☎ *03/6234 1903. Reservations required. Main courses: A$20–A$28 (US$16–US$22/£8–£11). AE, DC, MC, V. Open: Daily 6–10:30 p.m.*

Mures Upper Deck
$$$ City Centre   SEAFOOD

This large, bustling waterfront restaurant offers great views of bobbing yachts as well as fine seafood caught on the owner's own fishing boats. We recommend starting with a bowl of the signature Mures Smokey Chowder or some local oysters. Main courses could include grilled Atlantic salmon with an asparagus and smoked salmon terrine, or blue eye (a fish) pan-fried in a spice mix of cumin, fennel, and black pepper. A real treat is the seafood platter, costing A$50 (US$40/£20). The best dessert is the restaurant's famous summer pudding, which almost bursts with berries. The complex includes **Lower Deck,** a popular self-service family restaurant where you can dine well for under A$20 (US$16/£8).

See map p. 467. Between Victoria and Constitution docks, Hobart. ☎ *03/6231 2121.* www.mures.com.au. *Reservations recommended. Main courses: A$26–A$33 (US$21–US$26/£11–£13). AE, DC, MC, V. Open: Daily noon to 10 p.m.*

Exploring Hobart

The top attractions

In addition to walking around the waterfront and exploring the historic areas of Battery Point and Salamanca Square, you may want to save time for the following attractions.

Cadbury Chocolate Factory
Claremont

Eat chocolates until you burst on this Willy Wonka–type trip. Book well ahead, because chocolate tours are very popular. Keep in mind that you'll need to climb lots of stairs inside the factory, where you'll see chocolate being made. You can visit the factory on a ferry tour (see the "Cruising the Derwent" sidebar for more information).

Claremont, 16km (10 miles) north of Hobart. ☎ *1800/627 367 in Australia, or 03/6249 0333. Admission: A$13 (US$10/£5.20) adults, A$6.50 (US$5.20/£2.60) children. Open: Tours start Mon–Fri 9 a.m., 9:30 a.m., 10 a.m., 10:30 a.m., 11 a.m., noon, 1 p.m., and 1:30 p.m.*

Cascade Brewery Tours
South Hobart

Cascade Premium is one of the best beers in Australia. To see how this heady amber nectar is produced, head to Australia's oldest brewery and tag along on a two-hour tour, which includes tastings — and a stroll through the grand old Woodstock Gardens behind the factory. The tour involves lots of stairs.

Cascade Road, South Hobart. ☎ *03/6224 1117. Admission: A$18 (US$14/£7) adults, A$7 (US$5.60/£2.80) children 5–12, A$42 (US$34/£17) families. Open: Tours start Mon–Fri 9 a.m., 9:30 a.m., 10 a.m., 10:30 a.m., 11 a.m., noon, 1 p.m., and 1:30 p.m. Closed public holidays. Reservations required. Bus: 44, 46, or 49 (stop 18).*

Cruising the Derwent

Get out and explore the glorious Derwent River estuary on one of Hobart's boat tours.

Captain Fells Ferries (☎ **03/6223 5893**; www.captainfellshistoricferries. com.au) offers morning tea, lunch, afternoon, and dinner cruises. A dinner cruise on a historic ferry costs A$40 (US$32/£16) adults, A$110 (US$88/£44) families; lunch cruises are A$35 (US$28/£14) adults, A$85 (US$68/£34) families. A 90-minute Discovery Cruise departs at 10:30 a.m. and 2:30 p.m. and costs A$20 (US$16K£8) adults, A$50 (US40/£20) families.

The company also runs **Cadbury Factory Tours,** which include a double-decker bus transfer, a tour of the factory, a harbor cruise, and a two-course lunch for A$55 (US$44/£22) adults, A$140 (US$112/£56) families. These leave in the morning on most weekdays (check with the company for departure days and times). Cruises depart from Franklin Wharf behind the wooden cruise-sales booths beside Elizabeth Street Wharf at the bottom of Elizabeth Street.

Derwent River Cruises, Brook Street, Pier (☎ **03/6233 1914**; www.derwentriver cruises.com.au), offers a 75-minute cruise of the harbor daily at 10 a.m. (summer only), 11:30 a.m., and 2 p.m. It costs A$25 (US$20/£10) adults, A$12 (US$9.60/£4.80) children, A$66 (US$53/£27) families. It also offers a two-hour Storm Bay Cruise, which includes cliff views, tales of whales and history, and a view of Iron Pot lighthouse, the oldest lighthouse in Australia. It costs A$35 (US$28/£14) adults, A$18 (US$14/£7) children, A$90 (US$72/£36) families. It leaves at 3:30 p.m. between October 1 and May 31. The company also runs a cruise to Port Arthur.

Female Factory Historic Site and Island Produce Fudge Factory
South Hobart

This is an interesting stopover if you're visiting the Cascade Brewery or Mount Wellington. You get not only a trip around the successful fudge-making factory, but a guided tour around the remains of the women's prison next door. The tales told here will make the hairs on your neck stand on end — like the fact that 17 out of every 20 children born within the walls of the institution died soon after birth, and that women who died were tossed into an unmarked mass grave.

16 Degraves St., South Hobart. ☎ *03/6223 1559. Fax: 03/6223 1556.* www.female factory.com.au. *Admission: A$10 (US$8/£4) adults, A$5 (US$4/£2) children, A$25 (US$20/£10) families. MC, V. Open: Tours run Easter Tuesday to Dec 24 Mon–Fri 9:30 a.m. (closed weekends and public holidays); Dec 26 to Easter Monday daily 9:30 a.m., Mon–Fri 2 p.m.*

Royal Tasmanian Botanical Gardens
City Centre

Established in 1818, these gardens are known for English-style plant and tree layouts including a great conifer collection and a superb Japanese garden (better than some we've seen in Kyoto), and seasonal blooming plants. A busy road nearby somewhat disturbs the peaceful atmosphere. A restaurant provides lunch and teas. To walk here from the city center, partly along a pleasant lane known as Soldier's Walk, takes around 40 minutes — but it's badly signposted.

On the Queens Domain near Government House. ☎ *03/6234 6299. Free admission. Open: Daily 8 a.m.–6:30 p.m. (until 5 p.m. in winter).*

More cool things to see and do

If you have more time in Hobart, check out the following:

- ✔ **Bonorong Park Wildlife Centre,** Briggs Road, Brighton (☎ **03/ 6268 1184**), has plenty of wallabies, snakes, koalas, Tasmanian devils, and wombats. The Bush Tucker shed serves lunch, *billy tea* (tea brewed in a metal pot with a gum leaf thrown in), and *damper* (Australian-style campfire bread). The park is on the side of a steep hill. Take a bus to Glenorchy from the central bus terminal in Hobart (about 10 minutes), then take bus no. 125 or 126 to the park. Drive north on Route 1 to Brighton; it's about 25 minutes north of Hobart and is well signposted. Admission: A$11 (US$8.80/ £4.40) adults, A$6 (US$4.80/£2.40) children under 15. Open: Daily 9 a.m. to 5 p.m.

- ✔ The **Tasmanian Museum and Art Gallery,** 40 Macquarie St. (☎ **03/6211 4177**), is the place to find out more about Tasmania's Aboriginal heritage, its history since settlement, and the island's wildlife. The art gallery has an impressive collection of paintings by Tom Roberts and by several convict artists. The pride of the collection is *The Conciliation,* by Benjamin Duttereau, one of the most historically significant paints in Australia. Admission: Free. Open: Daily 10 a.m. to 5 p.m.

Living It Up after Dark

- ✔ Opened in 1829 as a tavern and a brothel frequented by whalers, **Knopwood's Retreat,** 39 Salamanca Place (☎ **03/6223 5808**), is still a raucous place to be on Friday and Saturday evenings, when crowds cram the historic interior and spill out onto the streets. Light lunches are popular throughout the week, and occasionally you'll find jazz or blues on the menu.

- ✔ A favorite drinking hole in Hobart is **Irish Murphy's,** 21 Salamanca Place (☎ **03/6223 1119**), an atmospheric pub with stone walls and lots of dark wood. Local bands play Friday and Saturday evenings.

- ✔ If you want to tempt Lady Luck, head to the **Wrest Point Casino,** in the Wrest Point Hotel, 410 Sandy Bay Rd. (☎ **03/6225 0112**), Australia's first legal gambling club. Smart, casual attire required (collared shirts for men).

Fast Facts: Hobart

Area Code

The area code in Tasmania is **03**.

American Express

There is no American Express office in Tasmania, but you can cash checks at post offices.

Doctor

City Doctors Travel Clinic, 93 Collins St. (☎ 03/6231 3003).

Emergencies

Call ☎ **000** for an ambulance, the police, or the fire department.

Hospitals

The Royal Hobart Hospital is at 48 Liverpool Street (☎ 03/6222 8423).

Internet Access

Service Tasmania, 134 Macquarie St. (☎ 1300/135 513), offers 30 minutes of free Internet access.

Newspapers/Magazines

The *Hobart Mercury* is the local newspaper.

Pharmacies

A central drugstore is Chemist on Collins, 93 Collins St., City Centre (☎ 03/6235 0257).

Police

The City Station is at 43 Liverpool St. (☎ 03/6230 2111).

Post Offices

The main post office is on the corner of Macquarie and Elizabeth streets. It's open Monday through Friday from 8:30 a.m. to 5:30 p.m.

Restrooms

Public restrooms are available at the Argyle Street Carpark, 36 Argyle St.; in the Cat and Fiddle Arcade, 51 Murray St.; at the Centrepoint Shopping Centre, 70 Murray St.; and in Franklin Square, off Elizabeth Street.

Transit Information

Metro Tas (☎ 13 22 01; www.metrotas.com.au) coordinates the local bus system.

Chapter 23

Exploring the Rest of Tasmania

*O*ne of the advantages of visiting Tasmania is that you can explore the entire state more easily than some of Australia's larger regions. After Hobart, you can easily get to the other major towns and historical sites, as well as the amazingly beautiful Freycinet National Park.

Convict Heritage in Port Arthur

Port Arthur (102km/63 miles southeast of Hobart on the Tasman Peninsula) houses the remains of Tasmania's largest penal colony — Australia's version of Devil's Island. You can spend a whole day in this picturesque yet haunting place.

From 1830 to 1877, Port Arthur was one of the harshest institutions of its type anywhere in the world. It was built to house the settlement's most notorious prisoners. Nearly 13,000 convicts found their way here, and nearly 2,000 died while incarcerated.

Getting there

Port Arthur is a one-and-a-half-hour drive from Hobart on the Lyell and Arthur highways. **Tassielink** (☎ **1300/300 520** in Australia, or 03/6230 8900) runs trips from Hobart to the former penal settlement on Tuesday, Wednesday (in summer only), Thursday, Friday, and Sunday. Tours cost A$90 (US$72/£36) adults, A$54 (US$43/£22) children 4 to 16. The trip includes a guided tour of the Port Arthur site.

Derwent River Cruises, Brook Street, Pier (☎ **03/6233 1914;** www.
derwentrivercruises.com.au), runs an exceptional tour to Port
Arthur. You travel the sea route of convicts transported from Hobart to
Port Arthur. The all-day journey includes a 2½-hour cruise along the
coastline, entrance to the site, another 20-minute cruise, and a return by
bus to Hobart. It costs A$149 (US$119/£69) adults, A$110 (US$88/£44)
children, A$434 (US$347/£174) families. The cruises run on Wednesdays,
Fridays, and Sundays from October 1 to May 31.

Exploring Port Arthur

The **Port Arthur Historic Site** (☎ **03/6251 2310;** www.portarthur.
org.au) has some 30 19th-century buildings. You can tour the remains
of the church, guard tower, model prison, and several other buildings.
Touring with a guide, who can describe what the buildings were used
for, is best. Don't miss the museum, which has a scale model of the complex, as well as leg irons and chains.

The site is open daily from 9 a.m. to 5 p.m.; admission is A$25 (US$20/
£10) adults, A$11 (US$8.80/£4.40) children 4 to 12, A$55 (US$44/£22) families. The admission price is good for two consecutive days and includes
a walking tour and a boat cruise. There is also a separate cruise to the
Isle of the Dead off the coast of Port Arthur twice a day; some 1,769 convicts and 180 free settlers were buried here, mostly in mass graves with
no headstones. The cruise costs an extra A$10 (US$8/£4) adults, A$6.50
(US$5.20/£2.60) children, A$29 (US$23/£12) families.

Lantern-lit **Ghost Tours of Port Arthur** leave at 6:30 p.m., 8:30 p.m., and
9:30 p.m. (8:30 p.m. only during the winter) and cost A$17 (US$14/£7)
adults, A$10 (US$8/£4) children, A$45 (US$36/£18) families (2 adults, up
to 6 children). Reservations are essential; call ☎ **1800/659 101** in
Australia.

The main feature of the visitor center is a fabulous **Interpretive Gallery,**
which takes visitors through the process of sentencing in England to
transportation to Van Diemen's Land. The gallery contains a courtroom,

Visiting Taz in his native land

Eighty kilometers (50 miles) from Hobart is the **Tasmanian Devil Conservation Park,** Port
Arthur Highway, Taranna (☎ **03/6250 3230;** www.tasmaniandevilpark.com), which
houses orphaned or injured native animals, including Tasmanian devils, quolls, kangaroos, eagles, and owls. The park is open daily from 9 a.m. to 5 p.m. Admission is A$12
(US$9.60/£4.80) adults, A$6 (US$4.80/£2.40) children, A$30 (US$24/£12) families. Tasmanian
devils are fed daily at 10 a.m., 11 a.m., and 5 p.m. The center is breeding devils with unusual
genes that could make them resistant to the facial tumor disease that's devastating the
population. If you want to help save the Tassie devil, go to the park's Web site.

a blacksmith's shop, a lunatic asylum, and more. Allow between three and four hours to explore the site and the gallery.

Allow at least one-and-a-half hours to enjoy the scenic drive from Hobart to Port Arthur. The drive along the Tasman and Arthur highways forms part of the **Convict Trail Touring Route** and takes in breathtaking seascapes, rolling farmlands and villages, vineyards, and artists' studios.

Exploring Freycinet National Park

The **Freycinet Peninsula** (206km/128miles northeast of Hobart) hangs down off the eastern coast of Tasmania. From Hobart it's about a three-hour drive to the park. The peninsula is a place of craggy pink-granite peaks, spectacular white beaches, wetlands, heathland, coastal dunes, and dry eucalyptus forests. This is the place to come to spot sea eagles, wallabies, seals, pods of dolphins, and humpback and southern right whales during their migration to and from the warmer waters of northern New South Wales from May through August.

The township of **Coles Bay** is the main staging post, and there are many **bushwalks** in the area. The **Moulting Lagoon Game Reserve** — an important breeding ground for black swans and wild ducks — is signposted along the highway into Coles Bay from Bicheno. Some 10,000 black swans inhabit the lake, so it's unusual *not* to see them. Spectacular **Wineglass Bay,** named one of the world's top ten beaches by *Outside* magazine, is an amazingly beautiful spot for a walk.

Getting there

There are no direct public buses from Hobart. **Tasmanian Redline Coaches** (☎ **1300/360 000** in Australia, or 03/6336 1446) run from 112 George St., Launceston, to Bicheno at 2 p.m. Monday through Thursday, and at 3:45 p.m. on Friday, and take under three hours. **Tassielink** (☎ **1300/300 520** in Australia, or 03/6272 6611; www.tigerline.com.au) runs buses from Launceston to Bicheno on Monday, Wednesday, Friday, and Sunday at 8:30 a.m. From Bicheno, catch a local bus run by **Bicheno Coach Services** (☎ **03/6257 0293,** or 0419/570 293 mobile) for the 35-minute trip to the park. Buses leave at 9 a.m. daily and 3 p.m. Sunday through Friday from the Freycinet Bakery and Cafe. Buses also meet every coach from Launceston, but you need to book in advance.

Tassielink (☎ **1300/300 520** in Australia, or 03/6230 8900) offers a day trip to Freycinet with an optional walking trip to Wineglass Bay from both Hobart and Launceston on Friday and Sunday year-round. It costs A$85 (US$68/£34) adults, A$51 (US$41/£21) children.

Getting information after you arrive

The **Visitor Information Centre** (☎ **03/6375 1333;** fax: 03/6375 1533) on the Tasman Highway at Bicheno can arrange tour bookings. Otherwise, the **Tasmanian Travel and Information Centre** in Hobart (☎ **03/6230 8383**) can supply you with maps and details. Daily entry to the park costs A$10 (US$8/£4) per vehicle.

Exploring the park

If you have time to do only one walk, head out from Freycinet Lodge on a 30-minute uphill hike past spectacularly beautiful pink-granite outcrops to **Wineglass Bay Lookout** for breathtaking views. You can then head down to Wineglass Bay itself and back up again. The walk takes around two-and-a-half hours.

Tasmanian Expeditions (☎ **1300/666 851** in Australia, or 03/6339 3999; www.tas-ex.com) offers a three-day trip from Launceston and back that includes two nights in cabins at Coles Bay. The trip includes guided walks to Wineglass Bay and Mount Amor. It costs A$690 (US$552/£276) and departs year-round on Wednesday. The company also offers 6- and 12-night walking, rafting, and cycling trips, as well as walking trips all over Tasmania.

Spending the night in the park

Camping is available for A$10 (US$8/£4) per tent, though water is scarce. Call the **Parks and Wildlife Service** (☎ **03/6257 0107**).

Freycinet Lodge
$$$

We can't praise this ecofriendly lodge enough. Comfortable one- and two-room cabins spread unobtrusively through the bush, connected by raised walking tracks. Each has a balcony, and the more expensive ones have huge Jacuzzis. Twenty cabins have their own kitchens. The main part of the lodge houses a lounge room and an excellent restaurant that sweeps out onto a veranda overlooking the limpid green waters of Great Oyster Bay. The lodge is right next to the white sands of Hazards Beach, and from here it's an easy stroll to the start of the Wineglass Bay walk.

*Freycinet National Park, Coles Bay, TAS 7215. ☎ **1800/420 155** or 03/6225 7000. Fax: 03/6257 0278. www.puretasmania.com.au. Free parking. Rack rates: A$190 (US$152/£76) standard cabin, A$225 (US$180/£90) cabin with Jacuzzi, A$255 (US$204/£102) deluxe cabin with Jacuzzi; extra adult A$54 (US$41/£21). Children under 14 free in parents' room. Check the Web site for packages. AE, DC, MC, V.*

Visiting Launceston, Tasmania's Second City

Tasmania's second-largest city is Australia's third oldest, after Sydney and Hobart. At the head of the Tamar River, 50km (31 miles) inland from the state's north coast, and surrounded by undulating farmland, Launceston is a pleasant city crammed with elegant Victorian and Georgian architecture and plenty of remnants of convict days.

Local and state governments are overseeing the chipping away of its great architectural heritage in favor of the usual parking garages and concrete monoliths. However, Launceston (pop. 104,000) is still one of Australia's most beautiful cities and has plenty of parks and churches. It's also the gateway to the wineries of the Tamar Valley, the highlands and alpine lakes of the north, and the stunning beaches to the east.

Getting there

Qantas (☎ 13 13 13 in Australia), **Virgin Blue** (☎ 13 67 89 in Australia), and **Jetstar** (☎ 13 15 38 in Australia) carry passengers from Sydney and Melbourne to Launceston. The **Airport Shuttle** (☎ 03/6343 6677) provides transportation between city hotels and the airport from 8:45 a.m. to 5 p.m. daily for A$11 (US$8/£4) adults, A$5 (US$4/£2) kids 4 to 16, each way.

Tasmanian Redline Coaches (☎ 1300/360 000 in Australia; www.tas redline.com.au) depart Hobart for Launceston several times daily (trip time: around 2 hours, 40 minutes). The one-way fare is around A$30 (US$24/£12).

The drive from Hobart to Launceston takes just over two hours on Highway 1.

Getting around

Launceston is easy to explore on foot. A must for any visitor is a stroll with **Launceston Historic Walks** (☎ 03/6331 3679; e-mail: harris.m@ bigpond.com), which leaves from the Gateway Tasmania Travel Centre Monday through Friday at 9:45 a.m. (Weekend walks can also be arranged.) The one-hour walk gives a fascinating insight into Launceston's history and costs A$15 (US$12/£6).

Tassielink (☎ 1300/300 520 in Australia, or 03/6230 8900) operates a half-day coach tour of the city on Monday, Wednesday, and Friday at 9:30 a.m. It costs A$51 (US$41/£21) adults, A$31 (US$25/£13) children.

Spending the night in Launceston

There are a couple of good hotels in Launceston, but we really recommend that you try to stay in one of the historic buildings remodeled into up-market guesthouses, apartments, or cottages.

Alice's Cottages & Spa Hideaways
$$ City Center

We highly recommend these delightful cottages: **Alice's Place,** which sleeps two, was made from bits and pieces of razed historic buildings; **Ivy Cottage** is a restored Georgian house (ca. 1831). Both are furnished with antiques and period bric-a-brac. Kitchens are fully equipped, and both units have Jacuzzis; they share a garden. Guests come and go as they please, and stay here on their own. (Check in at the reception area, 129 Balfour St.) Also available are **Alice's Hideaways,** five other cottages in a colonial Australian theme, some of which sleep four; and four cute cottages collectively known as **The Shambles.** A recent addition is **Aphrodites Deluxe Spa,** a large, regal setup with a formal dining room.

129 Balfour St., Launceston, TAS 7250. ☎ *03/6334 2231. Fax: 03/6334 2696.* www. cottagesofthecolony.com.au. *Rack rates: Alice's Place, Ivy Cottage, Alice's Hideaways all A$197 (US$157/£78); Shambles cottages A$160 (US$128/£64); Aphrodites A$230 (US$184/£92). Minimum 2-night stay. Rates include breakfast ingredients left in your fridge. AE, DC, MC, V.*

Hotel Grand Chancellor Launceston
$$$ City Center

This centrally located "grand" hotel is a short stroll from the main shopping precinct, public gardens, and other city features. The rooms are large and elegant and the restaurant is good. Standard rooms have two double beds or a king-size bed. There's a piano bar and a brasserie.

29 Cameron St., Launceston, TAS 7250. ☎ *1800/555 811 in Australia, or 03/6334 3434. Fax: 03/6331 7347. Rack rates: A$220 (US$176/£88) double, A$245 (US$196/£99) room with Jacuzzi, A$290–A$500 (US$232–US$400/£116–£200) suite. AE, DC, MC, V.*

Peppers Seaport Hotel
$$ Seaport

The hotel is part of a redevelopment of the Seaport Dock area — five minutes by car from downtown — which includes new restaurants, entertainment venues, and shopping facilities. The hotel is built on the site of an old dry dock and has been designed in the shape of a ship. The décor is luxurious and contemporary nautical in style, using soft, light colors, natural timbers, and chromes. Rooms are spacious and most have balconies looking over the river, or the town center to the mountains beyond. Each has a good kitchenette and an extra foldout sofa bed.

28 Seaport Blvd., Launceston, TAS 7250. ☎ *03/6345 3333. Fax: 03/6345 3300.* www. peppers.com.au. *Free parking. Rack rates: A$125 (US$100/£50) river-view double, A$120 (US$96/£48) city-view double, A$146–A$224 (US$116–US$195/£58–£98) suite. AE, DC, MC, V.*

York Mansions
$$$ City Center

Within the walls of the National Trust–classified York Mansions, built in 1840, are five spacious apartments, each with a distinct character. The Duke of York apartment is fashioned after a gentleman's drawing room, with rich leather sofa, antiques, and a collection of historical books. The light, airy Duchess of York unit has two bedrooms, hand-painted silk panels, and a Jacuzzi. Each apartment has its own kitchen, dining room, living room, bedrooms, bathroom, and laundry. A CD player and large-screen TV add modern touches. The ingredients for a hearty breakfast can be found in the refrigerator. There's also a delightful cottage garden.

9–11 York St., Launceston, TAS 7250. ☎ *03/6334 2933. Fax: 03/6334 2870.* www.york mansions.com.au. *Rack rates: A$216–A$242 (US$173–US$194/£87–£97). Rates include breakfast provisions. AE, DC, MC, V.*

Dining locally

Most places to eat in Launceston don't have a fixed closing time — they close when the last customer has eaten.

Fee & Me Restaurant
$$$ MODERN AUSTRALIAN

Perhaps the best restaurant in Launceston, Fee & Me is in a grand old mansion. Diners choose a selection from five categories, moving from light to rich. An extensive wine list complements selections. A five-course meal could go something like this: Tasmanian smoked salmon with salad, capers, and a poached egg; followed by chile oysters with coconut sauce and vermicelli noodles; then ricotta and goat cheese gnocchi with creamed tomato and red capsicum; followed by Asian-style duck on bok choy with citrus sauce; topped off with coffee and chicory soufflé.

Corner of Charles and Frederick streets. ☎ *03/6331 3195. Reservations recommended. Main courses: A$42 (US$34/£17) for 3 courses, A$48 (US$38/£19) for 4 courses, A$50 (US$40/£20) for 5 courses. AE, DC, MC, V. Open: Mon–Sat 7–10:30 p.m.*

Konditorei Cafe Manfred
$ BAKERY

This German patisserie had to move to larger premises to keep up with demand for its sensational cakes and breads. It also added an a la carte restaurant serving up the likes of pastas and steaks. Light meals include croissants, salads, and cakes. You can eat inside or outside.

106 George St. ☎ *03/6334 2490. Main courses: A$15 (US$7.20–US$14/£3.60–£7), light meals A$4–A$5 (US$3.20–US$4/£1.60–£2). AE, DC, MC, V. Open: Mon–Fri 9 a.m.–5:30 p.m., Sat 8:30 a.m.–4 p.m.*

Stillwater River Café
$$$$ MODERN AUSTRALIAN

This fabulous eatery is inside an old mill beside the Tamar River. Come here for a good breakfast, a casual lunch at one of the tables outside overlooking the river, or an atmospheric dinner. The dinner menu is fascinating, with all sorts of delicacies including abalone and sea urchin. Try the seared scallops or the Vietnamese sugar-cooked pork belly. The wine cellar brings up a good selection of Tasmanian wines.

Ritchies Mill (bottom of Paterson Street). ☎ *03/6331 4153.* www.stillwater.net. au. *Reservations recommended. Main courses: Lunch A$19–A$24 (US$15–US$19/*

£7.50–£10); dinner A$66 (US$53/£27) for 2 courses, A$91 (US$73/£37) for 3 courses; 6-course tasting menu A$98 (US$78/£39), A$139 (US$111/£56) including matching wines. AE, MC, V. Open: Daily 8 a.m.–10 p.m.

The top attraction

Cataract Gorge

The result of violent earthquakes some 40 million years ago, Cataract Gorge is a scenic area ten minutes from Launceston. The South Esk River flows through the gorge and collects in a lake traversed by a yellow suspension bridge and the longest single-span chairlift in the world. The hike to the Duck Reach Power Station takes about 45 minutes. Other walks in the area are shorter and easier. The **Gorge Restaurant (☎ 03/6331 3330)** and a kiosk serve meals with views from outdoor tables.

Open: Chairlift (☎ 03/6331 5915) daily 9 a.m.–4:30 p.m. (except June 23–Aug 11, when it operates Sat–Sun only). Admission: A$8.50 (US$6.80/£3.40) adults, A$6 (US$4.80/£2.40) children under 16.

More cool things to see and do

An interesting little store is the 1860s **Old Umbrella Shop,** 60 George St. (**☎ 03/6331 9248**). Umbrellas spanning the last 100 years are on display, and modern "brollies" and souvenirs are for sale. Admission is free and it's open Monday through Friday from 9 a.m. to 5 p.m., Saturday from 9 a.m. to noon.

Another place worth visiting is the **Queen Victoria Museum & Art Gallery,** 2 Wellington St. (**☎ 03/6323 3777**). Opened in honor of Queen Victoria's Golden Jubilee in 1891, this museum houses a large collection of stuffed wildlife, including the extinct Tasmanian tiger. Admission is free, and it's open daily from 10 a.m. to 5 p.m.

Exploring Cradle Mountain and Lake St. Clair National Park

The national park and World Heritage area, 175km (109 miles) northwest of Hobart, encompasses Cradle Mountain and Lake St. Clair. It's one of the most spectacular regions in Australia. The 1,545m (5,068-ft.) mountain dominates the north part of the island, and the long, deep lake is to its south. Between them lie steep slopes, button grass plains, alpine forests, lakes filled with trout, and several rivers. **Mount Ossa,** in the center of the park, is Tasmania's highest point at 1,617m (5,304 ft.). The **Overland Track,** links Cradle Mountain with Lake St. Clair and is the best known of Australia's walking trails.

Getting there

Tassielink (☎ **1300/300 520** in Australia, or 03/6272 6611; www.tiger line.com.au) runs buses to Cradle Mountain from Hobart, Launceston, Devonport, and Strahan. Its summer Overland Track service leaves from either Launceston or Hobart and drops off passengers at the beginning of the walk (Cradle Mountain), and picks them up at Lake St. Clair before returning to either Launceston or Hobart. It costs A$90 (US$72/£36) starting from Launceston and returning to Hobart; A$119 (US$95/£48) starting at and returning to Hobart; and A$110 (US$88/£44) starting at and returning to Launceston. Check the Web site for departure times.

Maxwells Cradle Mountain–Lake St. Clair Charter Bus and Taxi Service (☎/fax **03/6492 1431**) runs buses from Devonport and Launceston to Cradle Mountain. The fare starts at A$35 (US$28/£14). The buses also travel to other areas nearby, such as the Walls of Jerusalem, as well as Lake St. Clair. Buses also run from the Cradle Mountain camp-ground to the start of the Overland Track.

Finding information after you arrive

The park headquarters, **Cradle Mountain Visitor Centre** (☎ **03/6492 1133;** www.parks.tas.gov.au), on the northern edge of the park outside Cradle Mountain Lodge, offers the best information on walks and treks. It's open daily from 8 a.m. to 5 p.m. (until 6 p.m. in summer).

Exploring the park

Cradle Mountain Lodge runs a daily program of guided walks, *abseiling* (rappelling), rock-climbing, and trout-fishing excursions for lodge guests. The park has plenty of trails that can be attempted by people equipped with directions from the staff at the park headquarters. Of the shorter walks, the stroll to Pencil Pines and the 5km (3-mile) walk to Dove Lake are the most pleasant. Between June and October, it's sometimes possible to cross-country ski in the park.

The best-known hiking trail in Australia is the **Overland Track,** an 85km (53-mile) route between Cradle Mountain and Lake St. Clair. The trek takes five to ten days and goes through high alpine plateaus, button grass plains, heathland, and rain forests, and passes glacial lakes, ice-carved crags, and waterfalls.

Several companies offer guided walks of the Overland Track October through April. For those who want to do it solo, simple public huts (on a first-come, first-served basis) and camping areas are available.

> ✔ **Tasmanian Expeditions** (☎ **1800/030 230** in Australia, or 03/6334 3477; www.tas-ex.com) offers a full eight-day trek on the Overland Track from Launceston. The price is A$1,790 (US$1,432/£716), all-inclusive. These trips depart every Saturday between November and April, with extra trips from late December to the end of January.

✔ **Cradle Mountain Huts** (P.O. Box 1879, Launceston, TAS 7250; ☎ 03/6331 2006; www.cradlehuts.com.au) runs six-day walks for A$2,450 (US$1,960/£998). Rates are all-inclusive and include transfers to and from Launceston. Treks leave daily between Christmas and early February, and around five times a week between November and April.

Staying in style

Cradle Mountain Lodge
$$$ **Cradle Mountain**

Cradle Mountain Lodge is marvelous. Just minutes from your bed are giant buttresses of 1,500-year-old trees, moss forests, mountain ridges, pools and lakes, and hordes of marsupials. The cabins are comfortable, the food excellent, the staff friendly, and the open fireplaces well worth cuddling up in front of. Each modern wood cabin has a potbellied stove as well as an electric heater for chilly evenings, a shower, and a small kitchen. There are no telephones or TVs in the rooms. Spa cabins come with carpets, Jacuzzis, and balconies offering a variety of views. Two cabins have limited facilities for travelers with disabilities. Guests have the use of the casual main lodge where almost every room has a log fire.

G.P.O. Box 478, Sydney, NSW 2001. ☎ *13 24 69 in Australia, or 03/6492 1303. P&O Resorts:* ☎ *800-225-9849 in the U.S. and Canada; 020/7805-3875 in the U.K.; 1800/737 678 in Australia, or 02/9364 8900. Fax: 02/9299 2477.* www.cradlemountain lodge.com.au. *Rack rates: A$274 (US$219/£110) Pencil Pine cabin double, A$342 (US$274/£137) spa cabin double, A$418 (US$334/£117) spa suite; extra person A$58 (US$46/£23). Ask about winter packages. AE, DC, MC, V.*

Waldheim Cabins
$ **Cradle Mountain**

For a real wilderness experience, head to these cabins run by the Parks and Wildlife Service. Nestled between button grass plains and temperate rain forest, they're simple, affordable, and offer good access to walking tracks. Each heated cabin has bunk beds, basic cooking utensils, crockery, cutlery, and a gas stove. Each accommodates four or eight people; if your party is smaller, you won't have to share with strangers. Two outbuildings with sanitary facilities (composting toilets and showers) serve all the cabins. Power is provided for lighting between 6 and 11 p.m. only. Supplies and fuel can be bought at Cradle Mountain Lodge. Bring your own bed linen and toiletries.

Cradle Mountain Visitor Centre, P.O. Box 20, Sheffield, TAS 7306. ☎ *03/6492 1110. Fax: 03/6492 1120.* www.parks.tas.gov.au. *Rack rate: Cabin A$70 (US$56/£28) for 2 adults; A$25 (US$20/£10) additional adult, A$9.90 (US$7.90/£4) additional child 6–16. MC, V.*

Part VIII
The Part of Tens

The 5th Wave   By Rich Tennant

THE Didgeridoo Jazz Quartet
OPEN SET NIGHT

"Oh, sweet—someone's sitting in on bagpipe."

In this part . . .

This part is a potpourri of history and information about Australia. In Chapter 24, we visit ten sites where transported convicts and their jailers became the first European immigrants. Then we give you some unique Down Under expressions in Chapter 25, and a hint on whether they're a compliment or an insult!

Chapter 24

Ten Convict Connections

by Lee Mylne

In This Chapter
▶ Discovering Sydney's convict origins
▶ Visiting Tasmania's old penitentiaries
▶ Exploring historic prisons in Queensland and Western Australia

*F*or many Australians, convict heritage is something to be proud of. The first European settlers, who sailed into Sydney Cove on a fleet of 11 ships on January 26, 1788, were mostly in chains. Many were convicted of what today would be minor crimes (such as petty theft, carried out in order to survive the poverty they lived in) and transported to Australia for long periods, with little hope of returning to England. Along with the soldiers who accompanied them, they formed the basis of the new settlement, which would become Sydney, and later came to areas including Tasmania, Queensland, and Western Australia.

The decision to establish a penal colony in Australia was made by the British government in 1786. It chose Botany Bay, which had been recommended for settlement by Captain James Cook when he sailed along Australia's east coast in 1770. But within a week of arrival in 1788, Captain Arthur Phillip, the colony's first governor, decided to move the settlement to the more suitable Sydney Cove, naming it after First Lord of the Admiralty, Viscount Sydney. The last convicts were transported to New South Wales in 1840.

While you travel around Australia, you'll find plenty of reminders of the harsh life those first arrivals endured. Here, we fill you in on some sites you can visit today that still bear witness to the arrival of Europeans.

Fort Denison, Sydney Harbour

A tiny island in Sydney Harbour was used to imprison and execute criminals from the time of the arrival of the First Fleet in 1788. The island was known as "Pinchgut" by hungry convicts who spent time there. Just two weeks after the fleet arrived, Advocate General David Collins recorded that "three prisoners were tried, one for assault . . . he was sentenced to

150 lashes, a second, for taking some biscuit from another convict, was sentenced to a week's confinement on bread and water on a small rocky island near the entrance to the cove." In 1796 the body of convicted murderer Francis Morgan was hung from a gibbet post on Pinchgut Island as a lesson to serious offenders. The macabre spectacle was, as Collins recorded "an object of great terror to the natives . . . his clothes shaking in the wind, and the creaking of his irons. . . ." The Aborigines, who had known the island as **Mat-te-wan-ye** (rocky island), from then on shunned the place.

Around 1840, the island was converted into a fort to protect against possible Russian invasion during the Crimean War. Pinchgut became home to Fort Denison, which was completed in 1857. The island was named after Governor William Denison in 1862. It is now part of Sydney Harbour National Park and is accessible by tour.

Hyde Park Barracks, Sydney

The colony gained its first architect in 1814 when Francis Greenway was transported for forgery. Greenway designed numerous buildings both as a convict and after gaining his full pardon in 1819, among them Sydney's Hyde Park Barracks on Queens Square in Macquarie Street. Built by convict labor between 1817 and 1819, the barracks were first used as a dormitory for homeless convicts. In 1848, they became an immigration depot and were later used as a female asylum (1862–1886) and a courthouse (1887–1979). Today the building is a museum, with exhibits about the lives of convicts, the history of Australia's convict system, and other occupants of the building. It's a popular place for school groups, so bear that in mind when you're planning your visit and get there outside school hours.

Richmond Gaol, Tasmania

The first section of Australia's oldest convict *gaol* (pronounced *jail*), Richmond Gaol, north of Hobart, was built in 1825, with a second wing added in 1835 for women prisoners. This gaol was a harsh place, in which floggings were frequent and other punishments included solitary confinement and hard labor in chain gangs. Escapes by unrepentant and unbowed convicts were also common.

One of the gaol's most famous — and infamous — prisoners was Ikey Solomon, on whom Dickens is said to have based Fagin in *Oliver Twist*. The colonial hangman, Solomon Bleay, was also imprisoned at Richmond Gaol, being escorted to and from Hobart and Launceston (the only places of execution), when necessary, to carry out his duties.

Convicts were transported to the colony as an indentured workforce to build both public and private buildings. Convict chain gangs were accommodated at Richmond in 1830, sharing crowded cells and passageways with prisoners on far lesser charges.

Most female convicts in Tasmania worked as domestic servants. Those subsequently convicted of minor offences or en route to Hobart's female factory (see the following section) were held at Richmond Gaol. Many women were returned to the factory by dissatisfied masters, but some convict women committed minor offences to escape unsatisfactory situations. Ann Forest, for example, was given 14 days' solitary on bread and water for insolence and disobedience, a sentence twice repeated for refusing to return to her assignment and absenting herself without leave on her release. Finally, she was returned to Hobart.

After transportation of convicts to Tasmania ended in 1853, the gaol was taken over by the Municipal Police; it remained a prison until 1928. Today you can step inside a cell measuring just 1 x 2m (3 x 6 ft.), peer into chain-gang sleeping rooms, walk in the flogging yards, see the cook house and holding rooms, and see historical relics and documents.

Cascades Female Factory, Tasmania

One of five female factories in Tasmania, the Cascades Female Factory in South Hobart was a women's prison from 1828 to 1856, employing women in washing, sewing, carding, and spinning. It was designed to hold 700 female convicts and their children, though, at its overcrowded worst, it housed 1,200 women and children. Life here was tough and often short. Women who died were buried in an unmarked grave and the children incarcerated with their mothers suffered terribly. For every 20 infants born here, 17 died soon after birth.

After it ceased operation as a female factory in 1856, the institution continued as a jail from 1856 until 1877.

You can take a self-guided tour of the Female Factory Historic Site which allows you access to the memorial garden and the historic site, or a guided one-hour tour. Cascades Female Factory was the setting for Australian novelist Bryce Courtney's book *The Potato Factory*, which gives an insight into life for the transported women.

Port Arthur, Tasmania

Port Arthur was Tasmania's largest penal colony. Set on the shores of the Tasman Peninsula, the prison was built for the most notorious convicts — and was one of the harshest prisons in the world. From 1830 to 1877, nearly 13,000 convicts were incarcerated here and nearly 2,000 of them died here. Only a few ever managed to escape. Those who tried either perished in the attempt or were hunted down and hanged.

About 30 19th-century buildings are dotted around the Port Arthur Historic Site, including the remains of the church, guard tower, hospital, and officers' houses. The site's most imposing ruin, the penitentiary, was originally a flour mill and granary; it was converted into a penitentiary for more than 480 convicts in 1857.

Off the coast of Port Arthur is the Isle of the Dead, where around 1,770 convicts and 180 free settlers are buried, mostly in mass graves with no headstones.

Port Arthur's gruesome history has been added to by modern events. In 1996, the Port Arthur Historic Site became the scene of one of Australia's worst mass murders, when a Hobart man armed with three high-powered automatic firearms killed a total of 35 people. Dozens more were injured. The devastating events encouraged Australians to question laws on the private ownership of automatic and semiautomatic firearms and resulted in new gun control laws that are among the strictest in the world. The gunman was sentenced to life imprisonment with no eligibility for parole. Events of this terrible day remain forever with the staff at Port Arthur, many of whom lost close friends, colleagues, and family members. Because they still find it difficult and painful to talk about, visitors are requested not to ask their guide about these events, but to instead read the plaque at the Memorial Garden.

Maria Island, Tasmania

A penal settlement was established at Darlington, on Tasmania's Maria Island, in 1825. This was for convicts who committed offences within the colony, but who were not bad enough to be banished to Macquarie Harbour on Tasmania's west coast. The first 50 prisoners (all men) and soldiers were housed in bark huts and tents. Supplies were short and the men lived on "fish and fowl." Many suffered from scurvy and ulcers. But it can't have been all bad — it was later reported that some convicts deliberately committed minor offences to be sent to this island "of ease and pleasure." Many of the permanent buildings erected later, such as the Commissariat Store and the penitentiary, can be visited today. Frequent escape attempts and the opening of Port Arthur led to the abandonment of the settlement in 1832.

Only ten years later, in 1842, a second period of convict settlement on the island began. Probation stations for convicts were established at Darlington and Point Lesueur. Around 600 men were housed in existing and new buildings at Darlington, and you can stay in these today, in hostel-style accommodations for less than A$25 (US$20/£10) a night (for more information visit www.discovertasmania.com.au). At Point Lesueur, the ruins of the old cells still stand.

Maria Island's most famous prisoner was the Irish rebel William Smith O'Brien. A political prisoner convicted of high treason, O'Brien was a British Member of Parliament and an Irish freedom fighter. On arriving in 1849, O'Brien wrote, " . . . to find a gaol in one of the loveliest spots formed by the hand of Nature in one of her loneliest solitudes creates a revulsion of feeling I cannot describe." He spent less than a year on Maria Island before being moved to Port Arthur, but you can find a display devoted to his life and times in one of the penitentiary cells.

Maria Island is reached by ferry from Triabunna, about an hour's drive from Hobart along the east coast.

Fremantle Prison, Western Australia

This limestone jail was built by convict labor to house 1,000 inmates. The first convicts came to Western Australia at the request of local merchants and politicians to provide cheap labor for the building of roads, bridges, and jetties for the colony. The first ship carrying 75 convicts arrived at Fremantle on June 1, 1850.

Work on the prison began in 1852 and by 1855 enough was complete for the convicts to be transferred to the site from their temporary jail. The prison was completed by 1859. Six houses were constructed on the western side of the prison for the senior officers.

Cells have been re-created in the style of past periods of the jail's history. Among them you'll find the "escape-proof" cell of Joseph Bolitho Johns or "Moondyne Joe," one of the more colorful characters who spent years in and out of Fremantle Prison, after being initially transported from Wales in 1853 for stealing food.

Other features of interest include the gallows, workshops, chapel, hospital, jailers' houses, and cell walls featuring artwork by former inmates. The precinct also includes a women's prison and commissariat.

Fremantle Prison was the last convict establishment built in Australia, marking the end of transportation with the arrival of the convict ship *Hougoumont* in January 1868. By the time transportation ceased, more than 9,700 convicts had been transported to Western Australia. It remained a maximum-security prison until 1991.

St. Helena Island: "The Hell Hole of the Pacific"

From 1867 to 1932, a small island in Brisbane's Moreton Bay was known as "the hell hole of the Pacific" to the nearly 4,000 souls incarcerated there. Discipline on the prison island of St. Helena was iron-fisted, with severe punishments — the lash, the dark underground cells, the gag, and the shot drill — meted out to those who stepped out of line. Bars on the windows and leg irons were further deterrents. Tough measures were called for because St. Helena housed some of Australia's worst criminals. In

1891, for example, there were 17 murderers, 27 men convicted of manslaughter, 26 men convicted of stabbings and shootings, and countless others who had been convicted of assault, rape, and other violent crimes.

Because of this, St. Helena had to be secure — and it was. Drowning and shark attacks were fierce deterrents. Queensland's bushrangers — including the infamous Captain Starlight — murderers and thieves toiled together to build this unique prison system using locally quarried stone held together with cement made from the island's lime kiln. By the turn of the century, St. Helena had more than 300 prisoners, housed in a maze of buildings surrounded by a high wall. It operated as a self-sufficient settlement, and even exported some of its produce to the mainland, including bricks for many of Brisbane's buildings.

Today, the prison ruins are a tourist attraction, with a small museum in the restored and reconstructed Deputy Superintendent's Cottage. Entry is by guided tour only, and you can visit the ruins of the blacksmith shop, punishment yard, sugar mill, prisoners, warders and children's cemetery, lime kiln, as well as the olive grove.

Commissariat Store, Brisbane

Brisbane was a penal colony from 1825 until 1839. The original Moreton Bay convict station was established at Redcliffe in September 1824, but this site was abandoned after a few months in favor of the Brisbane site, 20km (13 miles) up the Brisbane River. By 1831, there were 1,066 convicts and 175 soldiers living here.

The Commissariat Store, in William Street, is believed to be Brisbane's first stone structure and is among the few remaining relics of Brisbane's convict era. It was constructed by convict laborers from 1828 to 1829 as a two-story building, with a third story added in 1913. The building now houses the Royal Historical Society of Queensland.

The Old Windmill, Brisbane

The only other convict-built structure remaining in Brisbane today (besides the Commissariat Store — see the preceding section) is the old windmill on Wickham Terrace. Built in 1828 under the command of the feared and loathed Captain Patrick Logan, the Commandant of the colony, the mill was constructed to grind maize.

Why, you may ask as you gaze at this "windmill," are there no sails on it? Well, it was originally fitted with heavy sails but due to a mechanical flaw, they failed to work properly. And this is where the convicts enter the picture again: Wind power was replaced by the "never-ending staircase" of a treadmill, where convicts were forced to work as punishment, almost as dreaded as the lash. The treadmill was used from 1829 to 1837, when the windmill was repaired.

At least one public hanging took place here, in 1841, with the projecting arms of the windmill used as a gallows. After free settlement, the windmill became a signal station in 1861, and later served as an observatory, a fire lookout, and a television transmission tower.

You can't enter the windmill, but you can admire the outside from Wickham Terrace, and most tour buses include it on their routes.

Chapter 25

Ten Expressions You Need to Know

In This Chapter

▶ Deciphering the meaning of Australian slang
▶ Hoping no one is insulting you

T
he Aussie version of the English language can be largely attributed to convicts who created new words and expressions to add color to their conversations or to conceal their ideas from the authorities. In this chapter, we introduce you to some common Australian expressions you may well come across.

Buckley's Chance

No chance at all, as in: "You've got Buckley's chance, mate!" Some claim it comes from the name of the convict William Buckley, who escaped from Port Phillip in 1803 and lived for 32 years with Aborigines.

Dag

Someone who dresses badly, as in: "He's a dag." Dags are clumps of matted wool and dung that hang around a sheep's rear end. The word *dag* (originally *daglock*) was a British dialect word that entered mainstream Australian English in the late 19th century.

Drongo

In the early 1920s, an Australian racehorse called Drongo came very close to winning major races, but in 37 starts he *never* won a race. Soon after the horse's retirement, racing fans started to use the term for other horses that were having similarly unlucky careers. Soon after, the term became more negative, and was applied also to people who were hopeless cases or used to describe a fool, a stupid person, or a simpleton. So if you're called a drongo, it's not a compliment!

Dunny

A toilet — though it's not one of the more polite versions of the word. The dunny was originally any outside toilet. The word comes from British dialect *dunnekin* meaning "dung-house."

Fair Dinkum

"It's true!" or "Is that true?", depending on the context and inflection. Some people believe it originated in the 1850s, during the Australian gold rushes, when thousands of Chinese laborers came to Australia in a bid to make their fortune. It's possibly derived from the Cantonese *ding kam,* meaning "top gold." It may also originate from the East Midlands dialect in England, where *dinkum* meant "hard work" or "fair work."

G'day

You've certainly heard this one! And it really is the standard Australian greeting, used at any time of the day or night, though it's not used as an alternative to *farewell,* as *good day* might be in other countries.

Hard Yakka

Hard work! This expression is derived from *yakka* — an Aboriginal word for "work," from a language once spoken in the Brisbane region.

Stubby

A short, squat beer bottle often encased in a *stubby holder* (a foam casing) in warmer climates. The stereotypical Australian male is often depicted drinking a stubby, while dressed in a pair of *stubbies* (the trade name for a pair of men's brief shorts).

Tucker

This common Aussie slang word refers to food, as in: "Fancy some tucker?" By the late 18th century, it had developed its association with the consumption of food and drink. So, a school canteen is a *tuckshop,* and *bush tucker* is wild food.

You Right?

"Do you need my help?" It's often used by salespeople and is the Australian equivalent of "Are you being served?" or "May I help you?"

Appendix

Quick Concierge

Fast Facts

American Express

To report lost or stolen traveler's checks or credit cards, call ☎ 1800/688 022 in Australia or 02/8223 9171.

The main American Express office in Sydney is at Level 3, 130 Pitt St., near Martin Place (☎ 02/9236 4200). It's open Monday through Friday from 8:30 a.m. to 5 p.m. and Saturday from 9 a.m. to noon.

Amex also has offices in Melbourne, Brisbane, Adelaide, and Perth. See individual chapters for opening hours and locations. In all states and territories, you can find American Express foreign exchange services within some Westpac Bank branches.

ATMs

ATMs, also called "cash machines" or "money machines" in Australia, are widely available in most towns and cities. The Cirrus (☎ 800-424-7787; www.mastercard.com) and PLUS (☎ 800-843-7587; www.visa.com) networks span the globe. Check the back of your card to see which network your bank is part of, and check online to find ATM locations.

Area Codes

Each Australian state has a different area code: **02** for New South Wales and the Australian Capital Territory; **07** for Queensland; **03** for Victoria and Tasmania; **08** for

South Australia, the Northern Territory, and Western Australia. You must dial the appropriate code if you're calling to a state other than the one you're in; however, you also need to use the code if you're calling outside the *city* you're in. For example if you're in Sydney, where the code is 02 and you want to call another New South Wales town, you still dial 02 before the number.

Credit Cards

Visa and MasterCard are universally accepted in Australia; American Express and Diners Club less so. Discover card is not accepted. If your card is lost or stolen, call the following Australian toll-free numbers: Visa, ☎ 1800/450 346 or 02/9251 3704; MasterCard, ☎ 1800/120 113; American Express, ☎ 1300/132 639 or 1800/688 022; Diners Club, ☎ 1300/360 060 or 03/8643 2210.

Currency Exchange

Travelex is one of Australia's major foreign exchange bureaus, with around 80 outlets around the country, including at all major airports and in the larger cities. You can find locations at www.travelex.com/au or by calling ☎ 1800/637 642.

Customs

When entering Australia, as well as when returning home, keep in mind Customs restrictions.

Australia is a signatory to the Convention on International Trade in Endangered Species (CITES), which restricts or bans the import of products made from protected wildlife. Examples of the restricted items are alligator, bear, coral, crocodile, giant clam, monkeys, wild cats, zebra, as well as American ginseng, some types of caviar, and orchid products. Banned items include ivory, rhinoceros products, sturgeon caviar, tortoise (marine turtle) shell, and tiger products. Keep this in mind if you stop in other countries en route to Australia, where souvenirs like these may be sold. Australian authorities may seize these items. (Some of these items are also banned in the U.S., Canada, and Great Britain, so check first before you leave your home country.)

Because Australia is an island, it is free of many agricultural and livestock diseases and invokes strict quarantine laws for importing plants, animals, and their products, including food. Dogs at Australian airports detect these products (as well as drugs). Amnesty trash bins are available before you reach the immigration counters for items such as fruit.

Don't be alarmed if, just before landing, the flight attendants spray the aircraft cabin (with products approved by the World Health Organization) to kill potentially disease-bearing insects. For more information on what is and is not allowed, contact the nearest Australian embassy or consulate, or Australia's Department of Agriculture, Fisheries, and Forestry, which runs the Australian Quarantine and Inspection Service (☎ 02/6272 3933; www.affa.gov.au). Its Web site has a list of restricted or banned foods, animal and plant products, and other items.

A helpful brochure, available from Australian consulates or Customs offices, as well as online, is *Know Before You Go.* For more

information, contact the Customs Information and Support Centre (☎ 1300/363 263 in Australia or 02/6275 6666) between 8 a.m. and 5 p.m., except public holidays, or check out www.customs.gov.au.

For clear summaries on what you can take home with you after a trip to Australia, check out the following:

U.S. citizens: Download the free pamphlet *Know Before You Go* online at www.cbp.gov or contact the U.S. Customs and Border Protection (CBP), 1300 Pennsylvania Ave. NW, Washington, DC 20229 (☎ 877-287-8667) and request the pamphlet.

Canadian citizens: Write for the booklet *I Declare,* issued by the Canada Border Services Agency (☎ 800-461-9999 in Canada, or 204-983-3500; www.cbsa-asfc.gc.ca).

U.K. Citizens: For information, contact HM Customs & Excise at ☎ 0845/010-9000 (020/8929-0152 from outside the U.K.) or consult its Web site at www.hmce.gov.uk.

Driving

In Australia, drive on the **left** side of the road. Seat belts are compulsory for everyone.

The speed limit is 50kmph (31 mph) or 60kmph (37 mph) in urban areas, 100kmph (62 mph) in most country areas, and sometimes 110kmph (68 mph) on freeways. In the Northern Territory, the speed limit is 130kmph (80 mph) on the Stuart, Arnhem, Barkly, and Victoria highways, while rural roads are designated 110kmph (68 mph) speed limits unless otherwise signposted.

The emergency breakdown assistance telephone number for every Australian auto club is ☎ 13 11 11 from anywhere in

Australia. It is billed as a local call. If you aren't a member of an auto club at home that has a reciprocal agreement with the Australian clubs, you'll have to join the Australian club on the spot before the club will tow or repair your car. Most car rental companies also have emergency assistance numbers.

Electricity

The current in Australia is 240 volts AC, 50 hertz. Sockets take two or three flat, not rounded, prongs. North Americans and Europeans will need to buy a converter before they leave home. (Don't wait until you get to Australia; Australian stores are likely to stock only converters to fit American and European outlets.) Some large hotels have 110V outlets for electric shavers (or dual voltage), and some may have converters you can borrow — but don't count on it. Power does not start automatically when you plug in an appliance; you need to flick the switch beside the socket to the "on" position.

Embassies and Consulates

Most diplomatic posts are in Australia's capital, Canberra. Embassies or consulates with posts in state capitals are listed in "Fast Facts" in the relevant state chapters of this book.

In case you lose your passport or have some other emergency, here's a list of addresses and phone numbers:

Britain: The high commission is on Commonwealth Avenue, Canberra, ACT 2601 (☎ 02/6270 6666). There are also consulates in Sydney, Melbourne, Brisbane, and Perth.

Canada: The high commission is on Commonwealth Avenue, Yarralumla, ACT 2600 (☎ 02/6270 4000). There are consulates in Sydney, Melbourne, and Perth.

Ireland: The embassy is at 20 Arkana St., Yarralumla, ACT 2600 (☎ 02/6273 3022). There are also consulates in Melbourne and Perth.

United States: The embassy is at 21 Moonah Place, Yarralumla, ACT 2600 (☎ 02/6214 5600). There are also consulates in Sydney, Melbourne, and Perth.

Emergencies

Dial ☎ 000 anywhere in Australia for police, ambulance, or the fire department. The call is free from public and private telephones. The TTY emergency number is ☎ 106.

Information

See "Where to Get More Information" later in this appendix, to find out where to get visitor information before you leave home.

Internet Access and Cybercafes

Internet access is available just about everywhere in Australia, including some small Outback towns, which generally have at least one cybercafe, coin-operated machines, or both. Coin-op terminals are available at larger airports. Major tourist towns, such as Darwin and Cairns, have whole streets full of cybercafes. Public libraries in small towns are often a good place to get Internet access, too.

Liquor Laws

The minimum legal drinking age is 18. Pubs are usually open daily from around 10 a.m. or noon, to 10 p.m. or midnight, although hours vary slightly from place to place. Random breath tests to catch drunk drivers are common, and drunk-driving laws are strictly enforced. Getting caught drunk behind the wheel will mean a court appearance. The maximum permitted blood alcohol level for driving is 0.05 percent.

Alcohol is sold in liquor stores, in the "bottle shops" attached to every pub, and in supermarkets in some states.

Maps

Two of the biggest map publishers in Australia are HEMA Maps (☎ 07/3340 0000; www.hemamaps.com.au) and Universal Publishers (☎ 1800/021 987 in Australia, or 02/9857 3700; www.universalpress-online.com). Both publish an extensive range of national, state, regional, and city maps.

HEMA has a strong list of regional maps, while Universal produces a complete range of street directories by city, region, or state under the UBD and Gregory's labels. HEMA produces four-wheel-drive and motorbike road atlases and many regional four-wheel-drive maps (good if you plan to go off the trails), an atlas of Australia's national parks, and maps to Kakadu and Lamington national parks.

Both companies produce national road atlases. Universal's UBD *Complete Motoring Atlas of Australia* publishes street maps of regional towns in each state.

Australian auto clubs, visitor information centers, bigger newsdealers, and bookstores are your best sources for maps. Gas stations usually only stock a limited local range. Maps published by state automobile associations will likely be free if you are a member of an affiliated auto club in your home country, but you'll have to pick them up on arrival. Remember to bring your auto club membership card to qualify for discounts or free maps.

Police

Dial ☎ 000 anywhere in Australia for police. This call is free from public and private telephones.

Post Office

For general information about postal services call ☎ 13 13 18 anywhere in Australia. A postcard costs A$1.25 (US$1/£0.50) to send anywhere in the world. A card will take up to six working days to reach the United States. Post boxes are red.

Safety

Australia is generally safe, but as anywhere else, it pays to keep your wits about you, particularly in major cities, such as Sydney.

Smoking

Australia has strict anti-smoking laws, so always ask if it's okay before you light up. Smoking is restricted or banned in most public places, including museums, cinemas, and theaters. Smoking in restaurants may be limited — Western Australia and New South Wales ban it altogether, and in many other states, restaurants have smoking and nonsmoking sections. In most states, there are total bans in pubs and clubs. South Australia will introduce these bans in 2008, joining Queensland, Tasmania, Western Australia, Victoria, the Australian Capital Territory, and New South Wales. Only in the Northern Territory can you still light up in some parts of a pub.

Taxes

Australia applies a 10 percent Goods and Services Tax (GST) on most products and services, including airline tickets bought within Australia (although your international airline tickets to Australia are not taxed, nor are domestic airline tickets for travel within Australia if you bought them outside Australia).

You can claim a refund of the GST through the Tourist Refund Scheme (TRS) — and also of a 14.5 percent Wine Equalisation Tax (WET) — if you've purchased more than A$300 (US$240/£120) from a single outlet, within the last 30 days before you leave. See Chapter 5 for details on how to claim your refund. Call the Australian Customs Service (☎ 1300/363 263 or 02/6275 6666) for more information. Items bought in duty-free stores will not be charged GST.

Basic groceries are not subject to the GST, but restaurant meals are.

Visitors to the Great Barrier Reef will be charged a "reef tax," officially known as the Environmental Management Charge, of A$5 (US$4/£2) per person every time you enter the Great Barrier Reef Marine Park.

Telephone

For directory assistance, dial ☎ 12455 for a number in Australia, and dial 1225 for numbers to all other countries.

To call Australia from the United States, dial the international access code **011** (or **00** from the U.K., Ireland, or New Zealand), then the country code **61,** followed by the city code (drop the **0** from any area code given in this book), and then the number. To make international calls from Australia, first dial **0011** and then the country code, followed by the area code and number. An international online telephone card such as ekit (www.ekit.com) will allow you to call overseas at much cheaper rates.

Numbers beginning with 1800 within Australia are toll-free, but calling a U.S. toll-free number from Australia is not toll-free. In fact, it costs the same as an overseas call.

Numbers starting with 13 or 1300 in Australia are charged at the local fee of A25¢ (US20¢/£0.10) per minute anywhere in Australia. Numbers beginning with 1900 (or 1901 and so on) are pay-for-service lines,

and you will be charged as much as A$5 (US$4/£2) a minute.

Telstra pay phones are found in most city streets, shopping centers, transport terminals, post offices, and along highways — even in some of the most remote areas of Australia. To find the nearest one, call ☎ 1800/011 433 or go to www.telstra.com.au/payphoneservices/index.htm. The cost of a local call from a pay phone is A$0.50 (US$0.40/£0.20), either in coins or by using a phone card. Some phones only take prepaid phone cards, which you can purchase from newsdealers and other retailers in denominations of A$5, A$10, and A$20, and are good for local, national, and international calls. There are no access numbers — you just insert the card and dial. Credit phones take most major credit cards. In addition to the pay phones in the usual booths, you may find some called "blue phones" or "gold phones" inside convenience stores.

Time Zone

Australian Eastern Standard Time (AEST or just EST) covers Queensland, New South Wales, the Australian Capital Territory, Victoria, and Tasmania. Central Standard Time (CST) is used in the Northern Territory and South Australia. Western Standard Time (WST) is the standard in Western Australia. When it's noon in New South Wales, the Australian Capital Territory, Victoria, Queensland, and Tasmania, it's 11:30 a.m. in South Australia and the Northern Territory, and 10 a.m. in Western Australia. All states except Queensland, the Northern Territory, and Western Australia observe daylight saving time, usually from the first Sunday in October to the first Sunday in April. However, not all states switch to daylight saving on the same day or in the same week.

Australia's east coast is GMT (Greenwich Mean Time) plus ten hours. When it's noon on the east coast, it's 2 a.m. in London (the same day) and 6 p.m. in Los Angeles and 9 p.m. in New York (the previous day). These times are based on standard time, so allow for daylight saving in the Australian summer, or in the country you're calling. New Zealand is two hours ahead of the east coast of Australia, except during

daylight saving, when it's three hours ahead of Queensland.

Weather Updates

Two good Web sites to keep you up to date with the weather where you're going are the Weather Channel (www.weather channel.com.au) and the Australian Bureau of Meteorology (www.bom. gov.au).

Toll-Free Numbers and Web Sites

Airlines

Air Canada
☎ 888-247-2262 in the U.S. and Canada
☎ 02/8248 5757 in Sydney or 1300/655 767 elsewhere in Australia
www.aircanada.com

Air New Zealand
☎ 800-262-1234 or 310-615-1111 in the U.S.
☎ 800-663-5494 in Canada
☎ 0800/737 000 in New Zealand
☎ 13 24 76 in Australia
www.airnewzealand.com

British Airways
☎ 800-247-9297 in the U.S.
☎ 0870/850-9850 in the U.K.
☎ 1300/767 177 in Australia
www.britishairways.com

Cathay Pacific
☎ 020/8834-8888 in the U.K.
☎ 13 17 47 in Australia
www.cathaypacific.com

Jetstar
☎ 13 15 38 in Australia, or 03/8341 4901
www.jetstar.com.au.

Malaysia Airlines
☎ 0870/607-9090 in the U.K.
☎ 13 26 27 in Australia
www.malaysiaairlines.com.my or www.malaysiaairlines.com/uk

Pacific Blue
☎ 13 16 45 in Australia, or 07/3295 2284
☎ 0800/670 000 in New Zealand
www.virginblue.com.au

Qantas
☎ 800-227-4500 in the U.S. and Canada
☎ 0845/774-7767 in the U.K.
☎ 13 13 13 in Australia
www.qantas.com.au

Regional Express
☎ 13 17 13 in Australia
www.regionalexpress.com.au

Singapore Airlines
☎ 0844/800-2380 in the U.K.
☎ 13 10 11 in Australia
www.singaporeair.com/uk

Thai Airways International
☎ 0870/606-0911 in the U.K.
☎ 1300/651 960 in Australia
www.thaiair.com

United Airlines
☎ 800-538-2929 in the U.S. and Canada
☎ 13 17 77 in Australia
www.united.com or www.united.ca

Virgin Blue
☎ 13 67 89 in Australia, or 07/3295 2296
www.virginblue.com.au

Major hotel and motel chains

Accor Asia Pacific
☎ 1300/656 565 in Australia, or 02/8584 8666
www.accorhotels.com.au

Hilton Hotels
☎ 800-445-8667 in the U.S. and Canada
☎ 0870/590-9090 in the U.K. and Ireland
☎ 0800/293 229 in Australia
www.hilton.com

Hyatt Hotels & Resorts
☎ 888-591-1234 in the U.S. and Canada
☎ 0845/888-1234 in the U.K.
☎ 13 12 34 in Australia
www.hyatt.com

Medina Serviced Apartments
☎ 1300/633 462 in Australia, or 02/9356 1000
www.medinaapartments.com.au

Mirvac Hotels & Resorts
☎ 13 15 15 in Australia
www.mirvachotels.com.au

Quest Serviced Apartments
☎ 1800/334 033 in Australia, or 03/9645 8357
www.questapartments.com.au

Radisson Hotels
☎ 888-201-1718 in the U.S.
☎ 800-333-3333 in Canada
☎ 0800/374-411 in the U.K.

☎ 1800/333 333 in Australia
www.radisson.com

Rendezvous Hotels
☎ 1800/088 888 in Australia
www.rendezvoushotels.com

Shangri-la Hotels and Resort
☎ 866-565-5050 in the U.S.
☎ 866-344-5050 in Canada
☎ 0800/028-3337 in the U.K.
☎ 1800/222 448 in Australia
www.shangri-la.com

Sheraton Hotels & Resorts
☎ 800-325-3535 in the U.S. and Canada
☎ 0800/325-3535 in the U.K. and Ireland
☎ 1800/073 535 in Australia
www.sheraton.com

Stamford Hotels & Resorts
☎ 1300/301 391 in Australia
www.stamford.com.au

Voyages Hotels & Resorts
☎ 1300/134 044 in Australia, or 02/8296 8010
www.voyages.com.au

Westin Hotels
☎ 800-937-8461 in the U.S.
☎ 1800/656 535 in Australia
www.westin.com.au

Major car rental agencies

Apollo Motorhome Holidays
☎ 1800/777 779 in Australia, or 07/3265 9200
www.apollocamper.com.au

Avis
☎ 800-230-4898 in the U.S. and Canada
☎ 8445/81 81 81 in the U.K.
☎ 13 63 33 in Australia
www.avis.com or www.avis.com.au

Britz Campervan Rentals
☎ 1800/331 454 in Australia, or
03/8379 8890
www.britz.com

Budget
☎ 800-472-3325 in the U.S.
☎ 800-268-8900 in Canada
☎ 8701/565-656 in the U.K.
☎ 1300/362 848 in Australia
www.budgetrentacar.com or
www.budget.com.au

Europcar
☎ 877-940-6900 in the U.S. and
Canada
☎ 0870/607-5000 in the U.K.
☎ 1300/13 13 90 in Australia, or
03/9330 6160
www.europcar.com or
www.europcar.com.au

Hertz
☎ 800-654-3001 in the U.S. and
Canada
☎ 0870/844-844 in the U.K.
☎ 13 30 39 in Australia
www.hertz.com or
www.hertz.com.au

Maui
☎ 1300/363 800 in Australia, or
03/8379 8891
www.maui.com.au

Red Spot Car Rentals
☎ 1300/668 810 in Australia, or
02/8303 2222
www.redspotrentals.com.au

Thrifty
☎ 800-847-4389 in the U.S. and
Canada
☎ 01494/751-540 in the U.K.
☎ 1300/367 227 in Australia
www.thrifty.com or
www.thrifty.com.au

Where to Get More Information

For more information on Australia, you can visit the tourist offices and Web sites listed in the following sections.

Official tourist offices

For general information about Australia, contact an office of Tourism Australia at one of the following addresses or on its Web site at www. australia.com. Tourism Australia's 133 "Aussie specialist" travel agents throughout North America are also listed, and you can search online by zip code or state to find one near you. Tourism Australia operates a Web site only — no phone lines.

- ✔ **In the United States:** 6100 Center Dr., Suite 1150, Los Angeles CA 90045 (☎ **310-695-3200**)

- ✔ **In Canada:** 111 Peter St., Suite 630, Toronto, Ontario M5V 2H1 (☎ **877-733-2878** or 416-408 0549)

- ✔ **In the United Kingdom:** Australia Centre, Australia House, 6th Floor, Melbourne Place (at The Strand), London, WC2B 4LG (☎ **020/7438 4601**)

State and territory tourism Web sites

The state tourism boards all have useful and user-friendly Web sites:

- ✔ **Australian Capital Tourism:** www.visitcanberra.com.au

- ✔ **Northern Territory Tourist Commission:** www.travelnt.com

- ✔ **South Australian Tourism Commission:** www.southaustralia.com

- ✔ **Tourism New South Wales:** www.visitnsw.com.au

- ✔ **Tourism Queensland:** www.destinationqueensland.com (for North American visitors) or www.queenslandholidays.com.au

- ✔ **Tourism Tasmania:** www.discovertasmania.com

- ✔ **Tourism Victoria:** www.visitvictoria.com

- ✔ **Western Australian Tourism Commission:** www.western australia.com

Tourist information for major cities

The following Tourist Information Centers and their Web sites provide information on hotels, restaurants, and attractions in cities and states around Australia:

- ✔ **Adelaide:** The South Australian Visitor & Travel Centre is at 18 King William St., Adelaide (☎ **1300/655 276** in Australia, or 08/8303 2033; www.southaustralia.com). There is also an information booth in the Rundle Mall (☎ **08/8203 7611**).

- ✔ **Alice Springs:** The Central Australian Tourism Industry Association (CATIA) Visitor Information Centre is at 60 Gregory Terrace, Alice Springs (☎ **08/8952 5800;** www.centralaustralian tourism.com).

- ✔ **Brisbane:** The Brisbane Visitor Information Centre is in the Queen Street Mall (☎ **07/3006 6290;** www.experiencebrisbane.com).

- ✔ **Cairns:** Tourism Tropical North Queensland runs the Gateway Discovery Centre, 51 The Esplanade, Cairns (☎ **07/4051 3588;** www.tropicalaustralia.com).

- ✔ **Canberra:** The Canberra Visitors' Centre is at 330 Northbourne Ave., Dickson (☎ **02/6205 0044;** www.visitcanberra.com.au).

- ✔ **Darwin:** Tourism Top End's visitor center is at Mitchell and Knuckey streets, Darwin (☎ **08/8936 2499;** www.tourismtop end.com.au).

- ✔ **Hobart:** The Tasmanian Travel and Information Centre is at 20 Davey St., Hobart (☎ **1300/655 145** in Australia, or 03/6230 8233; www.discovertasmania.com.au).

- **Melbourne:** The Melbourne Visitor Centre is in Federation Square (☎ 03/9658 9658; www.thatsmelbourne.com.au). Other good Web sites are www.visitmelbourne.com and www.onlymelbourne.com.au.

- **Perth:** The Western Australian Visitor Centre is in the Albert Facey House, 469 Wellington St., Perth (☎ 1300/361 351 in Australia, or 08/9483 1111; www.westernaustralia.com). The City of Perth's i-City Information Kiosk in the Murray Street Mall is another good source of information.

- **Sydney:** The Sydney Visitor Centre at The Rocks, First Floor, The Rocks Centre, Argyle and Playfair streets (☎ 02/9240 8788). There are several good Sydney Web sites, including www.sydneyvisitorcentre.com, www.sydneyaustralia.com, and www.sydney.citysearch.com.au.

National park visitor Web sites

The following sites give you information on national parks in Australia:

- **Department of Conservation and Land Management, Western Australia:** www.calm.wa.gov.au (for information on both national parks and marine parks)

- **Great Barrier Reef Marine Park Authority:** www.gbrmpa.gov.au or www.reefhq.com.au

- **Great Barrier Reef Visitor Bureau:** www.great-barrier-reef.com

- **Kakadu National Park:** www.environment.gov.au/parks/kakadu

- **New South Wales national parks:** www.nationalparks.nsw.gov.au

- **Northern Territory national parks:** www.nt.gov.au/ipe/pwcnt

- **Queensland national parks:** www.epa.qld.gov.au/parks_and_forests

- **South Australian national parks:** www.parks.sa.gov.au

- **Tasmanian national parks:** www.parks.tas.gov.au/natparks

- **Uluru-Kata Tjuta National Park:** www.environment.gov.au/parks/uluru

- **Victorian national parks:** www.parkweb.vic.gov.au

Index

• *N* •

• *O* •

• *X* •

• *Y* •

• *Z* •

BUSINESS, CAREERS & PERSONAL FINANCE

0-7645-5307-0

0-7645-5331-3 *†

Also available:
- Accounting For Dummies †
  0-7645-5314-3
- Business Plans Kit For Dummies †
  0-7645-5365-8
- Cover Letters For Dummies
  0-7645-5224-4
- Frugal Living For Dummies
  0-7645-5403-4
- Leadership For Dummies
  0-7645-5176-0
- Managing For Dummies
  0-7645-1771-6

- Marketing For Dummies
  0-7645-5600-2
- Personal Finance For Dummies *
  0-7645-2590-5
- Project Management
  For Dummies
  0-7645-5283-X
- Resumes For Dummies †
  0-7645-5471-9
- Selling For Dummies
  0-7645-5363-1
- Small Business Kit For Dummies *†
  0-7645-5093-4

HOME & BUSINESS COMPUTER BASICS

0-7645-4074-2

0-7645-3758-X

Also available:
- ACT! 6 For Dummies
  0-7645-2645-6
- iLife '04 All-in-One Desk Reference
  For Dummies
  0-7645-7347-0
- iPAQ For Dummies
  0-7645-6769-1
- Mac OS X Panther Timesaving
  Techniques For Dummies
  0-7645-5812-9
- Macs For Dummies
  0-7645-5656-8
- Microsoft Money 2004 For Dummies
  0-7645-4195-1

- Office 2003 All-in-One Desk
  Reference For Dummies
  0-7645-3883-7
- Outlook 2003 For Dummies
  0-7645-3759-8
- PCs For Dummies
  0-7645-4074-2
- TiVo For Dummies
  0-7645-6923-6
- Upgrading and Fixing PCs
  For Dummies
  0-7645-1665-5
- Windows XP Timesaving
  Techniques For Dummies
  0-7645-3748-2

FOOD, HOME, GARDEN, HOBBIES, MUSIC & PETS

0-7645-5295-3

0-7645-5232-5

Also available:
- Bass Guitar For Dummies
  0-7645-2487-9
- Diabetes Cookbook For Dummies
  0-7645-5230-9
- Gardening For Dummies *
  0-7645-5130-2
- Guitar For Dummies
  0-7645-5106-X
- Holiday Decorating For Dummies
  0-7645-2570-0
- Home Improvement All-in-One
  For Dummies
  0-7645-5680-0

- Knitting For Dummies
  0-7645-5395-X
- Piano For Dummies
  0-7645-5105-1
- Puppies For Dummies
  0-7645-5255-4
- Scrapbooking For Dummies
  0-7645-7208-3
- Senior Dogs For Dummies
  0-7645-5818-8
- Singing For Dummies
  0-7645-2475-5
- 30-Minute Meals For Dummies
  0-7645-2589-1

INTERNET & DIGITAL MEDIA

0-7645-1664-7

0-7645-6924-4

Also available:
- 2005 Online Shopping Directory
  For Dummies
  0-7645-7495-7
- CD & DVD Recording For Dummies
  0-7645-5956-7
- eBay For Dummies
  0-7645-5654-1
- Fighting Spam For Dummies
  0-7645-5965-6
- Genealogy Online For Dummies
  0-7645-5964-8
- Google For Dummies
  0-7645-4420-9

- Home Recording For Musicians
  For Dummies
  0-7645-1634-5
- The Internet For Dummies
  0-7645-4173-0
- iPod & iTunes For Dummies
  0-7645-7772-7
- Preventing Identity Theft
  For Dummies
  0-7645-7336-5
- Pro Tools All-in-One Desk
  Reference For Dummies
  0-7645-5714-9
- Roxio Easy Media Creator
  For Dummies
  0-7645-7131-1

* Separate Canadian edition also available
† Separate U.K. edition also available

Available wherever books are sold. For more information or to order direct: U.S. customers visit www.dummies.com or call 1-877-762-2974.
U.K. customers visit www.wileyeurope.com or call 0800 243407. Canadian customers visit www.wiley.ca or call 1-800-567-4797.

SPORTS, FITNESS, PARENTING, RELIGION & SPIRITUALITY

0-7645-5146-9   0-7645-5418-2

Also available:
- Adoption For Dummies
  0-7645-5488-3
- Basketball For Dummies
  0-7645-5248-1
- The Bible For Dummies
  0-7645-5296-1
- Buddhism For Dummies
  0-7645-5359-3
- Catholicism For Dummies
  0-7645-5391-7
- Hockey For Dummies
  0-7645-5228-7

- Judaism For Dummies
  0-7645-5299-6
- Martial Arts For Dummies
  0-7645-5358-5
- Pilates For Dummies
  0-7645-5397-6
- Religion For Dummies
  0-7645-5264-3
- Teaching Kids to Read
  For Dummies
  0-7645-4043-2
- Weight Training For Dummies
  0-7645-5168-X
- Yoga For Dummies
  0-7645-5117-5

TRAVEL

0-7645-5438-7   0-7645-5453-0

Also available:
- Alaska For Dummies
  0-7645-1761-9
- Arizona For Dummies
  0-7645-6938-4
- Cancún and the Yucatán
  For Dummies
  0-7645-2437-2
- Cruise Vacations For Dummies
  0-7645-6941-4
- Europe For Dummies
  0-7645-5456-5
- Ireland For Dummies
  0-7645-5455-7

- Las Vegas For Dummies
  0-7645-5448-4
- London For Dummies
  0-7645-4277-X
- New York City For Dummies
  0-7645-6945-7
- Paris For Dummies
  0-7645-5494-8
- RV Vacations For Dummies
  0-7645-5443-3
- Walt Disney World & Orlando
  For Dummies
  0-7645-6943-0

GRAPHICS, DESIGN & WEB DEVELOPMENT

0-7645-4345-8   0-7645-5589-8

Also available:
- Adobe Acrobat 6 PDF
  For Dummies
  0-7645-3760-1
- Building a Web Site For Dummies
  0-7645-7144-3
- Dreamweaver MX 2004
  For Dummies
  0-7645-4342-3
- FrontPage 2003 For Dummies
  0-7645-3882-9
- HTML 4 For Dummies
  0-7645-1995-6
- Illustrator CS For Dummies
  0-7645-4084-X

- Macromedia Flash MX 2004
  For Dummies
  0-7645-4358-X
- Photoshop 7 All-in-One Desk
  Reference For Dummies
  0-7645-1667-1
- Photoshop CS Timesaving
  Techniques For Dummies
  0-7645-6782-9
- PHP 5 For Dummies
  0-7645-4166-8
- PowerPoint 2003 For Dummies
  0-7645-3908-6
- QuarkXPress 6 For Dummies
  0-7645-2593-X

NETWORKING, SECURITY, PROGRAMMING & DATABASES

0-7645-6852-3   0-7645-5784-X

Also available:
- A+ Certification For Dummies
  0-7645-4187-0
- Access 2003 All-in-One Desk
  Reference For Dummies
  0-7645-3988-4
- Beginning Programming
  For Dummies
  0-7645-4997-9
- C For Dummies
  0-7645-7068-4
- Firewalls For Dummies
  0-7645-4048-3
- Home Networking For Dummies
  0-7645-42796

- Network Security For Dummies
  0-7645-1679-5
- Networking For Dummies
  0-7645-1677-9
- TCP/IP For Dummies
  0-7645-1760-0
- VBA For Dummies
  0-7645-3989-2
- Wireless All In-One Desk Reference
  For Dummies
  0-7645-7496-5
- Wireless Home Networking
  For Dummies
  0-7645-3910-8